Doug Reeser

PHYSICAL EDUCATION HANDBOOK

Life is a series of games—games of finding answers, finding amusement, persuading people, winning friends, raising families, and performing rituals. Some persons relish the game of life and enjoy all the sub-games to the hilt. Others play them grimly, with their eyes fixed on the scoreboard, too much concerned with staying ahead to enjoy the game.

DON ROBINSON *(Phi Delta Kappan)*

PHYSICAL EDUCATION HANDBOOK

EIGHTH EDITION

DON CASH SEATON
*Late Chairman, Department of Health,
Physical Education, and Recreation,
University of Kentucky*

NEIL SCHMOTTLACH
*Professor of Physical Education,
Ball State University*

JERRE L. McMANAMA
*Assistant Professor of Physical Education,
Ball State University*

IRENE A. CLAYTON
*Former Director of Physical Education,
Bryn Mawr College*

HOWARD C. LEIBEE
*Late Professor of Physical Education,
The University of Michigan*

LLOYD L. MESSERSMITH
*Late Professor of Physical Education,
Southern Methodist University*

 PRENTICE HALL, Englewood Cliffs, New Jersey 07632

Library of Congress Cataloging-in-Publication Data

Physical education handbook / Don Cash Seaton . . . [et al.].
— 8th ed.
p.   cm.
Includes bibliographical references.
ISBN 0-13-663097-9. — ISBN 0-13-666900-X (pbk.)
1. Physical education and training—Study and teaching.
I. Seaton, Don Cash, (date).
GV361.P49   1992
796′.07—dc20
91-24567
CIP

Acquisitions Editor: Ted Bolen
Editorial Supervision: Margaret Antonini
Interior Design: Hilda Tauber
Cover Designer: Ben Santora
Prepress Buyer: Herb Klein
Manufacturing Buyer: Patrice Fraccio
Editorial Assistant: Diane Schaible

Cover Photographs: Basketball players, David Johnson; Runners,
Brian Drake; Cyclists, Dave Black; Skiers, Lori Peek—all
SportsChrome. Swimmer, David Lissy—Focus on Sports.

Printed in the United States of America
10 9 8 7 6 5 4 3 2 1

ISBN 0-13-666900-X PBK

ISBN 0-13-663097-9

Prentice-Hall International (UK) Limited, *London*
Prentice-Hall of Australia Pty. Limited, *Sydney*
Prentice-Hall Canada Inc., *Toronto*
Prentice-Hall Hispanoamericana, S.A., *Mexico*
Prentice-Hall of India Private Limited, *New Delhi*
Prentice-Hall of Japan, Inc., *Tokyo*
Simon & Schuster Asia Pte. Ltd., *Singapore*
Editora Prentice-Hall do Brasil, Ltda., *Rio de Janeiro*

*This edition is dedicated
to the many people who would enjoy
a lifetime of active participation.*

CONTENTS

PREFACE

Teachers, recreational leaders, volunteer scout trainers, and similar personnel are often called upon to "start the ball rolling" or to teach an activity with which they are not completely familiar. Many instructors have only a few specializations and it would take them too long to master all the present offerings in physical education. Some activities, too, are more familiar to men than to women, and vice versa. Yet with the changes brought about by Title IX and laws regarding participation by special populations, today's teaching personnel must be able to give instruction in a great variety of activities. This is particularly true of individual and team sports such as golf, orienteering, cycling, speedball, flag football, field hockey, and soccer.

To meet these needs, the *Physical Education Handbook,* 8th edition, has been written to serve as a teaching and reference tool for several types of people: physical educators, student teachers, recreational leaders, sports enthusiasts, physical education majors, and all high school and college students who are interested in sports activities and physical fitness.

Previous users of the *Handbook* will find that a couple of activities have been dropped and three new activities have been added: swimming, pickle-ball, and speedball. In deciding which activities to include, we relied on a survey of previous users who expressed their needs. All the activities chapters have been revised where necessary and updated with new illustrations and the latest rules. Hints for special populations have been expanded and refined with the addition of suggested audio-visual materials.

In order to derive maximum utility from the *Handbook,* it is essential to begin with a careful study of the two introductory chapters. Chapter 1 covers four basic areas: (a) the historical development of physical education and sport, (b) the socio-logical aspects, (c) the mechanical (movement) aspects, and (d) the psychological aspects. Chapter 2 explains the principles and benefits of physical fitness programs, and gives suggestions relative to clothing, nutrition, and fitness workouts. These introductory chapters constitute the backbone and sinews of this manual; they provide both meaningful principles necessary for understanding and the practical suggestions needed in applying these principles to effective teaching and learning.

Format of the Activity Chapters

At the head of each chapter is a list of objectives highlighting its main concepts and features. These objectives are written in instructional terms to help the teacher in evaluating learner progress. The activities chapters open with a discussion of the nature and purpose of the specific activity and then present information regarding rules, equipment, playing field dimensions, organizational setups, and much more. A section called "Suggested Learning Sequence" outlines the teaching progression—beginner to intermediate—that is normally used in most schools. Although this section is highly recommended, the order may be varied to meet program and teacher needs, so long as concepts are properly interrelated and not fragmented.

The "Skills and Techniques" sections are designed for the beginner-to-intermediate levels of skill development (more advanced skills are often covered in selected references). Skill analysis is given in the form of "Learning Cues," while the "Practice Suggestions" offer specific aids to the teacher in formulating drills and planning lessons.

Other features include playing strategies, safety considerations, and terminology associated with the specific activity. A new section has been added to each chapter, where appropriate, called "Modifications for Special Populations," outlining suggestions for modifying skills or activities to meet special needs. At the end of each chapter is a list of selected references, including books, periodicals, and audiovisual materials to supplement the material found in the chapter.

Modifications for Special Populations

A new section has been added to each chapter, where appropriate, outlining suggestions for modifying skills or activities to meet special needs. These modifications are intended for general applications and are not suggested for specific disabilities and/or handicapping conditions. Considerations for adapted physical education require more detail in preparation and implementation and are beyond the scope of this book. The new section is divided into the following three categories:

Orthopedically Impaired—wheelchair users, crutch and cane users, e.g., spinal cord injuries, spina bifida; low mobility, e.g., cerebral palsy, amputations; poor muscular strength and endurance, e.g., muscular dystrophy, obesity.

Mentally Impaired—mild (IQ 53+); moderate (IQ 36–52).

Sensory Impaired—blind and visually impaired with visual acuity ranging from 20/200 (legally blind) to total blindness. Deaf and hard of hearing ranging from slight (27–40 db loss) to profound (91 db+ loss).

The following are some general considerations for modifying activities for special populations:

Balance

1. Keep the student at a low level, e.g., concentrate on wide base and low center of gravity.
2. Provide the student with support devices during ambulation, e.g., guide ropes, broom handles. If assistance is provided by a peer teacher, concentrate on support at the hips to allow freedom of arm swing.
3. Stress good body position with head and trunk as erect as possible.

Agility

1. Promote movement in activities but concentrate on controlled movement. Do not allow the students to move too fast and out of control.
2. Moving forward and backward in a straight line should be accomplished before asking the student to move in a circular path.

Coordination

1. Remember that as the teacher you have control over the size, shape, distance, and color of objects involved in an activity; select them wisely.
2. Accuracy tasks can frustrate certain special pop-

ulations, e.g., athetoid cerebral palsy; keep these tasks to a minimum.
3. Modify striking implements to provide a larger striking surface, e.g., paddles instead of baseball bats.
4. Tether objects to be struck or thrown, to avoid wasted time recovering them. Elastic straps from fabric stores work great for tethering balls to walkers or wheelchairs.
5. Make sure to use safety items, e.g., helmets, where needed.

Planning the Lesson

The following suggestions are offered to assist the instructor, recreational leader, or student teacher in planning a lesson or a unit of instruction.

1. Determine your *goal*. What would you like the learner to achieve at the conclusion of the lesson or unit of instruction?
2. Determine the *population* of your group. What are their ages, sex, characteristics (social, physical, emotional, mental)? What is their previous skill background in the activity or type of activity to be taught? What skills must they possess to begin their lesson?
3. Determine the *content* (skills, knowledge, strategy, etc.) based on the type of population represented.
4. Determine the *lesson* or *unit objectives* based on the lesson or unit content. Unit objectives will be broader whereas the lesson objective will be more specific.
5. Determine in what *sequence* the learning material may be presented most effectively. The "Suggested Learning Sequence" given in each activity of the *Handbook* is a good order to follow; or it can be altered to suit your needs and style of instruction.
6. Determine the *instructional equipment and supplies* (bats, balls, etc.) you will require.
7. Determine whether to supplement the lessons with *audio-visuals,* and select appropriate materials (see Appendix D).
8. Determine the *evaluation* plan for assessing (a) performance skill achievement and (b) mastery of instructional material.

Use of Audio-Visual Aids

Many visual aids are available in the physical activity area; the alert teacher will want to take advantage of these aids to increase teaching effectiveness. Many sporting organizations and professional organizations have produced audio-visual materials for a wide range of physical activities. The sources listed in Appendix D of this *Handbook* should enable any teacher to select appropriate materials. Before using any visual aids, however, you are urged to read the guidelines given at the head of Appendix D. A wise use of audio-visual materials will enrich and improve most instructional programs. The following guidelines are essential to consider as you plan to integrate audio-visual materials with your lesson.

1. Always preview the audio-visual aid before class use in order to become familiar with the material and to make sure it is appropriate for the lesson being taught.
2. Prepare the class in advance by pointing out the features that students should watch for and indicating how the aid will help them in the lesson.
3. After showing the aid, provide an opportunity for class discussion in order to clarify points and to emphasize important parts.
4. It is often advisable to view the film a second time. Some instructors find it helpful to show a film as an introduction to an activity and to rescreen it after students have had an opportunity to practice the activity or particular techniques. There is usually more interest in the second screening because the activity is now more meaningful to the students.
5. Be sure to provide a satisfactory room for viewing projected audio-visual aids. The effectiveness of a motion picture, for example, may be lost if students cannot see the picture easily or hear the commentary.
6. Provide students with the means of evaluating the contribution of the visual aid.

7. Be sure you know how to operate the projection equipment and always have things in readiness when the class arrives.

Coeducational Teaching

With a few exceptions, all activities described in this *Handbook* can be used in a coeducational setting. Specific ways to modify activities and rules in order to play on a coeducational basis are outlined in some of the chapters.

Use of the Appendices

In using this manual, we hope you will not overlook the valuable reference materials contained in the appendices. Appendix A lists sources of official rules by type of activity. Appendix B gives the specifics on how to conduct tournaments. Appendix C shows diagrams of athletic fields and playing courts. Appendix D provides guidelines on the use of audio-visual materials and a list of sources of such materials. Appendix E outlines several national health objectives for the year 2000, as formulated by the U.S. Department of Health and Human Services.

Whether you use the book for administering a program, planning a unit or lesson, directing a recreational activity, or for your own personal use, we hope this 8th edition will meet your needs and bring healthful enjoyment to all.

ACKNOWLEDGMENTS

We are indebted to the following professors and instructors who graciously contributed their knowledge and expertise to this revised edition:

DR. MARVIN GRAY, Ball State University
Historical Aspects of Physical Education

DR. ARNO WITTIG, Ball State University
Psychological Aspects of Physical Education

DR. GALE GEHLSEN, Ball State University
Mechanical Aspects of Physical Education

DR. LEONARD KAMINSKY, Ball State University
Physical Fitness Programs

JOHN WINGFIELD, Ball State University
Swimming

DR. SUNG-JAE PARK, Ball State University
Archery; Team Handball

WILLIAM NICHOLS, Ball State University
Badminton; Wrestling

DEBBIE POWERS, Ball State University
Basketball

SHARON BURGESS-TROXELL, Ball State University
Cycling

TERRY WHITT, Chicago State University
Dance (Folk, Square, Social, Modern)

DR. BARBARA CURCIO, Ball State University
Fencing

PENNY JUSTIN, Ball State University
Gymnastics

DALE SCRIVNOR, Ball State University
Golf

DR. RON DAVIS, Ball State University
Modifications for Special Populations

DR. WARREN VANDER HILL, Ball State University
Angling

KAREN FITZPATRICK, Ball State University
Field Hockey

TERRY HITCHCOCK, Muncie Central High School
Handball and Racquetball

JERRY RUSHTON, Ball State University
Orienteering; Track and Field

DR. MARILYN BUCK, Ball State University
Softball

SCOTT B. PERELMAN, University of Kansas
Tennis

DR. DAVID PEARSON, Ball State University
Weight Training

DR. CHARLES SIMONIAN, Ohio State University
Fencing

We also thank the following people for their valuable assistance:

WILLIAM RICHARDS, Head Tennis Coach, Ball State University, for his assistance on the Tennis chapter.

ANNA SHUNCK, Ball State University, for suggestions on the Handball and Racquetball chapter.

SAM ALFORD, Chairman, Physical Education Department, Chrysler High School, New Castle, Indiana, for use of the weight room and for providing students for photographs.

The high school and college students who gave willingly of their time to pose for photographs.

DONNA RIDER, Institute for Wellness, Ball State University, Muncie, Indiana, for the many hours spent typing and preparing the manuscript.

HILDA TAUBER, Prentice Hall, whose creative genius, sharp eye, and questioning mind helped to organize the eighth edition of the HANDBOOK into a workable form.

MARGARET ANTONINI, Prentice Hall, whose sharp eye helped guide us through the final revisions.

PHYSICAL
EDUCATION
HANDBOOK

1 UNDERSTANDING PHYSICAL EDUCATION

- ▶ *Historical Aspects*
- ▶ *Sociological Aspects*
- ▶ *Mechanical Aspects*
- ▶ *Psychological Aspects*
- ▶ *Objectives and Programs*

NATURE AND PURPOSE

What is physical education? Let's begin by saying what it is *not*. Physical education ("fizz ed" or "p.e." or "gym") does not mean punishing fitness and conditioning exercises ("no pain, no gain"), even at times inflicted as a form of punishment ("Give me 20 push-ups!"). Physical education is not merely free play or recreational time when no instruction need occur, nor is it a non-intellectual activity with no claim to a place in formal education.

Physical education, when planned and taught properly, is "education through the physical." That is, the activity serves as a medium through which a total learning experience takes place. Do you recall the first time you ever got up on water skis, or jogged a mile or two, or first rode a bicycle? If you have been successful at some relatively difficult and strenuous physical feat, what happened to your self-esteem as a result? In all likelihood your achievement created a more positive outlook of yourself. In addition, you may have been encouraged to try other types of activities. Researchers have determined that such experiences improve our total being. In other words, physical activity not only improves our physical health, but it enhances our emotional outlook, and even stimulates our intellectual activity and ability. In short, it improves our "wellness" in that it improves us totally.

Physical education focuses on the teaching of skills, the acquisition of knowledge, and the development of attitudes through movement. Most public

FIGURE 1-1   Some skills provide a lifetime of pleasurable activity.

schools, colleges, and universities recognize the importance of physical education by making it a part of the curriculum. School physical education and wellness programs provide each person with various opportunities—from the assessment of fitness levels and the appropriate activities that will help overcome personal weaknesses to the acquisition of lifetime fitness-type activities. Physical education remains a vital part of the total process of education that utilizes games, sports, aquatics, dance, and other vigorous activities to help the individual acheive the goals of education.

In Chapter 1 we will examine four important aspects of physical education, sport, and recreational activities: historical, sociological, mechanical, and psychological. This material provides the necessary background for understanding physical education as it relates to wellness. At the end of the chapter we outline specific objectives and discuss school programs.

HISTORICAL ASPECTS

History is much more than a description of what happened in the past. One of the best justifications for studying history was given by the British statesman Sir Winston Churchill, who is credited with "the farther backward you can see, the farther forward you can see." By understanding how physical education and sport programs developed, you can more readily comprehend contemporary events and be better able to anticipate new trends in physical education, sport, and wellness. In this chapter the terms "wellness," "physical education," and "sport" will be used frequently and while their meaning is generally related, they do have subtle differences which will be clarified later.

SPORT IN EARLIER CIVILIZATIONS

Primitive Cultures

During primitive times people were forced to engage in vigorous physical activities in order to survive. They hunted and fished for food and clothing and had to be alert against constant danger. For prehistoric people, movement was essential to staying alive. Running was considered an admirable physical trait, and those who were skillful at it were considered valuable members of the group. If some historical accounts are correct, the ability of some runners to cover long distances as couriers or to avoid capture was outstanding by even today's standards.

The Greeks

The first recognized culture in which sport played a significant role was Greece. Greeks saw sports participation, particularly in individual activities, as an important part of a young man's educational experience. The most popular activities consisted of boxing, wrestling, and track (which included the five-event pentathlon consisting of the discus, javelin, long jump, stade race, and wrestling). Track was the most prominent sport, and the 200-meter run or "stade" was probably the best-known event. At the peak of the Greek culture, sport participation was considered to be a noble and worthwhile endeavor, and this philosophy of sport was followed later in other cultures, including the United States.

The Romans

While sport was popular in Rome, spectating was emphasized over individual participation. The violent chariot races and brutal gladiatorial bouts were very popular and were sometimes sponsored by politicians in order to gain favor among the unemployed masses who migrated to Rome during difficult economic periods. The difference in sport philosophies between the Greeks and the Romans provides an interesting contrast. The Greeks believed in individual participation to benefit one's education whereas the Romans used more violent forms of sport to amuse and satisfy spectators. Which philosophy do you believe best depicts that of contemporary American intercollegiate and professional sport? Are we heading for a decline like Rome or do we favor the Greek system of individual participation for educational purposes?

EARLY AMERICAN PHYSICAL EDUCATION AND SPORT

In general, the Pilgrims who came to America discouraged sport and play activities as a waste of time and the work of the devil. The Protestant work ethic held that only hard work would develop the ideals of thriftiness, morality, and purity. In many cases, especially in Colonial New England, people who took part in sports and games, particularly on the Sabbath, were subject to arrest. Most sporting activities were utilitarian in that they served some particular life-giving function. For example, hunting and fishing were survival pursuits; few people, if any, thought of them as sporting or recreational activities. Some recreational sports did exist however, among the most popular being bowling, horse racing, skating, and various forms of ball games. The village tavern was the frequent scene of other less approved activities such as card playing, darts, and various games of chance, all of which were usually associated with gambling.

EARLY GYMNASTICS PROGRAMS

The Battle of the Systems

The first organized physical education programs that were introduced into American schools following the Civil War emphasized various culturally based gymnastics systems. These programs, which reflected the nationalistic philosophies of their native homelands, featured formal movement (sometimes referred to as "formal gymnastics") performed on various types of gymnastics equipment. Among the best known was the German system, or "heavy gymnastics," which stressed exercise routines on heavy nonmovable equipment performed with a background of patriotic music. Another popular form of exercise was the Swedish system, known as "light gymnastics," which emphasized graceful routines and more rhythmic activities sometimes performed with a lilting piano accompaniment.

As these programs gained prominence in the schools, some educators began to question the appropriateness of play-type activities in an educational setting. Critics insisted that schools were a place for the serious pursuit of scholarly activities such as mathematics, the sciences, languages, and religion. Those who favored the gymnastics programs in the schools maintained it was necessary for urban youngsters to exercise since they were faced with growing leisure time on their hands. Furthermore, they contended that it served as a way for young men to reduce their surplus energy and help keep them out of trouble. This philosophical debate over the appropriateness of physical activity in the schools and which gymnastics system could best achieve the most desirable results became known as the "Battle of the Systems."

Gradually the gymnastics systems faded in popularity due to their structured nature which lacked spontaneity and were replaced by an informal system of sports and games based loosely on the English system (a philosophical view that sports participation by amateur athletes has inherent educational benefits), but more closely associated with our natural instinct for play and movement. This concept was generally referred to as the "new physical education" and was promoted by leaders as an alternative based on acceptable educational objectives. As a result of the new movement, curricular offerings in physical education now began to include lifetime fitness and recreational pursuits as well as sport activities. Gradually, the term "physical education" began to refer to planned public school programs related to the development of motor skills, physical fitness, social attributes, and knowledge through instruction in various games, sports, and dance activities.

DEVELOPMENT OF AMATEUR AND COLLEGIATE SPORTS

During the 19th century, participation in amateur sport was limited primarily to the members of well-to-do families who belonged to the exclusive country clubs generally located along the East Coast. Sports such as tennis, golf, swimming, cricket, and track were most popular. Young men usually competed because it was believed this would help them become "gentlemen" and contribute to developing the necessary physical and social skills for future success. Young women occasionally took part in some of the less vigorous sports because it was feared that strenuous participation might result in an injury, particularly to the reproductive organs. Furthermore, women who participated in sports were expected to maintain their femininity at all times in order to make themselves more attractive to an eligible gentleman. Typically, formally-dressed women participated passively in sports such as archery, croquet, and tennis doubles, with the emphasis on the activity's social aspects. As the sons and daughters of the well-to-do left home to attend college, they took with them their desire to participate in various sports. Typically, during the latter part of the 19th century, universities were segregated by gender. At the men's universities, sports such as baseball, football, and later basketball, began to emerge where they rapidly became the focal point of many programs. Football aroused the most controversy due to the number of injuries and deaths that occurred from its brutal style of play. At the women's colleges, female physical educators maintained strict control over the growth of women's sports with activities being limited to field or sport days where the focus was on the development of social skills through modest participation in selected sports and games.

Equal Opportunities for Women

The gender separation pattern generally persisted until the 1960's, when changed societal norms gradually led to acceptance of girls and women into competitive sports. With this came the development of regulatory groups such as the Association of Intercollegiate Athletics for Women (AIAW), which supported athletic competition for women. Later, the passage of Title IX of the 1972 Educational Amendments Act by the federal government mandated that by 1975, all institutions of higher education receiving federal funding had to provide programs where females could receive an equal physical education and athletic participation opportunities. This law resulted in sweeping changes since it held that women could not be excluded from physical education or athletic programs on the basis of gender. Since that time, the upsurge of female participation in sport has been tremendous and, with the demise of the

AIAW, the National Collegiate Athletic Association (NCAA) became the major governing body for women's intercollegiate athletics. In most locales, female students enjoy the same competitive and participation rights and privileges as do the male students. There is no verifiable scientific evidence that the previously held fears have made women athletes more masculine, damaged their reproductive systems, or otherwise had any negative physiological or psychological effects on them. This has essentially put to rest the original notion that women athletes were too frail to stand the rigors of sport competition. Perhaps the major form of gender discrimination today is the number of males coaching women's teams and male athletic directors in influential leadership positions associated with women's athletic programs.

Opportunities for Handicapped Youth

A second significant historical event occurred in 1975, with the passage of the Education for All Handicapped Children Act (Public Law 94–142). This law gave every handicapped child the opportunity to be integrated into the regular physical education program, whenever appropriate. Programs had to be modified to meet the needs of the handicapped students who were now being "mainstreamed" into the regular classes. In effect, this law requires that all teachers must be prepared to work with handicapped youngsters and that virtually no one should be denied an opportunity to participate in a physical education or sports program.

FUTURE TRENDS

As we near the 21st century, it is clear that sport and recreational pursuits, and particularly fitness-wellness activities, will maintain their popularity. We will continue to see participation in a broader range of recreational activities such as hiking, backpacking, cross-country skiing, and variations of aquatic sports. And, in spite of fluctuations in the supply and price of gas, participation in a variety of motorized sports will continue. The love of motor vehicles remains strong, and Americans will be reluctant to give up motor sports entirely.

Further technological sophistication has resulted in a form of video sports in which the sights and sounds are simulated, yet remarkably realistic, as the player experiences such thrills as landing a jet on an aircraft carrier, piloting a spaceship, or driving a race car. Other forms of effect include flying a stunt plane, riding a roller coaster, and taking a submarine ride. According to the promoters, the experience virtually eliminates the possibilities of injury, death, or potential lawsuit. The drawback to such games is that they are passive, nonvigorous forms of diversion offering practically no fitness or wellness benefits. Nevertheless, they appear to be a part of the future.

Satellite communications systems will continue to develop the capacity for international sport audiences. Baseball and basketball are already played throughout much of the world, and soccer continues its rapid growth in the United States. Longer sport seasons will be the norm as new professional franchises will locate in mild climates or play in domed stadiums. More and more roofed stadiums will have retractable domes which can be opened when the weather permits. A new variety of natural grass has been developed which will grow in domed facilities and should be an advantage in reducing the incidence of turf-related injuries.

Furthermore, we can look for true world championships, due to professional team sponsorships moving away from the geographical concept and toward the multi-national corporation. Many professional teams will be located throughout the European and American continents as well as in some of the Pacific rim countries. How about a World Series played between the IBM Yankees and the Tokyo Giants? Or the Super Bowl being decided between the Mexico City Aztecs and the Royal Dutch Shell Rams? But perhaps by the time we enter the 21st Century, the World Series and the Super Bowl will have waned in popularity. Soccer is expected to continue its growth due to the international influence in this country. Furthermore, it is a relatively inexpensive, injury-free sport in which one of any physical size may participate.

SUMMARY

We have seen that sport participation was originally necessary for survival. Some countries began to use formalized gymnastics systems to promote nationalistic support. Later physical education and sport grew in popularity as a medium through which education might occur. While this viewpoint has been disputed, the "new physical education" concept began to grow in popularity since it reflected peoples' natural desire to participate in sport, games, and dance. More recently, federal laws mandated that women and the handicapped could not be denied their right to participate in physical education classes. The future will see technological development and international expansion being influential in the growth of physical education and sport as we move into the 21st century.

SELECTED REFERENCES

Betts, J.R. *America's Sporting Heritage: 1850–1950.* Reading, MA: Addison-Wesley Publishing Co., 1974.

Hackensmith, C.W. *History of Physical Education and Sport.* New York: Harper & Row, Publishers, 1966.

Rader, Benjamin G. *American Sports.* Englewood Cliffs, NJ: Prentice Hall, 1990.

Zeigler, E.F. *History of Physical Education and Sport.* Englewood Cliffs, NJ: Prentice Hall, 1979.

SOCIOLOGICAL ASPECTS

Sport is an important part of America's culture. It creates newspaper headlines, holds our attention on television, produces countless millions of dollars annually, and even influences international relations. Moreover, millions of people of all ages and abilities participate in a vast array of recreational and sport activities. Sport sociologists refer to this as the pervasiveness of sport. This means we can rarely escape participating, watching, talking or reading about sport in our society. Because sport permeates virtually every aspect of our culture, whether social, political, legal, economic, or educational, it is only natural that we should examine more closely selected parts of this phenomenon that is so influential in many lives.

Sport events reflect many of the same characteristics we observe in our daily lives and may thus be described as a microcosm of society. For example, both sport and society are concerned with material things such as salaries and benefits. And if discrimination toward women and minorities exists in sport, it exists also in society. The same may be said of unhealthy forms of competition, unequal distribution of power (such as the coach or leader having complete control over a team or a group of workers), incidences of violence, and so on.

AFRICAN AMERICANS IN SPORTS

The traditional American view has been that sport was one of the few areas where racial discrimination did not exist. Success in sports was generally believed to be based on one's athletic performance and not on ethnic background or socio-economic status. Indeed the relatively low percentage of black or African Americans in this country (12 to 14 percent) contrasts sharply with the disproportionately higher percentage of black athletes found in intercollegiate and professional basketball and football, and to some extent, baseball.

Despite the impressive number of participants, however, some scholars maintain that the African Americans' sport involvement is not free from racial prejudice. Perhaps the most outspoken of this group

is Dr. Harry Edwards, sociologist at the University of California, Berkeley. He is among those who argues that high school and collegiate African American athletes virtually ignore their educational development and devote countless hours to honing their athletic skills. Many of those athletes believe this will lead to a college athletic scholarship, which in turn, will result in a multi-million dollar professional contract with a hero status and lifelong financial security. The fact is that a pitifully small number attain success because the competition is fierce. Furthermore, the possibility of a career-ending injury or just plain bad luck can dash one's hopes in an instant. All too soon the vast majority find themselves back where they started with little education or marketable skills. Sports fans do not see the thousands of shattered dreams and broken hearts of the cast-off athletes whom Edwards refers to as "more bodies under the bridge." Spectators see only those who are giving "high fives" and shouting "Hi Mom!" in front of the TV camera after having just scored the winning touchdown. The idea that sport serves as a way to riches is a myth, for only a select few make it in a typically brief career.

While some progress is being made by athletic governing agencies, academic abuse persists at the public school and collegiate levels because athletes are sometimes encouraged to enroll in carefully selected courses solely in order to keep them eligible. Clearly, a careful balance must be maintained in order to develop marketable skills with a solid educational background for those high school and collegiate athletes who see themselves as future stars.

INTERNATIONAL SPORTS

As world travel becomes more common and international communication systems become more advanced, Americans are getting increased first-hand information about sports from other countries. We tend to think that the Super Bowl and World Series are major international events. While they may be growing in international popularity, they pale in comparison with the global attention of the World Cup soccer matches or the nearly month-long Tour de France cycling race, considered by many to be the world's most grueling athletic event.

In Canada and the Scandinavian countries hockey, skiing, and ice skating are very popular. In the Latin American countries soccer and baseball capture a great deal of attention. Some of the Far Eastern countries, such as Thailand, India, and Malaysia, consider badminton a major sport, second only to soccer. Volleyball is promoted widely in Russia as well as in China and Japan. Baseball is the Japanese national sport. In China, table tennis and basketball are among the most popular activities. In

Mexico and Spain, bullfighting and jai alai are national pastimes. As we become more aware of the traditions and customs of other lands, we better understand and appreciate how important a role sport plays throughout the world.

The Olympic Games

Among the widely-known international competitions are the Asian Games, the Pan American Games, the British Empire and Commonwealth Games, the World Maccabee Games, and the World University Games. But the oldest and most popular are the Olympic Games, first held in 776 B.C. at Olympia, Greece. They probably occurred every four years thereafter until A.D. 394 when the Roman Christian emperor Theodosius abolished the Games as sinful because they were traditionally held in honor of the Greek pagan gods.

The Modern Games were revived in 1896 by the Frenchman Baron Pierre de Coubertin, who believed they could serve as an instrument for peace and goodwill. It was his desire that the Modern Olympics be conducted in a spirit of fair play, free of political interference, and honor the achievements of athletes from around the world.

In many respects de Coubertin's ideals have not been realized, for the Olympic Games have been embroiled with many problems. Political disputes, some of which have resulted in boycotts, terrorist attacks, and the subsequent loss of life have marred the Games. There have also been disagreements over the amateur status of the athletes. And the Olympic Games have become so expensive to sponsor that many countries can no longer consider hosting the event.

Two major changes have occurred since the 1984 Games in Los Angeles which may help diffuse some of the problems. The first is the concept of corporate sponsorship, introduced at the 1984 Games, whereby various companies agreed to underwrite certain expenses. For example, one such company, McDonald's Restaurants, supported the construction of the aquatic facility, and hundreds of other companies made financial contributions in return for the privilege of having their products labeled "The Official Olympic . . . ."

A second change involves the question of amateur status. Historically, Olympic athletic eligibility held strictly to the amateur code, but gradually those standards have been relaxed and professional athletes have been allowed to participate. Currently, any amateur or professional athlete is eligible to participate in the Olympic Games. Whether these changes will work toward the potential promise of promoting international goodwill and understanding remains to be seen.

THE NEED FOR RECREATION

In the past few years there has been a growing awareness of the social implications of wellness, physical fitness, and sport activities. A nation's attitude toward its recreational and leisure time pursuits reveals a great deal about its lifestyle and cultural patterns. The type of sports that are popular reflect many socially related factors such as tradition, religious beliefs, geographical location, and economic status. Earlier we discussed how recreational pursuits were discouraged, but as time passed educational leaders began to call attention to the benefits of recreation and sport participation. Both the medical and physical education professions cited many of the physiological benefits of regular exercise. Social scientists and psychologists pointed out the advantages of acceptable leisure time pursuits from the standpoint of social development and psychological enhancement. And, contrary to the earlier belief, there was a gradual acceptance that meaningful leisure time activity could actually improve one's working efficiency.

Changing economic conditions and lifestyles further supported the concept that leisure time activity could be beneficial. As our society shifted from an agricultural to a more urban setting, manual outdoor farm work gave way to the indoor factory as-

FIGURE 1-2   Cross-country skiing provides a sharp test of endurance.

sembly line and sedentary office jobs. Technology took over, and jobs became routine and monotonous with little chance for self-expression. As the growing cities became more crowded, a major concern was the fatigue, tension, and stress, which undermined the physical and mental health of many citizens. Gradually, however, along with improved working conditions and salaries, people began to see the importance of recreational pursuits as a way to relax and unwind, and to restore themselves physically, mentally, and emotionally.

As various technological improvements—such as computers—make much of our work faster and more efficient, the work day and work week are shrinking. In some parts of the country, the four-day, forty-hour work week is standard. The mid-week, half-day or one-day break and extended vacations are also becoming more common. While we may seem busier than ever, most people are able to complete their routine work tasks much faster. Whether or not we actually have more leisure time is open to dispute among recreation and play scholars. Perhaps a more serious question is the extent to which we can appropriately use what leisure time we have. Some social scientists and philosophers believe that the way in which we use our time is the final test of a civilization. Since we are living longer than ever, it is important now to develop the habit of participating in fulfilling leisure-time activities so you can continue to enjoy them later in life.

While some activities are more vigorous than others, virtually any form of regular moderate forms of exercise can be beneficial. The benefits of recreational activities go beyond the purely physical. Even if your work is satisfying, you cannot perform at an efficient level indefinitely. Recreation offers a needed change from the work routine, an opportunity to relax, to be uplifted, to be "re-created," so you can return to work physically and mentally restored. Recreation makes a major contribution to our physical, psychological, and mental stability that is greatly needed today.

Sport and Television

No discussion on sport sociology would be complete without mentioning the influence of television on the popularity of sports in our culture. More than any other form of communication, television has been responsible for bringing sports into our homes, serving both as a form of entertainment and instruction. Recently, not only has cable television become an important factor in sports broadcasting, but innovations such as the instant replay, slow motion, reverse angle, and "chalk board" explanations, enhance popularity among viewers. Some sports have undergone some rule modifications (tennis tie-breaks, moving the hash marks in football, sudden death, and stroke scoring in golf), in order to accommodate the viewing public. Starting times, no matter how inconvenient for the athletes or the spectators at the contest, are established to attract the highest possible television viewing audience.

Some sports by their very nature do not fare well as a televised activity. The hockey puck is difficult to see on television and its continuous action makes it difficult to air commercials; consequently, the sport is more difficult to sell to prospective sponsors. Baseball does not lend itself well to telecasting due to its large playing area, and golf, skiing, and some motorized sports are among those sports that can suffer because the viewer cannot get a realistic perception of the activity. There are some signs that the viewing public has been oversaturated with televised professional football and that sport may have seen its best years. Professional basketball appears to have a bright future and is naturally suited to television with its relatively confined playing area and natural breaks for commercials. Likewise, soccer faces a bright future, but its non-stop action is not suitable for the necessary commercial breaks in television.

While sports on television may promote an inactive lifestyle, there are signs that we are moving in the direction of active participation. Each year more people are taking part in such sport and recreational activities as fitness walking, swimming, racquetball, tennis, golf, skiing, camping, and backpacking, to mention just a few. Both trends seem to be operating simultaneously—toward the spectating, inactive lifestyle on one hand and toward the participating, active lifestyle on the other. While something may be gained from watching someone else perform an activity (such as learning more about the game and appreciating the athlete's skill level), it is generally agreed that active participation offers more total benefits. One of the important ideas you can learn is that an active lifestyle can return healthful benefits many times over.

WELLNESS

Thus far in this chapter, the term "wellness" has been used in conjunction with physical education, sport, and recreation. More than any other fitness-related term, wellness is "in" for the '90's. Most authorities agree that the current interest in fitness is not a fad. Some call it a fitness renaissance . . . a re-birth or renewal of fitness. But the concept goes beyond commonly accepted views of fitness and health. Historically, fitness occasionally referred to "getting back into shape" after neglecting one's body. And health was traditionally viewed merely as the absence of disease. In other words, if you were not sick, you were healthy. In order to stay healthy, people all too often expected everything of their doctor and virtually nothing of themselves.

Research done by health educators and members of allied medical professions have amassed a considerable amount of scientific evidence that this philosophy is no longer acceptable. Wellness refers to a proactive (taking action) view of health in which one strives to develop a total lifestyle that results in a positive physical, mental, emotional, social, spiritual, and occupational state of being. The main feature of wellness is that to achieve it, you must work toward it—it will not just happen. In the wellness concept, you take responsibility for your personal well-being by pursuing a dynamic course of action to alter your lifestyle. The wellness philosophy refers to your entire being—designated as holistic—and all parts of that being are parallel and interrelated. This means we are concerned not only about exercise and fitness, but smoking, alcohol and drug usage, stress control, eating habits, and safety. Living a wellness lifestyle does require an effort, but it can be a joyous effort!

FUTURE SOCIOLOGICAL SPORT TRENDS

All socially-related factors point to the idea that sport will also constitute an important part of our lifestyles. Furthermore, the problems with sport will also constitute a microcosm of society's problems. Slowly, as the African American's social status improves, and as more professions become available, the focus on athletics as "a way out" will become a less desirable goal. The Latin American will likely succeed the African American in focusing on athletic competition with the sports of choice being soccer, baseball, basketball, and boxing. This will have an important positive impact on soccer growth in this country.

International sport will continue its prominence, and more professional and collegiate teams will enter this level of competition. The Olympic Games will maintain its role as the most popular form of international competition. Ironically the Olympics will continue to be plagued with political problems for that very reason. Those wishing to make a political statement will take advantage of that prominence and attempt to use the Olympic forum to enlist support for their causes.

The benefits of recreational activity will continue to be pointed out despite the fact that televised sports may continue to serve as an alluring deterrent to the active lifestyle. The wellness concept will become the primary focus of the '90's.

SUMMARY

We have pointed out how sport is pervasive and represents a microcosm of society. Pervasiveness refers to the notion that sport is an important aspect in all phases of our culture. Microcosm refers to the fact that within sport there exists similar types of societal issues. While the African American athlete is quite prominent in selected sports, this does not necessarily indicate that sport is free from discrimination. It would appear that the Latin American will become the main minority group involved in sport participation. International sport will increase in popularity and will continue to be a setting for political dispute. The popularity of televised sport will continue, although some sports may decline in popularity. While televised sports may serve as a deterrent to an active lifestyle, it is important that we learn fulfilling recreational activities for benefit to our total health.

SELECTED REFERENCES

Black Athletic Superiority: Fact or Fiction? Program on NBC Television, New York, NY, April, 1989.

Coakley, J. *Sport in Society: Issues and Controversies.* St. Louis: Times Mirror/Mosby Co., 1990.

Curry, T.J. and Jiobu, R.M. *Sports, a Social Perspective.* Englewood Cliffs, NJ: Prentice Hall, 1984.

de Grazia, S. *Of Time, Work and Leisure.* New York: Twentieth Century Fund, 1962.

Edwards, H. *Speech on Sport and Race.* DePauw University, Greencastle, IN, 1988.

Eitzen, D.S. and Sage, G.H. *Sociology of North American Sport.* Dubuque, IA: Wm. C. Brown Publishers, 1986.

Smith, R.A. *Sports and Freedom: The Rise of Big-Time College Athletics.* Oxford: Oxford University Press, 1988.

MECHANICAL ASPECTS

This section examines selected positions and movements found in everyday and sport activities such as standing, sitting, walking, lifting, carrying, pulling, pushing, running, jumping, throwing, catching, and striking. Discussion will focus on the mechanical aspects related to basic movement skills. The presentation is divided into two sections: the first part deals with static and semistatic activities for which balance considerations are the main concern; the second part describes dynamic activities which are dependent on force considerations.

BALANCE CONSIDERATIONS

Basic to all activity, both ordinary and sports-related, is an understanding of how the body maintains a balanced position. The degree of stability or balance a body possesses depends upon several factors including: (a) the area of the base of support, (b) the height of the center of gravity, and (c) the proximity of the center of gravity within the supporting base.

A balanced position is defined as a position wherein the center of gravity is placed over the support base. The center of gravity is the point around which the body balances in all directions. The base of support includes not only the feet in contact with the ground but also the area between the feet. If the center of gravity is placed outside the supporting base, balance is destroyed and downward motion results. Balance can be regained by reestablishing the support under the center of gravity. Locomotion, therefore, is accomplished by a continuous process of placing the center of gravity outside the base, thus losing balance and then regaining balance by placing the foot under the center of gravity.

The area of the base of support is an important stability factor. As the area of the base increases, balance increases. When standing in a side stride position, one has a greater degree of balance than in the feet together position. A side stride position increases balance in a lateral direction; a forward stride position increases balance in an anterior-posterior direction.

The degree of balance is also influenced by the height of the center of gravity: a low center of gravity increases balance, and a high center of gravity decreases balance. In athletic situations, an increase in balance is often accomplished by bending the knees to lower the height of the center of gravity.

If the center of gravity falls over the middle of the supporting base, equal balance on all sides of the body is established. However, if the center of gravity is placed over the back edge of the base, the degree of balance increases toward the front of the body and

decreases toward the back edge of the supporting base. In other words, as the horizontal distance from the center of gravity to the front edge of the support increases, balance increases. To stop quickly and maintain balance, the center of gravity should be moved to the back edge of the supporting base. To move quickly in the forward direction, the center of gravity should be placed toward the front edge of the base. This allows the balance to be destroyed very quickly because the center of gravity only has to be moved a short distance to be outside the supporting base.

Standing

Standing posture varies among individuals and is affected by such factors as health (including mental attitude), body build, and occupation. Although there is no single description of good standing posture, proper body alignment is an essential element. The body is not one solid mass, but is composed of a series of segments. Each segment is connected to the next segment by joints which are held together by muscle tendons and ligaments. If the segments of the trunk are stacked so that the line of gravity passes directly through the center of each segment, less stress will be placed upon the muscles and ligaments. There is little stress on the muscles and ligaments because the segments are perfectly balanced one over the other. Therefore, a good standing position is one in which each body segment is centered over the segment immediately below it (see Figure 1-3).

In the standing position with perfect alignment, a straight line should pass through the ear lobe,

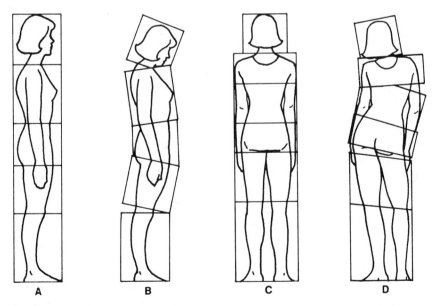

| A | B | C | D |

FIGURE 1-3   In (A) and (C) each segment is balanced above the segment below. In (B) and (D) the alignment is unbalanced.

center of shoulder joint, slightly behind the hip joint-ing, slightly in front of the center of the knee joint and in front of the ankle joint. The total picture of the best standing posture shows shallow curves of the upper and lower back, a slight tilt forward-upward of the pelvis to help decrease the curve of the lower back, the head back and the chin comfortably down, the abdominal wall flattened, the chest lifted and the shoulders relaxed and back. This posture is not only mechanically sound but also attractive in appearance.

In good standing position, the feet are usually placed parallel, four to six inches apart. Although some authorities consider a toeing-out position to be normal, those who advocate the parallel position appear to have sounder reasons. In this latter position, the base is firm in both forward-backward and lateral directions as compared with the weaker triangular foot position (smaller base) resulting from the toeing-out position. The parallel foot position also places less strain on the leg muscles, and the body weight can be transferred along the entire longitudinal arch of the foot.

Sitting

On the average, individuals spend over 60 percent of their waking hours in a sitting position. As in the standing position, body alignment and balance are the two essential considerations in sitting and in the act of getting into and out of a chair.

In preparing to sit down, stand near and in front of the chair. This is necessary so that in the act of sitting, the trunk and upper body will move in an almost erect position with the leg muscles controlling the action. As the body is lowered, the trunk should bend slightly forward from the hip joint. This will keep the center of gravity over the supporting base. The body weight should first be placed on the front edge of the chair, thus establishing a new base of support, and then pushed back in the seat (chair).

When sitting on a straight chair, full use should be made of the chair seat and the chair lower back for support. Sit with the buttocks well back into the seat with the body against the back of the chair. The upper torso should rest slightly against the upper back of the chair. Good body segment alignment, as in standing, is the major criteria for sitting.

To get up from the chair, reverse the order for sitting down. Place one leg in front of the other, slide forward, bend the trunk forward from the hips. When the center of gravity is over the feet, lift the body upward.

Lifting and Carrying

Considerations of balance and body alignment also apply in lifting and carrying. Keeping an aligned position will avoid strain and stress on muscles and joints.

When lifting an object from below, stand close to it, place one foot slightly in front of the other, keeping the back straight, the ankles, knees and hips flexed. In this position the entire body remains over the center of the supporting base. To straighten up, the strong leg muscles (not the weak back muscles) are used to lift the body and object to the erect position.

During lifting, the weight of the object alters the location of the body's center of gravity. The object is momentarily a part of the body and tends to move the body's center of gravity in the direction of the object. Therefore, a wider supporting base is required.

A weight carried on one side of the body should be carried close to the body with only a slight shift of the center of gravity. If the weight must be carried away from the body, raising the arm on the opposite side will move the center of gravity back toward the middle of the base. A weight carried in front of the body necessitates a backward shift of the center of gravity. The shift should be only enough to keep the center of gravity over the base. The most economical way to carry a load is on top of the head, directly in line with the body.

Pushing and Pulling

Many pushing and pulling tasks are not strenuous, but several involve the application of considerable force and make economy of effort and avoidance of strain prime considerations. The more nearly the body segments are aligned to apply the force of either pushing or pulling and the better the base over which the body moves, the easier the task. The height and weight of the object to be pushed or pulled determine the amount the body's center of gravity must be lowered. To push a heavy object, the hands should be placed in line with the object's center of gravity. The body should be in line with the arms. If the object tends to tip, the position of the hands must be lowered.

In pulling, the body should be inclined in the direction of motion. In this position the body exerts its force most economically by using the strong leg muscles. The force should be applied as nearly as possible in the direction of the desired movement. Whenever the force is applied at an angle to the line of movement, only the component of the force in the direction of movement is effective in accomplishing the desired result.

FORCE CONSIDERATIONS

All locomotor tasks (running, jumping, skipping, etc.) propel the body by applying a force against the ground. The force that actually moves the body is a reaction force (ground reaction force) which is reacting to the muscular force applied to the ground in accordance with Newton's Third Law: for every action there is an equal and opposite reaction. The greater the force pushing against the ground, the greater will be the reaction force pushing the body forward. Therefore, the key to increasing the vertical ground reaction force and thus increasing the speed of movement is the development of explosive leg movements. Explosive leg movements provide the body with a positive acceleration. This positive acceleration is directly proportional to increased ground reaction forces (Newton's Second Law).

The direction in which the force is applied is another factor that contributes to speed and efficiency of locomotion. In almost all locomotor tasks (except some forms of hopping and jumping), the muscular force is applied to the ground in a backward-downward direction; the reaction force results then in a forward and upward direction. The upward (vertical) component is effective in lifting and supporting the body against the pull of gravity; the forward (horizontal) force component results in the forward movement of the body. If the body can apply only a limited amount of force and if the force is exerted in two directions, then it is better to divide the force unequally, putting more force in the desired direction. In running and walking, where the vertical force is greater than the horizontal, the body appears to bounce upward with each step. A greater horizontal force provides more speed in the horizontal direction, giving the motion an appearance of smoothness. An increase in the forward lean allows the body to pull more backward than upward, thus increasing the horizontal force component.

In some locomotor activities (walking, skipping, galloping, and sliding), the forward foot strikes the ground well ahead of the body's center of gravity. This action exerts a backward and upward reaction force against the body. The backward component of this force provides a resisting action to the body's forward momentum and makes it possible to stop the forward progress. This retarding force component remains in action to a lessening degree until the foot is directly under the center of gravity. From this point until the foot leaves the ground, the propelling forward-upward reaction force is invoked.

Friction, a force which opposes motion, tends to influence the ground reaction force. In order to move the body forward, there must be sufficient friction between the foot and the ground to invoke the ground reaction force. Everyone knows that it is easier to walk or run on a hard, solid surface than on a slippery surface or on a surface which gives. In the latter situation, the foot slides backward against the surface or the surface moves, thereby reducing the ground reaction force. That is why rubber-soled shoes or cleats are used in athletics, to provide adequate friction, thereby assuring the best possible ground reaction force.

FIGURE 1-4   (A) Backward component or pushing force, (B) downward component of pushing force, (C) forward component of reaction force, (D) upward component of reaction force.

Walking

Walking is the process of locomotion in which the body weight is transferred from one forward swinging leg and foot to the other. It differs from other locomotor tasks in that at no time is there lack of contact with the floor. The outstanding characteristic of the walk is the period of double support. For clarity the walk will be described in terms of leg action and arm swing.

Leg Action.   From the double support position with one leg in front of the other, the back leg moves backward until it breaks contact with the ground. Then the knee and the hip begin to bend, starting the forward swing of the leg. The leg moves in the shape of an arc more or less. When the approximate midpoint of the arc is reached, there is more flexion of the knee and hip to permit clearance from the ground. The leg is then extended and the heel contacts the floor. As the heel of the swinging leg touches the floor, the leg extends; the body then shifts forward, and the cycle is repeated.

In ideal foot placement the toes are pointed straight ahead. This provides the best possible position to apply force in a direction opposite the desired movement. A toeing-in or a toeing-out position not only places undue stress on the ankle and knee joints but also is less efficient because the force is applied at an angle to the foot.

Arm Swing.   In walking, the arms hang relaxed at the sides and swing forward and backward in opposition to the leg movement. This oppositional action occurs in all movements and is controlled at the reflex level of the nervous system. It is possible to interfere with this reflex through conscious control of movement. However, it is not desirable to do so because this oppositional action of the arms and shoulder girdle counterbalance the rotation of the hips, and the resultant forces are applied straight ahead.

In efficient walking, the heel should first contact the ground (toes pointed straight ahead), the body weight should be transferred to the outer border of the foot and then the ball, followed by a push off from the toes. Foot placement is considered best when the inner border of each foot falls closely (within one to two inches) along an imaginary line. Care should be taken not to cross this line in a weaving motion.

In summary, a natural walk is one in which the arms and legs swing easily although the length of the stride and the frequency of steps taken will vary with the individual. The essential factors causing this variation are the individual's height, particularly the leg length, and speed of walking. An increase in walking speed is accomplished by either an increase in the stride length (distance covered per stride) or an increase in the frequency of steps or both. In most people the stride length is increased until a given acceleration, at which time stride length is decreased and the stride frequency increases.

There should be little up and down bouncing movement of the body caused by the vertical force component. Increased walking speed is also accompanied by an increased body inclination. Horizontal movement is facilitated by this position because (a) the body is more in line with the driving leg, (b) the center of gravity is shifted forward to the front edge of the supporting base and gravity is used to assist in overcoming the body's inertia, and (c) the stride length is increased from the center of gravity to the release.

Running

Running, like walking, is a locomotor task in which the body weight is transferred from one forward swinging foot to the other. Running differs from walking, however, in that there is a short period of non-support (no contact with the ground), whereas in walking there is always contact with the ground. Running is generally divided into three phases: (a) recovery phase, (b) support phase, and (c) driving phase.

The recovery phase starts the instant the rear or driving leg leaves the ground and ends when the same leg has moved forward and again contacts the ground beneath the individual's center of gravity. As the foot leaves the ground (the beginning of the recovery phase), the hip begins its forward movement and the lower leg folds up toward the upper leg. As the speed of running increases, there is a greater tendency for the heel to kick up toward the buttock. This kick-up action is not a fault as it was once thought. The kick-up shortens the lever of the leg and permits the swinging leg a smaller moment of inertia. The advantage of the small moment of inertia is that it can be moved very quickly without a great deal of muscular force.

As the leg continues forward in the recovery phase, the height to which the knee is lifted depends upon the running speed. The lift is highest in sprinting and lowest in jogging. The forward swinging leg reaches its highest point as the rear leg completes its full extension. After reaching the limit of its forward swing, the recovery leg (front leg) reverses its direction and moves the foot first forward and then downward. The recovery phase is completed as the foot strikes the ground. Several factors must be considered in the foot striking. First the foot should be placed under the center of gravity and moving backward at moment of contact. This positioning of the foot enables upward and forward ground reaction forces to be invoked. Overstriding is characterized by the foot contacting the ground in front of the center of gravity and by the forward movement of the foot at contact. The foot should be moving backward at the time of contact in order to invoke the forward ground reaction force. The contact of the foot in front of the center of gravity tends to create a backward driving force or blocking action which will determine the running momentum.

The support phase of running begins with the landing of the forward foot and ends when the center of gravity passes in front of the supporting foot. As the foot contacts the ground, the knee bends to absorb the shock of landing which is the first function of the support phase. The second function of the support phase is to arrest the body against the force of gravity. The final function of this phase is to move the body to a position for an effective driving phase.

The driving phase begins as the supporting phase ends—as the foot leaves the ground. In this phase, the body is propelled forward by exerting muscular leg force against the ground and behind the center of gravity. As the body progresses forward, the heel is lifted, the knee extends, and finally the ankle and toe extend well behind the body. Failure to obtain complete extension of the driving leg is a very common characteristic of the poor runner.

Arms. In running, the upper body (shoulders and arms) moves in opposition to the leg action in order to balance the rotation effect of the leg swing on the trunk. The upper arms move relatively straight backward and forward. However, the lower arms move in a slight cross body direction in front but do not cross an imaginary vertical plane bisecting the body into right and left halves.

In sprinting, the elbows tend to be bent at an angle of approximately 90 degrees. This angle increases as the hand swings in front of the body and decreases as the hand passes the hip to the rear. The smaller moment of inertia (small lever arm) allows the arms to be moved very rapidly. The amount of bend in the arms decreases as the running speed decreases. The distance that the arms are carried away from the side of the body (lateral distance) seems to be dependent on the width of the hips. The heavier the hips in relation to the arms, the farther from the body the arms must be carried. The hands are usually carried in a relaxed, cupped position.

Body Lean. When the rate of acceleration of a runner is the greatest, the forward lean of the trunk is the greatest. Thus a sprinter has a tremendous lean at the start of a race. From the instant the sprinter starts to reach top speed, the rate of acceleration is gradually diminished and the forward lean becomes less and less. The body lean at a uniform rate of speed is nearly erect. This slight lean is necessary in order to maintain balance; i.e., to keep the body from rotation or falling forward.

Stride Length-Stride Frequency. The speed at which a runner moves depends upon two factors: (a) the stride length and (b) the stride frequency. The stride length is the horizontal distance translated from the toe of one foot to the toe of the other foot. The frequency is the number of strides taken per unit of time. If a runner has a stride length of 2 meters per stride and a frequency of 3 strides per second, the running speed (distance per time) equals 6 meters per second. Any increase or decrease of these two elements will cause a corresponding change in the running speed. Biomechanics research over the past decade indicates that stride length is the major running speed factor at speeds from 3 to 6 m/s. At running speeds from 6 m/s to 11 m/s, stride length levels off and stride frequency becomes the important speed factor. The skilled runner has the ability to produce larger forces against the ground in a short period of time. Explosive leg strength is needed to produce large forces in a short period of time.

Jumping, Hopping, Leaping

The jump, hop, or leap are all forms of locomotion which involve projecting the body into the air. The hop is defined as any movement involving a takeoff and landing on the same foot. In the leap, there is a takeoff from one foot and a landing on the other foot. For the jump, the takeoff is from one foot or both feet, and the landing is on both feet simultaneously. Many sports skills involve a form of jumping, hopping, and/or leaping.

The essential factors to be considered in jumping, hopping, and leaping are: (a) initial force, (b) angle of takeoff, and (c) gravity.

In preparing to jump, hop, or leap, the legs bend in preparation for the strong, explosive leg action.

The depth of the bend of the legs (or crouch) depends upon the strength of the leg muscles and the nature of the sport skill. A deep crouch requires a great deal of leg strength and a long period of time to lift the body. Therefore, in most situations the crouch should never form a 90-degree angle at the knee. The angles between 65 and 90 degrees tend to produce the best jumps.

The initial force is produced by the explosive leg action pushing down against the ground. In accordance with Newton's Third Law, an equal and opposite ground reaction force is produced which pushes the body into the air. The height reached by the body's center of gravity is proportional to the magnitude of the vertical ground reaction forces at take off. An arm swing in an upward direction produces an increase in the ground reaction forces and a transfer of momentum.

If the purpose of the jump, hop, or leap is to move the body upward as far as possible (i.e., a vertical jump), all force should be applied straight down against the ground with the center of gravity directly over the feet. This will produce a ground reaction force with only a vertical component, and all energies are used to lift the body vertically. If however, the purpose of the task is to propel the body forward and upward, the force should be applied against the ground at an angle. The forward lean of the body and the arm swing forward contributed to this angle of projection. When the takeoff force is applied at a 45-degree angle, half of the ground reaction force is used to move the body upward and half is used to move the body forward. A higher angle of pushoff, for example 70 degrees, provides a greater vertical force than horizontal; a lower angle, for example 30 degrees, provides greater horizontal motion and less vertical motion. Thus the angle of takeoff is dependent upon the goal of the skill.

Once the body is projected into the air, gravity will slow its vertical velocity and bring the body back to earth. The height that a body will achieve is dependent only on the magnitude of the ground reaction force and the angle of application. An angle of projection of 90 degrees will provide the greatest amount of time in the air because all available force is in a direction to resist gravity. Any other angle divides the ground reaction force vertically and horizontally, producing less time in the air.

Any movement in the airborne phase of a jump, hop, or leap will create an equal and opposite reaction. However, it is possible to create a momentary pause at the high point of a jump by lowering the position of the center of gravity within the body. This may be achieved by lowering the arms or bending the legs at the top of the jump.

In landing from a jump, hop, or leap the force must be absorbed in order to avoid injury. A force can be absorbed by its gradual slowing over the greatest possible time and distance (i.e., giving with the force). Therefore, all joints of the legs must "give" in sequence as contact with the ground is made, in order to absorb the force.

Catching

Catching is a skill that requires the body to stop the momentum of a moving object. The mechanical considerations are (a) absorbing the force over the greatest possible distance; i.e., "give" and (b) absorbing the force over the greatest possible surface area.

The absorption of the force over the greatest possible distance involves exerting a force on the object in the opposite direction of the moving object. This can be accomplished by first, moving in line with the oncoming object; second, reaching out as far as possible to meet the object; and third, contacting and slowly allowing the object to move toward the body. A step taken in the direction of the oncoming object not only increases balance but also, for an increase in the distance and time, permits the object's velocity to be reduced.

For balls that are to be caught above the waist, the thumbs of both hands should be placed together and the fingers pointed upward. For objects to be caught below waist level, the little fingers should be placed together and pointed downward. These positions are important in order to avoid injury and to present the largest possible surface area. In baseball, the padded glove increases the area over which the force is received.

Throwing

Throwing an object involves the transfer of momentum from the body to the object. An object held in the hand acquires the speed and direction of the hand and, when released, continues to move at this velocity and in the same direction until acted upon by other forces, such as gravity and air resistance. Of primary concern are the methods for developing speed and controlling the direction of the hand.

The faster the hand is moving when a ball is released, the greater the speed of the throw. The speed of hand movement can be increased by increasing the period of time the ball is moving in the direction of the throw—in other words, increasing the length of the backswing. To increase the backswing: (a) turn the side opposite the throwing arm toward the direction of the throw, (b) rotate the body away from the direction of the throw, and (c) place the feet in a stride position with the foot opposite the throwing arm forward.

An essential factor to throwing velocity is the length of the external lever arm or the perpendicular distance from the axis of rotation to the throwing hand. Holding the ball in the finger tips and holding the arm farther away from the body are two ways to increase the lever arm.

The total effective force is the sum of the force produced by all the muscle groups contributing to the action. The contributing body parts brought into action in timed sequence provide more speed. The sequence is: step, rotate, throw. The step should be taken in the direction of the throw. The rotation refers to the rotation of the trunk, and the throw refers to the forward arm swing. Any movement of the body in the direction of the throw adds to the velocity of the throw. A run up or hop preceding the throw gives the body added momentum which is transferred to the thrown object. Follow through, a gradual reduction of the body's momentum, is essential to avoid injury and to insure maximum transfer of momentum to the object.

In addition to the speed of release, such factors as angle of release, air resistance, gravity, height of release, and spin will affect the distance an object can be thrown. For example, top spin on a ball will cause a ball to have a shorter period of flight. When throwing for distance, the ball must be released at an angle no greater than 45 degrees. The greater the distance the ball is released, above the ground, the lower the projectile angle should be. The angle of release should also be decreased when throwing against high air resistance.

Striking

As in throwing, the effectiveness of striking is judged in terms of the speed, distance and direction of the stuck object. All the factors that apply to a thrown ball apply similarly to striking. Momentum must be developed in the body, transferred to the hand and then to the implement held in the hand (or foot as in kicking) and then transferred to the ball or object.

The speed which can be developed by the striking implement depends upon: (a) the length of the striking implement, (b) the mass of the striking implement and the mass of the ball, (c) the velocity of the striking implement and the ball, (d) the firmness of the striking implement and the point of contact between the striking implement and the struck object at the time of contact.

A longer striking implement will provide a longer lever arm which will increase the struck object's velocity. The longer the implement the faster the distal end of the object will travel and more velocity will be imparted to the ball. However, the longer lever is more difficult to control. In many cases choking up on the striking implement will increase control but decrease the optimal velocity of the struck object.

The heavier the striking implement, up to the point of loss of movement speed, the greater the momentum transfer possible. If a bat, for example, is so heavy that the speed of the swing is reduced, the resulting momentum will be decreased rather than increased by weight. The opposite is true of the struck object, the lighter the object being struck, the greater the resultant velocity.

The firmer the striking surface, the greater the force imparted to the struck object. The striking implement must not be allowed to "give" at the moment of contact. Any loosening of the grip or lack of a firm wrist at contact will absorb and reduce the magnitude of the imparted force. If a flat open hand is used to strike a ball, as in volleyball, some of the force being transferred to the ball will be absorbed by the hand. The hand, constructed of many small bones and muscles, cannot be kept completely firm and absorbs some of the forces at contact. The use of a closed hand, or heel of the hand, provides a firmer striking surface.

The more nearly the ball is contacted in line with its center of gravity, the greater the force transferred to the ball in the desired direction. Any force applied at a distance from the object's center of gravity will create an angular force (spin) in addition to a reduced linear force. The angle at which the ball leaves the striking surface also depends upon the angle at which it hits the surface of the striking implement. The ball will generally rebound at an angle equal and opposite to the one with which it strikes the implement surface (the angle of incidence is equal to the angle of reflection).

In addition to the above factors, successful striking movements like throwing movements depend on the length of the backswing, number of contributing muscles, correct sequence of muscular contraction, weight shift, and follow through. Each factor contributes significantly to optimal striking ability.

The above mechanical aspects section was intended to provide an overview of movement biomechanics. For additional information, the reader should explore the selected references in the interrelated fields of anatomy, kinesiology, and biomechanics that are listed in the bibliography.

SELECTED REFERENCES

Adrian, M.J. and Cooper., J.M. *The Biomechanics of Human Movement.* Indianapolis, IN: Benchmark Press, Inc., 1989.

Enoka, R.M. *Neuromechanical Basis of Kinesiology.* Champaign, IL: Human Kinetics Books, 1988.

Gowitzke, B.A., and Milner, M. *Scientific Bases of Human Movement.* 3rd ed., Baltimore, MD: Williams and Wilkins, 1984.

Hay, J.G. *The Biomechanics of Sports Techniques.* 3rd ed., Englewood Cliffs, NJ: Prentice Hall, 1985.

Hay, J. and Reid, J.G. *Anatomy, Mechanics and Human Motion.* 2nd ed., Englewood Cliffs, NJ: Prentice Hall, 1988.

Kreighbaum, E. and Barthels, K.M. *Biomechanics.* 3rd ed., New York, NY: Macmillan Publishing Co., 1990.

Rasch, P.J. *Kinesiology and Applied Anatomy.* 7th ed., Philadelphia, PA: Lea and Febiger, 1989.

PSYCHOLOGICAL ASPECTS

Psychology is the study of behavior and cognitive processes. As such, it is concerned with all aspects of physical and mental behavior. There are many areas of study in psychology, but in this HANDBOOK we concentrate on principles that are most relevant for teachers and coaches, particularly those concerning motivation, learning, personality, and social interactions.

MOTIVATION

Whatever behavior is being studied, one important consideration is the motivation prompting it. *Motivation* is any condition that energizes, guides, and sustains responding. Motives may be unlearned, such as hunger or thirst, or learned, such as the desire for friendship or for accomplishment.

Needs and Drives. Psychologists view *needs* as the physiological or psychological deficits a person experiences; *drives* are the states resulting from needs. Motives are often viewed as the product of needs and drives.

Physiological needs include hunger or thirst, need for air, or need for relief from pain. Teachers and coaches may not be concerned with the first two, but the latter two provide good illustrations of problems that may prove important. For example, teaching swimming may be very difficult if the learner has a strong fear of suffocation and refuses to put his or her head in the water. And many runners experience painful "stitches" and simply stop practicing.

Psychological deficits may be more difficult to identify. If not expressed by the learner, it may be extremely hard for the instructor to realize the type of achievement "needed" and the resultant drive produced. For example, research has shown that key reasons for children's participation in sports include wanting to achieve improvement in skills and ability, have fun, and enjoy the social and sportsmanship aspects of the events. If the instructor believes that the children's primary desire is to win, the wrong kinds of achievements may be stressed and rewarded. Taking part in sports often is prompted by a desire to be "part of the group" for people of all ages. If the instructor fails to support this, an important psychological motive may not be satisfied. Children or adults who do not experience satisfaction may be likely to leave the learning (sport) situation and not return.

Level of Motivation.   Regardless of the type of motive being investigated, psychologists have tried to find ways to express the strength of the motive. This is sometimes accomplished by measuring *deprivation*, that is, how much time has passed since last satisfying the motive. A baseball player in an 0-for-24 slump would be thought to have experienced considerable deprivation and be likely to have a high level of motivation to get a hit.

Another quite common way of investigating the level of motivation is to use standardized tests. Many versions exist, some attempting to identify current motive states and others concentrating on what are thought of as enduring traits. For example, state anxiety is thought to be the prevailing level of anxiety being experienced as a result of conditions existing in the environment at the moment. By contrast, trait anxiety is thought of as a more permanent characteristic of an individual, a general way of responding in many different situations. As an illustration, recent research has shown that some players are actually more anxious in intra-team qualifying matches than when participating in conference championships. This form of state anxiety would be very important for a coach to identify.

Psychologists have studied the relationships between the level of motivation and the resultant performance. For many years, the results illustrated in Figure 1-5 were thought to represent the most common findings, often called the "inverted-U curve." Performance was thought to be best at moderate levels of motivation, with poorer performance expected when motive levels were low (laziness, for example) or too high ("choking").

More recently, psychologists have modified their beliefs about level of motivation, finding that each individual may have a best level of motivation for him or her. Based on the work of Russian psychologist Yuri Hanin, psychologists interested in sport behaviors now often talk about the zone of optimal

functioning (ZOF). The ZOF theory proposes that each person will perform best at a motivation level that matches individual characteristics; that is, while many people *will* show best performance when experiencing moderate levels of motivation, others will do equally well when highly aroused or when in a very relaxed or passive state. According to this theory, coaches who previously accepted the concept that all players should be "psyched up" before a competition should modify that concept to recognize that each player may need individualized consideration.

Functional Autonomy.   *Functional autonomy* refers to a situation where a response is first made to satisfy some external motivating condition, but after being repeated a number of times, comes to be motivating in and of itself. One example of functional autonomy found in physical education is that of jogging. Very few joggers start to jog because they really like it, rather, they are trying to get in shape, lose weight, quit smoking, or obey doctor's orders. Yet many joggers come to appreciate the jogging just for its own sake. Indeed, kept from exercising by bad weather, travel, job pressures, or other reasons, avid joggers often feel very deprived.

(Note: A number of studies have found that a vigorous bout of exercise is followed by improved mood state, the "feeling good" reaction to a work-out. While there are some questions as to whether such reactions can be experienced by all and questions regarding the causality of the mood state change, this phenomenon is one that teachers and coaches should recognize as a possibility.)

Conflict.   One other aspect of the study of motivation is that of *conflict*, a situation where two or more incompatible motives are operating at the same time. Resolving any conflict usually involves choosing a response that satisfies the strongest of the motives. Continuing with the jogging example mentioned above, the beginning jogger may experience significant conflict as he or she starts. Starting to exercise has the positive value of getting in shape, but possible negative values such as experiencing some pain or having to change one's daily schedule. Not starting has the positive values of maintaining a comfort level and not experiencing the pain, but the negative value of getting more and more out of shape. Obviously, teachers or exercise instructors will want to try to strengthen the motives and reinforce those aspects that lead the person to resolve such a conflict by choosing the exercise alternative.

LEARNING

Assuming a person is motivated to attempt some behavior, teachers and coaches must then facilitate learning the behavior properly. *Learning* is defined as a relatively permanent change in behavior that occurs as a result of experience. This definition does

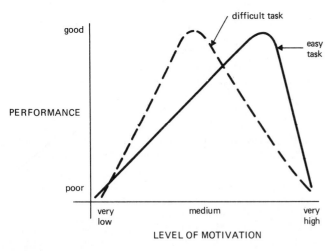

FIGURE 1-5

not negate the importance of physical development. Physical growth often is a necessary condition for learning to take place, but physical growth alone is not sufficient. Experience must also occur.

Learning–Performance Distinction. *Performance* is the actual behavior shown by the person. It must be recognized that what is observed does not necessarily reveal what has been learned. For example, a tennis player may have learned how to hit a "cut shot," but not be confronted with a situation that requires such a response. The observable performance would not show the learning.

A variation of the concern with performance has been the choice of *process*, or how a response is made, versus *product*, or what result turns out. This debate often is expressed as "That's not the right way to do that!" versus "But it works!" Teachers and coaches constantly are confronted with this concern. It is awfully hard to tell a player with a .375 batting average that "putting the foot in the bucket" is poor form. The product is successful, even though the process is not ideal.

Effects of Practice. Some people are able to realize the effects of poor form. Recently, one quite successful professional golfer decided that he needed to "rebuild" his swing in order to become even more successful. He sought a new teacher, changed his practice pattern, accomplished the swing changes, and found himself winning four major championships in the space of three years.

Many students and athletes grow up believing that "practice makes perfect." This is an inaccurate statement unless the response being performed *is* perfect or is being modified constantly to approach perfection. Instructors should recognize that a more appropriate viewpoint is that "practice makes *permanent*." As with the golfer, the instructor's task is to try to help any student-athlete make permanent the very best response possible.

REINFORCEMENT

The condition that satisfies a motive is called a reinforcer. Although often thought of as reward, psychologists use the term *reinforcement* in a broader sense, defining it as any condition that increases or maintains the strength of a response.

Positive Reinforcement. The conditions usually described as rewards are called *positive reinforcements*, events, which when present, increase or maintain the strength of the response. These may include anything from a few words of praise to stickers pasted on a football helmet.

Negative Reinforcement. Another form of reinforcement is called *negative reinforcement*, when the removal or absence of some stimulus increases or maintains the strength of a response. The unpleasant condition being removed is called an *aversive*

stimulus. Negative reinforcement is *not* punishment. *Punishment* occurs when a response *leads* to an aversive stimulus while negative reinforcement occurs when the aversive stimulus does not occur or is stopped.

Teachers and coaches often use negative reinforcement as well as punishers. Particularly good responses are reinforced by the removal of some unpleasant condition, for example, cancelling the laps to be run at the end of class or practice. On the other hand, if the responses have been especially poor, adding laps to the end of the class or practice represents punishment.

Extinction, Counterconditioning, and Spontaneous Recovery. When a response is no longer followed by a reinforcer, the response tends to become weaker. *Extinction* is both the procedure of no longer presenting the reinforcement and the result of this process, that is, the weakening of the response strength. When a replacement response is desired in the same stimulus situation, *counterconditioning*—reinforcing a substitute response—is often employed. Interestingly, sometimes there will be a reappearance of an extinguished response after a period of rest has followed the extinction procedure. This is called *spontaneous recovery* of the response and occurs when stimulus conditions provoke the response, although there is no reinforcement present.

All three of these principles should be familiar to instructors. For example, many young children learn to throw ineffectively, placing forward the foot on the same side of the body as the throwing hand. An instructor hoping to change this pattern may have to devote quite a bit of time to praising an appropriate response (counterconditioning) and extinguishing (not reinforcing) the less efficient pattern. Despite this instruction, sometimes after children have been away from class or competition for some time, the inefficient form may reappear. Just why this spontaneous recovery occurs is not understood. Regardless, instructors must realize that if it does, additional practice such as that described above will be necessary.

Partial Reinforcement Effect. One condition that works against extinction is partial reinforcement; that is, when a response is followed by reinforcement only part of the time. The result of partial reinforcement is called the partial reinforcement effect (PRE). Responses learned under partial reinforcement are more resistant to extinction than responses learned under continuous reinforcement.

This works to the advantage of the coach or teacher if the response is a productive or efficient one. However, an inefficient response such as the throwing response mentioned above will work some of the time. In such cases, eliminating the response may be quite difficult. This points to the need for effective instruction for motor responses very early in a child's life. When appropriate response patterns can be trained, they can become very resistant to extinction and probably will be maintained throughout life. On the other hand, lack of instruction or poor instruction may allow inefficient or inappropriate responses to be learned that will work against the pleasures and successes that could be experienced.

SHAPING

One of the most common ways of using reinforcement to improve athletic performance is to shape the preferred response. *Shaping* is defined as reinforcing closer and closer approximations of a desired behavior, for example, when teaching a young soccer player to make an instep kick. To begin, the player is encouraged whenever contact with the ball is made on the instep rather than the toe. Step-by- step, increasing proficiency is reinforced so that eventually the player can use either foot to make accurate, appropriate-speed kicks with a still or moving ball.

Modeling. *Modeling* occurs when a person observes the behavior of another, then performs some or all of that observed response. The instructor teaching the instep kick first demonstrates how it is done. The person learning then tries to imitate what has been seen. If combined with shaping, the instructor reinforces each imitation that gets closer to the ultimately desired performance.

Another concern in modeling is *vicarious learning*, which occurs when the learner observes both the response and the consequences of that response. For example, this is shown when the learner imitates the form of an expert archer who consistently hits the bullseye. In some cases, observing an unsuccessful response may instruct a student as to *avoid* making an ineffectual response. For example, if a companion attempts to cast a fishing line while standing too close to a tree and snags the line, the observer learns to avoid that response without actually having to perform it.

Superstitious Responding. Occasionally, a response is followed by a reinforcement that is *not* contingent upon the response being made, but the athlete comes to believe there is a contingency. The result, called *superstitious responding* because of this inaccurate belief, is repetition of the response pattern. Unfortunately, infrequent response-reinforcement sequences, although not contingent relationships, are enough to sustain the superstition, illustrating the partial reinforcement effect.

While many superstitions may be harmless, such as putting a sock on the left foot before putting one on the right foot when dressing for a game, the teacher or coach must guard against circumstances where the person believes a superstition so deeply that failure to satisfy the conditions produces an attitude of complete defeatism. The "now we can't win,

FIGURE 1-6 Modeling is an important instructional principle.

because you didn't follow the superstition" attitude can be extremely destructive, while in reality, it is completely false.

ATTENTION

Almost any sport or activity environment has many aspects of stimulation. Response acquisition may depend on the person's attention to the stimuli that are important for correct learning.

A popular way of conceptualizing attention in sport situations has been proposed by Robert Nideffer,[1] who suggests that attention can be viewed as having both width and direction. Width refers to whether the athlete must focus in a broad or narrow manner, while direction refers to having either an internal or external focus. Combining these two dimensions, sport activities can then be viewed as: broad-internal, such as the responsibilities of a coach who must pay attention to all aspects of what the team is doing and make decisions accordingly; broad-external, such as when a quarterback is trying to pick out a receiver among the many players on the field; narrow-internal, such as is required by the kind of focus used by weightlifters; and narrow-ex-

[1] R.M. Nideffer, A Test of Attentional and Interpersonal Style (1976). *Journal of Personality and Social Psychology, 34,* 394–404.

ternal, such as the responses required of a successful golfer.

Analysis of each physical activity or sport might help teachers and coaches instill appropriate attentional focus into players. For example, a golfer distracted by shadows or sounds while putting could be taught to focus only on the line of the putt and other relevant external cues. Eventually, the goal would be to reach a level of habitual responding where attending to the necessary and appropriate cues is done in a manner that makes correct responding automatic.

Generalization and Discrimination. Attention may be influenced by *stimulus generalization*—responding not only to the original stimulus, but to other similar stimuli—and *discrimination* (or *differentiation*), when the response is made to one stimulus, but not made to other stimuli that are judged to be dissimilar. Downhill skiing provides examples of both principles. The novice skier may judge all snow conditions to be the same, that is, generalize that all slopes have "snow." The more experienced skier may discriminate among the several different types of snow that can be encountered and adjust responses accordingly.

OTHER GENERAL ACQUISITION PRINCIPLES

While many factors such as those mentioned above influence acquisition, there are a number of other variables that affect learning. This section presents some that seem most appropriate for physical education.

Overlearning. *Overlearning* is associated with the "practice makes permanent" concept. If some criterion is used to decide when learning has occurred, overlearning refers to the amount of time or number of trials spent practicing beyond that criterion level. Even if the shortstop and second baseman seemingly have mastered the double play pivot, repeated practice will ensure the learning.

Transfer of Training. When task acquisition is affected by some previous learning, *transfer of training* has taken place. Teachers should strive for *positive transfer*, that is, when learning one task facilitates the acquisition of another. The throwing motion mentioned earlier provides a good example of positive transfer. The opposite hand-foot requirement can be transferred from throwing a ball to serving a volleyball, serving in tennis, or rolling a bowling ball. Some situations generate *negative transfer*, when already knowing one task interferes with the acquisition of a second. Something that seems as simple as learning the rules regarding out-of-bounds illustrates how negative transfer can occur. In baseball, tennis, soccer, and a number of other sports, on the line is inbounds. The ball must be completely beyond the line to be out-of-bounds.

But in football or basketball, on the line is out-of-bounds. Obviously, learning in one case may be detrimental to learning the same type of rule for some other sport. To further complicate the matter, some judgments involve *how much* over the line, as when a referee in wrestling must make a decision as to whether most of the body has or has not crossed the boundary line.

It should be noted that there will be some instances where no transfer takes place, either positive or negative, thus one task has no bearing upon another.

Knowledge of Results. Also called feedback, *knowledge of results* is the information about success or failure a person receives after performing some response. In general, knowledge of results facilitates acquisition of a response, especially if it is provided immediately after the response is made rather than delayed.

Many motor tasks provide knowledge of results automatically. If a person tries a new type of turn while skiing and falls, there is immediate feedback about the response. Other circumstances require the feedback provided by a coach or instructor (an outside observer) such as comments about position on the playing area or time elapsed for a particular distance.

A popular way to provide feedback information in classrooms and athletic situations is the use of film or videotape. One advantage of this type of feedback is that it can be used repeatedly, allowing the learner the certainty of understanding the point being made.

Distribution of Practice. A summary of research supports the finding that holding relatively short practice periods and distributing them over some period of time will produce the best acquisition of a response. This is often called *distributed practice*, as opposed to *massed practice* where practice periods are bunched together. (Note: The concern here is with acquiring a response; longer practice periods for already-learned responses may be necessary to obtain desired conditioning levels.)

Many teachers and coaches take advantage of distributed practice by scheduling a variety of tasks during any one session. The tasks may be repeated a number of times over several days, but are not practiced long enough in any one session to produce boredom or fatigue. Distributed practice also seems to allow for consolidation of learning to take place during the interim periods.

Active versus Passive Attitude. A principle that seems to apply to almost any acquisition situation in education and athletics is that an active approach to learning will produce better acquisition than will a *passive* attitude. However, it should be recognized that the activity may be physical or mental or both. Recent investigations in cognitive psychology have shown that some forms of both approaches may combine to produce improved acquisition and excellent performance. For example, athletes who combine active physical practice with *mental imagery*, the relatively passive mental rehearsal of a task, often appear to benefit. Those who create images about the response to be made and how it will be executed frequently show considerably improved performance when compared to athletes who use only active practice without employing imagery as well.

Coaches and teachers should explore the many possibilities that may lead to improved acquisition and performance. An illustration would be to use a videotape of an excellent performer as an introduction to a task (a potential modeling situation). After viewing the tape, the learners might then try to create mental images matching their intended performance to those seen in the tape. The positive transfer resulting from the modeling and imagery should produce better learning and performance of the response.

Context of Learning. Evidence indicates that people often develop what is called *state-dependent learning*, where the response is attached to the physical context in which it is learned. This factor is one that is important for both the acquisition and retention of the response. "Dress rehearsal" practices are conducted to try to satisfy this factor. Practicing in game uniforms, on the actual playing field or court to be used, or in other circumstances that match the conditions that will be used when retention is actually demanded may help maximize performance.

Coaches may have to allow for change of context as well. A recent popular movie showed the coach measuring the height of the basket and the distance from the basket to the free-throw line in order to prove to his team that the court on which they would later play was the same as those in arenas with smaller seating capacities where they had previously played.

RETENTION AND FORGETTING

Of major concern to instructors in all areas is whether responses that have been learned will be retained or forgotten. *Retention* is the storage of learning over some period of time, often called the *retention interval*. *Forgetting* refers to the loss of retention, or the inability to retrieve a response from storage. It should be noted that we must always measure retention in some manner, not forgetting. Forgetting is only inferred from what appears to not be retained.

Storage. *Storage*, or the maintenance of a memory over the retention interval, has several forms. All are well illustrated by the life-long activity of bicycling. Stimuli encountered while riding may be kept briefly in *sensory storage*, when information is held in an unprocessed form for several seconds or less. These might include such things as the visual scene, the sound of a car's horn, or the kinesthetic sensations produced by the seating position on the bicycle. Some stimuli may be incorporated into *short-term storage*, where information is given some initial processing then may be further processed or simply discarded. For example, the rider may be given directions and hold these in memory only long enough to execute them, or may further process that information into *long-term storage*, where information is encoded, rehearsed, or treated in some manner so that retention extends over some longer period of time. Long-term storage may last a lifetime, and the rider may always remember the appropriate way to follow the route. Of course, the act of riding the bicycle itself is good evidence for life-long, long-term storage of a series of responses. It has often been said that once one learns to ride a bicycle, the responses are never forgotten. Much evidence exists to indicate this is correct.

Athletics provide comparable examples—in football there are many sensory stimuli that must be evaluated, short-term storage of the play that has just been called which when used is then temporarily discarded, and long-term storage of all the plays and formations to be used over the course of a game or a season.

Failure to Retrieve. The two most common explanations for failure to retrieve information from storage are: (a) a person is given the wrong cue to initiate the retrieval; (b) the cue is correct, but some other, interfering response is produced instead. As an example of inappropriate retrieval cues, consider the dance instructor who asks her young students to "start with the pattern you learned last Friday." If they practiced two different dances at the last session, the students may be unable to make the correct response. They have not forgotten the dances, but are confused by the retrieval cues given.

Interference suggests that retention of one response conflicts or interferes with the retention of some other response. This may be previous learning interfering with the retention of something learned later (often called proactive interference) or later learning interfering with something learned before (called retroactive interference). In either case, more than one stored response can be elicited by the retrieval cue and, if the inappropriate response is given, forgetting will seem to have occurred. Professional football players traded from one team to another sometimes show the confusion associated with interference when they run or block incorrectly because the numbering system used by their previous team differs from the more recent one. The old learning interferes with the newly acquired learning and makes it appear that forgetting has occurred.

PROBLEM SOLVING IN PHYSICAL EDUCATION

The Problem Solving Sequence. *Problem solving*, that is, establishing a goal and then seeking ways to achieve that goal, is typified by a fairly common sequence of events. The five steps are (1) recognizing there is a problem, (2) defining the problem accurately, (3) producing hypotheses about the problem's solution, (4) testing the hypotheses, and (5) selecting the best solution.

Recognition that a problem exists may be a major step in initiating problem solving because, logically, lack of understanding stops the sequence before it gets started. For example, not realizing the rules of a game are misunderstood means the problem is not recognized and the game continues to be played incorrectly. If recognition occurs, defining the problem accurately requires identifying the most relevant concepts. When rules are misunderstood, discovering which are not grasped is essential if they are to be learned properly.

Once the areas to be worked on have been identified, hypotheses about how to resolve the problem can be generated. Generating as many solutions as possible before testing any or making judgments about any of the approaches may help to guarantee that the best possible solution will be found. For example, the teacher or coach may suggest holding rules classes, giving a rule book to each student or player, showing videotapes depicting the rules, or taking participants to a contest where the rules are being enforced properly. Each of these possible solutions might be suggested before any evaluation or decision was made.

Testing means that each hypothesis is either confirmed or disconfirmed. If disconfirmed, it is discarded as unworkable. If confirmed, the solution should be compared to any other confirmed ones to determine which is most acceptable. Taking the students to a contest might be an acceptable hypothesis, but prohibitively expensive when compared to renting a videotape. The latter solution would be more likely to be adopted.

Variables Affecting Problem Solving. The reader is invited to review earlier sections of this chapter and try to develop applications of the principles presented to a problem-solving situation. To illustrate the complexity of problem solving and how many variables may be important, consider the coach or teacher trying to teach novice swimmers to make a flip-turn. The heightened motivation level generated by submersion and disorientation may reduce performance effectiveness considerably. Repeated practice almost certainly will be needed. The teacher may use modeling as one solution and use the principles of shaping as well. Knowledge of results will show how a well-executed flip-turn reduces the turn-around time required at the end of the pool. Finally, interference may exist in the form of other rolling-motion activities or other turns the swimmers have learned previously. What may seem to be a fairly simple goal to achieve may actually be rather complicated and require thorough study before initiating a practice plan.

PERSONALITY AND SOCIAL CONCERNS IN PHYSICAL EDUCATION

While it is beyond the scope of the HANDBOOK to consider personality variables or social interactions in great detail, it should be recognized that the characteristics of each individual and the ways in which individuals interact will have pronounced effects on the behaviors seen in athletic situations. The study of personality considers the characteristics of each person individually, while social psychology studies the behavior of an individual within the group setting.

Personality. *Personality*, the enduring characteristics that represent a person's behavior, develops from the combined effects of environmental and hereditary influences. Aspects of personality that have been studied in relation to sport and physical activity include anxiety, aggression, gender role orientation, racial differences, mood states, and sociability. Concern has been with every level of participant, from the beginning child to the elite adult athlete.

Many of the topics overlap with those already discussed; for example, several researchers have devoted substantial study to the attributes of people who participate in high-risk sports such as hanggliding and parachuting. These people plainly operate at motivation levels unlike the typical person, and studies have identified them as being high in need for achievement, dominance, and courage, while low in need for order. They are often described as sensation-seeking or stress-seeking individuals, ones who appreciate high levels of arousal.

William Morgan and his associates have studied the mood states of elite athletes from a number of sports. Using a test called the *Profile of Mood States (POMS)*, Morgan has found that, in general, outstanding athletes show what he calls the "Iceberg Profile."[2] Scores on the tension, anger, depression, fatigue, and confusion scales of the POMS are lower than average, while scores on the vigor scale are considerably higher.

These examples illustrate the kinds of personality research being done in sport psychology. Characteristics are identified that appear to distinguish the type of person who will succeed in particular sport situations. Teachers and coaches should realize that personality variables may have pronounced influence on the activities chosen and the performance

---

[2] W.P. Morgan, Test of Champions: The Iceberg Profile (1986). *Psychology Today, 14* (2), 92–102, 108.

success of potential participants. They are encouraged to explore these possibilities more thoroughly through additional study.

Social Interaction. Many recreational pursuits, games, and organized sports involve the participation of more than one person at the same time. *Social interaction*, how people interact and what effects these interactions have on their behaviors, is of major importance in many sport circumstances. The phenomena of *social facilitation* and *social interference* refer to the effects the presence of an audience or crowd may have upon performance and provide good illustrations of social interaction.

Social facilitation means that the presence of others tends to make performance better than when others are not present; social interference refers to situations where the presence of others tends to make performance poorer than when others are not present. Obvious examples of these phenomena occur when performance is required in front of a class or when a crowd is present for an athletic contest.

In general, studies have shown that social facilitation is most likely to occur when the response to be performed is one that has been well learned. Social interference occurs more frequently with relatively new responses. Again, teachers or coaches who understand these results can try to establish conditions that create facilitation and avoid interference. The implied reinforcement of social facilitation or punishment of social interference can be expected to affect later performances.

Social Expectations. *Social expectations* may influence a person's behavior, especially when the behavior appears to occur in order to satisfy some previously expressed expectation. Instructors should be particularly careful to avoid repetitive demeaning remarks when dealing with behaviors that are easily changed. Comments such as "You'll never get it right" become the expectation and yield inadequate performances. Teachers and coaches must also guard against peer group ridicule, which can produce the same kind of effect. Correspondingly, establishing positive expectations often will generate improved performance. The "You're getting better. I know you'll get it soon" attitude can be expected to produce improved responding.

Competition and Cooperation. *Competition* is the attempt to do better than someone else. Competition often requires a positive attitude, whether the someone else involved is another person or the previous accomplishments of the person competing. Research indicates that a successful competitor strives for and expects accomplishments that an unsuccessful competitor does not. Additionally, studies have shown that anxiety about competition varies as a function of many variables including perceived threat, level of motivation, or gender role endorsement. Coaches may need to evaluate competitive anxiety before establishing contest strategies.

Cooperation refers to working with or helping someone else in hopes of achieving some mutual goal. Both competition and cooperation often are fostered by sport or game situations. In many cases, this refers to cooperation with teammates, but cooperation with officials, opponents, or even spectators may be a part of the sport or game situation.

One problem coaches or teachers often face is the competition versus cooperation dilemma. The person who has a high level of competitive motivation may find it difficult to cooperate with others, even though cooperation would facilitate pursuit of the goal desired. In effect, what the person experiences can be described as a social conflict, when two incompatible social motives are experienced at the same time. An example of this occurs when a player wishes to be a starter and must compete against teammates for the starting positions available, yet is required to cooperate by the very nature of the game. Convincing players that both competition and cooperation are possible simultaneously in such situations is difficult. Because social motives such as achievement and friendship can be extremely powerful and create social conflict circumstances, instructors are cautioned to evaluate such possibilities when working with their athletes.

SUMMARY

This brief look at psychological principles is sufficient to indicate the need for coaches and teachers to be aware of the many variables that may affect performance. The references listed below will help the reader explore in more detail those areas that are of particular interest.

SELECTED REFERENCES

Butt, D.S., *Psychology of Sport: The Behavior, Motivation, Personality, and Performance of Athletes*, 2nd ed. New York: Van Nostrand Reinhold Co., 1987. A comprehensive review of theory, research, and practice, with special emphasis on consulting and other "how to" topics.

Cox, R.H., *Sport Psychology: Concepts and Applications*, 2nd ed. Dubuque, IA: Wm. C. Brown, 1990. A thorough compilation of the basic topics of sport psychology.

LeUnes, A.D., and Nation, J.R., *Sport Psychology: An Introduction*, Nelson-Hall Inc., 1989. A comprehensive text that presents theory, research, and application in sport psychology.

Martens, R., *Coaches Guide to Sport Psychology*, Human Kinetics Publishers, 1987. Complete guidelines for implementing a psychological skills training program for coaches.

Martens, R., Vealey, S., and Burton, D., *Competitive Anxiety in Sport*, Human Kinetics Publishers, 1990. A review of the research using a particular measuring instrument, together with suggestions for future investigations.

Orlick, T., *Psyching for Sport: Mental Training for Athletes* and *Coaches Training Manual to Psyching for Sport*, Human Kinetics Publishers, 1987. Techniques for developing the psychological skills needed for sport competition; a package for applied sport psychology courses.

Journals

Journal of Sport & Exercise Psychology. Human Kinetics Publishers, Box 5076, Champaign, IL 61825-5076. In addition to a wide variety of papers, includes book reviews, commentaries, and a digest of related works found in other publications.

Other journals likely to contain work related to sport psychology include *The Sport Psychologist, Journal of Motor Behavior, Perceptual and Motor Skills, Journal of Teaching in Physical Education, Journal of Sport Science, Journal of Applied Psychology, The Physician and Sports Medicine, Research Quarterly,* and *International Journal of Sport Psychology.*

OBJECTIVES AND PROGRAMS

The well-planned physical education program has the potential to contribute in a number of ways to all phases of your educational development. Physical education's contribution is unique since it offers movement as the primary medium through which the educational process may occur.

OBJECTIVES OF PHYSICAL EDUCATION

Physical educators are in general agreement that a sound course will comprise the following three objectives:

1. Psychomotor Objectives. This refers to the dual role of skill improvement and fitness development that you should experience as a result of your participation in a physical education or wellness course. For example, if you are taking a swimming course, skill improvement would refer to your ability to become a more proficient swimmer as a result of planned class instruction and directed practice in that skill. Fitness development would refer to improvement in some of the commonly accepted fitness measures as a result of your class participation. In swimming class, you might notice how much more easily you can perform the skill as a result of your class experiences. This may be an indication that your cardiorespiratory system is adapting to the stress placed on it by the exertion from activity. It could also mean that your stroke technique has improved (skill development), and you are now moving

your body through the water more efficiently. Whatever the reason, both are desirable traits and constitute an important achievement for you and what physical education is all about. Of course, the same argument could be used for any other course you might be taking, whether soccer, fitness walking, dance, racquetball, etc.

2. Cognitive Objective. This refers to the accumulation of knowledge as well as the ability to think and interpret that knowledge. In a fitness walking class, for example, you might become involved in working with times in determining pace per mile walked. You will undoubtedly become involved in computing your target heart rate (as well as why this is important), which could include the correct way to determine your resting and maximum pulse rates. Closely associated with that is the matter of cardiac anatomy and physiology which might get you involved with appropriate nutrition and diet for a healthy heart. Nutritional study opens up other areas of exploration such as the metric system in understanding the amount of sodium or fat contained in a certain food product. Furthermore, we may be motivated to be a more well-informed consumer when we shop. Other possibilities in a class such as this might be appropriate walking shoe selection, proper clothing for hot or cold weather walking, warm-up and cool-down, appropriate times of the day to walk to avoid high air pollution levels, and so forth.

3. Affective Objective. This objective deals with the development of traits such as the individual's values, appreciations, attitudes, and interests. How might the affective objective be applied to an activity such as tennis, for example? Perhaps the most obvious example would deal with the matter of calling your opponent's shots as they land in your half of the court. For someone who does not have a background in the racket sports, this responsibility can be quite awesome. But it goes beyond that relatively obvious task. It could involve learning the importance of being the type of opponent or partner who makes playing tennis a pleasant experience as you play the game enthusiastically and to the best of your ability regardless of the conditions. You compliment others on their outstanding play. While you play competitively, your standard of conduct is within both the written word and the spirit of the rules. As a result of participating in tennis, you acquire habits of loyalty, cooperation, initiative, self-control and courtesy. You demonstrate a concept of fair play as it relates to others.

SCHOOL PHYSICAL EDUCATION PROGRAMS

Sound programs of physical education provide a systematic progression of movement experiences for the students as they develop and mature. Federal legislation mandates that learning experiences must be equally available to both genders (Title IX) as well as the disabled student (Public Law 94-142). These two laws were discussed previously in the Historical Aspects section of this chapter.

Elementary School. Programs of physical education at this level should provide a wide range of learning experiences for the youngsters. Unfortunately, good programs in the elementary schools are frequently lacking in quality, and one of the major concerns within the profession is the inactive lifestyle that many grade school youngsters now follow. Programs in the lower elementary grades should include large muscle, vigorous activity featuring such locomotor skills as walking, running, jumping, hopping, skipping, galloping, and leaping. Nonlocomotor skills such as bending, twisting, reaching, lifting, turning, lowering, and raising also characterize good programs. These movement skills can be incorporated in programs of dance, movement exploration, movement education, stunts and tumbling, rhythmics, fitness and wellness activities, and aquatics. These activities emphasize key elements such as self-expression, cooperation, coordination, body awareness in a variety of mediums, creativity, strength, endurance, flexibility, agility, balance, and spatial awareness. As the children move into the upper elementary grade levels, the emphasis should focus more on manipulative-type skill development. Children are taught the basic elements of a variety of physical activities, such as soccer, gymnastics, dance, swimming, fitness and wellness activities. The child's need to excel and compete can also be developed through the thoughtful planning of movement experiences. Sound programs of physical education at the elementary school level are crucial in developing a positive attitude toward an active, healthful lifestyle.

Middle School. Programs at this level should continue to emphasize the soundness in planning and instruction that characterized the elementary school physical education experience. Skill development at this level is more advanced and a broader range of activities are involved. Because this period is an age of rapid physical and social growth, challenging activities that provide an opportunity for the development of interpersonal relationships should be offered. Emphasis on team sports will enhance the development of social skills as would such coeducational activities as gymnastics and track and field. Furthermore, the inclusion of such fitness-wellness activities as swimming, jogging, cycling, and rhythms would make a significant contribution to the middle school youngster's educational development.

Senior High School. At this level, sound physical education programs are designed to answer the how and why of an activity. Attempts are made to design learning experiences that will help the students gain an understanding of mechanical principles and the effects of exercise on the body. It is also important that they understand concepts that deal with the role of physical education, sport and wellness in society and to make valued judgments about their own well-being. Interpersonal skill development can continue through participating in competitive activities and taking part in a wide variety of lifetime skills such as golf, tennis, fitness and wellness activities, aquatics, etc.

EXTRACURRICULAR PHYSICAL EDUCATION AND SPORT PROGRAMS

Aside from the instructional program in physical education, there are other opportunities for participation in selected sports on a more competitive level. Normally, such programs begin at the middle school level and extend through the college experience.

Intramural Sports. This program consists of individuals or teams from within a public school or college competing with others from the same school. The type of program offered can cover a complete range of activities from distance running and wrestling to bridge and archery. Intramural sports programs are voluntary, and the play is usually scheduled in the late afternoon or evening. Normally participants are not on a varsity team or they do not participate in the same intramural sport in which they are a varsity athlete. On college campuses, teams may come from fraternities, sororities, residence halls, other housing units, classes, clubs, etc. Unfortunately, due to a lack of funds, trained leadership, and adequate facilities, most high school intramural sports programs are not too strong.

Sports Clubs. This program consists of teams organized primarily at the collegiate level which compete in a variety of sports on an intercollegiate basis. Some club activities might include volleyball, rugby, softball, lacrosse, weightlifting, bowling, sailing, and ice hockey. While sports clubs' policy may vary, they usually receive the same type of university support as the varsity teams with one exception: its members do not receive varsity awards. Generally, sports clubs may have less strict eligibility regulations (some permit graduate students to play), and they may be funded in various ways such as through a student activities office or the athletic department. They are usually required to have some type of faculty sponsorship although there is usually more student leadership than on varsity teams. Sports clubs provide an excellent way for students to train in a particular sport and compete on a varsity-like level.

Interscholastic and Intercollegiate Athletics. Sometimes referred to as "varsity sports" (a shortened version of the word "university"), this program is an American educational tradition and is well established as a part of our culture. Interscholastic athletics refer to the public school programs where athletes leave the school to compete with a similarly organized team at either a host school or neutral location. Intercollegiate athletics is the same program, functioning in the same general fashion at the college or university level.

Varsity programs are found at all educational levels and are usually characterized by dedicated leadership, high levels of organizationally skilled participants, and an emphasis on competition. Unfortunately, such programs sometimes focus on a few skilled performers who in fact, represent only a small percentage of the student body. The educational value of such programs has been debated since their inception during the latter part of the 19th century. With appropriate leadership that supports a program of broad participation with the students' interests foremost, interscholastic and intercollegiate athletics have a great deal to offer as rich educational experiences. All too often, they do not achieve those objectives.

FUTURE OF PHYSICAL EDUCATION AND SPORT

While fitness, sport, and wellness activities are very popular, physical education, as we have described it in this chapter, struggles for acceptance. Currently, in all states, it is a public school course requirement; otherwise, it might well be dropped or offered on an elective basis. At the college and university level, required physical education is frequently offered on an elective basis. It appears the future of physical education will be enhanced if it can be offered as a course integrated with fitness and wellness-type concepts. Otherwise, the future may indeed be dim.

We have already addressed some aspects of the future of sport. In many areas of the country, interscholastic sports do not attract the following they once did. This may be attributed to the increased expense in sponsoring such activities, the high rate of injuries in some sports with the implicit legal ramifications, and the number of other pursuits now available to teenagers. In those areas, however, where sports constitute an important part of the cultural heritage of a community, they fulfill an important psychological need for those involved (not the least of which are the fans), and will likely remain firmly in place in those locations at both the high school or university level.

SUMMARY

Physical education is much more than just fitness and exercise or the psychomotor objective. While these are important objectives, the well-planned program has more to offer through the cognitive and affective objectives. Sound programs can take place from kindergarten through college, and various extracurricular sport-related activities, with sound leadership, can make a valuable contribution to your education. Such experiences can truly enhance your sense of wellness.

SELECTED REFERENCES

Bucher, C., and Wuest, D. *Foundations of Physical Education and Sport*. St. Louis: Times Mirror/Mosby Co., 1987.

Robbins, G., Powers, D., and Burgess-Troxell. *A Wellness Way of Life*. Dubuque, IA: Wm. C. Brown Publishers, 1991.

Siedentop, D. *Introduction to Physical Education, Fitness and Sport*. Toronto: Mayfield Publishing Co., 1990.

2 PHYSICAL FITNESS PROGRAMS

THIS CHAPTER DISCUSSES:

▶ *Skill-related versus health-related physical fitness.*
▶ *The need for and benefits of physical fitness.*
▶ *Components of the pre-exercise program screening.*
▶ *The principles of exercise training.*
▶ *Exercise for weight (fat) loss.*
▶ *Supplemental training programs (interval and circuit training).*

If ten people were asked to define physical fitness, it would not be surprising to get ten different answers that are all partially correct. This variation occurs because physical fitness can be categorized into two types—skill-related and health-related—with each type having various components. Skill-related physical fitness includes: power, speed, agility, balance, coordination, and reaction time. Prior to 1980, the majority of physical education programs evaluated primarily the skill-related components of physical fitness by using a battery of tests that included: sit-ups, pull-ups, shuttle run, 50-yard dash, softball throw, and 600-yard run/walk. However, beginning in 1980, the American Alliance for Health, Physical Education, Recreation, and Dance (AAHPERD) began using a health-related physical fitness test that included: a one-mile run/walk, skinfold measurements, sit and reach measurement, and a sit-up test.[1] In 1988, AAHPERD added a pull-up test to the assessment as part of their *Physical Best* program.[2] Health-related fitness includes the following five components:

1. *Cardiorespiratory Endurance*—the ability of the heart, respiratory and circulatory systems to supply oxygen and nutrients to, and to remove waste products from, the working muscles;
2. *Muscular Strength*—the ability of the muscles to exert a force to move an object or to develop tension to resist the movement of an object;
3. *Muscular Endurance*—the ability of a muscle to sustain repeated contractions or to maintain a submaximal contraction;

4. *Body Composition*—the relative proportion of body fat to fat-free body tissues (muscle, bone, organs);
5. *Flexibility*—the ability to move a body part fluidly through a complete range of motion about a joint.

The focus of this chapter will be on health-related physical fitness programs, specifically related to the cardiorespiratory endurance and body composition components (muscular strength, muscular endurance, and flexibility training will be discussed in later chapters). Information concerning the need for and benefits of health-related physical fitness will be presented. This will be followed by concerns for pre-exercise screening and then specific types of training programs will be presented.

CURRENT PHYSICAL FITNESS CHARACTERISTICS

The mechanization of many American industries in the early through mid-twentieth century decreased the occupational activity level of many individuals. As the technology explosion continued, the automation of products for home and recreation further decreased the activity levels of Americans. This has led to a substantial number of unfit Americans.

Youth. Data from the National Children and Youth Fitness Study II (NCYFS)[3] conducted in the mid-1980's revealed that a majority of the youth in the United States have low levels of physical fitness. Some specific findings were: that only 50 percent of the youth exercise at appropriate frequency, intensity, and duration to stimulate cardiorespiratory en-

[1] American Alliance for Health, Physical Education, Recreation and Dance: *AAHPERD Health-Related Physical Fitness Test Manual.* Washington, D.C., AAHPERD, 1980.
[2] American Alliance for Health, Physical Education, Recreation and Dance: *AAHPERD Physical Best Manual.* 1990 Association Drive, Reston, VA, AAHPERD, 1988.

[3] J.G. Ross and R.R. Pate, The National Children and Youth Fitness Study II: A Summary of Findings, *J. of Physical Educ., Recreation and Dance,* Nov./Dec.: 66–70, 1987.

durance, and this was supported by the finding that 50 percent or less of the children tested could run one mile in less than ten minutes; obesity (triceps skinfold > 85th percentile) increased 54 percent (6- to 11-year olds) and 39 percent (12- to 17-year olds) and superobesity (triceps skinfold > 95th percentile) increased 98 percent (6- to 11-year olds) and 64 percent (12- to 17-year olds) from 1965 to 1980.[4] Poor performances were also recorded for boys in flexibility and for girls in muscular strength and endurance.

Adults. The National Health Interview Survey in 1985, collected the following information concerning the exercise habits of adults in the United States: 28 percent were completely sedentary, 31 percent were irregularly active, 34 percent were active (but were not exercising at appropriate frequency, intensity, and duration to stimulate cardiorespiratory endurance), and only 7 percent were meeting criteria for appropriate physical activity.[5] Approximately one-third to one-half of adult Americans (depending on the criteria used) are overweight or obese.[6]

Consequences. The lack of physical fitness has been associated with a number of health problems. The term hypokinetic disease, meaning "a condition related to, or caused by, a lack of regular physical activity,"[7] has been used to describe this problem. Specific diseases and health problems associated with inactivity are: coronary heart disease, cancer, hypertension, hyperlipidemia, obesity, and low back pain/injury. Coronary heart disease (CHD) is the leading cause of death in the United States, accounting for 36 percent of all deaths. Cancer is the second leading cause, accounting for 22 percent of all deaths. Two of the three primary risk factors for CHD are associated with physical inactivity. The prevalence rate of these two (smoking being the third) in adult Americans is: 25 percent for high total cholesterol (>240 mg/dL); and approximately 33 percent for high blood pressure (>140/90 mmHg). Another health-related factor associated with physical inactivity is low back pain, with approximately 70 to 80 percent suffering from this malady.

BENEFITS OF PHYSICAL FITNESS

A regular exercise program will result in numerous physiological adaptations. A summary of some of the physiological changes that occur with aerobic exercise training is provided in Table 2-1. These changes

[4] S.L. Gortmaker, et al., Increasing Pediatric Obesity in the United States. *Am J Dis Child,* 141:535–540, 1987.

[5] C.J. Casperson, et al., Status of the 1990 Physical Fitness and Exercise Objectives—Evidence From NHIS 1985. *Pub Health Rep,* 101:587–592, 1986.

[6] W.J. Miller and T. Stephens, The Prevalence of Overweight and Obesity in Britain, Canada and the United States. *Am J Pub Health,* 77:38–41, 1987.

[7] D.K. Miller and T.E. Allen, *Fitness: A Lifetime Commitment.* 4th ed. (New York: Macmillan Publishing Co., 1990), p. 3.

TABLE 2-1 Physiological Effects of Training

At Rest	Increase	Decrease	No Change
During Rest and/or Submaximal Exercise			
Lactic acid accumulation		X	
Heart rate		X	
Stroke volume	X		
Cardiac output			X
VO$_2$			X
Fat utilization	X		
Ventilatory efficiency	X		
Carbohydrate utilization		X	
During Maximal Exercise			
Lactic acid accumulation	X		
Heart rate		X or	X
Stroke volume	X		
Cardiac output	X		
VO$_2$	X		
Ventilatory efficiency	X		
Other Changes			
Body Fat		X	
Serum cholesterol		X	
Serum triglycerides		X	
Serum high-density lipoproteins	X		
Serum low-density lipoproteins		X	
Resting metabolic rate	X or		X

allow the individual to function more efficiently when faced with everyday demands and stresses and also allow the individual to take on more total work. Physical fitness can be generically described as the ability to perform daily activities without undue fatigue.

Physiological Adaptations

The beneficial effects of exercise on the cardiovascular system are very evident. The heart, which in essence is a muscular pump, becomes stronger and more efficient. Cardiac output, the amount of blood pumped from the heart each minute, is a product of stroke volume and heart rate. The heart adapts to regular aerobic exercise training by increasing the amount of blood it pumps with each beat (stroke volume), thus becoming a stronger, more effective pump. Consequently, at submaximal workloads the heart does not have to beat as often, thus reducing the demand on the heart. One can easily recognize this training effect by simply monitoring the decrease in resting heart rate or the heart rate during a fixed submaximal work task. The body also responds by increasing the total blood volume and the hemoglobin content in the blood. These two adaptations allow the individual to deliver more blood and more oxygen to the working muscles during exercise.

Changes also take place within the muscles themselves. Basically, the "metabolic machinery" of the muscle cell is built up so that it can produce more energy. The muscle can extract more oxygen from the blood, and the enhanced circulation through the muscle helps to remove the additional waste products produced.

The physiological measure of these adaptations is that of maximal oxygen consumption (VO_2 max). This is also termed the individual's maximal aerobic power or the functional capacity (i.e., the maximal ability of the body to produce energy and thus perform work). Factors such as muscle fiber type make-up (determined by genetics) and pre-training VO_2 max level will determine the potential to improve one's maximal aerobic power; however, improvements in the range of 20 to 30 percent are possible following three months of appropriate aerobic training. Training will also increase the individual's "anaerobic threshold," the point in metabolism where lactic acid begins to accumulate in the blood. Lactic acid accumulation, with the resultant decrease in muscle and blood pH, is a key factor associated with fatigue. Increasing the anaerobic threshold allows the individual to work at a higher absolute submaximal workload without fatiguing.

Regular aerobic exercise training can also improve an overfat individual's body composition. Through training, the muscles and bones are stimulated which helps the body maintain muscle tissue and increase the integrity of bone. At the same time the increased energy expenditure of training promotes the loss of body fat stores. Exercise for weight loss will be discussed in more detail later in this chapter.

Blood lipids and hypertension are also favorably changed after regular aerobic exercise training. Total cholesterol, low-density lipoprotein (LDL), and especially triglycerides may all decrease, and high-density lipoprotein (HDL) can increase following training. The lipoproteins serve as carriers of lipids (fats) in blood and have been found to play a major role in the process of developing fatty deposits in walls of blood vessels. Basically, LDL is used to transport cholesterol from the liver to various tissues in the body to serve important purposes, such as structure of cell membranes. In excess, LDL can promote the development of atherosclerotic plaques within the coronary blood vessels. HDL's, on the other hand, function to transport unneeded cholesterol from the tissues to the liver. Thus, HDL's can prevent the build-up of fatty deposits in the blood vessels. It should be noted that recent evidence suggests that only individuals with unfavorably high total cholesterol and/or low HDL see marked improvement in these lipid concentrations following

aerobic training. Training can also help reduce blood pressure in those with borderline hypertension. Thus, the risk of coronary heart disease can be reduced by improving physical fitness.

Reduced Mortality. Evidence is mounting that physically fit individuals or those who are regularly active have a reduced death rate from coronary heart disease compared to the unfit and inactive population. The most recent findings from the Aerobic's Research Institute reported that the largest reduction in coronary heart disease deaths, as well as deaths from all causes, was between the lowest fitness category and those in the moderate fitness category.[8] This suggests that one does not have to be a "marathon runner" to obtain these benefits, in fact, those who regularly participate in a moderately vigorous aerobic exercise training program receive the greatest benefit.

PSYCHOLOGICAL AND SOCIOLOGICAL VALUES

Regular exercise affects not only the body but the mental and emotional states as well. Exercise can serve as an outlet for pent-up emotions through socially accepted channels. Stress, anxiety, and depression may be relieved by exercise, without the ills and side effects of mood-altering drugs. Physically fit individuals speak of their enhanced mental acuity, mental energy, concentration, and feelings of well-being. These feelings have been documented in several studies. In addition, physically fit individuals have an enhanced self-image, a definite sign of excellent mental health.

The late President Kennedy, an exponent of the strenuous life, summed it up in this way:

> Physical fitness is not only one of the most important keys to a healthy body, it is the basis of dynamic and creative intellectual activity. The relationship of the body and the activities of the mind is subtle and complex. Much is not yet understood, but we do know what the Greeks knew: that intelligence and skill can only function at the peak of their capacity when the body is healthy and strong; that hardy spirits and tough minds usually inhabit sound bodies.

In this sense, physical fitness is the basis of all the activities of our society. And if the body grows soft and inactive, if we fail to encourage physical development and prowess, we will undermine our capacity for thought, for work, and for the use of those skills vital to an expanding and complex America. Thus, the physical fitness of our citizens is a vital prerequisite to America's realization of its full poten-

[8] S.N. Blair, et. al., Physical Fitness and All-Cause Mortality: A Prospective Study of Healthy Men and Women. *JAMA*, 262:2395–2401, 1989.

tial as a nation, and to the opportunity of each individual citizen to make full and fruitful use of his capabilities.

PRE-EXERCISE SCREENING

Although exercise is a safe activity for most individuals, for some it should be avoided (at least temporarily), and for others some special considerations may need to be followed. In order to identify those who may have an unfavorable response to exercise, some simple procedures should be followed prior to beginning the physical activity. An essential procedure to use is a health history questionnaire which asks for items that could present problems during exercise (example: heart problems, diabetes, asthma, etc.). Many of these questionnaires have been published and most can use a closed answer, check-off type response format. However, one can construct their own questionnaire to fit their specific program needs.

A second step which is advisable, especially if concerns arise during the health history review, is a medical examination. This step becomes mandatory if programs are being designed for previously sedentary adults.

Finally, an assessment of the individual's current level of fitness should be made prior to beginning the training program. This allows designing the program to meet the individual's weaknesses and to provide an evaluation of the effectiveness of the training program. As mentioned previously, AAHPERD recommends a battery of tests to assess cardiorespiratory endurance, muscular strength and endurance, body composition, and flexibility of school-aged children in the *Physical Best* program. Alternative tests of cardiorespiratory endurance for college-aged students are a 1.5 mile run, a step test, and a submaximal cycle test. Likewise, muscular strength can be assessed by weight lifting tests. It should be noted that muscular strength, muscular endurance, and flexibility are specific to the muscle groups and joints being moved. Thus no one test can give an overall, total body measure of these components of fitness. A more complete fitness assessment of these components would include tests of various muscle groups and joints throughout the body.

When programs are being designed for adults, the guidelines established by the American College of Sports Medicine should be followed for screening individuals.[9] Depending on age and health status, recommendations are provided for the need for a physical exam and exercise testing prior to beginning an exercise program.

[9] American College of Sport Medicine. *Guidelines for Exercise Testing and Prescription*. 4th ed. (Philadelphia: Lea & Febiger, 1991).

EXERCISE PROGRAMMING

Regardless of the type of training to be used, all exercise training sessions should have the same basic structure of beginning with a *warm-up* period, proceeding with the specific type of training, and finishing with a *cool-down* period. The purpose of the warm-up is to prepare the body for the training session by gradually increasing the heart rate and blood circulation to the active musculature. Walking, calisthenic type of exercises, and stretching are appropriate warm-up activities. Although documentation is lacking, many believe that warm-up activities serve a preventative function against injury.

The cool-down helps restore the body to its pre-exercise condition. Initially the cool-down consists of walking, which is then followed by stretching exercises. It is believed that the cool-down is the optimal time for making flexibility improvements since the muscles are warm and the joints are most supple. Although many flexibility exercises are available, a basic routine would include: neck rotations, arm pull-overs, side stretches, one-legged sit and reach, hip and knee flexion, and ankle rotation (Figures 2-1 to 2-6).

FIGURE 2-1   Neck rotations.

FIGURE 2-2   Arm pull-overs.

FIGURE 2-3   Side stretches.

FIGURE 2-4   One-legged sit and reach.

FIGURE 2-5   Hip and knee flexion.

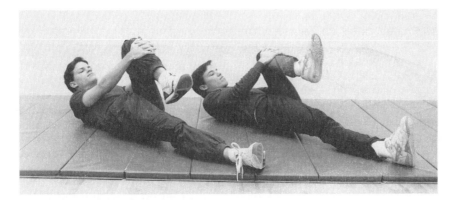

FIGURE 2-6   Ankle rotations.

When designing the training session of the program, the basic principles of specificity and overload, as well as individualization should be employed. The principle of *specificity* states that adaptations to training will be specific to the muscle groups trained, the specific movement patterns and speed of contractions used, and to the metabolic energy systems stressed. This principle is most applicable to training for sport; however, it is also important to consider when evaluating improvements in physical fitness. For example, cycling, jogging, and swimming are all appropriate activities to condition the cardiorespiratory systems. However, the one mile run/walk test will only accurately reflect cardiorespiratory improvements for those in a jogging program. Those in a cycling or swimming program would have their cardiorespiratory endurance underestimated with such a test. The *overload* principle means that in order for a muscle or system to adapt, it must be stressed beyond a level that it is normally accustomed to. The American College of Sports Medicine has established guidelines for applying the training overload, which are applicable to individuals of all ages. Overload is derived by manipulating the following factors: intensity, duration, and frequency.

Intensity.   Intensity refers to the percentage of the maximal capabilities that are being required for the activity. Research has established that for cardiorespiratory improvements, an intensity level of at least approximately 50 percent of VO_2 max must be achieved (note: severely deconditioned individuals will make improvements at lower intensities). Additional improvements are achieved through intensities up to 85 percent of VO_2 max, with optimal improvements being in the range of 70 to 80 percent. This intensity can be monitored by palpating a pulse rate during the exercise session. Pulse rates of approximately 75 to 85 percent of maximum are the equivalent of 70 to 80 percent of VO_2 max. Maximal heart rate can be measured during a maximal exercise test; however, an estimate can be made from the formula of 220 − age. For example, the training in-

tensity for a 15-year old would be calculated as follows:

$$(220 - 15) \times .75 = 154 \text{ bpm} - (220 - 15) \times .85 = 174 \text{ bpm}$$

It should be noted that the aged-predicted maximal heart may vary between ± 15 beats per minute, in some individuals, from the actual maximal heart rate.

To monitor the intensity of the exercise session, the individual should momentarily stop the exercise (after at least five minutes of activity) and immediately count the pulse rate. It is advisable to keep walking or walk in place during this time. The pulse can be palpated using the index and middle fingers at either the radial artery on the wrist or at one of the carotid arteries on either side of the neck (Figure 2-7). Some precautions need to be followed if the carotid artery is used. First, it is important to palpate only on one side of the neck (i.e., do not put the thumb on one side of the neck and the fingers on the other side). Also, the individual should not press too hard to palpate the carotid artery as a reflex lower-

FIGURE 2-7   Radial and carotid pulse palpitation.

ing of the heart rate could occur. The pulse count is taken for a ten-second count (start the count with zero), and the training range can be determined by dividing the training heart rate by 6 (examples: 154 ÷ 6 = 26; 174 ÷ 6 = 29). The pulse should also be monitored at the end of the training session. Exercising within the training heart rate range will produce optimal physiological adaptations. Highly motivated individuals sometimes have a tendency to train above the training heart rate range (i.e., the feeling that if some is good, then more must be better); however, this should be discouraged as the additional benefits are relatively small and the risk for injury increases at these high intensities.

Duration. The duration of the program is the amount of time spent in the training part of the exercise session (not including warm-up and cool-down time). The minimum duration necessary to stimulate physiological adaptations is 20 minutes, with further increases seen through 60 minutes of activity. The recommended duration range for most individuals is 30 to 40 minutes.

Frequency. The frequency of the training program refers to how often the training should take place, usually described in terms of days per week. Training needs to be performed at least three days per week to derive physiological benefits. Further increases are seen with more frequent training; however, for health-related physical fitness training more than five days per week is of little value. In fact, the body needs rest time between training sessions to make the adaptations. Training six to seven days per week increases the individual's risk for injury. It should be noted that these "off" days do not have to be totally sedentary, indeed alternative types of physical activities and recreation should be encouraged.

Individualization. Intensity, duration, and frequency of training are interrelated. This allows the capability of designing an exercise program to meet the individual's physical capabilities and psychological perceptions of the comfort of the exercise program. Also, factors such as availability of facilities, work or school schedules, weather, and medical restrictions can influence the exercise training program. To be effective, regular exercise must become an integral part of one's lifestyle.

If an intensity level of 75 to 85 percent HR max is found to be undesirably strenuous, the training program can be modified by reducing the intensity level to 65 to 75 percent and either increasing the duration by five to ten minutes per session or the frequency by one day per week.

Individualization can also take place by considering the type of exercise being utilized for the training. Aerobic exercise types are those that use the large muscle groups (i.e., legs or arms and legs) in a rhythmical, dynamic fashion. Activities such as walking, jogging, swimming, cycling, rowing, and cross-country skiing are examples of aerobic exercise types.

A final consideration is the need to begin an exercise program at the reduced intensity and duration and to progress slowly. As one becomes acquainted with the exercise program structure and techniques used, he or she can gradually increase the intensity and duration of the training session. This helps to reduce injuries at the beginning of the program and also increases the individual's self confidence. Table 2-2 represents an example of a start-up walk/jog pro-

TABLE 2-2   Two-week Walking/Jogging Program

WALKING PROGRAM

	Mon.	Tues.	Thur.	Fri.
First Week	Walk 20 min.	Walk 20 min.	Walk 24 min.	Walk 24 min.
Second Week	Walk 28 min.	Walk 28 min.	Walk 32 min.	Walk 32 min.

JOG-WALK PROGRAM

	Mon. and Tues.	Thur. and Fri.
First Week	Walk 20 min.	Walk 17 min.
	Jog/walk 1/2, 1/2, 1/2, 1/2	Jog/walk 1/2, 1/2, 1/2, 1/2, 1/2, 1/2
	Walk 10 min.	Walk 10 min.
Second Week	Walk 15 min.	Walk 12 min.
	Jog/walk 1/2, 1/2, 1/2, 1/2, 1/2, 1/2, 1/2, 1/2, 1/2	Jog/walk 1/2, 1/2, 1/2, 1/2, 1/2, 1/2
	Walk 10 min.	Walk 10 min.

*Note: 1/2 = 110 yds. or 30 to 45 sec. Individual should alternate on the Jog/Walk routine—i.e., Jog 1/2, Walk 1/2, Jog 1/2, etc.

JOGGING PROGRAM

	Mon.	Tues.	Thur.	Fri.
First Week	Jog 2 miles	Jog 4 miles	Jog 3 miles	Jog 5 miles
Second Week	Jog 3 miles	Jog 4 miles	Jog 2 miles	Jog 5 miles

gram. Dr. Bud Getchell, the founder of the Adult Fitness Program at Ball State University, has developed protocols for beginning and progressing in programs of walking, running, cycling, and swimming.[10]

Recreational Activities. A question that often is asked is if one can use recreational activities for training. In general, one should "get in shape to play the game, not play the game to get in shape." However, once an acceptable level of physical fitness is obtained, recreational activities can be useful as a supplement to the training program to maintain the desired level. Table 2-3 shows the caloric equivalents of different recreational activities as well as the standard aerobic training modes for comparison purposes. Recreational activities can provide the necessary variety to the training program to make the long-term commitment to regular exercise solid.

Exercise for Weight Loss. As mentioned previously, from a third to a half of adult Americans are overweight or obese. Body weight is determined by the balance between energy intake and energy expenditure (Figure 2-8). If intake exceeds expenditure, weight will increase, and if expenditure exceeds intake, weight will decrease. Although energy intake is easy to quantify and regulate (increase or decrease food intake), energy expenditure is more difficult to understand since the body can become more or less energy conservative, depending on how it responds to different stresses.

The goal for weight loss programs is the loss of excess body fat. Weight can be lost if energy intake is decreased (dieting), if energy expenditure is increased (principally by increased physical activity), or by both dieting and exercising. Intervention programs for obesity have not been very successful, as most have concentrated only on the energy intake side of the body weight balance equation. The majority of diet programs require substantial caloric restrictions that are actually counterproductive to long-term weight loss as they result in a decrease in resting metabolic rate (the largest component of daily energy expenditure). The more successful weight loss programs use the "exchange" principle for reducing calorie intake. They recommend that individuals exchange their intake of much of the dietary fat, which has 9 kcal/gm, for complex carbohydrates (fruits and vegetables), which have only 4 kcal/gm. This essentially reduces the energy intake but still allows the individual to consume *normal quantities* of food. Successful programs also realize that energy expenditure must be increased for long-term maintenance with weight loss. The types of activities used does not really matter; what is important is that the total amount of physical activity be increased. The increased physical activity level

TABLE 2-3 Energy Requirements of Various Activities

Activity		kcal/min. 123 lb.	kcal/min. 150 lb.
Aquatic Games		7.2	8.7
Archery		3.6	4.4
Badminton		5.4	6.6
Basketball		7.7	9.4
Bicycling		5.6	6.8
Bowling		3.7	4.0
Canoeing		2.5	3.0
Cycling	10 mile/hour	6.5	7.0
Football:Touch/Flag		5.4	6.0
Golf (walking)		4.8	5.8
Handball		7.8	9.5
Hiking		5.5	6.3
Racquetball		7.8	9.5
Running	12 min/mile	8.1	9.9
	11 min/mile	8.7	10.7
	10 min/mile	9.5	11.6
	9 min/mile	10.3	12.7
	8 min/mile	11.6	14.2
	7 min/mile	13.1	16.0
	6 min/mile	15.1	18.5
Skiing: Cross-Country		13.7	15.1
Skiing: Downhill		8.7	10.0
Soccer		7.8	9.5
Softball		3.6	4.7
Swimming		7.2	8.7
Table Tennis		3.8	4.6
Tennis		6.1	7.4
Volleyball		2.8	3.4

Note: A heavier person (150 vs. 123 lb.) must do more work to transport his/her body weight, thus requiring more energy

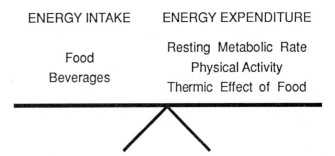

FIGURE 2-8 Body weight balance.

actually serves two purposes: (1) it results in an increase in caloric expenditure due directly to the activity; and (2) it maintains or may slightly increase the resting metabolic rate.

Estimates of how much weight should be lost can be made from the following equation:

[10] Bud Getchell, *The Fitness Book*. (Indianapolis: Benchmark Press, Inc., 1987).

$$\text{Desired Body Weight} = \frac{\text{Fat-free body weight}}{1 - (\text{desired body fat } \% \div 100)}$$

Note that this equation requires knowledge of the individual's body fat percentage and also what percent is a normal or desired body fat. For example, consider a 200 lb. man with a 25 percent body fat and a goal of 15 percent body fat. The desired body weight would be calculated as follows:

$$\frac{200 \ (1 - 25 \div 100)}{1 - (15 \div 100)} = \frac{150 \text{ lb.}}{0.85} = 175.5 \text{ lb.}$$

Thus, this individual would need to lose 23.5 of fat to achieve his desired body composition. Since one pound of fat holds 3,500 kcals, 82,250 kcals must be expended to achieve the desired goal. At first glance this may seem like an insurmountable task. However, success in weight (fat) loss programs is achieved by using the *long-haul* approach. For example, say this man exchanged one-third of his 133 gm of daily fat intake for carbohydrates; this would result in a daily decrease of 220 kcal/day [44 gm/day $\times$ (9 $-$ 4 kcal/gm)]. Additionally, he began a four-day/week exercise program and expended 300 kcal/session (approximately 2.5 miles of walking or jogging) and increased his daily activity level to expend an additional 100 kcal/day. Over a week he would have burned an additional 3,440 kcal or approximately the equivalent of 1 lb. of fat. Thus, it would take him about half a year to attain his goal; however, during this time he likely developed lifestyle dietary and exercise habits which will make long-term maintenance of his desired body weight much more likely. Additionally, the exercise training program would also improve total physical fitness. Note that the maximal safe rate of weight loss is 1 to 2 lb. per week. Losing weight more rapidly will involve losing fat-free weight and decreasing resting metabolic rate.

CLOTHING AND EQUIPMENT

Essentially the only piece of specialized clothing required for aerobic training is proper footwear. Good exercise shoes provide adequate support and cushioning to protect the feet and reduce the shock of the foot strike to the rest of the body (good shoes can take on a force of approximately three times the body weight). The running/walking shoe industry has gone high-tech with literally hundreds of different shoes available with variable features (outsole, midsole, heel counter, upper, foxing, toe box). One should shop for the shoes at a reputable dealer who has personnel that can explain the various features of the different types of shoes and thus assist in selecting the most appropriate shoe for the individual's needs.

In general, exercise clothing should be lightweight and should fit loosely. Fashionable exercise clothing has become very popular; however, care has to be taken to assure that the clothing is breathable and allows moisture to evaporate from the skin. Seasons will dictate how much to wear. In warm, humid weather it is important to expose as much body surface area as possible to allow sweat the opportunity to evaporate and thus help keep body temperature down. In cold weather, layering lightweight clothing is most advantageous since this allows removal of a layer (or two) as the body heat production increases. In extremely cold conditions, protection of the extremities is a must. A hat that covers the ears and either gloves or mittens are needed. Additionally, some individuals find using a breathing filter-type mask helpful to moisturize the cold, dry air.

One myth related to exercise clothing is that rubberized sweat suits are helpful for exercise and weight loss programs. It is true that one can lose a substantial amount of weight in an exercise session if a rubberized suit is worn. However, the weight lost is from body water, *not* body fat, and thus is quickly regained. Not only are these suits ineffective for reducing excess body fat, but they are also potentially dangerous as dehydration can cause body temperature to rise to dangerous levels.

Exercise equipment sales have been tremendous in recent years as claims that particular machines provide the "best" workout in the shortest period of time. Technological advances have allowed computer aided features such as monitors for heart rate, estimations of caloric expenditure, and interval type training sessions to be a part of some of these exercise devices. Indeed many of these exercise machines can make the exercise session more enjoyable by adding some variety to the workout. However, the individual must still perform the work (i.e., same specificity and overload principles apply) to achieve the physiological benefits. The other factor to consider is the expense of much of this equipment. Individuals should be counseled to test thoroughly a piece of equipment before purchasing it. Too often an individual purchases a piece of exercise equipment for home and only uses it for a short period of time before it is moved into a closet or out to the garage for storage.

SUPPLEMENTARY TRAINING

Once the major cardiorespiratory adaptations have been made, some individuals like to modify their training program for maintenance of the adaptations. A modification used is to supplement their regular aerobic training with one or two interval training sessions a week. *Interval training* involves doing repeated cycles of high intensity exercise followed by a brief recovery period. This type of training is used widely in athletics and can produce excellent fitness benefits. The principal advantage of this type of training is that it allows high quality training stimulus in a relatively short duration. For aerobic training, work intervals of .25, .5, and/or .75 miles are recommended, with a work:recovery ratio of 1:1 (i.e., if the work interval is 2 minutes, the recovery time is 2 minutes). These distances are run at a pace faster than the average time for that distance from the best time the individual can run a mile (example: if the best mile time is 8 minutes, the average .25 mile time is 2 minutes, thus the interval training pace for the .25 mile interval run would be less than 2 minutes). A complete description of interval training is beyond the scope of this chapter.[11]

Circuit training involves a series of exercises designed to improve muscular endurance and muscular strength that are completed within a set time frame. The individual moves quickly between each exercise station and then begins the next type of exercise. Some stations may involve aerobic exercise such as stationary cycling, running, rope skipping. These types of programs are useful ways to add some variety to the exercise program if it is becoming "stale" and also assure that the muscular strength and endurance components of fitness are stimulated. A typical circuit could involve two sets of the following exercise stations (one minute per station):

Station	Activity
1	jumping jacks
2	bicep curls
3	modified sit-ups
4	bench press
5	running in place
6	leg press
7	stationary cycling
8	tricep curls
9	rope skipping or bench stepping
10	leg curls

It is important to remember that appropriate program structure of beginning with a warm-up and finishing with a cool-down period also applies to these supplemental types of training.

CONCLUSION

A quote attributable to Hippocrates sums up the value of physical fitness:

All parts of the body which have a function, if used in moderation and exercised in labors in which each is accustomed, become thereby healthy, well-developed and age more slowly, but if unused and left idle they become liable to disease, defective in growth, and age quickly.[12]

TERMINOLOGY

Aerobic training   Exercise training performed at an intensity, duration, and frequency that stimulates adaptations of the aerobic energy system and the cardio-respiratory systems of the body.

Body composition   The evaluation of the components of the body (ex. water, muscle, bone, fat) with the determination of percentage of body fat the most common.

Calorie   A unit of energy.

Cool-down   A group of activities including walking, calisthenics, and flexibility exercises performed following the exercise training session to gradually return the body to its resting state.

Duration   The amount of time spent in one exercise training session.

Exchange principle   A diet modification that substitutes foods of lower caloric value, mainly high carbohydrate foods, for foods of higher caloric value (i.e., foods of high fat content).

Frequency   The number of training sessions performed in a fixed period of time, usually one week.

Intensity   The percentage of maximal capabilities that are being utilized (e.g. percentage of maximal heart rate).

Interval training   Exercise training sessions that are characterized by alternating periods of vigorous exercise (work interval) with periods of relief (low intensity exercise or rest interval).

Lipids   Substances that are not soluble in water. The most important blood lipids include cholesterol and triglyceride.

Lipoproteins   A compound formed by combining cholesterol and protein to allow the cholesterol to be soluble in fluid and thus transported in the blood.

Overload   An exercise training principle that states that adaptations to training will only take place when the activity stresses the body's systems beyond what it is normally accustomed to.

Specificity   An exercise training principle that states that adaptations to training are specific to the muscle groups utilized, the speed of contractions performed, the movement patterns employed, and the energy systems required to power the activity.

VO₂   The volume of oxygen consumed, used as an indirect measure of energy expenditure.

Warm-up   A group of activities including walking, calisthenics, and flexibility exercises performed prior to

[11] For more information on designing interval training workouts, see E.L. Fox, *Sports Physiology.* New York: CBS College Publishing, 1984, pp. 378–380.

[12] A.G. Wallace, Fitness, Health, and Longevity—A Question of Cause and Effect. *Inside Track,* 583, 1986.

the exercise training session to prepare the body for vigorous physical activity.

SELECTED REFERENCES

American College of Sports Medicine. *Resource Manual for Guidelines for Exercise Testing and Prescription.* Philadelphia: Lea & Febiger, 1988.

Katch, F.L. and McArdle, W.D. *Nutrition, Weight Control, and Exercise,* 3rd ed. Philadelphia: Lea & Febiger, 1988.

Pollock, M.L. and Wilmore, J.H. *Exercise in Health and Disease,* 2nd ed. Philadelphia: W. B. Saunders Co., 1990.

Powers, S.K. and Howley, E.T. *Exercise Physiology: Theory and Application to Fitness and Performance.* Dubuque, IA: W.B. Brown Publishers, 1990.

Prentice, W.E. and Bucher, C.A. *Fitness for College and Life,* 3rd ed. St. Louis, MO: Mosby Year Book, 1991.

3 ARCHERY

THIS CHAPTER WILL ENABLE YOU TO:

▶ *Identify and demonstrate the ten basic steps of shooting in target archery.*
▶ *Identify and demonstrate terms related to the bow and arrow.*
▶ *Understand the basic terminology associated with target archery.*
▶ *Identify and describe the rules associated with target archery.*
▶ *Identify and observe the necessary safety precautions.*

NATURE AND PURPOSE

For the past several years, not only has interest in archery grown tremendously throughout the world, but many schools and colleges include archery in their physical education programs. Consequently, archery has become a modern sport form. In the 1972 Olympic Games held at Munich, archery appeared as an Olympic event for the first time. Several archers from the United States have captured Olympic medals and medals from other international competitions.

Archery is an easy-to-learn activity, and it is possible for both sexes of all ages to develop proficiency in archery skills in a relatively short period of time. As an individual sport, it is relatively inexpensive and can be practiced year-round. The benefits of archery are both physical and emotional.

EQUIPMENT

Archery equipment as a whole is known as "tackle." The minimum essential tackle for the beginning archer includes: (1) a bow of correct length and weight, (2) one dozen matched arrows, (3) a finger tab or glove, (4) an arm guard, and (5) a target. The selection of a proper bow and matched arrows are the two most important steps for successful archery practice.

Bows

Bows are constructed of many materials including wood, fiberglass, or laminated wood core and fiberglass. To overcome the disadvantages of the wooden or fiberglass bow, a laminated (composite) bow was designed. This bow is smooth-shooting and is not subject to changes due to weather.

Bow weight refers to the weight in pounds required to bring a bow to full draw. The most important factor in determining bow weight is the individual archer's muscular strength. For the beginner, it is best to start with a bow that is easier to draw and handle rather than using "overbow." The bow weight may be gradually increased as the archer improves shooting technique and develops muscular strength. Table 3-1 shows the recommended bow weights according to the standards established by the Archery Manufacturers Organization.

Arrows

Arrows are made of wood, fiberglass, or aluminum. The least expensive, wooden arrows, are used by most beginning archers; glass and aluminum arrows are used by more advanced archers. Each type of arrow has it own advantages and disadvantages, but it is very important that one select arrows closely matched in weight, length, and stiffness (spine).

A beginner should start to shoot with arrows that are two inches longer than the needed proper

TABLE 3-1 Recommended Bow Weights.

	Under 20 lbs	20 lbs	25 lbs	30 lbs	35 lbs	40 lbs	Over 40 lbs
Children 6-12	X	X					
Teen (girl)		X	X				
Teen (boy)		X	X	X			
Women		X	X	X			
Men					X	X	X	
Hunting							X

length in case of an overdraw. To determine the proper length, one should place the nock of the arrow on the center of one's chest and extend arms full length forward, palms facing, so that the point of the arrow extends past the fingertips. When purchasing a bow and arrows, one should seek advice from an expert to determine the proper bow and arrows that fit best.

Arm Guards

Arm guards have two main functions: (1) the most important is to protect the bow arm from the slap of the bow string; (2) the other is to keep a long sleeve close to the arm so it will not interfere with the bow string. The arm guard is worn on the inside of the forearm below the elbow, near the wrist of the bow arm. The arm guard is usually made of leather with elastic straps to hold the guard on the forearm.

Finger Tabs or Gloves

Friction between the fingers and the bow string can produce not only soreness to the fingers, but it can also have effects on proper shooting. Tabs or gloves will protect the fingers and aid in developing a smooth and consistent release. Many beginners have difficulty in using finger tabs or gloves, but with a little patience and practice one can overcome this difficulty.

Target

A target consists of a target face, a mat, and a stand, and ready-made targets can be purchased from a sporting goods dealer. Schools and colleges usually use a 48-inch target face. Target mats are easily made from tightly compressed hay and should measure at least 50 × 50 inches.

RULES OF TARGET ARCHERY

1. Any bow except a crossbow may be used for competition.
2. Arrows should have a distinctive crest in order to distinguish each archer's arrow.
3. After the signal to shoot, arrows should be nocked.
4. Arrows that fall from the bow and cannot be reached with the bow from the shooting line are considered to be shot.
5. Only six arrows may be shot at the designated target; if more than six are shot, only the lowest six scores are counted, and any arrow(s) shot at any other target shall not be scored.
6. An archer should shoot from the longest distance first, the second longest distance next, and so forth.

7. Scores are recorded from the highest score to the lowest score.
8. Arrows should be retrieved only after the signal is given.

SCORING

The scoring values of target archery are 9 points for gold; 7 for red; 5 for blue; 3 for black; and 1 for white rings. An arrow that goes completely through the target or that bounces off the target counts 7 points regardless of the part of the target it passes or hits. An arrow that lands on the line between two rings counts as hitting the higher scoring ring.

All target archery rounds (competitions) are shot at a regulation 48-inch target face unless otherwise specified. The common target archery competitions are the American Round, Columbia Round, Hereford Round, York Round, Women's and Men's Metropolitan Rounds, and Scholastics Round. Each competition round differs in the number of arrows and the distance from which the arrows are shot.

For physical education classes, a modified institutional round should be implemented to enable a round to be completed within a given time period. For example, the Ball State Round consists of 12 ends: 4 ends each shooting from 20 yards, 25 yards, and 30 yards, and requiring approximately sixty minutes to complete. Each end consists of shooting 5 arrows. The scoring values of the Ball State Round are 5 points for gold; 4 points for red; 3 for blue; 2 for black; and 1 for white. This gives a maximum total of 300 points (5 arrows × 5 points × 12 ends = 300 points). If a class period is only forty-five minutes, a round should consist of 8 ends: 4 ends from 25 yards and 4 ends from 30 yards.

SUGGESTED LEARNING SEQUENCE

Open space with good lighting and a proper backdrop, well-organized lessons, and an emphasis on safety are all important aspects of creating a successful atmosphere for archery. Safety should be stressed from the very beginning. Instructions should include the care of the equipment (bow, bowstring, and arrows) and the ten essential steps for shooting described in this chapter. A good learning sequence is the following:

A. Introduction
B. Nature of the Activity
   1. Archery as a sport and family recreation
   2. Discussion of equipment
   3. Safety
C. Skills and Techniques—Ten Basic Steps of Shooting

Static Stage: Practice without arrows
1. Proper stance
2. Nocking the arrow
3. Setting the hook
4. Holding the bow
5. Raising the head
6. Raising the unit

Dynamic Stage: Practice with arrows
7. Drawing and anchoring
8. Aiming and holding
9. Releasing
10. Follow-through

Steps 7 and 8 should be practiced several times before moving into steps 9 and 10.

The first shooting practice should start from 15 yards, then 20 yards, 30 yards, and so on.

D. Rules and Scoring—Once some proficiency in shooting technique has been achieved, participants can be taught the rules governing target archery and the scoring method.

SKILLS AND TECHNIQUES

String the Bow

Push-pull Method

1. Take the bow handle in your left hand with the back of the bow toward you.
2. Holding the left arm in front of the body and angling the bow's upper limb toward the right, place the lower nock against the instep of the left foot, but not touching the ground.
3. Place the right hand on the upper limb just below the upper loop of the bowstring; then keeping both arms straight, pull with the left hand and push with the heel of the right hand, and slide the string into the upper nock with fingers. While stringing, keep your face away from the bow.

Step-through Method

1. Hold the bow in your right hand and the string with the other hand.
2. Place the back of the lower limb of the bow across the ankle of your left foot.
3. Step through the bow with your right leg.
4. Place the bow handle high on your right thigh.
5. Press the upper limb of the bow forward with the open right hand and slide the string in the nock with the left hand. Always check both notches for proper string insertion and alignment after each stringing.

Shooting: The Ten Basic Steps

Archers should always follow the ten basic steps of the shooting sequence in their proper order. Consistency is very important for becoming a good archer. Repetition of these ten steps will help you develop rhythm in shooting and help you become a satisfied archer. The steps described below are for the right-handed person; adjustments are required for left-handers.

Step 1—Establishing a Proper Stance

The stance establishes the foundation of good archery form; the square and open stances are the most commonly used. For both stances, the archer should spread both feet apart (approximately shoulder width) to achieve a comfortable feeling. The archer's weight should be equally distributed upon both feet, and the knees should be locked to maintain balance. Once you decide on a stance—either the square or open stance—you should take the same stance each time you shoot.

1. *Square Stance.* The square stance is recommended for beginning archers. In this stance, the archer's feet straddle the shooting line with both feet parallel to each other, and toes line up with the center of the target. The body should be upright with head turned toward the target (see Figure 3-1).
2. *Open (Oblique) Stance.* To assume the open stance, the archer draws the foot closer to the target back about 4 to 6 inches from the square stance. At the same time, hips and shoulders must also turn so that the body is at about a 45-degree angle to the target (see Figure 3-2). The open stance is recommended for advanced archers.

Step 2—Nocking the Arrow

Nocking the arrow means placing the arrow on the bowstring in preparation for drawing.

▶ **Learning Cues**

1. Hold the bow with the left hand and the palm of the bow hand facing the ground.

FIGURE 3–1 Square stance.

FIGURE 3–2 Open stance.

2. The right hand holding the shaft of the arrow, with index finger pointing upward, slip the nock onto the string at a 90-degree angle with the string. Make a small mark with ink on the string to ensure that the nocking is always done in the same place. If a bow with the nocking point is already fixed on the string, the arrow is usually nicked below the nocking point. After nocking, the archer makes sure there is no gap between the string and the throat of the nock.

Step 3—Setting the Hook

After nocking the arrow, the archer must establish a proper hook. The hook is set using three fingers (index, middle, and fourth fingers) of the archer's right hand. Hook first three fingers around the string at the first knuckles of these fingers. Hold the arrow lightly between index and middle fingers but do not squeeze the arrows (Figure 3-3). Thumb and little finger of the right hand should be touching each other over the palm. After shooting for a while the thumb and little finger should be relaxed. It is important to keep the back of the right hand straight.

Step 4—Establishing a Bow Hold

As in all other aspects of archery, consistency is also required in establishing a proper bow hold. First, extend your left arm at the shoulder height toward the target with left hand in a "handshake" position, then place the pivot point of the bow handle (midsection of the bow) in the "V" formed by the thumb and index finger. Now the handle of the bow should rest against the base of the thumb, and other fingers should be placed lightly around the handle. This keeps the bow from falling at release of the arrow. Make sure that you do not grip the bow. Before releasing the arrow, the elbow of the bow arm must be turned down to avoid slapping by the bowstring (Figure 3-4).

Step 5—Raising the Head

Before raising the unit (bow and arrow), the archer's head should be in a natural position turned to look directly at the center of the target without any tilt (Figure 3-5).

FIGURE 3–3 Setting the hook.

FIGURE 3–4 The bow hold.

FIGURE 3–5 Note head position.

Step 6—Raising the Unit

At this point, the archer has prepared mechanically for shooting by establishing a proper stance, nocking an arrow, setting the hook, establishing the grip, and raising the head. Now the archer is ready to do the dynamic parts of shooting. The archer raises the entire unit (bow with a nocked arrow) to shoulder height. The bow is now in an upright position facing the target, bow arm is extended toward target, and the drawing arm is forming an extension of the arrow. The elbow of the drawing arm is better slightly higher than lower in relation to the arrow (Figure 3-6).

Step 7—Drawing and Anchoring

Drawing is the act of pulling the bowstring into the shooting position, and anchoring is the point where the drawing hand is placed. The drawing and the anchoring should be done with one smooth deliberate motion.

▶ **Learning Cues—Drawing**

1. Before drawing, keep in mind that the three fingers of the drawing hand are just hooked onto the string at the first knuckles.
2. The drawing hand should be relaxed with special attention given to relaxing the back of the hand; elbow of the drawing arm should be slightly elevated.
3. The elbow of the drawing arm should be slightly elevated.

4. Now the archer draws the bow by letting the shoulder and back muscles do the pulling with one smooth and deliberate motion.
5. At the full draw, the string should make contact with the center of the nose, lips, and chin.

▶ **Learning Cues—Anchoring**

1. Anchoring must be done at the same point for each draw. This lets the arrow be drawn exactly the same distance and place each time.
2. The index finger of the drawing hand should be under the tip of the jawbone with the thumb relaxed against the neck (low anchor point).
3. While drawing, the archer should take a deep breath, exhale about half of the air and hold the rest until the arrow has been released (Figure 3-7).

Step 8—Aiming and Holding

Three methods of aiming in archery are by using a bow sight attached to the bow, by "point of aim," and by "instinctive shooting."

1. Shooting with a bow sight is the most accurate aiming technique. The archer should line up the string and bow sight with the center of the target. If the arrow hits high, move the sight up and if low, move the sight down. The sight can also be adjusted left or right.
2. Point-of-aim shooting is aiming at some spot with the point of the arrow. The spot may be in front of, on, or above the target. The selection of

FIGURE 3-6 Eyes on target, drawing arm slightly higher than arrow.

FIGURE 3-7 Anchoring.

the aiming spot depends upon the height of the archer, length of the arrow, and bow weight. When shots are low, move the spot up; when shots are high, move the spot down. String alignment is also important and should be done directly in front of the right eye and lined up vertical with the bow.

3. Instinctive shooting is shooting without a sight or point-of-aim marker. The archer's eyes are focused on the center of target and the bow arm will adjust itself toward target. Accuracy of this technique depends upon the archer's shooting form, eyesight, depth perception, and kinesthetic awareness.

Concentration may be the single most important part of aiming. You should hold your breath and relax a few seconds until the arrow is released. You should also be aware that the sight will oscillate while you are aiming, but make sure it oscillates within the target center.

Step 9—Release

Releasing the arrow should be done with unconscious effort. The archer simply relaxes the entire drawing hand and lets the string roll off the fingers by itself. No other parts of the body except the drawing hand should be moved. During the release, the archer must continue aiming and maintain the contraction of the upper back muscles. Furthermore, the archer should let neither the drawing hand move forward nor come off the anchor position to release the string.

Step 10—Follow-through

Follow-through is the act of maintaining the body position and mental condition assumed at release until the arrow hits the target. The bow arm is pushed slightly forward, and the drawing hand rubs the chin as it moves back behind the archer's neck. During the act of release and follow-through, the archer must continue aiming at the target center rather than following the flight of the arrow and keeping the tension of the upper back muscles (Figure 3-8).

Retrieving Arrows

To retrieve an arrow from the target, place the palm of your left hand against the target face with the arrow resting between the index and the middle finger, and push the target face lightly. With your right hand, grasp the arrow by the shaft close to the target and, twisting it slightly counterclockwise, pull the arrow directly backward. If the arrow goes through the target but the fletchings (feathers) remain inside the mat, go to the back of the target and pull the arrow carefully forward without any twisting motion.

FIGURE 3–8 Release and follow-through.

MODIFICATIONS FOR SPECIAL POPULATIONS

Orthopedically Impaired

1. Minimal modifications are needed for the wheelchair user with good upper body strength and coordination.
2. Students with grasping difficulties should consider commercially purchased assistive devices, e.g., trigger, wrist, and mouthpiece releases.
3. Wrist and elbow supports would also assist in aiming.

Mentally Impaired

Minimal modifications are needed.

Sensory Impaired

1. Blind students can be taught to feel the correct way to notch the arrow in the bow.
2. Place an audio signal at the target, e.g., bell, buzzer.
3. Secure a rope from the archer to the target to provide the blind student a guide for retrieving the arrows.
4. Make targets out of various textures or areas of the target out of various textures, e.g., velcro, sandpaper, or paper.

5. Deaf and hard of hearing students would require minimal adaptations.

HINTS FOR IMPROVING TECHNIQUE

Upon release, movements of certain parts of the body will cause faulty arrow flights. Be aware of these movements so that you can avoid them.

1. *High arrow flights are usually caused by:*
   a. Peeking (looking up to watch the arrow in flight)
   b. Heeling the bow (putting pressure on the low part of the bow handle with the low portion of the bow hand)
   c. Body leaning backward
   d. Overdraw (pulling arrows beyond normal anchor point)
2. *Low arrow flights are usually caused by:*
   a. Creeping (letting the drawing hand move forward before arrow is released)
   b. Overhold (maintaining the hold position too long)
   c. String hitting the arm guard upon release
   d. Hunching the shoulder of the bow arm
3. *Arrow flights to the left are usually caused by:*
   a. Cupping the drawing hand instead of having the back of the drawing hand relaxed and straight
   b. Bringing the string away from the face (anchor point) to release the arrow
   c. Improper alignment of the bow, body, or string
4. *Arrows falling off the arrow rest of the bow are caused by:*
   a. Pinching of the arrow nock with the fingers of the drawing hand. To remedy this, the archer should separate the index and middle fingers to insure a light touch with the nock, hook the string with the first knuckles of drawing fingers, and utilize back muscles to draw
   b. Tight finger tab
   c. Cupping of the drawing hand

SAFETY

Bows and arrows are weapons capable of inflicting serious injury and should be handled with care. Here are some specific precautions to follow. Remember that the continued enjoyment of archery depends upon everyone observing these safety rules.

1. Always check the bow and string to see if it is properly placed at both ends of the string notch before starting to shoot.
2. Shoot only at the target.
3. Don't draw the bow when anyone is between you and the target area.
4. Never allow anyone to retrieve arrows until all arrows have been shot.
5. Never shoot into the air or in any direction where it might destroy property or endanger life.
6. Always be sure that the area in back of the target is clear or has an adequate back stop.
7. Do not overdraw the bow.
8. Be sure arrows are of the correct length and stiffness for the bow.
9. Do not release a fully drawn bow without an arrow.
10. Obey all commands given for shooting and retrieving arrows.
11. Always wear an arm guard and finger tab to prevent injury.
12. Do not wear bulky clothing or dangling jewelry when shooting.
13. No fooling around or horseplay on the shooting line.
14. Never run with arrows in your hand; when carrying arrows, keep the pile ends toward the ground.
15. When you have finished shooting, stand behind the other archers until the end has been completed.

TERMINOLOGY

Addressing the target Standing ready to shoot with a proper shooting stance.
Anchor point Specific location on the archer's face to which the index finger comes while holding and aiming.
Archery golf An adaptation of the game of golf to the sport of archery. Players shoot for the holes, and score according to the number of shots required to hit the target.
Arm guard A piece of leather or plastic that is worn on the inside of the forearm to protect the arm from the bowstring.
Arrow plate A protective piece of hard material set into the bow where the arrow crosses it.
Arrow rest A small projection at the top of the bow handle where the arrow rests.
Back The side of the bow away from the shooter.
Bow arm The arm that holds the bow; this would be the left arm for a right-handed person.
Bow sight A device attached to the bow through which the archer sights when aiming.
Bow weight Designates the amount of effort (in pounds) needed to pull a bowstring a specific distance (usually 28 inches).
Cant The act of holding the bow tilted or slightly turned while shooting.
Cast The distance a bow can shoot an arrow.
Clout shooting A type of shooting that uses a target 48 feet in diameter, laid on the ground at a distance of 180 yards for men and 140 or 120 yards for women.

Usually 36 arrows (6 ends with 6 arrows) are shot per round.

Cock feather   Now called the "index feather." The feather that is set at a right angle to the arrow nock; differently colored than other two feathers.

Creeping   Letting the drawing hand move forward at the release.

Crest   The archer's identifying marks shown just below the fletchings on the arrow.

Draw   The act of pulling the bow string back into the anchor position.

End   A specified number of arrows shot at one time or from one position before retrieval of arrows.

Face   The part of the bow facing the shooter.

Finger tab   A leather flap worn on the drawing hand to protect the fingers and provide a smooth release of the bow string.

Fletchings   The feathers of the arrow, which give guidance to its flight.

Flight shooting   Shooting an arrow the farthest possible distance.

Handle   The grip at the midsection of the bow.

Hen feathers   The two feathers that are not set at right angles to the arrow nock. See *Cock feather.*

Hold   Steadily holding the arrow at full draw before release.

Instinctive shooting   Aiming and shooting instinctively, rather than using a bow sight or point-of-aim method.

Limbs   Upper and lower parts of the bow; divided by the handle.

Nock   The groove in the end of the arrow in which the string is placed.

Nocking point   The point on the string at which the arrow is placed.

Notch   The grooves of the upper and lower tips of the limbs into which the bow string is fitted.

Overbow   Using too strong a bow that is too powerful to pull a bowstring to proper distance.

Overdraw   Drawing the bow so that the pile of the arrow is inside the bow.

Petticoat   That part of the target face outside the white ring.

Pile (point)   The pointed metal tip of the arrow.

Pinch   To squeeze the nock of the arrow.

Plucking   Jerking the drawing hand laterally away from the face on the release, which will cause arrow flight to the left.

Point-blank range   The only distance from the target at which the point of aim is right on the bull's eye.

Point-of-aim   A method of aiming in which the pile of the arrow is aligned with the target.

Quiver   A receptacle for carrying or holding arrows.

Recurve bow   A bow that is curved on the ends.

Release   The act of letting the bowstring slip off the fingertips.

Round   The term used to indicate shooting a designated number of arrows at a designated distance or distances.

Roving   Archery game played outdoors in which natural targets (stumps, trees, bushes, etc.) are selected for competition.

Serving   The thread wrapped around the bowstring at the nocking point.

Shaft   The long, body part of the arrow.

Spine   The characteristic rigidity and flexibility of an arrow.

Tackle   Archery equipment referred to as a whole.

Target face   The painted front of a target, usually replaceable.

Trajectory   The path of the arrow in flight.

Vane   Plastic feather of an arrow.

SELECTED REFERENCES

Baier, P., Bowers, J., Fowkes, C.R.; and Schoch, S. *The National Archery Association Instructor's Manual.* 3rd ed. Colorado Springs, CO: National Archery Association of the United States, 1982.

Bavousett, F.L. *Beginning Target Archery.* College Station, TX: Unlimited Products, 1979.

Bavousett, F. and Beardsley, M. *Archery Lab Manual.* College Station, TX: Unlimited Products, 1979.

Driscoll, M.L. *Selected Archery Article.* 1st ed. Reston, VA: American Association for Health, Physical Education and Recreation, 1971.

Hadas, L. *Champions.* Panorama City, CA: L.F.H. Film Production, 1980.

Haywood, K. *Teaching Archery: Steps to Success.* Champaign, IL: Leisure Press, 1989.

Heath, E.G. *Archery: The Modern Approach.* 2nd ed. London and Boston: Faber and Faber, 1978.

Henderson, A. *Understanding Winning Archery.* Mequon, WI: In Target Communications, 1983.

Keaggy, D., Sr. *Power Archery.* 2nd ed. Drayton Plains, MI: Power Archery Products, 1968.

Kember-Smith, John. *Archery Today: Techniques and Philosophies in Action.* North Pomfret, VT: David and Charles, 1988.

Khouri, L.M. *Archery for the Visually Handicapped.* Thesis: Women's College, University of North Carolina, 1961.

Morisawa, J.S. *The Secret of the Target.* New York and London: Routledge, 1984.

McKinney, W.C. and McKinney, M.W. *Archery.* Dubuque, IA: Wm. C. Brown Publishers, 1985.

Patterson, W.F. *Encyclopedia of Archery.* New York: St. Martin's Press, 1984.

Pszczola, L. *Archery.* 2nd ed. Philadelphia: Saunders,1976.

Richardson, M.E. *Archery.* New York: McKay, 1979.

Solier, A. and Gyorbiro, Z. *Japanese Archery: Zen in Action.* New York and Tokyo: Walker/Weatherhill, 1969.

Target Archery With Easton Aluminum Shafts. Van Nuys, CA: Easton Aluminum Co., 1981.

Williams, J.C. *Archery for Beginners.* 2nd ed. Chicago: Contemporary Books, 1985.

Wise, L. *Tuning Your Compound Bow.* Mequon, WI: Target Communications, 1985.

Audio-Visual Materials

Advanced Shooting Techniques. Writ. A. Henderson. Athletic Institute: North Palm Beach, FL, 1978 (motion picture).

An Invitation to Archery. Writ. A. Henderson. Athletic Institute: North Palm Beach, FL, 1978 (motion picture).

Fundamentals of Archery: Basic Shooting Techniques. Writ. A. Henderson. Athletic Institute: North Palm Beach, FL, 1978 (motion picture).

Mastering the Bow and Arrow Sports. Writ. A. Henderson. Athletic Institute: North Palm Beach, FL, 1978 (motion picture).

4 BADMINTON

THIS CHAPTER WILL ENABLE YOU TO:

▶ *Understand the fundamental techniques in various strokes used in the game of badminton.*
▶ *Display an understanding of basic strategy in both singles and doubles.*
▶ *Identify and understand the basic rules for singles and doubles.*
▶ *Understand basic terminology used in the game of badminton.*

NATURE AND PURPOSE

The game of badminton has been around for a number of years. Historians believe that a very similar game (called *battledore*) was played in China over 2,000 years ago. However, badminton as it is presently known is believed to have originated from a game called *poona* that was played by English army officers stationed in India during the 17th century.

Badminton has steadily gained world-wide acceptance as being a very fast-paced, highly skilled, competitive game. This is substantiated by the fact that badminton has now been included as a full-fledged medal sport in the Olympic Games. Badminton in America is also rapidly growing in popularity. At the beginning level it is usually possible to keep the shuttle in play, which makes the game enjoyable and rewarding for most age groups. Singles, doubles or mixed doubles may be played; thus badminton is an excellent coeducational activity.

Although courts can be set up outdoors, competitive badminton is generally played indoors where the wind and elements will not affect the shuttle.

EQUIPMENT

The choice of equipment is important in badminton. High-quality rackets and shuttlecocks (birds) can have a favorable bearing on performance. When purchasing rackets and birds, buy the best you can afford.

Racket

Badminton rackets are quite light and can be made of wood, aluminum, metal, or synthetic material such as graphite or carbon. Synthetic rackets are quite popular now because of their extreme lightness and strength.

The price of rackets also varies. There are "playable" rackets that can be purchased from $20 to $35 (excellent for the beginner or physical education classes) and other higher quality rackets for the "competitive" player, ranging from $45 to $150. The racket can be strung with either nylon or gut. Nylon string is sufficient for the beginning player as it usually costs less and lasts longer than gut.

In any case choosing a racket is a matter of personal preference and you should use what feels comfortable, not what looks good.

Shuttlecock

The "official" shuttlecock, usually called *shuttle* or *bird,* is made from goose feathers which are placed in a cork head that is leather covered. Feather shuttles are quite expensive and can be damaged during play very quickly. They are used primarily in high-level tournament competition.

Shuttles are also made of either plastic or nylon. These shuttles last longer and are not as expensive as the feathered bird. There are several types of nylon or plastic birds that are very durable and excellent for class play.

BADMINTON COURT

The official badminton court (shown in Figures 4-1 and 4-2) is 44 feet long. The doubles court is 20 feet wide, while the singles court is 17 feet wide. The net is 5 feet at the center and 5 feet 1 inch at the posts. A "½ court" practice/drill arrangement is shown in Figure 4-3.

Overhead clearance is an important factor in

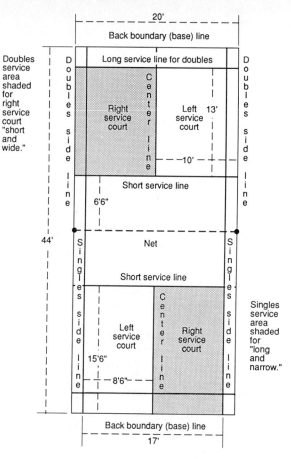

FIGURE 4-1 Badminton playing court. Top view.

setting up a badminton court. Generally speaking, an overhead clearance of less than 20 feet would not be considered conducive for playing the game effectively. A clearance of at least 30 feet is required for all national and international competition.

Serving Court—Singles

The serving court for singles is bounded by the short service line, the centerline, the singles sideline, and the back boundary line of the court. The server must stand within this court, feet not touching any lines, and serve diagonally over the net into his opponent's singles service court in order to have a legal serve.

Serving Court—Doubles

The serving court for doubles is bounded by the short service line, the centerline, the doubles sideline, and the long service line for doubles. The server must stand within this court, feet not touching any lines, and serve diagonally over the net into his opponent's doubles service court in order to have a legal serve.

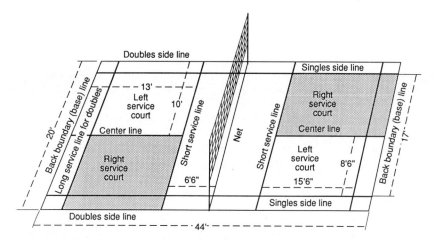

FIGURE 4-2 Badminton court. Side view.

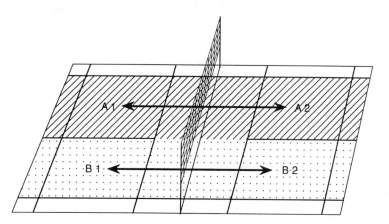

FIGURE 4-3 "½ court" practice/drill areas. A1 practices/drills with partner A2; B1 practices/drills with B2.

RULES OF BADMINTON

1. Toss for serve. Before a match begins, opponents can toss a coin, spin a racket, or toss a shuttle to determine who shall get the choice of "serve" or "side." If spinning a racket, identify a marking on the racket and have one person call the mark. If tossing a shuttle, the proper procedure is for one person to either hit or toss the shuttle in the air and let it land. The person towards whom the base of the shuttle is pointing gets the choice.

2. Men's singles and all doubles games are played to 15 points. Women's singles is played to 11 points. In a 15-point game, if the score becomes tied at 13–13, the player/team scoring 13 points first (the receivers) can elect to continue and finish the game to 15 points (which is termed "no set") or, they can elect to play 5 more points ("set") to finish the game. When tied at 14–14, the player/team scoring 14 points first can elect to continue and finish the game to 15 points, or they can elect to "set" the game at 3 points. In an 11-point game, if the game is tied at 9–9, the first player scoring 9 points has the choice of either finishing the game at 11 points ("no set"), or "setting" the game at 3 points. If the game is tied at 10–10, the choice would be either to finish the game at 11 points or to "set" the game at 2 points.
(NOTE: A player/team *does not* have to win by 2 points.)

3. The serve must be delivered into the diagonal service court and within its boundaries to be a legal serve. Any shuttle hitting the line is in. In singles the shuttle must land in the long, narrow court, in doubles it must land in the short, wide court. In doubles, once the serve has been returned, the full court (20 × 44 feet) is played.

4. The server is allowed only one trial to put the shuttle into play. The shuttle may hit the net and land in the proper court and be legal. In singles the service is made from the right service court whenever the server's score is an even number (0, 2, 4, etc.). Whenever the server's score is an odd number (1, 3, 5, etc.) the service is made from the left service court. In doubles the first serve is always started from the right court whenever a team acquires the service from their opponents. The server will alternate service courts each time a point is made or until the serve is lost. Only one "hand" is allowed the side beginning the serve in doubles the first "inning." Two hands are allowed each inning thereafter.

5. Matches consist of winning two out of three games. Players must change sides of the court after each game. The winner of the previous game starts the serve in the next game. If a third game is required, players will switch courts again at what is considered the half-way point: immediately after a player reaches 8 points in a 15-point game or immediately after a player reaches 6 points in an 11-point game.

6. It is a fault (loss of service or "hand out" for the serving side; or loss of point for the receiving side) when:
   a. Service is illegal, i.e., the shuttle is struck when above the waist, or the head of the racket is higher than the lowest finger of the racket hand when contact is made.
   b. Service or played shot lands outside the specified court, passes through or under the net, or hits a player or obstruction outside the court.
   c. If server or receiver is standing outside of the proper court upon delivery of the serve or balks in any way before the service. Only the person served to may return the shuttle.
   d. The server or receiver steps forward, lifts, or drags a foot during the delivery of the serve.
   e. The server misses the shuttle in attempting to serve.
   f. A player reaches over the net to contact a shuttle. (The follow-through, however, may break the plane of the net.)
   g. A player touches the net with the racket or any part of the body while the shuttle is deemed to be in play.
   h. A player contacts the shuttle twice in one swing. (Referred to as a "double hit.")
   i. A player fails to return the shuttle to the opponent's proper court. (The opposing player cannot hit, catch, or be struck by a doubtful shuttle and then call it "out.")
   j. On a doubles serve, the server's partner unsights the server (does not allow receivers to view the service).
   k. In doubles, a shuttle is hit by a player and the player's partner successively.
   l. A player prevents or hinders an opponent from making a legal stroke where the shuttle is followed over the net (racket follow-through of the striker).

SUGGESTED LEARNING SEQUENCE

After acquiring an understanding of the basic strategy, simplified rules, and court courtesies, playing should start immediately. Specific skills will be introduced as the learning sequence progresses. The following outline includes everything that needs to be covered, but the exact teaching sequence will vary according to circumstances.

A. Nature of the Game
   1. Demonstration or video of actual play (National or International competition)
   2. The playing court

B. The Singles Game
 1. Basic strategy
 2. Simplified rules and scoring
 3. Court courtesies
C. Grip
 1. Forehand
D. Play Games
E. Strokes
 1. Overhead clear
 2. Long serve
 3. Short serve
F. Introduce intra-class competition
 1. Ladder tournament
 2. Round robin, etc.
G. Strokes (continued)
 1. Smash
 2. Block (forehand and backhand)
H. Footwork and movement
 1. Backcourt
 2. Lateral (blocking)
 3. Forecourt
I. Strokes (continued)
 1. Around-the-head
  a. Clears
  b. Smashes
 2. Overhead drop
J. Grip
 1. Backhand
K. Strokes (continued)
 1. Net clears (forehand and backhand)
 2. Net drops (forehand and backhand)
L. The Doubles Game
 1. Basic strategy
 2. Simplified rules and scoring
 3. Alignments
  a. Side-by-side (defensive)
  b. Up-and-back (offensive)
  c. Circular rotation (combination of a and b
   above, depending upon the situation)

SKILLS AND TECHNIQUES

Many different skills and techniques must be utilized effectively to be a good, fundamentally sound badminton player. In this section we will describe each stroke or skill, and give learning cues and practice suggestions for each.

The Grips

Forehand. To acquire the proper grip for a forehand stroke, hold the racket by the shaft in the left hand with the face of the racket perpendicular to the floor and "shake hands" with the grip (Figure 4-4). Slide your hand down so that the fatty part rests comfortably against the "butt" of the handle. There will be a "V" formed by the juncture of your

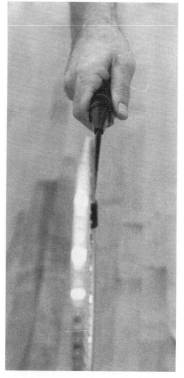

FIGURE 4-4
Forehand grip.

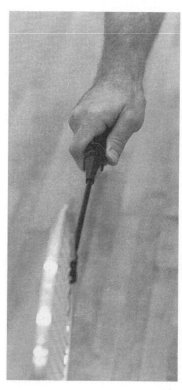

FIGURE 4-5
Backhand grip.

thumb and index finger. This "V" should be slightly to the left of center for right-handed players. Grasp the handle lightly with fingers spread slightly. The thumb wraps around the handle on the left side. Proper thumb placement is vital for stroking proficiently.

When not in the act of stroking the shuttle your grip should be relaxed and fairly loose. As you start your stroke you will tighten your grip somewhat—just enough to maintain control of the racket. The more forceful the shot the tighter the grip.

This same grip may be used for most backhand shots. For our purposes we will vary this grip only when stroking backhand net drops and net clears. (At the beginning level, asking players to change grips repeatedly during fast-paced volleys can be quite frustrating to most students).

Backhand. For backhand net drops and net clears you will move the racket a quarter turn clockwise from the forehand grip, so that your thumb moves farther behind the racket handle (Figure 4-5).

Home Base—Singles

"Home base" is referred to as the area in the court where a player would stand to best cover the entire court effectively. In singles it is in the center of the court—an equal distance to all four corners.

After each shot is hit the player should attempt to return to home base position as quickly as possible and prepare for their opponent's return. If you cannot return quickly enough prior to your opponent's return, you should stop, ready yourself, and then react to his or her return from wherever you are in the court. A player should not be moving at the moment an opponent contacts the shuttle.

The Ready Position

Moving efficiently around the court during play is of the utmost importance in badminton. Good movement begins with a proper "ready position." This is the position, or stance, a player should assume prior to maneuvering towards an opponent's return shot. The feet should be spread shoulder width apart or slightly wider, the knees slightly bent, and your weight on the balls of your feet ready for movement in any direction. A stagger stance with the racket-foot forward is used by most players (Figures 4-6 and 4-7).

Footwork

Efficient footwork is extremely important in badminton. You must be able to get to the shuttle as quickly as possible in order to set up for your next stroke. Generally speaking, long strides and lunging action should be emphasized in footwork. Using short steps to cover the court is time consuming and a waste of valuable energy.

For shots close to the net, the player should always lunge with the racket-side foot reaching towards the shuttle at the moment of contact.

For lateral shots, push off with the foot that is farthest away from the shuttle and lunge with the other—pushing off with your right foot if you are moving to the left.

For shots hit deep into the backcourt, backward strides should be used. It is important to turn the body sideways to the net when hitting the shuttle—non-racket shoulder facing the net. This will allow full rotation of the upper body and hips in generating power. More advanced players will use a scissors kick (switching the legs) while in the act of striking the shuttle. This allows them to push off with the non-racket side leg, gaining efficiency in returning to the home base position.

The Strokes

There are five basic groups of shots that should be learned at the beginning level of badminton: serves, clears, smashes, blocks, and drops. Each of these strokes is described below, followed by a sixth type: "around-the head" shots.

I. Serves

There are two basic badminton serves: the long serve, which is hit high and deep, and the short serve, which is hit low and short. The long serve is used primarily in singles play, and the short serve is used primarily in doubles play. The serving stances and areas are the same in both singles and doubles.

A. Long Serve (high and deep). The object of the long serve is simply to move your opponent as far away from the net as possible. In singles play this

FIGURE 4-6 Ready position. Front.

FIGURE 4-7 Ready position. Side.

FIGURE 4-10 Holding shuttle during service delivery.

FIGURE 4-8 Service stance.

would be to the baseline, and in doubles play it would be to the long service line for doubles.

When positioning yourself stand approximately three to four feet behind the short service line and close to the centerline (Figure 4-8). Face your opponent's diagonal service court, stagger your stance (right foot behind the left if you are right-handed) with your weight on the back foot, stand tall, and relax (knees slightly bent).

Hold the shuttle with your fingers and thumb wrapped gently around the feathers and cork base when starting the service (Figure 4-9). The shuttle

arm is flexed at approximately 90 degrees and positioned across the body towards the racket-shoulder. When released the shuttle is "set out" and dropped away from the body towards your racket-side. It should not be allowed to "tumble" (flipped end-over-end) or "waver" after it is released because these actions will cause inconsistent flight patterns. The shuttle should be released from approximately shoulder height (Figure 4-10).

The racket is in the backswing position with the racket head being held higher than the racket-hand. As you release the shuttle to start your serve, your weight shifts forward (to your front foot), and your racket is pulled down and through the shuttle (Figure 4-11). At the contact point your wrist snaps, and the forearm rotates upward and forward in the direction of your serve. Contact point is about knee level.

FIGURE 4-9 Holding shuttle for service delivery.

FIGURE 4-11 Long serve. After the shuttle is dropped, bring the racket downward and forward.

FIGURE 4-12 The follow-through position after a vigorous wrist snap and rotation of the forearm.

Hips and shoulders will rotate towards the net, and the racket-arm will finish across the body (Figure 4-12).

The long serve can be described as a basic underhand motion with a vigorous wrist snap and forearm rotation.

▶ **Learning Cues** (Figure 4–13)

1. Stand facing the receiver's court in a relaxed, upright, staggered serving stance.

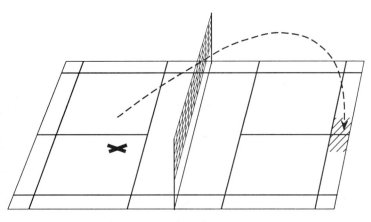

FIGURE 4-13 Long serve. Trajectory and target zones for singles play.

2. Make sure the racket wrist is cocked as much as possible in the backswing position, elbow fairly close to the body.
3. Drop the shuttle before starting the swing.
4. Drop the shuttle in front of and to the side of your body far enough away to force the hitting arm to reach for it slightly.
5. Be as relaxed as possible and try to generate maximum racket head acceleration by snapping the wrist and rotating the forearm at point of contact.
6. Contact shuttle at about knee height.
7. Hit the shuttle up and out.

▶ **Practice Suggestions**

Get as many shuttles as possible and hit the high, deep singles serve. You can practice serving diagonally if space permits, or you can practice serving straight across the net using the ½ court practice/play variation.

The two keys to look for are height and depth. Hit the shuttle high enough and hit it deeply enough to land in the back alley close to the base line. Remember, a long serve that is not high enough or deep enough will put you in a very defensive situation.

B. Short Serve (short and low).   The object of the short serve is to force your opponent to "lift" the shuttle. (Lifting the shuttle—resulting most often from underhand strokes—is considered to be defensive as it will allow the opponent an opportunity to return the "lifted" shuttle downward.)

When positioning yourself, stand approximately three to four feet behind the short service line and close to the centerline. Face your opponent's diagonal service court, stagger your stance (right foot behind the left if you are right-handed) with your weight on the back leg, stand tall, and relax (knees slightly bent).

The racket is in the backswing position with the racket head being held higher than the racket-hand. As you release the shuttle to start your serve, your weight shifts forward (to your front foot), and your racket is "pushed" (rather than pulled as in the long serve) through the shuttle (Figure 4-14). At the contact point your wrist remains cocked with the racket-arm following through forward (in the direction of your serve)—as if pushing from behind to guide it over the net (Figure 4-15). Contact point is about thigh level. Minimum hip or shoulder rotation is utilized.

The idea is to hit the shuttle so that it will stay low and drop just behind the short service line. Because little power is needed to achieve this, the wrist remains in the cocked position throughout the stroke. The shuttle should reach its maximum height at the net and then immediately start to drop.

FIGURE 4-14 Short serve. After the shuttle is dropped, bring the racket forward and push the shuttle toward the net.

FIGURE 4-15 Notice the short follow-through in the direction of the flight.

▶ **Learning Cues** (Figure 4-16)

1. Stand facing the receiver's court in a relaxed, upright, staggered serving stance.
2. Make sure the racket wrist is cocked as much as possible in the backswing position, elbow close to the body.
3. Drop the shuttle before starting the swing.
4. Drop the shuttle in front of and to the side of your body.
5. Be as relaxed as possible and try to "push" the shuttle rather than "hitting" it.
6. Contact shuttle at about thigh height.
7. Keep the shuttle as low and short as possible.

▶ **Practice Suggestions**

Get as many shuttles as possible and hit the short, low serve. You can practice serving diagonally if space permits, or you can practice serving straight across the net using the ½ court practice/play variation.

The two keys to look for are low clearance of the net and short in depth. Hit the shuttle low enough, and hit it short enough to land just past the short service line. Remember, a short serve that is not low enough will put you in a very defensive situation.

Return of Service: Singles. The position for returning serves in singles is approximately four feet

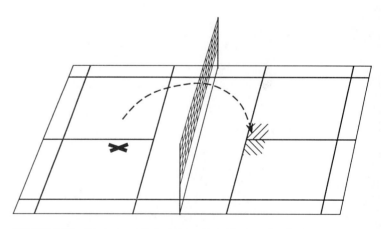

FIGURE 4-16 Short serve. Trajectory and target zones for singles and doubles play.

in back of the short service line (mid-court) and moved slightly to your backhand side in the service court. Your stance will be a slightly exaggerated stagger with the non-racket leg forward (Figures 4-17 and 4-18). Stand tall with the majority of your weight on the forward leg. Hold your racket in front of your body about chin high.

For returning a long serve (high and deep), push off with your forward leg and backstride to position yourself under the oncoming shuttle. To return a short serve (low and short), lunge forward by moving

FIGURE 4-17 Singles service return stance. Even court.

FIGURE 4-18 Singles service return stance. Odd court.

your back leg quickly to the net. As you lunge, reach out with your racket to contact the shuttle at its highest point.

Return of Service: Doubles. The position for returning serves in doubles is approximately one foot in back of the short service line and moved slightly to your backhand side in the service court. This position puts you much closer to the net than in

the singles return position. Your stance will be a slightly exaggerated stagger with the non-racket leg forward. Stand tall with the majority of your weight on the forward leg. Hold your racket in front of your body slightly higher than the position held for a normal singles return. This will allow you a quicker contact time for short serves—the serve that is used most often in doubles play.

The footwork used in returning doubles long serves is the same as that used for returning long serves in singles.

II. Clears

Clears are used as a defensive stroke to allow you time to return to the ready position and regroup; and to move your opponent as far away from the net as possible. There are two types of clears: overhead and underhand.

A. Overhead Clear. Overhead clears are usually taken from a backcourt position. From your home base position, move into a position under and slightly behind the oncoming shuttle. Prepare your racket for the stroke by bringing it back behind the shoulders into what is called the "back scratching" position: arm bent, elbow parallel to the floor (Figure 4-19).

With your racket shoulder now in line with the shuttle, extend the arm to meet the shuttle at the highest point possible (Figure 4-20). At the moment of contact your forearm rotates outward, and the wrist snaps quickly causing the racket head to accelerate and drive the shuttle upward and outward deep into your opponent's court. The racket head will be facing slightly upward at contact. Follow-through with the racket arm crossing your body in the direction of your non-racket side (Figure 4-21).

▶ **Learning Cues** (Figure 4-22)

1. Position yourself under and slightly behind the dropping shuttle.
2. Prepare the racket in the "back scratching" position.
3. As you swing upward, rotate the forearm and extend the arm as high as possible with the racket face pointing slightly upward.
4. At the moment of contact snap the wrist quickly.
5. Hit the shuttle high (18 to 20 feet) and deep into your opponent's backcourt area.
6. Follow-through across your body.

▶ **Practice Suggestions**

1. *Straight Clears using the ½ court area.* Partners hit continuous clears to each other attempting to get the shuttle into the back alley.
2. *Crosscourt Clears.* Partners hit continuous clears diagonally to each other working on distance and accuracy. Each partner attempts to get the shuttle into the back alley and corner of the singles court.

FIGURE 4-19   Overhead clear. Backswing (used for all overhead strokes).

FIGURE 4-20   Overhead clear. Contact.

FIGURE 4-21   Overhead clear. Follow-through.

3. *Side Alley Clears*. Partners hit continuous clears within the side alley boundaries working on accuracy and distance.

B. Forehand Underhand (Net) Clear. Underhand clears are usually taken from a forecourt position. When your opponent hits a drop shot into your forecourt, or close to the net, it forces you to "lift" the shuttle and go on the defensive. Hitting an underhand clear in this situation will serve the same purpose as hitting an overhead clear in a backcourt situation. That is, it will allow you time to return to the ready position and regroup; and, it will move your opponent as far away from the net as possible.

As the shuttle is dropping toward your forehand side and in the forecourt area, from the ready position take a short first step with your non-racket leg and then a long lunge to the shuttle with the racket leg.

Reach for the shuttle with the wrist slightly cocked and your racket arm in as high a position as necessary to contact the bird at its highest point possible. At the moment of contact rotate your forearm so that the racket is uncocked explosively up and through the shuttle (Figure 4-23). The follow-

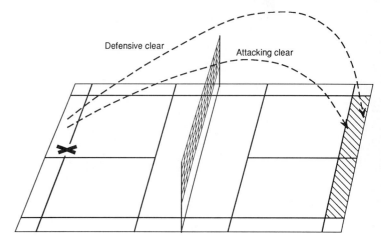

FIGURE 4-22   Overhead clears. Trajectory and target zone for singles play.

through is in the direction that you intended the shuttle to travel (Figure 4-24).

C. Backhand Underhand (Net) Clear. Change to a backhand grip. As the shuttle is drop-

FIGURE 4-23   Forehand net clear. Contact.

FIGURE 4-24   Forehand net clear. Follow-through.

FIGURE 4-25   Backhand net clear. Contact.

FIGURE 4-26   Backhand net clear. Follow-through.

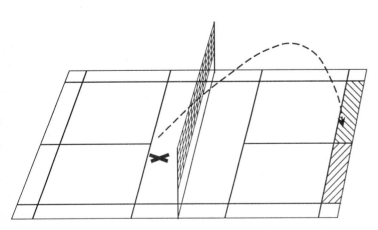

FIGURE 4-27   Net clear. Trajectory and target zones for singles play.

ping toward your backhand side and in the forecourt area, from the ready position take a short first step with your non-racket leg and then a long lunge to the shuttle with the racket leg.

Reach for the shuttle with the wrist slightly cocked and your racket arm in as high a position as necessary to contact the bird at its highest point possible. At the moment of contact rotate your forearm so that the racket is brought explosively up and through the shuttle (Figure 4-25). The follow-through is in the direction that you intended the shuttle to travel (Figure 4-26).

▶ **Learning Cues** (Figure 4-27)

1. Lunge to the shuttle with your racket leg forward at contact.
2. Contact the shuttle at the highest point possible.
3. Lift the shuttle with a hard, explosive wrist action.

4. Hit the shuttle high (18 to 20 feet) and deep into your opponent's backcourt area.

5. Follow-through in the direction you intended the shuttle to travel.

▶ **Practice Suggestions**

Straight underhand clears using the ½ court area.

One player hits overhead drops from the back alley, while the partner hits underhand clears from the net area.

NOTE: See overhead drop "Practice Suggestions" in section V: Drop Shots.

D. Attacking Clear. Attacking clears are used primarily to drive your opponent to the backcourt (farthest point from the net) after he or she has come very close to the net, and you think you can "clear" the shuttle over his racket for a winner. They are stroked similar to the clears discussed above except that the trajectory is lower. This lower trajectory will cause the shuttle to reach the floor sooner, and in turn put your opponent in a very defensive situation (see Figure 4-22).

III. Smashes

The smash is the basic offensive shot in badminton. It is a very powerful stroke that is used primarily for getting the shuttle to land on your opponent's side of the court as quickly as possible. However, if the shuttle does not land on their court and end the volley as expected, it will force your opponent to "lift" the shuttle—putting him or her in a very defensive situation. The smash is a shot that can be tremendously effective.

The body position is similar to the overhead clear stroke, with one exception: the shuttle should be lined up *ahead* of your racket-shoulder (Figure 4-28), farther ahead than the contact point of the overhead clear. By the same token the racket face must be angling downward as compared to upward for the overhead clear.

You should contact the shuttle at the highest point possible. The higher you contact the shuttle, the greater the angle down to your opponent's court. The greater the angle, the greater the chance you have for clearing the net. Your forearm and wrist will rotate and snap rapidly as the shuttle is contacted. Follow-through is similar to the overhead clear (Figure 4-29).

Unless you have an exceptionally strong smash, this stroke should only be used when you are in the front three-quarters of the court. Remember, smashing from the back alley area forces the shuttle to fly a greater distance to get to your opponent's side of

FIGURE 4-28 Smash. Notice that the contact point is in front of the racket shoulder.

FIGURE 4-29 Smash. Follow-through.

the court. This will allow your opponent more time to react to your smash and increase his or her chances of returning the shuttle with some control.

▶ **Learning Cues** (Figure 4-30)

As far as preparation and motion are concerned, the same learning cues apply to both the overhead clear and the smash. These additional key points apply to smashes:

1. Get into position so that contact can be made ahead of the racket-shoulder which is farther ahead than an overhead clear.
2. The racket face should be angling downward at contact.
3. Sharp downward angle is just as important as shuttle speed.

▶ **Practice Suggestions**

Straight smashes using the ½ court area. One player hits short, underhand clears while the partner returns them with smashes.

NOTE: Also see "Practice Suggestions" under Blocks, section IV.

IV. Blocks (Figures 4-31, 4-32, 4-33)

Blocks are used as a defensive stroke in response to an opponent's smash. They are used primarily for returning a smash in an emergency situation. However, if effectively stroked, a block can also change your defensive situation into an offensive situation. (An effective block will force your opponent to return the shuttle with an underhand stroke. Hopefully, this "lifting" action on the part of your opponent will enable you to regain the attack.)

The block shot is best accomplished by trying to get the racket head out in front of your body and to the shuttle as quickly as possible. Use the forehand grip (Figure 4-31). There is no backswing to this stroke, merely a slight push of the shuttle to have it rebound from the racket and barely clear the net.

FIGURE 4-31   Forehand block.

FIGURE 4-32   Backhand block.

FIGURE 4-33   High body block.

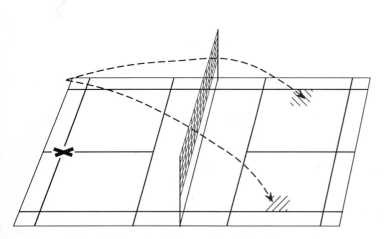

FIGURE 4-30   Smash. Trajectory and target zones for singles play.

The force of your push will depend upon the speed of your opponent's smash. The harder the smash the less the push. A mere rebound off of a stationary racket face—from a powerful smash—is often sufficient enough to accomplish this stroke. The object is to drop the shuttle over the net shallow in the opponent's forecourt.

▶ **Learning Cues** (Figure 4-34)

1. Do not try to take the racket back as this stroke does not require a backswing.
2. React as quickly as possible trying to get the racket head out in front of your body and to the shuttle.
3. Try to keep the shuttle low, barely clearing the net.
4. Do not swing at the shuttle. Merely block with a slight push.

▶ **Practice Suggestions**

1. *Smash and Block drill using the ½ court area.* One player hits a short, high underhand clear that the partner smashes. The returner attempts to block the smash and get it over the net shallow in the forecourt.
2. *2-1-1 Smash and Block drill* (½ court). Player (A) hits a short, high underhand clear to start the drill.
   The partner (B) overhead clears.
   (A) smashes.
   (B) blocks.
   (A) underhand (net) clears, and the drill continues.
   Sequence: underhand clear, overhead clear, smash, block, (repeat).
3. *3-1-1 Smash and Block drill* (½ court). Use the same sequence as the 2–1–1 except add in an extra overhead clear to this drill.
   Sequence: underhand clear, overhead clear, overhead clear, smash, block, (repeat).

V. Drop Shots

There are two types of drop shots: overhead and underhand. Underhand drop shots are taken from the forecourt area, often times close to the net, and are referred to as "net drops." Overhead drops are usually taken from the backcourt area and referred to as simply "drops." Drops are used to force your opponent to come to the net from his or her backcourt position; and, to force him or her to "lift" the shuttle for their return. They can be described as soft shots that barely clear the net and then drop quickly into the opponent's forecourt area—preferably in front of the short service line.

A. Overhead Drop. Overhead drops are usually taken from a backcourt position. The object is to make your opponent think that you are going to clear or smash, and then execute a soft stroke that gently drops the shuttle over the net. As stated

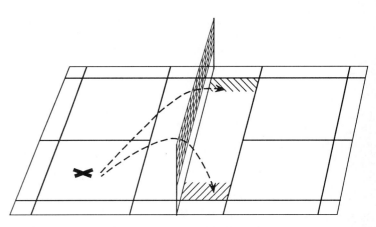

FIGURE 4-34 Block. Two flight patterns and target zones for blocking.

above, overhead drops are used to move your opponent to the forecourt; and, to force a "lifting" return of the shuttle. If stroked deceptively enough, overhead drops can put your opponent into such an off-balance position that a decent return from them would be extremely difficult.

The body position used is similar to the overhead clear. The shuttle is contacted in front of the body, but the racket head will slow instead of accelerating at the moment of impact. As in the smash, the racket face must be angling downward. Follow-through is across your body and towards the non-racket side.

This shot depends to a great extent on finesse and deception. A backswing, stroke, and follow-through that is similar to the clear or smash is very vital in the disguise of this stroke. Remember, *the shuttle is fully stroked and guided,* not pushed from the shoulder or tapped from a stiff, overhead, outstretched arm position.

▶ **Learning Cues** (Figure 4-35)

1. Get into position so that contact can be made in front of the body.

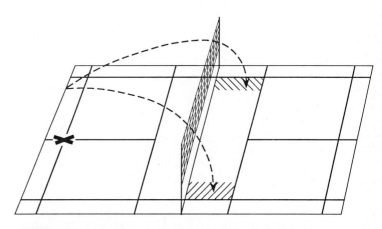

FIGURE 4-35 Overhead drop. Trajectory and target zones for singles play.

2. Racket preparation has to be the same as if you were going to clear or smash.
3. Slow the speed of the racket head just before contacting the shuttle.
4. The racket face should be angling slightly downward on impact.
5. Gently guide the shuttle over the net with your wrist action and follow-through.

▶ **Practice Suggestions**

1. *Continuous straight drops using the ½ court area.* One player hits underhand clears while the partner returns them with overhead drops.
2. *2–1 Overhead Drop drill* (½ court).
   Player (A) hits a short, high underhand clear to start the drill.
   The partner (B) overhead clears.
   (A) overhead drops, and the drill continues.
   Sequence: underhand clear, overhead clear, overhead drop, (repeat).
3. *3–1 Overhead Drop drill* (½ court). Use the same sequence as the 2–1 except add an extra overhead clear to this drill.
   Sequence: underhand clear, overhead clear, overhead clear, overhead drop, (repeat).
   NOTE: Also see net drop "Practice Suggestions," below.

B. Net Drop. Net (or underhand) drops are hit from the forecourt area and are used to draw your opponent close to the net after they have hit an overhead drop from their backcourt. They are also used to force an opponent to "lift" the shuttle.

Net drops taken on the forehand side are stroked using the forehand grip (Figure 4-36). Net drops taken on the backhand side are stroked using the backhand grip previously described (Figure 4-37). The object is to lift slightly or push the shuttle gently over the top of the net so that it falls below the white tape level as quickly as possible. If stroked properly the shuttle will fall very close to the net. This will force your opponent to travel the greatest distance possible from his or her present position in the court.

Getting to the shuttle quickly is of the utmost importance. The idea is to contact the shuttle as close to the top of the net as possible. The lower the contact point the more "lift" you will have to put on your shot. You would rather "push" your drop over the net than "lift" it over. Lifting the shuttle forces you into an uncertain defensive situation. Remember, a shuttle that is lifted too hard (too high) will put you in terrible trouble. A shuttle that is lifted too soft (not high enough) will result in a bird that didn't make it over the net. Pushing and guiding your net drop will eliminate the uncertainty of "lifting."

Lunge toward the shuttle with your racket-side leg. With your arm and racket out in front of your body and as high as necessary to contact the shuttle at its highest point, gently push and guide the shuttle over the net. Have the shuttle just barely clear the net so that your opponent will not have a chance to smash it back at you.

▶ **Learning Cues** (Figure 4-38)

1. Lunge with the racket-side leg toward the shuttle.
2. Contact the shuttle as near the top of the net as possible.
3. Gently push and guide the shuttle over the net.
4. Have the shuttle just barely clear the net.

FIGURE 4-36 Net drop. Forehand.

FIGURE 4-37 Net drop. Backhand.

▶ **Practice Suggestions**

1. *Toss and stroke drill using the ½ court area.* One player stands on the short service line and tosses a shuttle over the net, while the partner lunges toward the shuttle and net drops. Tosses should be directed to the forehand side for forehand practice, backhand side for backhand practice. The stroker should be in a ready position approximately two feet behind the short service line prior to each toss.
2. *Continuous net drops* (½ court). From behind the short service line, one player puts the shuttle into play with a short serve. Each player continues to hit net drops until a missed shot has occurred.
3. *2-1-1 Overhead Drop and Net Drop drill* (½ court).
   Player (A) hits an underhand clear to start the drill.
   The partner (B) overhead clears.
   (A) overhead drops.
   (B) net drops.
   (A) underhand clears, and the drill continues.
   Sequence: underhand clear, overhead clear, overhead drop, net drop, (repeat).
4. *3-1-1 Overhead Drop and Net Drop drill* (½ court). Use the same sequence as the 2–1–1 except add an extra overhead clear to this drill.
   Sequence: underhand clear, overhead clear, overhead clear, overhead drop, net drop, (repeat).

VI. Around-the-head Shots.

Around-the-head strokes are used in place of the conventional overhead "backhand" stroke—a shot usually considered to be weak and very defensive. "Around-the-heads" may be used for overhead clears, smashes, and overhead drops. If stroked properly they can be very powerful, attacking strokes. Although this stroke will be contacted on your backhand (non-racket) side, your grip will be a forehand grip.

Position yourself so that the shuttle is in alignment with your non-racket shoulder. The backswing is exactly the same as in the other overhead shots but the contact point will be over your non-racket shoulder (Figure 4-39). There will be a bending of the waist in the direction of the backhand side. The racket arm is extended as fully as is necessary to contact the shuttle at its highest point possible.

Remember, the only difference between around-the-head shots and other overheads is that the shuttle is contacted over the non-racket shoulder in all "around-the-heads."

At the beginning and intermediate levels, it is suggested that around-the-head strokes be strongly emphasized. This will not only encourage more aggressive stroking, but it will also deter players from stroking the weaker backhand shots (clears and drops) unnecessarily.

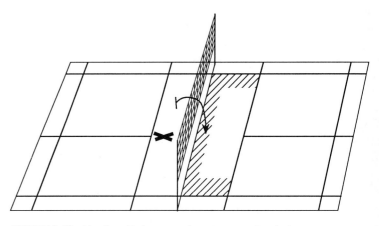

FIGURE 4-38 Net drop. Trajectory and target zones for singles play.

FIGURE 4-39 Around-the-head. Notice that the contact is on the backhand side of the body.

PLAYING STRATEGY

There is no set sequence of shots or strategic decisions that one can use to win a volley. However, with sound fundamentals, proficient strokes, and good strategy you will win many matches.

Basically, shots made from below net level (the white tape), or what is termed "lifted," are considered to be *defensive,* and those made from above the net level, or stroked downward, are considered to be *offensive.*

Basic Strategy

1. Force your opponent to move as far as possible to return a shot.
2. Use attacking strokes whenever you get a chance.
3. Return to "home base" after every shot.
4. Play to your opponent's weakest side—generally the backhand.
5. When in doubt, hit a high, deep clear and hope for a weak return.

Singles Strategy

The game of singles demands a great deal of determination, hustle, quick reactions, and patience. Outsmarting your opponent using good strategy, and outhustling him or her through mere determination is very exciting and rewarding.

Serving

1. A long serve (high and deep) to the backcourt area near the centerline is used the majority of the time. This serve will put your opponent as far away from the net as possible and will force him or her to hit a very strong return to put you at any disadvantage whatsoever. Directing your serve to the centerline will cut down the angle of return.
2. A short serve can be used if your opponent is standing too deep in his or her receiving court to return your serve. Or, short serves can be used if your opponent has a very effective smash from the backcourt area, and you want to eliminate a smash return directly off your serve.

Return of Service

1. Return serves with shots that are straight ahead. Crosscourt shots take longer to travel and need to be hit harder due to the extra distance they have to fly.
2. Your service return should move your opponent out of his or her home base position.
3. Long serves are generally returned with an overhead clear or a drop shot in the near corner.
4. Short serves are generally returned with an underhand clear or a net drop (push) to the near corner.

The Volley

1. Move your opponent to the various corners of the court by varying your shot selection. Moving your opponent out of his or her home base position and to the different corners of the court will increase your chances of forcing a weak return and lose control of the volley.
2. Move your opponent to the various corners of the court, in diagonal patterns if possible. Moving your opponent diagonally forces them to travel greater distances in covering the court.
3. Force your opponent to "lift" the shuttle as often as possible. This will decrease your opponent's chances for returning the shuttle with a strong stroke and increase your chances for staying on the attack (hitting the shuttle downward).
4. Build your game on a pattern of drops and clears. If you are patient, this pattern will eventually force your opponent to hit a weak return. Then, use your smash to put the volley away.
5. Take advantage of any weakness your opponent may have. The backhand is usually the weaker side, so direct your shots to that side.
6. In defending a smash, block it to the opposite side of where the smash was originated.
7. If your opponent is moving to cover an open spot on the court when you make your shot, play the bird to the position being vacated. The most difficult maneuver on the court is one that requires a quick change of direction in your movement. Retracing your steps demands the utmost agility and speed.
8. Do not play the sidelines too close with your shots. Give yourself about a three-foot "safety" variance inside the sideline to reduce your chances of hitting the shuttle out-of-bounds.
9. If late in the game, and you are trailing your opponent, you might want to switch to a more conservative type play. Direct your shots toward the center portion of the court. This will increase your chances of staying in-bounds and remaining "in the game." This does not, however, mean that you should become less aggressive in your stroking.

Doubles Strategy

It must be understood that doubles is a more complex game than singles. It is faster paced and demands considerable strategy and cohesive teamwork for partners to be effective. It is offense oriented, which means that attacking, energy-consuming strokes are used most of the time. With excellently placed strokes and long volleys, doubles can be a very strenuous game.

Serving

1. A short serve (low and short) to the "T" area (near corner) is used most of the time. This serve will force your opponents to "lift" the shuttle and will put them in a defensive situation directly off the serve.

2. Long serves (high, but not as deep as the singles long serve) can be used to move a strong fore-court player to the backcourt area, or they can be used to maneuver an opponent who has an ineffective smash to the backcourt. Remember, because long serves in doubles are not allowed to travel as far back into the playing court area as long serves in singles play, the long serve should be used very sparingly in doubles.

3. The server's partner should assume a position two feet forward of the long service line and straddling the centerline. This alignment is used in preparation for an attacking strategy (up-and-back).

Return of Service

1. The receiving position in doubles is slightly different for the receiver than in singles (see p. 54). From this doubles receiving position, short serves can be played very quickly. This will, in turn, increase the possibility of using attacking strokes for short service returns.

2. Rush short serves. As soon as the shuttle is served, step forward with the racket-foot and attempt to contact the shuttle while it is still above the net level. Stroke the shuttle downward if possible.

3. Drop returns should be directed to the near corner.

4. A push shot directed to the near side alley, mid-court depth, is an excellent return for a short serve.

5. Return long serves with a smash.

6. The receiver's partner should assume a position two feet forward of the long service line and straddling the centerline. This alignment is used in preparation for an attacking strategy (up-and-back).

The Volley

There are three basic alignments used for doubles play. These alignments are generally dependent upon the specific situation during the game or volley. There is a defensive alignment *side by side;* an offensive alignment, *up and back;* or, you can use a combination of these two alignments called *circular rotation.* Circular rotation depends largely upon the situation your team is in (offensive or defensive) during the point being played.

Side-by-side Alignment. This alignment is considered to be defensive. In this alignment, each partner is responsible for his or her half of the playing court (Figure 4-40). Whenever your opponents are in control of the volley (using attacking strokes or forcing you to "lift" the shuttle), the side-by-side alignment is the best strategy to use. With this alignment it will be harder for your opponents to stroke a smash past you because you and your partner will have the court covered laterally very efficiently. This alignment is also easy to understand and learn.

A disadvantage of this alignment is that it allows for a team to play to the weaker player. It would be to your advantage, if aligned in this formation, to get back to an attacking (offensive) situation as soon as possible. This can be accomplished by either blocking your opponent's smashes to the side alleys or front corners, forcing them to "lift" the shuttle to you; or net dropping their overhead drops to the front corners forcing them to "lift" and assume a defensive alignment. Remember, although the side-by-side alignment is a very effective defensive

FIGURE 4-40 Doubles side-by-side alignment.

FIGURE 4-41   Doubles up-and-back alignment.

alignment, doubles is an attacking game. Very few points can be won directly from defensive strokes or defensive alignments.

Up-and-back Alignment.   This alignment is considered to be offensive. In this alignment one partner is responsible for the forecourt area (sideline to sideline, from the net to the "T") while his or her partner is responsible for the midcourt and backcourt area (sideline to sideline). Both players are situated along the centerline of the court with one player positioned at the "T" and the other positioned approximately two feet forward of the long service line (Figure 4-41).

Whenever your team is in control of the volley (using attacking strokes or forcing your opponents to "lift" the shuttle), the up-and-back alignment is the best strategy to use. With this alignment it will be harder for your opponents to block a smash or net drop effectively, because one partner will have the forecourt covered very efficiently. It will also decrease the effectiveness of your opponent's clears in that your partner will have the backcourt covered.

A disadvantage of the up-and-back alignment is that it allows for a team to pass or drive a shot down the side alleys of the court.

The net player's (partner at the "T") responsibility is to intercept any shot by the opponents before that shot reaches his or her partner's midcourt or backcourt area. The net player is also responsible for stroking the shuttle downward, net dropping, or pushing the shuttle back over the net as quickly as possible from the forecourt area in response to an opponent's stroke. The net player should use any stroke that will keep the opponents in a defensive situation, or "lifting" the shuttle.

The backcourt player's responsibility is to attack the opponents with strokes that force "lifting" responses. Smashes and overhead drops used strategically will serve this purpose. He or she should direct these shots down the centerline or toward the side alleys. The backcourt partner should also direct these attacking strokes to the opponent that is the weaker player.

Remember, the up-and-back alignment is an offensive alignment and that doubles is an attacking game. Points can be won directly from attacking strokes with players in offensive alignments.

Combination (circular rotation).   The combination system combines the best of the other two systems, using the side-by-side alignment for defense and the up-and-back alignment for attacking. This system is generally used by more advanced players. It takes a great deal of teamwork, practice, and playing time to use this system effectively.

The basic principles to be followed in the combination system are as follows:

1. If the server serves short, the serving team will remain in the up-and-back alignment.
   Reason: A short serve forces your opponents to "lift" the shuttle. This will, in turn, allow the serving team to return the shuttle with downward, attacking strokes and keeping them in an offensive situation.
2. If the server serves long, the serving team will go to a side-by-side alignment. The server should drop back to his or her serving side. The partner will, in turn move to the opposite side.
   Reason: A long serve allows the opponents to return the shuttle with attacking strokes thereby putting your team in a defensive situation.

3. If the receiver of the serve is served short, and he or she net drops or pushes the shuttle downward back over the net, the receiving team should stay in an up-and-back alignment.
   Reason: The receiving team, with those returns, has just forced their opponents to start "lifting" the shuttle.
   If the receiver of the serve is served short, and he or she clears the shuttle, the receiving team should go to a side-by-side alignment.
   Reason: The receiving team has been forced to "lift" the shuttle. They are now in a defensive situation.
   If the receiver of the serve is served long, his partner should immediately go to the "T" to play the net, and the receiver should smash or overhead drop the shuttle to force his or her opponents to "lift." With these actions they have now assumed the up-and-back offensive alignment.

4. On any shot that gives the opponents the advantage and opportunity to smash or overhead drop, the team making the stroke should take up the defensive side-by-side alignment. The player making the shot should cover the half of the court from which the shot was made.

5. When reverting from a defensive alignment to an offensive alignment, the player taking a backcourt stroke (attacking) that initiates the change will stay in the backcourt "back" position. The partner will then move to the "up" position and guard the net from the "T." If the stroke that initiates the change is taken from a forecourt position, the player taking that stroke will move to the "up" position at the net. The partner will then move to the "back" position in the backcourt.

▶ **Learning Cues for Doubles Strategy**

1. Attack as often as possible. Hit the shuttle downward and force your opponents to "lift" the shuttle.
2. When attacking use the up-and-back alignment.
3. When "lifting" the shuttle use the side-by-side alignment.
4. Rush short serves. Attack them if possible.
5. Smash long serves.
6. When opponents are in a defensive alignment smash or overhead drop toward the centerline.
7. When opponents are in a defensive alignment, play to the weaker opponent.
8. When opponents are in an offensive alignment, direct your shots to the side alleys.
9. When you are in a defensive alignment, revert to an attacking situation as soon as the chance arises.
10. Use clears only in emergency situations. If you must clear, clear to the back corners.

PLAYING COURTESIES

Badminton emphasizes good sportsmanship and playing courtesies. Use good judgment at all times with regard to your own behavior as well as your attitude toward your opponent. Be cordial and respectful. As in any sport, be a good loser as well as a gracious winner. Try to maintain a positive rather than negative attitude creating a more enjoyable game for all participants. Some courtesies specific to badminton are:

1. If your opponent is unknown to you, introduce yourself and shake hands prior to the match.
2. The warm-up period should be gracious and uncompetitive.
3. The server should call the score prior to each serve—server's score first.
4. If in doubt about the shuttle's landing, always call it in favor of your opponent.
5. Inform your opponent of the call as quickly as possible.
6. Never question your opponent's calls.
7. If there is any question of your faulting, be sure to call it on yourself.
8. If a shuttle lands on your side and you are the receiver, pick it up and hit it back to the server so that he or she does not have to go out of his way to retrieve it.
9. Do not smash at your opponent if the point could be easily won by placing the shuttle elsewhere in the court.
10. Do not stall. Keep the play continuous.
11. If you are the receiver, get ready to receive the serve without any hesitation.
12. Compliment your opponent's exceptional shots.
13. Do not offer playing advice to your opponents.
14. Do not, under any circumstances, throw your racket or the shuttle in anger.
15. Always shake hands with your opponent after the match.

MODIFICATIONS FOR SPECIAL POPULATIONS

Orthopedically Impaired

1. See modifications discussed in Tennis and Handball/Racquetball.
2. If one team (doubles) has a wheelchair student, place a standard classroom chair in the opposite court for one of the able-bodied opponents. Position the seated students in the front court.

Mentally Impaired

See modifications discussed in Tennis, Handball/Racquetball.

Sensory Impaired

1. See modifications discussed in Tennis, Handball/Racquetball.

2. Blind students might practice using a tethered shuttlecock.

TERMINOLOGY

Alley   The 1½-foot-wide area on each side of the court that is used for doubles. Often referred to as the "side alley."

Around-the-head stroke   An overhead stroke used when hitting a forehand-like overhead stroke which is on the backhand side of the body.

Back alley   The area between the doubles long service line and the baseline.

Backcourt   The back third of the court.

Backhand   A stroke made on the non-racket side of the body.

Baseline   The back boundary line of the court.

Bird   Another name for the shuttlecock.

Block   A soft shot, used primarily in defense against a smash. Intercepting an opponent's smash and returning it back over the net.

Carry   Called when the shuttle stays on the racket during a stroke. It is legal if the racket follows the intended line of flight. Also referred to as a "throw."

Centerline   The mid-line separating the service courts.

Clear   A high shot that goes over your opponent's head and lands close to the baseline.

Combination alignment   Partners play both up-and-back and side-by-side during doubles games and/or volleys.

Crosscourt   A shot hit diagonally into the opposite court.

Defense   The team or player hitting the shuttle upwards (lifting), usually from an underhand stroke.

Double hit   An illegal shot in which the racket contacts the shuttle twice in one swing.

Doubles service court   The short, wide area to which the server must serve in doubles play.

Down-the-line shot   A shot hit straight ahead—usually down the sideline.

Drive   A hard driven shot that travels parallel to the floor. This shot clears the net but does not go high enough for your opponent to smash.

Drop   A shot that just clears the net, then falls close to it.

Face   The string area of the racket.

Fault   Any infraction of the rules. It results in the loss of serve or in a point for the server.

First serve   A term used in doubles play to indicate that the server is the "first server" during an inning.

Foot fault   Illegal position or movement of the feet by either the server or receiver.

Forecourt   The front area of the court, usually considered to be between the net and the short service line.

Forehand   Any stroke made on the racket side of the body.

Game point   The point which, if won, allows the server to win the game.

Hand in   The term used to indicate that the server retains the serve.

Hand out   The term used in doubles to show that one player has lost the service.

Home base   The position in the center of the court from which the player can best play any shot hit by an opponent.

Inning   The time during which a player or team holds service.

Let   The stopping of play due to some type of outside interference. The point is replayed.

Lifting the shuttle   To stroke the bird underhanded and hit it upward.

Long serve   A high, deep serve landing near the long service line in doubles or back boundary line (base line) in singles.

Love   The term used to indicate zero in scoring.

Match   A series of games. In badminton, winning two out of three games will win the match.

Match point   The point which, if won by the server, makes that person the winner of the match.

Midcourt   The middle third of the court, usually considered to be between the short service line and the long service line for doubles.

Net shot   A shot taken near the net.

Non-racket side   The opposite side of the hand holding the racket.

Offense   The team or player that is stroking the shuttle downward (attacking).

Overhead   A motion used to strike the shuttle when it is above the head.

Racket foot or leg   The foot or leg on the same side as the hand holding the racket.

Ready position   The position a player assumes to be ready to move in any direction.

Receiver   The player to whom the shuttle is served.

Second serve   In doubles, the term indicates that one partner has lost the serve, and the other partner is now serving.

Server   The player who puts the shuttle into play.

Setting   Choosing how many more points to play when certain tie scores are reached.

Short serve   A serve that barely clears the net and lands just beyond the short service line.

Shuttlecock (shuttle)   The feathered, plastic, or nylon object which is volleyed back and forth over the net.

Side Alley   See *Alley*.

Side-by-side   A defensive alignment used in doubles play. Each partner is responsible for one side of the court, from the net to the back boundary line.

Side out   When a player or team loses the serve.

Smash   An overhead stroke hit downward with great velocity and angle. The principal attacking stroke in badminton.

"T"   The intersection of the centerline and the short service line.

Underhand   A stroke that is hit upward when the shuttle has fallen below shoulder level.

Unsight   Illegal position taken by the server's partner so the receiver cannot see the shuttle as it is hit.

Up-and-back   An offensive alignment used in doubles. The "up" player is responsible for the forecourt and the "back" player is responsible for the midcourt and backcourt.

SELECTED REFERENCES

Annarino, A. *Individualized Instructional Program in Badminton.* Englewood Cliffs, NJ: Prentice Hall, 1973.

Davis, P. *The Badminton Coach: A Manual for Coaches, Teachers, and Players.* New Rochelle, NY: Sportshelf, 1976.

Davis, P. *Badminton Complete.* London: Kaye and Ward, 1967, revised 1982.

Davis, P. *Badminton, the Complete Practice Guide.* London: David and Charles, 1982.

Johnson, M.L. *Badminton.* Philadelphia: W.B. Saunders Co., 1974.

Paup, D.C. and Breen, J.L. *Winning Badminton.* Chicago: Athletic Institute, 1984.

Poole, J. *Badminton.* (Goodyear Physical Activities Series). Glenview, IL: Scott, Foresman and Co., 1982.

Wadood, T. and Tan, K. *Badminton Today.* St. Paul, MN: West Publishing Co., 1990.

Periodicals

Badminton U.S.A. United States Badminton Association, 501 W. Sixth Street, Papillion, NE 68046.

World Badminton. The International Badminton Federation, 24 Winchcombe House, Winchcombe Street, Cheltenham, Gloucestershire, England GL52 2NA.

Films and Videos

Badminton Movies. Louisville Badminton Supply, 9411 Westport Road, Louisville, KY 40222.

C.B.A. Video Library. Canadian Badminton Association, 333 River Road, Toronto, Ontario M4W 1J5, Canada.

U.S.B.A. Video Library. United States Badminton Association, 501 W. Sixth Street, Papillion, NE 68046.

5 BASKETBALL

THIS CHAPTER WILL ENABLE YOU TO:

▶ *Know the playing court, equipment, and basic rules of basketball.*
▶ *Practice and develop skill in the fundamentals of passing, dribbling, shooting, rebounding, individual offense, and individual defense.*
▶ *Identify the objectives and strategies of team offense and defense.*

NATURE AND PURPOSE

Basketball is an extremely popular game, played in all parts of the world and at every conceivable level. In America, the extremes are very evident—from rickety backboards attached to outdoor garages to multi-million dollar arenas that hold thousands of spectators. Basketball can be played at a highly organized level or very spontaneously at a neighborhood playground. Children can play on school teams beginning with elementary school, continuing through college. Highly skilled men and women can earn basketball scholarships to play for colleges and universities. There are amateur tournaments and professional leagues. The United States has a men's and women's Olympic Basketball Team. Recreationally, basketball is played in the YMCA, YWCA, Boys Club, church leagues, and community centers. It is a vital part of school intramural programs, sometimes even played coeducationally. Basketball presents the opportunity to learn ball skills, coordination, agility, and body control; participation in the game can contribute toward maintenance of an individual's total fitness. For these reasons, basketball is an attractive physical education class activity.

This originally American sport has very broad applications: large groups can participate at relatively low cost; the game can serve for competitive as well as recreational purposes; and it has the necessary appeal to make it a popular spectator sport.

Officially, a basketball team is composed of five players. However, in recreational play two, three, or four players can play a game. The purpose of the game is to score a larger total number of points than the opponent. The score is compiled by shooting the ball through the basket either from the field (called a field goal) or from the free-throw line (called a free-throw or a foul shot). The ball is passed, thrown, bounced, batted, or rolled from one player to another. A player in possession of the ball must maintain contact with the floor with one foot (called the pivot foot), unless the player is shooting, passing, or dribbling. Dribbling consists of a series of one-hand taps, causing the ball to bounce on the floor. Physical contact with an opponent can result in a foul if the contact impedes the desired movement of the player.

EQUIPMENT

The Ball. The official ball is spherical with a circumference of 29½ to 30 inches for men and 28½ to 29 inches for women. Smaller balls are available for younger participants. In competition, a ball of high-grade leather is used. Less expensive balls are made of rubber or synthetic materials.

The Basket. The basket consists of a simple metal ring, 18 inches in inside diameter. A white-cord net suspends from beneath the ring. The basket is securely attached to a rigid backboard. Most backboards used in competition are transparent glass and rectangular in shape. However, it is not uncommon for backboards to be fan-shaped and made of solid wood.

COURT OR FIELD OF PLAY

The playing area of basketball is called the court. The rectangular court measures a maximum of 94 feet long and 50 feet wide, or a minimum of 74 feet long and 42 feet wide. The baskets are suspended 10 feet above the floor at the endline of each court. The court has three restraining circles and two free-

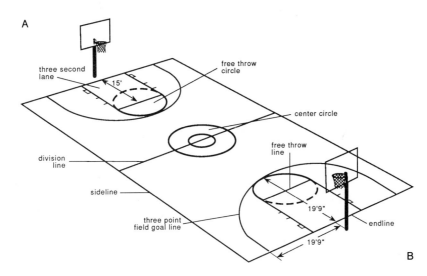

FIGURE 5-1   The basketball court.

throw areas (Figure 5-1). The court can be modified (made smaller) and the baskets lowered to accommodate younger participants. Basketball can be played on half of a court if large numbers of participants want to play in an intramural, class, or recreational situation.

BASIC RULES

Two or sometimes three on-the-court officials regulate a basketball game. The game is divided into 20-minute halves for college and university teams and 8-minute quarters for high school teams. Teams composed of players younger than high school age should have 6-minute quarters. The length of the game in a recreational, class, or intramural situation can be adjusted by shortening the quarters or halves, or by having "running time," wherein the clock does not stop on the dead balls.

There are slight variations of rules between high school and collegiate play, as well as between the men's and women's collegiate game. Nevertheless, there are basic rules of basketball governing play at any level.

Players

1. Even though only five players play at a time, any number of substitutions can be made at any dead ball during the game. Substitutes must report to the scorer and wait to be beckoned onto the court by an official.
2. One of the five players is the designated floor captain and may address the official on matters of interpretation or information. Any player may request a timeout.

Scoring and Timing

1. A goal is made when a live ball enters the basket from above and remains in or passes through except on a throw-in. A field goal counts *three points* if the shot is made by a player situated beyond the three-point field goal line. For a successful three-point field goal, the player must have one or both feet on the floor and be beyond the three-point line when attempting the shot. After releasing the ball, the shooter may land on or over the line. Touching the line before the release places the shooter in the two-point area.
2. A goal from the field other than from the three-point area counts *two points*.
3. When a free throw is awarded for fouls, each successful free throw counts *one point*.
4. If a player mistakenly scores a field goal in the opponent's basket, the goal is counted for the opponent.
5. Timeouts are restricted to a total of five. One additional timeout may be granted each team for each extra period of the game. A timeout lasts one minute and can only be requested during a dead ball or anytime by the team in possession of the ball.
6. If the score is tied at the end of regulation time, play continues an extra period. As many extra periods are played as necessary to break the tie.
7. The clock stops each time an official blows the whistle indicating a dead ball (violation personal foul, out-of-bounds). The clock keeps running after successful field goals.

Play

1. The ball is put into play at the beginning of the game and any overtime period by a jump ball in

the center circle between two opponents. Each subsequent quarter or half starts with the team entitled to possession given the ball at the center division line. In jump ball situations, other than at the start of the game and start of extra periods, teams will alternate taking the ball out-of-bounds. The team not obtaining control of the initial jump ball will start the alternating process. After each goal, the ball is put into play by the team that did not score from the out-of-bounds area at the end of the court at which the basket has been scored.

2. A player is out-of-bounds when touching the floor on or outside the boundary line.

3. The ball is out-of-bounds when it touches a player who is out-of-bounds or any other person, the floor, or any object on or outside a boundary, or the supports or back of the backboard.

4. The ball is caused to go out-of-bounds by the last player touching it before it goes out. The ball would be awarded out-of-bounds for a throw-in by the opposing team. The ball is awarded out-of-bounds after a violation, successful free-throw or field goal, or a common foul until the bonus rule goes into effect.

5. While the ball is alive, an offensive player cannot remain for more than three seconds in that part of the free-throw lane between the endline, the free-throw line, and the free-throw lane lines.

6. If two opponents are both firmly holding the ball, or an offensive ball handler is closely guarded by the defense for five seconds, a jump ball is called.

7. Violations include causing the ball to go out-of-bounds, double dribbling, running with the ball, kicking the ball (positive act), striking the ball with the fist, interfering with the basket, illegal throw-in (taking more than five seconds or stepping on the line), and the three-second lane rule.

8. Fouls are classified as: (a) *personal*—involving pushing, charging, tripping, holding, body contact; or (b) *technical*—involving delay of game, unsportsmanlike conduct, illegal entry, excessive timeouts. For personal fouls, the offender is charged with one foul; a fifth personal foul results in disqualification. The offended player is awarded:

a. one free-throw if the foul occurred during a field goal attempt and the basket was made.

b. two free-throws if the foul occurred during a field goal attempt and the basket was missed.

c. no free-throw, but the ball is awarded to the offended player's team out-of- bounds if it was before the fifth common team foul of the half (in a game played in quarters) or before the seventh common team foul of the half (in a game played in halves).

d. one free-throw plus a bonus free-throw if the first one is made, when the fifth common foul or seventh common foul (see above: c) has occurred. This is called the bonus rule.

For technical fouls, the offended team is awarded two free-throws as well as the ball out of bounds.

SUGGESTED LEARNING SEQUENCE—BEGINNERS

A. Conditioning and stretching
B. Purpose of the game and general game concepts
C. Basic rules
D. Fundamental skills:
  1. Pivoting
  2. Catching and holding the ball
  3. Passing—chest, bounce, overhead
  4. Dribbling—high speed, low control
  5. Shooting—one-handed set, layup
  6. Rebounding—position, jumping
E. Individual offense:
  1. Cutting—V-cut, front
  2. Driving
F. Individual defense:
  1. Basic stance and movement
  2. Guarding a player with the ball
  3. Guarding a player without a ball
G. Team play:
  1. *Offense*—basic concepts on how to attack a player-to-player defense
  2. *Defense*—player-to-player
  3. *Other*—jump ball alignment, free-throw alignment

SUGGESTED LEARNING SEQUENCE—INTERMEDIATES

A. Conditioning and stretching
B. Additional rules
C. Review beginners unit
D. Intermediate skills:
  1. Passing—one-hand bounce, baseball
  2. Dribbling—crossover, reverse (spin)
  3. Shooting—free throw, jump shot, layup from various angles
  4. Rebounding—blocking out, outlet
E. Individual offense:
  1. Cutting—backdoor (reverse)
  2. Fakes and feints
F. Individual defense:
  1. Defense against a player one pass away and two passes away
  2. Denial defense
  3. Defense against a ball handler
G. Team play:
  1. *Offense*—basic concepts on how to attack a zone defense

2. *Defense*—combatting picks and screens, zones
3. *Other*—fast break, in-bounds plays

SKILLS AND TECHNIQUES

Pivoting

Pivoting is the only legal maneuvering a player standing and holding the ball is allowed. One foot (the pivot foot) must be kept at its point of contact with the floor, while the other foot can step in any direction. A good technique for the beginner is to imagine that a spike has been driven through the pivot foot into the floor; this would afford faking movements with the opposite foot, but the spike can be removed only through dribbling, passing, or shooting. Illegally moving the pivot foot or taking too many steps while stopping constitutes "traveling." The result is a loss of possession of the ball for that team.

Passing

Good passing is necessary in order to maintain possession of the ball and be able to move into scoring position. The key to an effective offense is accuracy in passing and passing is the quickest way to move the ball, thus allowing the offense to catch the defense off balance or out of position.

Chest Pass. This pass is probably the most commonly used pass. The ball is held in both hands, the finders spread on the sides of the ball with the thumbs behind the ball. Held about chest high with the elbows held comfortably at the sides of the body, the ball is released by extending the arms fully, snapping the wrists, and stepping in the direction of the pass. The palms should be facing downward or slightly outward with the elbow chest high on the follow-through. The chest pass should be received chest high.

Bounce Pass. This pass is a short distance pass used to avoid a deflection or interception when a player is being closely guarded. It is executed in the same manner as the chest pass except the ball is bounced into the hands of the receiver. The ball should bounce at approximately two-thirds of the distance between the passer and receiver, and should rebound waist high. This pass can also be released with one hand by stepping out with the free foot to either side of a close defender and bouncing the ball around him. It is also possible to make this pass directly off of the dribble.

Overhead Pass. This pass is used to pass over a defensive player, usually to a post player or a cutter. The ball is held overhead with both hands, thumbs under the ball and fingers spread on the sides of the ball (Figure 5-2A). The passer steps forward toward the intended receiver and transfers the

FIGURE 5-2 The overhead pass.

body weight to the front foot. The arms, which are slightly bent, are brought forward sharply, with a snap of the wrists releasing the ball (Figure 5-2B). This pass is best utilized by a player who is taller than the defending opponent.

One-Hand Overhead Pass (Baseball Pass). This pass is used most frequently to cover long distances, especially in initiating the fastbreak. When this pass is thrown with the right hand, the ball is brought back to the right ear, close to the head, with the fingers well spread in back of the ball. The left hand can steady the ball when it is in this position, ready to be thrown. The weight of the body is shifted to the right rear foot as the ball is brought back. The weight shifts forward to the left foot as the right arm is brought forward to release the ball. The ball is released about one foot in front of the body with the wrist snapping forward and downward.

▶ Learning Cues for Passing

1. Passes should be crisp, but not too hard to catch.
2. Use a pass appropriate for the specific situation.
3. Take a step in the direction of the pass.
4. Weight should be balanced when passing.
5. Do not "telegraph" the pass; be deceptive with your eyes.
6. Aim to hit your receiver between the waist and shoulders.
7. A fake before you pass may cause your defender to move, creating a better passing lane.
8. Put as little spin as possible on the pass.
9. Pass to the side of your teammate away from the defender.
10. Always pass ahead of a running teammate.
11. Learn to catch and pass in one motion.

Catching and Holding the Ball

Possession of the ball is so important that receiving and holding the ball are as essential as passing. A player should attempt to catch every pass regardless of how it is thrown. To help eliminate deflections, a player should cut sharply toward each pass to meet it, with the hands held out in front of the body to provide a target and to maintain balance when moving in any direction to meet the ball. It is also possible to hold one hand up in the air (the hand

furthest from your defender) to provide a high target for a pass (Figure 5-3). The ball should be caught with the pads of the fingers and brought toward the body to protect it before dribbling, passing, or shooting. If a player must stand for a few moments in possession of the ball, it is best to step back slightly with your free foot, away from your defender, pulling the ball back with you. This places your body between the ball and the defender for added protection.

▶ Learning Cues for Catching and Holding the Ball

1. Provide the passer with a target by holding a hand up or both hands forward.
2. Move to meet passes thrown to you.
3. Hands should be comfortably spread and relaxed when catching.
4. Keep elbows flexed, not stiff, enabling absorption of the impact of the thrown ball.
5. Watch the ball all of the way into your hands.
6. Pull the ball in close to your body for protection.
7. Whenever possible, catch with two hands to ensure control.

▶ Practice Suggestions for Passing and Catching

1. Stand approximately 8 feet from a wall. Execute different passes against the wall, concentrating on form and accuracy.
2. With a partner, stand in positions as either two guards, or as a guard and a forward. Pass back and forth, faking before each pass and practicing deception. Add two defenders. Add a cut to the basket after each pass to receive a return pass.
3. To practice the baseball pass, stand 30 feet from a partner. Pass back and forth. To practice this pass on the move, both players position themselves near the backboard. One player rebounds the ball off the board, dribbles toward the side-

FIGURE 5-3 Preparing to catch a pass against a defender.

line, and releases a baseball pass to the other player cutting downcourt. Add defenders.

4. Three-player weave: Three players start on the endline approximately 15 feet apart. The player in the middle has a ball. He passes to a wing and subsequently cuts behind him. This receiver, in turn, passes to the third player and cuts behind him. The three players continue passing and moving downcourt. Vary the passes. Add one, two, or three defenders.

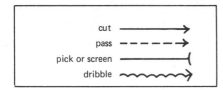

KEY TO MANEUVERS

cut	——————▶
pass	– – – – –▶
pick or screen	——————⊢
dribble	∿∿∿∿∿▶

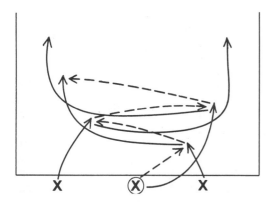

FIGURE 5-4   Three-player weave.

5. Variation: Five-player weave.

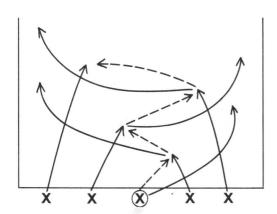

FIGURE 5-5   Five-player weave.

6. Four corner passing: With players in a box formation, one player makes a long pass to the first player in the next line. She follows her pass and receives a shorter pass back. She hands off to the same player and goes to the end of that line. Continue with a long pass to the next corner.

Variation: Add another ball. Start them in opposite corners.

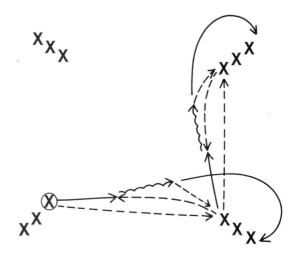

FIGURE 5-6   Four-corner passing.

7. Shotgun passing: One player stands apart from a half-circle of teammates who are arranged so that two players are just in the peripheral vision of the single player. Using two balls, the half-circle players and the single player pass very quickly back and forth.

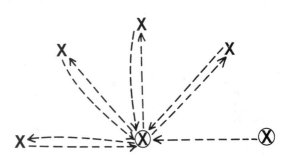

FIGURE 5-7   Shotgun passing.

8. Reaction pass drill: One partner has a ball, while the other player stands approximately 15 feet away with his back turned to the ball. The player with the ball calls out the other player's first name, followed by a pass to the player. Upon hearing his name, the player quickly turns and attempts to catch the ball and gain control of it. The pass should vary, making the receiver jump, reach, stoop, etc. to secure every pass.

9. Monkey in the middle: Players form a circle with one player ("monkey") in the middle. Using one ball and any type of pass, a player in the circle attempts to get the ball to any other player in the circle, other than the two players immediately adjacent to her. The "monkey" attempts to touch, deflect, or intercept the pass, at which time she changes place with the passer.

10. Shuttle pass drill: Form two lines in a shuttle formation. The first player in one of the lines has

a ball. The first person in the opposite line defends as the player attempts to pass across to the other line. Continue passing between the two lines with the passer each time becoming the next defender.

Dribbling

Dribbling is slower than passing as a means of moving the ball. Therefore it should not be overused. The dribble should be used only to: (1) penetrate or drive toward the basket; (2) create a better passing lane; (3) get out of a crowd; and (4) bring the ball down the court. A good rule to remember is never to dribble the ball when a pass can be completed successfully.

With the hand cupped, the pads of the fingers control the direction of the ball, while the wrist and finger flexion provide the force. The ball should be pushed downward and slightly forward, with the body in a crouched position. The opposite arm and forward foot should provide protection between the ball and the opponent. There are basically two types of dribbles that are identifiable by observing the rebounding height of the ball and the proximity of the defender. These are the high-speed dribble and the low-control dribble.

High-Speed Dribble. The high-speed dribble is used when a player is unguarded and moving quickly—leading a fastbreak, driving to the basket, bringing the ball down the court without opposition. The body is erect with only a slight forward crouch. The ball rebounds between the waist and chest. The dribbling arm pushes the ball forward and slightly to the side of the body. A full running stride is used, limited only by the dribbler's ability to control the ball.

Low-Control Dribble. This dribble is used when a player is closely guarded or in a congested area. Both the body and the ball should be kept low (Figure 5-8). The ball should rebound knee high and close to the dribbling side of the body. The more frequent contact with the ball allows for control and change of direction when under pressure.

Cross-over Dribble. In order to change directions, the crossover dribble can be used. It is effective only if the defender is guarding loosely. The dribbler simply pushes the ball to the floor so that it rebounds across in front of the body to the opposite hand. This must be done very quickly and with only one low bounce in order to avoid an interception. The shoulder opposite the dribbling hand should always be lowered and brought forward to protect the ball. The dribbler can now continue dribbling in the opposite direction.

Reverse (Spin) Dribble. The reserve dribble allows a player to change directions against an opponent who is guarding closely. It provides good pro-

FIGURE 5-8 Low-control dribble.

tection for the ball, but forces the dribbler to turn away from the basket and lose visual contact with teammates (Figure 5-9). To execute the reverse while dribbling with the right hand: plant the left foot, spin or pivot away from the defender, and rotate the head quickly to the right as the right foot swings out past the defender. Only one bounce of the ball is necessary to switch the dribble from the right hand to the left hand. The dribbler then continues dribbling toward the left with the left hand.

▶ **Learning Cues for Dribbling**

1. Keep your eyes and head up, facing the basket and your teammates as much as possible.
2. Be able to dribble with either hand.
3. Protect the ball with your body and opposite arm.
4. Control the dribble with your fingers and wrist: not the palm.
5. Push the ball; do not slap it.
6. Keep your knees bent for balance.
7. Dribble with the right hand when dribbling to the right, and dribble with the left hand when dribbling to the left, *especially* when being guarded.

▶ **Practice Suggestions for Dribbling and Ball Handling**

(Work to keep your head up during all dribbling and ball handling drills.)

1. Rotate the ball around the body, starting with the head. Go all the way down around the legs, and back up.
2. Rotate the ball around each ankle—right and left. Rotate the ball in a figure 8 around the ankles in a continuous motion.
3. Dribble the ball around the legs in a figure 8. Keep the ball low.

FIGURE 5-9   Reverse (spin) dribble.

4. Straddle flip: With the legs shoulder width apart, hold the ball low in front with both hands. Flip it up slightly between your legs, bringing your hands around behind the legs to catch the ball before it hits the ground. Flip it up again and bring the hands back to the front. Repeat as quickly as you can. *Variation:* Start with the hands alternately on the ball—one in front and one in back. Flip the ball up, alternating the hands quickly.

5. Dribble the ball around your body while on one knee, both knees, sitting, lying.

6. Standing two feet from a wall, tap the ball with the right or left hand high against the wall. *Variation:* Tap two balls simultaneously.

7. Circle keepaway: Within the boundaries of a restraining circle, try to dribble and maintain possession of a ball while another player attempts to steal it. *Variation:* Both players have a ball, trying to dribble *and* steal the other player's ball.

8. On a half court, try to dribble and maintain possession of a ball while two or three players try to pursue and steal the ball.

9. Dribble tag: On a half court, with all players dribbling a ball, play "tag." *Variations:* (a) More than one player is "it." (b) Restrict all players to use their nondominant hand.

10. Column dribbling drills (players at the endline in three columns): Dribble the full length of the court:
    a. In a zigzag pattern, executing a crossover dribble or a reverse dribble at each corner.
    b. Doing a crossover, reverse, or stop on the coach's signal.
    c. Going around obstacles.
    d. Against a defender, trying to steal the ball.

Shooting

The primary objective of the game of basketball is to score goals. Therefore all players should be able to shoot. Being able to shoot a variety of shots from varying distances increases the effectiveness of any player.

Point of Aim.   There are two targets that can be used in aiming at a basket—the rim, or a spot on the backboard for a bank shot. The easiest point of aim for a beginner is the rim of the basket, due to its permanent position from anywhere on the floor. The player should concentrate on dropping the ball just beyond the front of the rim. The bank shot is typically used when a player is positioned at a 24–45 degree angle on either side of the basket. A spot on the backboard is sighted with the purpose of allowing the ball to hit this spot and rebound into the basket. Selecting the correct spot and judging the force to put on the ball makes this a skill for experienced players. A square box is painted on most backboards

FIGURE 5-10 One-handed set shot.

forward-backward stride position with the foot under the shooting hand slightly forward. The ankles, knees, and hips should be slightly flexed with the weight easily balanced over the feet, and the shoulders square to the basket (Figure 5-10A). The ball is held below the chin (sighting the basket over the ball), or above the forehead (sighting the basket below the ball). It might be noted that the higher the ball is held, the less chance the defense has of blocking the shot. The ball should be held with the fingers, never in the palms of the hands. The shooting hand is behind and slightly under the ball with the fingers spread and wrist cocked (hyper-extended). The non-shooting or guide hand is placed on the side and slightly under the ball with fingers spread. In executing the shot, the legs extend upward while the shooting arm extends toward the basket (Figure 5-10B). The wrist flexes forward, while the guide hand comes off of the ball. The wrist flexion releases the ball, with the fingertips coming off last, creating a slight backspin on the ball. A proper follow-through should have the guide hand held high, with the palm of the shooting hand facing the floor. The one-handed set shot is also used by most players when shooting free-throws.

Jump Shot.   The jump shot is a very effective offensive weapon, due to its high point of release. The initial body position and the placement of the hands on the ball are the same as in the one-handed set shot. The shooter jumps into the air by pushing off with both legs. The ball is brought high above the forehead. At the apex of the jump, the body should be in a near-stationary, balanced position (Figure 5-11). Keeping the eyes focused on the basket, the shooting arm is uncocked and releases the ball with the same action as the one-handed position. Since the force for the jump shot is supplied primarily by the arms and wrist, the range of this shot is limited, as compared to the set shot which incorporates leg power as well as arm strength.

Lay-up.   This shot is one of the highest percentage shots in the game, due to its closeness of range. It is used when a player has received a pass close to the basket, or has driven past the defense near the goal. It is best executed on a diagonal in relation to the basket, using the backboard to bank the ball in. At the last dribble the ball is firmly grasped with the fingers of both hands, and carried above the head. When shooting with the right hand, the take-off should occur with the left foot, while the right knee thrusts upward to achieve maximum height. At the same moment, the ball is set in the shooting hand and the left hand falls away. The shooting arm and fingers extend upward to "lay" the ball against the backboard. A proficient basketball player will develop the ability to shoot a lay-up with either hand being the dominant hand—the left hand when on the left side of the basket, the right hand when on the right side.

to aid in spot selection. In aiming, the brain sights the target, computes the distance, and determines the correct trajectory to put on the ball. It is important for the eyes to be focused on the target before each shot, during the release, and after the follow-through. It is obvious why shooting demands so much practice.

One-Handed Set Shot.   This shot is used for most long shots. The feet should be positioned in a

FIGURE 5-11 Jump shot.

▶ **Learning Cues for Shooting**

1. Knees should bend to help generate power and provide balance.
2. Eyes should be focused on the target before, during, and after the shot.
3. Fingertips should control every shot.
4. Use the backboard to bank a shot from an angle.
5. Maintain body balance; try not to lean or fall.
6. The shooting hand should follow through toward the basket after releasing the ball.
7. Backspin on the ball is desirable.
8. Generally, a higher arc on the ball results in greater accuracy and a better bounce off the rim if the shot is missed.

▶ **Practice Suggestions for Shooting**

1. Add shooting to various passing and dribbling drills.
2. Column shooting drills (two lines of players facing the basket):
   a. One line shoots lay-ups; the other line rebounds. Vary the angles for the lay-ups. Add defensive pressure from the rebounding line.
   b. Same as (a), only use jump shots or set shots.
3. Around-the-world shooting: One player shoots, moving to a new spot after each shot, while another player rebounds and quickly passes to the shooter. *Variations:* (a) The passer-rebounder applies defensive pressure on each shot. (b) Have two rebounders and two balls, so the shooter must move and shoot quicker.
4. Shuffle and shoot: Using two balls, a player shuffles between two spots, picking up the ball at each spot and shooting. Two rebounders work at rebounding the balls and replacing them at each spot.

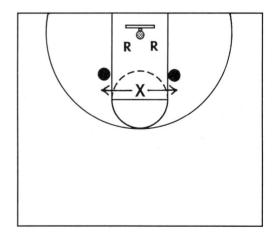

FIGURE 5-12 Shuffle and shoot.

5. One-on-one: A player passes the ball to a player being guarded. The receiver practices various shots against the defender. *Variations:* (a) The

receiver "posts up" to practice hook shots and moves with her back to the basket. (b) The receiver is allowed to use the passer again if she gets stuck.

6. Rebound-pass-shoot drill: Player X shoots from one of the spots, after receiving a pass from the passer. The rebounder rebounds and passes the ball to the passer. In the meantime, the shooter has moved to the next spot, ready to receive the pass there. Use two balls to make the action even more continuous. Vary the shooting spots and passing angle.

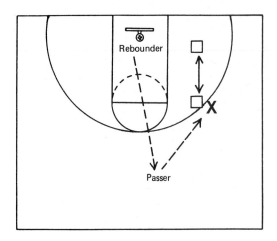

FIGURE 5-13   Rebound—pass—shoot.

7. Follow the leader: Each player has a ball. One leader is designated. The leader shoots from various spots, while every player follows him or her.
8. Competitive shooting: Two teams compete against each other from various shooting spots. *Variations:* (a) Timed shooting. (b) Designated number of completed shots. (c) Least number of misses. (d) First team to finish.

Rebounding

Rebounding is gaining possession of the ball after an unsuccessful shooting attempt. Since approximately 60 percent of field goal attempts are missed, rebounding skill is essential to any team. Rebounding is categorized as being either defensive (at your opponent's basket), or offensive (at your own team's basket). The keys to effective rebounding are positioning, aggressiveness, and timing of the jump.

Positioning for the rebound is called "blocking out" or "boxing out" (Figure 5-14). The defensive player has a distinct advantage here, already being closer to the basket. With anticipation and a quick move, however, the offensive player can gain the inside position. Blocking out is done by pivoting to face the basket, putting the opponent behind you. It is important here to spread the feet far apart, bend the legs, lower the hips, and hold the elbows out away

FIGURE 5-14   Blocking out.

from the body. This helps to create a stable position, not allowing an opponent to get around. Since both the offensive player and the defensive player want the inside position, a player must be very aggressive in order to maintain this desired position. This means the player that is blocking out must slide and maintain physical contact with his opponent until the rebound is secured.

Once the inside position is attained, the player must observe the ball, and anticipate how and where it will rebound off of the rim or backboard. The player should jump high and grasp the ball firmly with both hands (Figure 5-15). On the downward move, after getting the ball, spread the legs and hold the ball high and away from the opponents. If it is a defensive rebound, pass (outlet) the ball away from the basket to a teammate near the sideline, or dribble the ball out away from the basket. An offensive rebound should be tipped back up to the basket, shot back up after landing on the ground or passed to a teammate in better shooting position.

▶ **Learning Cues for Rebounding**

1. Work hard to attain or maintain the inside position closest to the basket.
2. Do not get pushed too far under the basket or backboard.
3. Be aggressive.
4. Jumping:
   a. Initiate the jump with the arms.
   b. Explode off of the floor by bending the legs.

FIGURE 5-15   Rebounding. Note the blockout by the other player.

c. Reach high with both arms extended.
d. Time the jump in order to grasp the ball as high as possible, attempting to keep the ball on line with the forehead.

5. Go for the ball; do not let it merely fall into your hands.
6. Keep a firm hold on the ball, jerking it down and away from any nearby opponents.
7. Land with feet comfortably spread and elbows out.
8. After landing, hold the ball high to keep opponents from getting it.
9. For a defensive rebound, get the ball away from the basket quickly (outlet). For an offensive rebound, try to get an immediate score out of it.

▶ **Practice Suggestions for Rebounding**

1. Standing 20 to 25 feet from a partner, have her toss a ball high into the air toward you. Jump high and grasp the ball firmly with both hands, bringing it down aggressively.
2. Standing in front of the backboard, toss the ball high against the board. Jump and grasp the rebound, concentrating on good rebounding form. *Variations:* (a) Execute an outlet pass after rebounding (defensive rebound). (b) Shoot or tip the ball into the basket (offensive rebound).
3. Second effort drill: Stand in front of the backboard with a partner holding a ball behind you. On your partner's command, jump high into the air as if rebounding. After you have jumped, the partner tosses the ball against the board, forcing you to spring back up immediately to rebound.
4. Circle blockout: Place a ball in the center of a restraining circle. Align three pairs of players around the outside of the circle—facing each other (one inside player with her back to the ball). On the whistle, the player on the inside turns and blocks out the other player, trying to keep her from touching the ball for approxi-

mately five seconds. *Variation:* Place a ball on the floor near each pair. Have each player block out her opponent from their ball for 30 seconds.

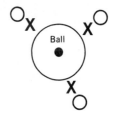

FIGURE 5-16   Circle blockout.

5. Three-on-three block out: With three offensive players and three defensive players positioned around the basket, the coach shoots the ball. Both teams attempt to secure the rebound. The offensive player should shoot the ball again or tip it in, while the defensive player should outlet the ball.

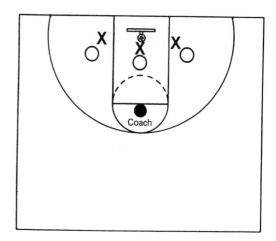

FIGURE 5-17   Three-on-three blockout.

FIGURE 5-18 Jab step.

Individual Offense

To be a good basketball player, you must always be a threat to the opponents when your team has possession of the ball. This means being able to score when the ball is in your hands, as well as being able to move effectively on the floor without the ball in order to free yourself or a teammate.

Driving. Driving is a means of getting past opponents by faking them off balance, accelerating, and dribbling hard past them. It is important to dribble with the hand farthest from the defender when driving. Fakes can be executed with the head, ball, or free foot. By holding the ball close to your body, away from the defender, a series of "jab" steps with the free foot may lure the opponent off balance so that you can drive (Figure 5-18). It is essential that a player not dribble immediately after receiving a pass. This would eliminate the fake and drive—a prime individual offensive weapon.

Cutting. Cutting is sharp, angular movement involving starting, stopping, and changes of direction, which enables a player without the ball to get free from defenders. All cuts should be preceded by a fake in the opposite direction. Cuts can be in front of the defender (front cut) or behind a defender (reverse or backdoor cut). A V-cut is a sharp, angular cut (in the shape of a V) used to clear an area for a pass.

All offensive movement should be purposeful—not aimless, wasted motion. An offensive player with the ball is constantly looking for open shots, passes, or drives. An offensive player without the ball is cutting and moving to get free, or to set a screen for a teammate. Of course, offensive team patterns or plays are a means of regulating and structuring every player's movement on the floor.

Individual Defense

Defense involves preventing a team from scoring, or, at least, limiting the maneuvering ability of the offensive team. Defense is as important as offense, but is considered less glamorous than scoring baskets. It requires hard work, concentration, and determination. Body balance is the key to good defense. The feet must be ready to move, preventing leaning and reaching with the upper body. It is a general rule (with only a few exceptions) that a defensive player should try to stay positioned between the offensive opponent and the basket. Foot movement is accomplished by sliding, keeping the feet as close to the floor as possible to enable quick shifts in direction.

There are two general situations to consider in individual defense: guarding a player with the ball (a ball handler), and guarding a player without the ball.

Defense Against a Player With the Ball. Note the fundamental defensive stance (Figure 5-19) of the player: weight low and evenly distributed on the balls of the feet, head up, knees flexed, arms flexed, hands relatively close to the body, palms up. The eyes should be focused on the opponent's hips rather than on the eyes or the ball. This prevents being faked out of position. Rather than reaching with the hands, a player should constantly be sliding the feet to maintain good body position. The arms should extend upward or outward from the body only

FIGURE 5-19   Defensive stance.

FIGURE 5-20   Defense against players without the ball. Note the "help" position defensive player.

to deflect a pass or a shot. The distance between the defensive player and the ball handler depends on the quickness and shooting range of the offensive player. Once a player stops dribbling, a very close defensive position should be established, with arms extended to prevent passes or a shot.

Defense Against a Player Without the Ball.   It makes sense that a player without the ball is not an immediate scoring threat. Thus, in playing defense, you must work hard to prevent your opponent from *receiving* the ball. This is accomplished by keeping the player you are guarding and the ball in view at all times. Also, one arm should constantly be extended between the ball and your defender to "deny" the pass (Figure 5-20). If your opponent is not close enough to the ball to receive a pass, you may have to open up your body position, using your peripheral vision to keep the ball and your opponent in view. This position allows you to "help out" a teammate who has been beaten by an offensive player. Again, like defending a ball handler, you try to dictate and thwart your opponent's moves.

▶ **Practice Suggestions for Individual Offense and Defense**

(Either the *offensive* or *defensive* portion can be emphasized.)

1. Cutting: B attempts to free himself for a pass from A by executing V-cuts, front cuts, or reverse cuts (backdoors). X works to deny the pass.
2. Individual Offense: After receiving a pass from A, B must do three offensive maneuvers en route to the basket for a shot (Example: jab step, reverse dribble, head fake.) May add a defender.

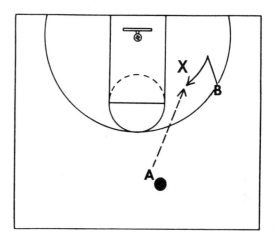

FIGURE 5-21   Cutting.

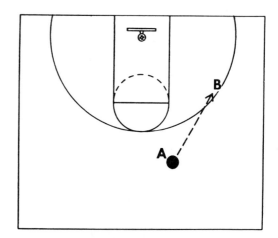

FIGURE 5-22   Individual offense.

3. Zigzag: Divide the court into thirds. Staying in her third of the court, the offensive player dribbles in a zigzag pattern down the floor. The defensive player stays with her, practicing good defensive form and position. *Variation:* The dribbler stops her dribble en route, making the defensive player move closer, straighten, and extend her arms.

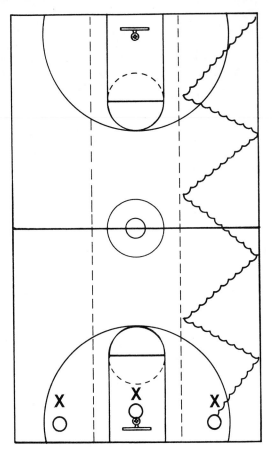

FIGURE 5-23   Zigzag.

4. Denial Defense: Both defensive players (X) work hard to deny any pass to the player they are guarding. A and B pass the ball back and forth trying to get it to the Os.

FIGURE 5-24   Denial defense.

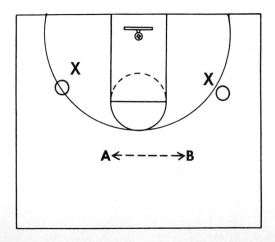

5. Denial in a Box: Within a 10 to 15 foot square, X must work hard to deny B from receiving a pass from A.

FIGURE 5-25   Denial in a box.

PLAYING STRATEGY

Team Offense

Offensive tactics in basketball vary according to the defensive tactics employed by the opposing team. Thus the offensive patterns will vary in order that the most efficient attack may be developed against the particular defense. Generally speaking, there are two types of offense: (1) that which is employed against the player-to-player defense, and (2) that which is employed against the zone defense.

Offense Against a Player-to-Player Defense. The offense used against the player-to-player defense is a combination of passing and player movement. Even though the offense consists of five players, it is most common for only two or three players to work together for a shot while the others employ decoying or rebounding roles. Against a player-to-player defense, it only takes one defensive player to falter to enable an open shot for the opposing offensive player. Working together to accomplish this, it is possible to do a give-and-go and a variety of screens and picks. These maneuvers employ only two or three players and confuse the defense, putting them out of good defensive position. Of course, individual offensive moves such as cutting and driving may be incorporated also.

These maneuvers can be incorporated into set plays, or used spontaneously in a freelance situation.

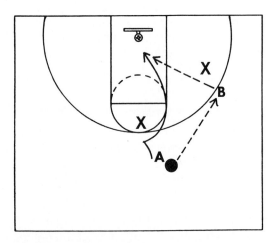

FIGURE 5-26   Give-and-go.

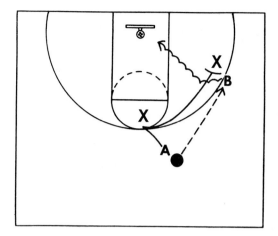

FIGURE 5-27 Pick.

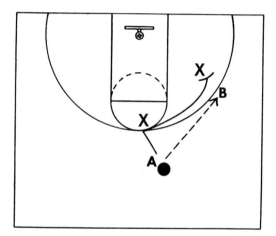

FIGURE 5-28 Screen.

Thus, five-player plays are actually a combination of two- and three-player maneuvers.

Offense Against a Zone Defense. The offense used against the zone defense is primarily one of moving the ball with short, quick passes to force the defensive players out of their assigned positions in order that a good shot may be taken. The offensive players move to positions that will force the defense to alter their zone and thus weaken its strength. Even if an offensive player gets past a defender, in a zone defense there is another defender waiting to cover. Therefore, the following principles should guide the offense in defeating the zone defense:

1. Quick passing
2. Outside shooting
3. Penetrate the zone with a dribble or a pass, then quickly pass out to a free teammate
4. Cut through the zone, splitting two defenders
5. Overload one side of the zone with more offensive players than defensive players
6. Dribble very sparingly
7. Screen a shifting defensive player

Team Defense

The Zone Defense. This style of defense calls for the placement of the defensive players in designated areas in and around the defensive basket in order to give a maximum protection against good shots. The alignments are numbered. The alignment selected must take into consideration the size, speed, and abilities of the players, as well as the area of the court desired to be covered. The most common zone defenses are the 1-3-1, the 1-2-2, the 3-2, the 2-1-2,

FIGURE 5-29 1-3-1 zone defense.

and the 2-3. Each player in zone defense is assigned a certain area on the court to cover, and guards only that offensive player who comes into that area. The defense shifts in relation to the ball, rather than in relation to the position of the offensive players. The zone defense is valuable in securing rebounds, in cutting off inside shooting against taller opponents, and in protecting players who are tired, weak defensively, or in foul trouble.

The Player-to-Player Defense. The principle behind the player-to-player defense is the assignment of each player to guard one offensive player, and thus the area element that is prominent in the zone defense is eliminated. Instead of shifting as a unit in relation to the position of the ball, each player must follow one player all over the defensive court. This defense takes extraordinary skill, stamina, and teamwork, since any free offensive player is a scoring threat. Since the offensive team will be working screens, picks, and cuts to free a teammate, the defense must communicate and have tactics to avoid such maneuvers. One such tactic involves immediate on-the-floor switching of defensive assignments if an offensive player has gotten free. Another tactic involves defensive players allowing room for each other to slide through picks and screens, enabling them to stay with their assigned players.

The Pressing Defense. In recent years, pressing defenses have taken on great significance at all levels of basketball competition. The main objectives of pressing defenses are to harass opponents into ball-handling errors, to force opponents into changing their game strategy, and to force the offensive team to use up valuable time in bringing the ball down the court. The press can be administered full-court, ¾ court, or ½ court, and can incorporate zone or player-to-player principles.

MODIFICATIONS FOR SPECIAL POPULATIONS

Orthopedically Impaired

1. Contact the National Wheelchair Basketball Association in Lexington, Kentucky for the rules of wheelchair basketball.
2. Students with grasp and release difficulties could practice dropping smaller balls into hoops, wastebaskets, buckets.
3. Consider utilizing commercial "Nerf Basketball" games for severely impaired students.
4. Establish the rule that the student using a wheelchair must touch the ball, e.g., pass from a teammate, before a shot is taken from his/her team.

Mentally Impaired

1. Contact Special Olympics for their manual on basketball rules.

2. Concentrate on the concepts of offense and defense in the earlier lessons. Allow "traveling" violations if it reinforces the concept of the game in the early stages of learning. Specific rules about the game will evolve as the unit continues.

Sensory Impaired

1. Try blindfolding the sighted students in class.
2. Position a student near the basket as the designated shooter in a stationary position. Rotate a sighted and a blind or visually impaired student through that position. A shot must be taken from that position every two trips down the court.
3. Minimal modifications needed for the deaf and hard of hearing.

TERMINOLOGY

Backcourt players (Guards)   Players who set up a team's offensive pattern; usually the smaller players on the team or the best ball handlers.

Backdoor   An offensive maneuver whereby a player cuts toward the baseline to the basket, behind the defenders, and receives a pass for a field goal attempt.

Baseline   The endline.

Blocking out (Boxing out)   A term used to designate a player's position under the backboard which prevents an opposing player from achieving good rebounding position.

Charging   Personal contact against the body of a defensive opponent by a player with the ball.

Corner players (Forwards)   Tall players who are responsible for the rebounding and shooting phases of the team's operation. They make up the sides of the offensive set-up.

Cut   A quick offensive move by a player trying to get free for a pass.

Denial defense   Aggressive individual defense where the defensive player works hard to keep the offensive player from receiving a pass.

Double foul   When two opponents commit personal fouls against each other at the same time. The result is a throw-in for the team entitled, as a result of the alternating jump ball process.

Dribble   Ball movement by a player in control who throws or taps the ball in the air or onto the floor and then touches it. The dribble ends when the dribbler touches the ball with both hands simultaneously, permits it to come to rest while in contact with it, or loses control.

Drive   An aggressive move toward the basket by a player with the ball.

Fake (Feint)   Using a deceptive move with the ball to pull the defensive player out of position.

Fastbreak   Moving the ball quickly downcourt in order to score before the defense can set up.

Field goal   A basket scored from the field.

Freelance   No structure or set plays in the offense.

Free throw The privilege given a player to score one or two points by unhindered shots for a goal from within the free throw circle and behind the free throw line.

Give-and-go A maneuver in which the offensive player makes a pass to a teammate, and then immediately cuts in toward the basket for a return pass.

Held ball Occurs when two opponents have one or both hands firmly on the ball, and neither can gain possession without undue roughness. The result is a throw-in for the team entitled, as a result of the alternating jump ball process.

Inside player (Center, Post, Pivot) Most often the tallest player on the team. This player is situated near the basket, around the three-second lane area, and is responsible for rebounding and close-range shooting.

Jump ball A method of putting the ball into play to start the game or any overtime periods by tossing it up between two opponents in the center circle. In jump ball situations that occur (due to held ball, double foul, etc.), once the game has begun teams will alternate taking the ball out-of-bounds. The team not obtaining control of the initial jump ball will start the alternating process.

Outlet pass A term used to designate a direct pass from a rebounder to a teammate, with the main objective being the start of a fastbreak.

Overtime period An extra period of playing time (5 minutes in college; 3 minutes in high school) played if the score is tied at the end of the regulation game.

Personal foul A player foul which involves contact with an opponent while the ball is alive or after the ball is in possession of a player for a throw-in.

Pick A special type of screen where a player stands so the defensive player slides to make contact, freeing an offensive teammate for a shot or drive.

Pivot Takes place when a player who is holding the ball steps once or more than once in any direction with the same foot; the other foot, called the pivot foot, being kept at its point of contact with the floor. Also, another term for the inside player.

Posting up A player cutting to the three-second lane area, pausing, and anticipating a pass.

Rebound A term usually applied when the ball bounces off the backboard or basket.

Restraining circles Three circles of six-foot radius, one located in the center of the court and one located at each of the free-throw lines.

Running time Not letting the clock stop for fouls or violations, usually used in a recreational situation.

Screen An offensive maneuver where a player is positioned between the defender and a teammate in order to free the teammate for an uncontested shot.

Switching A reversal of defensive guarding assignments.

Technical foul A noncontact foul by a player, team, or coach for unsportsmanlike behavior or failure to abide by rules regarding submission of lineups, uniform numbering, and substitution procedures.

Telegraphing a pass Indicating where you are going to pass by looking or signaling.

Throw-in A method of putting the ball in play from out-of-bounds.

Traveling When a player in possession of the ball within bounds progresses illegally in any direction.

Violation An infraction of the rules resulting in a throw-in from out-of-bounds for the opponents.

SELECTED REFERENCES

AAHPERD: Basketball Skills Test Manual, AAHPERD Publication, P.O. Box 704, Waldorf, MD 20604, 1984.

Atkins, K. and Rainey, R. *Winning Basketball Drills.* West Nyack, NY: Parker Publishing Co., Inc., 1985.

Basketball Rule Book, published yearly by the National Federation of State High School Associations, 11724 Plaza Circle, Box 20626, Kansas City, MO, 64195.

Garfinkel, H. (ed.) *Five-Star Basketball Drills.* Grand Rapids, MI: Masters Press, 1987.

Harkins, H.L. *Basketball's Winning Zone Offenses.* Waukesha, WI: MacGregor Sports Education, 1988.

Head S. and Jennings, P. and D. *Basketball.* Dubuque, IA: Wm. C. Brown Publishers, 1991.

Krause, J.V. and Brennan, S.J. *Basketball Resource Guide.* 2nd ed., Champaign, IL: Leisure Press, 1990.

Murrey, B. (ed.) *Individual Fundamentals.* Waukesha, WI: MacGregor Sports Education, 1988.

Murrey, B., (ed.) *Zone Defense.* Waukesha, WI: MacGregor Sports Education, 1987.

NCAA Men's and Women's Basketball Rules and Interpretations, published yearly by The National Collegiate Athletic Association, P.O. Box 1906, Mission, KS, 66201.

Smith, D., and Spear, B. *Basketball—Multiple Offense and Defense.* Englewood Cliffs, NJ: Prentice Hall, 1982.

Walker, A.L. and Donahue, J. *The New Option Offense for Winning Basketball.* Champaign, IL: Leisure Press, 1988.

Wilkes, G. *Basketball.* 5th ed. (P.E. Activities Series). Dubuque, IA: Wm. C. Brown Publishers, 1984.

Wooden, J. *Practical Modern Basketball.* 2nd ed. New York: John Wiley and Sons, 1980.

Periodicals

The Basketball Bulletin, The National Association of Basketball Coaches (NABC), P.O. Box 307, Branford, CT 06405.

Basketball Clinic, Princeton Educational Publishers, CN 5245, Princeton, NJ 08540.

Basketball Digest, Century Publishing Company, 1020 Church St., Evanston, IL 60201.

Coaching Clinic, Parker Publishing Company, US Highway 9W, Englewood Cliffs, NJ 07632.

Coaching Women's Basketball, published jointly by the Women's Basketball Coaches Association (WBCA) and Human Kinetics Publishers, Inc., Box 5076, Champaign, IL 61820.

National Wheelchair Basketball Association Newsletter, 110 Seaton Building, University of Kentucky, Lexington, KY 40506.

Scholastic Coach, Scholastic, Inc., 1290 Wall St., Lyndhurst, NJ 07071.

Audio-Visual Materials

"Power Basics of Basketball." 80-minute ½" VHS tape. A step-by-step guide to dribbling, passing, blocking, shooting, and defensive play. Hosts are Bill Walton, Walt Hazzard, and Greg Lee. Available from Video Sports, Dept. S. 8720 Villa La Jolla Dr., Suite 110, La Jolla, CA 92037.

The following are available from The Athletic Institute, 200 Castlewood Drive, North Palm Beach, FL 64195:

"Becoming a Basketball Player" by Hall Wissel. Five 20-minute ½" VHS tapes that offer a sound program of drills to help players develop in five key areas: ball handling, shooting, offensive moves off the dribble, defense, and rebounding.

"Basketball in the 90's" by Lute Olson. Two 50-minute ½" VHS tapes that teach post and perimeter players the right moves.

Basketball Series, Nos. 1–5. Each is 20-minute ½" VHS:

No. 1: "Ball Handling"—techniques and drills for ball handling, passing, catching, and dribbling.

No. 2: "Shooting"—focuses on all shooting skills, with challenging drills.

No. 3: "Offensive Moves"—from footwork to faking, teaches moves to make players offensive threats.

No. 4: "Offensive Moves Off Dribble"—power moves, reverses, and change of pace moves to enhance offensive play.

No. 5: "Defense and Rebounding"—develops defensive techniques and rebounding skills.

(Other organizations that distribute basketball-related visual resources are listed below.) Contact each organization for a current listing of titles/materials:

AAHPERD Educational Media Sources. 1201 16th St., N.W., Washington, DC 20036.

Bob Knight Basketball Aids, Inc., 1113 South High St., Bloomington, IN 47401.

Converse, 55 Fordham Road, Wilmington, MA 01887.

MacGregor Sports Education Library. 2236B Blue Mound Road, Waukesha, WI 53186.

Pro Keds Lessons from Lehmann, P.O. Box 157, Riverside, NJ 08075.

National Instructional Sports Videos, P.O. Box 8188, Cranston, RI 02920.

6 BOWLING

THIS CHAPTER WILL ENABLE YOU TO:

▶ *Select a proper fitting bowling ball and a pair of bowling shoes.*
▶ *Bowl a game according to the official rules of the American Bowling Congress.*
▶ *Practice and use the four-step approach and delivery, the straight ball, and the hook ball.*
▶ *Score a complete game using the appropriate symbols to indicate the line score.*
▶ *Improve your strategy by converting spares.*
▶ *Understand the terminology, observe safety rules, and utilize proper etiquette associated with the sport.*

NATURE AND PURPOSE

Bowling appeals to people of all ages and is easily adapted for special populations. Because a relatively small expenditure of energy is required in bowling, it is not an activity that lends itself to the development of physical fitness. However, participants may bowl for years after more strenuous activities have been abandoned, and fortunately, any person who has a degree of motor fitness can enjoy bowling as a lifetime sport.

The typical bowling center of today has become an almost 24-hour enterprise. It caters to housewives leagues in the morning, to junior leagues in the afternoon, to leagues (separate or mixed) for men and women in the evening, and to late night-early morning bowlers who work the second shift. Most establishments are clean and well kept, thus providing suitable entertainment places for the whole family.

The modern game of tenpins is played on indoor wooden lanes, 60 feet long from the foul line to the center of the number one pin, and 41 or not more than 42 inches wide (see Figure 6-1). The tenpins are set up (or "spotted") in a diamond formation on pin spots 12 inches apart, center to center (Figure 6-2A). A regulation tenpin is 15 inches high, with a diameter of 2¼ inches at the base. Pins are constructed of clear, hard maple and are usually coated with a plastic outer covering. They must conform to American Bowling Congress specifications. The object of the game is to roll the ball down the lane and knock down all the pins located in the diamond formation.

The lane is bordered on either side by gutters that prevent an errant ball from moving into another adjacent lane. It is constructed of two types of wood: maple, a hardwood to take the constant punishment of the ball, and pine, a soft wood that aids in gripping the ball. As shown in Figure 6-2B, a lane has several

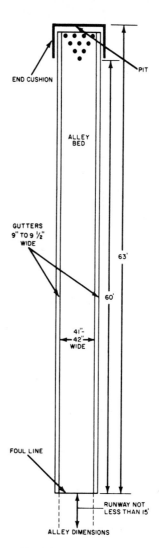

FIGURE 6-1 Lane dimensions.

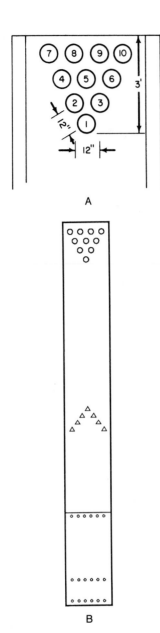

FIGURE 6-2 (A) Position and number of pins. (B) Lane markings.

markings, some of which appear to be off the lane (the approach area). All of the marks serve as points of reference for the bowler. The initial sets of dots, found in the approach area, serve as a point of reference for the bowler. The set of points in arrow formation beyond the foul line serve as a point of reference for aiming the ball.

EQUIPMENT AND FACILITIES

Bowling is one of the few sports that a participant can enjoy without having to buy expensive equipment. For the recreational or occasional bowler,

bowling centers provide "house balls," and shoes may be rented for a small fee. However, if you are planning to become a regular bowler, it is best to own your own equipment. Studies that have been conducted indicate that men and women who own their own equipment have higher bowling averages. Basically, all the bowler needs is a ball, a carrying bag, and a good pair of bowling shoes.

For a school physical education class, it would be expensive and impractical to have bowling lanes in the gymnasium. Several companies manufacture bowling sets consisting of plastic bowling pins, a plastic sheet on which to place the pins for proper distance and placement, and a hollow rubber bowling ball containing several holes so the learner can properly fit the ball to the hand. Markings and distances can be measured and painted on the floor with a water-based paint for easy removal. Many techniques can be learned in the gymnasium before proceeding to the bowling center.

Bowling Ball

Choosing a Ball. Bowling balls are made of hard rubber or plastic and come in a variety of colors. The hard rubber ball is black and is the type of ball found in most bowling centers. Although all bowling balls are the same size, 27 inches in diameter, the weight varies from 8 to 16 pounds. When selecting a ball, the beginner should choose the weight that feels most comfortable. Young junior bowlers use a light ball, women generally use a ball that weighs 10 to 13 pounds, and men usually use a ball weighing 14 to 16 pounds. The primary considerations in making your decision should be comfort and how well you can control the ball. If you consistently use a house ball, find a ball that best fits you. House balls are marked with an identification number and the weight; try to use the same ball each time you bowl.

Fitting the Ball. It is also important to select a ball equipped with holes that fit your fingers. Balls are drilled with three holes, one for the thumb and two for the third and fourth fingers. If you buy your own ball, the ball is fitted to your hand span. This ensures a proper fit that will allow you to handle the ball fairly easily. The holes should be large enough for the fingers to slip in and out with ease. The thumb hole should be comfortably loose. The bowler should be able to turn the ball around the thumb without binding, grabbing, or excessive rubbing of the skin.

To determine the proper fit, the bowler must decide the type of grip that will be used. There are three grips: the conventional, the semi-fingertip, and the full fingertip. Advanced bowlers use the latter two grips; beginners should use the conventional grip since it is the easiest to control. To determine proper hand span for the conventional grip, place the

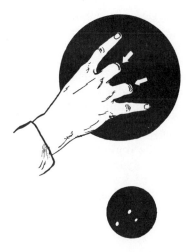

FIGURE 6-3 Position of fingers in three-hole ball.

thumb completely in the thumb hole, keeping the fingers relaxed and spread over the finger holes. The crease of the second joint of the two middle fingers should extend ¼ inch beyond the inside edge of the finger holes (Figure 6-3). The finger holes are cut at a certain pitch or angle to aid the bowler in grasping the ball.

In practice bowling sets used in most schools, the hollow rubber ball generally comes with several finger holes in order to accommodate the various hand spans.

Bowling Shoes

Another important item in the bowler's list of equipment is proper footwear. At first glance, both shoes of a pair of bowling shoes look the same. Closer inspection of the soles of the shoe will reveal a difference. For the right-handed bowler the left shoe should have a leather sole to facilitate sliding at the release point, and a rubber heel; the right shoe should have a rubber sole with a leather tip, and a rubber heel. For the left-handed bowler the order is reversed. Most bowling centers have rental shoes for both right-handed and left-handed bowlers.

For the physical education class, it is important that students wear smooth-soled shoes which enable sliding during the approach and release. Crepe soles or heavy-treaded rubber soles such as used in jogging shoes would be inappropriate.

Ball Bag

The serious bowler and the bowler who owns equipment should have a bag in which to store and carry the ball. Bags come in a variety of materials; those made of plastic, vinyl, or canvas are the least expensive. Many discount department stores have bags on sale regularly.

BASIC RULES

In league or tournament play, two contiguous lanes are used, and the bowling of ten complete frames on these lanes constitutes an official game. Members of contesting teams successively and in regular order bowl one frame on one lane and the next frame on the other lane, so alternating frames until the game is completed. Each player bowls two balls in each frame. If a strike is made on the first ball, the second ball is not rolled (except that in the tenth frame if a strike or spare is made, the player immediately rolls on the same lane the additional balls or ball to which the strike or spare entitles him).

In case of a tie game, each team bowls an extra complete frame on the same lane in which the tenth frame was bowled. The extra frame is bowled and scored in exactly the same manner as the tenth frame. If a tie still exists at the completion of the first extra frame, the teams must change lanes for the additional frames that may be required to determine the winner.

It is a foul if a bowler permits any part of his foot, hand, or arm, while in contact with the lanes or runways, to rest upon or extend beyond the foul line at any time after the ball leaves the bowler's hands and passes beyond the foul line. No count is made on a foul ball, and any pins knocked down are immediately respotted. A foul ball counts as a ball bowled by the player. If a player commits a foul which is apparent to both captains, one or more members of each of the opposing teams competing in a league or tournament on the same pair of lanes where the foul is committed, and the foul is not seen by the foul judge or umpire, or recorded by an automatic foul detecting device, a foul shall nevertheless be declared and so recorded.

Pinfall—Legal

Every ball delivered by the player shall count, unless declared a dead ball. Pins must then be respotted after the cause for declaring such dead ball has been removed.

1. Pins knocked down by another pin or pins rebounding in play from the side partition or rear cushion are counted as pins down.
2. If, when rolling at a full setup or in order to make a spare, it is discovered immediately after the ball has been delivered that one or more pins are improperly set, although not missing, the ball and resulting pinfall shall be counted. It is each player's responsibility to detect any misplacement of pins and have the setup corrected before he bowls.
3. Pins knocked down by a fair ball, and which remain lying on the lane or in the gutters, or which lean so as to touch kickbacks or side partitions, are termed dead wood and counted as pins down,

and must be removed before the next ball is bowled.

Pinfall—Illegal

When any of the following incidents occur, the ball counts as a ball rolled, but pins knocked down shall not count.

1. When pins are knocked down or displaced by a ball which leaves the lanes before reaching the pins.
2. When a ball rebounds from the rear cushion.
3. When pins come in contact with the body, arms, or legs of a pinsetter and rebound.
4. A standing pin which falls upon removing dead wood or which is knocked down by a pinsetter or mechanical pinsetting equipment shall not count and must be replaced on the pin spot where it originally stood before delivery of the ball.
5. Pins which are bowled off the lane, rebound, and remain standing on the lane must be counted as pins standing.
6. If in delivering the ball a foul is committed, any pins knocked down by such delivery shall not be counted.

Bowling on Wrong Lane

When only one player or the leadoff players of both teams bowl on the wrong lane and the error is discovered before another player has bowled, a dead ball shall be declared and the player, or players, required to bowl on the correct lane. When more than one player on the same team has rolled on the wrong lane, the game shall be completed without adjustment, and the next game shall be started on the correctly scheduled lane.

SCORING

All players should learn how to score. It adds considerably to the enjoyment of the game if the player can keep an accurate record of the score as the game progresses. There are ten numbered boxes on the score sheet to correspond to the ten frames in a game. At the top of each frame box are two small squares in which to write the number of pins toppled with the first ball and the second ball. Some simple scoring rules must be remembered in order to score a game accurately.

1. The score that is entered from box to box is cumulative; i.e., it represents the total number of pins toppled up to that point.
2. If a bowler does not get a strike or spare in any frame, scoring is just a matter of adding on the number of pins knocked down in each frame.

3. If all pins are knocked down with the first ball, it is called a *strike* and a cross (X) is marked in the small square in the upper right-hand corner of the frame box. The strike will count 10 pins plus the number of pins knocked down on the next two successive balls. A score will not be entered in the frame box until those two balls have been rolled.
4. If all pins are knocked down with two balls, it is called a *spare* and is indicated by a diagonal mark (/). The spare will count 10 pins plus the number of pins knocked down on the next ball rolled. A score will not be entered in the frame box until the next ball has been rolled.

Frame	1st Ball	2nd Ball	Total Score
1.	7 pins Enter score in first square	2 pins	9 pins
2.	5 pins	3 pins	17—cumulative score of first two frames: 9 + 8 = 17
3.	Strike. Enter (X) in first square		46—2 strikes (20) + 9 pins (see frame five) + 17 = 46
4.	Strike (X)		65—Strike (10) + 9 + 46 = 65
5.	9 pins—add to the two consecutive strikes	Miss (−) no pins	74 (65 + 9)
6.	8 pins	Spare. Enter (/) in second square	89—Spare (10) + 5 pins + 74 = 89
7.	5 pins—add to spare from frame six	4 pins	89 + 9 pins = 98
8.	9 pins	(−) no pins	98 + 9 = 107
9.	7 pins—a split	(O) no pins, missed converting the split	107 + 7 = 114
10.	Strike (X)—Player rolls two more balls, which are also strikes		114 + 3 strikes (30) = 144

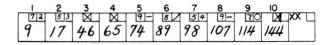

FIGURE 6-4 Scoring example and score sheet of a complete game.

5. If you spare or strike in the tenth frame, then you roll one more ball if a spare, or two more balls if a strike, and add that to your total score.

In order to illustrate scoring we will score a hypothetical game. But first let's review the symbols used and the scoring procedure.

(X) Indicates a *strike*: 10 plus the score of the next two balls.

(/) Indicates a *spare*: 10 plus the score of the next ball rolled.

(O) Indicates a *split*: score will depend on number of remaining pins knocked down by next ball rolled.

(Ø) Indicates a *converted split*: 10 plus the score of the next ball rolled.

(-) Indicates a *miss* or *error*: no score.

(F) Indicates a *foul*: no score.

(G) Indicates a *gutter ball*.

The score sheet of a completed game is shown and analyzed in Figure 6-4.

SUGGESTED LEARNING SEQUENCE

A. Nature of the game
   1. Equipment
   2. Fitting a bowling ball
   3. Safety: Lane courtesy
B. Techniques. Rules should be introduced early in the learning progression to coincide with specific techniques.
   1. Stance
   2. Approach
   3. Straight ball
   4. Hook ball
C. Scoring. May be introduced as the situation warrants and is most appropriate.
D. Strategy
   1. Pin bowling and Spot bowling
   2. Making spares

SKILLS AND TECHNIQUES

Bowling is a relatively easy game to learn, but like all sporting activities it is important to learn the techniques involved in order to develop consistency. For the physical education teacher, much of the technique involving the grip, stance, approach, and release can be taught in the gymnasium. The two basic skills to be learned are the swing coordinated with a specific number of steps.

The Stance

There is no definite or prescribed stance assumed by all bowlers preparatory for the start of the approach. However, there are some important points to remember.

1. Hold the ball with both hands in front of the body. For a man this may be waist high, for a woman a little higher in order to attain a longer swing for increased speed.
2. The feet are spread slightly apart, weight evenly distributed, perhaps one foot slightly ahead of the other.
3. Most of the weight of the ball should be supported by the nonthrowing hand at this point.
4. The ball is gripped with the thumb in a 12 o'clock position for a straight ball or the 10 o'clock position for a hook ball.

The Approach

Bowlers vary in the number of steps taken in the approach. The number of steps range from three to five, but most experts recommend the four-step approach. The beginning bowler should experiment with the delivery and determine which works best. The following discussion will center around the four-step approach for the right-handed bowler. The left-handed bowler will reverse the starting procedure.

In proper execution of the approach, the bowler will take a series of steps in a smooth, rhythmical manner, and will end with a slide and follow-through as the ball is released. Women bowlers begin on the 12-foot line with feet straddling the second dot from the right for right-handers or the second dot from the left for left-handers. The eyes should be fixed on the second arrow from the right (right-hander) or left (left-hander) located on the lane. Men will begin the approach approximately 18 inches farther back from the 12-foot line. As the steps are taken and the delivery is executed, it is important for the bowler to walk in a straight line. Let the dots near the foul line be your guide.

▶ Learning Cues

Step 1. The push away. Step with the right foot and at the same time push the ball out to an arm's length in front of the body. Do not overextend the push away or loss of balance and direction may result.

Step 2. The ball moves to the bottom of the arc on the downswing as the left foot completes the second step.

Step 3. The ball reaches the top of the backswing (shoulder high), as the right foot completes the third step. The ball must swing in a straight line, shoulders square to the foul line.

Step 4. As the last step is taken the ball swings forward, the wrist is firm, and the ball is released toward the target. The nonthrowing hand will help serve as a means of balance. The left toe will be pointing at the target.

If the timing is correct the ball is released out in front of the body and laid rather than dropped on the lane. The bowling ball, when properly delivered, has a double motion. When first released it slides and revolves, sliding in the direction toward the pins. After sliding a distance, once it reaches the nonoiled surface, friction increases, and the ball begins to revolve, causing it to hook, roll straight, or back up, depending on the type of ball that is thrown.

▶ **Practice Suggestions**

1. Allow students to move to the ball rack and demonstrate proper technique for picking up the ball.
2. Pick up the ball and assume a good, well-balanced stance with ball held comfortably and in proper position.
3. From a designated line on the floor or on the approach try a four-step approach without the ball. To determine the length of your approach, move to a position short of the foul line and take four steps toward the beginning position. Try to coordinate steps, arm swing, follow-through without the ball. Check the line from step one to step four.
4. Bellisimo recommends a one-step delivery with a ball.[1] Place students in a position to take the last step. Allow them to first take a practice swing with a ball, then allow students to take the last step and delivery. Concentrate on a straight pendulum swing and a good follow-through with the hand finishing high.
5. Allow bowlers to try a four-step approach and delivery using the ball (Figure 6-5).

The Straight Ball

Beginning bowlers should concentrate first on perfecting a straight ball before attempting to roll a hook. It is also recommended that the woman bowler who lacks ball speed continue the use of a straight ball.

Learning Cues

1. The thumb should be held in a 12 o'clock position with the fingers underneath the ball.
2. The hand position should be maintained throughout the swing, with no arm rotation during release of the ball.

3. The wrist remains firm, the palm faces the pins as the ball is delivered; maintain a straight follow-through.
4. The ball should be started from the right side of the lane and directed toward the 1–3 pocket.

The Hook Ball

Most good bowlers use a hook ball; beginning bowlers will want to learn this delivery as soon as possible. To obtain maximum pin action, the ball should strike the pins at an angle, but the angle of the straight ball is limited by the width of the alley. The straight ball revolves forward, but the hook ball revolves at an angle, thus giving it greater pin splash or action by imparting a revolving action to the pins. This delivery is sometimes called the "handshake" delivery because the position of the hand is similar to that used in an ordinary handshake.

▶ **Learning Cues**

1. The wrist is firm, the thumb is in a 10:30 o'clock position. This position must be maintained throughout the swing.
2. As the ball is released, the thumb comes out first, the fingers lift and impart a rotational effect to the ball.
3. Release the ball with the V formed by the thumb and forefinger pointing toward the target.
4. The hand should be carried upward and forward toward the pins in the follow-through. Do not side-wheel, twist the arm, or intentionally spin the ball.

There are two other types of deliveries: the curve ball and the backup ball. However, because of the difficulty of controlling them, they are not recommended for the beginning bowler.

▶ **Practice Suggestions**

1. For the physical education class, use partners. Roll a straight ball or a hook using a hollow plastic ball to each other. Concentrate on proper wrist and hand position as well as swing consistency.
2. At the lanes, practice the swing first, holding the ball in the correct position. Some experts recommend rolling the ball back and forth between partners to practice the proper release technique.
3. The bowler will continue to roll the ball over the second arrow from the right (right-hander). However, experiment with your starting position by moving over one or two boards toward the left to find the most consistent path for your hook (Figure 6-6).

[1] L. Bellisimo and J. Bennett, *The Bowler's Manual,* 4th ed. (Englewood Cliffs, NJ: Prentice Hall, 1982), p. 10.

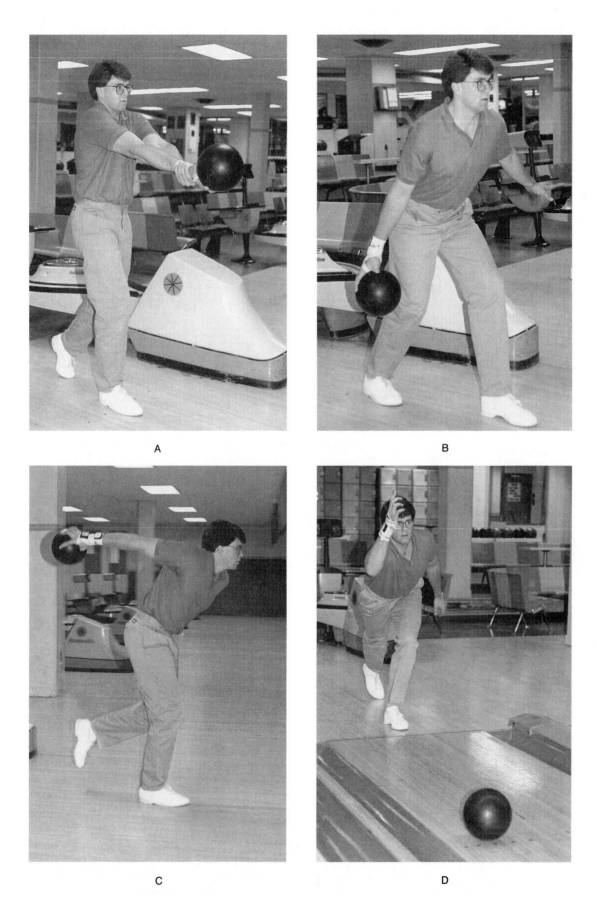

A

B

C

D

FIGURE 6-5   Four-step approach. Note shoulders squarely facing the pins.

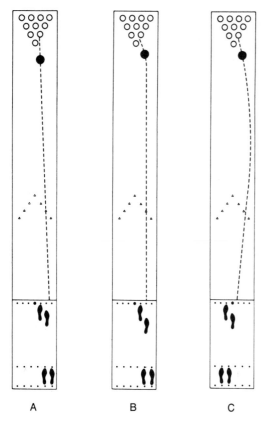

FIGURE 6-6 Path of (A) straight ball, (B) hook ball, (C) curve ball.

PLAYING STRATEGY

Spot Bowling and Pin Bowling

An individual sport, bowling has no complicated playing strategies similar to those found in many team sports. You should plan your game so as to knock down the greatest number of pins possible. This is accomplished by individual control and accuracy, rather than cooperation with teammates in the execution of plays.

Playing strategy should include, first, a mastery of a definite approach and delivery style. The good bowler will settle upon a definite pattern as early as possible, making every effort to throw each ball with the same motion. Most bowlers are classified as "spot" or "pin" bowlers. The spot bowler selects a spot on the alley a few feet from the foul line and attempts to roll the first ball in each frame over that spot. The pin bowler looks at the pins while approaching and making the delivery. Whether you prefer throwing a hook or a straight ball, follow your selected style on all balls and concentrate on developing accuracy with a smooth and rhythmical delivery.

Spares

To bowl a good score, the bowler must pick up spares consistently. Accuracy is essential for good spare bowling. Unlike rolling a strike ball, the spare may force the bowler to vary the starting position and the spot over which the ball may be rolled. For the right-handed bowler, pins left on the right side of the lane such as the 1, 3, 6, 10 or 3, 5, 6, 9, 10, the starting position should be on the left side of the lane. For pins on the left side, the ball will be delivered from the right side of the lane. Pins that are left one directly behind another should be hit head-on; otherwise, the bowler runs the risk of having the ball glance off the front pin, thereby missing the rear pin. Conversion of spares will make a marked difference in your scores; practice and experience are two important factors in increasing the score.

MODIFICATIONS FOR SPECIAL POPULATIONS

Orthopedically Impaired

1. Use commercially adapted bowling ramps made from the following: wood, aluminium, plastic.
2. Use push sticks, either commercial or homemade.
3. Use special bowling ball made with retractable handles.

Mentally Impaired

1. Show video tapes of bowlers with additional visual cues, e.g., pictures, magazines.
2. Reinforce students with additional tactile and kinesthetic input during delivery.
3. Allow additional practice time.

Sensory Impaired

1. Use variations on the approach:
   a. Carpet squares for footwork or carpet strip for the entire approach.
   b. Secure a rope from start of approach to a chair or stool placed at the end of the approach for visually impaired.

OTHER CONSIDERATIONS

Lane Etiquette

As in other sporting activities, certain playing courtesies should be extended to your bowling competitors and teammates.

1. Do not talk to or otherwise disturb a bowler who is on the approach and ready to bowl.
2. Do not walk in front of a bowler to secure your ball from the rack when the bowler is ready to bowl. Wait for your ball to return.

3. When bowlers on adjacent lanes are both ready to bowl, the one on the right (as you face the pins) should always be permitted to bowl first.
4. Do not use a ball that is the personal property of an individual unless you have the owner's permission to do so.
5. Be at your post, ready to bowl when your turn comes.
6. After delivering the ball and noting the result, turn and walk back immediately to the rear of the runway, being careful to stay in your approach lane.
7. Do not argue with the foul line judge over divisions even though you think an unjust call has been made against you.
8. Be punctual when scheduled to bowl. Nothing upsets a team more than having to wait for a late member.
9. Control your temper. Public exhibition of anger disturbs fellow bowlers and detracts from your efficiency.

Safety

Bowling is a relatively safe activity. Accidents are few, and good common sense will prevent them from occurring. The following are a few guidelines for safe bowling.

1. With a large class, plan formations well in advance so there is plenty of space between each participant during the approach, backswing, forward swing, and follow-through.
2. Be aware of people around you; swing the ball only on the designated alley.
3. Check to make sure the approaches are free of oily or rough substances that may interfere with the approach.
4. Use a towel to wipe the ball or dry your hands before each roll. A ball can become oily from the lanes, and the oil may get on your hands.
5. When picking up the ball from the rack, always keep your palms parallel to the sides of the bowling rack (Figure 6-7).
6. Be aware of your fellow competitors; make sure the approach area is cleared before rolling the ball.
7. If students are used to set the pins, make sure the pinsetter is clear of the alley before rolling the ball.

TERMINOLOGY

Anchor   The person who shoots last on a team.
Baby split   The 1-7 or 3-10 railroads.
Backup   A reverse hook. A backup rotates toward the right for a right- handed bowler.
Bed posts   The 7-10 railroad.
Blow   An error; missing a spare that is not a split.
Box   The same as a frame.
Brooklyn   A crossover ball, one that strikes in the 1-2 pocket.
Bucket   The 2-4-5-8 or 3-5-6-9 leaves.
Cherry   Chopping off the front pin on a spare.
Crossover   Same as a Brooklyn.
Double   Two strikes in succession.
Double pinochle   The 7-6 and 4-10 split.
Dutch 200 (Dutchman)   A score of 200 made by alternating strikes and spares for entire game.
Error   Same as a "blow." Failure to make a spare that is not a split.
Foul   To touch or go beyond the foul line in delivering the ball.
Frame   The box in which scores are entered. There are ten frames to each game.
Gutter ball   A ball that drops into either gutter.
Handicap   A bonus score or score adjustment awarded to an individual or team based on averages.
Head pin   The number one pin.
High hit   Hitting the head pin full in the face or head-on.
Hook   A ball that breaks to the left for a right-handed bowler. For a left-hander a hook ball breaks to the right.
Jersey side   Same as a Brooklyn.
Kegler   Synonym for bowler, derived from the German: *Kegel* (game of ninepins).
Lane   A bowling alley.
Leave   Pin or pins left standing after a throw.
Light hit   Hitting the head pin lightly to the right or left side.
Line   A complete game as recorded on the score sheet.
Mark   Obtaining a strike or spare.
Open frame   A frame in which no mark is made; at least

FIGURE 6-7   Proper method of picking up a ball from the rack.

one pin remains standing after rolling both balls in a frame.

Pocket Space between the head pin and pins on either side.

Railroad Another term for a split. There are several kinds.

Sleeper A pin hidden from view.

Spare All pins knocked down on two balls.

Split A leave, after the first ball has been thrown, in which the number one pin plus a second pin are down, and seven pins remain standing. Indicated by 0 on score sheet.

Spot A place on the alley at which a bowler aims.

Strike All pins knocked down on the first ball.

Striking out Obtaining three strikes in the last frame.

Tap When a pin is left standing on an apparently perfect hit.

Turkey Three strikes in a row.

SELECTED REFERENCES

American Association for Health, Physical Education, Recreation, and Dance: Division of Girls' and Women's Sport. *Official Bowling, Fencing and Golf Guide* (current ed.). Washington, D.C.: AAHPERD.

American Bowling Congress. *ABC Bowling Guide* (current ed.). Milwaukee: American Bowling Congress, 1572 East Capitol Drive.

Bellisimo, L. and Bennett, J. *The Bowlers Manual.* 4th ed. Englewood Cliffs, NJ.: Prentice Hall, 1982.

Costello, P. and Glossbrenner, A. *Bowling.* New York: Mason/Charter, 1977.

Grinfelds, V. and Hultstrand, B. *Right Down Your Alley.* 2d ed. Champaign, IL.: Leisure Press, 1985.

Scott, T.M. and Carpenter, C.L. *Bowling Everyone.* Winston-Salem, NC.: Hunter Books, 1985.

Showers, N.E. *Bowling.* Santa Monica, CA.: Goodyear Publishing Co., 1980.

Strickland, R.H. *Bowling—Steps to Success.* Champaign, IL.: Leisure Press, 1989.

Audio-Visual Materials

RMI Media Productions, 2807 W. 47th St., Shawnee Mission, KS., 66205. *Earl Anthony on Beginning Bowling* (½ inch VHS or Beta video, 61 minutes). Features selection equipment, proper delivery and common errors to avoid.

Athletic Institute, 200 Castlewood Dr., North Palm Beach, FL., 33408. *Four Steps to Better Bowling Series* (¾ or ½ inch video). Focuses on strikes and spares, fundamentals of footwork, fundamentals of armswing, shoe and ball selection and scoring, and approach and delivery.

7 CYCLING

THIS CHAPTER WILL ENABLE YOU TO:

▶ *Use proper hand signals and follow bicycle safety rules.*
▶ *Discuss the advantages and disadvantages of one-, three-speed, 10–18 speed, and all-terrain (mountain) bicycles.*
▶ *Select and fit a bicycle to individual needs.*
▶ *Select equipment for everyday riding and repair.*
▶ *Describe and apply the gearing theory to everyday cycling.*
▶ *Demonstrate techniques for safe and efficient cycling in city and country, including ankling, balancing, body positioning, braking, cadence, emergency stops, group riding, mounting and dismounting, maneuvering, pacing, short radius turning, and straight roadside riding.*

NATURE AND PURPOSE

Bicycling is a wonderful lifetime activity. It can be enjoyed by young and old alike and is a great family recreational pastime. Cycling offers relaxation, fitness, and occasional vacation touring or camping. A bicycle is not only a vehicle for pleasure and sport, but also a means of transportation to work or school —a role it has long played for millions of people throughout the world. While it is not likely to replace the automobile in this country, the bicycle is relatively inexpensive, durable, cheap to operate and maintain. It does not use up natural resources nor pollute the atmosphere. This chapter will introduce the fundamentals of cycling. Racing enthusiasts will find sources on competitive cycling among the Selected References.

BICYCLES AND EQUIPMENT

Bicycles come in various models, styles and colors, and with different components. They are priced from under $200 to over $1,000. Bicycles include touring, racing, all-terrain and utility models. When buying a bike, shop at a local bike store for the best selection and service. A dealer will help you choose a bike based on the type of riding you want to do.

10–18 Speed (Derailleur) Touring and Racing Bikes. If you want to cycle for fitness and perhaps weekend bike trips, choose a sport or touring 10-speed (now sometimes with 12 to 18 gears). A touring model is durable with a flexible frame that absorbs shock, a wide range of gears for climbing hills, caliper hand brakes, and padded seat. Dropped handlebars take some weight off the seat and allow a wide range of riding positions. Avoid a racing model unless you plan to race. Racing bikes are built for

FIGURE 7-1 Touring is fun and provides an excellent way to exercise.

speed, with stiffer frames, less shock absorption, a narrow range of gears, and less padding.

All-Terrain (Mountain) Bike. An all-terrain (mountain) bike, while heavy and slow on the open road, is best if off-road exploring is your goal. It is also fine for commuting or riding around town, but not recommended for extended tours. All-terrain bikes have at least 18 gears, high ground clearance, fat, knobby tires, upright handlebars, and sturdy frames.

Utility Bikes. Utility bikes with heavy frames, upright handlebars, wide tires, and wide, padded seats are less expensive, can take more abuse, and require less upkeep than 10–18 speed models. The one-speed adult cruiser with its balloon tires is easy to handle and gives a very smooth ride. It is fine for off-road riding. The three-speed bike has lighter wheels, hand brakes, and gears which can be shifted when stopped. It is good for commuting around town, but is not good for long trips or climbing many hills.

Basic Parts of a Bicycle

The touring bicycle shown in Figure 7-2 illustrates the basic parts of the bicycle:

1. *Frame.* Heavy frames are welded steel. Better, costlier frames are double-butted, lugged and brazed alloy. Frames come in different shapes and sizes, and determine the quality of the bike.
2. *Brakes.* Either center- or side-pull hand caliper brakes are good on derailleur bikes. Coaster (pedal) brakes are used on one-speed models.
3. *Wheels* consist of hubs, spokes, rims and tires, come in standard, touring, and racing versions.
4. *Tires* come in two basic types. Clinchers are durable and inexpensive (recommended). A liner can be inserted between tire and tube to prevent punctures. Tubulars (sew-ups) are not advised

for the general bicyclist. While thinner and lighter, they are expensive and very prone to punctures.

5. *Handlebars* come in raised or dropped styles, and either version can be fitted on any bike. Upright bars allow good vision and are comfortable for many people. Dropped bars take shock off the spine and weight off the seat while allowing a wider range of riding positions. Handlebar padding may be added to reduce road shock, preventing arm and hand soreness.
6. *Crank set* in better bikes is alloy and cotterless (uses bolts or nuts to attach the crank arm to the axle).
7. *Derailleur* is a gear-changing device which lifts and pulls the chain from sprocket to sprocket. If you don't like shifting, click shifting is now widely available. It finds gears automatically, so you don't have to feel around for the next one.
8. *Pedals.* Rubber tread pedals are cheap. Metal platform or thin cage pedals allow use of toe clips.
9. *Saddle* (Seat). Leather or plastic, narrow or wide, padded or not, the seat should be comfortable right away.

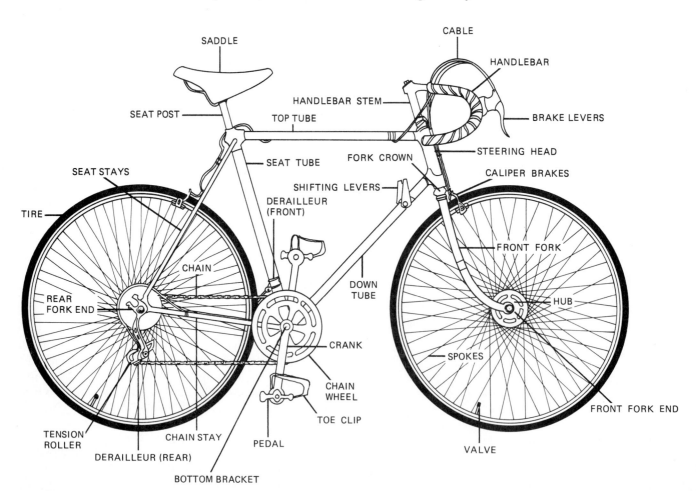

FIGURE 7-2 Parts of a bicycle.

Bicycle Inspection Checklist

Name _____

Bicycle make & model _____

Serial No. _____

	OK	FIX

FRAME SIZE
Can you straddle frame with both feet flat on the ground? ___ ___
(Should be 1 to 2 inch space between crotch and top bar.)

SADDLE
Horizontal adjustment—Nose of the saddle should be 1 to 3 inches behind a vertical line drawn through the crank hanger. A cyclist 5′ 6″ tall would position saddle 1 inch back; 5′ 10″ tall: 2 inches back; and 6′ 3″ tall: 3 inches back. ___ ___
Vertical adjustment—Sit on bike with heel on pedal at lowest position. Knee should be straight, so when toe is on pedal, knee is slightly bent. ___ ___
Tilt—Should be horizontal or slightly downtilted. ___ ___
Is saddle tight and in good condition? ___ ___

HANDLEBARS
Vertical adjustment—Top bar should be level with nose of saddle. ___ ___
Horizontal adjustment—Place elbow on nose of saddle. Outstretched fingertips should just touch center of handlebars. (Length of stem may need to be changed.) ___ ___
In line with wheel and symmetrical ___ ___
Tight, no horizontal or vertical movement ___ ___
Tubing ends plugged, grips tight ___ ___

TIRE PRESSURE
Check. Correct pressure for this bike is ___ ___
(Correct tire pressure is embossed on side of tire.)
Check once a week.

BOLTS
Check bolts for looseness. Recheck monthly. ___ ___

HAND BRAKES
Adequate space between lever and handlebar when engaged? (If not, tighten cable.) ___ ___
Cable: Should be taut, with no kinks, rust, or frayed ends. ___ ___
Brake shoes: Tight? Openings face rear? ___ ___
Level with and no more than ¼″ from rim? ___ ___
At least ³⁄₁₆″ rubber remaining? (Replace if needed.) ___ ___
Test operation of each brake separately.
Must hold without catching: Front ___ ___
                                          Rear ___ ___

WHEELS
Spin each wheel. It should run true (no wobbles) ___ ___
Should have no binding or looseness (bearings) ___ ___
Centered between forks (and chain stays in rear) ___ ___
Rim: Not dented or kinked? ___ ___
Spokes: All intact and tight? ___ ___
Tire: Properly seated? Tread? ___ ___

DERAILLEURS
Turn bike upside down or have partner lift rear wheel while you crank pedal and shift through first the front then rear gears. (Shift only while pedal is turning!) Derailleur should shift chain smoothly from one sprocket to the next without skipping a gear, catching, or throwing chain off. ___ ___
Chain condition (Clean with silicone spray if dirty.) ___ ___
Sprocket teeth intact, not bent or broken. ___ ___

PEDALS
Shake and spin to check bearings: no looseness or binding. ___ ___
Pedals intact and tight? ___ ___
Tread intact and tight? ___ ___
Press down on both pedals at once. Tight? ___ ___

REMARKS:

_____

G. Robbins, D. Powers, and S. Burgess, *A Wellness Way of Life* (Dubuque, IA: Wm. C. Brown Publishing Co., 1991), pp. 329–330.

▶ **Learning Tips**

1. See how many different types of bicycle components you can identify on different bicycles in class.

2. Visit a local bike shop and have the owner explain the advantages of different types of bicycle components.

Fitting the Bicycle

A properly set up and well-maintained bike is a pleasure to ride, easier to control, and important in accident prevention. The most common problem for beginners is riding with the seat too low. Complete the Bicycle Inspection Checklist above to check the fit of your bike and to see if any preventive maintenance needs to be done before you hit the road.

▶ **Practice Suggestions**

1. Check seat height. Locate the bolt under the seat which loosens the seat post. Mark on the stem current height, then, if needed, change seat height, and set at correct height and tighten bolt.
2. Locate bolts which adjust seat tilt. Loosen and remove saddle, then replace and retighten bolts.
3. Locate quick release levers for front and rear brakes. Release front lever and squeeze front brakes. Close lever. Recheck front brakes.
4. Locate quick release levers for front and rear wheels. Loosen front brake, release front wheel, remove. Replace front wheel, center between brake shoes, and close brake lever.

GENERAL MAINTENANCE TIPS

Regardless of the type of bicycle you have, it must be kept in good working order. Preventive maintenance, tightening loose bolts before they fall off, and lubricating cables before they rust and stick is better than finding yourself stuck miles from home with a broken bike. If you are not mechanically inclined, consult your local bike shop for a spring tuneup. Then, at least once a month, make the following checks: Investigate rattles and tighten loose bolts, if needed. Check tire pressure and inflate to the recommended pressure embossed on the sidewall. Lubricate cables and moving parts with a silicone lubricant like WD-40. Also spray the chain and clean it off by holding a rag against it as you turn the pedals. If anything is bent or broken, like spokes, rims, brakes or gears, take it to a bicycle mechanic for repairs.

On the other hand, if you like learning how things work, you can save money and time by doing much of your own maintenance. The following tools are recommended: tire patch kit, tire irons, adjustable wrench or set of crescent wrenches (best), third hand (for brakes), screwdriver, tire gauge, silicone lubricant, tire pump. Several of the listed bike books provide a complete section on bike repairs and should be consulted.

▶ **Practice Suggestions**

1. Use wrench to check and tighten any loose bolts.
2. Lubricate cables and inside cable housing with spray silicone lubricant. Spray and wipe chain to clean. Spray pivot points of levers and calipers, but *do not spray bike rims.*
3. Use tire pressure gauge to check tire pressure. Find recommended pressure on tire sidewall and inflate carefully to correct pressure.

ACCESSORIES AND CLOTHING

The most important accessory, a bicycle helmet, should be worn every ride. Make sure that it is approved by the American National Standards Institute (ANSI) or the Snell Memorial Foundation. It should contain a dense liner made from stiff polystyrene which absorbs most of the impact in a crash. It should fit snugly and be fastened securely with the chin strap.

Toe clips are good because they enable a rider to pull up as well as push down each pedal stroke. However, they do take some getting used to, and must be worn loosely at first so you can get your foot out quickly. Some new safety pedals work like quick-release ski bindings, releasing the shoe with a twist of the foot.

Avoid the "suicide" or "safety" brake levers positioned on the top of handlebars. They decrease braking power and increase the distance needed to stop.

Other equipment that is recommended includes lock and chain, a water bottle, bike bag, tools, and gloves. Bicycles operated at night must have a headlamp that is visible from a distance of at least 500 feet to the front. New bicycles must have front, rear, pedal, and side reflectors. A patch kit, tire irons and pump are useful for fixing flats on the road. If you encounter dogs frequently, you may wish to carry dog repellent spray.

Clothing worn depends on weather conditions. In warm weather, regular or bicycling shorts and a t-shirt are ideal. Also remember to wear SPF 15 sunscreen. In cool weather, tights, t-shirts, sweatshirt or jersey, and windbreaker (or warmups) can be layered to keep you comfortable. Gloves are essential, and a stocking cap can be worn under the helmet and pulled down over the ears. If you wear long pants, you will need pants clips or a rubberband to keep them out of your chain. Rain calls for a rain cape, though a large plastic garbage bag may suffice in a pinch.

RULES OF THE ROAD AND SAFETY CONSIDERATIONS

A bicycle is not a toy but a means of transportation. Bicycle drivers are subject to the same traffic laws as automobile drivers. In most bicycle-automobile accidents, it is the bicyclist who is at fault. Riding on the road requires maturity, knowledge, and ability to follow rules of the road. The police issue traffic tickets to careless cyclists. Rules for safe cycling include:

1. Wear an ANSI or Snell approved bicycle helmet and brightly colored clothing for maximum visibility in traffic.

2. Obey all traffic regulations, stop signs, stop signals, one-way streets, and traffic control signs.
3. Keep to the right side of the road, drive with the traffic in a straight line, and ride single file.
4. Never hitch a ride on other vehicles or carry other riders or packages which obstruct vision or interfere with proper control of the bicycle.
5. Always use proper hand signals to indicate turning or stopping.
6. Avoid cycling at night, but if you must do so, wear light or reflective clothing and use lights and reflectors on your bike.
7. Watch for doors opening from parked cars, for drain grates, wet leaves, potholes, stones, glass or other obstacles on the road, and for pedestrians. Cross railroad tracks at a 90 degree angle to avoid catching the wheel in the tracks.
8. Be sure your brakes are operating efficiently and keep your bicycle in perfect mechanical condition.
9. In rainy weather, caliper brakes lose up to 90 percent of their stopping power. Allow extra stopping distance and don't take corners too fast. Pump the brakes occasionally to wipe water off the wheel rims.
10. Keep alert. Look out for cars pulling out into traffic or turning. Listen for traffic approaching out of your line of vision. Anticipate traffic conditions rather than simply reacting to them.

Road Signs. The cyclist should be familiar with traffic signs and markings, which may be found in a driver's manual. Refer to the driver's manual for rules regarding cycling specific to your state.

Dogs running loose are potential hazards. If you see a dog at a distance, you can probably outrun it. If threatened, you might scare him off with water from your bottle, or stop, keeping the bike between you and the dog, and walk away slowly. Most dogs will leave you alone if ignored. Under no circumstances should you kick the dog.

Group Riding

When riding as part of a group, the front rider should call and signal (point to) road hazards such as holes, loose gravel, bumps, etc. (Figure 7-3). The rear rider can call "car back" to alert the group when an overtaking car is approaching. Although experienced riders may draft off each other to cut wind resistance, novice riders should avoid overlapping wheels, because a sudden unexpected swerve could cause both to crash.

Hand Signals. *Always* use hand signals when turning or stopping to alert other drivers to your intentions and to allow them time to react appropriately. Automobile drivers can anticipate moves and give a cyclist more respect and maneuvering room

FIGURE 7-3 Front rider signals road hazard.

FIGURE 7-4 Hand signal—left turn.

FIGURE 7-5 Hand signal—stop or slow down.

when they use hand signals than when they simply stop without warning or suddenly cut across traffic.

▶ **Practice Suggestions**

1. a. Ride a mapped route. Practice braking, and signaling before every intersection or stoplight.
   b. Stop or slow. Downshift into a lower gear, signal with the left hand, then squeeze the brakes.
   c. Turns. Downshift and slow down before turning. Keep the right hand on or near the brake at all times, make sure traffic is clear both ways, signal the appropriate turn with the left hand, then proceed when safe. Do not brake while turning.
2. Ride route in groups of three to six. Have front rider call road hazards and rear rider call approaching traffic. Switch group positions at intervals so each person rides front and rear. Discuss different road hazards encountered.
3. Before riding route on which dog may be encountered, discuss strategies for dealing with dogs.

SUGGESTED LEARNING SEQUENCE

A basic learning progression for the beginning cyclist is listed below.

1. Bike safety inspection (complete checklist)
2. Rules of the road (signaling, group riding)
3. General practice skills for bicycling
4. Physical fitness
5. Parts of the bicycle and terminology
6. Preventive maintenance and adjustment
7. Bicycle selection
8. Bicycle clothing and accessories
9. Clubs, organizations, racing, touring, bikeways, etc.

SKILLS AND TECHNIQUES

Mounting and Dismounting

When mounting, straddle the frame, place one foot on the pedal, raise the pedal to a high position, then push off and sit down on the saddle. You may dismount from a stationary or moving bike. For a stationary dismount, coast and brake with one pedal high and one low. Stop, step down first with the higher foot. When both feet are on the ground, swing one leg over the top bar. For a moving dismount, coast with one pedal low, bring the other foot over the frame and downward as you leave the saddle, then apply the brakes and touch the ground.

Mounting and Dismounting with Toe Clips

After mastering mounting and dismounting, if you wish to ride with toe clips, you will want to practice getting your feet into and out of them. Toe clips keep the ball of the foot firmly centered over the pedal. They may seem more trouble than they're worth at first, but most people who make an effort to use them feel they are indispensable.

Mounting. Practice in an open area where you are not likely to run into anything. You may first wish to use just the clip without the strap. Straddle the frame, place one toe in the clip, push off, and get going a few strokes, then use your unclipped toe to flip the pedal so you can slip your toe into the clip. While you are doing this you must steer the bike straight.

Dismounting. Use just the clips or keep straps loose. Stop and slide the foot on the higher pedal backwards, not sideways out of the clip. Practice stopping quickly and taking the feet out of the clips without looking at the pedals.

Control and Balance

Cycling on the road requires straight-line riding, ability to maneuver quickly around obstacles, ability to stop quickly without skidding or being tossed over the handlebars, and ability to glance back at traffic without losing balance. To set up a practice course, locate an empty parking lot or other flat surface, and use chalk and sponges or empty milk cartons to mark lanes.

▶ **Practice Suggestions**

1. *Balance.* Pedal 50 feet very slowly within a two-foot wide boundary taking as much time as you can with feet remaining on the pedals and moving only in a forward direction.
2. *Speed and Coordination.* Begin 30 feet before the starting line and pedal quickly through a course that is eight feet wide but gradually narrows to two feet during the 50-foot run.
3. *Steering.* Place sponges 10 feet apart on each side of a 50-foot line. Weave in and out of the line of sponges with both front and rear wheels without knocking them over. Experienced cyclists steer by leaning the body as well as turning the handlebars.
4. *Left and Right Spiral.* Follow a spiral to the center without touching any lines on the two-foot-wide course. This tests left and right turning skill and balance.
5. *Emergency Braking.* Caliper brakes are so powerful that they can throw you over the front handlebars if applied forcefully. To brake safely, keep your weight far back in the saddle while

applying both brakes simultaneously, just below the point where they skid. Pedal at average speed toward a goal and stop the bicycle 10 feet short of a marked line without skidding.

6. *Evasion.* Set up 12 sponges in a pattern as follows:

Place one sponge, then four feet later two sponges one foot apart. Ride around the single sponge, then between the pairs of sponges. A skilled cyclist should be able to quickly skirt an obstacle, yet remain on course.

7. *Checking Traffic.* Signaling turns requires that the rider first glance back at traffic without steering off course or losing balance. Ride a straight line in a chalked-off lane, and on signal, look back over the left shoulder and tell your partner how many fingers he or she is holding up.

8. *Signaling and Turning.* Quickly glance back over the left shoulder to check traffic without wobbling; downshift; demonstrate proper signals for turns in both directions or stopping; then execute the maneuver.

Gearing and Cadence

When you can skillfully mount and dismount, start and stop, ride a straight line and make turns, you are ready to use the gears. The purpose of gearing is to be able to maintain a steady pedalling cadence, regardless of terrain, wind, or weather conditions.

There are several gearing errors commonly made by beginners. Many people gear too high and pedal too slowly. They don't feel like they're doing any work unless they're pushing against resistance. This is inefficient and can produce sore knees. It is better to pedal quickly against less resistance in lower gears. While beginners may pedal at a cadence of 60–70 rpm, experienced tourists often maintain cadences of 90–100 rpm.

Second, in climbing a hill, beginners often wait to shift until they're halfway up the hill and pedalling cadence has slowed. To maintain your cadence, downshift in advance of need.

Finally, beginners seldom downshift when approaching stop signs or stop lights. They end up having to stand up on the pedals to get going again. While it takes practice to coordinate the downshift, signal, and braking, it is more efficient and kinder to the knees to pull away from an intersection in a low gear, upshifting as speed increases.

▶ **Practice Suggestions**

1. *Gearing.* To practice shifting gears:
   a. On a straight road with little traffic, maintain normal pedalling cadence (about 65 rpm) but ease up on the pedal pressure.
   b. Without taking your eyes off the road, move a shift lever slightly forward or back. You will hear a brief rattle, then a click as the chain moves to another sprocket. If the rattling continues, the chain is between gears. Adjust the lever until there is no noise from the chain.
   c. Shift through several gears using first the left, then the right shift levers, until you can shift into a higher or lower gear by feel.
   d. To achieve the lowest gear, the chain must be on the innermost chainwheels (small front and large rear). In the highest gear, the chain will be on the outermost chainwheels (large front and small rear). Avoid using the large front-large rear or small front-small rear chainwheel combinations. These force the chain to cross at the most extreme angle, producing excessive wear and tear on the chain.
2. *Cadence.* While cycling at a steady cadence, time and count your pedal strokes for one minute. How does your cadence compare to the suggested cadence?
3. *Hill Climbing.* Ride a course which includes one or more hills. As you approach each hill, keep well to the right. Try to downshift early enough so that you maintain an even cadence as you climb the hill and keep your hands on top of the brake hoods. You can lean forward and either pull on the handlebars with each push of the pedals or practice standing up on the pedals for maximum power. As you pick up speed on the downhill side, get down low and keep your weight well back in the saddle. Pump the brakes on-off to control speed.
4. *Ankling.* Ankling involves applying equal force with the foot pushing and pulling throughout the pedalling cycle. Adding toe clips and straps enables you to pull on the upstroke as well as push on the downstroke, doubling pedalling efficiency.

▶ **Practice Suggestion**

During part of a ride, concentrate on ankling technique.

MODIFICATIONS FOR SPECIAL POPULATIONS

Orthopedically Impaired

1. Allow the wheelchair user to propel his or her wheelchair with the hands.
2. Commercial armcrank and rowcycles are available for persons with lower extremity injuries.

3. Use adult tricycles for balance deficiencies.
4. Depending on age groups, use scooter boards with arm propulsion in the gymnasium.
5. Use of stationary cycles is advised for balance deficiencies.

Mentally Impaired

1. Very little modifications are needed. Use of peer teachers is advised.
2. Use adult tricycles for balance.

Sensory Impaired

1. Use of tandem cycles is advised for blind or visually impaired.
2. Use of stationary cycles is advised for balance deficiencies.

CYCLING FOR PHYSICAL FITNESS

Bicycling offers all the benefits of any cardiorespiratory activity, plus it is non-impact. However, the bicycle is so efficient, that cycling short distances won't get you in shape. You'll have to put in some effort and sustain a training heart rate of 150–160 beats per minute (age 20 and under) if you want to improve your aerobic capacity. The sample workouts below are a good way to begin.

Sample Workout Program

Directions: Ride the recommended number of days and time at your training heart rate; rest one day between rides.

Weeks	Beginning

1. Ride 3 days × 15 minutes
2. Ride 3 days × 20 minutes
3. Ride 3 days × 25 minutes
4. Ride 3 days × 30 minutes
5. Ride 3 days × 35 minutes

Intermediate

6. Ride 4 days × 30 minutes
7. Ride 4 days × 35 minutes
8. Ride 4 days × 40 minutes
9. Ride 4 days × 45 minutes

Maintenance

10. Ride 3–5 days × 40–60 minutes

Physical Fitness Evaluation. Take a five-mile time trial and record your time. After 8 to 12 weeks repeat the ride and see how your time compares with the first trial.

The route, weather conditions, time of day, and type of clothing worn should be similar on both rides in order to make a valid comparison.

TERMINOLOGY

Ankling Pedaling technique in which the foot applies equal force on both the upstroke and downstroke.
Bikeway Paths or roads designated as bicycle routes.
Cadence Pedaling at a constant pace; around 65–85 pedal revolutions per minute (RPM) for beginners, around 95–100 for tourists, and 120 and up for racers.
Caliper brakes Hand brakes.
Clincher Common tire and tube combination rim.
Coaster brakes Foot-activated internal hub rear brakes.
Derailleur Device which moves the chain from one gear to another.
Down tube Part of frame extending from the steering head to the bottom bracket.
Head tube Tube holding front fork assembly.
Saddle Seat.
Seat tube Part of frame extending from the bottom bracket to the seat.
Toe clips Metal cages or straps which hold the foot on the pedal.
Top tube Part of frame extending horizontally from the head tube to the seat tube.
Tubular tire (Sew up) Tire glued to rim of bike.
Wheel Includes the hub, rim, spokes, and tire.

SELECTED REFERENCES

Ballantine, R. *Richard's New Bicycle Book.* Rev. ed. New York: Ballantine Books, Div. of Random House, 1987.

Bicycling Magazine Staff, ed., *Bicycling's Complete Guide to Bicycle Maintenance and Repair.* Emmaus, PA: Rodale Press, Inc., 1986.

———, *Bicycle Touring.* Emmaus, PA: Rodale Press, Inc., 1985.

———, *Training for Endurance.* Emmaus, PA: Rodale Press, Inc., 1989.

Burke, E.R. *Science of Cycling.* Champaign, IL.: Leisure Press, Div. of Hutman Kinetics Publishers, Inc., 1986.

Cuthbertson, T. *Anybody's Bike Book.* Berkeley, CA.: Ten Speed Press, 1988.

Howard, J., et al. *Cyclists Companion.* Bergenfield, NJ.: Greene, Div. of Penguin USA, 1987.

Hughes, T. *The Cycle Tourer's Handbook.* N. Pomfret, VT.: David & Charles Inc., 1988.

LeMond, Greg. *Greg LeMond's Pocket Guide to Bicycle Maintenance and Repair.* New York: Perigee Books, Putnam Pub. Group, 1988.

Sloane, E.A. *The Complete Book of Bicycling.* St. Louis, MO.: Fireside Books, Div. of Warren H. Greene, Inc., 1988.

Sloane, E.A. *Sloane's Handy Pocket Guide to Bicycle Repair.* St. Louis, MO.: Fireside Books, Div. of Warren H. Greene, Inc., 1988.

Snowling, S. and Evans, K. *Bicycle Mechanics.* Champaign, IL.: Leisure Press, Div. of Human Kinetics Publishers, Inc., 1990.

Van der Plas, R. *Bicycle Fitness Book: Riding Your Bike for Health & Fitness.* Mill Valley, CA.: Bicycle Books, Inc., 1989.

Periodicals

Bicycle Guide. 9/yr. Raber Publishing, Boston, MA 02116.

Bicycle Guide's Complete Cycling Fitness. Raber Publishing, Boston, MA 02116. (All fitness levels.)

Bicycle USA. 9/yr. League of American Wheelman, 6707 Whitestone Rd., Ste. 209, Baltimore, MD 21207. (General, beginning to advanced.)

Bicycling. 10/yr. Rodale Press, Inc. 33 E. Minor St., Emmaus, PA 18049. (General, beginning.)

Audio-Visual Materials

AIMS Media. 6901 Woodley Ave., Van Nuys, CA 91406. Telephone 1–800–367–2467. *Bicycle Driving Tactics.* 14 min. *Bicycling for Physical Fitness, Health & Recreation.* 14 min. *Bikes Are Back.* 9 min. *Bicycle Basics.* 10 min. *Get to Know Your Ten Speed.* 19 min.

Beacon Films. An Hschul Group Company, 930 Pinter Ave., Evanston, IL 60202. Telephone 1–800–323–5448. *Bike Style.*

Centron Education Films, Supplementary Education Group, Simon & Schuster, 108 Wilmot Rd., Deerfield, IL 60015. Telephone 1–800–323–5343. *Safe Bicycling in Traffic.* 1981. 19 min.

Do-It-Yourself, Inc. 5250 77 Center Dr. , Suite 340, Charlotte, NC 28210. *Anybody's Bike Video—Bicycle Repair, Vol. 1.* 40 min. *Bike Tripping.* 40 min.

Iowa State University. 121 Pearson Hall, Media Resources Center, Ames, IA, 50011. *Bicycling Safely on the Road.* 25 min.

National Safety Council. 425 N. Michigan Ave., Chicago, IL 60611. *Bike Safety: Making the Right Moves.* 15 min.

Pyramid Film and Video. 2801 Colorado Ave., Santa Monica, CA 90404. Telephone 213–828–7577. *Everything About Bicycles.* 15 min.

Organizations and Clubs

American Bicycle Association. P.O. Box 718, Chandler, AZ 85244. (Off-road bicycle racing.)

American Cycling Union. C/o Estelle G. Black, P.O. Box 6099, Newark, NJ 07106. (Cycling for recreation and competition.)

America's Freedom Ride. C/o Vineberg Communications, 61–20 Grand Central Pkwy., B-800, Forest Hills, NY 11375. (Bicycle tours.)

Bicycle Federation of America. 1818 R St., N.W., Washington, DC 20009. (Promotes bicycle transportation, recreation, and programs.)

Bicycle Network. P.O. Box 8194, Philadelphia, PA 19101. (Advocates bicycle transportation.)

Bicycle Transportation Action. 308 E. 79th St., NY, NY 10021. (Promotes bicycles as transportation.)

Bikecentennial: The Bicycle Travel Association. P.O. Box 8308, Missoula, MT 59807. (Researches and maps bicycle touring routes.)

International Bicycle Touring Society. P.O. Box 6979, San Diego, CA 92106. (Bicycle tours.)

League of American Wheelmen. 67 Whitestone Rd., Suite 209, Baltimore, MD 21207. (Bicyclists and clubs.)

National Bicycle League. P.O. Box 729, Dublin, OH 43017. (BMX racing.)

National Off-Road Bicycle Association, P.O. Box 1901, Chandler, AZ 85244. (Promotes off-road bicycling.)

8 DANCE

> ▶ *Folk Dance*
>
> ▶ *Modern Dance*
>
> ▶ *Social Dance*
>
> ▶ *Square Dance*

NATURE AND PURPOSE

Dance can be defined as any patterned, rhythmic movement of the human body in space and time as a means of expression.

Since prehistoric times, humans have always had the desire to dance. Today that desire is still with us: people dance (1) for self-expressive purposes; (2) for religious, ritualistic, or ceremonial purposes; and (3) to entertain or please others. Dance will never die because it is constantly being reborn through different dancers, different environments, and different cultures.

Unlike other art forms, the art of dance is the only art form whose sole necessary tool is the human body. As with other structured or creative physical activities, it is important not only to understand the objectives and basic patterns of dance, but to practice the skills necessary to achieve a level of proficiency in this highly-expressive art form.

This chapter will look at four forms of dance commonly taught in educational institutions: folk dance, modern dance, social dance, and square dance. Other popular dance forms such as ballet, tap, and jazz dance are not included because of space limitations.

MOVEMENTS COMMON TO ALL DANCES

All forms of dance involve movement. Although dance movement may at times be confined only to the body (nonlocomotor or axial movement), more commonly it requires the use of various forms of locomotion in which the body weight is transferred to the feet or from one foot to the other. All forms of locomotion can be reduced to five fundamental steps: walk, run, leap, jump, and hop. Any other type of lo-

comotor activity is a combination of these basic steps. Closely related to the five fundamental steps are the skip, slide, and gallop, and often reference is made to the eight fundamental means of locomotion.

Walk. The weight is transferred from one foot to the other, alternately, one foot always being in contact with the ground. The usual foot action is a transfer of weight from the heel to the ball of one foot, during which time the other leg is pushing off, then swinging through to assume its position in the sequence of action.

Run. The speed of the walk is increased, and there is a brief period when neither foot is in contact with the ground. A run is usually a quicker progression than a walk.

Leap. A leap is a spring into the air by means of a strong push-off from one foot, returning to the ground or the opposite foot. The leap differs from the run in that more energy is needed, and there is a longer period between transfer of weight due to a longer period of suspension in the air. The leap may be done either for height or for distance.

Jump. The body springs into the air by a two foot take-off, landing on two feet. Other types of jumps that you might see include: (1) a single foot take-off, landing on two feet, and (2) a two foot take-off landing on one foot. A jump may be made for either height or distance.

Hop. A hop is a spring into the air by means of a strong push-off from one foot, returning to the group on the same foot.

Graphic Representation. A walk, leap, jump, and hop are all done to an even beat, sometimes designated as long, and represented graphical as

━━━━   ━━━━   ━━━━

etc. A run can take just as much time, but is usually twice as fast and represented as

— — —

In relation to the long beat, it is shown

— — — — — —
▬▬▬   ▬▬▬   ▬▬▬

etc. Should the pattern become uneven (long-short), each of the three remaining related forms of locomotion would fit into this rhythm: skip, slide, gallop. The graphic representation would be

— — — —

which total time is equivalent to one beat, thus

▬▬▬ — ▬▬▬ —

Skip. A combination of a step and a hop, done to an uneven beat in which the step is given the long time-value (——) and the hop the short value (—):

step hop step hop step hop step hop
▬▬▬ — ▬▬▬ — ▬▬▬ — ▬▬▬ —

Note: Were each part given equal time-value, a step-hop would result instead of a skip:

▬▬▬ ▬▬▬ ▬▬▬ ▬▬▬
 step   hop   step   hop

In performing the skip, there is a feeling of elevation resulting from the natural tendency to swing the free leg forward and upward.

Slide. The weight is transferred from one foot to the other by means of a step on one foot followed by a quick drawing up of the other foot with an immediate transfer of weight to it resulting in a sideward movement.

Gallop. A gallop is similar to a slide, except the gallop moves forward, and the foot executing the leap is brought up to but not beyond the foot that has completed the step. The leap, a forward movement, is done with slight height; distance is not a factor.

FOLK DANCE

A BRIEF HISTORY

They are of all ages, from all societal levels, and have vastly different backgrounds, yet individuals gather to participate in the shared activity of folk dance. Since the early 1940's in the United States, there has been increased interest and participation in international folk dance. This activity has become a common element in education, recreation groups, dance clubs, and senior citizen programs.

Folk dances are sequences of movements, formations, and rhythmic patterns which have been created by people of different cultures. Although many of these international dances have the same steps and movement patterns, the stylization and the purposes for these particular dances are what adds to the rich cultural expression of each dance. Most dances are performed solely for recreational purposes; however, some international folk dances are performed for ritualistic ceremonies or for celebrating special occasions (Figure 8-1).

FIGURE 8-1 International folk dancers enjoy the exhilaration of this rhythmic group activity.

SUGGESTED LEARNING SEQUENCE

The following progression is recommended for beginners. Each step will be fully described below.

1. Two-Step
2. Schottische
3. Polka
4. Mazurka
5. Waltz Box

Basic Folk Dance Steps

The following abbreviations and terms (also used in social dance) will be used in describing the basic folk dance steps:

Fwd = Forward
Back = Backward
Q = Quick
S = Slow
L = Left
R = Right
FD = Forward Diagonal

The term "close" is commonly used in folk and spiral dance to mean that the free foot is moved toward the supporting foot. The free foot then becomes the supporting foot, and the supporting foot is now free to move.

Learning Cues

Two-Step. Three steps are taken in the rhythm quick, quick, slow, using four counts. Thus, step left, closing step right to left, step left, and hold. The pattern may be repeated starting with the right foot.

1	2	3	4
Step QL	Close QR	Step SL	Hold

Schottische. This four-count pattern is most frequently done by taking three small steps followed by a hop, each using one count. It is an easy, smooth pattern that is sometimes done with small runs instead of steps.

1	2	3	4
Step L	Step R	Step L	Hop L

Polka. Two long-short intervals based upon two counts make up the timing for one polka step. Depending on which part of this step one selects as a starting point, a polka becomes either (a) a hop-step-close-step or (b) a step-close-step-hop. The polka that is performed most is the (a) type.

(a)	&	1	&	2
	Hop L	Step R	Close L	Step R
(b)	&	3	&	4
	Hop R	Step L	Close R	Step L

Mazurka. This step is commonly executed diagonally forward and requires three even, long counts to be performed once. A gliding step is taken with the left foot to the front diagonal on count one, a closing step is taken with the right foot to the right, and a hop is taken with the right foot on count three. At the time of the hop, the left leg swings out, then the left knee immediately bends so that the foot comes close to the right shinbone. The left foot is then lowered to prepare for the next mazurka step. This is a strong, vigorous step, done continuously to the same diagonal unless a variation is introduced.

1	2	3
Step FDL	Close R	Hop R

Waltz Box. This step is a six-count pattern consisting of step, step, close, step, step, close. It must be remembered that the weight is evenly transferred from one foot to the other. Thus, step forward with the left foot, step side with the right foot, closing step left to right, step backward with the right foot, step side with the left foot, and closing step right to left.

1	2	3
Step Forward L	Step Side R	Close L
4	5	6
Step Backward R	Step Side L	Close R

Combinations of the above noted basic folk dance steps are then used to perform specific international folk dances. Stylization, formations, and music allow these basic steps to become more exciting to perform and to watch.

▶ **Practice Suggestions**

1. The primary concern of the teacher should be the selection of dances which are suited to the level of ability of the dancers. While there are many values of international folk dancing, it should also be a joyous activity. There is no better way to discourage students and to create dislike for the activity than to attempt to teach beginners a long, complicated dance.
2. Before teaching a new dance, the teacher should review the basic step or steps that are involved. Basic steps may be practiced in an open, a single or double circle, moving counterclockwise, which is the most common line of direction in international folk dances.
3. The teacher should be thoroughly familiar with the dance and the music before attempting to present the material. A short background introduction to the dance may be given, which should include the dance's native country, but students should get into the activity as soon as possible. The teacher should then demonstrate the complete dance to music.
4. In the starting formation, the teacher can break

down the parts of the dance into small units while verbalizing with one descriptive word for each action. If necessary, this may be done somewhat slower, speeding up until the skill approximates the rhythm of the dance. In beginning any dance part, the teacher might give a two-word signal such as "Ready, and . . ." to alert dancers and allow for reaction time. When combining a part, the teacher may cue the dancers as to what will be next. Upon completion of the dance, corrections in skill, techniques, or stylization may be given to the entire group. When the dance is repeated, any errors may be corrected individually.

Suggested Folk Dances for Beginners

Dance	Basic Step
Alunelul	Walk
Black Forest Mazurka	Mazurka
Doublebska Polka	Polka
Hora	Walk
Jugo	Schottische
Kalvelis	Polka
Korobushka	Schottische
Laz Bar	Two-Step
Little Man in a Fix	Waltz Box
Miserlou	Two-Step
Polka zu Dreien	Polka
Salty Dog Rag	Schottische

MODERN DANCE

BRIEF HISTORY

Unlike three types of dance discussed in this chapter, modern dance is considered to be an art form on a par with painting, sculpture, music, and ballet. It began as an American art form around the turn of the century when Isadora Duncan presented modern dance to general audiences as an experimental movement away from the restrictions of classical ballet. Other dancers followed suit: Ruth St. Denis, Ted Shawn, Mary Wigman, Doris Humphrey, Charles Weidman, Martha Graham, and Hanya Holm. The last four people mentioned were labelled the "four pioneers of modern dance" because during their studies at the Bennington College Summer School of Dance in the 1930's, each of them discovered their own unique approaches to modern dance technique and choreography which are still used and performed in educational institutions and on the stage.

There are numerous modern dancers and choreographers who followed and each made individual statements through technique and choreographic

FIGURE 8-2   Dancers using the whole body as an instrument for expression.

principles. Today, modern dance encompasses an even broader spectrum of techniques and thematic concepts which continually reflect the social and political issues and technical aspects of our time.

Many colleges and universities now offer undergraduate majors and minors in modern dance, and some offer advanced degrees. For many students who are not looking to dance as a professional career, this dance form offers an opportunity to develop a strong, supple, well-coordinated body, and to use the whole body as an instrument of expression (Figure 8-2). In this section, the beginner will obtain some basic understanding of the elements of modern dance, and practical suggestions for technique, improvisation, and choreography.

PRINCIPLES OF MOVEMENT

Movement Determined by the Body Structure

Students of dance must train their instrument—their body—to be as fully responsive as possible to the demands of beautiful, skilled movements. Flexibility, coordination, strength, control, and balance are among the basic tools one should acquire in technique classes. These abilities also enable the dancer to perform special skills such as complex turns, spirals, and falls. The beginning dancer should be guided in the correct alignment of the body to enable freedom and clarity of movement. Each bony portion of the body should be lined up directly over or under another. The head is held level and tall above relaxed (not collapsed) shoulders, under which is a very high (not forward) chest, narrow waist, and pulled-up abdomen. The hips are aligned directly under the chest, not pushed forward or backward.

The legs are pulled up straight, not locked or hyper-extended. The body weight is held up from the center of each relaxed foot. The posterior and anterior torso should be high and strong enough to allow the extremities to remain relaxed and free to move. Nothing should be "gripping." Poor posture or alignment not only hampers technical facility, but can ultimately lead to sprains and dislocations or can aggravate other injuries.

The beginner should be encouraged to use the body as freely and fully as possible. This develops an appreciation of movement and a realization of actually dancing. Later, as the body becomes more finely "tuned," the dancer is trained to control specific parts of the body for subtler, more refined expression. The modern dancer has many ways to portray the emotional and psychological content of a performance, and searches for ways to move to modern, dissonant, and rhythmically complex music and sounds. An acute kinesthetic sense must develop in the dancer so that the sensation of movement, the visual shape, becomes the guidepost. Depth, quality, and dynamics of the sensation are conveyed by the dancer for the observer, creating an enriching experience shared by both. Beside such training, the dancer should clearly comprehend the number of ways a human being can move. These may be categorized as a nonlocomotor (or axial) movements and locomotor movements.

Nonlocomotor (or axial) movements occur in space but do not transport the body from place to place. They generally include:

1. Flexion—bending
2. Extension—raising or stretching
3. Rotation—twisting
4. Adduction—moving a body segment toward the central axis of the body
5. Abduction—moving a body segment away from the central axis of the body
6. Circumduction—circling the entire torso or any body part
7. A combination of the above

Locomotor movements (as described at the beginning of this chapter) involve moving with the feet from one place to another space. Again, they are walk, run, leap, jump and hop, along with skip, slide, and gallop.

Movement Determined by the Environment and the Demands of Dance

There are a number of elements of movement that can be analyzed. We move within a specific rhythmic structure, and with a variety of muscular forces, all having relationship to physical forces such as gravity, acceleration, and momentum. We move in space making designs, and through space by means of locomotor patterns.

Rhythm. The rhythmic structure organizes the movement into repeatable units of time. Rhythm is composed essentially of both force and time factors. Dynamics is a frequently preferred term for describing the relationship between force and time. Rhythmic factors include:

1. Tempo—variation from fast to slow.
2. Underlying beat—the steady pulse inherent in a particular movement phase. Three ways to arrive at a basic beat are through:
   a. Metric or movement counts determined by the accompaniment.
   b. Breath rhythm determined by the intervals of inhalation—exhalation and carried like a pulse through the body.
   c. Emotional rhythm determined by the inner motivation of the dancer and the expressive content of the work.
3. Phrase—sequence of long and short beats with a feeling of unity, an idea suggested but not complete in itself, though having its own beginning and dynamic line followed by a pause before a new phrase begins.
4. Accent—emphasis given in movement, sound, force, space, tempo in the beat. Silence, or arrested movement, can be as much an accent as a loud sound or abrupt movement.
5. Syncopation—an unexpected or displaced accent in the general pattern. This engenders surprise and excitement as heard in jazz or felt in clapping two beats while walking three in the same given time.

   — — —   walk

   —— ——   clap

   ————   time length

Force. Force conveys the quality, texture, or kinesthetic and emotional energy underlying a dance. Energy or force is that factor which enables one to feel the qualitative differences. Muscles and joints are capable of moving with varying degrees and combinations of forces; each is as different as the texture of velvet is from silk or tweed. These forces may be generally expressed as:

1. Sustained—an evenly timed, controlled flow of energy. The muscles resist gravity in varying degrees from very, very strong to light and airy. There is an equalization of muscle tension, as in movements requiring careful balance or slow motion.
2. Swing—an alternate swaying, suspended, to-and-fro use of energy. There is a passive acceleration as the dancer gives in to gravity and a more active retardation and suspension as the dancer completes the arc of the swing. The swing has a characteristic beat of three for each phase.
3. Ballistic—a piston-like thrusting use of energy.

The dancer attacks out against gravity and re-covers with an equal action before momentum is overcome. There is a gradual dying down of the movement between the two attacks. Such movements usually have an underlying beat of two and need far more energy than does the relaxed swing. A series of vigorous jumps and leaps would require ballistic force.

4. Percussive—a sharp, explosive use of energy. The muscles fixate against gravity as the movement comes to an abrupt halt, rather than "following through." The halt usually occurs in one beat, though the preceding and following movements may be in any other quality and time. Percussive moments are the strongest peaks of a movement. Much of the excitement felt in watching jazz dance is due to a continual use of percussive energy.

5. Vibratory—a continuous back-and-forth use of energy. Short, percussive movements done very rapidly produce this effect but are difficult to prolong because of the high tension and control required to keep them even.

6. Collapsing—a letting go of muscular energy. The dancer's body (or a part of it) gives in to the force of gravity. To recover from a collapse requires any other use of energy called for to convey the idea in mind. A true collapse occurs in one time interval, a long or short beat.

Space.   This special element limits and defines the movement through the factors of:

1. Direction
   a. Line of motion—forward, backward, side-ward, diagonal, turning, circular.
   b. Focus—use of eyes or a body part, such as a leg, to emphasize a point of attention.
2. Range
   a. Distance covered—by locomotion.
   b. Degree and number of joint actions—in axial movement, from narrow to broad. For example, a greeting by a slight nod or a deep, sweeping bow.
3. Levels—low through high.
4. Body facing—front, side, diagonal, back, up, down—all in relation to the location of the front of the given work space.

▶ **Practice Suggestions**

Dance classes are conducted in various manners, but they all consist of the same basic elements. There is a time for warm-up, locomotor and nonloco-motor (axial) combinations, creative endeavors, and concluding activities. The student learns how the elements of rhythm, (time) force, and space can be used in dance during these class experiments.

Warm-up.   The warm-up often consists of easy stretches and large muscle movements through their full range of motion, then progresses to the smaller, more specific muscle groups. Warming up at the beginning of the class allows the body temperature to rise and can help to protect the body from injury. Stretching within the warm-up helps the dancer gain flexibility, control and balance in movement, and also places emphasis on correct body alignment necessary to execute the movement.

It is important to execute the warm-up exercises in a dance-like manner so that the students realize the relationship between the warm-up and actual dancing. Warm-ups vary in intensity and acceleration but have a common factor of being in motion, always attempting to increase the range of motion.

Locomotor Movement.   Locomotor movements enable the student to discover space. The use of change in direction, level, and focus for basic movements creates an awareness of the emotional expressions possible and of the dimensions of movements to fill the shape of the space. Locomotor and nonlocomotor (axial) movements are combined to develop the balance and control stressed in the warm-up. These movement phrases aid in exploring movement combinations which can create possible sections of dance compositions.

The beginning dance student finds satisfaction in completing movement sequences using familiar and unfamiliar material. Combining walks, runs, falls, rolls, and pauses allows the student to experiment with the changes in force and rhythm, and to become comfortable with the floor through contact with all parts of the body and not just the feet. This often represses the fear of injury many beginners have when working on a base floor and also broadens their experience in movement. The beginner must be guided in creative activities through a series of movement problems ranging from the simple to the complex.

Improvisation.   Improvisation can be an exciting creative experience for dance students because it allows them to spontaneously express their inner feelings, in their own style, through movement. Therefore, it is essential to create a comfortable atmosphere of freedom for exploration to take place. The dancer should be familiar with all areas of the space and be aware of the other persons in the space. Improvisation may take place employing a large group of dancers or an individual. One example of developing a series of movement explorations is by working with a circle and the parts of a circle. Circular floor patterns, large and small, may be shown by using basic locomotor movements such as walks, runs, or leaps. The full circles patterns then can be changed to half- circles with full circles, sometimes developing into spirals. This same series may be executed by isolating different parts of the body from rounded shapes into angles and including different levels or directions (Figure 8-3).

FIGURE 8-3 Dancers exploring angular shapes.

Improvisation may be an end in itself or a tool for developing choreography. It is important during improvisation that the student learn to make decisions in movement sequences, to recreate patterns explored, and to develop new technique and styles through the use of rhythms (time), space, and force.

Conclusion.   The concluding activity of a class session varies with the material presented. It may include stretches to relax and cool down the body or a presentation of movement sequences developed during the time period. Students become aware of the dramatic implications of movement through observation. Discussion concerning the sequences and causes of the effectiveness increase awareness plus appreciation in the student for other dances and dancers.

Warm-Up and Stretching Techniques

Listed below are a few specific ideas for class use.

A. Bend Series
  1. Stand tall with the feet parallel and hip distance apart; arms rest comfortably on each side of the body.
  2. While breathing out, allow the head to easily drop forward, resting the chin on the breast bone.
  3. Round the shoulders so that the spine curves forward. Continue to allow the arms to hang loosely from the shoulders. The body is still vertically aligned from the waist down.
  4. Bend the knees, keeping the heels on the floor, and lower the entire body until the fingertips touch the floor.
  5. Unbend the knees, while the fingertips are still touching the floor, by raising the hips toward the ceiling. Be sure that the knees do not lock or overextend.

  6. Reverse this entire process until the body has returned to its original erect position.
B. Foot Series
  1. Stand tall with the feet parallel and a few inches apart; arms rest comfortably to the side; legs are straight, but not locked.
  2. Extend the right leg forward until only the ball of the foot and toes touch the floor.
  3. Push the toes to a point, stretching the top of the foot.
  4. Pull back onto the ball of the foot.
  5. Bend both knees, placing the heels on the floor and making sure that the weight is evenly distributed on both feet.(The legs and feet are in fourth position parallel plié using ballet terminology.)
  6. Extend both legs, making sure the knees are not locked, and rise onto the balls of the feet.(The legs are now in fourth position parallel relevé, in ballet terminology.)
  7. Plié again (in fourth position parallel).
  8. Point the right foot, straightening both legs, but not locking the knees.
  9. Pull the right foot back into parallel position keeping the legs straight.
  10. Repeat on the left foot and execute as many repetitions as desired.
      Note: Cue words for this series are : "ball of the foot, point, ball of the foot, plié, relevé, plié, point, pull back."
C. Leg Swing Series
  1. Stand tall on a slightly turned-out and straight left leg, with the right leg extended to the back.
  2. Swing the right leg forward and backward easily from the hip with a relaxed knee and foot for 7 counts; then step forward onto a straight and slightly turned-out right leg on count 8. Left leg should now be extended to the back.
  3. Repeat the swing with the left leg.
  4. This series can also be done with 3 counts of swings and a step on count 4, or 1 swing forward with a step on count 2.
  5. The arms may be placed to the sides as an extension of the shoulders, or they may move in opposition to the motion of the swinging leg.

These are examples of parts of a warm-up which need to be combined with other techniques to prepare the body for vigorous activity. It is essential to sufficiently warm-up the feet and legs if leaps, jumps, and hops are to be stressed during the class session. A warm-up does not necessarily consist of only axial movements. Locomotor combinations of the walk using pliés and relevés, lunges and leg swings also may be used. Variations on stretches may be executed by working with a partner and using specific parts of the body, such as the ribs, hips, shoulders, or knees as the impulse for the stretch. The partner acts as an opposing force and also serves as protection against injury in case the dancer who is stretching begins to topple over.

Locomotor Patterns

Listed below are a few examples of locomotor patterns for class use.

A. Slide Series
  1. Slide to the right and then the left in diminishing counts of 8-4-2-1.
  2. Three slides, then half-turn on the fourth slide.
  3. Three slides then a full turn jump on the fourth slide.
B. Triplet Series
  A triplet is three forward steps with an accent on the first step, which is usually done in plié.
  1. Triplets moving forward.
  2. Two triplets forward and a turning triplet.
  3. Two triplets, a turning triplet, a reach in relevé to one side and a side fall in the opposite direction.
C. Hop Series
  1. Three runs forward then hop.
  2. Three runs then turn the hop.
  3. Two steps and a hop.
  4. Step, hop, step, leap.

Locomotor movements should include the use of the arms in a variety of ways to complement and contrast the basic movements. Arms may move in opposition to each other, in parallel positions, in a static pose, or only one arm moving at a time. The beginning student often has difficulty coordinating the arms with other dance movements; therefore, simplicity in arm positions is essential until some mastery of the movement has been accomplished. The challenge of different arm, leg, and torso movements and their combinations stimulates the dance student to strive for achievement and more complexity of movement.

Creative Activities—Improvisation

Listed below are a few suggestions for creative activities or improvisational exercise.

A. Individual dancers create an intricate floor pattern to fit a designated space. This activity may initially only use a walking pattern, but could eventually develop a series of locomotor movements and patterns.
B. Individual dancers explore the elements of weight and weightlessness. For example, one group of dancers could improvise pushing a heavy boulder uphill, while another group improvises the weightlessness of blowing a feather or dancing on the moon.
C. Dancers pair off and face their partner. One per-

FIGURE 8-4 Dancers use points of attachment to create an interesting design for composition.

son leads and the other person follows in a series of simple, mirrored axial (nonlocomotor) movements. The follower must attempt to imitate exactly the movements of the leader. After the dancers have switched roles, the teacher may then advise them to use levels and to begin incorporating locomotor movements into their mirroring activity.

Ideas for creative activities evolve from numerous sources. The beginning dancer may wish to work with a basic movement such as the swing and discover how the parts of the body swing, then combine these swings with changes in focus and level, then the changes in rhythm and then how the movement develops as a locomotor or axial action.

The images and impulses for the movement may be abstract or literal in nature. A prop such as a rope, a cape, or a box may be used to stimulate activity. Exploring movement using various points of attachment with another person or persons can be interesting and create awareness of dancing with other dancers (Figure 8-4).

The problems presented to stimulate creativity must be clearly designed and have specific goals, especially for the beginner. Improvisation and exploration of movement should develop an expansion of emotional expression as well as technical accomplishment.

ELEMENTS OF CHOREOGRAPHY

As in music, painting, and the other arts, dance must have both subject and structure-content and form. The subject may be something as concrete as a story or character study (representative, denotative) or as abstract as an emotional or mood idea (manifestative, connotative). Movement itself is often used as an initial stimulus to begin a dance; the gestures, principles of movement, and kinesthetic experience of the dancer will suggest further material. For example, the performer may move forward three steps with the arms raised, then discover that the arms could be used by moving them in small areas. This may then suggest a leg gesture of a similar style the next time a forward movement is used; this could be executed in five beats, then with stronger tension and a different focus. Eventually, a whole phrase or dance assumes shape.

Modern dancers have been experimenting with many abstract ideas as subject matter. Among these, a student may find interest in explorations of physical principles, such as the movement and structure of the atom, and the effects of centrifugal force on the body. Atonal and twelve-tone music, as well as sounds from nature, cities, and electronic machines, are other fields of interest. The use of objects such as elastic ropes or chairs; innovations in costume design and material such as stretchable tent-shaped dresses; and stage sets such as slanting boards or scaffolds—all of these suggestions open up the many possibilities for original and meaningful dances. There is virtually little in life that could not be the source of creative work. A student may find that nature ideas—the wind, seas, birds, fire, the seasons—suggest qualities and themes that can become a full-length work. Themes based on work, play, routine-farming, a basketball game, geometric shapes—are all fruitful sources for beginning choreographers.

After this subject has been chosen, the dancer must begin to find the movements expressed as a theme or basic material from which many of the later combinations will come. Improvisation is one of the most valuable tools for discovering movement. The student simply moves spontaneously with or without music, then employs dramatic actions or dances freely with other persons. Gradually, the movements will be molded into a concrete, rhythmic, spatial form. New ideas will arise from work on the dance itself. One should take care to be specific about what one is trying to say. It is important to develop good work habits, including the ability to make decisions, to change something, and to stay with the problem at hand until it is resolved. Sometimes it is helpful to ask someone to observe parts of a dance composition to determine whether or not the feeling or message is really being conveyed through the movement.

Another way to begin a dance is within an already set form. Literary forms such as poetry, plays, and short stories may be used. Musical forms lend themselves well to dance; for example, ABA, rondo, ABC, theme and variations. Different instruments in a quartet may be copied in movement—the oboe, drum, violin, and flute, for example. Early musical dance forms such as the pavane, gigue, or gavotte, can bring excellent results.

Aesthetic Principles

Whether or not a dancer works within a set framework, the overall design is still the prime concern. Some of the following aesthetic principles should be observed not only in a finished dance but in any art work.

1. Balance: Alternations of length, energy, symmetrical and asymmetrical designs.
2. Repetition: Needed for familiarity of the themes; for making one "whole" of a piece, for emphasis.
3. Contrast: In force, time, space; needed for interest, heightened drama.
4. Unity: Again, to make a dance a satisfying whole structure.
5. Sequence: Phrases and sections needed to follow each other for coherence.
6. Transition: The way in which movements and phrases change from one to another. Transitional movements must not be important within themselves, but should be smooth and part of the dance proper.
7. Variety: For interest by manipulating any principle or dramatic idea.
8. Climax: A structural high point in a dance; present in a classical approach to composition, needed for developing the conclusion of the dance.

In today's dance theater, the more experimental avant-garde choreographers often depart from many of these principles. The novice, however, will produce more fruitful results when given disciplines to follow.

To compose a dance, the beginning student may find it best to use one or only a few dancers and stay within the limits of an idea small in scope and length. It is wise to select an idea about which the student has some knowledge or experience. As in any art, simplicity and honesty in staying with one idea, no matter how limited it may seem at first, are necessities in learning the discipline demanded by dance. Choreographing for a large number can become as complex as writing for a symphony orchestra. Too many philosophical ideas incorporated into a dance tend to weaken the real value of the piece. The value lies in the movements, not in words. The medium of the dance is movement; its province is one in which moods, feelings, and meaningful activities in space and time can put into visual forms what words cannot express. Every human being who can move can find personal and shared values in the dance.

SOCIAL DANCE

BRIEF HISTORY

Social or ballroom dancing really began in the United States at the time of World War I with the introduction of many new forms of couple dances. The Charleston was followed by a series of "jitterbug" dances and the Latin-American rhythms which were performed to big swing bands. Rock and roll music influenced an individual type of dance which led to performances of disco. Novelty and fad dances seem to fill a need at a particular time and may reflect changing trends in music. They may stimulate interest and participation, but they seldom last long enough to merit a place in the repertory of traditional social dances. The following discussion focuses on basic elements used in social dance.

DANCE POSITIONS

Closed. (Used in Waltz, Fox-trot and Polka). Partners face each other, standing toe to toe, looking over each other's right shoulder, the man facing the line of direction. With this style arm (left), the man's left hand holds the woman's right hand at about shoulder height, arms are relaxed and slightly bent at elbows. With his lead arm (right), the man's fingers are closed and on the woman's back slightly above her waist. The woman's left hand is placed on the man's right shoulder (Figure 8-5).

In Latin dances (tango, samba, merengue), rumba, mambo, and cha cha cha, the man's lead arm (hand on partner's back) should be above the small of the back, and the elbow should be slightly higher than in the above-mentioned closed dance position. The man's style arm (left) is also placed higher when performed.

Semi-Open. From closed position partners turn slightly away from one another looking in line of direction—man's right and lady's left sides are near each other (Figure 8-6).

Open. From semi-open position, turn apart so that both are facing in line of direction.

Reverse Open. Partners turn so that both are facing in reverse line of direction—man's left and woman's right sides are near each other. Man's right arm and woman's left arm may hang down at side (Figure 8-7).

Line of Direction

In general, couples move about the floor in a counterclockwise circle known as the line of direction (LOD). Couples may, however, move forward, back-

FIGURE 8-5 Closed position.

FIGURE 8-6 Semi-open position.

FIGURE 8-7 Reverse open position.

ward, or sideward within this pattern; and, there are many new dance steps in which the couples dance in much the same spot.

Style and Etiquette

Every type of dance is performed with a certain style. The particular dance form, its tempo, and rhythm determine the style with which a particular dance is executed.

A man asks a woman to dance in a simple and direct way: "May I have the next dance?" or "Will you dance with me?" are the two customary approaches. It is polite to escort the woman to and from the floor and to thank her for the dance. Usually a man may cut in on a couple at a private party, but at a public dance, cutting in is not condoned. Dancers should always be courteous and well-mannered on the dance floor.

How to Lead and Follow

The man must indicate his steps and lead sufficiently in advance so that the woman can follow with confidence. He does this primarily with his upper torso, shoulders, and right arm and hand. The right hand becomes the steering rudder.

The woman's principal method of following is to remain relaxed so that her partner may guide her easily.

SUGGESTED LEARNING SEQUENCE

There is no set sequence for learning basic social dance patterns. The teacher might consider the interests and ages of the students, variety in rhythm, available music, and then select the order of dances that best fits the students. The following dances are described below in detail:

>Fox- trot
>Waltz
>Tango
>Rumba
>Cha Cha Cha
>Jitter bug

All steps indicated as slow (S) use two beats of the music, and all steps indicated as quick (Q) use one beat of the music. Unless otherwise indicated, the steps described are for the man's (or lead) part; the woman's is opposite. For example, the man's "forward left" would mean the woman's "backward right." (Note: Review the abbreviations listed in the Folk Dance section, page 108.)

Fox-trot (4/4 Time)

The fox-trot is an American ballroom dance first performed to ragtime music by Harry Fox in a 1913

musical. A fox-trot may vary in tempo, but for beginning students, a slower version is more appropriate. Although it began as a trotting dance, the fox-trot developed into the smoother, gliding dance that is performed today.

Magic Step. Basic Rhythmic Pattern: S S Q Q

1. Closed Position
   Fwd left-S
   Fwd right-S
   Side left-Q
   Close right to left-Q

LEAD CUE: Lift right arm, lean forward.

2. Semi-open Position
   Side left-S
   Cross right over left-S
   Side left-Q (return to closed position)
   Closed right to left-Q

LEAD CUES:
   Pressure with heel of right hand.
   Pressure with finger tips of right hand.

3. Turn-Under
   Man's part same as semi-open position
   Lady's part:
   Side R: start to turn under R arm-S
   Complete turn under R arm onto L foot-S
   Side R-Q (return to closed position)
   Close L to R-Q
   Lady's right and man's left hands are released during turn.

Box Step. Basic Rhythmic Pattern: S Q Q
   Fwd L-S
   Side R-Q
   Close L to R-Q
   Back R-S
   Side L-Q
   Close R to L-Q

Waltz (3/4 Time)

The waltz is the oldest form of ballroom dance, and it is credited as being the first of its kind to be performed in the basic closed-couple dance position. It was not accepted when first introduced in America; however, composers such as Johann Strauss, Von Weber, and Franz Shubert gave the waltz a dignified grace through their smooth and flowing musical styles.

It is important to note that the heels stay off the ground when performing this dance pattern.

Basic Rhythmic Pattern: Q Q Q

1. Box step
   Same as Fox-trot except each step is Q.
2. Crossover
   Do one-half Box
   Cross R over L (semi-open position)

Slide L (return to closed position)
Close R

LEAD CUES:
Pressure with heel of right hand.
Pressure with finger tips.

Tango (4/4 or 2/4 Time)

Some scholars believe the tango is derived from the "milongo," a dance that originated in Andulusia, Spain; others feel that the tango's roots lie in an Iberian gypsy dance resembling flamenco. Regardless of its beginnings, the tango is characterized by low, lingering steps followed by quick directional changes.

Basic Rhythmic Pattern: S S Q Q S

1. Basic step (closed position)
   Fwd L-S
   Fwd R-S
   Fwd L-Q
   Fwd R-Q
   Draw L to R, weight remaining on R-S
2. Semi-open Position
   Side L-S
   Cross R over L-S
   Fwd L-Q
   Side R-Q
   Draw L to R-S

LEAD CUES:
Pressure with heel of right hand.
Pressure with finger tips.

Rumba (4/4 Time)

The rumba came to America in the late 1920's from Cuba. This Latin American dance was originally performed by African slaves living in South America. One of the main characteristics of the rumba is the smooth lateral swaying of the hips, a movement known as Cuban Motion.

Basic Rhythmic Pattern: Q Q S

1. Box (closed position)
   Side L-Q
   Close R-Q
   Fwd L-S
   Side R-Q
   Close L-Q
   Back R-S
2. Cuban Walk
   Walking forward or backward in the Q Q S rhythm.

Cha Cha Cha (4/4 Time)

The cha cha cha, which is a combination of the swing and mambo, became popular during the 1950's. The cha cha cha has Mexican, Afro-Cuban and American influences, and was probably named after the three quick rhythmic sounds that the feet make when executing the steps. Like the rumba, the cha cha cha uses Cuban Motion.

Basic Rhythmic Pattern: S S Q Q S

1. Basic Step (closed position)
   Dancing toward each other with hands held:
   Fwd L-S, Back R-S
   Back L-Q, Back R-Q
   Back L-S, Back R-S
   Fwd L-S, Fwd R-Q
   Fwd L-Q, Fwd R-S
2. Cross Step
   Cross L-S (reverse open position) Man's L and Lady's R hands joined
   In place R-S
   Side L-Q, Close R-Q, Side L-S
   Cross R-S (open position) Man's R and Lady's L hands joined
   In place L-S
   Side R-Q, Close L-Q, Side R-S

Jitterbug (4/4 Time)

The jitterbug evolved from the lindy hop, an American novelty dance that was named after the famous pilot, Charles Lindbergh, in 1927. As the movement of the lindy hop evolved into more exaggerated hopping sequences, viewers remarked that the dancers looked like "jittery bugs," thus giving the jitterbug its name.

Basic Rhythmic Pattern: S S Q Q

1. Basic Step (closed position)
   Touch L, then take weight on L-S
   Place R, then take weight on R-S
   Back L-Q (semi-open position)
   Fwd R-Q (return to closed position)
2. Basic Turn Man's Part same as Basic Step
   Lady's Part:
   Start to turn to R under R arm on R foot-S
   Complete turn under R arm on L foot-S
   Back R-facing partner-Q
   Fwd L-Q
   Start to turn to L under R arm on R foot-S
   Complete turn under R arm on L foot-S
   Back R-facing partner-Q
   Fwd L-Q

LEAD CUES:
Pressure with heel of right hand.
Pressure with finger tips.

Once the basic step patterns are learned the teacher may introduce variations or the students may be encouraged to create their own modifications.

▶ **Practice Suggestions**

Since leading and following are basic elements for partner dances, the teacher should introduce them by using a simple dance walk. Today's young persons are not accustomed to dancing in contact with a partner, traveling on a dance floor, or following a definite basic step. The teacher, therefore, should try to begin in a fundamental manner.

Using a free formation, the basic step of any social dance should be learned without a partner. The teacher, prior to presenting the foot pattern, might have students clap hands to the music which will be used for the dance, because being able to recognize the underlying rhythm is essential. The basic step pattern should be performed next with partners, all couples moving in line of direction. While the individuals keep dancing, the teacher may give verbal cues in relation to position, rhythm, or step pattern. If necessary, individual assistance may be continued through additional demonstration or dancing with the student. Students may receive extra ideas or be encouraged to create variations with partners learning together.

In the teaching of social dance, it is important to provide a relaxed learning atmosphere; to suggest and implement partner changes; to build confidence through words of encouragement; and to give opportunities for everyone to practice good social etiquette.

SQUARE DANCE

A BRIEF HISTORY

Although square dancing originated in 17th century England with the English country dances (as well as the French contra dances), square dance has been labeled "America's Folk Dance." (Note: Some scholars believe that the dances of the American Indian are the true American folk dances.)

The early New England colonists brought with them these pompous and precise line dances where the couples faced each other. However, as American square dance evolved, the less rigid and the more recreational and social these dances became. In fact, square dancing was one of the most popular and satisfying forms of social recreation because it was something in which all generations could participate and enjoy.

The "caller" was introduced to American square dance in the early 19th century. The caller enabled dancing participants to execute the basic patterns without having to memorize the dances. Square dance calling requires a good deal of practice, understanding, voice control, and ability to handle large groups. Anyone who attempts calling must have a distinct and pleasant voice, a sense of timing so that the calls will immediately precede the figure and produce continuity in the dance, and a thorough knowledge of the dance figures. Excellent recordings of square dance music with calls are also available.

Although there have been radical changes in the calls, style, and music of contemporary square dance, the basic patterns and figures have been standardized, making it possible to enjoy this popular recreational art form all over the United States and abroad (Figure 8-8). Today, this popularity has created avenues in the competing commercial market for professionally-trained callers, square dance retreats and vacations, and square dance clothing and accessories, for those who desire the latest square dance fashions.

SUGGESTED LEARNING SEQUENCE

Honor	Couple Promenade
Shuffle	Grand Right and Left
Forward and Back	Star Left (Right)
Do-sa-do	Pass Through
Seesaw	Ladies Chain
Allemande Left (Right)	Right and Left Through
Swing	Square Positions
Promenade Single File	Half Promenade

These steps, terms, and figures are described below, along with a few other important square dance terms, in alphabetical order. The number of counts usually used to fully execute the figures, and steps are also indicated where appropriate.

Square Dance Terms, Figures, and Steps

Allemande Left. Man gives his left hand to the woman on his left. With left hands joined, they shuffle around one another (exchanging places) and then both return to place. This figure is sometimes followed by an allemande right, in which the man executes the same figure but with his partner. More frequently, the allemande left is followed by a grand right and left (8 counts).

Circle Left (or Right). Three or more dancers circle to the left or right, as directed. Hands are joined with elbow comfortably bent so that the hands are above the elbow, man's palm up, woman's palm down (16 counts for a full circle, 8 counts for half).

Corner. The person to the man's left or the woman's right is the corner person.

Courtesy Turn. The man takes the woman's left hand in his left, then places his right hand in her right which is at her back, waist high. Turning counterclockwise, the man backs up and the woman walks forward one half turn.

FIGURE 8-8   Square dancing has become a popular recreational art from in the United States and abroad.

Do-sa-do.   Do-sa-do is a French term meaning back to back. Two dancers face each other and advance passing right shoulders. Each person slides behind the other person passing them, then moves backward into place (8 counts).

Forward and Back.   The persons or couples designated move four steps into the center of the circle, then move four steps backward out of the circle (8 counts).

Grand Right and Left.   In a square or circle formation, the partners face and take right hands. Men going counterclockwise and then women clockwise, each partner moves ahead giving the left hand to the next person and pulling by giving the right hand to the next person and pulling by, giving the left to the next, and stop. In square formation, the original partners will now be facing each other and ready for the next call (16 counts).

Honor.   The men bow while the women curtsey to their partners (or to the "corner" person, depending on the call). "Honor your partner" is an acknowledgement of your partner usually at the beginning of a dance.

Ladies Chains:

A. *Two Ladies Chain.* With couples facing each other, men stand still as the women shuffle forward, take right hands, pull by them, then give the left hand to the opposite man who completes a courtesy turn (8 counts).
B. *Four Ladies Chain or Ladies Grand Chain.* In square formation, all four women star right and move clockwise to their opposite man who gives them a courtesy turn (8 counts). Partner. The woman on the man's right, the man on the woman's left. Sometimes partners are changed temporarily before returning to the original partners.

Pass Through.   Two facing couples move forward, pass right shoulders, and remain facing in the same direction until the next call.

Promenade:

A. *Couple Promenade.* The most commonly used promenade in square dancing is the couple promenade. Standing side by side, couples join left hands, then join right hands on top of their left hands. The couple then moves forward in a counterclockwise direction.
B. *Half Promenade.* Two couples, indicated by the call, use a couple promenade position to move counterclockwise and exchange positions in the square (8 counts).
C. *Promenade Single File.* Dancers face counterclockwise and move one behind the other.

   Right and Left Thru. With couples facing, each person gives a right hand to the person opposite them and pulls by. The left hand is immediately given to the partner, and each couple does a courtesy turn (8 counts).

Seesaw.   Two dancers face and pass left

shoulders. Each slides to the left while back to back, then backs up to original position (8 counts).

Separate.   Each dancer turns his back on his partner, then they move in opposite directions. This movement is followed by a directional call.

Shuffle.   A walking pattern in which the feet alternately slide in short, smooth steps along the floor in time with the music. A shuffle step is executed in an even rhythm, unlike the boisterous skip or hop of the early square dances which is now regarded as an unacceptable style.

Square Positions.   A square is an arrangement of four couples who stand facing the center in a square formation. The couples are numbered consecutively to the right, beginning with couple number 1, whose backs are closest to the music or caller. Couples 1 and 3 are the "head couples;" couples 2 and 4 are the "side couples."

Star Left (or Right).   If couples or ladies star, those involved touch fingers of the designated hand, elbows bent, and shuffle forward. If men star, each turns the designated side toward the center of the star, and with an overhand grip, takes the wrist of the man in front of him. Dancers move around the circle to return to their original positions (8 counts).

Swing.   This is a modified social dance position in partners. The man's left arm is extended to the side, his right arm around the woman's waist. The woman puts her right hand in the man's left, her left hand is on the man's shoulder. They stand to the side so that right hips and right feet are in line with one another and almost touching. Using the right foot somewhat as a pivot, they push with the left foot so that partners circle about in place, in a clockwise direction. As the swing is performed, partners look at each other and lean away, which results in a quick, vigorous turn (8 counts).

▶ **Practice Suggestions**

1. The most common mistake made by the inexperienced square dance teacher is selecting a specific square dance and then directing the dancers to walk through the basic movements and figures of the dance. The movements from these dances require a great deal of practice and probably cannot be performed with music, resulting in uninteresting drills more than an enjoyable dance. Basic calls should be taught in a single circle. This method enables the teacher to see quickly all dancers, to use music immediately, and to eliminate the necessity for a specific number of students for squares. A simple dance to music can begin, for example with:

   Honor your partner
   Honor your corner
   Join hands, circle left, circle right
   Walk into the middle
   Come right back

2. When the movements can be done effectively, teach a Do-sa-do, Seesaw, Swing, Allemande Left, and a Couple Promenade. All calls may be combined then in varied sequence or in the following manner:

   Face your corner do a Do-sa-do
   Seesaw your partner
   Join hands, circle right
   Circle left
   Face the center, go forward and back
   Allemande left your corner
   Allemande right your partner
   Swing your corner
   Swing your partner and promenade
   Go single file
   Face the center
   (Repeat)

3. A Grand Right and Left may be taught by designating a certain number of hands until a new partner is reached. For example, a right hand to the partner would be "one" and a left to the next would be "two." Any number may be chosen, but seven hands enables the dancers to learn the principle involved and eliminates the confusion of counting a large number of hands. Once the Grand Right and Left is mastered, an Allemande Left with the corner may precede this figure. These movements are ready to be combined with those already learned.

4. The group of dancers may then move smoothly from the single circle formation to a double circle with partners facing. One may direct calls already acquired to make dancers comfortable in this new formation, for instance:

   Honor your partner
   Do-sa-do your opposite
   Swing your partner
   Circle left, Circle right
   Allemande right your partner
   Allemande left your opposite
   Do-sa-do your partner
   Seesaw your opposite
   Swing your partner

5. In the double circle formation, Star Left and Right and Pass Thru may be taught rapidly. This permits dancers to work with different couples while being at ease with the basic calls. Two Ladies Chain and Right and Left Thru may be added to the figures. All basic calls except the Grand Right and Left and the promenades may be combined to music.

The teacher will be able to teach the square formation using previously taught calls and may add more advanced figures as the selected dances below require. Many of these are performed to music that has a familiar melody; therefore, the callers may choose to sing their calls. Happy dancing!

Selected Square Dances for Beginners

Big Daddy
Buffalo Girls
Gentle on My Mind
If You Knew Susie
Little Ole Winemaker
Little Red Wagon
Marina Just Because
Oh, Johnny
Ragtime Banjo Ball
Winchester Cathedral

MODIFICATIONS FOR SPECIAL POPULATIONS

Orthopedically Impaired

1. Keep movement patterns slow and avoid quick changes for the students with ambulation difficulties, e.g., cerebral palsy, amputees.
2. Keep tempo of the music moderate.
3. Emphasize concepts of high, low, soft, hard, rough, smooth, etc., and have students interpret movements.
4. Minimal modifications are needed in square dance for students using a wheelchair, e.g., larger work area.

Mentally Impaired

1. Follow suggestions for Orthopedically Impaired above.
2. Keep concepts and movement patterns simple.

Sensory Impaired

1. Use peer teachers for blind students.
2. Individual considerations need to be made on the appropriateness of dance for the deaf and/or hard of hearing student.

SELECTED REFERENCES

Folk Dance

Bambra, A. and Webster, M. *Teaching Folk Dancing.* London: B.T. Batsford, 1972.

Evans, J. *Let's Dance: A Movement Approach to Folk Dance.* Toronto, Ontario Can. Ed. Media Ltd. Publishers, 1985.

Gilbert, C. *International Folk Dance at a Glance.* Minneapolis: Burgess Publishing Group, 1974.

Harn's, J.A., et al. *Dance a While: Handbook of Folk, Square, Contra, and Social Dance.* 6th ed. New York: Macmillan Publishing Co., 1988.

Lidster, M.D. and Tambunni, D.H. *Folk Dance Progressions.* Belmont, CA: Wadsworth Publishing Co., 1965.

Mynatt, C.V. and Kaimar, B.D. *Folk Dancing for Students and Teachers,* Dubuque, IA: Wm. C. Brown Publishers, 1975.

Weikart, Phyllis S. *Teaching Movement and Dance: Intermediate Folk Dance.* Ypsilanti, MI: High/Scope Press, 1984.

Modern Dance

Anderson, J. *Ballet and Modern Dance: A Concise History.* Princeton: Princeton Book Co., 1986.

Blom, L.A. and Chaplin, T.L. *The Moment of Movement: Dance Improvisation.* Pittsburgh: University of Pittsburgh Press, 1988.

Cheney, G. *Basic Concepts in Modern Dance: A Creative Approach.* 3rd ed., Princeton, NJ: Princeton Book Co., 1989.

Duffy, N.W. *Modern Dance: An Adult Beginner's Guide.* Englewood Cliffs, NJ: Prentice Hall, 1982.

Hawkins, A.M. *Creating Through Dance.* 2nd ed. Pennington, NJ: Princeton Book Co., 1988.

Minton, S.C. *Choreography: A Basic Approach Using Improvisation.* Champaign, IL: Human Kinetics Publishers, 1986.

Morgenroth, J. *Dance Improvisations.* Pittsburgh: University of Pittsburgh Press, 1987.

Penrod, J. and Plastino, J.G. *The Dancer Prepares: Modern Dance for Beginners.* 3rd ed. Mountain View, CA: Mayfield Publishing Co., 1990.

Social (Ballroom) Dance

Dow, A. *The Official Guide to Ballroom Dancing.* Secaucus, NJ: Chartuell Books, Inc., 1980.

Ellfeldt, L., et al. *This Is Ballroom Dance.* Palo Alto, CA: National Press Books, 1974.

Fallon, D.J. and Kuchenmeister, S.A. *The Art of Ballroom Dance.* Minneapolis: Burgess Publishing Co., 1977.

Harris, J.A., et al. *Dance a While: Handbook of Folk, Square, Contra, and Social Dance.* 6th ed. New York: Macmillan Publishing Co., 1988.

Moore, A. *Ballroom Dancing.* 9th ed. London: A & C Black, 1986.

Schild, M. *Social Dance.* Dubuque, IA: Wm. C. Brown Publishers, 1985.

White, B. *Ballroom Dancebook for Teachers.* New York: David McKay Company, Inc., 1962.

Square Dance

Greene, H. *Square and Folk Dancing: A Complete Guide for Students, Teachers, and Callers.* New York: Harper and Row, 1984.

Harris, J.A., et al. *Dance a While: Handbook of Folk, Square, Contra, and Social Dance.* 6th ed. New York: Macmillan Publishing Co., 1988.

Jenson, C.R. and Jenson, M.B. *Square Dancing.* Provo, UT: Brigham Young University Press, 1973.

Phillis, P.A. *Contemporary Square Dance.* Dubuque, IA: Wm. C. Brown Co. Publishers., 1968.

Schild, M.M. *Square Dancing Everyone.* Winston-Salem, NC: Hunter Textbooks, Inc., 1987.

Stultz, S.J. *Contemporary Square Dance.* Minneapolis, MN: Burgess Publishing Co., 1974.

Sweet, R. *Let's Create 'Old Tyme' Square Dancing.* Hazardville, CT, 1966.

Additional Sources

Diggins, D. *Tap Technique.* Sante Fe, NM.: Teal Press, 1988.

Emery, L.F. *Black Dance from 1619 to Today.* 2nd ed. Princeton, NJ: Princeton Book Co., 1988.

Kislan, R. *Hoofing on Broadway.* New York: Prentice Hall, 1987.

Kraines, M.G. and Kan, E. *Jump Into Jazz.* 2nd ed. Mountain View, CA: Mayfield Publishing Co., 1990.

Music Sources

Big "O" Record Service, P.O. Box 786, Springfield, VA 22150.

Dance Record Dist/Folkraft Records, 10 Fenwick Street, Newark, NJ 07114.

Dansounds, P.O. 27618, Philadelphia, PA 19118.

Fair 'N Square Records, 816 Forest Hills Dr. SW, Rochester, MN 55901.

Square Dance Record Roundup, Inc., 957 Sheridan Blvd., Denver, CO 80214.

Tape & Record Service, 3508 Palm Beach Blvd., Ft. Myers, FL 33905.

9 FENCING

THIS CHAPTER WILL ENABLE YOU TO:

▶ Identify the types of equipment used in foil fencing, and name the parts of the French foil.
▶ Perform some of the basic skills of foil fencing while participating in a bout, including the grip, salute, on-guard, advance, retreat, lunge, defense, parries, engagements, and attacks.
▶ Identify and apply some of the basic strategies used during a foil fencing bout.
▶ Identify and apply the rules of foil fencing as participant or as a spectator.
▶ Officiate as a judge at a bout and apply the rules.
▶ Know and use the proper safety precautions.
▶ Define and use the terminology generally associated with foil fencing.

NATURE AND PURPOSE

Modern fencing is a combat sport practiced by men and women of all ages from 8 to 80 and at every level from novice to Olympic. A fencing bout retains many of the characteristics of a real fight but without the attendant dangers usually associated with the use of swords. The foils used in fencing are not sharp, and the fencer scores a point by touching an opponent anywhere on the torso.

To touch the opponent without being touched is the object of the game. In days long past, a duelist certainly knew when he had been touched by a sharp sword. In modern foil competition, the weapons are wired so that when a touch lands, a scoring box shows a light and a buzzer sounds. Such equipment is now required at most competitions, but in the typical physical education class it is impractical and expensive to use the electrical foil. In such classes, student judges stand alongside the fencers and watch for touches.

Fencing is for everyone—from the bespectacled youngster who loves to play video games to the quick-footed, athletically inclined youngster who loves to play sports of all kinds. Both should be given the opportunity to experience the thrills of matching one's fencing wit and skill on the narrow strip of combat where each will be able to find fulfillment and common values.

Fencing offers them the complete sport, one that involves the total person—mind, body, spirit. It is a game of grace, speed, and especially finesse that tests the body's coordination and stamina along with the mind's acuity and guile. Fencing is the thinking person's sport that eschews brute force—not unlike chess on a strip.

For most people, fencing is a new athletic experience and even the early lessons are fun. At first, the emphasis is on footwork, body position, and main-taining correct distance. As these are mastered, concentration shifts to the proper use of the foil. By the end of a course, a student can expect to do some actual fencing and to know some of the rules and terms of the sport. Bouting experience with a wide variety of opponents is an important part of any fencer's development; therefore, after the basic skills are learned, the student should seek opportunities to test these skills against other fencers.

EQUIPMENT

Weapons

The three types of competitive weapons used are the épée, the sabre, and the foil (Figure 9-1). The épée, a direct descendant of the rapier, has a large bell guard. Touches may be made only with the tip of

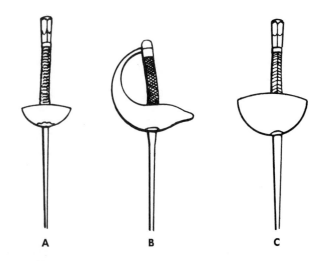

A   B   C

FIGURE 9-1   Types of weapons: (A) French foil, (B) sabre, (C) épeé.

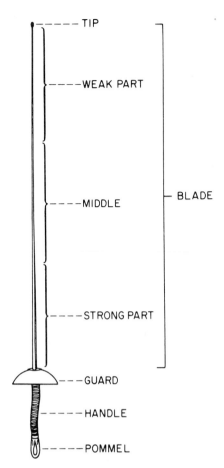

FIGURE 9-2   Parts of the French foil.

FIGURE 9-3   Fencing cart loaded with equipment.

the épée, and the entire body is valid target. The sabre (or saber) is principally a slashing weapon, although the tip may also be used; the target area includes all body parts above the hips. The foil is a light thrusting weapon, and the target area is the torso. This chapter will deal with the French foil, because most teachers favor its use by beginners. Figure 9-2 shows the parts of the French foil.

The foil is the modern version of the dueling rapier. It weighs 17 ounces and has a flexible blade 35 to 36 inches long. The total length of the weapon cannot exceed 43 inches.

Foil grips are right- or left-handed, and the teacher might mark them as such to expedite issue. The foil tip should be covered with adhesive tape or a rubber tip, and a slight downward bend should have been worked into the first one-third of the blade.

Protective Wear

The usual class equipment that ensures the maximum amount of protection consists of a mask, a bib, a foil, a jacket, an optional glove, and breast protectors for women. The mask comes in three sizes: small, medium, and large. A quilted cotton canvas bib attaches to the mask to protect the neck and throat. The jacket sizes are small, medium, large, and extra large. A separate plastron or underarm garment is worn underneath the jacket. Women must wear breast protectors.

The glove worn by a fencer is usually leather with a padded gauntlet. The gauntlet should be long enough to cover the end of the jacket sleeve so the point of an opponent's foil will not slide inside the sleeve. The beginner may wear any type of glove during the initial stage of learning in order to get used to the "feel" of a glove on the hand.

All the equipment needed for a fencing class can be stored on the fencing cart as pictured in Figure 9-3. The rolling cart, which measures 40 inches wide, 64 inches high, and 14 inches deep, can be built by your woodworking shop at minimum expense. The utilitarian nature of the cart is such that it holds maximum equipment neatly while taking up a minimal amount of space. The 1×2 inch boards on the front of the cart act as racks for 5 masks each, while the top flat surface has one-inch holes drilled 2½ inches apart in order to accommodate up to 20 foils. Each hole is numbered for a corresponding numbered foil. The pegs at the upper back provide a place on which the numbered jackets are to be hung. The bibs and breast plates can be stored on the top surface behind the foils. This cart can be the answer to all of your class equipment problems, for it can store all of the equipment needed for a class of 20 students.

RULES AND PLAYING AREA

Fencing rules are identical for both men and women; however, men do not normally compete against women.

Touches and Target. In foil fencing the target is the body exclusive of the head and appendages. It begins at the top of the jacket collar and extends in front down to the groin and in back to the top of the hips. The sleeve seams mark the side limits.

A valid touch is one made with the foil point on valid target area. Contact made with the side of the blade never counts and is simply referred to as a slap or plaqué. If the point slides along the target without momentarily fixing, it does not count and is known as a passé. Touches made with the point on invalid target areas (mask, legs, arms) are called "off-target" and do not count but do cause the bout to be stopped.

Playing Area. For class purposes, any large room will serve very well for instruction and bouting. When judged bouts are held, boundaries can be quickly marked with masking tape. Precise measurement is seldom needed, and a rectangular strip 46 feet by 6 feet should be laid out. Two on-guard lines need to be marked 6 feet in both directions from the center, and warning lines are placed 6 feet from each end. A diagram of a regulation strip is shown in Figure 9-4.

At the start of a bout and also after each scored point, the fencers begin at the on-guard lines and must remain on the strip during the bout. Stepping off the side with both feet is a violation. The director stops the bout and positions the fencer on the strip one meter farther back from where he or she went off. One foot out only halts the bout until position is regained. Whenever the rear foot of a retreating fencer reaches a warning line, the director calls a halt and informs the fencer about being on the meter line. This warns the fencer that continued retreat beyond the end line with both feet will result in a point being awarded. If the warned fencer has regained his or her own on-guard line before crossing the warning line a second time, the warning is repeated each time.

Officiating

In nonelectric fencing, a foil jury is composed of a director and four side judges. Two judges stand beside each fencer and watch for touches made against the opposing fencer. The director maintains a central position in order to observe the entire jury as well as the competitors (Figure 9-5). The judges and the director must move around as the fencers move, so as to maintain their relative positions.

The director is in total control of the bout and

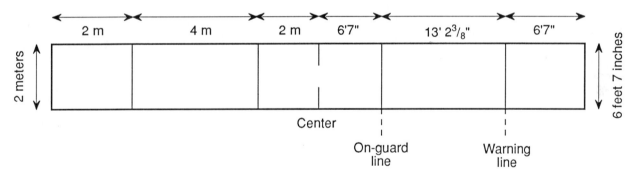

FIGURE 9-4 Foil strip measurements, in meters and in feet.

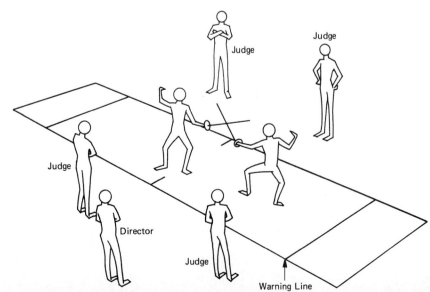

FIGURE 9-5 Positions of jury for nonelectric foil. (Adapted from Charles Simonian, *Basic Foil Fencing.* Kendall/Hunt Publishing Company, 1979.)

gives the orders to fence or to halt. The commands a director uses to start or restart the bout are: "On guard;" "Fencer's ready;" "Fence." A fencer indicates readiness by a nodding of the head. Whenever a bout is halted, unless a touch or penalty is awarded, fencers hold their ground. The director's duties include: inspecting equipment; supervising judges, scorers and timers; directing bout; awarding touches; and penalizing offenses. Often during the bout the director will command "halt," to award touches, issue warnings, or stop the action if it becomes too dangerous or too confused to follow.

There are four judges in each bout; two stand on each side of the strip about two feet left of the director to observe the fencer on the right and vice versa. The judge's primary responsibility is to observe when a touch is made on either valid or invalid target and to signal by raising an arm to indicate that a touch landed. While the director also watches for touches, it is the sole responsibility of the director to determine which fencer had the right of way (explained below) in any situation where both fencers received touches at about the same time.

When a judge raises a hand, the director immediately calls a halt and proceeds to analyze the action just completed. As each step is described, the director polls the two judges from whose side the action was initiated. The analysis and voting continue until a decision has been reached to award or not to award a point.

Votes. Judges may only reply with one of the following answers:

1. The judge will vote *no* if the attack missed or was parried.
2. The vote is *yes* if the attacking point clearly fixed on valid target.
3. The vote is *abstain* if the judge could not see the action clearly or is unsure of a touch.
4. The vote is *yes*, but *invalid* if the point was seen to fix on invalid target.

The vote of each judge is worth one point, while that of the director is 1 ½ points. Thus, if two judges have agreed on the vote, they could override a contrary vote of the director by 2 to 1 ½. If the director and one judge have the same opinion about the touch, they prevail over the other judge by 2 ½ to 1. An abstention carries no point value in the voting. If the two judges have contradictory opinions while the director abstains, there is a one to one tie that results in a *doubtful touch* decision, and no point is awarded.

If the jury decides that a particular action landed on invalid target, no further voting is needed, and fencing is resumed. In other words, any touch on invalid area stops the action and nullifies any other touches that might have landed during that phase. There is no penalty for invalid (off-target) hits.

Scoring. Each time the director awards a point, that point is recorded next to the name of the fencer who was hit. Therefore, the fencer with the lower score at any time is leading in the bout. When one fencer has been hit five times, the bout ends. The bout may also end if time expires, and the winner will be the fencer who led at that moment. When time runs out, enough points are added to the scores of each fencer to bring the loser's score up to five points.

Time limits are seldom used in informal or intramural meets. Where time limits are in effect, the competitors will need to be aware of the time that is allowed. Normally, a one-minute warning is given as the limit is approaching.

Types of Competitions

Most amateur meets are run on either a pool or a direct elimination system. In a pool, each fencer meets every other fencer in the pool in a specified order, with the winner having the best won–lost record. In the direct elimination format, the fencer advances with a win or is out of the competition with a loss.

Men's intercollegiate meets consist of a total of 27 bouts, nine in each of the three weapons. Each team has three men per weapon who fence against the three men from the opposing team.

Women's intercollegiate teams usually have four women in foil who meet each of the opponent's four entries. Thus 16 bouts are fought, and the team having the majority of wins is the winner. In the event of a tie in bouts won, there is a count of the number of touches scored by and against each team.

SUGGESTED LEARNING SEQUENCE

The skills should be learned in the order outlined below. A beginner can fence effectively if the skills through the *one-two* are learned. The counterparries, the double, the beat, and the low line offense and defense can be added when more time is available.

A. Nature and Purpose of Foil Fencing
   1. Equipment requirements
   2. Safety considerations
B. Rules. A discussion of rules and officiating practice can begin when most appropriate and applicable to a situation. This discussion should be ongoing throughout the learning sequence.
C. Terminology. A discussion of terminology, like rules, is most meaningful in the learning experience when dealing with that particular reference to a term at a given time. The learning of the language of foil fencing should occur throughout each segment.

D. Skills and Techniques
  1. Gripping the foil
  2. Salute
  3. On-Guard
  4. Advance
  5. Retreat
  6. Lunge
  7. Guard Positions and Engagements
  8. Defense
  9. Right of Way
  10. Advance Lunge
  11. Disengagement Attack
  12. Compound Parries
  13. One-Two
  14. Counter Parries
  15. Double
  16. Low Line Parries
  17. Beat Attack
E. Strategies. Beginning strategies should be discussed once the fencer begins engaging in elementary bouts and at times most meaningful to the learner.

FOIL SKILLS AND TECHNIQUES

While it is much more fun to fence than to practice, you must realize that fencing too often and too soon will lead to bad habits. Fencing requires self-control and correct execution of skills, and there is no shortcut to success. Therefore it is important to spend a large portion of class time doing drills to perfect the lunge, the footwork, and the blade skills. Some fencing must be done in order to relate the drills to the reality of the bout.

Gripping the Foil

Most beginners learn to fence with the French foil. As shown in Figure 9-6, the thumb and forefinger oppose one another on the broad surfaces of the handle, while the remaining three fingers rest lightly along the side. There is slight curvature to the rectangular handle, and the curves should be directed toward the palm and toward the thumb. The following instructions are addressed to right-handed students.

▶ **Learning Cues**

1. Curve of the handle to the thumb side.
2. Index finger and thumb on handle near pad of bell guard.
3. The three remaining fingers rest lightly on the handle.
4. The forearm should be at approximately a 45-degree angle from the elbow joint.

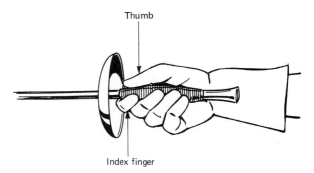

FIGURE 9-6 Gripping the French foil (right-handed).

Salute

It is customary to salute your opponent or partner before a bout or a practice session. Stand erect with the heels together, the right foot pointing straight ahead and the rear foot placed at a right angle to the lead foot. From this position, bring the foil bell up to eye level and then smartly straighten the elbow to swing the foil downward.

On-Guard

Flex your foil arm enough to bring the foil point up to face level while maintaining a fairly straight line between the blade and your forearm. Bend the non-foil arm and raise your elbow to about shoulder height; the forearm should be vertical and the wrist flexed and relaxed. While holding the arms in this position, take a short step forward, and bend both knees to a slight squat as in Figure 9-7.

This on-guard stance is designed to permit movement in either forward or rearward direction and to allow the effective launching of an attack.

FIGURE 9-7 The on-guard stance.

Your body weight should be evenly distributed onto both legs, and your feet should be spaced somewhere between 14 and 18 inches apart. The heels are in line and the feet are held at a right angle.

▶ **Learning Cues**

1. Feet must be in line, weight evenly distributed on both legs; feet are 14 to 18 inches apart.
2. Flex the foil arm enough to bring the foil up to the face level while maintaining a fairly straight line between the blade and forearm.
3. Bend the left arm and raise the elbow to about shoulder height; the forearm should be vertical and the wrist flexed and relaxed.
4. While holding the arms in this position, take a short step forward and bend both knees to a slight squat.

▶ **Practice Suggestions**

1. Place students on a line, check grip, have them go through a routine of the salute and then assume on-guard positions.
2. An effective drill for advance and retreat involves a leading partner who advances or retreats one or more steps at a time while the follower reacts and moves accordingly. Footwork should be varied so that the steps are sometimes slow and sometimes fast. Step lengths should range from quite short to fairly long.

Advance

Whenever the opponent is too far away, one or more steps forward need to be taken. This is done by moving first the front foot a few inches forward and then the rear foot an equal distance. Neither foot should slide on the floor.

Retreat

If the opponent is too close, the fencer will need to take one or more steps backward. The rear foot will move first, followed by the front foot.

Footwork must be responsive to the opponent's movements. The ability to change direction quickly in order to maintain fencing distance is very important.

Lunge

When two fencers maintain the correct fencing distance, neither can hit the other by merely reaching out with the arm and foil. It will be necessary to take a long stretching step with the front foot in order to be able to touch the target with the foil tip. This is known as the *lunge* (Figure 9-8). Start by extending your foil arm toward the opponent. Your foil hand will be shoulder high, and the tip of the foil will

FIGURE 9-8 The lunge. (Courtesy of the Athletic Institute.)

be aimed at your opponent's chest. Next, lift the front foot, toes first, while simultaneously straightening your rear knee and swinging your non-foil arm to the rear in a large arc. The lunge ends with the front foot landing well out ahead, while the rear foot remains where it was in the on-guard stance.

If the lunge results in a touch, it makes no real difference how the fencer recovers. But if the attack fails, it is most important that the fencer be able to recover quickly to a defensive position. This is done by bending the rear knee while pushing hard with the front foot. As the legs complete the recovery, the arms return to their proper positions in the on-guard stance.

The lunge is one of the most important movements in fencing and must be practiced diligently. The first lunges made by a beginner should be of medium length, because the muscles might be injured if long lunges are attempted before the student has the necessary flexibility. The need to fully extend the foil arm just before lifting the front foot must be stressed. A bout director must decide who the attacker is at any given time and does this by observing which fencer extended first to present a definite threat to the opponent. In other words, which fencer had the right of way. When two touches land at approximately the same time, the fencer who first extended will receive the priority in the decision.

▶ **Learning Cues**

1. The foil arm is first extended toward the opponent.
2. The front foot, toes first, are lifted while simultaneously straightening the rear knee and swinging the non-foil arm to the rear in a large arc.
3. The front foot lands well out ahead while the rear foot remains anchored as in an on-guard position.

4. To recover, the rear knee is bent while pushing off with the front foot.

▶ Practice Suggestions

NOTE: In preparation for the sudden lunging movement forward, it is important to do a series of stretching exercises giving particular attention to the major muscle groups of the leg and back.

1. Begin with students in a line in an on-guard position. Practice taking short to medium steps, then gradually lengthen the forward step.
2. With a partner, practice lunge at a partner then recover to guard.
3. With a partner, practice an advance-lunge-recover-and-retreat sequence.

Guard Positions and Engagements

In the on-guard stance, the foil arm can be held pretty much anywhere—to the right, to the left, low or high. Normally it is best to hold the foil in the *sixth guard position*, which is identical to the *simple parry six* position shown in Figure 9-9. From this guard, the fencer may use the strong parry four. If the fencer chooses to stand on-guard while maintaining contact with the blade of the opponent, the blades are said to be *engaged*. Engagement numbers derive from the numbers of the comparable parries. For example, if your opponent's blade is to the left of your own, the contact is termed a *fourth engagement*.

Defense

When attacked, a fencer generally has two options: one is to retreat and cause the attack to fall short, and the other is to deflect the attacking blade. If the attacking blade is to the left of your own, move your foil sharply to the left just enough to contact and deflect the blade away from your target. This is known as the *simple parry four* (Figure 9-10), the most common and strongest of the eight simple parries. Deflection of the attacker's blade to the right is made with the *parry six* (Figure 9-9). In both of these parries, the hand and blade should move horizontally right or left; the tip and the hand do not change level, and the elbow remains bent.

Following a successful parry, the defender has the opportunity to make a counterattack through the use of a *riposte*. This may be a simple reaching out to touch the opponent, but if the attacker is quick enough to recover after having been parried, the defender may have to lunge to score with the riposte.

Right of Way

Any time that there is a single touch landing, the director has no problem in awarding the touch. However, if both fencers hit at the same time, the director must decide which, if either, had the right of way. An attack is correctly made and has the right of way when the foil arm is fully extended as the lunge begins. The opponent must take defensive action by retreating or parrying. If the parry is successful, the

FIGURE 9-9 The simple parry six.

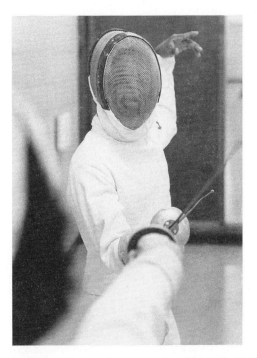

FIGURE 9-10 The simple parry four. (Photos by Ted Rice.)

right of way now passes to the defender who may riposte, and the former attacker is obliged to take some defensive action. Thus the right of way can change back and forth several times in any given flurry of action.

Suggestions for Practice Bouts

Students could have some early bout experience as soon as the skills and rules described above have been learned. In a practice bout without judges, two fencers get on guard a few feet apart and begin to fence. After a bit of maneuvering, perhaps one will chance a lunge. The opponent might step back, parry, or be hit. If the parry is made, the defender may fail to riposte immediately, thereby losing right of way, and either fencer may initiate the next attack. However, if the riposte is attempted, the new defender may recover, parry, or be hit. If both fencers attack correctly at the same moment and both touch, neither hit is counted. It is very helpful for the students to acknowledge being touched by halting any further action, but this is not required by the rules.

Advance Lunge

Since defenders often retreat to avoid being touched by a lunging fencer, the attacker may put together an advance and a lunge in order to reach the target. There should be no pause between the advance and the lunge, and the right of way should be obtained by extending the foil arm during the advance. The beginner should be careful to make the advance only long enough to make up for the distance that the defender will retreat.

Disengagement Attacks

When a fencer's direct attacks are being repeatedly parried, it will soon occur to the attacker that the parry must somehow be avoided. One method for doing this is by means of a two-part action called the *disengagement*. The first move is the extension of the foil arm to give the impression that a direct attack is being started. If this feint convinces the defender of the need to parry, the attacker then deceives the parry by lowering the point and then raising it again as the parry goes past. This disengagement is of course followed by a lunge to complete the attack.

Properly executed, the disengagement avoids any blade contact by the defender. The foil arm remains extended throughout. As the attacker, you have to convince the defender that your initial extension is a real attack that must be parried. However, when you are the defender, you must not parry a mere feint. Until you learn to distinguish between a feint and a real threat, your first response to an attack should be to retreat.

▶ **Learning Cues**

1. Extend arm to give illusion of an attack.
2. As a parry is made, lower the blade and then return it to a raised position.
3. Follow-up with a lunge to complete the attack.

▶ **Practice Suggestion**

For developing disengagement skills as well as defending skills, there is a very effective drill in which the defender may not retreat but may parry four or six. The attacker is permitted the options of direct lunge or disengagement lunge. In this drill, a well-made disengagement should touch, because the defender will be convinced that the feint is really an attack to be parried. On the other hand, a poorly made feint should get no response from the defender, and the disengagement will be easily parried. To avoid guessing by the defender, it is important for the attacker to make a number of direct attacks in a row, all of which will be parried.

Compound Parries

As an attacker's disengagement is being attempted, the defender may parry a second or even a third time in an effort to contact and deflect the blade. Combinations of parries are termed *compound parries*, and these are reflexive responses by a defender who realizes that his initial parry failed to make contact.

One-Two

A pair of parries can be deceived by an attacker who makes two disengagement movements. The first disengagement serves as a feint to draw a defender's second parry which is then deceived by the second disengagement. As with most attacks, the foil arm should remain extended throughout so as to maintain the right of way.

Counter Parries

Defensive variety is necessary against more skilled opponents. Constant use of simple parries will be answered by disengagements and one-twos. Against a direct lunge, a defender in the sixth guard position may make a clockwise rotation of his or her foil in order to contact and carry the attacking blade to a sixth parry. From a fourth guard position, the rotation is counterclockwise and terminates in a parry four.

Double

Against an opponent who utilizes counter parries, the attacker must deceive such parries by first making a feint of a direct thrust to draw the counter parry. As the parry is being made, the attacker's foil must circle in the same direction as that of the counter parry. By the use of the double, blade contact is avoided, and the accompanying lunge should deliver the touch to the target.

Low Line Parries

When an attack is aimed at the lower target, the normal parries four and six cannot be used. Instead, the defender should lower the point and move the foil hand in the direction of the attacking blade in order to deflect it. The *parry seven* is used against attacks to the lower left side (Figure 9-11), while the *parry eight* is used when the threat is to the lower right target area (Figure 9-12). As with the high parries, the hand should move horizontally and remain higher than elbow level.

Low line parries may be deceived by feinting to a low target and then disengaging to a high target. Similarly, an attack may begin with a high feint and terminate with a disengagement to the low target.

▶ **Practice Suggestions**

1. With a partner, practice counter parrying of attacks. (In this instance, the drill requires one fencer to attack in a predetermined manner in order that the one practicing the parry can have an opportunity to experiment with and learn the actual execution of the parry.)
2. Practice low line parries with a partner.

3. With a partner, practice the riposte from the parry. The partner should attack while the defender practices execution of riposte.
4. Practice riposte from disengagement.

NOTE: Once single skills have been well learned, drills that encourage a combination of the elements of the lunge, attack, parry, riposte, disengagement, advanced lunge, beat, advance, and retreat should be practiced.

Beat Attack

When an opponent is standing on-guard with an extended arm and a threatening point directed at your chest, a beat action can be used to remove this right of way. The *beat* is a sharp blow to the defending blade to knock it aside momentarily and create an opening for an attack. Be careful not to wind up and thereby telegraph your intention to beat.

STRATEGIES

1. Your first concern should be to make it difficult for your opponent to hit you. The maintenance of good and consistent distance is important, so never let your opponent get closer than full lunge distance unless it is part of your game plan.
2. A retreat is the simplest and most effective defense against any attack; use it more often than you use your parries.

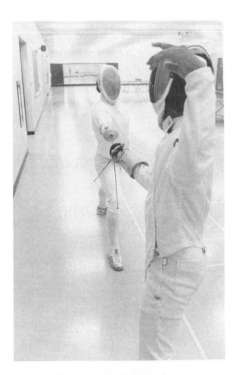

FIGURE 9-11 The simple parry seven being made by the near fencer.

FIGURE 9-12 The simple parry eight being made by the far fencer.

3. Offensively, you must analyze what your opponent is doing to stop your attacks. You cannot devise a good attack plan if you have not been able to recognize the defense being used against you.

4. Generally speaking, use the simplest attack that has a chance of scoring. Get more complex only if the opponent forces you to.

5. Attack with confidence as though you expect to hit. Too often the beginner is unsure and attacks timidly.

6. When you parry, the right of way is yours only if you riposte immediately. Be unpredictable in your defense—sometimes parry, sometimes retreat.

7. Remember that every fencer is different, and you must adjust your game accordingly. Unorthodox fencers and left-handers can be problems, and experience with a variety of opponents is necessary for anyone who wishes to become a good fencer.

8. Use each practice bout as an opportunity to improve your observational and fencing techniques. Don't try to win at the cost of damaging your hard-earned fundamental skills. In practice bouts it is better to lose while perfecting a particular skill or strategy than to win by resorting to sloppy tactics. Above all, enjoy each bout, and be sure to shake hands afterwards.

MODIFICATIONS FOR SPECIAL POPULATIONS

Orthopedically Impaired

1. Wheelchair users may compete from their chairs.
2. If only one student needs a wheelchair, let the opponent use a regular classroom chair.
3. Students on crutches, canes, or walkers can use modified foils, such as whiffleball bats with a soft protective tip. As an alternative, a crutch or cane with a soft protective covering over the tip can be used instead of the foil.

Mentally Impaired

1. Color code the opponent's body areas, e.g., trunk high, low, to reinforce appropriate target areas.
2. Allow additional practice sessions to reinforce safety precautions.

Sensory Impaired

1. Individual evaluation must be made as to the appropriateness of fencing for the blind student. Blind students might compete against stationary targets that would provide audio feedbacks based on position of score, e.g., high, too low, out of range.
2. Minimal modifications would be needed for the deaf and hard of hearing. Instructional consider-

ations would include ability to use sign language, videos, pictures.

SAFETY CONSIDERATIONS

Fencing ranks among the safest of all sports, but common sense must be exercised at all times. The following safety measures should be adhered to while participating in this sport.

1. Any time that partners face one another, a mask must be worn.
2. The tip of the foil must be covered with adhesive tape or a rubber tip.
3. Watch out for broken blades. A blade can break at the slightest touch and the jagged end cause injury.
4. Masks that show rust or weak places and jackets that are torn should be discarded.
5. A fencing half-jacket or full jacket should be worn in class; sweatshirts offer no protection against a broken blade.

TERMINOLOGY

Advance A step taken toward an opponent while remaining on-guard.

Advance lunge An attack that combines an advance and a lunge.

Attack The initial forward movement of the weapon with an extended arm to threaten the opponent's valid target.

Beat attack A sharp blow given to the opponent's blade to create an opening for an attack.

Bout A competition between two fencers.

Corps-à-corps Physical contact between two fencers at close quarters.

Counter parry A circular parry that deflects an attacking blade into a line opposite that of a simple parry.

Cutover A disengagement attack in which the blade is lifted over the defender's foil. Also called a *coupé*.

Deceive To offensively avoid contact by a defender's blade.

Director The official in charge of a jury. In Europe the director is called the president.

Disengagement An attack in which the blade passes under the defender's foil.

Double An attack comprised of a feint followed by a complete circle around the defender's counter parry.

Double touch A situation in which both fencers have equal right of way and both have landed touches. No point is awarded.

Doubtful touch This is the decision whenever the polling of the jury does not produce a majority opinion. No point is awarded.

Engagement A held contact of blades when neither fencer is attacking.

Épée One of the three competitive weapons. The bell is

large and the entire body is a valid target; there is no right of way. Only the electrical version is used in meets.

Feint Any movement of the blade or body that obtains a parry or other reaction from an opponent.

F.I.E. Fédération Internationale d'Escrime—the world governing body for amateur fencing.

Flèche (pronounced *flesh*) An attack in which the rear foot crosses in front of the leading foot. It is often followed by a short run because of the momentum developed. Potentially dangerous, this attack is not recommended for beginners.

Infighting Close combat that is permitted so long as there is no body contact or other violations such as use of the left hand or turning the back.

Invitation Any deliberate exposure of target that is intended to draw an opponent's attack.

Judge An official who stands beside one fencer to watch for touches made upon the other fencer.

Jury Consists of the director and the four judges in a match or tournament.

Line A target area; may be referred to as high or low, inside or outside. "In-line" defines a defender's position when the arm is fully extended and the point is threatening.

Low line That part of the target below the defender's hand level in the on-guard stance.

Lunge A means of delivering a touch by moving the leading foot substantially forward while the rear foot remains stationary.

Maître d'armes Fencing master: a coach who has undergone a period of formal training and has passed an accrediting examination.

Match A contest between two teams in any weapon. A series of bouts between the fencers of two different teams.

Meet A full tournament between teams or individuals. A series of matches, bouts, or pools of bouts.

N.F.C.A.A. National Fencing Coaches Association of America.

On-guard The position assumed by a fencer when ready to fence.

One-two An attack made up of two disengagements.

Parry Deflection of an attacking blade. It is *simple* if it moves directly to the blade and *counter* if it describes a circle.

Phrase Any unbroken series of offensive and defensive exchanges.

Pool A group of fencers who compete in round-robins.

Redoublement A new action made after the original attack is parried but no riposte is forthcoming.

Remise An immediate continuation of an attack that has been parried. A touch by remise can be allowed only if the riposte misses or is delayed.

Retreat A step taken backward away from an opponent.

Right of way A fundamental rule in foil and sabre that determines which fencer has priority in a phrase.

Riposte The return action that follows a successful parry.

Sabre (saber) One of the three competitive weapons. The cutting edge is used more often than the point, and the target area is all parts of the body above the hip level, including the head and arms.

Salle d'armes Fencing school or club.

Salute A universal gesture used before practice or a bout. A simple version is the raising of the weapon to a vertical position, bell at face level.

Strip The fencing area. It may be of any material and is marked with the boundary and warning lines. In electric foil and épée fencing, the strip may be covered with wire mesh that grounds touches made on the floor.

U.S.F.A. United States Fencing Association, the governing body that organizes U.S. fencing competitions and develops rules.

SELECTED REFERENCES

American Fencing Magazine. Colorado Springs, CO: United States Fencing Association, Inc., 1990.

Bower, M. *Foil Fencing.* Dubuque, IA: Wm. C. Brown Publishers, 1990.

Gaugler, W.M. *Fencing Everyone.* Winston-Salem, NC: Hunter Textbooks, Inc., 1987.

Shaff, J. *Fencing.* New York: Atheneum, 1982.

Simonian, C. *Basic Foil Fencing.* Dubuque, IA: Kendall-Hunt Publishing Company, 1982.

U.S.F.A. Rules Book. Colorado Springs, CO: United States Fencing Association, Inc., 1990.

10 FIELD HOCKEY

THIS CHAPTER WILL ENABLE YOU TO:

▶ *Identify the field markings.*
▶ *Describe the basic rules of the game.*
▶ *Analyze and demonstrate the techniques of holding the stick, dribbling, the hit, fielding, various passes, the tackle, the dodge, the penalty corner, the free hit, defense hit, and push in.*
▶ *Identify and describe the common goalkeeping techniques.*
▶ *Describe basic offensive and defensive tactics.*
▶ *Understand and use the basic terminology.*

NATURE AND PURPOSE

Field hockey, recognized as one of the most popular sports throughout the world, is an Olympic sport for both men and women. In the United States it has been played predominantly by women; however, men do play in various locations. The United States Field Hockey Association, through its sponsorship of youth hockey programs, encourages both girls and boys to become involved in the sport.

The game is played by two teams of 11 players usually designated as forwards, midfielders (links), defensive backs, sweeper, and goalie. The forwards are offensive players and therefore must be quick, possess good stickwork and ball control skills, and must shoot well. The midfielders serve as links transforming the game from defense to offense. Midfielders must be in good physical condition to play both offense and defense; they must be good playmakers to set up the forwards and sure tacklers to stop the offensive thrust of the opponent. Defensive backs must be aggressive and possess good marking skills in addition to being strong tacklers. The sweeper, the last line before the goalie, directs play and shores up the defense. Sweepers must have patience, good fielding skills, and a "nose" for the ball. The last link in the defensive chain is the goalie who must have catlike reflexes and be aggressive. Although some players are by nature offensive or defensive, an emphasis should be placed on total team offense and defense.

Field hockey has changed significantly in recent years. Although a traditional 5–3–2–1–G alignment is still used, most teams are moving to a style of play that is more characteristic of soccer. Spectators may expect to see a variety of system alignments (3–3–3–1–G, 4–2–3–1–G) being employed by a team based on the talents of individual players (Figure 10-1).

Each player carries a hockey stick, which is the

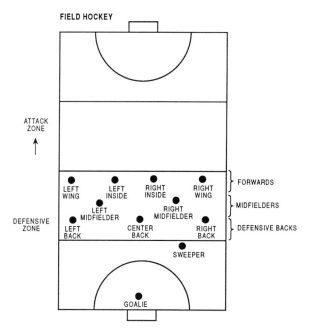

FIELD HOCKEY

FIGURE 10-1 Starting alignment of 4-3-2-1-G. Note team balance (depth), possible passing routes, and opportunities for 2-on-1 or 3-on-2 situations.

only means employed to move the ball in this game. The one exception to this rule is that the goalkeeper has kicking privileges.

Goals count one point and can be scored only if an attacker's stick touches the ball inside the striking circle. The official game is played in two periods of 30 minutes each, and 5 minutes between halves, at which time the teams change ends. NOTE: There is some variance in rules for high school, college, and international play.

Because of the vigorous nature of the game and the skill, coordination, and conditioning needed, field hockey is an acceptable activity for both boys

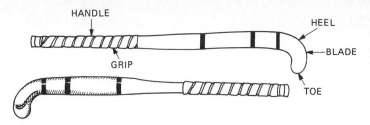

FIGURE 10-2 The hockey stick, right and left view.

and girls and men and women in a school or college physical education program. Whether played by all boys, all girls, or on a coeducational basis, it is important to emphasize the rules of play, particularly those governing the hockey stick. Emphasis should also be placed on the wearing of shin guards and other protective gear.

For coeducational play, any or all of the following rule modifications may be made:

1. Use a larger, softer rubber ball rather than the official field hockey ball (especially in youth hockey).
2. Place girls at every other position to encourage passes to boys and/or to girls.
3. Reduce the size of the field and the number of players (6 on 6) so the emphasis is on skill rather than on speed or strength.
4. Let all penalty shots be taken by girls, the corner pass by boys (or vice versa).
5. Eliminate the hit and allow only a push.
6. Eliminate the flick when shooting at goal.

As in soccer, an indoor version of field hockey has become very popular. Indoor hockey is played on a gym floor (similar to street hockey) with 6 players on a team. With large classes, use the additional players for sideline play. There are rule modifications involved with indoor play (see Appendix A, Field Hockey, USFHA), the most significant of which eliminates the hit and thereby encourages controlled passing with a push pass. Indoor hockey can be an excellent rainy day or cold weather activity as well as a complete unit.

EQUIPMENT

The Ball

The official ball is hard and slightly larger than a baseball. For class purposes a seamless polyurethane ball is most practical.

The Stick

The hockey stick ranges from 26 inches (youth sizes) to 37 inches in length and generally weighs from 16 to 23 ounces. The thin portion above the heel has a wrapping (usually fiberglass although other materials are used) around the wood to give greater strength to this critical area. The blade is generally made of mulberry wood and is somewhat shorter today than it used to be. The left side of the blade is flat and is used for contact with the ball. The right side of the blade is rounded and may not be used for contact with the ball at any time (Figure 10-2).

When selecting the stick, it is important that the handle be comfortable, thin, and strong. The stick should be light enough to facilitate technique and ease of control. To determine the suitable stick length, the individual should stand, grasp the stick as for a hit, and swing it in front of the body. The stick should "feel" comfortable and should not hit the ground behind the ball at contact. For elementary age physical education classes there are junior hockey sticks available which are shorter and lighter than typical adult sticks.

Shin Guards and Pads

Light shin guards are wise protection for all field players. The padding should cover the ankle bone as well as the shins. Goalkeeper's pads should cover the leg from the thigh down. In addition to pads, kickers are worn to provide padding over the goalie's field shoe. Required protection for goalies also includes a helmet with a face guard and throat protector. Chest and elbow pads are also encouraged.

PLAYING FIELD

The field is about the size of a football field, 100 yards long and 60 yards wide, with a goal at each end (Figure 10-3). Goal posts are 4 yards apart and 7

FIGURE 10-3 The hockey field.

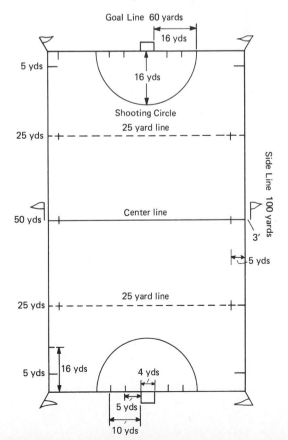

feet high, joined by a cross bar. The posts and cross bars should have a square front and be painted white. The goal is usually enclosed with a net or screening.

The striking circle is placed on the field by starting with a straight line drawn 16 yards in front of the goal and 4 yards long. This line is continued to the end line by quarter-circle arcs of a 16-yard radius with the goal posts as centers.

BASIC RULES

The following basic rules may require modification for coeducational play and perhaps additional rules for safety.

Fouls

1. Taking part in the game without a stick.
2. Using the rounded side of the stick.
3. Advancing a ball off the body. NOTE: Only the goalkeeper is permitted to kick the ball or block the ball with the body. The goalie shall not be penalized if the ball is deflected off the body, provided it is not dangerous to another player and the goalie contacts the ball within the striking circle.
4. Hitting the ball in a dangerous manner (i.e., into a player at close range, a hard hit that rises, or a ball that is hit on the fly).
5. Using the stick in a dangerous manner (i.e., following through into another player, tripping, or slashing).
6. Obstruction: placing the body (feet, shoulder, or any part) between an opponent and the ball. A player may not obstruct an opponent from playing the ball.
7. Stick obstruction: interfering with an opponent's stick (i.e., strike, hook, hold).
8. Pushing, charging, shoving, tripping, or in any way interfering with an opponent.
9. Offsides: When within a team's offensive 25 yards a player may not be ahead of the ball unless there are two defenders between the player and the goal. This does not prevent a player running forward to meet a pass after the ball has been hit.

Penalties for Fouls

A. Outside the circle. A free hit is awarded to the team fouled against on the spot of the foul.
B. Inside the circle.
   1. Foul by the attack—a defense hit which is outside the circle and 16 yards out from the end line. This also applies when the foul occurs outside the circle but within 16 yards of the offensive goal. The 16-yard distance is designated by a hash mark on the sideline.
   2. Foul by the defense.
      a. A penalty corner is awarded to the attacking team.
      b. A penalty stroke is awarded if the foul stopped a sure goal or was flagrant.

Out-of-bounds Play

In all cases the line is considered "in the field of play" whether it be the circle, sideline, end, or goal line. The umpire must decide which team touched the ball last, since there is no provision in the rules for co-responsibility (off two sticks).

A. Over the sideline. A hit-in (hit or push) by a member of the team opposite that of the player who last touched the ball before it crossed the sideline.
B. Over the end line but not between the goal posts.
   1. Off the attack—a defense hit.
   2. Off the defense.
      a. When the ball is unintentionally hit over the end line—a long hit.
      b. When the ball is intentionally hit over the end line—a penalty corner.
      c. Over the end line between the goal posts.
         (1) A legal goal when the ball was touched by the stick of an attack inside the striking circle. Play resumed by a push back on the center line. The goal counts even if the ball was last touched by the stick or person of the defense.
         (2) When the ball was not touched by a stick of the attack inside the circle and:
            (a) was touched by a stick of the defense—a long hit is awarded.
            (b) was last touched by a stick of the attack—a defense hit is awarded.

SUGGESTED LEARNING SEQUENCE

There are numerous ways to arrange the sequence of skill development for field hockey. In the one proposed, dribbling and passing skills are introduced early along with teaching students to move into space and use support passing to beat a defender. Fielding should be taught with the push pass and hit so that students can stop a ball coming towards them. As a general guide, it is best to introduce a technique along with its definition, a rule that may apply, and some strategy involved.

A. Nature and purpose
B. Conditioning aspects—plan drills and exercises that might be related to movements found in field hockey. Emphasis of all areas of fitness, particularly upper body (forearm, wrist) strength, agility, speed and flexibility.
   1. Circuit training with stickwork
   2. Footwork and acceleration moves

C. Basic game concepts
 1. Field of play
 2. Use of equipment
 3. Playing courtesies
D. Skills and strategy—introduce rules and terminology as well as combination skills and strategies at most appropriate times.
 1. Skills
  a. Gripping the stick
  b. Dribbling
  c. Push pass and fielding
  d. Hitting
  e. Flicking
  f. Dodging
  g. Tackling
  h. Goalkeeping
 2. Tactics and strategy
  a. Offensive playing hints and passing combinations
  b. Defensive playing hints
  c. Game tactics: Push back, free hit, defense hit, hit-in, penalty corner, penalty stroke, long hit.

SKILLS AND TECHNIQUES

The proper relationship between ball and feet is most important and can only be gained by always practicing skills while one is moving. The essence of stickwork is footwork. Make the feet assume the proper relationship to the ball, not the ball to the feet. Be able to see the ball while also scanning the field for open space and passing options.

Gripping the Stick

There are three basic grips used in field hockey. The fundamental position is used for the basic dribble as well as hitting, pushing, and fielding. A grip change is required for reverse stick contact on the ball as in the Indian dribble. A third grip is used in defensive play.

1. *Fundamental position.* With the heel of the stick resting on the ground in front of the body, allow the top of the handle to fall into the fingers of the left hand. This is basically a handshake position on the stick. Place the right hand 6 to 8 inches below the left. Grip the stick easily so the V formed by the thumb and index finger of both hands is in line with the toe of the stick (Figure 10-4).
2. *Indian dribble grip.* A slight variation of the fundamental grip occurs when the player executes an Indian dribble or any reverse stick action of the ball. In this grip the left hand slides right slightly. To assure correct positioning, place the stick flatside on the ground, reach down and place the V of the left hand on top of the stick (Figure 10-5). The right hand assumes its normal positioning. This grip allows the left hand to rotate the stick over the ball. The right simply acts as a sleeve allowing the stick to rotate in it.
3. *Defensive grip.* Slide the left hand slightly left from the fundamental position. In this grip the V of the left hand comes on the handle when the flat side of the stick is up (Figure 10-6).

FIGURE 10-4 Fundamental grip. Note the handshake positioning on the stick with V of left hand on side of stick when toe is up.

FIGURE 10-5 Assuming correct positioning for the Indian dribble grip. Note V of left hand is on rounded side of stick.

FIGURE 10-6 Defensive grip. Note the V of left hand is on flat side of stick.

FIGURE 10-7 Dribble position. Ball is on the stick in front of the body. Player's eyes scan ahead.

▶ **Learning Cues**

1. The stick must be held firmly but comfortably.
2. Adjust grip appropriately according to the skill executed.

Dribbling

In the dribble the fundamental grip position is used with the body in a crouched position for running. The stick is on the ball which is in front of the body and slightly off to the right side (Figure 10-7). The arms are relaxed and away from the body with the right arm extended beyond the left. The ball is moved forward by the stick as the player begins to run. The feet should stay behind the ball, and a change of direction is initiated by accelerating the feet in that direction. The ball should be kept close to the stick unless a player is in open field, in which case the ball can be pushed slightly ahead.

Indian Zigzag Dribble.   This dribble is generally used in crowded areas and before attempting to move around an opponent. The ball is positioned in front of the body and is rolled over on alternate sides by the use of forehand and reverse stick taps (Figure 10-8). This movement uses the Indian dribble grip. The zigzag motion with the stick around the

FIGURE 10-8   Zigzag dribble: forehand action on the ball; stick rolls over ball with reverse stick action.

ball allows the dribbler to disguise the dribble with faking moves, making it difficult for the opponent to tackle.

▶ **Learning Cues**

1. Keep the feet behind the ball.
2. Stay low and reach out for the ball.
3. Keep the stick close to the ball. Move the ball by accelerating with the feet.

▶ **Practice Suggestions**

1. Begin by moving in a straight line—push the ball ahead with an emphasis on footwork and ball control. Concentrate on staying low by bending at the knees and keeping the head up. As they dribble, have the students call out the number of fingers held up by the teacher.
2. Move on diagonals and into open space with a change of direction. Emphasize that the feet initiate the action when changing direction.
3. Practice the technique of the Indian dribble stationary, then in a straight line, with direction change and around cones.
4. Use a designated grid area with 6 to 10 students and have them dribble around each other. Encourage dribbling into open space. Place cones in the grid and see how many cones the students can dribble to in one minute.

Fielding the Ball

The ball should be fielded or controlled when it comes to a player before it is passed or played. A "two touch" sequence is used when thinking about fielding and passing. The first touch stops the ball, and the immediate second touch advances the ball. The right hand slides further down the stick (Figure 10-9).

▶ **Learning Cues**

1. Line the body up behind an approaching ball in a low position.
2. Let the ball come to the stick. Absorb the ball by having a "soft" right hand. Control deflections.
3. The left hand angles forward to trap the ball in the stick. Second touch the ball with pass or dribble.

▶ **Practice Suggestions**

1. Have a partner roll a ball to a player with a stick. Emphasize lining up, absorbing, and trapping the ball.
2. Have a partner field a ball pushed or hit from another.
3. Introduce fielding on the move, i.e., shuttle passing, passing down the field with a partner.
4. Introduce a passive defender and play two-versus-one keep-away. Later, as proficiency in fielding is gained, add an active defender.
5. Add passing drills that encourage give-and-go passing, i.e., player A receives a pass from player B, A passes back to B, cutting to receive and hit on goal.

Push Passing

The push pass is used for short, accurate passing or shooting when there is no time or necessity to hit the ball. The pass can be executed quickly off the dribble or after receiving a pass. There is no backswing on this skill because the stick stays on the ball as it is pushed forward. The approach on this skill involves starting with the left shoulder and foot forward in the direction of the pass, and the body in a low position (Figure 10-10). The ball should be contacted opposite the left foot.

FIGURE 10-9 Fielding the ball. Left hand angles forward as right hand absorbs the ball.

FIGURE 10-10 Push pass positioning: left shoulder in direction of pass and low positioning.

▶ **Learning Cues**

1. With the body in the correct approach position, extend the arms out away from the body. A firm right arm pushes the ball out while the left wrist pulls the stick back.
2. Transfer the body weight from back to front foot and finish with the head over a bent left knee.
3. The right hand pushes the stick through to the intended direction of the pass.

▶ **Practice Suggestions**

1. In a stationary position, push pass with a partner. Emphasize arm extension and follow-through.
2. Pass the ball off the dribble to a partner as in a shuttle formation.
3. Move into give-and-go passing and keep-away as presented in #4, #5 for fielding.

Hitting

The hit is a strong, hard skill for passing and shooting. The fundamental grip position is used, but the hands need to be brought together at the top of the stick. The stick swings in a perpendicular plane with a hip to hip pendulum-like motion in the direction the ball is to travel. The ball should be contacted opposite the left foot. On the backswing and follow-through, the toe of the stick is up (Figure 10-11). This is primarily a left-sided skill with a straight left arm pulling the stick through with a weight transfer onto the front (left) foot. To be assured of an accurate hit, allow the hands to guide the stick in the direction of pass.

FIGURE 10-11 The hit. Note the backswing and the beginning of weight transfer.

▶ **Learning Cues**

1. Bring hands together (fundamental grip position).
2. Transfer the weight to front foot. Initiate a left arm pull.
3. Let the arms swing freely.
4. Follow through with arms to intended direction of pass. Right hand helps guide the stick as the left arm pulls through.

▶ **Practice Suggestions**

1. Let the arms swing the stick in a pendulum fashion. Recognize a relaxed and freely flowing arm position. Practice left arm swings.
2. Hit to a fence (or rebound board) and follow through with the stick to the fence.
3. In a stationary position practice the hit with a partner. Add hitting on the move (i.e., shuttle, passing down the field, dribbling, and hitting on the goal).

Flicking

There is also no backswing on this skill, which is executed like the push pass. However, in the flick the ball is slightly in front of the body so the stick can be placed under the ball. The left hand brings the top of the stick back and behind the right hand, which causes the stick face to open. Therefore, when the stroke is executed the ball will rise with the height depending on the angle of the stick. The flick is used as a technique for lifting the ball over a defender's stick, for penalty strokes, and for shooting. The flick is especially valuable for shooting at close range since the ball comes off the ground. It is possible to execute the flick with a moving ball, but it is more difficult.

▶ **Learning Cues**

1. The stroke and follow-through are executed like the push pass.
2. Angle the stick by bringing the left hand back behind the right. This opens the stick face up and causes the ball to lift up.

▶ **Practice Suggestions**

1. In a stationary position practice the flick with a partner or into the goal.
2. Flick the ball to goal off a dribble.
3. Practice penalty strokes.

Dodging

The dodge is used when a player in possession of the ball wishes to evade an opponent who is approaching from the front. Because this technique is so useful, players should learn a variety of dodges. It is particularly important for beginners to learn how

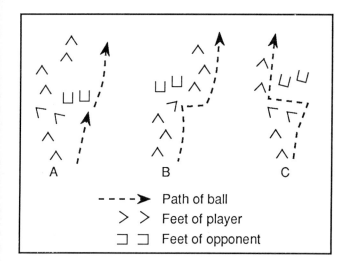

FIGURE 10-12   Diagrams of dodges: (A) non-stick side dodge, (B) reverse stick dodge, (C) pull left dodge.

to dodge, thereby avoiding the natural tendency to move directly into an opponent—which is illegal. Teachers should introduce dodging at an early stage in the unit and provide for continued practice.

Non-Stick Side Dodge.   The player in possession of the ball sends the ball ahead and close to the non-stick side of the approaching opponent. The player runs to the stick side of the opponent. In other words, the ball goes right, and the player goes left (Figure 10-12A). This dodge (which is sometimes called Y dodge) is easily executed and very successful because it is played to the opponent's non-stick side. However, control of the ball is important as possession is temporarily lost.

Reverse Stick Dodge.   Before the opponent can reach the ball, the player in possession pulls the ball with a reverse stick action laterally to the right. After this move, the player accelerates forward by the opponent (Figure 10-12B). The advantage of this dodge is it also goes to the non-stick side of the opponent, but with the player remaining in possession of the ball at all times. However, it is a more difficult dodge to execute.

Pull to the Left.   On this dodge both the ball and player go to the left of the approaching opponent. Shortly before the ball is within reach of the opponent, the player pulls the ball laterally to the left past the opponent's stick (Figure 10-12C). Upon completion of this move, the player should accelerate forward by the opponent. During this dodge the ball remains in the player's possession; however, the timing must be accurate and the ball must be played laterally left, not diagonally, to avoid the opponent's stick.

▶ **Learning Cues**

1. Execute the dodge just before the opponent is within reach of the ball. Remember that both

players are moving, thus this point will be considerably farther away than expected.
2. Keep the ball in control on the dodge to assure player possession.
3. Execute the dodge right off the dribble. Accelerate by the defender and cut in behind the defender to eliminate opponent recovery.
4. On lateral pulls turn the feet and run with the ball. Avoid slide stepping.

▶ **Practice Suggestions**

1. Practice dodge moves against a cone or a stationary defender. Be sure to emphasize lateral pulls as needed and footwork.
2. Dodge a passive defender who is standing but may use a stick to reach. Encourage early dodging by going against a defender using an ice hockey stick to extend the reach. The player must dodge before getting within a stick's reach of the opponent.
3. Carry this into one-versus-one play with an aggressive defender.

Tackling

The tackle is a technique used in attempting to take the ball away from an opponent. The key to becoming an accomplished tackler is preparation and patience.

In the preparation a defender must establish a basic athletic stance: feet shoulder width apart, knees flexed slightly, head up with eyes watching the ball, and feet moving. The stick is between the feet, down low to the ground in a defensive grip to permit proper stick action on the tackle (Figure 10-13). As the opponent approaches, the defender

FIGURE 10-13   Defensive positioning. Note the stick is down with player in a balanced position.

should establish an overplaying position (to the left of the opponent) which forces the opponent to dribble into the defender's stick side. If the opponent dribbles to the right, the defender must quickly move the feet to constitute forcing the opponent right. If the opponent does get to the non-stick side (left) of the defender, the tackle must be made with a reverse stick, which is more difficult.

The defender's feet must be moving and giving with the opponent before a tackle can be made. This will allow the defender to be patient, and find the opportune time to steal the ball from the opponent. Caution must be made to avoid overcommitment and lunging which makes the defender susceptible to being beaten with an opponent's dodge.

There are two basic approaches to tackling:

1. *Jab Tackle* (Figure 10-14)
   As the defender retreats with the opponent, extend the stick with the left hand to jab under the ball. If the attempt is unsuccessful, resume the position of two hands on the stick and attempt again. Fake jabs may be successful in confusing the opponent.
2. *Block Tackle* (Figure 10-15)
   The defender gives with the opponent, stick down, and allows the opponent to bring the ball to the defender. For this tackle the stick is held with the fundamental grip, and the defender extends the stick with two hands to block the ball. Avoid swinging and chopping with the stick.

▶ **Learning Cues**

1. Overplay to force opponent to the stick side.
2. Keep the feet moving with the opponent. Time the tackle so it is unexpected.
3. Continually jab and retreat, pressuring the ball.

▶ **Practice Suggestions**

1. Without sticks and balls, have the defenders practice footwork against an opponent.

2. Have a defender move with an opponent who is dribbling straight ahead with the ball. The defender may not tackle, but should watch for the appropriate time to tackle. The defender can also make jab fakes.
3. Allow a defender to make a tackle against an opponent moving at half speed. Incorporate block and jab tackles.
4. Move into one-versus-one play with the defender tackling an aggressive dribbler. After the defender tackles and assumes possession, accelerate away from the opponent. Can also build in a passing option after possession is gained.

Goalkeeping

Goalkeeping requires different skills from other positions. The goalkeeper must be agile, quick, and have good concentration and anticipation. The goalie is well protected with a mask, gloves, pads for the legs, and padded kickers which go over the regular field shoe. The goalie has the privilege of using the feet for stopping and directing the ball and may also stop the ball with the hand and other parts of the body, as long as it is not batted or deflected in a dangerous manner.

Stance. A basic athletic stance with a few modifications would describe the goalie stance. The feet are shoulder width apart, weight evenly distributed on the balls of the feet, legs slightly flexed, a slight lean forward, the arms hanging in front with the forearms parallel to the ground. Grasp the stick with palms facing out; the blade will be up and slightly pointing away from the right goal post. The head should be up watching the ball.

Goalkeeping Principles. The goalkeeper is the last line of defense. There are three important principles to follow and practice.[1]

---

[1] V. Gros. *Inside Field Hockey* (Chicago: Contemporary Books, 1979), pp. 58–59.

FIGURE 10-14 Jab tackle.

FIGURE 10-15 Block tackle.

1. In order to defend the goal line, the goalkeeper moves with small steps on an arc from post to post. This allows the goalkeeper to narrow the angle to goal and thereby eliminate shooting space.
2. The goalkeeper should be set when a shot is made. This will allow the goalie to react to the shot. If moving on the shot, the goalie could be caught off balance and unable to change direction to react to the ball.
3. The goalkeeper should line up with the ball; i.e., the ball should be in line with the goalkeeper and the goal line.

Technique. The beginning goalkeeper should meet the ball with legs together and "give" on impact so the ball drops almost dead. It is then cleared with the inside of the foot or the toe, hard and accurately, to a space away from the opponent (usually along the sideline) or to a teammate ready to receive and relay the ball up the field. On the kick to clear the ball, the goalie must have the head over the ball and hold a balanced position (Figure 10-16). After contact the knee follows through upward to bring the foot back into place alongside the other. With more experience, the goalie may learn to step out and redirect the ball with one foot, especially a well-directed shot that is impossible to get behind with two feet. The stick is used only for emergency clears.

FIGURE 10-16 Goalkeeper clear. Note the head over the ball and high knee follow-through.

▶ **Practice Suggestions**

Students should always wear protective equipment when practicing goalkeeping or in a scrimmage.

1. Reaction drills. Roll balls to the right, straight on, and to the left one at a time but quickly after each goalie clear. Emphasis is on getting behind the ball and maintaining balance and control.
2. Practice the application of basic goalkeeping principles. This can be accomplished by having a player push or hit on goal. Use caution to avoid players hitting when in very close to the goalie; instead encourage players to use the more accurate push pass rather than the hit.
3. Place a goalie in the goal area with a 3-on-3 or 5-on-5 scrimmage situation. Emphasis should be placed on clearing the ball into space away from the rushing attack.

PLAYING STRATEGIES

Offensive Strategy

Once the ball is in a team's possession, the players on that team must think about advancing the ball toward the goal. Advancement is executed by dribbling and through a series of passes. No matter what formation is being used, the following key principles must be employed if the attack is to be successful.

1. *Movement in Space.*
   a. Players with the ball—a player in possession should move the ball into free space. This movement should result in the drawing of a defender, in which case the player should look for further options.
   b. Players off the ball—the responsibility here is for a player off the ball to move into a helping position for the player with the ball. These players are in a "support" role and need to position themselves in open space where the ball can be passed. A player standing behind a defender is considered in "dead space" where a teammate will have to pass through the defender in order to make the pass.
2. *Passing.* The ability to execute an accurate and well-paced pass to a teammate is the very essence of field hockey. Passing includes the responsibilities discussed earlier of moving the ball to open space and support play. Teams that employ a hit-and-chase style of play will have minimal opportunities to establish a cohesive offensive plan. The team having the ability to make accurate, precise passes and maintain possession of the ball will have the most scoring opportunities and will control the tempo of the game.
   At any time during a game a player should have 2 to 3 avenues available to execute a pass if

the team has established good field balance and depth (i.e., relationship of forwards, midfielders, and defense). Considerable practice time should be allowed for passing in combinations of 2, 3, or 4 players. Drills should be developed that include two-versus-one, three-versus-two, or four-versus-three situations where the passer and players without the ball must confront and get around a defender.

3. *Scoring Ability.* The team that wins is the team scoring the most goals. A constant offensive pressure employed by all members of the team will usually result in more scoring opportunities. Players must be able to get shots off quickly and accurately, and follow up on rebounds.

4. *Individual Ball Control.* Although creating space and passing are the most essential elements of the game, there are circumstances where an offensive player must be able to get by a defender (one-versus-one) while carrying the ball. Successful dodging, acceleration, stick and body fakes while maintaining tight ball control are necessities in developing success in the one-versus-one situation.

Defensive Strategies

Once the ball is in the possession of the opposing team, then all players on the team without the ball must focus on defensive strategy. Defense involves total concentration on the game and an awareness of the offensive players in the vicinity. In addition to the principles previously discussed, the good defender must understand several others.

1. *Pressure on the ball.* The first responsibility on defense is to provide constant pressure to the player in possession of the ball. When applying this pressure it is important to channel the offensive player to a specific direction. In most instances this should result in forcing the opposing player to the strong side or stick side. An exception would occur with left side defensive players who generally would channel the opponent to the sideline.

2. *Marking.* The second responsibility on defense is to apply pressure on the next opponent most likely to gain possession of the ball. Being able to mark an opponent without the ball in order to prevent that player from receiving a pass or to decoy that player is good defensive strategy. In such a position it is important to know the position of the ball and the location of your own goal. The defensive player should stand ball side and goal side of the opponent when marking.

3. *Covering.* If an offensive player gets behind a defender assigned coverage, then another defender must be prepared to move in and accept the responsibility. The sweeper is most frequently found in a covering role. Once the opponent

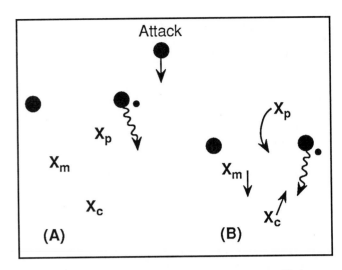

FIGURE 10-17 Defensive roles: (A) X_p pressure player with the ball; X_m marking ball side, X_c covering goal side; (B) when X_p is beaten and X_c moves to pick up the free offensive player while X_p recovers.

moves past a defender, it is important for that defender to switch into an unoccupied position (to cover) or to recover and catch the attacker (Figure 10-17).

4. *Transition.* Being able to switch from offense to defense without a moment's delay is going to save valuable yards. It may also make the difference in regaining possession of a ball momentarily lost and turning it back to your advantage. The reverse is also true in changing from defense to offense. Upon changing possession the defense needs to accelerate immediately into space looking for passing options.

Situational Game Tactics

Push Back. The game is started with a push back at the beginning, at half time, and after a goal.

Formation. Both teams line up in any manner on their own respective halves. The individual taking the push back must straddle the center line. All opposing players must be 5 yards away.

Execution. The ball must be moved backwards (any distance before advancing forward). Emphasis must be placed on an accurate, well-paced pass.

Penalty Stroke. The penalty stroke is awarded to the attacking team when a foul (intentional or unintentional) is committed by the defending team inside the circle and a sure goal is prevented, or for a flagrant foul inside the circle.

Formation. The penalty shot is taken at a point 7 yards from the center of the goal line. Aside from the shorter and opposing goalie, the remaining players must remain outside the circle behind the 25-yard line until the ball is played.

The Play. The goalkeeper should be in a ready position on the goal line, not leaving the goal line or moving the feet until the ball is played. The player (on the 7-yard spot) taking the penalty shot must use a flick or a push (no backswing allowed). The referee asks the goalie, then the shooter if each player is ready and then whistles for the play to begin. The shooter has five seconds in which to execute the stroke and is allowed one stride to the ball before shooting. Faking or any other deceptive moves by either player are not allowed. After a successful goal, the play is restarted by a push back. If the try is unsuccessful, the defense is awarded a free hit from the 16-yard area.

Penalty Corner. This formation is awarded as an advantage to the attacking team. It occurs when the ball goes over the end line off a defender's stick with no attempt being made to keep it in the field of play, or when the defense fouls in the circle.

Formation. The ball is placed on the end line 10 yards from the nearer goal post on either side of the goal, according to the choice of the attacking team. A member of the attacking team hits the ball out to a designated teammate on the circle. Other attacking players arrange themselves around the circle and, when the ball is hit, move in to rush the shot and play any rebounds. There need to be additional players backing up the forwards to provide support in case the ball is missed or is hit out of the circle by the defense (Figure 10-18A).

The defending team has five players (including the goalie) who start with sticks and bodies behind the end line. No player may be nearer than 5 yards to the player hitting the ball out. These players may move as soon as the ball is hit. Usually a zone formation (Figure 10-18B) is used to defend against the initial shot. The other six members of the defending team are behind the 50-yard line, and may not cross it until the ball is hit out.

The zone formation usually involves a rusher who pressures the initial shot. This player must approach in a stick-to-stick position (defender on attack) to avoid being hit with the shot. A trailer also follows out stick-to-stick but behind the rusher in case that individual is beat. A cover moves by the goalie to assist with any rebounds and to get the ball out of scoring range. The goalie moves out from the goal line to narrow the angle and play the shot. Last but certainly not least is a post player who positions on the goal line (to the goalie's non-stick side) to stop any shots that may get past the goalie. Once support from other players is available, the defense moves into marking position on the opponents.

The Play. The designated offensive player pushes or hits the ball along the ground to a teammate who must stop the ball. After the stop the ball should be hit to goal or passed to another teammate to hit to goal. In circumstances where field hockey is played on astroturf, a corner frequently involves a stick stop. In this case after the ball is hit out, a teammate stops the ball for a second player to hit immediately. A variety of alignments and plays can be

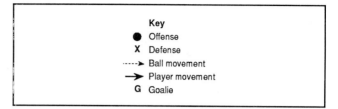

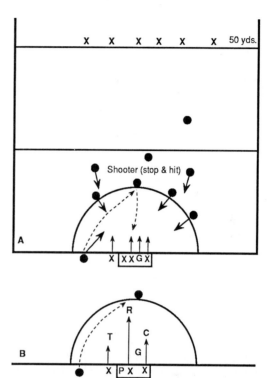

FIGURE 10-18 (A) Formation for penalty corner, (B) defensive zone alignment with rusher, trailer, cover, post, and goalie.

developed to assist in getting a shot off to goal. However, the success of a corner basically lies in a good initial pass, consequent stop, and hard, accurate hit to goal.

Free Hit. A free hit is awarded to the opposite team when a foul is committed anywhere on the field, except inside the circle (in which case a defensive hit or penalty corner is awarded according to the circumstances).

Formation. For a free hit outside the circle, the ball is placed on the spot where the breach occurred and is usually played by a midfielder or defensive player of the team fouled against. However, a forward can also play the ball especially if it can resume play quickly and help gain an advantage. For any free hit, all opposing players must stand 5 yards away. Within a team's offensive 25 yards, teammates must be 5 yards away as well. The ball must be motionless before the hit can be taken.

The Play. The player taking the free hit may hit or push pass the ball. In high school play the ball may also be lifted, but in college play the ball must remain on the ground. After taking a free hit, a player may not play the ball again until it has been touched by another player. When possible, a free hit should be taken quickly, so as to take full advantage of the penalty, before the opposing team gets placed to block the play. A free hit should be passed to a teammate or into open space for a teammate to run immediately onto the ball.

Defense Hit. A defense hit is awarded to the defending team when an attacking player hits the ball over the end line or commits a foul within the attacking 16-yard area.

Formation. The ball is placed 16 yards from the end line exactly opposite the spot where it left the field of play (and should be outside the circle). It is usually taken by a defensive player in whose area the ball is placed. The ball must be motionless, and all opposing players shall be at least 5 yards away.

The Play. The ball is put in play as for a free hit.

Hit-In. When the ball has completely rolled over the sideline by one team, the opposing team is awarded a hit-in.

Formation. The ball is placed on the sideline and can be hit or pushed in by any member of a team. The hitter may have the feet in bounds or over the sideline as the hit-in is being executed. The defending team must remain 5 yards away from the ball.

The Play. Successful execution will result when the hit-in is made quickly since the defenders are 5 yards away. Once the whistle blows indicating the out-of-bounds, the hit or push may be executed without another whistle to start play. The premium is on getting the ball to the point where it crossed the line and getting it in play. Once the ball is hit by the player, it cannot be played again by the same player until it is touched by another player.

Long Hit. A long hit is awarded to the attacking team when the ball is hit unintentionally over the end line by a defending player.

Formation. The ball is placed on a hash mark on the end line, 5 yards in from the sideline. Any team member may hit or push the ball into play, and opposing team members must position themselves 5 yards away.

The Play. The player taking the hit will try to direct the ball onto a teammate's stick or try to hit the ball across to the goal mouth if an opening is available. NOTE: A team cannot score directly off of a long hit. The defending team will attempt to block the hit with one or more players, while other players attempt to deny the ball to the opponent.

MODIFICATIONS FOR SPECIAL POPULATIONS

Orthopedically Impaired

Students who use wheelchairs will have to play in a gymnasium. Floor hockey is the recommended modification for mobility-impaired students. Contact Special Olympics for the rules of floor hockey and play hockey.

Mentally Impaired

1. Follow suggestions for Orthopedically Impaired.
2. Keep concepts and movement patterns simple.

Sensory Impaired

1. Use peer teachers for blind students.
2. Individual evaluations should be made as to the appropriateness of field hockey for blind or visually impaired students.

TERMINOLOGY

Advancing Foul committed when the ball rebounds from a player's body (i.e., kicked).

Covering A back-up defensive position used to support a teammate who is beaten or to pick up a free player moving into attack position.

Defense hit Term used to denote how play is resumed when the attacking team hits the ball over the end line or commits a foul within the attacking 16-yard area. The ball is placed 16 yards from the end line opposite the spot where it left the field or the foul was committed.

Dodge Play used to evade an opponent while maintaining control of the ball.

Dribble A skill used to move the ball on the field while maintaining constant control.

Fielding Controlling an approaching ball before it is passed or played.

Flick A skill which causes the ball to lift off the ground in a controlled fashion. Useful for shooting, lifting the ball over an opponent's stick, and in penalty strokes.

Foul Infringement of rules. Penalty may be a free hit, penalty corner, or penalty stroke.

Free hit A method used to restart play following certain infringements of rules. It is taken by a player on the team fouled against.

Hit A skill used to pass the ball which provides power and distance. This skill involves backswing into the ball.

Long hit A method used to restart play after the ball is hit unintentionally over the end line by the defending team.

Marking Guarding an opponent which is performed with ball side—goal side defensive positioning.

Non-stick side A player's left side, which is not easily defended by the stick.

Obstruction A foul made by placing the body between the opponent and the ball so as to interfere with the opponent's effort to play or reach the ball.

Offside A foul committed by a player receiving the ball while in an illegal position.

Penalty corner The play awarded to the attacking team for a foul by the defense inside the circle or when the defense intentionally hits the ball over the end line.

Penalty stroke A shot awarded to the attacking team

when a defensive player commits a foul to prevent a sure goal or flagrantly fouls the opponent in the circle.

Push back   Technique used to start a game at the beginning or at half time and to restart play after a goal.

Push pass   A skill used to pass the ball that is accurate and easy to receive. This skill has no backswing as the stick starts on the ball and extends forward.

Reverse stick   Turning the stick over to play a ball on the left.

Stick side   A player's right side where the stick can easily be extended to play the ball.

Tackle   A skill used to dislodge the ball from an opponent.

SELECTED REFERENCES

Coaching Hockey the Australian Way. The official coaching manual of the Australian Hockey Association. Suite 1, 36 Park St., South Melbourne, Australia. 1991.

USFHA Manual for Coaches. The official manual of the United States Field Hockey Association. Available from National Office, 1750 E. Boulder St., Colorado Springs, CO.

Wein, H. *The Science of Field Hockey*. Pelham Books LTD. London. 1973.

*Whitaker, D. *Coaching Hockey*. The Croowood Press. Ramsbury, Marlborough, Wiltshire. Great Britain. 1986.

Periodicals

Eagle. Published by USFHA, National Office, 1750 E. Boulder St., Colorado Springs, CO.

Audio-Visual Materials

Field Hockey: The Basic Skills. Produced and distributed by Tasmanian Film Corporation. Morris Video (distributor in U.S.), Tasmania, Australia.

Field Hockey Level I Skills. Produced by the Canadian Field Hockey Association, 333 River Rd., Vanier, Ontario, Canada.

Hockey. The Skill Revolution. Sponsored by Esanda Finance. Produced by Video Coach.

---

*Sources marked by an asterisk are available from Longstreth Sporting Goods, P.O. Box 475, Old Schuylkill Rd., Parkerford, PA 19457.

11 FOOTBALL: TOUCH AND FLAG

THIS CHAPTER WILL ENABLE YOU TO:

▶ *Discuss the key points of the games of touch and flag football.*
▶ *Identify the differences in equipment, rules, and strategy between flag football and touch football.*
▶ *Describe the rules governing play.*
▶ *Analyze and demonstrate the various skills and techniques including the stance, passing, catching, blocking, tackling, and kicking.*
▶ *Describe the offensive and defensive strategies utilized.*
▶ *Take proper safety precautions.*
▶ *Use the basic terminology associated with the game.*

NATURE AND PURPOSE

Touch Football

The object of the game of touch football (and its variation, flag football) is to advance the ball over the opponent's goal line without being "tackled." Points are awarded for a touchdown (6 points), a point after touchdown (1 point by kicking, 2 points by running or passing), a field goal (3 points), a safety (2 points), a forfeit (1 point), and by penetration in the event of a tie (1 point).

Informal games of touch football are often played in areas any size large enough to give the players running and passing room. In schools and recreation leagues, where the game is played on an organized basis, a regulation football field equipped with goal posts and yard lines is used. A regulation football is used, but players are not required to wear the heavy official football equipment because tackling is not permitted. Runners are stopped by a touch with one or both hands instead of a tackle. The fact that expensive equipment is not needed makes this game appropriate for use in recreational programs and in schools where funds are not available to outfit a regular football team.

The game retains most of the fundamentals of regular football, which gives it a popular appeal in the fall, when sport pages are filled with news about forward passes, touchdowns, and long runs. An official touch football team is usually composed of seven players, but variations (from five to eleven players) may be used with very little rules adaptation. The game provides an opportunity for the individual interested in football to duplicate in a relatively safe situation many of the skills utilized by widely publicized members of the gridiron game. Most present-day versions of the game resemble regulation football to the extent that names of positions of players, running and passing plays, punting, place-kicking, first downs, and scoring are used in touch football. The tackling element is eliminated in favor of the touch, and in most versions of touch football certain limitations are placed on blocking. In many cases no limitations are placed on eligibility of pass receivers, making it possible for any player to receive a forward pass. This factor makes the game more interesting to players on the line of scrimmage, who seldom have an opportunity to score or handle the ball in regulation football.

Flag Football

Flag football is a variation of touch football in which cloth or plastic flags are worn on both hips by all players. The flag is detached or stripped from a belt (worn by all players) by the defensive player in lieu of a touch. Flags are generally 12 to 15 inches long and 2 inches wide and are attached to the belt by an adhesive substance such as Velcro or by plastic snaps (Figure 11-1). A different colored flag is used by each team.

The basic rules governing flag football are similar to those used in touch football. Holding an opponent or holding onto the flag to prevent detachment are common infractions found in flag football and must be closely regulated. Some contend that utilization of the detachable flag in lieu of the one- or two-handed touch tends to minimize roughness in team play. Officiating is easier in flag than in touch football, since detachment of the flag is readily discernible while there may be arguments regarding the touch.

From a strategic standpoint, flag football would appear to orient itself better to all around offensive and defensive strategy because of the increased difficulty in detaching a flag. Teams will be more prone

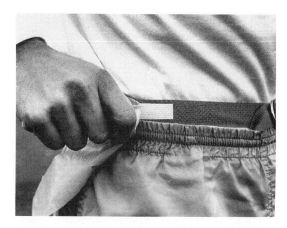

FIGURE 11-1 Flag and belt worn in flag football. Flag is attached with velcro.

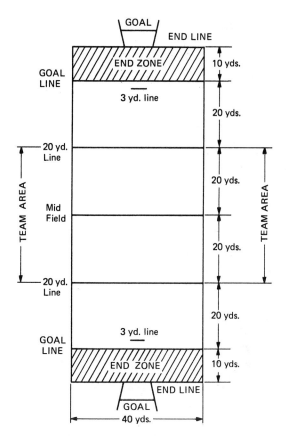

FIGURE 11-2 The touch and flag football field.

to include a more balanced running and passing attack; defenses will have to be designed to prevent both strategies.

In order to minimize hazardous play in flag football, the following precautionary measures are suggested:

1. Eliminate the blocking, tackling, or holding the ball carrier by a defensive player attempting to secure the flag.
2. Defensive players must maintain contact with the ground when attempting to secure the flag —no jumping or diving.
3. The ball carrier may not employ a straight-arm or utilize body contact against a defensive player in order to prevent him from securing the flag.

BASIC RULES

The rules for touch football and flag football are generally the same. However, when playing flag football, the rules for blocking, fumbling, and tackling must be strictly enforced. In flag football, any ball carrier without two flags is considered tackled.

Playing Field and Equipment

Playing Field. An official touch football and flag football field is 40 yards wide by 100 yards long (Figure 11-2). The field is divided into four 20-yard zones and two end zones, each 10 yards in depth.

Goals. Goal posts are not a necessity; however, lack of goal posts eliminates points after touchdown by kicking and field goals. In these cases, points after touchdown are gained by running or passing.

Uniform. No special uniform is required. The use of football helmets and football pads is prohibited, although tennis shoes or soccer shoes with molded rubber cleats may be used.

Ball. A regulation leather or rubber-coated football can be used. It is recommended that a junior-sized football be used by younger children.

Flags. Flags should measure 12 to 15 inches in length and 2 inches in width. They can be made of cloth and tucked in the elastic top of the gym trunks if belts are not available.

Length of Game. Four ten- to twelve-minute periods constitute a game with a one-minute rest between periods and a five-minute rest between halves. Games may also be divided into two twenty-minute halves with a five-minute rest period.

Overtime. Tie games may be decided by one of the following methods:

1. Award the game to the team with the greatest number of penetrations inside the opponent's 20-yard line.
2. Award the game to team with greatest number of first downs.
3. Give each team four downs from the 20-yard line and award the game to the team advancing the ball the farthest.

Forfeits. If a team is not ready to play within ten minutes after scheduled starting time, the opponents are awarded the win on a forfeit. Teams refusing to resume play after an order to do so by the referee forfeit to opponents.

Timeout. Each team is allowed two timeouts per half. Timeouts are also taken under the following conditions:

1. When ball goes out of bounds.
2. After a score is made.
3. While a penalty is being enforced.
4. At the discretion of the referee.
5. At the end of each period.

Scoring. Scoring is the same as in regulation football:

touchdown:	6 points
field goal:	3 points
safety:	2 points
point after touchdown:	1 point (by kick, 2 points by run or pass)

Players and Officials

Players. A team consists of seven players, although fewer or more players may be used by mutual consent. The offensive team must have at least three men on the line of scrimmage when the ball is put in play.

Substitutes. Any number of substitutions may be made at any time during the game. Substitutes must report to the referee.

Officials. Officials consist of a referee, an umpire, and linesmen.

Playing Regulations

Starting the Game. A toss of a coin by the referee determines which team has the choice of kicking off, receiving, or goals. The loser of the toss has the choice of remaining options. Privileges of choice are reversed at the beginning of the third period.

Putting the Ball in Play. The ball is put in play at the start of the game, after a score, and at the beginning of the third period by a place kick from the kicker's 20-yard line. Defensive team members must be 10 yards away when the ball is kicked, and members of the kicking team must be behind the ball. If the ball does not go 10 yards, it must be kicked again. If the ball goes out of bounds after 10 yards, the opponent has a choice of beginning play where it went out of bounds or on their own 20-yard line. If the ball is kicked into the end zone and the opponents elect not to run it out, play begins on their 20-yard line.

Fumbled Ball. A fumbled ball at any time is dead and belongs to the team that fumbled the ball at the point of the fumble, the down and point to be gained remaining the same. A fumbled forward pass is ruled as an incomplete pass.

Downed Ball. The ball is dead and the player downed when an opponent touches him with one hand somewhere between his shoulders and his knees. In flag football, the ball is downed or player tackled when one flag is detached from the belt or the ball carrier loses a flag.

First Downs. A team has four chances to move the ball from one 20-yard zone to the next. If a team does not advance the ball from one zone to the next in four downs, the ball goes to the opponents at that spot.

Passing. The following regulations govern passing:

1. All players on both teams are eligible to catch passes.
2. Forward passes may be thrown from any point back of the line of scrimmage, and lateral passes may be thrown anywhere on playing field.
3. Any number of passes may be thrown in a series of downs.

Penalties

5-Yard Penalty Infractions (from line of scrimmage):
   Offside
   Delay of game
   Less than three players on line of scrimmage
   Illegal motion or shift
   Illegal forward pass

15-Yard Penalty Infractions (from spot of foul):
   Illegal use of hands
   Illegal block
   Unnecessary roughness (push, tackle, shove, trip, holding)
   Unsportsmanlike conduct
   Clipping
   Pass interference

Flagrant violations of rules should be met with automatic disqualification.

RULES FOR COEDUCATIONAL FLAG FOOTBALL

Coeducational flag football is becoming an increasingly popular game. Many variations and modifications can be used. Modifications can be found in *Rules for Coeducational Activities and Sports,* published by the American Alliance of Health, Physical Education, Recreation, and Dance, 1977 and 1980.

SUGGESTED LEARNING SEQUENCE

A. Nature and Purpose of Touch Football/Flag Football

B. Conditioning Aspects—plan drills and exercises that might be related to movements of touch and flag football.
C. Basic Game Concepts
   1. Field of play
   2. Equipment
   3. Safety
   4. Playing courtesies
D. Rules/Coeducational Rules—rules should be introduced when appropriate and at a time that relates to a specific skill or strategy. This does not mean that all rules must be discussed at one time.
E. Skills and Techniques—skills should be taught in combinations whenever possible; the sequence that skills are taught is up to the individual preference of the instructor.
   1. Stances
      a. Three-point stance
      b. Upright stance
   2. Ball Carrying
   3. Passing and Receiving
      a. Pass Patterns
   4. Kicking
      a. Punting
      b. Place kick
      c. Kickoff
   5. Blocking
   6. Tackling
      a. Touch
      b. Flag detachment
   7. Centering
      a. Direct snap
      b. Long snap
F. Strategies—offensive game concepts as well as defensive game concepts should be introduced as early as possible so that skills can be practiced within the context of a game.

   1. Offense
      a. T-formation
      b. Shotgun formation
      c. Single wing
   2. Defense
      a. Pass defense—pass rush
      b. Running defense
G. Game Play

SKILLS AND TECHNIQUES

The techniques and fundamental skills associated with touch football and flag football are identical to regular football in most instances. There are two areas, however, where touch and flag football differ from the parent game; these are in tackling and blocking. The tackle in touch football refers to a touch between the shoulders and knees, while the tackle in flag football refers to the detachment or stripping of a flag by an opponent from a belt that circles the waist. In both touch and flag football, players cannot leave their feet when blocking. There are other skills that all players must work on since the skills will be used regardless of the position played.

Stances

The stance will vary according to the position played and the function of either the offense or defense. Generally speaking, the three-point stance is used by the players on the line on offense and defense and sometimes by the offensive backs. The upright stance may be used by linebackers, defensive backs, and sometimes, the offensive backs. (See Figure 11-3.)

FIGURE 11-3 Stance: the players on the line are in a three-point stance; the backs are in an upright stance.

▶ **Learning Cues—Three-Point Stance**

1. Feet are shoulder width apart, one foot slightly ahead of the other in a heel-toe relationship.
2. The supporting arm hangs vertically, the back is nearly horizontal, head is up looking ahead, weight is on support hand.
3. The free arm rests on the knee of the forward leg.

▶ **Learning Cues—Upright Stance**

1. Foot position is much the same as in the three-point stance.
2. Hands are placed just above the knees, back is slightly bent on the waist, head is up, focused downfield.
3. Weight is on balls of the feet.

Ball Carrying

Because of the rules governing play, most players have an opportunity at one time or another to carry the football. The effective ball carrier is one who can start quickly, change direction, dodge, side-step, and execute fakes that will throw the defensive player off stride. It is important for the ball carrier to follow the blockers in order to elude the defensive players.

▶ **Learning Cues** (See Figure 11-4)

1. Carry ball in outside arm furthest from the defensive player.
2. One end of the football is placed in the armpit and the other end is held in the palm of the hand with fingers spread comfortably around the end to provide a firm grip.

▶ **Practice Suggestions**

1. Align a ball carrier facing a defensive player standing 10 yards away. On the signal, have the ball carrier run toward the defensive player, changing the ball as the player changes direction.
2. Same type of formation, have the ball carrier run toward the defensive player using a series of fakes to try to avoid being tackled.
3. Using a blocker, have a ball carrier try to set up the block on the defensive player by following the interference and setting up a series of fakes.

Passing

The forward pass assumes an important role in touch football and flag football since rules permit everyone to be an eligible receiver. A good passing attack will loosen up the defense and allow the running game to become more effective. There are two types of passes commonly used: the forward pass and the lateral pass. The lateral pass may be thrown in an overhand motion or it may be "pitched" to a player in an underhand motion. The lateral, which cannot be thrown forward, adds much interest and excitement to the game since it can be used anywhere on the field.

▶ **Learning Cues—Forward Pass**

1. Ball is gripped by the hand on the top; the thumb is opposite the middle finger, the other fingers are spread on the laces (Figure 11-5).
2. As ball is brought up behind the ear, plant the rear foot, step with the opposite foot in the direction of throw as the arm is brought forward.
3. The wrist is snapped downward and palm of throwing hand is rotated outward as the ball is released, thus giving the ball a spiral motion.

FIGURE 11-5 Proper grip for a forward pass. Note that the middle finger and the thumb are opposite.

FIGURE 11-4 Proper way to carry a ball.

▶ **Practice Suggestions**

1. Place players opposite each other and throw ball back and forth. Begin at a distance of 10 yards and move further away.
2. After you have reviewed certain pass receiver patterns, form two lines, have a player center the ball back to the quarterback, receivers go out for a pass. First begin with short passes and then progress to longer passes.
3. Same formation as #2 but add two defensive linesmen; force quarterback to throw on the run. Another variation is to add two defensive backs and attempt to complete a pass.

Receiving

Pass receivers should become adept at eluding their opponents by dodging, faking, and using a change of pace that will enable them to move past the defensive player. It is important for the pass receiver to focus in on the ball as soon as it leaves the passer's hand, watching all the way to his own hands. Some basic fundamentals must be remembered.

▶ **Learning Cues**

1. Palms face out, thumbs toward the incoming pass. Catch with the hands and pull into the body.
2. On passes above the chest, thumbs are turned in; below the waist, thumbs are turned out (see Figures 11-6 and 11-7).

3. As the receiver moves away from the passer, fingers are extended, thumbs are turned out; give with ball on contact.
4. On passes caught over either shoulder, the thumbs are turned out; the arm on the ballside (nearest the body) is held below the shoulder, the forearm is held at eye level (Figure 11-8).

▶ **Practice Suggestions**

1. Form two parallel lines and have passes thrown above chest and below chest to pass receivers.
2. Two lines, passer drops back and throws pass over the receiver's head for over-the-shoulder catch.
3. Two lines, receivers practice pass patterns and catches. Add defensive backs as a variation.

Kicking

The kicking game consists of kickoffs to begin play, punting, and place kicks.

▶ **Learning Cues—Punting**

1. The punter stands 13 yards behind the line of scrimmage awaiting the center snap; the kicking foot is slightly ahead of the non-kicking foot, arms are relaxed, palms open and up, trunk is slightly flexed.
2. Follow the ball into the hands; the ball is held in the hand of the kicking foot toward the end and underneath. The other hand is placed on the ball with laces up to the front and side. The ball

FIGURE 11-6 Catching the ball above the chest—thumbs turned in.

FIGURE 11-7 Catching the ball below the waist—thumbs turned out.

FIGURE 11-8 Catching the football over the shoulder.

should be slightly tipped, nose downward just below the chest.

3. The kick and step is a step with the right foot, a hop with the left, and a follow-through with the right leg. The kicking foot may finish above the head.

4. The ball is released with the non-kicking hand and guided to the correct position of the foot by the kicking hand prior to release.

Place Kicking and Extra Point.   There are two types of place kicks, the traditional head-on approach and the soccer style instep kick, which is described in the chapter on Soccer. Some key points to remember for the traditional kick are:

1. Assume a stance two steps behind the spot of the kick; the right foot takes a longer step and the left foot a short step.

2. The non-kicking foot is placed approximately two feet behind and a foot to the side of the ball.

3. With the head down and eyes on the contact point, the body leaning forward, the right leg follows through with a definite leg snap coming at the contact point.

4. The ball is contacted just below the center of the football; the leg should be extended at impact.

The Kickoff.   The kickoff follows the same mechanics except the kicker is stationed 8 to 10 yards behind the ball prior to kickoff. Practice and timing are essential in executing the correct form for the place kick during a kickoff.

Blocking

Since the player is not permitted to leave the feet in executing a block, the player must become adept at maintaining balance while retaining a position between the defensive person and the ball carrier. It is important to try to maintain contact with the defensive player and draw him away from the ball carrier. The blocker is not allowed to hold the defensive person, so the hands must be held in close to the body at all times.

▶ **Learning Cues**

1. Assume a three-point stance opposite your opponent; the initial steps are short, choppy steps to the opponent.

2. Body is in a semi-crouch position, the shoulder and forearms make contact with the opponent's midsection, the head is placed between your opponent and the ball carrier.

3. Drive your opponent away from the ball carrier; use short, choppy steps.

▶ **Practice Suggestions**

1. Form two parallel lines 2 yards apart. On the signal, block right or block left; the blocker attempts to maintain contact on a blocking position for 3 to 4 seconds.

2. With a center, a ball carrier, defensive player, and offensive player, on signal the ball carrier runs behind the blocker and cuts right or left, depending on the direction of the block.

Tackling

Tackling is the term used to denote the touching of a ball carrier to stop play or, in flag football, the detachment or stripping of the flag to stop play. An important point to remember is that, for the tackle to be valid, both feet of the tackler must be on the ground. A legal touch is between the shoulder and knee of the opponent. The game may be played using a one-hand touch or it may be increased in difficulty by making it a two-hand touch game (Figure 11-9). In flag football, one flag must be detached from the belt (Figure 11-10). Body balance and control of body movement and speed are important factors to practice.

FIGURE 11-9   Tackling—a two-handed touch above the waist.

FIGURE 11-10 Tackling, flag football style. The ball carrier's hand may not protect the flag.

Centering

The center plays an important part in touch and flag football. The center snap is executed at close range (direct snap) if a team uses a T-formation, at longer range if a team uses a shotgun or single wing, and at still longer range on punts and extra point tries. Note that in touch or flag football if the center snaps the ball on the ground before getting to the receiver, it is a dead ball.

▶ **Learning Cues—Direct Snap** (Figures 11-11, 11-12)

1. Feet are shoulder width apart, bend at the waist, knees flexed, arms hanging comfortably in front, head up.
2. Quarterback places hands under the crotch of the center, fingers spread, heels of palms together.
3. The center places one hand on top of the ball (laces up) and the other hand alongside and toward the end of the ball. On the signal the arms are rolled toward the quarterback, the ball is snapped back to the quarterback, with the right hand turning the ball a quarter right turn so the ball is placed in the quarterback's hands on its side.

▶ **Learning Cues—Long Snap** (Figure 11-13)

1. Same starting position, although weight may be forward and head lower than the buttocks.
2. Arms are swept toward the receiver, wrist snap to impart spiral on the ball.

FIGURE 11-11 The snap. Note quarter turn of the ball as it is given to the quarterback.

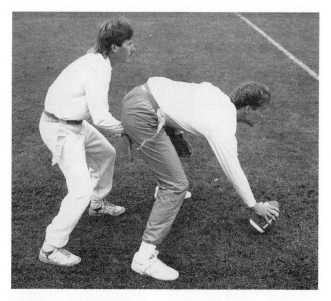

FIGURE 11-12 The direct snap.

FIGURE 11-13   The long snap.

STRATEGY FOR TOUCH OR FLAG FOOTBALL

Offensive Strategy

Touch football permits the use of a wide range of offensive plays because of the emphasis on passing and the fact that everyone is eligible to receive a pass. In arranging the offensive strategy, a team should plan a signal system that will denote the kind of play to be used (pass, run, punt), who is to carry the ball, and where the ball is to go. Plays should be kept as simple as possible. Numbers may be em-

ployed to represent the type of play, the player executing the play or carrying the ball, and the side of the line where the play is to go. The line may be numbered with odd numbers on the left side and even numbers on the right (Figure 11-14). The backs may be numbered: 1—quarterback, 2—right halfback, 3—fullback, and 4—left halfback. Thus, after the ball has been centered, the signal "Run 14" indicates a running play through the number 4 hole, with the number 1 back carrying the ball.

Offensive strategy should combine running and passing plays in order to create confusion to the defense. It is not good strategy to constantly employ all passing plays or all running plays. Try to keep the defense guessing; attempt running plays on second down with a lot of yards to go for first down.

Offensive Formations.   There are a number of formations that can be created by the offense as long as three people line up on the line of scrimmage before the ball is snapped. Three common formations used in touch football and flag football include (1) the T-formation, (2) the shotgun formation, and (3) the single wing formation (Figure 11-15).

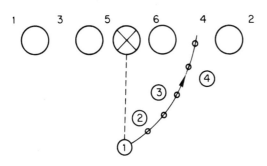

FIGURE 11-14   Numbers for offensive holes.

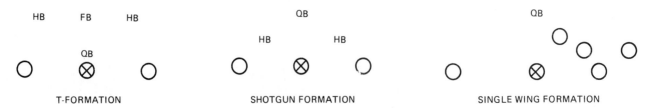

FIGURE 11-15   Types of offensive formations.

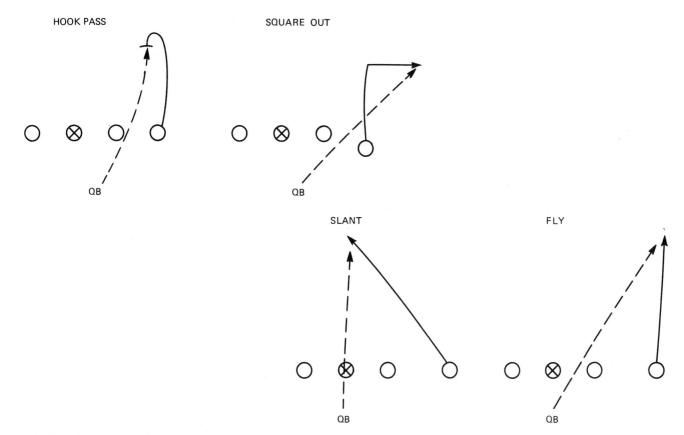

FIGURE 11-16 Types of pass patterns.

Defensive Strategy

Teams should agree on a plan for the pass and the run defense. For a passing defense, certain players on the line of scrimmage should be assigned to rush the passer, while other players drop back to help the defensive backs cover possible receivers. Generally a person-to-person assignment is made for the deep pass receiver while a zone defense is employed by the remaining defensive players to watch for the short pass receivers. Figure 11-16 illustrates four types of pass patterns.

▶ **Defensive Hints**

1. Assign rushers to contain the passer or runner inside, not allowing the ball carrier the opportunity to break outside the defensive containment.
2. Learn to recognize the opponent's formations and most effective players; set up your defenses accordingly.
3. Listen to see if an opponent is continually using the same cadence; time your rush to the cadence occasionally.
4. Defensive backs should not turn their backs on the pass receiver; learn to run backwards or sidewards so that you can always see the ball and the pass receiver.
5. Use different pass rushers to confuse the offense; send in linebackers at times as an element of surprise.

▶ **Offensive Hints**

1. Keep defense guessing by varying running and passing plays.
2. If the defensive secondary plays deep, use many of your players in short passing patterns. When the defensive draws in, use the deep pass.
3. If you receive a long penalty, do not try to make it up on one play; use a run and perhaps some short passes.
4. Change your cadence occasionally to pull the defensive team offside.
5. Utilize a quick kick on third down to get your team out of a defensive hole.
6. Let your field position help dictate the type of plays you will use—long passes are dangerous near your own goal line; plays involving deception are best in the vicinity of midfield; use quick hitting or pass plays near your opponent's goal line.

MODIFICATIONS FOR SPECIAL POPULATIONS

Orthopedically Impaired

1. For wheelchair users, games would have to be modified to be played on the gymnasium floor, and a foam rubber football is recommended.

Able-bodied students could use scooters in the sitting position. No modifications would be needed for throwing and catching for students with functional upper body skills. Forward passes to students using powerized wheelchairs would be completed by striking with the football any part of the wheelchair above the waist area, e.g., chair arms, seat back.

2. Students using crutches, canes, and walkers should be able to participate on an outdoor or indoor field. These students could be positioned as defensive linemen and coached to raise their assistive devices to block forward passes. Quarterbacks would not be allowed to move when throwing against this defense.

Mentally Impaired

1. Play the games with smaller numbers, (e.g., fewer than five on a team) to help minimize confusion and increase participation.
2. Make sure to use some means of designating team players in play demonstrations, e.g., green and red pennies.
3. Stationary lead-up games might be helpful, e.g., stationary passing relays the length of the field.

Sensory Impaired

1. Blind/visually impaired could be the designated center and blocker.
2. Blind/visually impaired students could play quarterback without using a center snap. Using a "double pass" system the student would be required to pass the ball to a sighted teammate before the defensive rush could occur, with the sighted player serving as the second quarterback.
3. Minimal modifications would be needed for the deaf or hearing impaired. Develop some visual system for stoppage of play, e.g., cue cards, waving of towel.

SAFETY

Observance of the following safety precautions will minimize the incidence of injuries.

1. Do not wear any equipment possessing sharp or projecting surfaces that may injure teammates or opponents. This includes rings, belt buckles, and watches.
2. Use rules that prevent leaving the feet in executing the block.
3. Declare the ball dead on all fumbles.
4. See that the playing area is smooth and free from holes and projecting objects that may prove a hazard.
5. Use competent officials who enforce the rules and eliminate rough play.

6. Be sure adequate treatment is available for players in case of injury during play.
7. Players who wear glasses should wear a headband or eyeglass guard.

TERMINOLOGY

Backs   Players on the team who ordinarily carry or pass the ball on offense. Stationed behind the linemen.

Backward pass   Play in which the ball is thrown or passed in any direction except toward the opponent's goal. Any player may make a backward pass.

Balanced line   An offensive formation which has an equal number of linemen on each side of the center. Line is unbalanced if more linemen are on one side of center than the other.

Block   Action of offensive linemen and backs in which they use their bodies to ward off defensive players from the ball carrier.

Bootleg play   An offensive play in which a back fakes handling the ball to a teammate, conceals it on his hip, and turns in the opposite direction.

Brush blocking   Momentary blocking by an offensive player.

Button hook   A forward pass play in which the receiver runs toward the defender, turns, and runs back toward passer to receive the pass.

Clipping   A blocking action in which a player throws his body across the back of the leg(s) of a player not carrying the ball. This can cause injury, and is a personal foul.

Cross-buck   An offensive play in which two backs cross paths in moving toward the line of scrimmage, one faking to receive the ball and the other actually taking the ball.

Cut-back   An offensive maneuver in which the back starts wide and then cuts back toward center of the line.

End around   An offensive maneuver in which one end wheels around, takes the ball from a teammate, and attempts to run for a gain.

Fair catch   A player may make a fair catch on a kickoff, return kick, or kick from scrimmage by raising his hand clearly above his head before making the catch. He may not be tackled, and must not take more than two steps after receiving the ball. The ball is put in play from the spot of the catch by a free kick or scrimmage.

Flanker   An offensive maneuver in which a player lines up nearer the sideline than a designated opponent.

Flat pass   A forward pass that travels chiefly in a lateral direction and is usually thrown with a flat trajectory.

Forward pass   An offensive play in which the ball is thrown toward the line of scrimmage.

Handoff   An offensive play in which one back hands the ball off to another back who attempts to advance the ball.

Lateral pass   An offensive play in which the ball is passed sideward or backward to the line of scrimmage.

Line of scrimmage   An imaginary line, or vertical plane, passing through the end of the ball nearest a team's goal line and parallel to the goal lines. Thus there is a line of scrimmage for each team, and the area between the two lines is called the neutral zone. Any player of either team is offside if he encroaches upon the neutral zone before the ball is snapped.

Naked reverse   An offensive play in which the ball carrier takes the ball from another back and attempts to advance without benefit of backfield blockers.

Neutral zone   The imaginary line which passes between the lines of scrimmage for each team. Either team is offside if it moves across the neutral zone before the ball is snapped.

Offside   When an offensive player is ahead of the ball before it is snapped. (The penalty is five yards.)

Safety   A score made when a free ball, or one in possession of a player defending his own goal, becomes dead behind the goal, provided the impetus which caused it to cross the goal was supplied by the defending team.

Screen pass   An offensive maneuver in which a wave of eligible receivers converge in area where a pass is to be thrown.

Shotgun offense   A formation in which the quarterback lines up five to six yards behind the center. Usually one or both halfbacks may line up one to two yards on either side of the quarterback and one yard in front of the quarterback.

Shovel pass   An offensive maneuver in which a pass is thrown, underhand, usually forward to a back behind the line of scrimmage.

Touchback   When the ball becomes dead behind the opponent's goal line legally in possession of a player guarding his own goal, provided the impetus which caused it to cross the goal line was supplied by an opponent. No points are scored on the play, and the ball is put in play by a scrimmage at the 20-yard line.

SELECTED REFERENCES

American Association for Health, Physical Education, and Recreation, *Rules for Coeducational Activities and Sports.* Revised ed. Washington, DC: AAHPER Publications, 1980.

American Association for Health, Physical Education, and Recreation, Division for Girls' and Women's Sports. *Soccer-Speedball-Flag Football Guide.* Current ed. Washington, DC: AAHPER.

Armbruster, D.A.; Erwin, L.; and Musker, F.F. *Basic Skills in Sports for Men and Women.* 5th ed. St. Louis, MI: C.V. Mosby Company, 1971.

Dintiman, G.B. and Barrow, L.M. *A Comprehensive Manual of Physical Education Activities for Men.* Englewood Cliffs, NJ: Prentice Hall, 1970.

Frommer, H. *Sports Lingo: A Dictionary of the Language of Sports.* New York: Atheneum, 1979.

Dowell, L.J. *Handbook of Teaching and Coaching Points for Basic Physical Education Skills.* Springfield, IL: Charles C. Thomas, Publisher, 1974.

Little, M.; Dowell, L.; and Jeter, J. *Recreational Football: Flag and Touch for Class and Intramurals,* Minneapolis: Burgess, 1977.

Mood, D., et al. *Sports and Recreational Activities for Men and Women.* Latest ed. St. Louis: Times-Mirror Mosby, 1987.

National College Physical Education Association. *Touch Football—Official National Touch Football Rules.* Current ed. Chicago: The Athletic Institute.

Stanbury, D. and DeSantis, F. *Touch Football.* New York: Sterling Publishing Co., Inc., 1979.

Skills Testing

Brace, D.K. *Skills Test Manual: Football.* Washington, DC: American Association for Health, Physical Education, and Recreation, 1965.

Hewate, C. and Reynolds, J. "Flag Football." *Soccer-Speedball-Flag Football Guide.* Washington, DC: American Association for Health, Physical Education, and Recreation, 1972.

Audio-Visual Materials

Clearvue Inc., 5711 Milwaukee Ave., Chicago, IL 60646 *Touch/Flag Football II: Rules of the Game* (Filmstrip/Guide).

Clearvue Inc., 5711 Milwaukee Ave., Chicago, IL 60646 *Touch/Flag Football I: How to Play* (Filmstrip/Guide).

AIMS Media, Inc., 6901 Woodley Ave., Van Nuys, CA 91406. *Playing Touch Football* (¾ or ½ inch video, 12 minutes).

12 GOLF

THIS CHAPTER WILL ENABLE YOU TO:

▶ *Identify the parts and features of a golf course.*
▶ *Identify the various clubs and other equipment, know their function and proper care.*
▶ *Describe and after practice execute the following skills: grip, stand, swing (irons and woods), pitch, chip, and sand shots, putting, and various golf exercises.*
▶ *Identify and carry out the courtesies associated with the sport.*
▶ *State and interpret the major official rules of golf.*

NATURE AND PURPOSE

One of the greatest advantages of golf lies in the age range of those who are able to participate. Both young boys and girls and mature men and women can be found participating at many golf courses. In recent years the United States Golf Association has sponsored Junior Golf Programs (ages 9 to 17); therefore, more and more children are becoming interested in playing at a very early age. Many private and public golf courses have extensive instructional programs for the junior golfer and sponsor golf tournaments all summer long. Most public and private clubs have also set aside specific playing times for the juniors in order to encourage their participation.

Golf may be played by strokes or by holes. The objective is to play a ball from a teeing area to a hole, a prescribed distance from the tee, in the fewest strokes possible. An official round is eighteen holes. In stroke play, the winner is the person taking the fewest number of strokes over an entire eighteen holes of play. Each hole receives a rating of par determined by the length of the hole (see Figure 12-1). In match play, or play by holes, the winner is the golfer who wins the greater number of holes despite the final total in strokes. Stroke play is considered more exacting, since each shot is of equal value, whereas in match play, a loss of two or more strokes on a hole may be recouped by a one-stroke victory on a later hole.

Golf is one of the few sports that allows a handicapping system among participants. Handicapping is a means of equalizing competition among golfers of differing abilities. The player with the lower average score is required to give strokes to the higher average golfer. In stroke play the higher average player subtracts these strokes from his total to get a *net* score. This is compared with the other player's *gross* or total score to determine the winner. In most

FIGURE 12-1 Directions for computing par on a golf course.

For Men	
Par 3	Up to 250 yards, inclusive
Par 4	251 to 470 yards, inclusive
Par 5	471 yards and over

For Women	
Par 3	Up to 210 yards, inclusive
Par 4	211 to 400 yards, inclusive
Par 5	401 to 575 yards, inclusive
Par 6	576 yards and over

handicap play the strokes are usually computed in relation to the difference between par and the average score of the player. Thus, many can compete in a tournament on a handicap basis. In match play the strokes are subtracted from the higher average player's score on holes designated as the most difficult. That is, a handicap of five would allow the player to subtract one stroke from his score on the five most difficult holes.

THE COURSE

The course is the whole area within which play is permitted, and it is the duty of authorities in charge of the course to define its boundaries accurately. Most courses consist of eighteen holes; however, there are many nine-hole courses. Golf scores are based on eighteen holes of play, with the par usually varying between 70 and 72. Each hole consists of many common components and some not so common components (see Figure 12-2). A player tees a ball up on a wooden tee in the teeing area, in line with or no more than two club lengths behind the tee markers. Generally there are three sets of markers on a tee: the farthest from the hole are for championship play; the middle markers are generally for men; and the markers closest to the hole are where women initiate play. From the tee, the golfer hits to a fairly well-groomed area called the fairway and from there, hits to a closely cut area of the hole called the green. Generally the area to the right and left of the fairway where the grass is long and other obstacles may be found is known as the rough. Most courses include obstacles such as sand traps, bunkers, water hazards, out-of-bounds, and trees placed in strategic positions to penalize a poor shot made by a golfer. There are specific rules governing play that the golfer must understand when confronted by one of these obstacles. These are discussed below under "Rules of Golf."

SCORING

Figure 12-3 represents a typical score card. The golfer will note the yardage given for each hole dependent on the set of markers from which play is initiated. Also included is information on the course rating, the par designation for a particular hole, as well as the hole's difficulty as expressed in men's or women's handicap. Thus the hole having the men's handicap designation of 7 (hole number 6) means that it is the seventh hardest hole on the course. If the golfer had a handicap of 7, he would be given a deduction of 1 stroke from his score in order to equalize the competition. In this example, the golfer would also receive a stroke deduction on holes 7, 11, 2, 13, 1, and 12.

The par designation is the number of strokes that an expert would take to play a hole. It is usually

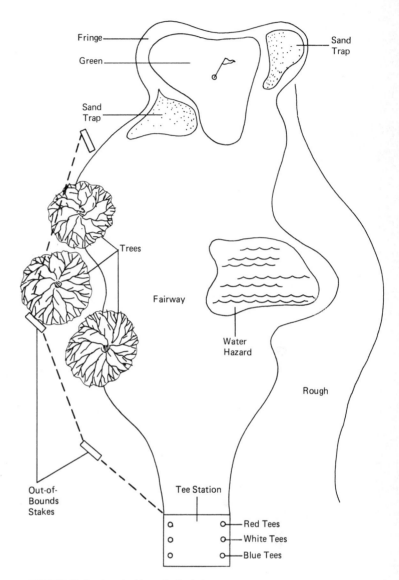

FIGURE 12-2 A typical layout of a hole.

SCORE CARD

HOLE	1	2	3	4	5	6	7	8	9	OUT	10	11	12	13	14	15	16	17	18	IN	Total
Championship BLUE	440	545	250	350	175	385	420	385	480	3430	520	440	525	420	205	350	385	185	405	3435	6865
Men's WHITE	365	515	245	325	160	380	415	350	455	3210	450	420	510	405	150	325	380	180	395	3215	6425
PAR	4	5	3	4	3	4	4	4	5	36	5	4	5	4	3	4	4	3	4	36	72
Men's Handicap	5	3	13	15	17	7	1	11	9		12	2	6	4	18	14	10	16	8		
Won + Lost − Halved 0																					
Women's YELLOW	360	490	245	320	160	365	410	350	440	3140	440	405	510	405	150	320	370	175	395	3170	6315
PAR	4	5	4	4	3	4	5	4	5	38	5	5	5	5	3	4	4	3	4	38	76
Women's Handicap	5	1	17	9	15	7	11	13	3		4	10	2	16	18	12	8	14	6		

COURSE RATING 70.5

DATE _____   PLAYER _____   ATTEST _____

FIGURE 12-3 Score card.

the number of shots from the tee to the green plus two strokes for putting. Thus an expert playing a par four hole would take two shots to reach the green and two putts to hit the ball into the hole. Sometimes a golfer will hit a ball from the tee into the hole in less than par. A score of 1 under par is a birdie, 2 under par is called an eagle, 3 under par on a par five is a double eagle, and 2 under on a par three is a hole in one, the golfer's dream.

EQUIPMENT

Clubs

A set of golf clubs consists of woods, irons, and a putter. The beginner may not wish to invest in a complete set of expensive clubs, and can initially get along with less expensive clubs. A minimum set should contain two woods, four irons, and a putter. The recommended choices would be a driver and a number 3 wood, the 3, 5, 7, and 9 irons, and a putter. While it is possible to obtain a full set by gradually adding the missing clubs, such as the number 4 and 5 woods and the 2, 4, 6, and 8 irons, as well as the sand wedge, a better plan is to play with the basic set until a fairly high level of skill is reached. At that time a golf professional should be consulted to fit the player with a better and completely matched set of 14 clubs. The most popular 14 clubs are the driver, numbers 3 and 5 woods, numbers 2 through 9 irons, a pitching wedge, a sand wedge, and a putter. A set of clubs may cost anywhere from around $75 to several hundred dollars. Generally the beginning golfer can purchase a starter set for approximately $100 to $175.

The Putter.   The putter is a golf club carried by all golfers; it is used primarily on the putting green to hit the ball into the cup. Today there are as many putter designs as there are golfers. The putter comes in various sizes, shapes, and colors. In choosing a putter, the key points to look for, according to the noted golf instructor Dick Aultman, are first, that the putter when soled flat on the ground allows you to look directly over the putting line; secondly, that it should be simple to aim, and thus, that it be easy to control.[1]

Choosing Clubs

Golf clubs are precision instruments and vary in design for men, women, and children. A golfer's shotmaking ability is affected by many factors directly related to the construction of the golf club. Among these factors are swingweight, length of the club, shaft flexibility, clubhead design, and the grip.

Swingweight.   Determined by a swingweight

[1] Dick Aultman, "Golf Primer," *Golf Digest* (May 1979), p. 113.

scale, swingweight is the relationship among the weights of a club's component parts—grip, shaft, and head. Scales to measure swingweight may be found in most pro shops. Swingweights are usually designated by the symbols C and D followed by a number ranging from 0 to 9. Women usually use a lightweight club that has a swingweight of C4 to C7; stronger women might use a C9 or even move to the D classification. Men's clubs start at D0; an average male golfer would use a swingweight of D0 to D4. Children's clubs are generally lighter.

Club Length.   An important point to remember is that the higher the *number* of the club, the shorter the club's *length*. The woods have the longest shafts while the 9 iron, pitching wedge, and sand wedge have the shortest shafts.

In addition, the shorter clubs have a more sharply-angled club face (greater degree of loft). The combination of club length and club loft determine in part the distance a golf ball can be hit under normal conditions. If a golfer can execute a good shot each time, there is an approximate ten-yard difference between each club used. Figure 12-5 indicates the degrees of loft of specific clubs.

Women's golf clubs are one to two inches shorter than men's clubs and children's clubs are shorter still. Some companies today are making fully matched sets of junior clubs, but they are quite expensive.

Shaft Flexibility.   Matching the correct shaft flexibility to a golfer's swing is important. Most men golfers should use a golf club with a shaft flexibility rating of R, meaning regular. This shaft is also recommended for stronger women players. An S shaft means stiff and should be used by stronger male players. Most women golfers will use a golf club with an L (Lady) rated shaft because these shafts have more flexibility.

Clubhead Design.   In recent years significant advances have been made in clubhead design in both woods and irons. The topic is too extensive and technical for discussion here. Almost any golf clubs can be used to get you started. When your skill level increases, you can consult a local golf professional for the latest clubhead information.

Grip.   Grips are generally made of synthetic rubber, although other materials such as leather or cord are also used. The standard size grip put on the club in the factory can be changed to accommodate different hand sizes. A good general rule is, "If it feels right, it probably is."

Balls and Tees

Golf Balls.   Golf balls come in a variety of types and in a wide price range. Beginners do not need to buy the most expensive ball.

Golf balls have two kinds of covers. Balata is a soft rubber cover which damages easily but is pre-

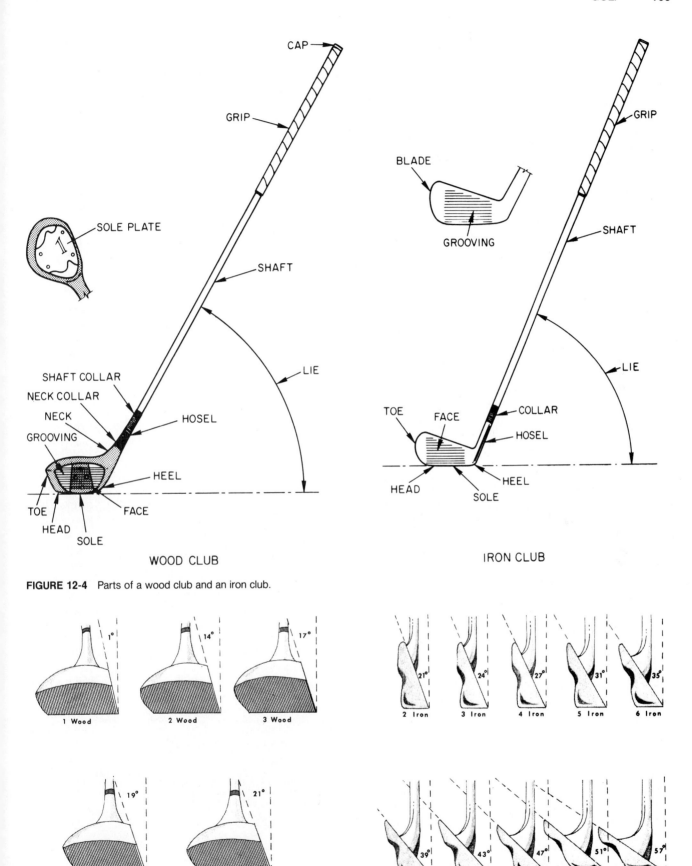

FIGURE 12-4 Parts of a wood club and an iron club.

FIGURE 12-5 Club lofts. The loft of any one club will vary a few degrees. The manufacturers' recommendations are shown here.

ferred by better golfers because they claim it has better feel. Surlyn is a sturdier cover made of plastic and some golfers claim surlyn-covered balls can be hit farther. Beginning golfers should use a surlyn-covered ball at first, and may have a different preference as skill develops.

The inside of a golf ball can be manufactured in two ways: (a) A small rubber core is covered by a thin rubber string wound tightly around the core; (b) The center of a golf ball can consist of synthetic material. Combinations of both styles of covers and insides are available.

Tees. Tees are made of wood and come in various lengths; the standard is 2⅛ inches. Tees made of other materials should be avoided.

SUGGESTED LEARNING SEQUENCE

Golf can be taught a number of different ways and from various starting points. Many of the skills can be learned and practiced indoors as well as outdoors. The availability of space and equipment (clubs, balls, screens, rugs, or mats) are important factors to consider. For beginning golfers, audio-visual aids can play a significant role in the learning process, for they reinforce many of the concepts explained during the initial stages of instruction. Another point to remember is that psychomotor and cognitive material is much better learned when presented together at the appropriate time. For example, etiquette and the rules governing play on the putting green are more meaningful during a lesson on putting than during a lesson devoted to the rules of golf. Finally, it is important to become proficient in the basic swing techniques before attempting to move on to the more advanced skills and techniques.

A. Introduction to Golf
  1. Nature and purpose of the game
  2. Choosing the right equipment
  3. Care of equipment
B. Etiquette and Rules of Golf. These should be introduced as deemed most appropriate for learning during different class intervals.
C. Skills and Techniques. Golf skills are best learned starting with the shorter clubs. Putting should be introduced very early. As skill increases the longer clubs can be introduced with the wood clubs coming last. Chipping can be introduced following putting and full swing fundamentals.
  1. Putting. Grip, stance, alignment, pendulum stroke, lag putting, short putts, reading greens, rules and etiquette.
  2. Pre-swing fundamentals. Grip, club face alignment, body alignment, stance, target selection and strategy.

  3. Full Swing techniques. Take-away, backswing, downswing, follow-through, balance and tempo.
  4. Special shots. Chipping, pitch and run, sand trap shots.
  5. Strategy of golf. Best taught on the golf course during play, or as deemed most appropriate for learning.

SKILLS AND TECHNIQUES

Preswing Fundamentals

It is very important to have a good understanding of the preswing fundamentals. These fundamentals, grip, club face alignment, body alignment, stance and target selection, should be mastered before proceeding with the swing fundamentals. These fundamentals should be reviewed before every practice session and before playing a round of golf. Should a swing problem occur during a round of golf, a review of these fundamentals most often will solve the swing problem.

The Grip

The correct grip is the most important fundamental skill to be learned by golfers of any skill level. It can determine in great part the path of your swing, and consequently the directional flight of the ball. There are three types of grips used in golf: the overlapping (or Vardon) grip, the interlocking grip, and the ten-finger grip (Figure 12-6). The overlapping grip is the one most commonly used. In this grip the little finger of the right hand overlaps the index finger of the left hand. The interlocking grip is used by the golfer who has small hands and short fingers. In this grip the little finger of the right hand *inter-*

FIGURE 12-6 Types of grips, from left to right: the interlocking, the overlapping, and the ten-finger grip.

locks with the index finger of the left hand. Both grips have the advantage of having the hands work as a unit, because the hands are joined together. The ten-finger grip is used by the golfer who has small hands; it is used frequently by beginning junior golfers. The ten-finger grip enables the golfer to take a strong hold, but there is a tendency for the hands to slip apart at times.

When assuming a grip, the fact that it may not feel comfortable is no reason for the golfer to think that it is incorrect. However, the grip should not feel like a vise; rather it should feel firm yet somewhat relaxed. Tenseness in the grip will cause a restricted swing; the golf swing should flow.

▶ **Learning Cues—Overlapping Grip (Right-handed Golfer)**

1. A good golf grip starts by using the same hand position used when standing erect. As you stand erect with your arms hanging freely from your sides, notice how both hands turn slightly inward (Figure 12-7A). Extend your left hand and arm as though to shake hands. Close the thumb next to the first finger. The line formed by the thumb and first finger should be pointing toward the right eye. The back of the left hand should be pointing in the direction you want the ball to travel.

2. Extend your right hand in the same manner as above. Close the right thumb next to the first finger. This line formed by the thumb and first finger should also point toward the right eye. The palm of the right hand should be pointing in the direction you want the ball to travel.

3. Extend both hands at the same time as de-scribed above. Place the right hand slightly forward of the left hand. (The right hand will be below the left hand when gripping the club). The palms of your hands should be facing each other (Figure 12-7B). The lines formed by the thumb and first finger of each hand should be pointing at the right eye. Later you may want to strengthen the grip by pointing the lines toward the right shoulder as most women golfers do. You may want to weaken the grip by pointing the lines toward your nose if your hands are very strong.

4. Using a 7 iron or a 5 iron, attempt to grip the club. Be sure the sole of the club is flat on the ground and the club face is pointed toward the direction you want the ball to travel. Place the left hand on first, using the correct hand position. Grip firmly with the last three fingers of the left hand. The thumb and index finger grip with less pressure. Use both palm and fingers to hold the club firmly and securely, but do not squeeze too hard. (Figure 12-7C).

5. The left hand grip, for a right-handed golfer, should see the end of the club cross the palm of the hand from the base of the index finger, diagonally to the heel of the hand (Figure 12-8A). Closing the fingers around the club will insure a good firm grip. Left-handed golfers will use the same grip using their right hand.

6. The right hand grip is mainly a finger tip grip. First place the two middle fingers on the club next to the index finger of the left hand (Figure 12-8B). Use only fingertips. Overlap the little finger between the index and middle finger of the left hand. The index finger of the right hand is formed like a trigger finger and placed gently

A   B   C

FIGURE 12-7   Assuming the grip: (A) natural hand position, (B) natural hand position—arms extended, (C) natural hand position—golf grip.

FIGURE 12-8   (A) Left-hand grip—fingers, palm.

FIGURE 12-9   A grip aid helps place hands in perfect grip.

(B) Right-hand grip—two middle fingers.

on the club. Let the thumb find a natural place as you form the line mentioned above. The palm of the right hand covers the left thumb but does not touch the golf club.

7. Close the right hand; the life line of the right palm should be placed over the left thumb.
8. The palms should face each other; the line formed by the index finger and thumb of the right hand should also point toward the right eye; the club face should be square to the line of flight.

▶ **Practice Suggestions**

1. Place class in groups of two. One student works on acquiring a correct golf grip aided by the second student.
2. Grip with the left hand only. Hold the 7 iron at arm's length using only the left arm and hand. Remove all of the fingers from the club except the index finger. The club will be held with only this finger and the base of the hand.
3. Have the student helper attempt to pull the club from the golfer's grip. The club should not come out easily if at all. If the grip is incorrect, the club will be very difficult to hold at arm's length and can be removed easily by the student helper.

4. Correct right hand position must be observed by a qualified instructor.
5. Grip aids can be purchased and placed on a dowel rod. Grip aids come pre-molded for both right- and left-hand golfers. Normal, strong, or weak grips are also available. Home practice with a grip aid will speed learning (Figure 12-9).

The Stance and Address

The stance and address first involve assuming a good grip. Next, the feet, hips, and shoulders are properly aligned along with the club face. The stance is completed with two bends and a tilt. The first bend is in the waist, the second bend is at the knees, and the right shoulder is dropped to form a tilt.

Although there are three styles of stances, the square stance is used by most golfers for most all shots (Figure 12-10). The open stance is used for special shots, such as a sand trap shot. The closed stance is usually used to compensate for certain types of body builds. The open and closed stances can produce altered ball flight patterns such as a slice or a hook.

▶ **Learning Cues**

1. Always choose a target before attempting the address and stance. Stand in line with the ball and target and draw an imaginary line from the ball to the target. A second imaginary line must be drawn parallel to the first line. These two lines must run parallel and not converge.
2. After securing a correct grip, place the club face on the target line with the bottom of the club face at a right angle to the line.
3. The second line is used to align your feet, hips, and shoulders at a right angle to the club face. The feet, hips, and shoulders should be pointing in the same direction.
4. In a good stance the arms will hang freely from

FIGURE 12-10 Three types of stances, left to right: open, square, and closed.

the shoulders and straight down. Standing too far from the ball will cause a poor swing plane, and poor shots will result.

Ball position is determined somewhat by experimentation. As a general rule, the golf ball will be placed near the inside of the left heel for all full swing shots. You may need to move the ball nearer the center of your stance for the shorter clubs. Place the ball right of center for special shots or unusual circumstances (Figure 12-11).

Swing

The swing is a long, large elliptical circle. The radius of the circle is the firm left arm and the club. The left arm, wrist, and hand must be in control from the takeaway, through the backswing, especially at the beginning of the downswing and on into the follow-through. Any undue influence by the right arm or hand will distort the swing circle and ruin the shot.

Swing the club back and up as far as you can, maintaining your balance. The right knee should remain inside the right foot during the backswing. The wrists will fall into a cocked position with the thumbs under the shaft. This will occur near the top of the backswing. You will have turned your back to the target, but your head has remained steady. Your right elbow will be pointed downward.

The forward swing is started by replacing the left heel in the original address position. You should strive for the feeling of stepping into the shot. Your left heel may not come off the ground for all clubs, but the feeling of stepping into the shot is the same for all clubs. As you step into the shot, you must keep your head positioned behind the ball. Avoid anxiety and an urge of the right shoulder to take over the swing.

FIGURE 12-11 Ball positions.

The wrists will remain cocked during the beginning of the downswing. They will uncock automatically without thinking about it.

During the forward swing you should have a sensation of the right side working underneath the left side causing a bowing action in the waist. With the irons, you should feel as though you are swinging down and through, and with the woods, you should feel a more level swing.

The entire swing lasts but a short time and does not require complicated thought processes. If you follow the above description of a golf swing and with good tempo, you will have the sensation of swinging the club through the ball and down the target line. The swing will finish as you face the target with most of your weight on the left foot. The right foot will turn up on the toes. Your hands will finish high, and the weight will be equally distributed between the outside of the left foot and the right toes.

Although we frequently think of the adage "practice makes perfect," the truth is that "practice makes permanent." Therefore, haphazard practice is worse than no practice at all. Plan your practices well, concentrating on one phase of the swing at a time. Remember that you will probably get worse as your mind and body attempt to learn or relearn this new skill. Be patient and give yourself time to succeed.

▶ **Learning Cues** (Figure 12-12)

A. *Takeaway.* The takeaway is the act of moving the club away from the ball. The length of the takeaway is determined by how far the club moves away from the ball yet remains close to the ground. The longer the club, the longer the takeaway. The speed of the takeaway also determines the overall tempo of the entire golf swing.
   1. With the left hand, wrist and arm in control, start moving the club straight back away from the ball. Do not pull the club inside the target line. The club will eventually begin an inside route as the club rises from the ground and is lifted into the backswing.
B. *Backswing.* This is not really a swing, but the act of turning and lifting the club into position.
   1. With the left arm still in control, begin coiling the body as you lift the club upward. The left shoulder will begin turning to a behind-the-ball position.

2. As the club reaches waist level, you should see the left arm still firm and in control. The right elbow has begun to hinge. The left knee has begun to turn inward. The right leg is still braced, with the knee turned inward to prevent a lateral sway and loss of balance. The head has also begun to rotate slightly, but does not move laterally.

C. *At the Top.*
   1. The club should be horizontal for the longer clubs, near horizontal for shorter clubs. The left side is still in control. The thumbs are under the shaft to support the club.
   2. Sometime during the backswing, usually near the finish, the wrists move to a cocked position. This action should happen naturally and is caused by the speed of the backswing.
   3. Your back should be turned to the target. The head will have continued to rotate but with no lateral movement. The right elbow is pointing toward the ground.
   4. The right leg has remained in the braced position. The left knee has turned inward, and the left heel may have been pulled off the ground.

D. *Downswing*
   1. The initial movement is made by replacing the left heel. A feeling of stepping into the swing should occur. As you step into the swing, the

A

B

FIGURE 12-12 Swing sequence: (A) takeaway, (B) backswing, (C) at the top, (D) follow-through.

hips will begin to slide on a parallel line to the target line.

2. With the left side still in control, you should pull the club on a downward angle. You will attempt to swing down and through the ball.
3. The right side is active as it works under the left side. You will feel a bowing sensation in the waist.
4. The wrists will uncock naturally; correct timing of the wrist cock will be obtained by practice.
5. The head must remain behind the ball. Swing the club beyond your face before you allow head movement.

E. *Follow-through.* The follow-through is a reaction to all that has gone on before. If all has gone well, the hands will finish high, and you should be facing the target. You will be equally balanced between the outside of your left foot and the toes of the right foot.

▶ **Practice Suggestions**

Many warm-up exercises can be used that approximate the rhythm and pattern of a full swing. In addition, golf is a target game and therefore a target should be selected and used as a reference in all drills.

A. Without a Ball or Club
1. Assume a golf stance and grip, arms hanging straight down from your shoulders, knees and waist bent slightly. On command, pivot and swing to a position with arms horizontal to the ground. Stop and check for correct balance and body position. Continue on to the top of the backswing and stop. Execute a downswing, stopping at a point where the ball would be struck. Finally, finish the swing. Each stop should be examined for correct body balance and position.
2. With a towel rolled and grasped at either end, assume a stance, then execute a golf swing. (A golf club can be used.) Make sure your weight is kept inside the rear foot on the backswing. Avoid excessive lateral movement.

B. With a Club and Ball
1. Assume a golf stance. Note the position of your left foot. Next, place your left foot next to your right foot. From this position, execute a backswing and come to a stop. The downswing is started by lifting your left foot from the ground and beginning to step this foot toward its original position. At the same time, begin to pull downward with your left arm. Complete the swing by replacing the left foot in its original position. Correct execution will teach

C

D

FIGURE 12-12 (cont.)

the sensation of weight transfer in the golf swing. Practice this drill without a ball first until you gain control. Add the ball to the drill only after you have good balance and control.

2. To learn control of the clubface, choke down on a 7 iron. Put your feet together and practice hitting balls. When a majority of the balls are flying toward your target, try a regular grip or move to a longer club. This drill can be used with any club including the woods.

3. Stand on the left foot only, using the right toes only for balance. Hit balls toward a target from this position. This drill simulates body position at ball contact.

SUITING CLUBS TO SHOTS

Woods

The woods are used for the longest shots in golf. The driver, the longest club, is used for shots from the teeing ground on the longer holes. The first shot on every hole may be teed.

The 3 and 5 woods are also used for distance. They may be used for teeing off, but their primary use is from the fairway. They do not afford as much distance as the driver, but are more accurate. A near perfect lie is necessary when using a wood from the fairway or rough. If in doubt as to the lie, it is best to use an iron.

Long Irons

The 2, 3, and 4 irons are considered the long irons. They produce less distance than the woods but are more accurate. Most long par 3 holes require a long iron for the first shot. These clubs are good for fairway and rough shots. They can also be substituted for a wood in a bad lie situation.

Some golfers find the long irons too difficult to use. A 7 wood can substitute for the 2 and 3 irons, leaving room for an extra club.

Medium Irons

This name applies to the 5, 6, and 7 irons. Remember, as the number becomes higher, so does the flight of the shot produced. Increased height gives less distance and less roll, but more accuracy.

Medium irons are versatile and can be used for several different kinds of shots. Par 3 golf holes of medium length require a medium iron for the first shot. On any hole, the medium irons should be considered as you near the 150-yard marker. A medium iron is a good choice from a fairway bunker with a large front lip. Near the green, if you desire a shot to land on the green and roll towards the hole, a medium iron works well. From deep rough, these clubs can get you back in play.

When first learning the golf swing, the medium irons are an excellent choice as the clubs with which to begin. Most golf drills require a medium iron.

Short Irons

This category includes the 8, 9, and pitching wedge (10 iron). These are the most accurate of all the irons and are used inside the 150-yard marker. Since the shots will fly much higher, you can expect less roll. You may now shoot more towards a specific target, such as the green or the hole, rather than a landing area.

During your practice sessions, learn how far the shortest club in your set will travel with a full swing under normal circumstances. On the golf course, once you are located at a distance that requires less than a full swing, adjustments will have to be made.

To curtail distance, first open your stance slightly. This will help shorten the backswing. Choking down on the club can also reduce distance. Narrow the stance in conjunction with the short irons for shorter shots. See Chip Shots and Pitch Shots for further ideas.

SPECIAL SHOTS

The short approach shots discussed in this section—the pitch, chip, sand shot, and putt—are frequently called the golfer's scoring strokes. A high percentage of shots taken during a round of golf consists of these four types; therefore, the more proficient you become, the lower your scores will become. One of the key elements in these shots involves "feel"; consequently, the shots must be practiced frequently in order to develop a comfortable feeling. Most of these shots, with the exception of a fairway sand shot, are executed near the green or on the green itself.

Pitch Shot

The pitch shot is characterized as a high flying, minimum roll type shot. This shot is generally executed with a high lofted iron such as the 8, 9 or pitching wedge. Less than a full swing is required.

The pitch shot is a good choice for a golfer faced with a hazard, sand or water, blocking the entry to the green. Many golfers use the pitch shot as a substitute for the chip shot, even though it is more difficult (Figure 12-13).

▶ **Learning Cues**

1. Assume a square or open stance. Use your normal grip.
2. The feet are moved closer together.
3. Play the ball slightly left of center.
4. Pick the club up early in the backswing by cocking the wrists.

FIGURE 12-13 Pitch shot.

FIGURE 12-14 Chip shot.

5. Swing down and through, making sure the hands do not stop at ball impact.

Chip Shot

The chip shot is characterized as a low flying, maximum roll type shot. Generally, the ball will be in the air one-third of the time, rolling two-thirds of the time. Any club—5 iron through pitching wedge —may be used. More lofted clubs produce less roll.

Most instructors suggest that the beginning golfer select one club, 7 or 9 iron, to develop the necessary experience. Since the chip shot is largely roll, the shot must be treated much like a putt. Select a landing spot, then read the green to the hole (Figure 12-14).

▶ **Learning Cues**

1. Narrow stance, square or slightly open.
2. Normal grip. Some golfers prefer a putting grip.
3. Play ball left of center. Hands, head, and weight center must be in front of ball. This delofts the club, allowing maximum roll.
4. Keep lower body movement to a minimum, especially on the backswing.

▶ **Practice Suggestions**

1. Experiment with different clubs at 10-yard intervals starting 10 yards from the green.

2. Hit pitch shots over a barrier, such as your golf bag.
3. Hit chip shots onto a practice green. Notice how far the ball rolls using different clubs.
4. Practice both chip shots and pitch shots with the same club. Note how changes are made to produce each shot.

Sand Shot

The sand shot is usually a difficult shot for the beginner to master because sand does not have the firmness of the fairway nor does the ball set up as it does on grass. A specially designed club called a sand wedge is used to execute the shot. Again, the element of "feel" can determine success. Getting out of a sand trap requires various strategies. With traps that are flat, near the green, and with no lip, the beginner might try putting the ball out of the trap, provided the ball is not buried. For shots with a low lip near the green, the golfer may try a chip shot. However, for shots in a deep trap and with the ball buried in the sand, the golfer must execute an explosion shot. Remember, a golfer may not ground a club in a trap without incurring a penalty.

▶ **Learning Cues**

1. Address the ball with an open stance. Wiggle the feet into the sand to secure a good foothold and prevent slipping.

FIGURE 12-15   Sand shot.

2. The ball is played right of center. Preshift some weight forward prior to the swing, but maintain your head position behind the ball during the entire swing. Open the club face slightly.
3. Cock the wrists early in the backswing, much like the pitch shot. Focus on a spot an inch or so behind the ball.
4. Explode the clubhead onto the spot behind the ball. You must hit sand—not the ball.
5. Be sure to keep the clubhead traveling through the sand, under the ball, and into a good finish (Figure 12-15).

The Putt

Putting is probably the most important phase of the game, and too often one of the most neglected. Concentration and confidence are two of the primary requirements for good putting, and can be gained best through practice of fundamental techniques. Forms of putting differ widely, but basic fundamentals are much the same.

▶ Learning Cues

1. Grip the club with your fingers, palms facing each other and in line with the putter face. All five fingers of the bottom hand grip the club. Overlap the index finger of the top hand (Figure 12-16).
2. Any stance that is comfortable and allows you to place your eyes directly over the ball is acceptable.

FIGURE 12-16   Putting grip. Note overlap of index finger.

3. Both elbows must be bent to allow you to stand close to the ball. You must also crouch down slightly for comfort.
4. The ball is played left of center. The putting stance may seem awkward at first, but give it a chance (Figure 12-17).
5. The backswing should be kept low. It is initiated with the arms with little or no wrist break.
6. The forward stroke should return along the same line, keeping the putter face square to the intended putting line.

FIGURE 12-17   Putting stance: (A) front view, (B) from behind.

The Sweetspot. This name is given to an eighth-inch wide vertical area located on the face of the putter. The most successful putts occur when the sweetspot strikes the center of the ball. Missing the sweetspot towards the heel of the putter will cause the loss of distance and some control. Missing the sweetspot towards the toe of the putter will cause even more loss of distance and even more loss of control.

Of all putting fundamentals, striking the sweetspot to the center of the ball ranks as the most important. Regardless of which putting style you choose or change to later, striking the sweetspot to the center of the ball will always be your number one goal.

Finding the Sweetspot. To find the sweetspot, hold your putterhead in front of your face, putter face facing you, using your thumb and first finger. Using a golf ball, begin dinging the putter's face. Find the area that will allow you to drive the putter straight back and forth with no gyrations or shaft vibrations. Note the spot. Make a line on top of the putter to align with this sweetspot. Some putters already have a line marked for you; this line may or may not be correct.

The Putting Stroke. The putting stroke can be described as a sweeping motion. There should be no lower body movement. Your head should also be kept still until the putt is well on its way. The amount of wrist break depends on the individual. Generally, the closer to the hole, the less wrist break needed to putt. Be sure to keep your hands moving with the putt. Many beginners stop the hands at ball impact causing mis-hit putts.

Finally, learn to read the greens. A putt seldom rolls perfectly straight to the hole unless it is a very short putt. Since no green is perfectly flat, study which way the ball will turn and to what degree. The most important factor in reading a green is judging distance. Misjudging distance and missing the sweetspot are the main causes of missed putts.

Judging distance on a putt must include factors along with distance. How fast the ball will roll on a green can be affected by the grass length. Greens are mowed early each day and are much faster early in the morning after being mowed. Soft greens are usually slower than hard greens. A putt traveling downhill will roll much farther than one going uphill. In some areas, the grain of the grass is a factor to be considered. Since putting can account for nearly half or more of your total strokes, be sure to devote plenty of time to developing your putting skills.

HELPFUL HINTS

1. Always select a target when planning any shot or putt. Stand at least ten feet behind the ball, plan your shot, then choose a club.
2. During the swing, concentrate on ball contact and direction rather than distance.
3. Know what club to use from 150 yards. Generally, men can add or subtract 10 yards and women 7 yards when choosing clubs for other distances.
4. For downhill shots, use a lofted club, wide stance, and play the ball back in the stance.
5. For uphill shots, use a less lofted club than normal, wide stance for balance, and play the ball forward in the stance. In both uphill and down-

hill shots, adjust your shoulder position and swing to match the contour of the hill.

6. For sidehill shots with the ball above your feet, take more club than normal, but choke down and swing easy. Expect the ball to travel in the direction of the contour of the hill.

7. For a sidehill shot with the ball below your feet, take more club than normal and plan to use a short, easy swing. This is one of the more difficult trouble shots in golf.

8. Consider weather conditions when planning shots. A golf ball will fly farther in warm, dry air. Consider the velocity and direction of the wind and how it will affect your ball flight.

9. Do not practice swing before you hit a normal shot. Use a practice swing after you have made a poor swing, and only if it will not delay play.

10. Practice swing may be used before playing an unusual or difficult shot to help determine how the normal swing must be altered.

11. Immediately after you play, analyze your game. Decide which part of your game needs the most practice or more instruction.

12. Most amateur golfers make three mistakes. First, they underclub themselves, then overswing, and finally overestimate their ability. Try to play within your own abilities and when in trouble, get back in play. Avoid attempting the miracle shot. It is better to accept a score of one or two strokes over par on a hole, rather than a very large score made by using poor judgment.

MODIFICATIONS FOR SPECIAL POPULATIONS

Orthopedically Impaired

1. Allow wheelchair users to play from their chairs using a standard position for striking, e.g., perpendicular to the ball. Reposition striking position to accommodate swing, e.g., facing the green and striking with one arm if necessary.

2. If outdoor facilities are not accessible, e.g., rough terrain or orthopedic condition too severe, develop an indoor putting course. Use carpet remnants for greens and tees, and boards for side rails.

3. Modify the length of the club.

Mentally Impaired

1. Keep the concept of the game simple, do not stress various club selections for various conditions, e.g., suggest that a student use a selection of driver from the tee, an iron for the fairway, and putter for the green.

2. Refer to #2 in Orthopedically Impaired above.

Sensory Impaired

1. Allow blind students to "feel" someone complete a golf swing.

2. Allow the blind student to pace off the distance on the putting surface to the hole.

SAFETY CONSIDERATIONS

Golf can be a dangerous game if attention is not given to your play and the play of others. Whether golf is being played in a class situation, on a practice range, or while playing a round, basic safety rules must be observed.

1. Never hit a shot until you are sure those in front of you are out of your range. If you hit another player, you may be liable for damages.

2. Never swing a club, especially on the tees, unless you are sure no one is standing close to you.

3. If the warning "Fore" is given, it is often dangerous to turn to see where the ball is coming from. It is best to cover the head for protection and turn away from the direction of the warning.

4. In the event of a thunderstorm, it is not wise to remain outdoors. Shelter should be sought in a closed building protected against lightning. Large or small unprotected buildings are alternatives in the order given. If remaining outdoors is unavoidable, keep away from open spaces and hilltops, from isolated trees, wire fences, and small shelters in exposed locations. Shelter may also be sought in caves, depressions or deep valleys and canyons, the foot of a cliff, or in a dense stand of trees. Umbrellas held overhead in exposed places are dangerous.

5. Never practice in an area where others are playing. Most golf courses have special practice areas.

6. Never hit practice shots while playing a round. It not only wastes time but is dangerous.

7. Only one person should hit at a time. The person farthest from the hole should play first.

8. Knowing and applying the rules of golf and golfing etiquette will increase your safety on a golf course.

9. Carry a towel and wipe hands dry, particularly on hot, humid days and rainy days.

10. Know the distances of specific clubs and distances you can hit the ball.

In Class—Rules for the Instructor:

1. Plan the lesson well in advance, checking such things as formation, target areas, methods of retrieval.

2. Allow no one to swing a club unless instructed to do so.

3. Provide plenty of space between golfers.

4. If stations are used, provide for adequate distance between groups.

In Class—Rules for the Student:

1. Do not retrieve a golf ball until asked to do so; never step out of line to pick up "muffed" shot.
2. Do not walk too close behind other golfers swinging the golf club.
3. If working with a partner, stand in front and to the side of your partner, not behind.
4. Listen to instruction, follow prescribed rules.

ETIQUETTE AND PLAYING COURTESIES

Since golf is a polite game with a well-defined code of ethics, it is important for every golfer to observe common courtesies while on the course.

In General, While Playing the Course:

1. Be polite at all times; know the rules of golf so decisions can be made quickly without causing undue delay.
2. Be aware of the local rules and regulations that govern play on a course.
3. Do not hit practice shots between regular shots —it is an infraction of the rules.
4. Abstain from obscene language, loud talk, and club throwing.
5. Plan ahead and be ready to play your next shot without undue delay. The player farthest from the flag stick shoots first.
6. Do not talk, move around, stand too close or directly in line of a shot when another player is preparing to shoot.
7. Never play a shot until the group ahead is completely out of range.
8. While looking for a lost ball, do not unduly delay the play of others. Allow a group playing behind you to go through by signalling them to do so and do not resume play until they are out of range.
9. After each shot, pick up the divot or loose grass and replace it with your hand in the divot mark. Pat it down with your foot.
10. Fill holes made in bunkers and smooth the sand after playing from a trap. Be sure to rake all sand traps upon leaving them.
11. Keep pull carts and motorized carts off the green area.
12. Yell "Fore" if a ball is in danger of striking another person.
13. The person having the honor (lowest score on the preceding hole) tees up first.
14. Notify your partners when you wish to change a golf ball.

On the Putting Green:

1. As soon as a hole has been completed, the player should leave the green. Do not total the scores and record them on the green.
2. Allow the person farthest from the hole to putt first.
3. When lifting a ball on the green, mark it with a coin.
4. Never lay a bag of clubs down on the green.
5. Do not throw the flag stick off to the side. Always lay it down gently, away from all play, and replace it when the hole has been completed.
6. Do not damage the hole with the stick or by standing too close to the hole.
7. Repair ball marks on the green.
8. Upon completion of the hole, the group should move off the green to record scores.
9. Do not drag your feet or in any way scuff the green.

RULES OF GOLF

The rules of golf have been developed and are periodically upgraded by two coordinating bodies—the United States Golf Association (USGA) and the Royal and Ancient Golf Club of St. Andrews, Scotland. The rules undergo continual study and are revised by these two bodies every four years. The USGA publishes a rule book each year and offers it for sale at a minimal cost. It is strongly recommended that serious students obtain a copy. A booklet entitled *Easy Way to Learn Golf Rules* is available at a minimal cost from the National Golf Foundation.

Local Rules

In constructing the rules which uniformly govern all golf play in the United States, the United States Golf Association recognizes that certain local conditions such as climate, variable physical conditions, and characteristics of golf courses may necessitate modifications of the rules. These modifications are termed Local Rules and are designed to protect the golf course and make the game more enjoyable. A player is responsible for becoming acquainted with the Local Rules before playing. Sources of information concerning Local Rules include the golf professional, the score card, golf course bulletin board, and players familiar with the golf course.

The United States Golf Association limits the extent to which Local Rules may modify the USGA rules. Players should refer to the United States Golf Association Rules of Golf Appendix to familiarize themselves with the limitations.

Summary of Important Golf Rules

1. A player may have a maximum of 14 clubs in the golf bag at any one time. Penalty for exceeding the maximum: disqualification.

2. A player must tee up his ball between the tee markers or anywhere in the rectangle two club lengths behind them. Violation of the rule: two-stroke penalty.

3. An intentional swing at the ball must be counted as a stroke, even if the player "wiffs" it.

4. A ball is considered lost outside of a hazard if not retrieved in five minutes.

5. A ball must be played as it lies except as provided for in the rules.

6. Loose impediments such as leaves, sticks (anything of nature lying around) may be removed outside of a hazard, so long as the ball does not move.

7. Relief from man-made obstructions, drop the ball within one club length of point of nearest relief without penalty, but no closer to the hole. See rule book for exceptions.

8. If a player hits a ball out-of-bounds, the player must take a one-stroke penalty and play the ball from the original spot.

9. When a ball is hit into a water hazard, the player may drop a ball behind the hazard, keeping the spot at which the ball crossed the hazard between himself and the hole. Penalty: one stroke.

10. A player, while in the act of putting on the green, whose ball hits another player's ball or the flag stick, is assessed a two-stroke penalty. Putting from off the green is not considered a putt.

TERMINOLOGY

Ace   A hole in one.

Address   The position taken by a player in preparing to start a stroke.

Apron   The area immediately surrounding the green.

Banana ball   A slice

Best ball tournament   Competition in which the better score of a partnership on each hole is used as the team score.

Birdie   The score of one under par on a hole.

Bogey   A score of one over par on a hole (United States rules). In countries playing the British rules, a bogey is the score an average golfer should make on a hole; on easier holes, par and bogey might be the same score.

Casual water   Temporary accumulation of water which is not recognized as a hazard on the course.

Course rating   The comparative difficulty of a specific course. Usually computed by a committee of a local association in order to have uniform handicapping for all courses within a district.

Divot   Sod cut with the clubhead when executing or attempting to execute a shot.

Dogleg   A hole which has a sharp bend in the fairway.

Driver   Number 1 wood.

Eagle   A score for a hole played in two strokes under par.

Fairway   The course between the teeing ground and the putting green, exclusive of hazards.

Flag   Banner on top of the flagstick identifying the cup.

Fore   A warning cry to anyone of a stroke about to be played or one that has been played.

Go to school   Learning the roll of a green by watching a previous putt over the same area.

Ground under repair   Any portion of the course so marked that includes material piled for removal or a hole made by a greenskeeper.

Hazard   Any bunker, water hazard, or lateral water hazard.

Hole   Small cup sunk into the green, into which the golf ball is hit. The hole is 4 ¼ inches in diameter and at least 4 inches deep.

Honor   The side entitled to play first from the teeing ground is said to have the honor. This is usually determined by a coin flip on the first tee. Once play begins, the player having the lowest score on the previous hole is said to have the honor thereafter.

Hook   A ball in flight that curves from right to left (for a right-handed golfer).

Lie   The position of the ball on the playing ground. Also refers to the angle of the clubhead.

Loft   The slope given to the face of a golf club to aid in knocking the ball in a high curve.

Loose impediments   Natural objects not fixed or growing and not adhering to the ball, and including stones not solidly embedded, leaves, twigs, branches, and the like, dung, worms, and insects, and casts or heaps made by them.

Match play   Competition in which the winner is decided by the number of holes won.

Mulligan   Permitting a second hit of a badly played ball—usually on a tee shot. (Not permitted under the rules but by mutual agreement in friendly matches.)

Obstruction   An artificial object erected, placed, or left on a course and not an integral part of the course.

Par   The standard score for a hole.

Pull-shot   To hit a ball straight, but to the left of the target (for a right-handed golfer).

Push-shot   To hit a ball straight, but to the right of the target (for a right-handed golfer).

Rough   The unmowed terrain on either side of the fairway.

Scotch foursome   A competitive round in which two partners play the same ball, taking alternate shots.

Slice   A ball in flight that curves from left to right (for a right-handed person).

Stroke play (medal play)   Competition in which the winner is decided by the total number of strokes taken from a specific number of rounds, not by individual holes won, as in match play.

Summer rules   Playing the ball as it lies from tee through green.

Teeing ground   The starting place for the hole to be played.

Trap   A hazard, technically known as a bunker.

Waggle   Body or club action prior to starting the swing.

Wedge   A heavy iron club that is used to loft the ball high into the air. It is also used for special situations, such as getting out of heavy grass or sand.

Winter rules   The privilege of improving the lie of the ball on the fairway of the hole being played.

SELECTED REFERENCES

Aultman, D. *The Masters of Golf: Learning Their Methods.* New York: Atheneum, 1989.

Hogan, B. *Free Lessons: The Modern Fundamentals of Golf.* Trumbull, CT: Golf Digest/Tennis, Inc., 1985.

Lopez, N. *The Complete Golfer.* Chicago, IL: Contemporary Books, Inc., 1988.

National Golf Foundation. *The Easy Way to Learn Golf Rules.* Jupiter, FL: National Golf Foundation, 1986.

Nicklaus, J. *My 55 Ways to Lower Your Golf Score.* New York: Simon and Schuster, 1985.

Oritz, H. and Farley, D. *Six Days to Better Golf: The Secret of Learning the Golf Swing.* New York: Harper and Row, 1988.

Owens, De De. *The American Coaching Effectiveness Program.* Champaign, IL: Leisure Press, 1991.

Palmer, A. *Play Great Golf: Mastering the Fundamentals of Your Game.* Garden City, NY: Doubleday, 1987.

Snead, J.C. and Johnson, J.L. *Golf Today.* St. Paul: West Pub. Co., 1989.

Watson, T. and Hannigan, F. *The New Rules of Golf.* Latest ed. New York: Random House.

Wiren, G. with T. Dawson. *Golf's Common Errors and What to Do About Them.* Chicago: Contemporary Books, Inc., 1987.

Wiren, G. *Golf: Building a Solid Game.* Englewood Cliffs, NJ: Prentice Hall, 1987.

Audio-Visual Materials

Other excellent material and films can be obtained by writing to:

National Golf Foundation, 200 Castlewood Dr., North Palm Beach, FL 33408.

United States Golf Association, Golf House, Library Corner Rd., Far Hills, NJ 07931.

13 GYMNASTICS AND TUMBLING

THIS CHAPTER WILL ENABLE YOU TO:

▶ Understand gymnastics as a competitive sport.
▶ Identify the various events which comprise competition in gymnastics for men and women.
▶ Appreciate the importance of acquiring safety attitudes and habits in gymnastics.
▶ Understand how to introduce a tumbling and/or gymnastics unit in the classroom.
▶ Identify basic body positions, grasps, and moves used in beginning tumbling and gymnastics.

NATURE AND PURPOSE

Many people find it hard to think of gymnastics as a sport. It does not have the same tangible, competitive aspect that spectators see in other sporting events. We cannot yell "defense" or "get the ball," nor can we measure the performance of the gymnast with a stop watch or measuring tape. Gymnastics is the performance of a routine on a piece of apparatus. The routine is a combination of stunts and moves that have been practiced and improved over a period of time. The gymnast is actually competing against himself (herself), trying to improve upon the last performance. The sport of gymnastics involves individual effort; however, the gymnast's score is added to that of his teammates to obtain a team score.

One reason that makes it difficult for the uninformed spectator to grasp the concept of gymnastics is that there is no scoreboard or clock to watch during a gymnastic performance. In gymnastics it is not only *what* is performed, but *how* it is performed that is important.

Gymnastics, like figure skating and diving, are judged by qualified individuals. Although judging may sometimes seem too subjective, there are specific guidelines that judges must use in scoring. A judge is considering the difficulty, the execution, and the composition of the routine. These three aspects are fundamental in scoring, but other areas also enter into a score—among them amplitude, creativity, elegance, risk, etc.

All parts of the body benefit in the sport of gymnastics. It promotes strength, agility, flexibility, coordination, kinesthetic sense, and balance. Furthermore mastery of a stunt or routine develops more than the physical aspects; it also improves the participant's self-image.

THE PARTICIPANT

As in other sports, size may determine the future and success of a gymnast. However, in gymnastics someone small in stature is more likely to succeed than the usual stereotyped 6'5", 220 lb. athlete. This does not mean that a tall gymnast will be unsuccessful, but generally a gymnast is shorter than 5'10".

Today's gymnast must be above average in strength for his or her height and weight. Flexibility is another needed physical attribute. Also required are a good kinesthetic sense (awareness of where one's body and body parts are in space), and a sense of balance. In addition, a well-developed sense of timing along with good coordination are important.

Cardiorespiratory endurance does not play as vital a role in gymnastics as in other sports; however, a gymnast must have muscle endurance. Although a gymnastic routine may last only from one to two minutes, the abdominal or quadricep muscles may be contracted throughout that time. Also, a gymnast must have muscle power to be able to use the body and muscle groups with explosive force. Timing plays a part with the burst of energy, but unless the strength is there to call upon, the gymnast may end up on the floor.

Along with the physical attributes, there are also psychological aspects to be considered. The participant is individualistic, self-motivated, confident, and self-assured. The sport involves perseverance and a drive for perfection. The gymnast is subject to taking risks but not to the extent that safety is sacrificed.

Gymnastics is a team sport, but as a member of a team a gymnast is also competing against his or her teammates. As previously mentioned, a gymnast is actually competing against himself, always striving to perfect his routine. The individual's score will not only determine his or her place among the competitors, but also will be added to the team scores to determine their final standing.

THE COMPETITION

The gymnastic meet is an event in which more than one thing is happening at once. In large meets all pieces of equipment may be worked at once. Judges will be at every station, and the gymnasts rotate to each station to perform.

On a smaller scale, for instance a women's college meet, you may have the balance beam and floor exercise being judged at the same time by different sets of judges. Later, the uneven bars and vaulting are judged. There are usually two judges per event at these meets. One set of judges may score the balance beam and unevens, while the other set will judge the floor exercise and vaulting.

At a gymnastic meet, the judges watch and score the performance. The average of scores is flashed (open scoring) or a runner will take the score to the scorer's table (closed scoring) where it will be tallied. Individual gymnasts' scores are added together to form a team score. A gymnast may score differently on each piece of equipment. For instance, he may be first on the pommel horse and third in vaulting, etc.

The "all-around" event comprises a total of the scores of a gymnast who competed in every event. The gymnast who wins the all-around is considered the top gymnast of the meet. A gymnast who does not compete all-around is called a specialist and may work only the floor exercise and vaulting. In most countries gymnasts are always all-around. Only in the United States do we continue to have gymnastic specialists and many argue this system enables more people to participate.

Each piece of equipment or event is unique, requiring a different strength from the gymnast. For example, a performer on the still rings would require more upper body strength than someone working floor exercise. However, the gymnast who specializes on rings may not be as flexible as the floor exercise specialist. Balance beam requires the athlete to have some dance background and a good sense of balance, while vaulting centers more on the gymnast's speed and explosive power. The all-around gymnast is able to compete in all areas at the meet.

THE RULES AND JUDGING

Most judges have been certified to judge gymnastics by one of the governing bodies of gymnastics. There are five main national groups that have developed the rules for gymnastics:

The National Collegiate Athletic Association (NCAA)

The National Association of Intercollegiate Athletics (NAIA)

The United States Gymnastic Federation (USGF)

The Amateur Athletic Union (AAU)

The National Federation of State High School Associations (NFSHSA)

Each of these organizations provides the guidelines that colleges, conferences, high schools, and clubs follow in competition. However, during national championships they must adhere to a specific set of national rules.

In 1968 the Fédération Internationale Gymnastique (FIG), or International Gymnastic Federation, published a Code of Points which has been the basis for the rules in gymnastics. Although it is not possible to state the universal rules, we will specify the rules that apply in each meet or competition described below.

Unless otherwise agreed upon by the teams involved, the men's gymnastic competition has six events and the women's four events:

Men	Women
1. Floor Exercise	1. Floor Exercise
2. Horizontal Bar	2. Balance Beam
3. Parallel Bars	3. Uneven Parallel Bars
4. Pommel Horse	4. Vault
5. Rings	
6. Vault	

For both men and women there is also the all-around event, which is the total of either the men's six events or the women's four events.

To qualify as a judge, one must first be certified. To earn certification involves passing a written test, attending workshops, and paying a fee for certification. A judge must be aware of the rules of the meet and the sport of gymnastics. He or she must try to watch the performance with complete concentration and be as objective as possible. Judges consider three major areas when scoring a gymnastic routine:

Difficulty (what has been performed). Most stunts have been given a difficulty value that the judges have learned.

Composition (the way the routine is put together). Each event has certain requirements that must be incorporated in a routine.

Execution (how the routine is performed). These three areas make up the greatest part of a judge's score sheet.

Depending on the level of competition, the judge may have a point with which he or she may judge risk, elegance, amplitude, etc. Usually deductions are made on the floor exercise area each time the gymnast goes out of bounds. Deductions are also made for falls, spotting, and not meeting time requirements on balance beam and floor exercise.

One other aspect of judging that is usually seen in private clubs is *compulsory routines*. This is a routine that is constructed for each piece of equipment at different skill levels. A gymnast learns the routine for his or her skill level and competes against other gymnasts at the same level, performing the same routine. As the gymnast becomes more skilled, he or she may move to harder "class levels" and learn more difficult compulsory routines. When judging this type of competition, the judge has also learned the routine and is aware of the specific deductions.

The type of routines used in the Olympics or in intercollegiate meets are routines constructed by the gymnast and are called *optional routines*. These routines contain certain difficulties, but each routine is as different in composition as each gymnast.

SUGGESTED LEARNING SEQUENCE

A. Stretching, sit-ups and push-ups
B. Introduction—nature and purpose
C. Basic rules and safety conditions
D. Fundamental Skills
   1. Tumbling
     a. Forward Roll
     b. Backward Roll
     c. Tripod Balance
     d. Headstand
     e. Prone Headstand
     f. Kip (neckspring)
     g. Cartwheel
     h. Round-off
     i. Back Walkover
     j. Front Walkover
     k. Headstand and Forward Roll
     l. Tinsica
     m. Valdez
     n. Back Handspring
     o. Elementary Combination
   2. Pommel Horse
     a. Feint
     b. Front Support and Swing
     c. Single Leg Circle Forward
     d. Simple Travel
     e. Elementary Combination
   3. Vaulting
     a. Squat Vault
     b. Straddle Vault
     c. Front Vault
     d. Rear Vault
     e. Stoop Vault
     f. Thief Vault
     g. Handspring Vault
     h. Elementary Combination
   4. Rings
     a. Inverted Hang
     b. Nest Hang
     c. Forward Single Leg Cut
     d. Backward Double Leg Cut Dismount
     e. Elementary Combination
   5. High Bar
     a. Backward Hip Circle
     b. Knee Circle
     c. Kip
     d. Squat Dismount from Support
     e. Elementary Combination
   6. Parallel Bars
     a. Forward Hand Walk
     b. Hip Roll
     c. Corkscrew Mount
     d. Flank Dismount
     e. Elementary Combination
   7. Uneven Parallel Bars
     a. Back Hip Pullover
     b. Mill Circle
     c. Pop-up
     d. Straddle Sole Circle
     e. Elementary Combination
   8. Balance Beam
     a. Squat Mount
     b. Chassé
     c. Back Shoulder Roll
     d. Arabesque
     e. Leap
     f. Forward Roll
     g. Cartwheel Dismount
     h. Elementary Combinations

SKILLS AND TECHNIQUES

Basic gymnastic teams refer to body positioning utilized in many of the events. A simple understanding of the basic body positions helps performance. Following are the positions used when performing different stunts in a routine:

1. *Tuck*—The knees and hips are bent, and the head is in a chin-down position.
2. *Pike*—The legs are straight, but the torso is bent at the hips.
3. *Layout*—The entire body is straight.
4. *Puck*—This position is a combination of tuck and pike. There is only a slight bend in the knees.

There are also different grasps used when working the pieces of equipment. The grasps are generally changed a number of times in a routine.

1. *Over grasp*—The palms of the hand are on top of the bar (Figure 13-1).
2. *Under grasp*—The palms of the hand are under the bar (Figure 13-2).
3. *Mixed grasp*—One hand is an over grasp, and the other hand is in an under grasp.

The following are specific terms for the way the body moves in gymnastics:

FIGURE 13-1 Over grasp.

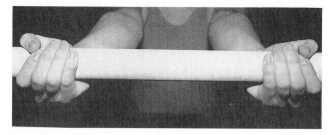

FIGURE 13-2 Under grasp.

1. *Somersault*—This is a rotation around a horizontal axis. The somersault could be in the tuck, pike or layout position.
2. *Twist*—A rotation around a vertical axis. Again, it can be done in different body positions or in combination with a somersault.
3. *Kip*—The kipping action is a skill involving the flexing of the body and then finishing in the extended position. It is done quickly and is used in all events.
4. *Extension*—This is the opposite of the kip because you extend first and then achieve the move due to flexion. A good example of the use of extension would be a back handspring.

In order for the beginning gymnast to master some elementary combinations, a learning series (Practice Suggestions) is given at the end of each apparatus and tumbling section.

MEN'S GYMNASTICS

Although both women and men vault and work floor exercises, the way they perform in these areas is completely different. We will describe first the six men's gymnastics events and then the four women's events.

Pommel Horse

The pommel horse is 64 inches long and 14 inches wide. It stands 45½ inches tall with two handles extending up from the leather body. The height of the handles is 4¾ inches, which makes the overall height 50 inches. The pommel horse is divided into three sections: the left end, as you face it, is called the neck; the middle is called the saddle; and the right end is called the croup. All three areas must be worked in a routine, without hesitations or stops, or else deductions are made by the judges. The pommel horse requires a great deal of upper body strength and balance and is considered by many to be the most difficult men's event. This is one event in gymnastics where a spotter only seems to be in the way. Because of the scissor and leg circles, there is a greater chance of the spotter being injured than the performer.

▶ **Learning Cues**

Feint A feint is used on the pommel horse primarily to initiate movement. A feint helps the gymnast gain momentum to perform a stunt. The gymnast would swing one or both legs in the direction opposite to which the stunt is performed. Many think of a feint as an extra swing or pumping action. In competition, a feint is considered unnecessary movement and its use would result in points being deducted.

Front Support and Swing (Figure 13-3). Jump to a front support. Hands are in an over grasp on the pommels. The arms are straight, and the body is straight with the legs spread wide apart. The swing is initiated from the hips, going side to side. The entire body moves side to side so the swing encompasses the shoulder joint as well as the hips. The gymnast tries to attain as much height as possible on the swing. There is a slight shift of weight as the body swings from pommel to pommel.

Single Leg Circle Forward (Figure 13-4). This can most easily be learned by placing the right hand on the pommel and the left hand on the neck of the horse. Jump to a straight arm support and immediately begin the move. Bring the right leg to the left between the horse and the left leg, twisting the hips slightly and leaning on the right arm. Bring the right leg over the neck of the horse and under the left hand which regrasps the pommel (neck of the horse)

FIGURE 13-3 Front support and swing.

FIGURE 13-4 Single leg circle forward.

after the left leg passes under it. Continue the right leg circling by passing under the right hand and over the croup. This is considered one circle. It should be rhythmic and repeated, making continuous clockwise circles. There is a certain timing to this movement that helps with the momentum and support, making it much like a pendulum swinging.

Simple Travel-Through. Though this is called a simple travel, it is anything but simple and requires a lot of practice to master. Begin by placing the left hand on the neck and the right hand on the left pommel. Jump to a front support. Swing the left leg forward, cutting away the left hand and replacing it. Swing the right leg forward; now both legs are forward. The right hand is between the legs with the left hand balancing on the neck. Swing the left leg back and shift the weight to the right hand and the pommel. The left hand regrasps the left pommel. Both hands are now on the pommel. Swing the right leg back and regrasp the right pommel again by shifting weight. This travel is repeated. Swing the left leg forward and under the left hand which replaces itself on the pommel. Swing the right leg forward and again the right hand is between the legs. Swing the left leg back and shift the body weight to regrasp the right pommel with the right hand. Swing the right leg back and shift the right hand off the pommel to the croup. At this point the performer can dismount, having performed a simple travel. When the gymnast is moving from the neck to the pommels, it is considered an uphill travel, and when moving from the pommels to the croup, it is considered downhill.

▶ **Practice Suggestions**

Jump to front support, single leg circle forward, simple travel, dismount.

Vaulting

The pommel horse may be used in this event. Remove the pommels and tape the holes to prevent any injury to the fingers. The horse is placed with the croup nearest the vaulter at a height of 53 inches. The male gymnast's hands must land only in the middle area of the horse to prevent a .5 deduction in competition.

When working with a beginning gymnast, it is advisable to lower and turn the horse sideways. The women gymnasts vault with the horse in this position, and it is much less intimidating to a beginner. The horse can be lowered to a height comparable to the gymnast's skill level.

The other piece of equipment used in vaulting is the spring board or reuther board. It is placed in front of the horse, and the gymnast hits the board with both feet to initiate the take-off over the horse. The pre-flight is the time between hitting the board until the gymnast touches the horse. The vault is performed and then the after-flight begins until landing. All three phases of the vault are judged. The run to the board is not judged. Judging begins with the board take-off.

▶ **Learning Cues**

Flank Vault (Figure 13-5). The flank vault is so named because the side (flank) of the body passes over the horse. The flank vault is performed by swinging upward from the board and swinging the body and legs to the right over the horse. The right hand is cut away and the left hand leaves the horse just before landing. The gymnast lands facing forward. To spot this vault, the spotter is on the side opposite the passing legs. The spotter helps support and keep the arm of the vaulter stationary by grasp-

FIGURE 13-5 Flank vault.

ing above the elbow. The spotter moves with the gymnast as he or she passes over the horse.

Front Vault. As with the flank vault, the front vault is so named because the front of the body passes over the horse. On take-off the body makes a quarter turn to the left. The legs swing up to the right so that the front of the body passes over the horse. The right arm supports most of the weight, and the left arm pulls out to counteract the legs. The right arm leaves the horse just before landing. The gymnast lands with his left side to the horse. The spotter again stands away from the legs and helps support the shoulders.

Rear Vault (Figure 13-6). The rear of the body passes over the horse. On take-off from the board, the hands hit the horse, and the body quarter turns to the right as the legs are swinging sideward. The rear of the body is passing over the horse, and the legs are parallel to the floor. The right hand leaves

the horse on the quarter turn, and the left hand releases as the body passes over. The right hand reaches for the horse on the landing for stability. The gymnast lands with the right side toward the horse. The spotter grasps the arm closest to him (away from the legs), moves with the gymnast, and releases the arm when the vault is being completed.

The Thief Vault. The thief vault is different from most vaults because it doesn't use a two-foot take-off. The take-off is from one foot, as the other foot swings upward the take-off foot joins it. Both legs pass over the horse followed by the rear. The hands touch the horse as the body passes over in a sitting position. The hands give a downward and backward push. Two spotters are used for the thief vault: one spotter stands on the vaulter's side to support the gymnast's shoulder and arm in case it is needed; the other spotter stands on the board side of the vault to help prevent a fall backward in case the vaulter does not clear the horse.

FIGURE 13-6 Rear vault.

Rings

In competition the rings are called still rings. The performer not only controls his body movement but that of the rings. It is important in a learning situation to have plenty of mats below the ring station. Women lack the upper body strength to compete on the rings; however, the stunts listed here can be taught to both men and women because they do not rely on a great deal of upper body strength.

▶ **Learning Cues**

Inverted Hang (Figure 13-7). Jump to grasp the rings and at the same time flex the arms and tuck the knees to the chest. Lean back with the upper body and stay in a squat position until the head is down, arms are straight, and the inverted position is attained. Extend the legs, using the ropes to stabilize the body if needed, then bring the legs together. The inverted hang can be done in a squat position or a straight position. To return to a starting position, simply flex at the hips and slowly bring the upper body forward. The spotting is either one or two spotters on each side of the performer. Grasp the performer's wrist, and with the other hand assist by lifting up and back if help is needed. Once the inverted hang has been attained, remain near the performer to steady him by placing a hand in front and back.

Nest Hang (Figure 13-8). Jump to hang and bring the feet up to the rings in a tuck position. Hook the feet through the rings and then push the body

through the arms by arching the back. Raise the head. Return by reversing the process. Spotting is done by grasping the performer's wrist and supporting his mid-section in case the feet slip out of the rings.

Forward Single Leg Cut and Catch. Attain an inverted squat hang and straighten legs. The position is an inverted pike with the legs parallel to the floor. Both legs are going to move quickly forward with the left leg straddling out to cut away the left hand from the ring. Regrasp the ring with the left hand as the legs move down to a hang. The performer keeps the arms slightly flexed and bears the weight on the right arm before releasing the left. Keep the ring as still as possible on the release and look for the ring on the regrasp. The spotter supports the performer's upper back and hips after he has reached the pike position. The spotter can help by lifting once the "cut" has been made so the performer can regrasp the ring.

Backward Double Leg Cut Dismount. The rings must be high enough so that the performer cannot reach the floor in a hang. Momentum is the key to successfully completing this dismount. In a hanging position, arch and flex the body to gain some momentum and then raise the legs up and back over the head, bending at the hips. As the feet approach the arms, straddle the legs and look back with the head. Release the rings and raise the chest as the momentum carries the performer to a stand. For the beginner, two spotters are advisable. The

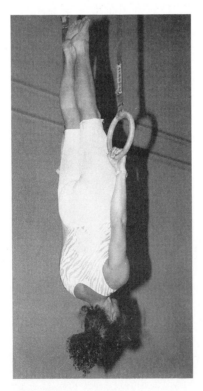

FIGURE 13-7 Inverted hang.

FIGURE 13-8 Nest hang.

spotter on the left side uses his right hand under the performer's shoulder and the left hand on his back. It is important to support the shoulder especially if momentum is lost or the performer releases the rings too soon.

▶ **Practice Suggestions**

Swing to an inverted hang, nest hang, forward single leg cut and catch, backward double leg cut dismount.

High Bar (Horizontal Bar)

The high bar is perhaps the most exciting piece of equipment to watch the male gymnast work. It has constant motion and moves quickly so that the spectator is often left wondering, upon completion of a routine, what the gymnast actually did! The steel bar is 7'10½" wide and is 8'4⅜" off the floor. A routine flows with no stops or pauses. The stunts performed on the high bar are much like the stunts performed on the women's uneven bars. If there is no high bar available, the top bar of the unevens can be used to learn beginning moves. Spotting of the performer on the high bar is virtually impossible without a spotting belt attached to the ceiling with pulleys. Spotting without a belt means that the spotter is in a position to catch the performer when difficulty arises.

Chalk (magnesium carbonate) is used when working the high bar to prevent the performer from slipping when hands are sweaty.

▶ **Learning Cues**

The following movements can be spotted by lowering the bar. These are beginning moves with which the student can attain success.

Backward Hip Circle (Figure 13-9).   The performer jumps to a straight arm support. The hands are in an over grasp. Cast the legs back by flexing at the hips, lifting the heels backward (legs straight and toes pointed) toward the ceiling. As the body comes back to the bar, the head and upper body drop back, and the momentum helps the hips circle around the bar. Keep the hips next to the bar. The spotter or spotters are next to the performer. If standing on the performer's right side, the spotter helps secure the performer's arm with his left hand and uses his right hand to help guide and lift the performer's hips as he circles the bar.

Knee Circle.   To prepare for a knee circle, the performer jumps to a front support and then lifts the right leg over the bar and between the hands. The performer sits on the right leg as he changes his hands or an under grasp. The performer circles the bar with the knee by moving in a forward motion. Before this can happen, he raises the hips so the bar is placed in the bend of the knee. Once in position, the performer lifts his head and chest to begin the forward motion. He circles and returns to the sitting position on the right thigh. The arms cannot collapse in the circling motion, and the head and chest remain up. The spotting for this act requires almost as much technique as the stunt itself. The spotter or spotters stand beside the performer. If the spotter is on the performer's right side, he uses his right hand to reach under and around the bar to grasp the performer's wrist. The grasp used is inverted, and the knuckles will be facing the spotter. The left hand helps support and lift the performer on the back as he circles the bar. The performer may want to chalk the back of the knee to prevent chafing.

Kip (Figure 13-10).   There are many variations of a kip (glide kip, drop kip, reverse kip, etc.). The

FIGURE 13-9 Backward hip circle.

FIGURE 13-10   Kip.

kip can be used as a mount, a stunt within a routine, or a connecting move between stunts. A kip requires strength, but the key is timing. It usually takes a lot of practice to master. Stand facing the bar with hands in an over grasp. Jump, flexing the hips, and bring the ankles forward. As the body swings slightly forward, prepare to whip the legs out and downward. The reaction to the whip with the legs is an upward motion; bear down with the arms and end in a front support. The spotter is on the performer's side and has a sense of timing to assist with the kip. The spotter on the right side of the performer places his left hand on the performer's back and the right hand on his calves. Move with the performer. Help lift the legs and after whip, lift lower back.

Squat Dismount from Support.   From a straight arm support, cast the legs back and tuck the knees to the chest. At the same time, move the feet between the arms and over the bar. Land facing forward in a standing position. Once the momentum is established from the cast, the body continues forward with the head up. The spotters are on either side of the performer in front of the bar he is going to squat over. With the spotter's closest hand, grasp the performer's wrist, and with the other hand grasp his upper arm. Spotters need to move with the performer on the dismount.

▶ **Practice Suggestions**

Jump to front support, backward hip circle, squat dismount from support.

Parallel Bars

Only men compete on the parallel bars, but there is no reason why women cannot successfully learn to work the parallel bars, too. The parallel bars are wooden bars measuring 11′6″ in length, and they are adjustable in height from 5′7″ to 5′9″ and in width from 18″ to 20″. Many beginners lower the bars and adjust the width according to the length of their forearm and hand.

▶ **Learning Cues**

Forward Hand Walk.   Jump to a straight arm support between the bars and move one hand at a time down the bars in a walking motion. Keep the head up and do not let the shoulders depress or sag. Take short hand steps and transfer the weight to the opposite arm on each movement. The spotter grasps the performer's thigh under the bar to support or lift if the performer becomes fatigued.

Hip Roll.   Sit in a straddle seat in the middle of the bars and place both hands in an over grasp on the right bar. The right hand is the hand closest to the right leg. Lower the upper body and bring the head and shoulders under the right bar. At the same time lift the right leg, maintaining the straddle position, and roll across the hips on the left bar. Still in the straddle position, the performer rolls across the right thigh as the left leg crosses over to the right bar. The upper body lifts as the performer ends in a straddle seat, facing the opposite direction from which he or she started. The spotting for this is done from underneath the bars at the shoulders to support the performer, and another spotter may be helpful in guiding the leg placement.

Corkscrew Mount (Figure 13-11).   This is a fun mount to teach beginners. The name matches the movement of the body, and the success rate is great. Stand facing the middle of one side of the bars. Grasp the near bar with the right hand in an under grasp and the left hand in an over grasp. Jump, lifting the legs toward the far bar, landing on the back

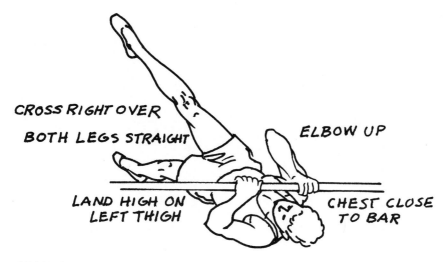

CROSS RIGHT OVER

BOTH LEGS STRAIGHT

ELBOW UP

LAND HIGH ON LEFT THIGH

CHEST CLOSE TO BAR

FIGURE 13-11 Corkscrew mount.

of the left thigh. Begin turning over the bar with the right leg extended and moving downward toward the bar where the hands are grasped. As the legs are twisting, the chest and head stay near and under the grasped bar. When the legs are straddling the bars, the upper body rotates, and the left hand releases to grasp the far bar. Push up with both hands to finish in a straddle seat. Spotting, like the hip roll, is done from under the bar, but this time supports the performer's hips. Again, it may be helpful as a teaching aid to have another spotter helping to guide the performer's legs.

Flank Dismount. Jump to a straight arm support. The body is between the bars. Begin swinging. When the legs are forward, lean on the left arm and release the right hand. Pass the body over the bar, making a quarter turn, and pushing off with the left hand to land with the back toward the bar. The spotter stands to the outside and slightly behind the performer. Grasp the performer's left arm at the wrist with the spotter's left hand and above the elbow with the right. As the performer dismounts the spotter would help guide him over the bar.

▶ **Practice Suggestions**

Corkscrew mount, hip roll, flank dismount.

Floor Exercise

The floor exercise mat is 42′ by 42′ and at least one inch thick. The floor exercise event is the longest of the men's events, lasting 1 minute and 30 seconds. Along with tumbling, the performer displays strength, agility, and balance. The routine moves smoothly and covers all the corners and area of the mat. (Tumbling dominates the floor exercise routine and will be covered later in this chapter.)

WOMEN'S GYMNASTICS

Women's competitive gymnastics consists of four events. Two of the events are timed (balance beam and floor exercise) and must be completed in the allotted time to avoid score deduction. Both balance beam and floor exercise require dance and tumbling. The uneven bars are similar to the men's horizontal bar. The use of two bars reduces the need for upper body strength on the part of the woman gymnast. The uneven bars require circling moves, changes of direction, and changes in hand grips. Lastly, the vault is performed with the vault positioned sideways. The run and take-off are like the men's vault. The women's performance in gymnastics centers around dance and the ability of the gymnast to perform difficult moves with ease. Unlike the men's gymnastic performance, a woman gymnast does not display strength throughout her routines.

Uneven Parallel Bars

This event is done with two parallel bars at different heights. The top bar is 7′6½″ above the floor, and the lower bar is 4′11″ high. The width between the bars can be adjusted out to 2′9⅞″. Routines are constructed to flow smoothly without stops or pauses.

▶ **Learning Cues**

Back Hip Pullover (Figure 13-12). Stand between the bars with the hands shoulder-width apart in an over grasp. Keeping the shoulders and chest close to the bar, kick one leg forward, up and back over the bar. As the first leg travels up, the second leg joins it, and the head drops back. The performer pulls the hips back over the bar and ends in a

FIGURE 13-12   Back hip pullover.

straight arm support. The spotter stands on the opposite side of the bar as the performer. The spotter on the performer's right places her left hand on the performer's lower back and helps lift the legs with the right hand.

Mill Circle (Figure 13-13). The mill circle is very much like the knee circle explained on the horizontal bar. The difference is that the knee is not bent during the stunt. The performer is astride the bar with both legs straight. The bar is resting on the front of the back thigh. The hands are in an under grasp. Keeping the bar in place on the back thigh, the performer lifts her hips up and thrusts the chest forward with the head up. Remaining in this position, circle the bar and finish in the starting position. The spotter stands on the same side of the bar as the back leg of the performer. If the spotter is on the performer's left, she uses her left hand to reach under the bar and grasp the performer's wrist in a reverse grip. As the performer circles the bar, the spotter helps lift the hips with the right hand.

Pop Up. This is an elementary transition from the low bar to the high bar. As the performer jumps to a long hang on the high bar, hands are in an over grasp. Place the left foot on the low bar with the knee bent. The right leg is straight, toe pointed on top of the low bar. The move is very much like a back hip pullover. As the left foot pushes off the lower bar, the head drops back and the arms pull the hips to the high bar. The right leg joins the left as they circle the high bar ending in a straight arm support on that high bar. The performer keeps the hips close to the high bar and thinks of lifting them up and over the bar. The spotter stands on either side of the performer. The spotter will help lift the hips up and

FIGURE 13-13   Mill circle.

back over the bar. On completion, grasp the calves of the performer to help steady the straight arm support.

Straddle Sole Circle Underswing Dismount (Figure 13-14). To learn this dismount the performer stands between the bars facing out. Grasp the

FIGURE 13-14   Straddle sole circle dismount.

bar in an over grip and jump up, placing the soles of the feet on the bar outside of the hands. The arms and legs remain straight as the body swings downward. The arms are pulling against the bar to keep the feet on as the performer circles under the bar. As the height of the swing is reached, the feet release from the bar and extend outward to land. The body follows in an arched position. The spotting for this move is done at the outside of the low bar. Because of the straddle position, the spotter reaches in for the upper body after the feet have passed. The spotter helps lift the upper body on the landing and follows the completed move.

▶ **Practice Suggestions**

Back hip pullover, mill circle, straddle sole circle underswing dismount.

Balance Beam

The balance beam is 3⅞″ wide, 16′4″ long, and 3′11¼″ above the ground. The gymnast is required to work from end to end on the beam, using tumbling, dance, and poses. The event is timed and the routine must be completed in 1 minute and 30 seconds to avoid penalty. A deduction is also made for each fall, and the gymnast is allowed only 10 seconds to remount the beam after a fall.

▶ **Learning Cues**

The beam should be lowered when teaching beginning students, and lines on the floor can often be utilized for beginners.

Squat Mount.   Place the spring board at a right angle to the beam. Stand on the board with the hands shoulder-width apart on the beam. Jump from the board, pressing down on the beam. At the same time, raise the hips and tuck the knees to the chest, placing the feet on the beam. The spotter stands on the opposite side of the beam and grasps the performer's upper arms to prevent her from falling forward.

Back Shoulder Roll (Figure 13-15).   Lie back on the beam and drop the head to one side. The hand closest to the face is placed on top of the beam, and the other hand is under the beam. Bring the legs back over the head to the beam, bending one knee to place on the beam. The hand under the beam moves to the top of the beam and the both hands push up. End in a knee scale. The spotter is on the opposite side of the performer's head. Facing the direction of the roll, the spotter grasps the performer's hips and guides them until the knee scale is attained.

Forward Roll.   Standing on the beam, bend at the waist and extend the arms to grasp the beam. Lower the upper body to the beam by bending the arms. Tuck the head by pressing the chin to the chest. Raise the hips, roll to the back of the neck and continue forward. Allow one leg to bend and place the foot on the beam as the other leg extends forward. Complete the roll by coming to a stand. The spotter stands to one side of beam and guides the performer's hips. Follow the performer until balanced.

Leap.   The leap is the transfer of weight from one foot to the other with neither foot touching the

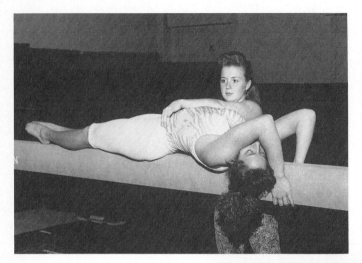

FIGURE 13-15 Back shoulder roll.

beam during the transfer. A leap is actually an isolated running step. The beginner may be hesitant to leave the beam for much height. Arms are out to the side at shoulder level for balance. Try to spot the end of the beam with the eyes and not look directly down. Spotters are on either side of the beam with the near arm extended toward the performer. The performer can then use the spotter's arms for balance when needed.

Chassé (Figure 13-16).   The right leg is in front of the left and remains in front throughout. Step forward with the right leg and bring the left leg from behind to take its place. The weight shifts from the right to the left as right leg is replaced with the left. Continue again, stepping forward with the right, and repeat. Spotter again walks along the side of the beam as the performer travels down the beam.

Arabesque (Figure 13-17).   This is generally considered a momentary balance or pose. Step forward on one leg and lift the other leg to the rear as high as possible. Chest and head are raised by arching the back. Extend the arms to the side. The arms

may be changed to different positions. Be creative. Use spotters on either side of the beam if needed.

Cartwheel Dismount.   In order to do a cartwheel dismount, the performer should first be able to do a good cartwheel on the floor. Stand approximately one step back from the end of the beam. Execute a cartwheel, placing the hands at the end of the beam. Legs travel overhead and land together, much like a round-off (see Tumbling: Round-Off on page 196). The performer ends facing the beam for better balance. Arms remain straight and push off to land. The spotter may want to stand on a bench or a stable chair to approximate the performer's height. Stand on the side of the beam at the performer's back when the cartwheel is performed. If the performer is placing his right hand down first, the spotter will cross his arms with the right arm on top and grasp the performer's waist. The spotter moves with the performer and as the cartwheel is done his arms uncross and end with the left over right. Reverse when spotting is on the other side.

FIGURE 13-16 Chassé.

FIGURE 13-17 Arabesque.

▶ **Practice Suggestions**

Squat mount, leap, forward roll, cartwheel dismount.

Vaulting

When teaching a beginner to vault, you should begin with the run and hurdle step. An instructor may want to first use the take-off board without the horse. The student can run, use the two-foot take-off, and land on a layer of mats. The hurdle step precedes the two-foot take-off. The hurdle is a step onto one foot in front of the board and a two-foot jump onto the board. The take-off from the board is explosive. With practice, the run and take-off become second nature, and the gymnast concentrates on the actual vault.

In women's vaulting the horse is sideways and 47 inches high. Women can perform two separate vaults, but only the better vault is scored.

▶ **Learning Cues**

Squat Vault (Figure 13-18).   The lead up to a squat vault could be a squat mount onto the horse. After leaving the spring board, tuck the knees to the chest and place the hands on the horse. Land in a squat position on top of the horse. As soon as the student masters the squat mount, she can try the vault. The performer will again draw the knees to the chest, but as the hands land on the horse, she pushes downward and keeps the head and chest up. Pass over the horse in the squat position to land facing forward. The spotter is on the far side of the horse, ready to grasp the performer above the elbows if she should need assistance.

The Straddle Vault.   The lead up to the vault can be the straddle mount. After hitting the spring board, the performer straddles (spreads the legs) and lands in a straddle position on top of the horse. The head is up with the feet and hands in contact with the horse. The spotter is in front of the performer on the opposite side of the horse, grasping the upper arms, to prevent her from falling forward. The vault

FIGURE 13-18 Squat vault.

FIGURE 13-19 Stoop vault.

is done the same way as the mount only the hands push downward and the performer clears the horse. The head remains up, and the hips travel in a forward motion over the horse. The spotter is in front of the performer, ready to grasp the upper arms if the performer should catch a toe while passing over the horse. If the performer clears the horse, the spotter moves quickly out of the way.

Stoop Vault (Figure 13-19). This vault is very much like the squat vault except the legs are kept straight. The hips are raised high enough to clear the feet between the hands. The head is up, and again the performer is pushing down against the horse with the hands. As the hips travel forward, the chest lifts upward to prepare for the landing. The spotter stays to the side to assist by grasping the performer's upper arm.

Handspring (Figure 13-20). This is a more difficult vault to master than the previous vaults because the performer needs a great deal of momentum to accomplish the handspring properly. The performer must have a good approach and take-off. The hips bend slightly on the take-off as the hips and legs pass overhead. The arms remain straight, and the head is aligned between the arms. There is a push on the horse which actually originates from the shoulders to the hands. The contact with the horse is short and explosive. The after-flight is approximately the same distance as the pre-flight. The spotter stands on the far side of the horse. Beginners

should have spotters on each side. Grasp the performer's shoulder and upper arm to prevent the arms from folding. Sometimes a spotter can also stand between the springboard and horse, lifting the vaulter's hips to attain the needed height.

Floor Exercise

Floor exercise for women is similar to the men's event in that the same equipment is used and the routine lasts no more than one and a half minutes. However, the requirements for the women's floor exercise are considerably different. The women's routine is choreographed to music, which must be instrumental only. Women must show dance skills, tumbling, and acrobatic skills, and they must work on the floor level sometime in the routine. The difficulties required in the composition of the routine may be derived from a gymnast's dance skills as well as from her tumbling. The beginning tumbling skills in floor exercise will be covered in the tumbling section.

Tumbling

Tumbling does not require the use of apparatus. Mats of different thicknesses are used as the tumbling stunts become more difficult or in the learning process of a certain skill. School programs from elementary through high school would do well to in-

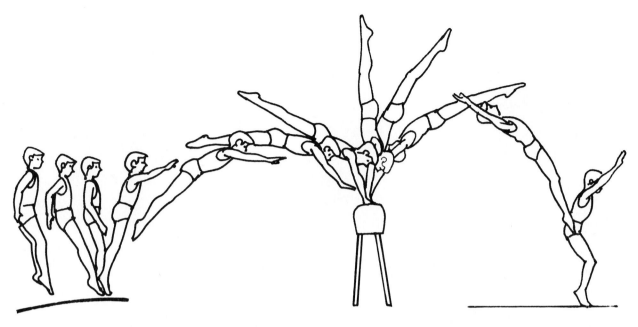

FIGURE 13-20   Handspring.

clude a tumbling unit in their curriculum. Most tumbling stunts require some courage and determination to accomplish, thus a student can gain self-confidence by mastering these new skills. The physical attributes attained through tumbling are increased balance, agility, coordination, and flexibility. Tumbling units can incorporate partner stunts, pyramids, and tumbling routines for variation.

The squad method of teaching a tumbling unit has been highly successful. Six to eight students on each mat is the preferred number. The mats are placed in a three-sided square or horseshoe formation, with the demonstration mat at the open side. The instructor can demonstrate or have a student demonstrate and then let the class practice the skill. Always explain and show spotting techniques.

There are many ways of evaluating a tumbling unit. The instructor can compose a short routine that all students must perform, or the students can compose their own routines which must include certain tumbling stunts. The instructor can evaluate certain predetermined tumbling skills at the end of the unit and may find it beneficial to have a testing day every three or four days in the tumbling unit. On this day, the students may choose to be evaluated on skills they have mastered. The more skills they master by the end of the unit, the better the evaluation. The instructor can be creative in his or her methods of teaching stunts and tumbling, and in evaluations. The important thing to remember is that each student should feel successful. The stunts introduced must be challenging and yet not be too difficult so the majority of students can master them by the end of the unit. A good instructor will keep the entire class involved and be generous with praise.

▶ **Learning Cues**

Forward Roll (Figure 13-21).   The forward roll is one of the basic skills in tumbling. The student squats and places the hands, shoulder width apart, on the mat. Next, tuck the chin to the chest, bend the arms and raise the hips. The back of the head touches the mat and continues to roll onto the feet to a stand. The hands *do not* touch the mat again. Some students find it helpful to grasp the shins and tuck more tightly on the roll. The spotter assists by placing one hand on the head (not the neck) and the other on the upper legs. The hand on the head keeps the chin tucked, and the hand on the upper legs assists with the roll.

Backward Roll.   The backward roll is another basic skill and is sometimes more difficult to master than the forward roll. Again, the student begins in a squat position. The hands begin on the mat, but as the backward roll starts, they move upward to the shoulders, fingers pointing back and palms up. It is essential that the chin be tucked. The hands reach back and are placed on the mat beside the head, under the shoulders. As the hips come over the head, the hands push off the floor. Remain tucked, never allowing the knees to touch the mat, and land on the feet. The spotter may have a more difficult time helping the student complete the roll. If possible, try to lift the hips as the roll begins. Many students will roll backward crooked. This usually indicates they are not pushing evenly with both hands at the same time.

Tripod Balance (Figure 13-22).   Place the hands, shoulder width apart, on the mat. The head is placed on the mat to make the third point of a trian-

FIGURE 13-21   Forward roll.

gle with equal sides. The balance is done on the roof of the forehead, not the crown of the head. Raise the hips and place the knees, one at a time, on the elbows. Balance. The spotter is behind the student to steady him or her at the hips.

Headstand.   The headstand can be done out of the tripod balance. Straighten both legs, with toes pointed, slowly. Once the balance is achieved, return to the tripod slowly. The spotter stands behind the student, making sure that the balance is maintained by steadying the legs. This stunt is readily adaptable to a uniform count, so that everyone can try it at once; e.g.:

1. Hands down
2. Head down

FIGURE 13-22   Tripod balance.

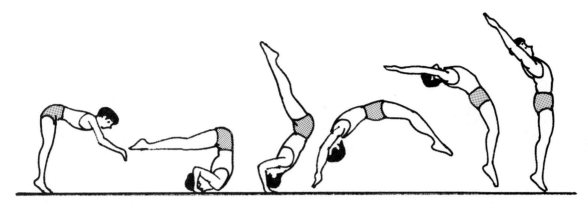

FIGURE 13-23   Kip (neck spring).

3. Legs up (tripod forward)
4. Headstand
5. Legs Down
6. Head up

Make sure that students are far enough apart that a loss of balance won't cause an injury.

Prone Headstand.   Begin in a prone position, lying flat on the mat with the hands placed under the shoulders, fingers pointing forward. Pressing down with the hands, lift and bend at the hips. Keep the legs straight and raise the hips as if a string attached to the ceiling was pulling them up. Drag the feet along the mat. At the same time, place the forehead on the mat. Once the hips are overhead, raise the legs into a headstand. Once balance has been achieved, reverse the procedure, or roll out of the headstand by tucking the chin to the chest and rolling. The spotter stands behind the student and helps him maintain his balance. If the student has trouble lifting the legs off the floor, pull the hips slightly toward the spotter. Continue to spot at the hips when the student returns to the starting position.

Kip (Neck Spring) (Figure 13-23).   Lying on the back, flex at the hips and bring the legs straight back so the knees are over the face. The hands are beside the head under the shoulders (same position as a backward roll). The hips begin to move slightly forward toward the floor and just at the off-balance moment, the legs snap upward and forward. Simultaneously, the hands push against the floor, and the feet come under the student to land on the mat. The hips must be kept high, and the legs remain straight on the whip. The spotter must have a feel for the timing of this stunt in order to help the student effectively. Kneel on the student's left side and place the left hand on the small of the back and the right hand on the upper arm. Help the student feel the slight movement forward before the whip. Lift at the small of the back on the whip and continue lifting with the right hand as the student stands.

Cartwheel (Figure 13-24A).   The cartwheel is a basic move in tumbling, and the student can visualize the spokes of a wheel when performing this move. The cartwheel is performed to either side (usually there is a preference). Stand with the right side to the mat. The legs are spread slightly more than shoulder width apart and arms are overhead. Bend sideways, placing the right hand (straight arm) on the mat and at the same time raise the left leg up, followed by the right, as the left hand goes down onto the mat. The left foot follows and then the

A

FIGURE 13-24A   Cartwheel.

B

FIGURE 13-24B   Spotting the cartwheel.

right foot arrives. As the feet are landing, the hands are coming off the mat. As with a wheel, the spokes (hands and feet) move in a straight line and hit the floor in an even count. The cartwheel can be modified by beginning facing the mat and bending forward instead of sidewards. The hand and foot placement are the same. The spotter (Figure 13-24B) always stands to the student's back to avoid being struck by his legs. If the student is going to his left, the spotter grasps the student's hips with the left arm crossed over the right. Move with the student, lifting at the hips as needed. Reverse hand placement if performing to the left.

Round-Off.   The round-off should be attempted after the cartwheel has been mastered. The round-off is done from a short run. Perform as if doing a cartwheel and as the legs are overhead, snap together and quarter-turn the trunk. The legs snap down together, and the hands push off the floor together (mule kick). The student will end facing the direction from which he or she started. The hands and feet are not in contact with the floor at the same time. It is difficult to spot a round-off because the student must learn to snap down and push off. If the cartwheel has been sufficiently mastered, there is little chance of injury. Verbal cues will be the greatest aid to the student in learning a round-off.

Back Walkover (Figure 13-25).   This stunt requires back flexibility. Stand with hands stretched up overhead, abdomen pulled in and the torso stretched. One foot is pointed in front of the body, and all the weight is on the back foot. Stretch up and look back, keeping the arms on either side of the head. As the head and shoulders move back and down toward the floor, the support leg may bend slightly, the pointed toe lifts off the floor and travels back. The legs remain split and move over the in-

FIGURE 13-25   Back walkover.

verted torso to the floor. As the first foot lands, the hands push off the floor. The spotters may kneel or stand. If there is only one spotter, stand on the side of the forward leg. Place the closest hand on the student's back and the other hand on the back of the lead leg as it goes over.

Front Walkover.   The front walkover requires even more flexibility than the back walkover and therefore is considered more difficult by many. Essentially it is the reverse of the back walkover. Stand with the hands overhead and one foot pointed forward. Place the hands on the mat, shoulder width apart. The weight transfers to the front foot as the back leg raises behind and upward. The leg continues to travel overhead, and the legs are in a split position. The back leg becomes the lead leg or the leg that will contact the floor first. As the foot lands, the hands push off the floor. There is no period of flight. The leg that is still moving through the air drives downward and forward, with the upper body trailing behind. The spotter supports the student throughout the walkover. It may be easiest to kneel beside the student, supporting the shoulders with one hand and the small of the back with the other.

Handstand to Forward Roll.   To achieve a handstand, the student places the hands shoulder width apart on the mat and kicks one leg back and up overhead. The other leg quickly raises upward to join the first. The head remains aligned with the rest of the body, ears next to the arms. A tight, straight body makes maintaining a balance easier. After the balance is maintained, the student shifts the shoulders to the back to create a loss of balance. At the same time tuck the chin to the chest and slowly bend the arms, lowering the upper body toward the floor. As the back of the head contacts the floor, begin the roll by tucking the legs to the chest. Finish the roll to a stand. The spotter stands to the side of the student moving slightly to the back as he kicks to the handstand. Spotting at the legs helps the student attain balance. When the roll begins, the spotter makes sure the student is leaning off balance in the direction of the roll before the head begins to lower toward the ground. The spotter helps control the momentum of the roll by controlling the legs of the student.

Tinsica.   The tinsica is a cross between a cartwheel and a front walkover. It is advisable that the student be able to do both before trying the tinsica. The student begins with the hands overhead and the preferred foot forward. Place the same hand down on the mat in front of the foot that is forward. As the back leg rises, the other hand is placed ahead of the hand on the mat. The back leg continues overhead, followed by the forward foot which has pushed off. The legs remain spread apart, and the student walks out of the stunt, one leg landing at a time. The student visualizes doing a front walkover on a balance beam with the hands and feet landing in a cartwheel-type rhythm. The hands and feet arrive at four different times, moving forward in a straight line. The spotter kneels and supports the student's back and upper body at the shoulder, moving and lifting with the student as the tinsica is being attempted.

Valdez (Figure 13-26).   Sitting on the floor, extend the left leg and bend the right knee, placing the right foot close to the buttocks. The right hand is placed on the floor behind the buttocks with the fingertips pointing away from the body. With a vigorous push off the right foot, swing the left arm back from the shoulder (backward and upward) and place the left hand on the floor. The legs remain split as they proceed overhead, finishing as if doing a back walkover. The right hand, which is on the floor, executes a half-turn during the inverted period. This usually happens naturally as the valdez is being performed. The spotter kneels beside the student on the side of the extended leg. Place the hand nearest the student's back on the lower back and the other hand on the extended leg's upper thigh. As the push-up and back is made by the student, the spotter lifts and guides the leg back and over.

Back Handspring (Figure 13-27).   This tumbling stunt should be taught with two good spotters. The student stands with the feet shoulder-width apart and the arms extended in front, shoulder level. Lower backward as if to sit in a chair. When balance is lost, push against the floor with the legs and vigorously swing the arms up and back, stopping beside the head. The head looks back when the arms begin the move upward; however, it is best not to overemphasize this aspect in order to prevent the student from traveling straight back. The motion is explosive, and the body is extended as the hips thrust upward. The back arches slightly as the hands reach for the mat. When the hands hit the mat, they push off and the legs snap down after having passed through the overhead inverted position. The spotters stand on either side of the student. The spotter on the student's right places his left hand on the student's lower back and the right hand on the back of the upper thigh. The spotter on the student's left reverses the hand placement. The spotters are careful not to lift the student through the handspring but rather to provide support. In order to master the back handspring, the student must "feel" the sense of timing that is needed. The spotters can help by providing the security needed in attempting a backward tumbling move.

▶ **Practice Suggestions**

Prone headstand, tripod, forward roll, cartwheel, handstand, forward roll, round-off.

FIGURE 13-26   Valdez.

FIGURE 13-27   Back handspring.

SAFETY CONSIDERATIONS

The nature of tumbling and gymnastics makes safety a major concern of those supervising the program. It is recommended that the participant warm up before beginning any work on the equipment. Warming up helps prevent muscle pulls and strains and makes an individual aware of his or her body's limitations. Stunts often require assistance (spotting), which aids in safety. The facility, equipment, and area organization can also assist in providing a safe environment.

Spotting

The purpose of spotting is to aid the gymnast to master a stunt safely. This aid can be either manual or employ a spotting belt.

A participant should not attempt a new stunt without having performed the progressions and lead-ups and without the confidence and ability required to succeed. The spotter should only be used as assistant or teaching aid, not as a guarantee of protection from injury.

Manual manipulation—the use of hands and/or body to assist the performer—is a valuable learning tool for students of gymnastics. A good spotter can apply just the right amount of support and protection needed. Of course it helps if the spotter has also tried the stunts, but that is not always necessary. A person can be an excellent spotter without ever having trained as a gymnast.

The Spotting Belt. The "hands-on" method of spotting seems preferable to the spotting belt, but for hazardous stunts the belt is a necessary safeguard. The belt fastens around the performer and has ropes on either side which are attached with hooks that swivel. The spotters stand on either side of the performer and hold the ropes. Depending on the stunt, the spotters move and lift with the ropes to assist or secure the performer. With the belt it is much harder to attain the feel of the stunt and the timing may not be as precise, but safety is always assured.

There is also an overhead spotting belt which is attached to the ceiling through pulleys. Only one individual assists the gymnast. The overhead belt can be helpful on the balance beam, high bar, and floor exercise (if it can travel). The spotter *must* have experience with this type of spotting method because it requires a good sense of timing for both the gymnast and spotter.

Facility and Equipment

Having the proper facility and equipment is important in providing a safe environment. Most schools use the gymnasium, which has plenty of space and overhead clearance. Equipment cannot be too close to existing walls or other pieces of equipment. For example, there must be ample distance for the run and pre-flight in vaulting, but also for the after-flight of the vault. The high bar and uneven parallel bars need overhead clearance. A low ceiling limits the use of these pieces of equipment.

Gymnastic equipment is expensive and must be kept in good repair, not only for safety reasons, but to prolong its life. Individuals need to be instructed in how to adjust settings and properly move the equipment. It is a good idea to show those involved how each piece is set up and to have safety checks done on each piece of equipment before performing.

Those responsible must continually emphasize that the gymnasium and equipment may not be used without proper supervision. No one should be allowed on the equipment at any time without prior permission from the instructor, coach, or supervisor.

Organization

To provide a safe, controllable learning environment for a gymnastics unit the instructor can organize the class into squads. By dividing a class into groups and then instructing by either rotation or at each station, the instructor can make sure a safe teaching progression of skills is used.

Teach the lead-ups and fundamentals of each skill before progressing. This not only makes it easier for the participant to learn and master the more difficult skills, but also is a safety factor. One of the main reasons participants are injured in the gymnastic or tumbling units is due to the individual not understanding the skill he or she is executing. Mind and body cannot work together unless they both have a basic understanding of the skill. This can only be accomplished through lead-up and mastery of elementary progressions. The responsibility ultimately lies with the instructor's knowledge of these progressions. The "Selected References" section listed in this chapter provides resources for enhancing one's knowledge of proper progressions for any of the stunts and apparatus.

MODIFICATIONS FOR SPECIAL POPULATIONS

Orthopedically Impaired

1. Create obstacle courses using gym mats draped over classroom chairs, balance beams, and similar apparatus, and allow wheelchair users to travel the course out of their wheelchair. Emphasis should be placed on traveling over, under, around, and through the course. (Consult with the adapted physical educator and/or physical therapist before removing the student from the wheelchair.)
2. Students using canes and/or crutches should be able to participate with upper body activities, e.g., parallel bars.

Mentally Impaired

1. Contact the Special Olympics for their gymnastics units.
2. Contact AIM, Adventures in Movement for the Handicapped, Inc., in Dayton, OH. (See Paciorek and Jones, 1989, listed in Selected References.)

Sensory Impaired

1. Use peer teachers for blind students.
2. Contact the United States Association of Blind Athletes in Muskogee, OK. (See Paciorek and Jones, 1989.)

TERMINOLOGY

Balance   The body weight is supported by the hands, upper arms, head or forearms in an inverted position, with the shoulders above the point of support.

Dismount   A stunt that moves the performer from the apparatus to a stand on the floor. Also the last moves of a floor exercise routine.

Grasp   The placement of hands upon a piece of apparatus with the thumb and fingers wrapped around.

Hang   A position on a piece of apparatus in which the weight is borne by the hands, knees, etc. with the shoulders below the base of support.

Layout   The entire body is straight.

Mixed grasp   A grasp in which one hand is in an over grasp position and one hand is in an under grasp position.

Mount   A stunt that moves the performer from a stand on the floor to the apparatus. Also can be the first moves of a floor exercise routine.

Over grasp   A grasp in which the palms of the hand are on top of the bar.

Pike   The legs are straight with the body bent at the hips.

Puck   A combination of the tuck and pike, bent at the hips with a slight bend in the knees.

Routine   A combination of stunts in a series. A routine contains a mount, stunts, and ends with a dismount.

Seat   A position on a piece of apparatus in which the weight is borne by the thighs or buttocks: *Straddle seat*—legs apart with the weight borne evenly. *Side seat*—legs are together with the weight borne by the buttocks or legs on one side of the apparatus.

Somersault   The rotation of the body in the air around the horizontal axis.

Stand   A fixed position with the body weight supported by the feet.

Support   A position on a piece of apparatus in which the weight is supported by the hands or arms with the shoulders above the base of support.

Tuck   The knees and hips are bent, with the head in a chin-down position.

Twist   The rotation of the body around the vertical axis.

Under grasp   A grasp in which the palms of the hand are under the bar.

SELECTED REFERENCES

Carter, E. R. *Gymnastics for Girls and Women.* Englewood Cliffs, NJ: Prentice Hall, 1969.

Drury, B. J. et al. *Gymnastics for Women.* 3rd ed. Palo Alto, CA: National Press, 1970.

Kalakian, L. H. et al. *Men's Gymnastics.* Boston, MA: Allyn and Bacon, Inc., 1973.

Murray, M. *Women's Gymnastics: Coach, Participant, Spectator.* Boston, MA: Allyn and Bacon, Inc., 1979.

Paciorek, M. J. and J. A. Jones, *Sports and Recreation for the Disabled.* Indianapolis, IN: Benchmark, Inc., 1989.

Ryser, O. et al. *A Manual for Tumbling and Apparatus Stunts.* 8th ed. Dubuque, IA: Wm. C. Brown Co., 1990.

Taylor, B. et al. *Olympic Gymnastics for Men and Women.* Englewood Cliffs, NJ: Prentice Hall, 1972.

14 HANDBALL AND RACQUETBALL

THIS CHAPTER WILL ENABLE YOU TO:

▶ *Select equipment necessary to play handball and racquetball.*
▶ *Identify and put into practice the rules governing handball and racquetball.*
▶ *Identify and develop the basic skills, namely the forehand stroke, the backhand stroke, the serve, and the back wall shot.*
▶ *Employ the basic strategy necessary to play the game.*
▶ *Identify and put into practice the safety considerations necessary for a successful game of handball or racquetball.*

NATURE AND PURPOSE

Handball and racquetball are related competitive sports in which the hand (or a racquet) is used to serve and return the ball. In their principal variations these games can be played by two opponents (as a singles game), by three opponents (as a cut-throat game), or by two opposing pairs of players (as a doubles game). In this chapter, all that is said about handball also applies to racquetball, unless otherwise stated.

Although the game can be played on one or three walls, the four-wall enclosed court provides perhaps the greatest challenge to skill and the most competition. Primarily the four-wall game will be discussed here, but most of its related description is meaningful to the other variations of the game.

The first side scoring 21 points wins the game (in racquetball, first side to reach 15 points), and the first side winning two games wins the match. The third game, or tie-breaker, is usually played to only 11 points. There is no tie score nor requirement to win by two points, as in some games.

A player may use either the right or left hand for hitting the ball (or holding the racquet), but only one hand at a time may be used to play the ball, and the ball must be struck only once in each instance.

PLAYING AREA AND EQUIPMENT

Court. The standard four-wall handball court is 40 feet long × 20 feet wide × 20 feet high (Figure 14-1). An outdoor single-wall court is 34 feet long ×

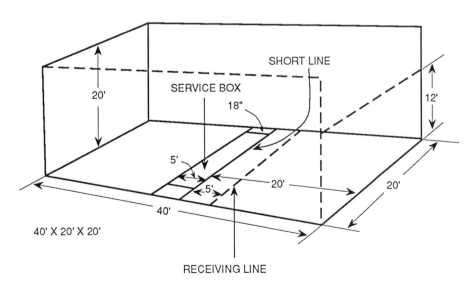

FIGURE 14-1 Four-wall handball court. The dotted line behind the short service line is for racquetball (receiving cue).

20 feet wide × 16 feet high (Figure 14-2). The four-wall court is divided into a front court and a back court of equal dimensions by a line called the *short line,* running parallel to the front wall. Five feet in front of the short line is another parallel line called the *service line.* Eighteen inches from and parallel with each side wall a line is drawn to form a box, termed the *service box,* where the partner of the serve (in doubles) must stand while the ball is being served.

The racquetball court has a *receiving line* which is marked as a broken line parallel to the short line. The back edge should be five feet from the back edge of the short line.

Ball. The handball is made of black rubber, has a diameter of 1⅞ inches and weighs 2.3 ounces. In racquetball a blue seamless rubber ball is used that is 2¼ inches in diameter and weighs approximately 1.4 ounces. If one-wall handball is to be played in a physical education class, it would be advisable to use the racquetball ball.

Gloves. The rules of handball require that gloves be worn. This is not only for protection but to keep perspiration off the ball as much as possible. In racquetball, gloves are not required by the rules; however, many players prefer to wear them for a better grip and reduced slippage due to perspiration.

Racquet. The racquetball racquet length must not exceed 21 inches. There should be a thong attached to the bottom of the racquet handle that should slip over the player's wrist to secure the racquet to the wrist. The racquet frame may be of any material judged to be safe; popular types are made of aluminum, steel, fiber glass, graphite or a combination of materials. The strings of the racquet must be gut, monofilament, nylon, graphite, plastic or a combination of these. Whatever the material, it should not leave a mark or deface the ball. The frame comes in three sizes—regular, mid-size or full size. The

price of the racquets ranges from $20 to $200. For physical education classes, a less expensive solution is to use wooden paddle racquets that cost much less.

Eyeguards. Eyeguards should be required of all racquetball players. Guards are available in various price ranges and styles.

BASIC RULES

A strong point in favor of handball is the simplicity of the rules governing the game. Any person can become familiar with the basic rules in one or two class sessions. In 1958 the Amateur Athletic Union, the U.S. Handball Association, and the YMCA agreed upon a unified set of handball rules that would be applicable throughout the country, and in 1959 these rules were adopted by the Jewish Welfare Board. A summary of the latest rules is given below.

The Game

In the act of serving, the server drops the ball on the floor (between the short and service lines), and on the first rebound the ball is struck in such a manner that it will first hit the front wall and on the rebound land upon the floor back of the short line, either before or after striking one of the side walls. After the ball is legally served, one of the receiving team players returns the ball by striking it either on the fly or on the first bounce so that it will strike the front wall before striking the floor, either directly or after having struck one or both of the side walls, back wall, ceiling, or any combination of these surfaces. The receiving side then returns the ball to the front wall, and play continues until one side is unable to return the ball legally, which will then constitute either a point or a handout.

Playing Regulations

The choice for the right to serve is decided by the toss of a coin, and the player or side winning the toss starts the first and third games. The server may stand any place in the service zone. When the server or serving side loses the service, he or they become the receiver and the receiver the server; they alternate in this fashion in all subsequent services of the game. The serve must be made within the service area; stepping on the line, but not beyond, is permitted. In serving, the ball must be bounced on the floor and struck on its first rebound from the floor. If the server attempts to hit the ball on this rebound, and fails, he is out. The server may not bounce the ball more than one time in the service zone in making a service. Violation of this rule retires the server. A server may not serve until his opponent has had a fair opportunity to get placed. The server's partner, in doubles, must stand within the service box with

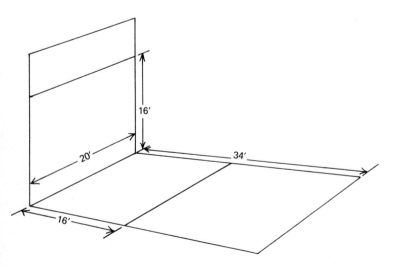

FIGURE 14-2 One-wall handball court.

his back to the side wall, both feet on the floor, until the ball passes the short line on its return from the front wall.

If a player's partner is hit by a served fly ball while standing in the service box, it counts as a "dead ball" without penalty, but does not eliminate any short or long fault preceding this service. If one is hit by a served ball on the bounce, it is a short ball. If the served ball should pass behind the partner and strike the floor back of the short line, it is a dead ball.

In doubles the side starting each game is allowed one handout only. After that both partners are permitted to serve. Players in doubles must follow the same order of service throughout the game. It is not necessary for players to alternate serves to their opponents.

If a ball is swung at and missed, it may be played again, providing it is hit before bouncing twice on the floor. If a player swings at and completely misses the ball and if in his, or his partner's attempt to again play the ball there is an unintentional interference by an opponent, it shall be a hinder. If the completely missed ball should on the fly or first bounce strike an opponent, it is a penalty against the opponent—a point, or handout, as the case may be.

Receiving Service

The receiver or receivers must stand at least five feet back of the short line while the ball is being served. In racquetball, the receiver stands behind the receiving line while the ball is served. The receiver may play the ball on the first bounce or volley it, provided he or she does not cross the short line. The receiver may not play an illegally served ball.

Illegal Service

Any two of the following serves in succession retires the server:

1. When the served ball hits the front wall and fails to strike the floor back of the short line on the fly.
2. When a served ball hits the front wall and two side walls before striking the floor.
3. When a served ball hits the front wall, side wall, and back wall before striking the floor.
4. When a served ball hits the front wall, then the ceiling or back wall before striking the floor.
5. When the server steps beyond the short line or service line in the act of serving.
6. Failure of the server to properly return a ball in play.
7. A served ball hitting the ceiling, floor, or side walls before striking a front wall.
8. A served ball which hits the front and side wall, or front wall and floor, or front wall and ceiling at the same time (crotch ball).

NOTE: In racquetball, #7 and #8 do not apply; the server gets only one attempt.

SUGGESTED LEARNING SEQUENCE

A. Introduction
   1. Origin and development
   2. Equipment
   3. Safety
B. Rules and Procedures of Play
   1. Playing area
   2. Scoring
   3. Serving
   4. Hinders
C. Skills and Techniques
   1. Forehand shot (sidearm stroke)
   2. Overhead stroke
   3. Overhead ceiling shot
   4. Back wall shot
   5. Backhand shot (Racquetball)
   6. Service
      a. Forehand serve
      b. Drive serve
      c. Lob serve
      d. Z serve
   7. Kill shot
D. Playing Strategy

SKILLS AND TECHNIQUES

Forehand or Sidearm Stroke

The forehand stroke is the primary offensive stroke in handball and its mastery is essential in order to achieve a winning game. The most efficient stroke occurs at knee height and is similar to the motion of bending over to skip a flat stone across a body of water or throw a sidearm pitch in baseball.

▶ Learning Cues

1. Position your body as if you were a baseball batter, facing the side wall.
2. Raise the striking hand to the height of your ear in a "cocked" position (Figure 14-3).
3. As the ball is struck, step forward with the front foot, shifting weight from back to front foot (Figure 14-4).
4. Simultaneously with the step, drop your striking shoulder, rotate your body to enable your forearm and hand to move forward in a plane parallel to the floor.
5. Contact the ball at the vertical center of your body.
6. The wrist moves past the elbow in a snapping motion.
7. Ball is struck by the hand at the base of the fingers or in the "sweet" part of the racquet.
8. Follow-through ahead of the front knee.

FIGURE 14-3 ''Cocked'' position, forehand.

FIGURE 14-4 Contact point, forehand stroke.

▶ **Practice Suggestions**

1. Stand facing the side wall in a ready position. Bounce the ball in front of you easily, striking the ball as it rebounds at about knee level. Start a series of practice shots near the short line,

then move back five feet and hit a series, then back five feet more, and so on.
2. Stand facing the side wall (five feet away) in a ready position. Toss the ball easily against the side wall so that the ball will rebound up from the floor into a striking position for a forehand shot.

Overhead Stroke

The overhead stroke is used to strike the ball at eye level or higher and is very similar to a baseball catcher's throw or a quarterback's pass in football.

▶ **Learning Cues**

1. Position toes toward the side wall and open shoulders to the front wall.
2. Weight is on the rear foot.
3. Bring cupped hand to the ear, cocked (Figure 14-5).
4. Weight shifts to the front foot as the arm moves up and forward.
5. Ball is struck above and in front of the head.
6. Ball is struck by the fingers with a wrist snap.
7. Follow-through in the direction you wish the ball to take (Figure 14-6).

▶ **Practice Suggestions**

1. Stand in a ready position deep in the court. Bounce the ball vigorously on the floor so that it rebounds up into a striking position for the overhead.

FIGURE 14-5 Overhead ''cocked'' position.

FIGURE 14-6 Overhead follow-through.

2. From a position deep in the court, throw the ball high against the front wall so that it bounces high to you, returning it with an overhead stroke. Move your body as soon as possible to the striking position.

Overhead Ceiling Shot

The overhead ceiling shot, fundamental to racquetball, can be used effectively as either an offensive or defensive strategy. While it can be hit with the side arm, forehand, backhand or underhand strokes, the overhand ceiling shot is described here. The motion is very similar to a tennis serve, the objective being to hit the ceiling first, the front wall, the floor and then land deep in the court.

▶ Learning Cues

1. The body should be facing the side wall and shoulders open to the front wall.
2. The weight is on the rear foot and will transfer forward as the contact and follow-through are executed.
3. The racquet arm is cocked, elbow up and racquet dropped behind.
4. The non-hitting arm should be pointed upward, overhead almost pointing to the ball.
5. As the racquet arm snaps upward, the ball should be contacted at the midline of the body. Too far behind will cause the ball to hit the ceiling directly overhead and too far forward will cause the ball to hit the front wall.

6. Follow-through in the direction you wish the ball to take.

▶ Practice Suggestions

1. Throw ball against the ceiling to get the feel of the ball rebounding off the ceiling, then front wall and the floor.
2. Toss ball overhead, using the same drill as #1, gradually increase the force at point of contact.
3. Repeat drill #2 and begin placing the ball in different parts of the court, trying to hit the ball consistently to the corner of the back court.

Back Wall Shot

The back wall shot, unique to handball and racquetball, rebounds from the front wall to the floor and then off the back wall before the opponent can get into position to play the ball. If you want to become an above average player you have to learn to play this shot successfully. The stroke most applicable for the back wall shot is the forehand stroke in which the forearm is swung parallel to the floor. This offers a balanced and powerful method of hitting the ball.

▶ Learning Cues

1. Face the back wall or the area of the back wall that the ball is in.
2. Move the ball toward the front wall.
3. As the ball rebounds from the wall and begins to descend, pivot on your right foot (for a right hand shot) and turn your body, stepping toward the front wall.
4. Hand and arm locked above the ear.
5. Strike the ball at the vertical mid-point of your body.
6. Let the ball drop as low as possible.
7. Follow-through in the direction you want the ball to follow.

▶ Practice Suggestions

1. Facing the back wall, toss the ball against the back wall, letting it bounce toward the front wall from the floor. Move with the ball, positioning yourself for a back wall shot.
2. Facing the back wall, toss the ball against the floor to the back wall, but before it bounces on the floor, position yourself for a back wall shot.

Backhand Shot

While the handball player needs to develop both hands equally well in playing both sides of the court, the racquetball player must learn to use the backhand shot. The backhand shot is similar to a tennis backhand, but the stroke is much shorter and uses more wrist snap.

▶ Learning Cues

1. Position your body by facing the side wall (opposite side of the forehand stroke).
2. Rotate the racquet in your hand one-eighth of a turn toward the front wall.
3. Cock the racquet back near the ear, pelvis turned (Figure 14-7).
4. As the ball is struck, step forward with the front foot, shifting the weight from the back leg to the front leg.
5. Simultaneously with the step, bring the racquet forward and contact the ball in line with the front foot, but away from the body (Figure 14-8).
6. As the ball is struck, uncock the wrist, snapping the ball towards the front wall.

▶ Practice Suggestions

1. Standing at mid-court, facing the side wall, bounce the ball easily into the backhand hitting area. Hit a series of shots from this area, back up five feet, hit another series, back up another five feet, and repeat.
2. Stand at mid-court, facing the side wall. Toss the ball easily against the side wall so that the ball rebounds up from the floor into the striking area for a backhand shot. Repeat this series from deeper in the court.

Service

The service, the beginning stroke of each point, must be placed successfully in order to continue the point, but the service can also be an offensive weapon if developed to its potential. You may serve from anywhere in the service area, the most advantageous spot being in the center, so that you may direct your serve to either side. You must drop the ball into the serving zone, strike it on the first rebound, causing the ball to strike the front wall and rebound over the short line and land on the floor.

Drive Serve. The drive serve is a low, hard serve placed so that it returns close to the side wall and drops dead in the back corner; or a low, hard serve that strikes the floor and wall just behind the short line. If possible, the drive serve should not rebound off the back wall, thereby giving your opponent a back wall shot. The drive serve should be struck with the same techniques described in the forehand stroke.

Lob Serve. The lob serve is a high ball placed on the front wall which permits the ball to return in an arc, hugging the side wall, and striking the floor a few feet past the short line in such a manner that the ball rebounds again and drops gently into the corner. The lob serve may be struck either with an underhand or an overhead stroke, the underhand stroke being generally easier to develop in the beginning.

Z Serve. This serve is named from the Z pattern formed by the ball. Standing near the left wall

FIGURE 14-7 Backhand "cocked" position.

FIGURE 14-8 Backhand positions on contact.

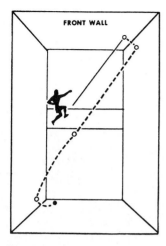

FIGURE 14-9 The Z serve.

of the service area, serve the ball so that it strikes the extreme right side of the front wall a few feet from the corner, approximately four feet above the floor. It should then strike the right wall, angle past in front of the server, strike the floor, and finally strike the left side wall from which it spins off nearly parallel to the back wall (Figure 14-9). The Z serve should be struck with a low forehand, almost underhand stroke. The Z serve could also be executed from the right side of the service area.

Kill Shots

A "kill" shot is actually of such a low placement that there is little or no possibility of a return. Generally hit with a forehand stroke, you do not hit "down" on the ball but let the ball drop to knee height before contacting it with a powerful stroke. Kills can either be front wall kills or corner kills. The front wall kill is stroked straight ahead, hitting so low on the front wall that the ball bounces twice before your opponent can hit it. The corner kill is hit low, but is aimed toward either corner formed by the front and side walls. The ball should strike either the front or side wall, and then it immediately will carom into the side or front wall, producing an angled return that is low and considerably slowed by the ball striking the two wall surfaces.

PLAYING STRATEGY

Handball and racquetball are games in which a premium is placed on analyzing the opponent's strengths and weaknesses. Some players are unable to use their left hand with much effectiveness in handball or they have not developed a strong backhand shot in racquetball. When facing such an opponent, a player should direct a majority of the shots so the opponent is placed at a disadvantage. Players should vary their strategy by employing fast balls al-

ternated with lobs (high, soft shots) in sufficient frequency to get the opponent off balance. The change of pace is particularly effective on the serve, and many good players use it to advantage. In playing doubles, partners should agree on the area that each is to cover and assign the areas so each player may take advantage of any particular strong points they may have.

Players should work for a desirable position on the court. It is usually good strategy to maintain a position in the well—near middle of the court and close enough to enable one to play low balls and corner shots. By skillfully placing shots, a player can keep an opponent in such a position that he or she will be at a disadvantage in returning crosscourt angle shots. Think ahead and make the first play a forerunner to a second or third play that will result in an error by the opponent, or afford the opportunity to place a passing or kill shot. If an opponent persists in playing close to the front wall, he or she can be driven out of position by high lob shots that go overhead but do not strike the back wall with sufficient force to rebound any distance. In the final analysis, a careful scrutiny of your opponent's style of play is the first step in planning a campaign that will be most effective. Identify his or her weak points and take advantage of them.

MODIFICATIONS FOR SPECIAL POPULATIONS

Orthopedically Impaired

1. Follow rules from Wheelchair Racquetball Association and allow wheelchair user two bounces before a return shot is required.
2. Tether a ball to an assistive device, e.g., walker, crutch, for mobility impaired students.
3. Use a larger size ball or one made of different material, e.g., nerf ball.
4. Use of velcro strapping to secure racquets to hand during play.
5. Use of flat paddle-type boards secured to hand instead of racquets for striking.
6. Commercial extension devices are available for amputees and others with grip limitations.

Mentally Impaired

1. Reduce the court size and responsibility to court coverage.
2. Use one-walled courts or stations in the gymnasium.
3. Refer to #3 Orthopedically Impaired above.

Sensory Impaired

1. Individual considerations need to be made on the appropriateness of handball/racquetball for blind students. Lead-up games might allow the student to roll or throw an audio ball against a wall to practice movement and appropriate posi-

tioning. Place small bells inside whiffleballs and use as audio ball.

2. Minimal modifications would be needed for the deaf and/or hard of hearing. Instructional considerations would be the same as previously mentioned, e.g., use of sign language, videos, pictures.

OTHER CONSIDERATIONS

Helpful Hints—Handball

1. Practice "kills" alone. Play the ball around an imaginary opponent and work on the various arm strokes.
2. If your hands swell from playing, soak them in hot water before entering the court, and swelling will be minimized.
3. Gloves are worn by a majority of handball players. Your enjoyment of the game will be increased if you wear a pair of gloves that fit your hands well. Always hang gloves up to dry after using them.
4. Do not rush the ball. Wait for it, and you will not only save energy but play a better game.
5. Control is more desirable than speed.
6. Serve each ball so that it is difficult for the opponent to return it. Try to get several ace serves in each game.
7. A ball hit close to the floor has less bounce and is more difficult to return. The forehand stroke is best for this shot; practice regularly on this play.
8. Watch good players and pattern your play after those who have mastered the game.
9. As a playing courtesy, the opponent is entitled to a fair and unobstructed opportunity to play the ball.
10. If there is any doubt about a play, it is advisable to play the point over.

Helpful Hints—Racquetball

1. "Think" your serve before serving it; you have 10 seconds—use them.
2. Back out of the serving zone as soon as the ball crosses the short line, keeping your eye on the ball the entire rally.
3. Remain in a set position until you see if your shot will be a forehand or a backhand, then turn facing the correct side wall and move to properly align yourself to take your shot.
4. Return to center court. Try to place your shots to keep your opponent out of center court so you can remain there.
5. Place the ball away from your opponent.
6. Try to get the ball to take two bounces before reaching the back wall.
7. Hit with 80 percent power for control.

8. Running around the forehand and backhand will pin you against the side walls.
9. Your shoulder level should equal the ball height.
10. Let any ball at chest level in center court go past you and play it off the back wall.

SAFETY CONSIDERATIONS

1. Dress properly for the game. Always wear rubber-soled shoes to ensure firm footing.
2. Always warm up thoroughly before beginning competition.
3. Do not play a dead ball, because your opponent may turn and get struck in the face.
4. Do not deliberately hit an opponent with the ball in the hope that he will call a hinder on the play. You may both get hurt, and ill feeling will develop.
5. After you play the ball to the back court, do not watch the ball; you may get hit in the face by a returning ball.
6. Allow your opponents room to make the play. Don't crowd or you may be struck.
7. Wear eyeguards at all times.

TERMINOLOGY

Ace   A service which completely eludes the receiver.

Back wall shot   A shot made from a rebound off the back wall.

Box   See **Service box.**

Ceiling shot   A shot striking the ceiling first, then the front wall.

Crotch   The juncture of any two playing surfaces, as between the floor and any wall.

Crotch shot   A ball that strikes the front wall and floor simultaneously. Not good.

Cut throat   A three-man game in which the server plays against the other two players, with each player keeping an individual score. Not played in official competition.

Drive shot   A power shot against the front wall which rebounds fast, low, and in a straight line.

Fault   An illegally served ball.

Handout   Retiring the server who fails to serve legally or when the serving team fails to return a ball that is in play.

Hinder   Accidental interference or obstruction of the flight of the ball during play. Point will be played again.

Kill   A ball directed to the front wall in such a way that it rebounds so close to the floor that it is impossible to return.

Passing shot   A placement driven out of opponent's reach on either side.

Rally   Continuous pay of the ball by opponents.

Receiving line   The receiving line is a broken line parallel to the short line on a racquetball court. The back edge of the receiving line is five feet from the back edge of the short line.

Run-around shot Ball that strikes one side wall, the rear wall, and other side wall.

Safety zone The safety zone is a five-foot area bounded by the back edge of the short line and receiving line. The zone is only observed during the serve in racquetball.

Screen A hinder due to an obstruction of vision by opponent.

Server Person (or persons, in doubles) in the "hand-in" position and eligible to serve.

Service box Area within the service zone bounded by the side wall and a parallel line 18 inches away; denotes where server's partner must stand in doubles when the serve is being made.

Service court The area in which the ball must land when returning from the front wall on the serve.

Service line The service line is parallel to and five feet in front of the short line. The front line of the service zone.

Service zone The area where the server must stand when serving the ball. Located between the service line and the short line, usually five feet wide, and extending across the court.

Short line A line on the floor parallel to front wall and equidistant from front and back wall. Serve must carry over this line on its return from the front wall.

Shoot To attempt kill shots.

Side out The loss of serve by a player or team.

Throng Strap attached to the bottom handle of the racquetball racquet which is worn around the player's wrist.

Volley To return the ball to the front wall before it bounces on the floor.

Z-ball A defensive shot that strikes three walls before touching the floor. The ball strikes the front wall, a sidewall and then the opposite side wall.

SELECTED REFERENCES

Allsen, P. and Witbeck, A.R. *Racquetball*. Dubuque, IA: William C. Brown, 1981.

Amateur Athletic Union. *Official Handball Rules*. current ed. 231 West 58th Street, New York, NY 10019.

American Amateur Racquetball Association. *Official 1990–91 Rulebook*. 815 N. Weber, Suite 203, Colorado Springs, CO 80903.

Blumfield, C., and Barstow, J.N. *Off the Wall*. New York: Dial Press, 1978.

Fabian, L. *Racquetball: Strategies for Winning*. Dubuque, IA: Eddie Bowers, 1986.

MacClean, N. *Platform Tennis, Racquetball and Paddleball*. New York: Drake Publishers, 1977.

Mand, C.L. *Handball Fundamentals*. Columbus, OH: Charles E. Merill Publishing Co., 1976.

McFarland, W.J. and Smith, P. *Sports Illustrated Handball*. Philadelphia: Lippincott, 1976.

Mood, D., et. al. *Recreational Activities*. St. Louis: Times Mirror/Mosby, 1987.

Pahgrazi, R.P. *Racquetball*. IL: Scott Foresman, 1986.

Sauser, J. and Shay, A. *Beginning Racquetball Drills*. Chicago: Contemporary Books, 1981.

Turner, E. and Hogan, M. *Winning Racquetball*. Champaign: Leisure Press, 1988.

15 ORIENTEERING

NATURE AND PURPOSE

Orienteering is a cross-country type of activity in which the participant utilizes topographic map reading skills and follows directions by compass or other means to navigate over unfamiliar terrain. The skills of orienteering can be used to enjoy many outdoor pursuits such as camping, backpacking, hiking, cross-country skiing, fishing, and hunting, or for competing in the sport of orienteering. Called "the thinking sport," competitive orienteering requires great mental acuity, problem solving and decision making, along with cardiorespiratory fitness, as the orienteer can cover distances from two up to ten miles in navigating an orienteering course. With today's back-to-nature interests by people of all ages, orienteering skills can be valuable in improving environmental awareness and self-reliance in the out-of-doors.

Participants of all ages and levels of ability can take part in orienteering as a recreational activity or competitive sport. In competitive orienteering, courses with various degrees of difficulty are set up to allow for differences in skill levels; therefore, all participants can achieve success. For many, just completing the course can be a satisfying experience.

Orienteering is an excellent coeducational activity. The techniques and skills can be easily taught to both boys and girls and men and women. The environmental setting makes for social acceptance. Since outstanding physical ability is not necessarily the limiting factor, girls often achieve the same success as boys.

Competitive Orienteering

Point-to-point or cross-country orienteering is the most common type of competition. This event requires the competitors to navigate through a prescribed series of control points shown on a topographic orienteering map (Figure 15-1), with all competitors visiting the controls in the same order. At the start of the event, competitors receive a clue card (Figure 15-2). The clue card identifies the control markers by letter code and describes a prominent feature in which the control marker has been set. The competitors leave the starting line at equal intervals of time, for example, one-minute intervals, so that the event becomes for each a contest of route selection and physical skills with the time to complete the course determining the order of finish. To insure that each competitor has visited the control markers, a code or punch is located at each control and must be marked on a competitor's scorecard (Figure 15-3). In competitive orienteering, courses of different levels of difficulty are set up to allow for the differences in navigational and physical skill abilities of the contestants. These courses are designated by colors: white, yellow, orange, green, red, and blue, with white and yellow being for the novice, orange and green for the intermediate, and red and blue for the advanced orienteer. Course difficulty is determined by the number of controls, distance between the controls, and the difficulty of the placement of the controls in the field. For example, compare the distance between controls and the total distance of the red course shown in Figure 15-4 with the distances of the white course shown in Figure 15-1. The red course is obviously much more difficult.

EQUIPMENT

Maps. The most essential item of equipment for successful orienteering is the map. For children just beginning, a map of a schoolyard, local park, or forest preserve, drawn to scale, is sufficient; however, for the advanced orienteer, large-scale topo-

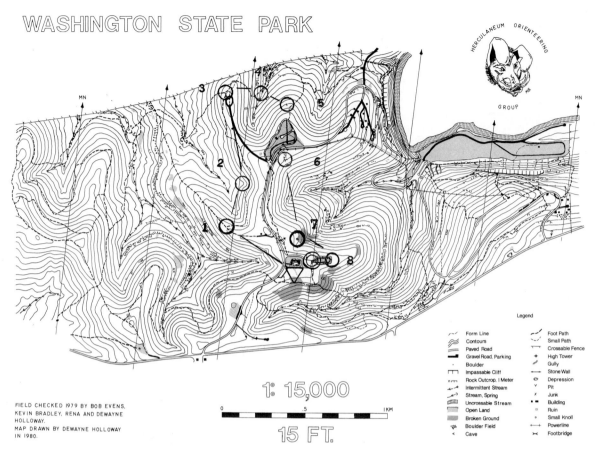

FIGURE 15-1   Topographic orienteering map showing a white course used by beginning orienteers. (Map courtesy of the St. Louis Orienteering Club and Dewayne Holloway.)

Day 1 White Course 2.7 km.

1	(WA)	The trail junction
2	(WB)	The re-entrant (head)
3	(WC)	The trail junction
4	(WD)	The re-entrant
5	(WP)	The junk
6	(WE)	The fence corner
7	(WF)	The depression
8	(HW)	The earth bank

Follow streamers to finish

FIGURE 15-2   Competitors' clue card for the white course. (Courtesy of the St. Louis Orienteering Club and Dewayne Holloway.)

ROSE ORIENTEERING CLUB CONTROL CARD

Name

Course   Class

Finish
Start
Elapsed

11	12	13	14	15	16	17	18	19	20
1	2	3	4	5	6	7	8	9	10

FIGURE 15-3   Competitors' score card. (Courtesy Rose Orienteering Club.)

---

graphic maps showing selected man-made and natural features are necessary. These topographic maps, usually drawn on a scale of 1:24,000, are produced by the United States Geological Survey (USGS) of the Department of the Interior. Recently, more accurate and highly developed orienteering maps have been produced. These maps, usually drawn on a scale of 1:15,000 and developed from current aerial photographs, have been accurately field checked and printed in the standard international orienteering colors: blue (water features), black (man-made features), green (vegetation features), brown (contour features), and yellow (clear areas). Although colored maps are more meaningful and precise, black-and-white maps can be successfully used and are less expensive.

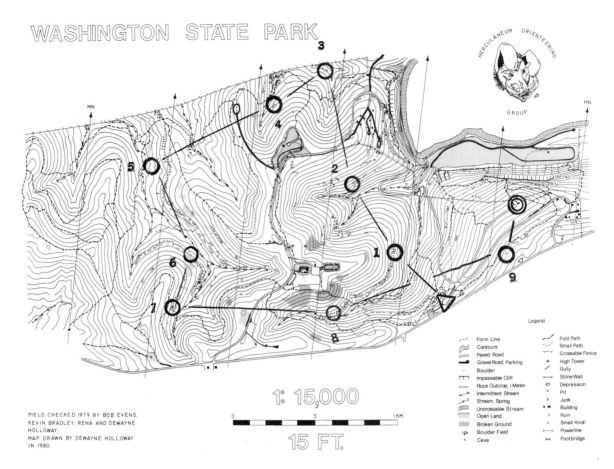

FIGURE 15-4 Topographic orienteering map showing a red course used by advanced orienteers. (Map courtesy of the St. Louis Orienteering Club and Dewayne Holloway.)

Orienteering maps provide the following important information to the orienteer:

1. *Map Scale.* Each map contains a certain scale which is proportional between a distance on the map and the actual distances in the field. For example, a scale of 1:15,000 on a topographical map means that one unit of distance on the map equals 15,000 units of actual distance in the field. A bar scale representing map distance is located in the margin of the map.

2. *Directions.* The top of an orienteering map represents geographic north; therefore, the other cardinal directions are: south (the bottom), east (the right), and west (the left). Most orienteering maps will have the magnetic-north lines already drawn on the map. These lines, called the declination lines, represent the degree difference between the magnetic north direction and true north direction. The angle of declination on USGS topographic maps can be found in the margin.

3. *Elevation Features.* A topographic map is distinguished from a planemetric map (roadmap) in showing the shape and elevation changes of the terrain by brown contour lines. Each of these lines represents a constant elevation, in feet or meters, above sea level. The space between each line on a topographic map represents a vertical distance called the contour interval. The contour interval is given below the bar scale at the bottom of the map sheet. In areas of the United States with little elevation, the contour interval will be 5 to 10 meters (or feet) to more accurately represent the land features, while contour intervals of 10 to 20 meters (or feet) are found in more mountainous areas.

4. *Other Map Features.* Other important man-made or natural features such as power lines, roads, trails, bridges, buildings, fences, boulders, cliffs, streams, lakes, marshes, or ponds are also shown on the map. These features are either drawn to actual scale or displayed symbolically with the description of each symbol found in the map's legend (see Figure 15-1).

Compass. The second most essential item of equipment for successful orienteering is the compass. The protractor type compass with the liquid-filled housing (Figure 15-5) is the most widely used compass in orienteering today because it permits the orienteer to take a bearing and measure its distance

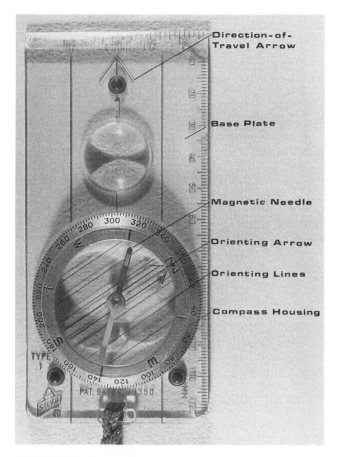

Direction-of-Travel Arrow

Base Plate

Magnetic Needle

Orienting Arrow

Orienting Lines

Compass Housing

FIGURE 15-5 The protractor compass.

quickly and accurately. The parts of the compass and their basic function are as follows.

1. *Base Plate.* The transparent rectangular plate on which the compass housing is mounted is called the base plate. The front edge and one of the side edges are marked off in inches and millimeters for measuring map scale or distance.
2. *Compass Housing.* The degree markings are found on the outer rim of the rotating compass housing. Each mark represents one degree, and they are numbered in intervals of 20. (It should be noted that 0° and 360° coincide and are both north.) Once the compass is set correctly, the degree bearing is taken at the index pointer on the rim of the housing.
3. *Orienting Arrow.* Located inside the compass housing is the orienting or north-seeking arrow. Its function is to assist in orienting the compass. The compass is oriented by holding the compass in such a way that the orienting arrow is lined up with the magnetic needle, both of which will be pointed north.
4. *Magnetic Needle.* The free floating needle located inside the compass housing is called the magnetic needle. The north end is painted red

and always points to magnetic north unless affected by a metal object.

5. *Orienting Lines.* Located inside the compass housing and running parallel to the orienting arrow are the orienting lines. These lines assist in determining declination by setting them parallel to the magnetic lines on the map, with north on the compass pointing to north on the map.
6. *Direction-of-Travel Arrow.* At the upper end of the base plate is located the direction-of-travel arrow which is used for determining the direction of travel when the compass is oriented.

SUGGESTED LEARNING SEQUENCE

Whole Method

The direct or whole method is recommended for teaching younger children and novice orienteers. In this method beginners walk or run an orienteering course in the field with suitable terrain as their first introduction to orienteering. The only preliminary learning prior to this field work is a knowledge of map symbols, an understanding of how to "orient the map," and the ability to map read by using the thumb—the first basic skills of orienteering.

It is important during these first learning sessions that orienteering courses be set that are good illustrations of those points that are to be learned. Therefore, the course-setter must understand that during the first few sessions, the courses should be set in such a way that the beginner needs only to follow roads, edges of fields, trails, and other similar objects.

The course-setter must never be enticed to set what we might normally call "good" controls, but instead, must always keep in mind that they are trying to show what the map symbols and definitions mean. The control points should be typical for the symbol and definition. All controls should be so distinct that no one can be uncertain as to what is meant.

The following factors must be carefully attended to when course-setting:

1. *Terrain.* There must be lots of trails, open country, roads, and similarly distinct and easily read features. Then it is important to make proper use of these.
2. *Map.* The map should be drawn according to the norms, have the correct colors, be easily read, and preferably be 1:15,000 although it is possible to use 1:24,000. (It is a good idea to enlarge the normal maps for beginner courses).
3. *Control choice.* The aim of the control was mentioned already. Besides the above points, the control should be such that even without a compass, the novice can match the map with the terrain and find the control.

4. *Route choice.* Route choice, as we usually mean it, should not be introduced at the novice level. There are lots of things which must be learned before you start on route choice. "Route choice" that comes in a later part of the course means only that the novice for example, chooses the correct path at a path junction.
5. *Orienting the map.* The controls and the legs between controls should be such that the novice can always match (orient) the map with the terrain without using his compass. It is important that he or she be taught always to have the map oriented. This is the most important point in the entire course, and it should be introduced right from the beginning.

After these basic techniques and skills are mastered and confidence gained, more advanced techniques and skills such as a knowledge of contour lines, map scale, handling a compass, measuring distance, use of attack points, off-aiming, and pace counting may be introduced.

Part-Whole Method

While the "whole" method of teaching is often used with children and novice orienteers, the most widely used and accepted method of teaching is the "part-whole method." In this method the basic and advanced techniques and skills of using the map, the compass, and map and compass together are taught in a classroom/field setting before the orienteer attempts to navigate an orienteering course. In attempting to navigate an orienteering course, an orienteer using this method should start with a novice yellow or white course (such as shown in Figure 15-1) gradually progressing to an intermediate, orange or green, and then to a more advanced blue or red course (such as Figure 15-4), once the basic orienteering skills and techniques are mastered.

SKILLS AND TECHNIQUES

Map Reading. Since the map is the primary tool for navigation in orienteering, it is essential to teach basic map reading techniques and skills first.

1. *Orienting the Map.* Orienting the map simply means keeping the map turned so that north on the map corresponds to north in the field regardless of the direction the orienteer travels. Orienting the map can be done either by inspecting the surroundings and aligning the terrain features with those on the map or by using the compass. The steps in using the compass to orient the map are as follows:
   a. Set the compass dial at 360°. Then place the compass on the map with the edge of the base plate parallel to one of the magnetic north

lines, making sure the direction-of-travel arrow points north.
   b. Rotate the map and compass until the magnetic needle is over the orienting arrow. The map is now oriented with respect to magnetic north.
2. *Map Reading by Thumb.* In using this technique the map should be folded so that it can be easily held and read as only the immediate area in which you are orienteering is showing. The tip of the thumb is then placed on the map corresponding to the place in the field where you are standing and pointing in the direction you will travel. As the orienteer travels along, the thumb is moved to the place on the map corresponding to the location in the field where the orienteer has traveled. This technique assists in keeping the map reader oriented, as the terrain features that lie ahead can be easily analyzed and checked.

Compass Reading. The compass can be used with a map or by itself. For the beginning orienteer, the steps in taking a bearing and traveling with the compass by itself should be taught first. These steps are as follows:

1. The orienteer stands facing in the direction of the intended destination. With the direction-of-travel arrow pointed in this direction, the compass housing is turned until the north end of the orienting arrow is lined up with the north end of the magnetic needle.
2. Once the compass is set, the orienteer picks out a prominent feature such as a tree or hilltop in line with the direction-of-travel arrow. He or she travels to that feature, takes another bearing, and continues toward the desired destination.

Additional Procedures. Taking a bearing and traveling with a compass and map involve additional procedures and should be done with precision. Three basic steps are used in this process:

1. Put the edge of the base plate from the present place of location to the intended destination, making sure the direction-of-travel arrow is pointing in the direction of travel (see Figure 15-6).
2. Turn the compass housing until the orienting lines are parallel to the magnetic lines and the orienting arrow is pointing north on the map (see Figure 15-7). When magnetic north lines are not present, the orienting lines can be set parallel with the meridian lines—the lines running true north to south. In this case the declination (angle of difference in degrees between true north and magnetic north) must be added or subtracted to the final bearing. This degree difference is given in the margin on topographic maps. To decide whether to add or subtract,

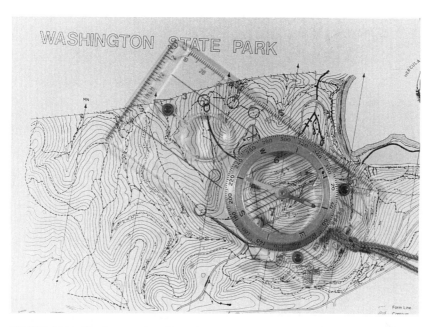

FIGURE 15-6   The first step in taking a bearing with compass.

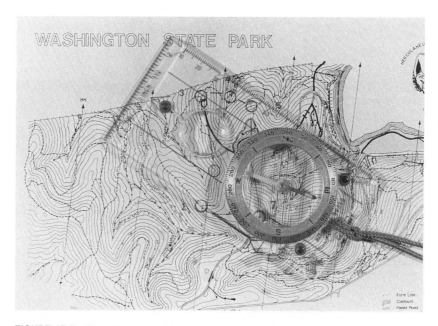

FIGURE 15-7   The second step in taking a bearing with compass.

think of the rhyme "East is least and West is best." If the angle of declination is *east*, the degree of declination is *subtracted; if the declination is west,* it is *added.*

3. The final important step is to turn yourself until the north end of the magnetic needle points to the north end of the orienting arrows (Figure 15-8).

COMPETITIVE STRATEGIES

In competitive orienteering the orienteer must know special techniques and skills in order to select the fastest and least tiring route between control points.

1. *Pace Counting.* Pace counting involves a two-step approach:

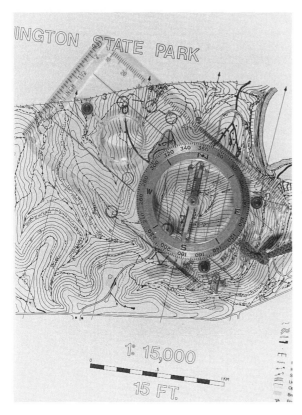

FIGURE 15-8 The third step in taking a bearing with compass.

FIGURE 15-9 A young orienteer using her map and compass takes a bearing to the next control point.

a. In step one, the orienteer measures the distance on the map by using the marked edge of the compass and the map bar scale.

b. Step two involves measuring the distance in the field by pace counting. In pace counting, you count your double step, or each time the same foot hits the ground. This can be practiced by measuring an exact 100 yards or 100 meters over different terrain and counting the number of double steps taken in covering this distance.

2. *Attack Points.* Sometimes called secondary controls, these are large, prominent features such as a cliff, building, bridge, trail junction, or other features near the control which can easily be found and identified on the map. Finding an attack point makes the final approach to the control much easier.

3. *Check Points.* After finalizing the route the orienteer should visualize certain prominent features (check points) she will see along the way which will indicate she is on the correct route.

4. *Handrails.* Linear features running parallel to the direction of a control point or an attack point are called handrails. These can take the form of natural features such as a stream, the edge of a field, a ridge or man-made feature such as a road, trail, fence or power line. Handrails are used by

FIGURE 15-10 After checking the map and setting her compass, the orienteer has selected the woods trail to the next control.

the orienteer as a natural guide to follow toward the control point.

5. *Catching Features.* Long features running crosswise to the orienteer's direction of travel are called catching or collecting features. These features can assist the orienteer in navigation, as upon reaching the catcher the orienteer needs only to turn in the proper direction and follow it until the attack or control point is reached. These "catchers" include the same linear features described as handrails.

6. *Aiming Off.* When control or attack points are located on linear features such as roads, streams, fences, etc., the orienteer aims off, that is, sets the compass toward a point 40 to 60 meters to the right or left of the control point rather than right at it, so that upon arriving at the linear feature he knows exactly which way he must turn, right or left, to find the control point.

MODIFICATIONS FOR SPECIAL POPULATIONS

Orthopedically Impaired

Work on special "searches" within the gymnasium using maps, and other coded documents. Designate each wall in the gym a color and have the students follow the colored map, e.g., travel to the yellow wall, then the green wall and find the hidden treasure.

Mentally Impaired

Have the students work on making special compasses to learn North, South, East, and West, e.g., color code the directions.

Sensory Impaired

1. Use peer teachers for blind students.
2. Use visual cues, e.g., posters, notebooks, etc., for the deaf and/or hearing impaired.

SAFETY CONSIDERATIONS

While orienteering is a relatively safe activity, there are some precautions which must be followed:

1. Orienteers should be cautioned to avoid potentially dangerous obstructions and features shown on the map such as cliffs, rock faces, barbed wire fences, or deep rivers and streams.
2. The orienteer should be instructed to wear protective clothing when heavy brambles, briar patches, or thick vegetation exist in the terrain.
3. Before embarking on a course, a safety bearing should be given which will lead the orienteer to a large catching feature such as a road, trail, etc., in the event he or she becomes lost or totally disoriented.

TERMINOLOGY

Aiming off   A technique in which the orienteer purposely aims to one side of a control point so that he or she will know which way to turn.

Attack point   A large, prominent visible feature both on the map and in the field, from which the final approach of attack to the control can be made.

Bearing   Sometimes called an azimuth, it is a direction measured in degrees from north with a compass.

Cardinal points   The four basic directions on a compass: north, south, east, and west.

Catching feature   A long, natural or made-made feature running perpendicular to the orienteer's direction-of-travel.

Contour interval   The vertical distance in height between contour lines on a topographic map.

Control   Marker of two colors—usually red and white or orange and white—placed in the field before the orienteering meet starts; used for locating control points on the map.

Control description   A word description for the location of a control point.

Declination   The degree difference between the magnetic north direction and the true north direction.

Handrail   Linear features running parallel to an orienteer's direction of travel which are used to navigate to a control or an attack point.

Magnetic north   The direction to the magnetic north pole located north of Hudson Bay.

Map symbols   Designs found in the legend on a map; used to indicate landscape features.

Meridians   Real lines on the map or imaginary lines in the terrain running true north to true south.

Orienteering   The skill or the process of finding your way in the field with map and compass combined.

Orienting the compass   Turning the compass until north on the compass is the same as north in the field.

Orienting the map   Turning the map until north on the map corresponds to north in the field.

Pace counting   Method used to measure distance in the field by counting each time the same foot strikes the ground.

Scale   A proportion between a distance on the map and the actual distance in the field.

Topographic map   A map showing elevation changes by means of contour lines.

True north   Geographic north (the North Pole).

SELECTED REFERENCES

Disley, J. "Your Way with Map and Compass." Burlington, Ontario: Silva® Orienteering Services, 1971.

Gilchrist, J. "Teaching Orienteering." Binghamton, NY: Silva® Orienteering Services, 1991.

Kjellstrom, B. *Be Expert with Map and Compass.* NY: Macmillan, 1976.

McNeill, C., Ransden, G., and Renfro, T. *Teaching Orienteering.* Perthshire, England: Harvey's Publishing, 1987.

Instructional Pamphlets

"Orienteering" (A Boy Scout Merit Badge Booklet).

"Learn Orienteering."

"So You Want to Know About Orienteering."

(All of the above pamphlets are published yearly through Silva® Orienteering Services USA—See "Training Aids and Orienteering Equipment" below for address.)

Audio-Visual Materials

The following materials are available from the International Film Bureau, Inc., 332 South Michigan Ave., Chicago, IL 60604. Phone (312) 427–4545.)

Color Films (rental or purchase):

1. "Orienteering" (10 minutes).
2. "Invisible Force of Direction" (21 minutes).

3. "What Makes Them Run" (20 minutes).
4. "By Map and Compass"

Filmstrips and Slide Series:

1. "Adventures with Map and Compass."
2. "Map and Compass Clinic Kit."
3. "Orienteering—What's That?"

Training Aids and Orienteering Equipment

Silva® Orienteering Services USA, P.O. Box 1604, Binghamton, NY 13902.

Topographic Maps

National Cartographic Information Center, 507 National Center, Reston, VA 22092.

Organizations

United States Orienteering Federation, P.O. Box 1039, Ballwin, MO 63011.

Canadian Orienteering Federation, 355 River Rd., Vanier, Ontario, KIL 8B9.

16 RECREATIONAL SPORTS

> ▶ *Angling*
>   ▶ *Horseshoes*
>   ▶ *Pickle-ball*
>   ▶ *Shuffleboard*
>   ▶ *Table Tennis*

ANGLING

NATURE AND PURPOSE

Angling is fishing for sport. More specifically, it is the use of the skill of casting to catch fish. Angling has increased steadily in popularity and today countless people of all ages engage in the sport. Over thirty million fishing licenses are issued in the United States each year, and millions of people fish without a license. With so many participants it is quite possible that more money is spent on angling than on any other sport. Wherever fish and water are to be found, anyone can enjoy this lifetime recreational activity.

The basic skill in learning to become an angler is casting. Despite the fact that this is a relatively simple skill, very few master it because they neither learn under proper guidance, nor do they take the time to practice the skill once they have acquired it.

There are two types of casting: fly and bait or spin casting. There are some similarities between the two, but they employ different tackle and very different techniques. In *fly casting,* a longer, more flexible rod is used, the line is controlled from the hand, and the light fly is propelled entirely by the weight of the line. The technique of fly casting makes it possible to use small, light "lures"; i.e., artificial flies, and to cast with a great deal of precision and accuracy. *Bait/spin casting* requires a shorter, less flexible rod. Distance is gained by the weight of the bait or lure and the line is controlled at the reel.

EQUIPMENT

Fly Casting Tackle

The beginner should try to enlist the assistance of an experienced fly fisher to help with the selection of proper equipment. With the recent upsurge of interest in fly casting and fly fishing, this should not be a difficult task since most fly fishers are willing to provide basic instruction as well as other information about getting started in this recreational activity.

Rod. The most important piece of equipment is the rod. Fly rods come in different lengths and have different actions. An 8½ or 9 foot graphite rod with a medium to fast action is probably the best choice for the beginner.

Reel. A single action fly reel is recommended. This reel should have an adjustable drag (a mechanism that increases or decreases the resistance on a line once a fish is hooked), an interchangeable spool, and the capacity to hold enough backing line in order to play the fish. Figure 16-1 shows some types of reels.

Line. The manufacturer's recommendations of line size for the rod should be closely followed. Fly lines today are usually constructed of a core of braided dacron or nylon fibers covered by a plastic or some other synthetic coating. They come in various tapers (thicknesses) and weight. To balance an 8½ or 9 foot rod properly, the beginner should select a weight forward floating line in a six or seven weight. These lines would be listed as a WF6F or WF7F on the manufacturer's box.

FIGURE 16-1   Types of reels.

Bait/Spin Casting Tackle

Once again, the advice of an experienced bait/spin caster is invaluable and would save the beginner a great deal of time in getting started.

Rod.   The beginner should select a rod that is 5 to 6 feet long, and has a medium action. Most rods are constructed of fiberglass, graphite, or some combination of the two.

Bait-Casting Reel.   The beginner should select a "level-wind" reel, meaning that the line is wrapped evenly on the spool. The reel should fit the length and action of the rod.

Spinning Reel.   Spinning reels are divided into two general classes. In the *open type,* the spool upon which the line coils has no cover, leaving the spool and line fully exposed. In the *cone type,* a cone covers the spool and line to protect the line from dirt and to prevent its being touched by lures, twigs, weeds, and other foreign objects. The line passes through a hole in the center of the cup, directly in front of the axis of the spool shaft.

The action of the reel spool is the basic difference between the spinning, spin-casting, and standard bait-casting outfit. The spool of a spinning reel does not rotate to release the line on the cast or to respool it during the retrieve. On most reels, it advances and recedes as the line is being coiled on, in order to spool the line uniformly—but it never rotates. On the cast, the line slips off the exposed end of the spool. This action can best be visualized by thinking of a spool of thread. If one end of the spool of thread is held firmly

in one hand and the thread end grasped by the other hand and stripped off straight over the opposite end of the spool, the action would be similar to that of the spinning line leaving the reel. The spool also remains stationary on the retrieve. A metal "finger" rotates around the spool, picking up the line and placing it back around the spool.

Line.   Generally speaking, a light to medium monofilament line is recommended for the beginner. When putting the line on a spinning reel, it is very important to follow the manufacturer's instructions carefully in order to avoid twisting the line. Usually a braided monofilament line is used for the bait-casting (level-wind) reel because many fishermen feel it is less likely to backlash.

SKILLS AND TECHNIQUES

The ability to cast the line onto the water is the most important skill the angler must learn. Indeed, the development of a good casting stroke is the key to success in any type of fishing. As the various techniques are described in this section you will notice some similarities in the use of the fly rod, bait-casting rod, and spinning rod; however, there are important differences. Reference will be made to the positioning of the casting arm in relation to the hands on a clock. Most of the movements center on the ten o'clock and two o'clock positions. Therefore, if you think of the movement in terms of the hands of a clock face, you should have relatively little difficulty

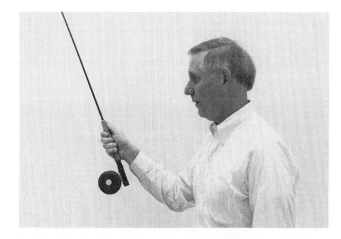
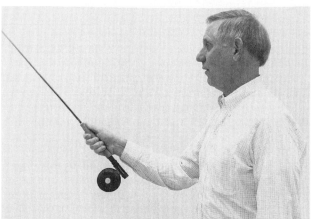
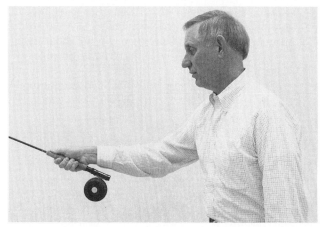

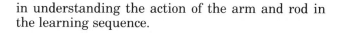

FIGURE 16-2 Overhead fly cast. Note wrist is firm not fixed.

in understanding the action of the arm and rod in the learning sequence.

Fly Casting

There are two important things to remember when learning to fly cast: first, the right hand will grip the handle and become part of the execution of the cast; and second, the other hand must control the feed of the line as the cast is being made. After sufficient practice, the sequence and action of the two hands will become smooth and rhythmical. (Left-handed individuals should reverse the described procedure.) Another key point for the beginner to remember is that the cast is primarily a result of the action of the hand and the forearm and less of the wrist.

To practice the cast, begin by pulling 15 to 20 feet of line from the tip of the rod and place it on the ground in front of you. Grip the rod on the handle with the thumb placed on top in line with the rod. Wrap the fingers comfortably around the handle. The wrist is bent until it becomes a parallel extension of the forearm. The stroke itself is best executed between the ten o'clock and two o'clock positions. The greatest problem novice flycasters have is using their wrist too much, resulting in a casting action like a "buggy whip" (Figure 16-2).

▶ **Learning Cues**

1. Begin by lifting the tip up, rapidly accelerate from the ten o'clock to one o'clock position. The space between the wrist and handle opens slightly.
2. The rod stops at the one o'clock position, and the line drifts behind the shoulder. Wait until the line is almost completely unrolled, then begin the forward cast.
3. Accelerate the rod forward to the ten o'clock position, stop quickly and allow the line to unroll forward. The line should land softly on the surface as the follow-through is completed.
4. Since the basic principle of fly casting is to cast ("roll" and "unroll") loops of line, the beginner should watch the back cast to be certain that these loops are "rolling" and "unrolling" properly. Indeed, fly casting is a recreational skill

that requires the caster to apply equal power to *both* the back cast and the forward cast. Even more specifically, a proper forward cast is impossible to execute after an incorrect back cast.

▶ **Practice Suggestions**

The left hand plays an important role in the cast as it feeds line to the rod on the forward cast or draws line from the reel during a false cast.

1. Slack is taken, and the line is grasped between the thumb and forefinger and stripped (drawn) from the reel. Repeat this action two or three times so additional coils are formed.
2. At the end of the forward cast, the line is released from the coil in the left hand, the loop nearest the ends of the finger being released first. It is important to keep the loops separated.
3. As soon as sufficient line is drawn for the length of the cast, complete the cast, releasing the loops of line referred to previously. The release of these loops of line into the cast is called "shooting the line" and is usually used to add distance to the cast.

Bait Casting

The grip for bait casting is different in that the thumb must be placed on the spool flange for the conventional type, and the reel turned sidewise so that the handle points straight up. The index finger should grip the finger trigger while the other fingers grasp the handle firmly but not rigidly.

In fishing, a good caster learns to cast from any position and with either hand. In target casting, which is the only method of learning accuracy, the caster may stand directly facing the target or slightly sidewise, with the right side (if casting right-handed) toward the target and the right foot slightly advanced. The arms should be held in a relaxed "natural" position with the elbow at or near the side. The target should be aligned by looking at it through the top of the tip.

The overhead casting action has two parts: the backward and the forward motion. Each is equally important.

▶ **Learning Cues**

1. Stand comfortably; the elbow should be clear of the body while the forearm becomes an extension of the rod.
2. Bring the rod up quickly and stop at a two o'clock position; the weight on the lure will bend the rod further back.
3. With no hesitation bring the rod swiftly to a ten o'clock position, and ease the thumb off the line on the spool.
4. While the lure is in flight, gently apply pressure with the thumb braking the spool, and allow the

rod to follow-through in the direction of the line of flight. The spool is braked to a complete stop as the lure reaches the surface of the water. The rod must be shifted to the left hand in order to retrieve the plug. The right hand then grasps the handle of the reel and begins to reel in the line. The method of retrieving depends on the type of bait being used. Often the manufacturer supplies printed instructions on proper manipulation so the angler may secure the best results from each type.

Spin Casting

Remembering that there are two types of spinning reels, the open and the cone type, the cast for both is made in the same manner as with the bait casting outfit. The only difference is in the control of the line during the cast. With the closed-type reel, the thumb button is pressed then released at the ten o'clock position, and the left hand helps to feather the line and eventually brake it. With the spinning outfit, the caster places pressure upon the line between the forefinger and the rod grip *after* the line has left the spool.

In starting the cast, the line (ahead of the reel) is held firmly against the rod grip with the forefinger of the hand with which the cast is made. While holding the line securely, the pick-up bail or finger is released and moved aside so that it will not interfere with the line during the cast. This is done by turning the handle very slightly in reverse, by pressing a release button, or as required for the particular make of reel. The pressure upon the line is released at the same time and in the same manner as the thumb pressure upon the spool would be released with a bait-casting outfit. During the flight of the lure, control is exercised by decreasing or increasing the index finger pressure on the line against the cork grip.

As with the conventional rod and reel, the direct overhead cast is recommended until proficiency with the new outfit is acquired.

▶ **Practice Suggestions**

The beginning angler must learn not only accuracy and form but also develop a "feel" for the casting technique being learned. Distance is secondary in the beginning. Use a dummy lure (no barbs) when practicing. *Teaching Note:* In all instances, whether dealing with beginners or more advanced anglers, make sure there is adequate space between participants. Single line formations with a two or three arms' length between participants are safest.

1. Pick up the rod and practice the forearm and wrist action without casting.
2. For a class, place a series of plastic hoops at a standard distance and have students hit the tar-

get. As proficiency is gained, move the hoops to varying distances, designate high scores for those hoops farthest away and lower scores for those that are nearest to the angler. Individual and team competition can be promoted.

3. Since many people fish from a boat, bring a bench or low-backed chairs to class so students can practice each method of casting from a sitting position.

SKILL TESTING—SKISH

Skish is a dry-land game designed to improve one's skill in casting with regular bait/spin casting and fly casting tackle. It is an excellent way for all casters to master the skills of accuracy and the control of distance.

Bait Casting. Bait-casting rules call for the plug not to exceed five-eighths of an ounce, and the line must be no smaller than nine-pound test. Ten targets, rings not to exceed 30 inches, are randomly scattered with distances unknown to the caster. The closest target is not less than 40 nor more than 45 feet from the casting box (4 × 4 feet), while the farthest one should not be more than 80 nor less than 70 feet away. Each target has its own casting box, and the contestants move from box to box, taking two casts at each target (Figure 16-3).

Scoring: 6 points are scored for a perfect cast on first trial; 4 points for a perfect cast on second trial. The cast must fall within the target to score. In the event of a tie score, the one having the greatest number of points on initial casts is declared the winner.

Fly Casting. Fly-casting rules for regular fly-casting tackle require a fly tied in approved dry fly style with the hook broken off back of the barb. Five targets are placed at distances unknown to the casters, between 20 and 40 feet from the casting boxes.

First round. The caster must start with fly in hand and no slack in the line, and is given two and one-half minutes at each target to make three casts.

Scoring: 5 points are scored for a perfect cast on first trial; 3 points for a perfect cast on second trial; 2 points for a perfect cast on third trial, and a maximum score is 50 points. (On water, the fly must rest on the water until the judge calls for the score.)

Second round. The time limit is one and one-half minutes (90 seconds) for each target. The caster roll casts until a "perfect" has been scored on all five targets or until the official calls time. Time begins when the fly drops on the surface. Each perfect score counts 5 points, with a possible score of 25.

Third round—with fly. The time limit is one to one and one-half minutes. The caster starts with fly in the hand and no slack in the line. To begin, the caster extends the line to the nearest target by false casting, and time begins when the fly drops on the surface as a measured cast. Two casts are made, without false casts, at each of the five targets from left to right, stripping the necessary line and shooting it to reach each target.

Scoring: 3 points are scored for a perfect cast on first trial; 2 points for a perfect cast on second trial. The maximum possible score is 25 points. In case of a tie, the caster having made the greatest number of initial perfects is declared the winner.

MODIFICATIONS FOR SPECIAL POPULATIONS

Orthopedically Impaired

Modifications must be considered for several aspects of fishing, baiting the hook, holding and casting, reeling, and removing the catch. Several adaptations can be made for grasping the rod (see sections on Handball/Racquetball and Tennis). Electronic devices exist to help casting and reeling; however, the simplest modification would be to eliminate these sub-tasks and use a simple "cane pole" arrangement.

Mentally Impaired

Minimal modifications are needed.

Sensory Impaired

Minimal modifications are needed.

SAFETY CONSIDERATIONS

1. *All* anglers should carry or have access to a first aid kit at all times. Hooks, whether on flies or lures, occasionally end up in one part or another of an angler's anatomy!
2. Anglers must be constantly aware of the dangers of being in the sun too long. Use a sunscreen or sunblocker, wear a hat (which is also good to ward off hooks on errant casts), and polaroid sunglasses—for safety and to see fish.

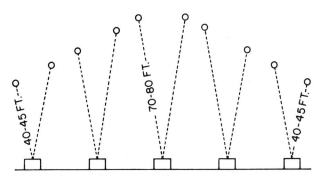

FIGURE 16-3 Skill testing set up or skish game using 10 targets and 5 stations.

3. Anglers often, probably too often, fish in places where there are lots of insects, especially of the flying variety. Be certain to carry appropriate repellent.
4. Wading with boots in unknown waters or wearing them in a boat is hazardous, and the angler must avoid such risks.

TERMINOLOGY

Back cast   Drawing the rod back; the initial movement in the cast.

Backing line   Thin braided line put on the reel before the fly line to fill up the spool and for insurance against a fish making a long run.

Backlash   A faulty casting technique that results in a tangling of the line.

Bait casting   The throwing and placing of a lure and line from the rod and reel.

Dry fly fishing   Casting a surface fly so that it resembles an insect on the water.

False cast   A fly casting cast where line is held in the air and not allowed to fall to the surface. Usually used to increase the length of a dry cast, or a fly change direction.

Ferrules   The connections between the sections of the rod.

Fly   Natural and/or synthetic materials tied on hooks.

Fly casting   Throwing a line with an artificial lure by means of a fly rod.

Forward cast   The last movement forward with the rod that throws the lure or the fly to the desired spot.

Guides   Small loops on the rod through which the line is run.

Leader   The strong, transparent material that connects the line to the hook or lure.

Level-wind reel   A reel which has a carriage that distributes the line evenly on the spool.

Lure   Artificial or natural bait used to attract fish. A hook or hooks is/are attached to the lure.

Net   A device to take the fish safely out of the water.

Power stroke   The brief time in fly casting between the forward and backward cast when power is applied by the caster.

Reel   The mechanism which winds or unwinds the line.

Reel seat   The part of the rod handle to which the reel is attached.

Rod tip   The top end of the rod.

Roll cast   A fly cast in which line is rolled out over a surface without utilizing a backcast.

Shoot   Feeding out extra line during a fly casting forward or backward cast. Also used to increase the distance of a cast.

Spinner   Artificial lure that spins when it is drawn through the water.

Spoon   Artificial lure shaped something like a spoon.

Strike   When a fish grasps the lure or fly as well as the angler's response to set the hook.

Tackle   Fishing gear; usually refers only to the rod and reel.

Thumbing   Controlling the speed of the cast by means of thumb pressure on the reel.

SELECTED REFERENCES

Cooper, G. and Haas, E. *Wade a Little Deeper, Dear: A Woman's Guide to Fly Fishing.* New York: Nick Lyons Books, 1989.

Gerlach, R. *The Complete Book of Casting.* New York: Winchester Press, 1975.

Knap, J.J. *Fishing Secrets.* New York: Crown Publishers, Inc., 1977.

McClane, A.J. *Secrets of Successful Fishing.* New York: Henry Holt, 1979.

National Association of Angling and Casting Clubs. *By-Laws, Rules and Regulations of Casting.* current ed. University City, MO: NAACC.

National Skish Board. *National Skish Guide.* latest ed. Washington, D.C.: NSB (Bond Building).

Rosenbaur, T. *The Orvis Fly-Fishing Guide.* New York: Nick Lyons Books, 1984.

Rosenthal, M. *The Freshwater Fishing Book.* New York: Macmillan, 1989.

Wright, L. *First Cast: The Beginner's Guide to Fly Fishing.* New York: Simon and Schuster, 1987.

Videos

Dierks, R. *Introduction to Fishing.* Prior Lakes, MN. Mintex Entertainment.

Krieger, M. *The Essence of Fly Casting.* Sebastopol, CA: Sonoma Video Productions.

Scientific Anglers. *Fly Fishing Made Easy.* Minneapolis, MN: 3M Sportsman Video Collection.

Note: The number of videos on all aspects of angling increases monthly. We urge you to check fishing publications for the latest releases.

HORSESHOES

NATURE AND PURPOSE

Horseshoe pitching has been popular for a long time both as a recreational and competitive sport. The formation of the National Horseshoe Pitchers Association in 1921 has given rise to chapters in nearly every state as well as Canada. The NHPA sanctions local and regional meets for men, women, boys and girls. A World Tournament is held each year for Men and Women while a Junior Boys and Junior Girls World Champion is also decided.

The game is played by pitching horseshoes toward a metal stake some 40 feet (30 for women and juniors) from the pitching point. Points are scored for shoes landing closest to the stake, providing the shoe is not farther than six inches from the stake. A ringer (shoe which encircles stake) counts three points. The winner is the player who first scores 21 points (informal play) or 50 points (official tournament competition). Players alternate in throwing shoes, with the player who scored one or more points on the previous pitch throwing first. In singles play the players move from stake to stake after each throw, but in doubles one partner is stationed at each stake and makes all throws from there.

PLAYING AREA AND EQUIPMENT

The Court. The official horseshoe court (see Figure 16-4) is 50 × 10 feet with one-inch metal stakes placed 40 feet apart (30 feet for women and juniors). The stakes are centered in a 6 × 6 foot pitcher's box. For informal recreational games, the distance between stakes may be arranged to fit the available space. If courts are to be built on a school ground, it is advisable to build back stops behind each pitcher's box to prevent the horseshoes from rebounding into a student. In schools that lack the space or do not wish to build permanent courts, temporary ones can be built in a place of convenience.

Horseshoes. Horseshoes may be bought at local hardware stores or discount department stores, or may be specially ordered from a number of companies approved by the NHPA. For schools, several physical education and recreation equipment companies sell either official metal shoes or indoor and outdoor rubber horseshoes that are used with wooden stakes. An official shoe should not exceed 7¼ inches in width and 7⅝ inches in length, and should weigh no more than 2 pounds 10 ounces. The opening can be no more than 3½ inches from point to point.

BASIC RULES

The National Horseshoe Pitchers Association establishes the official rules of horseshoe pitching. The simplified rules are listed below.

1. A game is divided into innings, and each contestant pitches two shoes in each inning. A game lasts 25 innings (50 shoes pitched by each person).
2. The choice of the first pitch to start the game is decided by the toss of a shoe or a coin.
3. A shoe that has left the pitcher's hand is ruled a pitched shoe.
4. A pitcher's opponent must stand behind the person in action and may not interfere with the pitch in any way.
5. A contestant may not walk to the opposite stake or be informed of the position of the shoes until the inning is completed.
6. Shoes thrown when a foul has been committed are considered shoes pitched; however, they may not receive any point value. Fouls may be assessed for the following:
   a. Illegal delivery of shoe.
   b. Failure of opponent to stay behind the pitcher, or his interfering in any way with the opponent while he or she is in the act of pitching.
   c. Touching thrown shoes before a measurement has been made.
   d. Thrown shoes which strike part of the pitcher's box or land outside the foul lines and which then rebound into the box.
   e. Stepping on or over the foul line.
7. Ties are broken by pitching an extra inning(s).

Scoring

1. The shoe nearest to the stake scores one point, providing it is within six inches of the stake.
2. Two shoes closer than opponent's shoe score two points.
3. One ringer scores three points and two ringers, six points.

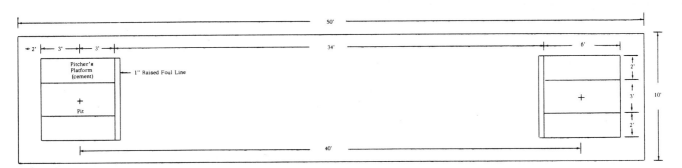

FIGURE 16-4 The official horseshoes court.

4. A player having two ringers to one by his opponent scores three points.
5. All shoes equally distant from the stake count as ties and no points are scored.
6. A leaning shoe has the same value as that of a shoe lying on the ground and in contact with the stake.

SKILLS AND TECHNIQUES

Players must stand behind the foul line on the pitching platform when pitching. Most players assume a starting stance with the pitching arm closest to the stake and in a position which permits a forward step in the act of delivery of the shoe. The number of turns which the shoe takes in flight usually determines the style of grip to be used. Regardless of the grip used, there are several factors common to all pitches:

1. The shoe should be held parallel to the ground which calks down.
2. The rotation of the shoe should be clockwise.
3. The open end of the shoe should face the stake when landing.

There are four standard methods of delivery, so the beginner should do some experimenting to determine which method is best for him or her.

1. In the single turn delivery (see Figure 16-5) the open face of the shoe is directed toward the stake.
2. In the one and one-quarter turn delivery (see Figure 16-6), the open end of the shoe faces the pitcher's left and the thumb is across the top.
3. In the one and one-half turn delivery (see Figure 16-7), the open end of the shoe faces the pitcher.
4. In the one and three-quarters delivery (see Figure 16-8), the open end of the shoe faces the pitcher's right and either of two shoe holding methods may be used.

▶ **Learning Cues**

1. Weight evenly distributed on both feet in the stance, step off on opposite foot, knees bent, eyes on the target, shoulders square to target.
2. While slightly leaning forward, the arm remains straight and falls down and back and retraces the same arc on the forward swing. The pitch must be smooth and rhythmical.

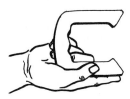

FIGURE 16-5   The single turn delivery.

FIGURE 16-6   The one and one-quarter turn delivery.

FIGURE 16-7   The one and one-half turn delivery.

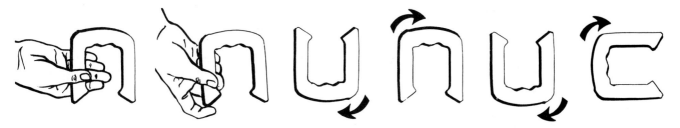

FIGURE 16-8 The one and three-quarter turn delivery. Two different grips are illustrated.

3. At the release the body and arm extend giving proper lift, the forearm rolls in order to turn the shoe.

▶ **Practice Suggestions**

1. Experiment with various deliveries; usually the one and one-quarter turn delivery is best for a beginner.
2. Practice the step and throw without a shoe then add the shoe. Partner should check to see that arc is straight and shoulders square and delivery is rhythmical.
3. Juniors and school age children might start closer to the stake and work their way back to 30 feet.

SAFETY

1. Stand well away from the pitching court when not involved.
2. Be aware of people around you when swinging the horseshoe. Pitch only in the designated area.
3. If setting up courts for a class, make sure there is adequate distance between courts to compensate for erratic throws of beginners.

COURTESIES

1. Observe all the rules.
2. Do not disturb a person who is in the process of pitching.
3. Keep emotions under control.
4. Be aware of the game and the position in the game so you are ready to pitch when your turn comes.

MODIFICATIONS FOR SPECIAL POPULATIONS

Orthopedically Impaired

1. Able-bodied students can be placed in a regular classroom chair if mainstreamed with students using a wheelchair.
2. Distances can be shortened.

3. The target for the horseshoe can be placed next to the student with grasp and release difficulties.
4. Small rings can be made from old jump ropes to replace the actual horseshoe or hula hoops can be used for more severe mobility impairments.

Mentally Impaired

Minimal modifications are needed.

Sensory Impaired

1. Some type of audio device can be placed as the target, e.g., buzzer or bell, and positioned inside of a hula hoop. Blind and/or visually impaired students could toss bean bags instead of horseshoes for inside the hoop.
2. No modifications should be needed for the deaf and/or hard of hearing.

TERMINOLOGY

Calks Raised areas on the heels and toes of one side of the pitching shoe that tend to make the shoe less likely to skid when striking the surface of the pit area.

Double ringer Two successive shoes which encircle the stake by the same player in the same inning.

Flipped-up shoe Flipping shoe in air to determine which player takes the first pitch. Instead of calling heads or tails, a player calls smooth or rough.

Heel The ends of the prongs on each side of the open end of the shoe.

Inning The pitching of two shoes by each player.

Leaner (also **Hobber**) Shoe which leans against a stake.

Pit The area in which the shoe lands.

Pitcher box The area which includes the pitching platform and the pit.

Ringer A shoe that encircles the stake.

SELECTED REFERENCES

National Horseshoe Pitchers Association of America. *Official Rules for Horseshoe Pitching.* Current ed. Federation of 54 State Associations in the U.S. and Canada. (Contact local association for state address.)

Reno, O.W. *Pitching Championship Horseshoes.* 2nd ed. New York: A.S. Barnes and Company, 1975.

The Horseshoe Pitchers' News Digest, published monthly, P.O. Box 1606, Aurora, IL 60507.

PICKLE-BALL

NATURE AND PURPOSE

Pickle-ball is a fast-paced, fun-filled game for individuals of all ages. Developed first as a recreational backyard game, it has found its popularity among racquet enthusiasts and in physical education programs. Combining the court markings and dimensions of badminton, skills associated with tennis, a net which is three feet high, solid wooden racquets, and a plastic whiffle ball, the game can be played in a singles format or doubles format. The premium is on ball placement rather than strength or size of the players. For this reason, it can be played as a coeducational activity, and a recreational activity by boys and girls and men and women. The winner of the game is that player or team first to reach 11 points; however, an individual or team must win by a margin of two points.

Pickle-ball can be played in a number of venues; the surface of the court must be hard enough so that the plastic ball will bounce. Therefore, it is not unusual to see pickle-ball courts set up inside on a gymnasium floor or on a concrete or blacktop playground surface. While official pickle-ball equipment can be purchased at a reasonable price from a number of physical education equipment suppliers or from Pickle-Ball Inc. in Seattle, Washington, the square-headed paddles can be made from a good quality plywood, a piece of nylon for a safety strap and wooden handles. Whiffleballs the size of a baseball or softball may also be used and generally the smaller the ball, the quicker the game. A badminton net strung across a series of wooden standards 36 inches high will meet the requirements of the net needed for the game. Because the equipment is relatively inexpensive, pickle-ball is an attractive game not only for class but for recreation and intramural tournament play.

The game itself uses skills associated with tennis. Some physical education instructors use the game as a good skill developer for the forehand and backhand drives, lobs and volleys. Because the player has to bend his knees to get low enough to stroke the ball properly, it is a good developer for this element of tennis. The game is played on a court the same dimensions as a badminton doubles court. While the service areas retain their markings, the pickle-ball court has a non-volley zone seven feet on either side of the net. For the gymnasium which has a permanent badminton court painted on it, the short service area may serve as the non-volley zone.

Most important of all, it is a safe game not requiring size or strength to enjoy. The fact is, the person who has difficulty with tennis, racquetball or handball because of the speed of the ball, will find greater success with the moderately paced pickle-ball game.

BASIC RULES

1. **Court.** The size of the court is 20 × 44 feet for both doubles and singles. The net is hung at 36 inches on ends, and hangs 34 inches in the middle. When laying out a court, allow adequate space—3 to 5 feet at each end and 1 to 2 feet at the sides—of the court boundary lines for player movement. However, it should be noted that many families play pickle-ball with little or no back and side court and enjoy the game.
2. **Serve.** Player must keep one foot behind the back line when serving. The serve is made underhand. The paddle must pass below the waist. The server must hit the ball in the air on the

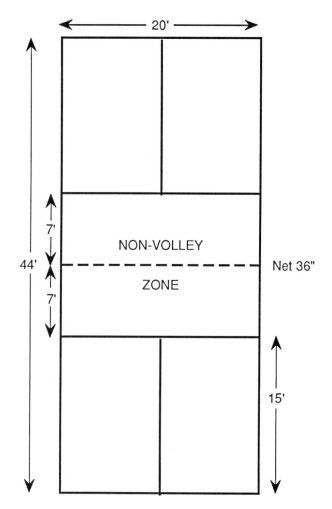

FIGURE 16-9 Official pickle-ball court. Note the non-volley zones. Diagrams courtesy of Pickle-Ball, Inc., Seattle, WA.

serve. Bouncing the ball before hitting it is not allowed. The service is made diagonally cross court and must clear the non-volley zone. Only one serve attempt is allowed, except if the ball touches the net on the serve and lands in the proper service court. Then the serve may be taken over. At the start of each new game, the first serving team is allowed only *one* fault before giving up the ball to the opponents. Thereafter, both members of each team will serve and fault before the ball is turned over to the opposing team. When the receiving team wins the serve, the player in the right hand court will always start play.

3. **Volley.** To volley a ball means to hit it in the air without first letting it bounce. All volleying must be done with player's feet *behind* the non-

volley zone line (Figure 16-10). NOTE: It is a fault if the player steps over the line on his volley follow-through.

4. **Double Bounce Rule.** Each team must play their first shot off the bounce. That is, the receiving team must let the serve bounce, and the serving team must let the return of the serve bounce before playing it. After the two bounces have occurred, the ball can be either volleyed or played off the bounce (see Figure 16-11).

5. **Fault**:
   a. Hitting the ball out-of-bounds.
   b. Not clearing net.
   c. Stepping into the non-volley zone and volleying the ball.
   d. Volleying the ball before it has bounced once on each side of the net, as outlined in Rule 4.

6. **Scoring.** A team shall score a point only when serving. A player who is serving shall continue to do so until a fault is made by his or her team. The game is played to 11 points; however, a team must win by 2 points.

Position of Players for Doubles at Start of Game

Determining Serving Team. Players may toss a coin or rally the ball until a fault is made. Winner of the toss or rally has the option of serving first or not serving first.

Doubles Play. Two alternate positions for players are shown in Figures 16-12 and 16-13.

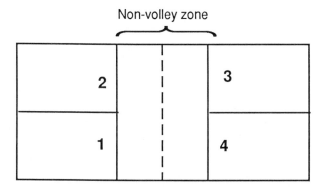

FIGURE 16-10 Position of players at net when volleying.

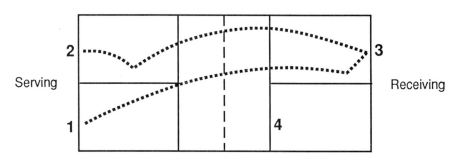

FIGURE 16-11 Illustration of double bounce rule.

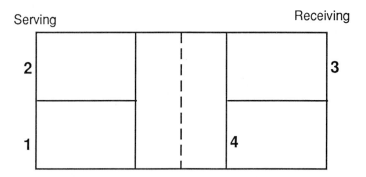

FIGURE 16-12 Position of players for doubles at start of game.

A

B

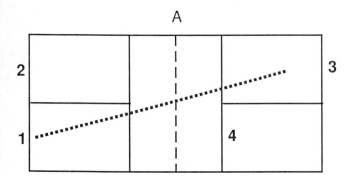

FIGURE 16-13 Doubles play.

a. Player 1 in RIGHT-HAND court serves diagonally across court to receiver (3) in opposite RIGHT-HAND court. The ball must clear the non-volley zone and land in the right-hand serving court. The receiver (3) must let the ball bounce before returning the serve. Serving team must *also* let the return bounce before playing it (Rule #4: Double Bounce Rule). After the two bounces have occurred, the ball may then be either volleyed or played off the bounce until a fault is made.

b. If the fault is made by the receiving team, a point is scored by the serving team. When the serving team wins a point, its players will switch courts and the *same* player will continue to serve. When the serving team makes its first fault, players will stay in the same court, and the second partner will then serve. When they make their second fault they will stay in the same courts and turn the ball over to the other team. Players switch courts only after scoring. A ball landing on any line is considered good.

Singles Play.   All rules apply with the following exception: When serving in singles, each player serves from the RIGHT-HAND court when his score is zero or an even number, and from the LEFT-HAND court when his score is odd numbered.

EQUIPMENT

Paddle

The official pickle-ball racquet is generally made of hardwood or a good quality plywood. The squared-off head should not exceed 8 inches in width nor 15 1/2 inches in length. A racquetball paddle, any strung paddle or paddle with holes is not legal. A cord should be attached to the butt end of the handle for safety purposes; the wrist should be inserted through the cord so the paddle does not come off during play (Figure 16-14).

Balls

The official perforated ball used in pickle-ball is 3 inches in diameter. Various sized whiffle balls may

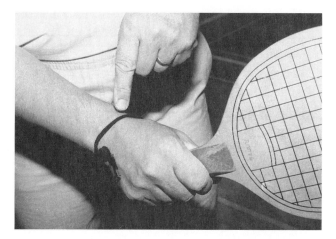

FIGURE 16-14 Note cord around wrist to prevent paddle from slipping from hand.

be used in a physical education class. Generally the larger the ball, the slower the game. For smaller children, the larger ball is easier to strike and to "watch" into the hitting area.

Net

A badminton or a tennis net may be used in the game of pickle-ball. Wooden standards may be constructed and strung across a gymnasium floor to make up several pickle-ball courts for class play.

SUGGESTED LEARNING SEQUENCE

A. Nature and purpose of pickle-ball
B. Acquaint players with equipment, court size
C. Skills and Techniques. Relate skills to tennis techniques; use drills to develop forehand and backhand drives, lobs, service, and volleys. Use practice drills using rebound volleying against a wall; play mini-games using only the forehand or backhand. Combine game-like drills as you begin introducing rules of the game.
  1. Grip, stance, and footwork
  2. Forehand and backhand drives

3. Service—lob, drive
4. Volley—forehand and backhand
5. Lob
D. Rules of the Game. Introduce the rules when appropriate; introduce the non-volley zone and rules governing net play as soon as possible.
E. Strategy can be introduced with a skill as soon as appropriate levels of skill are attained. Game-like drills which combine elements of strategy and are introduced early help the player learn more quickly.
F. Game Play

SKILLS AND TECHNIQUES

The techniques and skills required to play pickle-ball are identical for the most part with those used in tennis. Refer to Chapter 23 for the skill breakdowns for the eastern grip, the stance or ready position, forehand and backhand drives, the forehand and backhand volley, and the lob. Good footwork is also essential in pickle-ball. For movement to the ball requiring two steps or less, slide your feet into position. Use drills placing the player in a ready position and sliding the feet from side-to-side in that position. For balls hit further away, such as the lob over the head to the back court, turn and run to the ball while looking over the shoulder toward the net to note where opponents may be moving.

Service. There are two types of service. The first drives the ball over the net in a flat arc while the second type of service results in an arc best describing a lob. When initiating the serve, there are three important rules to remember: (1) the paddle must pass below the waist in the serving motion; (2) the ball must be dropped and hit out of the air; and (3) one foot must remain behind the back line.

Lob Serve. The lob serve (Figure 16-15) is used as a defensive technique to keep the opponents in the back court area. This high arcing serve will tend to bounce higher and keep the opponent in a defensive mode.

▶ **Learning Cues**

1. Standing with the paddle side foot behind the other and facing the net, the body is in a ready position.
2. The weight is transferred from the back foot to front foot, the ball is dropped just forward of the front foot.
3. The paddle arm swings forward and with the face of the paddle perpendicular to the direction of the serve, the paddle makes contact with the ball opposite the front foot.
4. The arm continues forward and upward giving the ball the necessary lift for a high arcing serve.

Drive Serve. The drive serve (Figure 16-16) is an effective defensive serve when executed correctly. This low, flat arcing serve will land deep in the opponent's back court, forcing the player away from the volley zone.

▶ **Learning Cues**

1. Standing with the paddle side foot behind the other and facing the net, the body assumes a ready position (knees flexed, bent at waist).

FIGURE 16-15 The lob serve. Note paddle makes contact with ball below waist.

FIGURE 16-16 The drive serve.

2. The weight is transferred from the back foot to the forward foot, the ball is dropped opposite the forward foot.
3. The paddle arm swings forward, the wrist is cocked.
4. At contact opposite the front foot, the wrist is snapped through, and the forearm is pronated as the follow-through is executed.

▶ **Practice Suggestions**

It is important to emphasize that the serve must be in play in order to score points; therefore, consistent serving is essential to the game. Practice serves for 5 to 7 minutes at the beginning of each class period. Zones can be outlined on the floor and serves directed toward specific zones. Players will get a feel for how hard to hit the two serves.

The key to the lob serve is the height and depth of the serve. Standards with a badminton net placed across the back of the non-volley zone at a height of 10 to 15 feet will force the server to practice hitting the ball high enough to carry to the back court.

The key to the drive serve is also the height and depth. For helpful practice, use standards with a string across the court at a height of 4 to 5 feet above official net height; direct the server to hit the ball over the regulation net height but below the string.

Practice drills for the other strokes can be adapted from the Tennis chapter.

PLAYING STRATEGY

1. Serves are most effective when hit into the far back court and into the corners. It is best to vary the serve, however, to keep your opponent off balance.

2. To receive the serve, place yourself in a ready position behind the back line; this enables you to return either a drive serve or lob serve. Return the service in the back court and corners. Vary the placement of the shot so your opponent is forced to hit a backhand or a forehand.
3. Force your opponent to move from side-to-side and up and back.
4. In doubles, try to take control of the net by forcing your opponents to hit shots from the backline.
5. In doubles, hit the ball down the center of the court occasionally; this forces opponents to make choices which sometimes puts them out of position to hit the return.
6. Use a lob shot occasionally when you have drawn your opponent to the net. However, if you and your opponent are near the net, use a lob as a defensive technique to allow you to get back into position.

MODIFICATIONS FOR SPECIAL POPULATIONS

Orthopedically Impaired

See modifications discussed in Tennis and in Handball/Racquetball.

Mentally Impaired

Minimal modifications are needed.

Sensory Impaired

See modifications discussed in Tennis and in Handball/Racquetball.

SAFETY CONSIDERATIONS

1. Always wear the strap around your wrist so if the paddle slips from your hands, it stays with you.
2. Warm up properly before starting the game. Stretching exercises for the shoulder girdle, hamstrings, and abductors of the legs are recommended.
3. Get used to calling for the ball so as to minimize contact with your doubles partner.

TERMINOLOGY

Approach shot A shot hit inside the baseline while approaching the net.
Backcourt The area near the non-volley zone and baseline.
Backhand Stroke hit on the opposite side of the hand holding the paddle.
Baseline The end line of the pickel-ball court.
Down-the-line A shot hit near a sideline which travels close to, and parallel to, the same line from where it was initially hit.
Drive A low shot that is hit near the opponent's backcourt.
Drop shot A ground stroke hit in such a way that the ball drops just over the net into the non-volley zone.
Error A mistake made by a player during competition.
Fault A serve which lands out of bounds or court area.
Foot fault Failure on the server's part to keep at least one foot behind the baseline during the serve.
Forehand The shot hit on the right side of a right-handed player.
Game A game is determined in pickle-ball when one side has reached 11 points; however a team must win by two points.
Half-volley A ball hit only inches from the court surface after the initial bounce.
Let Any point that must be replayed.
Let serve A serve that touches the top of the net and falls in the proper service court; it must be replayed.
Lob A ball hit sufficiently high to pass over the reach of an opponent that falls within the court.
Non-volley zone The 7-foot area on either side of the net. A player may not step into the non-volley zone to play a ball before it bounces or on the follow-through of a stroke.
Pace The speed of the ball.
Passing shot The shot which passes beyond the reach of the net player and lands inbounds.
Placement A shot hit inbounds and untouched by an opponent.
Poach To cross over into your partner's territory to play a ball normally played by your partner.
Serve The lob or drive stroke used to put a ball into play at the beginning of the point. The serve must be using an underhand motion.

Smash A shot hit forcefully from above the player's head.
Volley To hit the ball in the air before it bounces on the court.

SELECTED REFERENCES

Curtis, J.M. *Pickle-Ball for Player and Teacher.* 2nd ed. Englewood, CO: Morton Publishing, 1989.
Pickle-Ball Incorporated. Rules and other publications, 3131 Western Ave., Seattle, WA 98121.
Squires, D. *The Other Racquet Sports.* New York: McGraw-Hill, 1978.

SHUFFLEBOARD

NATURE AND PURPOSE

Shuffleboard may be played by two people *(singles)* or by four *(doubles)*. The game is played by propelling round wooden discs by means of a cue stick with a curved end over a hard, smooth surface on which the outlines of the court have been drawn.

The Court. The court is 52 feet long and 6 feet wide, with a triangular target and scoring diagram at each end (see Figure 16-17). One end of the court is designated as the Head of Court and the other as the Foot of Court.

Equipment. Each player is provided with a cue stick measuring 6 feet 3 inches maximum; it must have no metal parts touching the playing surface. There are two sets of discs, four in each set, one set painted red and the other black. The discs must be 6 inches in diameter, weigh not less than 11½ ounces nor more than 15 ounces, with thickness ranging from ¾ inch to 1 inch. Shuffleboard can be easily adapted to many types of surfaces; shuffleboard courts can be painted on the floors of classrooms, gymnasiums, hallways, sidewalks, or other concrete surfaces found at schools. Shuffleboard sets are available from most suppliers of physical education and recreation equipment at a very reasonable price. The discs are usually made of a durable composition material that can be used both indoors and outdoors.

Choice of disc color is made by playing one disc to the farthest deadline, with player of the disc closest to it receiving his choice of colors. In starting a game, the owner of red discs shoots first, followed by black, then by red, alternating thus until all discs are shot. In singles play, after all discs are shot from Head of Court, the players walk to Foot of Court and, after tallying the score, continue play toward Head of Court with owner of black discs shooting first.

In doubles, with two players at each end of the

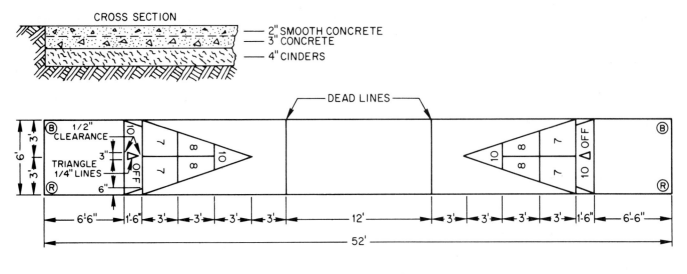

FIGURE 16-17 Shuffleboard court.

court, a game is started with the owners of red discs shooting all discs first from the Head of Court, followed by owners of black discs. Owners of red discs again shoot first from the Foot of Court, followed by black. On the second round, owners of black discs shoot first at each end of the court, followed by owners of red discs. Playing of all discs from one end of the court and back constitutes a round, so in doubles play the lead in starting to shoot changes after each round, while in singles play the lead changes after each half round.

BASIC RULES

Scoring. The scoring area contains one 10-point area, two 8-point areas, two 7-point areas, and one 10-off area. In order to count, a disc must lie entirely within one of the scoring areas with no part of the disc touching any side line, except that the separation line in the 10-off area is not considered. A game may end at 50, 75, or 100 points. Play continues until all discs have been shot, even if game point has been reached during the early part of a half round. In doubles, if a tie score results at game point or over, two additional rounds are played. If the score is still tied, play continues as outlined. In singles, one additional round is played to determine the winner in a tie game. In match play, the winner is determined on the basis of the best two out of three games.

Penalties. From 5 to 10 points are deducted from the player's score for certain infractions of

playing rules. Five points are deducted for the following infractions:

1. All discs not in respective half of 10-off area when ready to shoot.
2. Discs not played from respective half of 10-off (red played from right side, black from left).
3. Players stepping on or over baseline in making their shot.
4. Players not remaining seated when play is toward their end of the court.
5. Interfering in any way with opponent while he or she is making a play.
6. Players touching live discs at any time.

Ten points are deducted for the following infractions:

1. Player making hesitation or hook shot.
2. Player making remarks to disconcert opponent.
3. Making any remarks which may be construed as coaching a partner while making a play.
4. Player shooting before opponent's disc has come to rest.

Playing Rules. A disc returning or remaining on the court after having struck any object other than a live disc is called a *dead disc* and shall be removed from the court before the play is resumed. If a dead disc strikes a live disc, that half round shall be replayed. A disc that stops in the area between farthest deadline and starting point shall be considered dead and be removed from the court. Any disc that stops just beyond the farthest baseline shall be moved a distance of at least eight inches from baseline. Any disc stopping more than halfway over sidelines, or which rests or leans on the edge, shall be removed from the court.

SKILLS AND TECHNIQUES

The skills involved in playing shuffleboard are very few; however, it is a game requiring the development of touch—to know just how hard to push the disc. It is extremely important for the shuffleboard player to "read" the surface on which the game is being played, since the disc will react with different speeds on different surfaces. In executing the push or forward thrust of the cue, it is important to place the cue against the disc before the pushing action begins. Do not jab at the disc, because this will result in a loss of power. A few important points must be remembered about the push.

▶ Learning Cues

1. The handle is held at the end, weight forward on the feet, body slightly leaning forward (Figure 16-18A).
2. Push by straightening out the elbow, the opposite foot steps forward, the arm straightens and follows-through toward the target, with knees flexed (Figure 16-18B).

▶ Practice Suggestions

1. Have students line up in squads, one behind the other. Place one student at the end of the court to retrieve discs and push them back to students awaiting their turn. Rotate students from pushing position to retrieving position.
2. Place discs in different scoring areas, and allow the students to practice pushing the disc out of the area with their own disc.
3. Practice shooting for position. Develop "feel" for the push by attempting to push the disc to various boxes. Begin with no competition and then add competition.

MODIFICATIONS FOR SPECIAL POPULATIONS

Orthopedically Impaired

See modifications discussed in Field Hockey, Chapter 10.

Mentally Impaired

Minimal modifications are needed.

Sensory Impaired

See modifications discussed in Field Hockey.

TERMINOLOGY

Cue Stick used to propel discs toward the target.
Dead disc A disc that returns to or remains on the court after having struck an object other than another "live disc." Disc is also dead that stops between farthest deadline and starting line.
Foot of court That end of the court opposite the head.
Head of court That end of the court from which play starts to begin a match.
Hesitation shot This is illegal—the forward motion of the disc must be continuous (no stopping and restarting during the attempt).
Round The playing of all discs from one end of court and back constitutes a round.

FIGURE 16-18 Execution of the push in shuffleboard.

SELECTED REFERENCES

American Association for Health, Physical Education, and Recreation. *Official N.A.G.W.S. Recreational Games and Volleyball Guide.* Current ed. Washington, D.C.: AAHPER.

National Shuffleboard Association. *Official Rules.* Kissimmee, FL: NSA, Inc., 1965.

TABLE TENNIS

NATURE AND PURPOSE

Table tennis (popularly called Ping-Pong) may be played by two or four people. Equipment consists of a table with a smooth playing surface, a net, balls, and rackets (also called paddles). The game may be played by both old and young and seems destined to remain one of our most popular recreational activities.

EQUIPMENT

The equipment necessary to play table tennis is of simple construction and relatively inexpensive. School physical education programs can have rackets and tables made by the industrial arts department at a very nominal fee. Many physical education and recreation supply companies sell table tennis sets and balls for a very reasonable price. Obviously, as the competitive level and skill increases, more expensive rackets may be wanted.

Table. The table is 9 feet long and 5 feet wide, with a height of 30 inches from floor to top surface (Figure 16-19). Most tables are made of three-quarter inch pressed wood or good quality plywood,

but other materials can be used. Tables that come in halves and have a collapsible undercarriage are easy to store. Some are constructed so that one half can be folded up into a backdrop and used for a rebound wall in practicing various strokes.

Net. The playing surface is divided by a net secured in the center and parallel to the end lines. The top edge of the net is 6 inches above the playing surface.

Balls. The balls are constructed of celluloid, hollow, 4 1/2 to 4 3/4 inches in circumference, and weigh between 37 and 41 grains. A good ball should be perfectly round and without wobble when spinning. The United States Table Tennis Association seal of approval on a ball is a good indication of quality.

Racket. A variety of rackets (paddles) can be purchased at most sporting goods stores. Some have grips that will fit your hand size. All have a rubber or sponge covering of some type that covers the playing surface. A covering of inverted sponge is most used and is recommended for all levels of players.

BASIC RULES

Singles Game

Scoring. The winner of a match is the player who first scores 21 points, unless both players have 20 points, in which case the winner must gain a two-point lead in order to win. The choice of ends and service at the start of the game shall be decided by toss.

Change of Ends and Service. A game is started with the server making five consecutive services. The receiver follows with five services, each player alternating in this fashion for the duration of the game, unless the score becomes 20-all, in which case the receiver will make one serve, followed by the original server with one serve, then the receiver, and

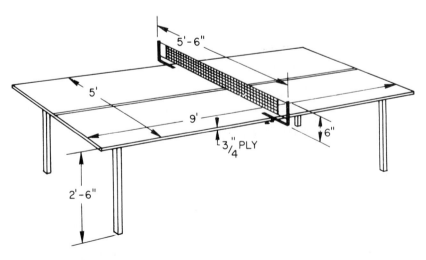

FIGURE 16-19 Table tennis table.

so on, until a winner is declared. If the match consists of only one game, or in the deciding game of a match, the players change ends at the score of 10. The player who started at one end of the table in one game starts at the other end in the immediately subsequent game.

The Service. The service is delivered by releasing the ball, without imparting any spin upon release, and striking it with the paddle outside the boundary of the court near server's end. Finger spins and rubbing the ball against the racket face are illegal. Any spin imparted to the ball must come from action of the racket upon impact with the ball. The ball shall be struck so that it first drops into server's court and then into receiver's court by passing directly over or around the net.

A Good Return. A ball having been served or returned in play shall be struck by the player so that it passes directly over or around the net and lands in opponent's court; if the ball, during play, returns of its own impetus over or around the net, it may be played the same as a returned ball.

Let Ball. The served ball shall be a let if it touches the net or its supports, and later lands in receiver's court. A let shall also be declared when a serve is made before the receiver is ready, unless the receiver makes an effort to strike the ball. It is a let if either player, because of conditions not under his control, is prevented from making a serve or a return.

Either player shall lose the point:

1. If he or she fails to make a good service, unless a let is declared.
2. If a good service or a good return is made by an opponent and he or she fails to make a good return.
3. If racket, or any part of player or clothing, touches the net or its supports while the ball is in play.
4. If the player moves the table in any way while playing the ball.
5. If a player's free hand touches the table while the ball is in play.
6. If, at any time, he or she volleys the ball. (A volley consists of hitting the ball before it has bounced.)

Doubles Game

The rules for singles games apply to doubles except as indicated below.

Service Line. A one-eighth inch white line drawn down the center of the table parallel to the side lines is called the service line.

A Good Service. The ball must touch first the server's right-half court or the center line on his side of the net, and then, passing directly over or around the net, touch the receiver's right-half court or the center line on his side of the net.

Choice of Order of Play. The pair who has the right to serve the first five services in any game shall decide which partner shall do so, and the opposing pair shall then decide similarly which shall first be the receiver.

Order of Service. Each server shall serve for five points. At the end of each term of service, the one who was receiving becomes the server, and the partner of the previous server becomes the receiver. This sequence of the receiver becoming the server and the partner of the previous server becoming the receiver continues until the end of the game or the score of 20-all. At the score of 20-all, the sequence of serving and receiving shall continue uninterrupted except that each player shall serve only one point in turn, and the serve alternates after each point until the end of the game.

Order of Play. After the server makes a good service, a good return is made by the receiver, then by the partner of the server, then by the partner of the receiver, and then by the server, and thereafter each player, in that sequence, shall make a good return.

SKILLS AND TECHNIQUES

Table tennis requires much concentration and excellent reactions. Because of the close similarity to tennis, the basic fundamentals regarding stroking the ball may be applied in some instances. The discussion in this section will deal with some of the beginning skills needed to get the player started.

Grip

The most common grip used by a majority of players is the "shake hands" grip used in tennis (Figure 16-20). The great Chinese players use a grip known as the penholder grip (Figure 16-21); however, this style of grip is usually best only for an attacking type of game.

▶ **Learning Cues**

1. With the racket perpendicular to the floor, grasp the racket as you would shake hands.
2. The last three fingers wrap around the handle and the forefinger lies close to the lower edge of the racket face.

Strokes

The forehand and backhand push shot should be mastered by the beginner before playing the game. For the right-handed player, the forehand stroke should be used when the ball approaches from the

FIGURE 16-20 Standard "shake hands" grip.

FIGURE 16-21 Penholder grip.

FIGURE 16-22 A good ready position.

right, and the backhand when the ball approaches from the left. Preparatory to any stroke the player should assume a good athletic stance in a ready position (Figure 16-22). The knees are bent, weight is evenly distributed on the forward half of the foot, arms are in front of the body, elbows bent, racket held parallel to the ground.

When executing both shots, it is important to remember that the ball is directed over the net by a pushing action, not a hitting action. Variations in arm movement and wrist movement will allow spin to be imparted to the ball.

▶ **Learning Cues:** Backhand Push (Figures 16-23, 16-24)

1. The ball is played in front of the body at the point of highest contact.

2. As the ball approaches, the right arm is drawn back by pivoting at the elbow, the right shoulder back by pivoting past the elbow, the right shoulder turns and is pointed toward the table.
3. Push the racket forward toward the ball, extend arm in a horizontal plane.
4. Body weight transfers from back foot to forward foot throughout the stroke.

▶ **Learning Cues:** Forehand Push (Figure 16-25)

1. As the ball approaches, the racket is drawn back; shoulders turn so the left shoulder is pointed toward the table.
2. Push the racket forward toward the ball, arm extended in a horizontal plane; shoulders return.

FIGURE 16-23 Position of the hand in backhand push.

FIGURE 16-24 Position of body during backhand push shot.

FIGURE 16-25 Position during forehand push shot. Note the left shoulder is pointing toward the table.

FIGURE 16-26 Ready to serve on the forehand side.

3. Body weight transfers from the back foot to the forward foot throughout the stroke.

Serves

It is important for the beginner to remember that the ball may not be served from the palm of the hand. In addition the ball must contact the server's side of the table first.

▶ **Learning Cues:** Topspin Serve (Forehand Side)

1. The body assumes a stance three quarters sideways to the table, the ball rests on the fingers of the left hand, racket assumes position of a forehand push shot (Figure 16-26).
2. The ball is tossed upward, the racket face

FIGURE 16-27 A folding table can be used as a rebound wall for practice.

(slightly closed) comes forward and continues forward after the contact.

3. As the racket face follows-through, it rolls over the top of the ball thus imparting topspin to the ball.

The mechanics for a backhand topspin serve will be essentially the same except the serve is initiated from the left side for the right-handed player.

▶ **Practice Suggestions**

1. If a folding table is available, fold up one side perpendicularly, so that it can be used as a re-bound wall to practice strokes and serves (Figure 16-27).
2. Practice the toss (6 to 8 inches high) needed for the serve, concentrating on a smooth, rhythmical toss.
3. Practice against a wall, either letting the ball bounce once or volleying the ball as long as possible. As a variation, mark a target (circle or square) on the wall and try to hit the ball into the target.
4. To develop a feel for the racket and ball, continuously tap the ball upward off the face of the racket, then downward, while walking. Note the importance of concentration as this drill is executed.
5. When practicing the strokes and the serve, equal amounts of time must be given to developing skills on the backhand side as well as the forehand side.

MODIFICATIONS FOR SPECIAL POPULATIONS

Orthopedically Impaired

1. See modifications discussed in Tennis and in Handball/Racquetball.
2. Set up a modified table-top tetherball game. Tether a small whiffleball with a string to a 12

to 16 inch vertical dowel rod. Use a large square piece of cardboard strapped to the student's hand instead of a regulation paddle.

Mentally Impaired

Minimal modifications are needed.

Sensory Impaired

See modifications discussed in Tennis and in Handball/Racquetball.

TERMINOLOGY

Ace A service that completely eludes the receiver.

Advantage (ad) Next point made after a deuce score. It is "advantage out" if the receiver wins it and "advantage in" if the server wins. The player wins the match who first wins a point after gaining "advantage."

All Term used to denote an equal score; e.g., 20-all.

Backhand Stroke frequently used by right-handed player when returning a ball hit to his left. The paddle is held so that the back of the hand faces the ball; the ball is usually hit with side of paddle opposite the side used in the forehand.

Backspin A ball hit so that top of ball rotates toward stroker, bottom moving away.

Block shot A half-volley.

Dead ball A ball is dead if a let is called, if the ball bounces twice on the table, and at the conclusion of a point or rally.

Deuce When the score is even at 20-all. To win, a player must score two consecutive points.

Drop shot A shot played so softly that it dies before opponent can reach it, or places him at a disadvantage if he does play it.

Finger spin An illegal procedure whereby spin is imparted to the ball by the fingers in serving.

Forehand A stroke or volley made in such a fashion that the palm is the leading part of the movement. Usually hit with the opposite face of the paddle than that used in backhand. In this stroke the left foot of a right-handed player is toward the table.

Let Means "play the point over" and occurs when the ball strikes the top of net and falls into correct service court, also if a ball breaks or if a player is interfered with by an official or spectator.

Mixed doubles Doubles game in which each team has one man and one woman player.

Push shot A ball struck with a pushing motion of the paddle near the top of the bounce so that no spin is placed on the ball.

Service court In singles, the entire table area on the receiver's side, 5 by 4½ feet. In doubles, the table is divided by a center line so each service court is 4½ by 2½ feet.

Slice A stroke in which the ball is stroked late so that it tends to spin in a direction away from the paddle.

Topspin A ball stroked so that the top spins forward in the direction of flight. Is the opposite of backspin or underspin.

Volley Illegal stroking of ball while it is in the air and before it has touched the table.

SELECTED REFERENCES

American Association for Health, Physical Education, and Recreation. *Official N.A.G.W.S. Individual Sports Guide.* Current ed. Washington, D.C.: AAHPER.

DeWitt, R.T. and Dugan, K. *Teaching Individual and Team Sports.* 2nd ed. Englewood Cliffs, NJ: Prentice Hall, 1972.

Miles, D. *Sports Illustrated Table Tennis.* Philadelphia: J.B. Lippincott Co., 1974.

Sklorz, M. *Table Tennis.* Yorkshire, England: E.P. Publishing Limited, 1973.

Varner, M. and Harrison, J.R. *Table Tennis.* Dubuque, IA: Wm. C. Brown Company, Publishers, 1968.

United States Table Tennis Association. *Table Tennis For You.* current ed. Philadelphia: USTTA.

17 SKIING: CROSS-COUNTRY

THIS CHAPTER WILL ENABLE YOU TO:

▶ Select equipment best suited to your needs.
▶ Consider the advantages and disadvantages of waxless skis and waxable skis, and know how to wax them.
▶ Understand and apply the concept of "layering" in clothing.
▶ Perform the techniques of getting up from a fall, poling, turning, and striding while moving on flat, downhill, and uphill terrains.
▶ Know what safety precautions to observe when cross-country skiing.

NATURE AND PURPOSE

The great increase in popularity enjoyed by cross-country skiing can be attributed to many factors. *First* is the relative ease with which Nordic skiing can be learned. To move from one point to another, the skier only has to initiate a walking action, thus it is a very natural activity. Unlike Alpine skiing, the touring skier has no lines to wait in, no crowds to endure, no long rides to the ski area, and no tow tickets to purchase. *Second,* the individual can engage in ski touring almost any place where there is no traffic: a country road, over fields, through woods, on hills, or on prepared tracks—these are all appropriate places to cross-country ski. *Third,* there are no age or sex limits; touring provides a good, clean form of recreation for all. It is not uncommon to find family groups—children, parents, and grandparents—gathering on a crisp, winter weekend day to ski tour in local and state parks, woods, or other scenic areas. In addition, many touring centers or local clubs in the United States now sponsor Citizens Races of varying distances, much like the marathons engaged in by many joggers. The purpose of the Citizens Races is not only competition but the opportunity to participate with hundreds of other people and to test yourself.[1] *Fourth,* ski touring is an excellent physical conditioner, especially when performed in a smooth, rhythmic manner over a prolonged period of time. Research studies indicate that the cross-country skier expends a great deal of energy in this physically demanding sport. *Finally,* ski touring equipment is reasonably priced at the beginner level; many stores offer ski packages that include bind-

ings, boots, poles, and skis for under $100. For the person who wishes to try out the activity, several outdoor stores or state parks will rent the necessary equipment for less than $10 a day.

School Programs. Several high school and college physical education programs include cross-country skiing as part of the regular curriculum. Many stores and state parks will rent equipment to schools for a reasonable price and in some instances will provide basic instruction. Many of the beginning techniques can be learned in two or three sessions, so the student can soon participate on flat and slightly rolling terrain. Obviously the more rugged terrain and steeper hills and valleys require more advanced techniques that take longer to develop. Although advanced techniques are beyond the scope of this chapter, information may be found among the Selected References.

Handicapped Programs. Cross-country skiing is an activity that also appeals to the blind and the partially sighted, the deaf, and the one-legged skier. Instruction programs for the handicapped enable special populations to enjoy this wonderful form of exercise and recreation. Several organizations that can supply additional information are listed in the Selected References.

EQUIPMENT

Ten years ago the individual interested in ski touring would have found a limited selection of equipment from which to choose. Today, however, almost every Alpine ski manufacturer has added a line of ski touring equipment. For the beginning skier the selection process can indeed be mystifying and frustrating; therefore, it is best to consult an expert before buying any equipment. The most important consideration for the beginner is that the equipment

---

[1] Further information about the Citizens Race can be obtained by writing to the Citizen and Club Cross-Country Racing Committee, United States Ski Association, 1726 Champa Street, Denver, CO 80202.

function properly and serve the skier through and after the initial stages of learning and participation.

Skis

When selecting cross-country skis, it is important to understand that they are categorized according to their use. *Racing skis,* which are narrow (35 to 45 mm) and very light, are designed specifically for competitive skiing. *Mid-touring skis* are heavier and slightly wider (40 to 50 mm). Beginners, novices, and recreational skiers frequently use the mid-touring ski. The *touring ski* is still wider (45 to 60 mm) and heavier than the racing or mid-touring ski. Many beginners learn on this type of ski because it is heavier, provides greater stability, and can withstand greater abuse. Many learn-to-ski programs rent this type of ski to the beginner. The touring ski is also used by the expert for deep powder skiing, because the extra width helps keep the ski above the surface rather than sinking into the snow.

Skis come in assorted lengths and should be selected according to your body build and sex. The following is a general guide to use in selecting proper ski length. While standing on the floor, raise your arm straight up. For a woman or girl, the tip of the ski should come to the wrist; for a man or boy, the tip should come to mid-palm of the hand (Figure 17-1). If you are a heavy person, consider a stiffer ski; if you are light, consider a more flexible ski.

One very important factor is whether to choose the waxable or waxless type of ski. Cross-country skis are designed to grip the snow's surface in order to obtain a good forward motion. The gripping action of the ski bottom to the snow results from the use of various waxes (the points of the snow flakes actually penetrate the wax to allow it to grip when pressure is applied to the kick zone) or, in the case of waxless skis, a specially designed indented surface that grips the snow (Figure 17-2). Although cross-country skis are generally made of a combination of wood and synthetic materials, most bottom surfaces are synthetic rather than wood, making them more impervious to moisture.

The waxless ski is easy to maintain and for that reason would perhaps better serve the occasional skier. There are, however, some disadvantages to this type of surface. The waxless bottom is not as adaptable to changing snow conditions as waxable skis. Application of different waxes in the kick zone is generally not possible, thus prohibiting maximum gripping performance. Additionally, the waxless ski sacrifices high level performance and speed. However, a majority of beginners and recreational skiers find the waxless type ski to be very satisfactory for their purposes.

Waxable skis are used by the ski purist and by the skier who wants the fun of waxing skis. The obvious advantage is that different waxes can be applied for different snow conditions, thus insuring a good

FIGURE 17-1 Determining proper ski length. Tip comes to mid-palm for men and to the wrist for women.

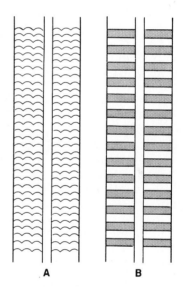

FIGURE 17-2 Types of bottom surfaces found on "waxless" cross-country skis: (A) fish scale pattern, (B) step pattern.

kick and glide. Waxing skis takes time and requires some basic knowledge of snow conditions. It is also an additional expense and bother that some skiers would rather do without. Waxing is described in detail at the end of this chapter.

Bindings

Bindings enable the boot to be attached to the ski. There are several types: some have cables that go around the bottom of the boot; others have cables that clamp the top of the boot to the ski. For the beginner and recreational skier the traditional three-pin binding is most commonly used (Figure 17-3). It

FIGURE 17-3   A three-pin binding.

FIGURE 17-4   A clamp binding found on some newer systems.

consists of three pins which are projected or inserted into the sole at the toe end of the boot; a metal bar or clamp called a bale is then pushed down and held by a projection on the binding. The bale can generally be released by applying pressure to the projection on the bar or clamp. Most toe bindings are made of metal, although some manufacturers have developed a plastic binding. All bindings are "norm fitted;" that is, they will fit any size boot. There are various norm sizes. The general size for the recreational skier is either a 75 mm nordic norm (width of the toe boot) or a 50 mm nordic norm. Newer, more sophisticated binding systems are available which may use a different design to secure the boot to the binding. Most, however, require some type of clamp to secure the boot to the ski (Figure 17-4). Bindings can be purchased separately, but it is best that they be mounted by an expert.

Boots

A proper-fitting boot is perhaps the key to successful cross-country skiing. Boots should be selected on the basis of comfort to the skier. The boot should be flexible enough across the crease so that it does not cut off circulation to the toes or cut across the toes. The skier should try the boot on, wearing the socks used for skiing. The heel of the boot should be snug, there should not be much side-to-side flexibility, and there should be plenty of room in the toes. Generally, a space about the width of a finger at the end of the big toe indicates proper length.

A light touring boot is best for the beginner and recreational skier (Figure 17-5). This boot is usually made of leather and comes in either a low cut or a high cut (gives more warmth), and should be set in a reinforced plastic or metal plate. Boots usually range

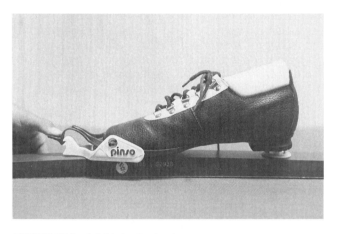

FIGURE 17-5   A light, touring boot.

in price from $20 and up. Before the first use it is important to apply a waterproofing conditioner and let the boots dry well. If properly taken care of, boots will last for several years.

Poles

Poles are used to aid in propelling the skier forward or as a means of balance and support. The pole consists of a grip, a strap, a basket, and a metal point that is bent to facilitate extraction from the snow. The poles can be made of a carbon fiber material, fiberglass, aluminium, or bamboo (Tonkin poles). Since poles tend to take a lot of abuse, the bamboo pole is the least durable. Most skiers prefer the fiber material pole which can be found in most stores.

The three key factors to look for when selecting a pair of poles are the length, the type of strap, and the size of the basket. To check for proper length, as you stand on the floor, the pole should fit snugly under the armpit (Figure 17-6). A pole that is too long or too short will hinder the skier's movement. The strap should be adjustable in order to allow the skier to make adjustments to the size of the gloves or mittens worn on the hand. Baskets, which are generally made of plastic, should be a medium size. Large baskets are used for deep powder snow, whereas smaller baskets are used by the competitive racer. Poles usually begin at $10.

Clothing

In addition to comfortable boots, what clothing to wear and how much are very important considerations. Remember that cross-country skiing involves total body movement and a great expenditure of energy. As a result, tremendous amounts of heat can be generated, and therefore overdressing will result in overheating. The best way to dress, as recommended by many experts, is on the "layering" principle; i.e., by wearing layers of loose-fitting clothing. Layering enables the skier to add or subtract articles of clothing according to the prevailing weather conditions. The following are important points to remember in selecting suitable ski wear.

1. A non-moisture absorbing layer (polypropolene material) should be worn next to the skin. This enables moisture and perspiration to pass out to your middle layer of clothing.
2. Avoid fabrics that do not breathe because they tend to hold in heat and moisture. Fabrics that are water repellent are preferable to fabrics that are waterproof.
3. Outer garments should be of a nonabsorbent material. Occasionally a skier falls and then snow clings to the material and may wet the inside layers.
4. Since much heat is lost through the head, wear a warm woolen knit hat or head covering big enough to be pulled down over the ears.
5. Loose-fitting pants or knickers are recommended to allow freedom of movement. A wool sweater or turtleneck shirt plus a nylon shell will keep the skier warm and dry under most conditions.
6. Wear a light inner pair of cotton socks and a pair of woolen knee length socks on top to keep the feet and legs warm and dry.
7. Wear mittens with a down fill or a light wool lining and a leather outer shell. Leather gloves with a warm lining are preferred by many because they give better control in handling the poles.

Other accessories include gaiters, an outer covering that keeps the lower legs dry (Figure 17-7); a fanny pack or knapsack to carry emergency materials, a repair kit, waxes, or extra clothes; and insu-

FIGURE 17-6 Judging the length of the ski pole. It should fit snugly beneath the armpit.

FIGURE 17-7 A pair of gaiters helps keep boots and ankles dry.

lated vests. The cost of these items varies with the type and the quality. The important thing to remember, no matter what you spend, is that the layering of loose-fitting garments permits the cross-country skier to adapt to all types of weather conditions.

SUGGESTED LEARNING SEQUENCE

Cross-country skiing can take place during various weather conditions and on different types of terrain (uphill, downhill, the flat), The sequence suggested here begins on the flat, preferably with prepared tracks, and then proceeds to the uphill and downhill. The skills and techniques described are for the beginner to beginner-intermediate level of recreational cross-country skiing.

A. Nature and Purpose
   1. Ski touring as a recreational sport
   2. Selecting equipment
   3. How to dress—what to wear
   4. Safety—introduced at appropriate times, when most meaningful
B. Conditioning—should begin prior to instruction on the slopes and should continue during the ski season
C. Waxing Techniques
D. Skills and Techniques
   1. On the Flat
      a. Getting up from a fall
      b. Diagonal stride
      c. Diagonal stride/Single poling
      d. Double poling
      e. Double poling/Stride
      f. Kick turn
   2. Uphill
      a. Diagonal stride
      b. Side step
      c. Traversing
      d. Herringbone
   3. Downhill
      a. Straight running
      b. Snow plow turn
      c. Step turn
      d. Traversing

SKILLS AND TECHNIQUES

The skills and techniques discussed in this section are for the beginner and beginner-intermediate recreational cross-country skier. There are several pre-techniques that can be practiced prior to beginning on the snow. These can be done on a carpeted area. If waxable skis are used, they should be free of wax.

▶ **Practice Suggestions:** Carpeted Area

1. Familiarize yourself with how the binding on the ski works. Put on the boots and insert the toe in the binding so that the three pins are inserted into the three holes at the bottom of the toe.
2. With both skis on, side step; move the tails of the skis keeping the tips fairly stationary, move around in a circle.
3. Slide the skis forward, approximating a walking action. Get the feel of the opposite arm and leg moving forward as the skis slide forward.
4. Learn to grasp the pole properly (Figure 17-8). Insert the hand through the strap, with thumb up, grasp the strap and pole grip. The skier should feel pressure at the bottom of the V of the thumb and index finger if gripping properly. As the arm pushes backward during the poling phase, the hand will release the pole; however, pressure of the strap should always be felt at the junction of thumb and index finger.

FIGURE 17-8 Grasping the pole. The strap lies beneath the palm of the hand.

5. Lift one ski then the other to note the action of the ski to boot and to develop a sense of balance. Because the heel is free from the binding, often the tail will fall causing the beginner to catch the snow and fall during side stepping or a kick turn.

FIGURE 17-9 Getting up from a fall. Note the skier rolls to his knees, with knees straddling the uphill ski.

Skiing on the Flat

It is best to start learning to cross-country ski on the flat. A facility that has pre-made tracks aids the beginner by placing the skis in the proper track while skiing. (When skiing alone in the wilderness you are not very likely to find any pre-laid tracks.) If no tracks are available, any flat ground with a shallow covering of powder snow will also serve the purpose.

Getting Up from a Fall. All skiers at one time or another find themselves on the ground either as a result of a fall or as a deliberate means of slowing down. If on a hill or flat, the following method will enable you to resume a standing position (Figure 17-9).

▶ **Learning Cues**

1. Holding a pole in each hand, assume a position perpendicular to your skis. If you are on a hillside, the skis must also be perpendicular to the slope with the skis on the downhill side. Now tuck the knees up under the body.
2. Roll to a kneeling position on the skis, poles planted and held to either side for stability.

3. Slide one ski forward so one knee is at a 90-degree angle, then merely stand up.

Diagonal Stride—Single Poling

The diagonal stride is to cross-country skiing as walking is to moving forward. The diagonal stride is a smooth, vigorous, rhythmical walking action that must be mastered by all beginners (Figure 17-10). Opposite arm and leg action are used just as when walking in a vigorous fashion, while the other arm and leg serve as a counterbalance to maintain proper body position. The stride involves a kick (push off) of the ski and forward slide followed by the repeat action of the other ski as it is brought forward. A planting and downward and backward push of the ski pole aids the glide forward. This skill is used on flats and going up slight inclines. An accentuated motion can be used for moving up steeper inclines.

▶ **Learning Cues**

1. The head is looking up and forward; body leans forward slightly, knees are comfortably flexed, weight is forward over the center of the skis on the balls of the feet.

FIGURE 17-10   The diagonal stride. Note weight is forward, knees are flexed.

2. The right arm reaches forward as left leg slides forward. Place left pole opposite the left foot, push downward and backward with pole and push off with right foot. As glide slows, repeat action on opposite side.
3. From the pole plant the arm will extend behind as the push is completed, knees remaining flexed through the action. The pole is released from the snow, and the arm is swung forward as the pole is regripped.

Double Poling/Kick

Double poling is a variation used as a change of pace from the single poling done with the diagonal stride. It is a powerful action that may be used when the skiing surface is crusty or a bit icy. Both arms are brought forward, the poles are planted opposite the toes, and a vigorous downward and backward

FIGURE 17-11   Double poling. Note compression of the back and extension of the arms upon completion.

push of the arms combined with a bending and compression of the upper body forward at the waist is initiated (Figure 17-11). The arms travel past the hips, and the hands are released from the poles. A kick or stride may be added to this movement by simultaneously sliding the right or left ski forward as the arms swing forward. The opposite leg initiates the kick; near the end of the push the poles are planted and

FIGURE 17-12 The double pole and kick.

arms and upper body execute the double poling technique (Figure 17-12).

▶ **Learning Cues**

1. Weight should be evenly distributed on both skis, knees flexed, weight on balls of the feet.
2. As the arms are brought forward and poles are planted, the arms will be slightly flexed at the elbow.

3. The upper back is compressed forward at the waist as the arms continue to push downward and backward through extension.

Kick Turn

The kick turn is a technique used to change the skier to an opposite direction while standing on the flat or hillside. Although it may appear difficult, it is quite easy for the beginning skier to master.

▶ **Learning Cues**

1. While standing with the skis together, plant poles (used as balance) behind the body.
2. Turn body to the right, pick up the right ski and turn so it faces opposite direction of the left ski.
3. With weight on the right ski, pick up the left ski, swing it around so that it is parallel to the right ski.

▶ **Practice Suggestions:** On the Flat

1. Without poles, begin by walking with the skis, to develop a sense of balance and rhythm. Emphasis should be on sliding the skis forward.
2. Without poles, kick (push off) on one ski and return to starting position, then push off with the opposite ski. Combine a kick (push) followed immediately by the same action of the opposite ski. Add a vigorous pumping action with arms to approximate action used with using single poling.
3. Combine poling with the diagonal stride. Emphasis should be on the forward plant opposite the foot with one pole while the other arm is fully extended behind and then the consequent downward push and extension of arm. The same drill may be used to practice double poling.
4. To practice double poling with a stride, begin by striding with only the left or right leg until you feel comfortable coordinating the kick, pole plant and push; then add alternating strides.
5. Practice kick turn on flat without poles, then try using poles. Next proceed to the hillside and practice there.

Moving Uphill

Obviously not all cross-country skiing is done on a flat surface. The skier must learn to negotiate slopes as well. The easiest method for going uphill is using the diagonal stride described above. Where the slope is fairly steep, the action resembles a running motion with little or no glide during the concluding phases of the stride; thus the kick and stride will be shorter. It is important to remember to keep the weight well forward and knees flexed as you are moving uphill.

Side Stepping. When the beginning skier encounters a slope too steep to execute by means of the diagonal stride, the side stepping skill may be used for moving uphill.

▶ **Learning Cues**

1. Assume a position crosswise to the hill.
2. With the edges pressing into the side of the hill, step off with the downhill ski, step up with the uphill ski.
3. Use the downhill pole to help push off with the downhill ski, keeping weight into the hill.

Traverse. Traversing is another means to travel uphill. Traversing is merely a diagonal stride combined with a slight uphill movement. The skier strides toward a point, then executing either a kick turn or turn using a herringbone side stepping action, changes direction going uphill across the face of the slope. The skier actually will move back and forth across the face of the hill while moving uphill toward the top.

▶ **Learning Cues**

1. Setting the skis crosswise to the hill, move forward using a diagonal stride. The movement is slightly uphill.
2. Weight should be forward, keeping the edges of the skis set into the hill. The steeper the hill, the greater amount of edge setting will be necessary.

The Herringbone.   Although the herringbone is the most tiring way to climb a hill, it must be used when climbing up a steeper slope. The technique can best be described as a series of V's made by an alternating series of steps in which the ski tips are spread apart and the tails are kept fairly close together (Figure 17-13). In a V position, the poles are planted behind the skis; the edge of the skis are set with weight on the inside edge. As the right foot picks up the ski, the right pole is planted and used to maintain balance and push off; the process is then repeated on the other side.

FIGURE 17-13   The herringbone climb, a method of climbing uphill.

▶ **Learning Cues**

1. With weight forward and knees flexed, spread tips of skis apart and keep heels together.
2. Set the weight on the inside edges by shifting weight to inside of each foot.
3. Plant pole behind skis; step up, plant the other pole, and step up.

▶ **Practice Suggestions**

For the beginning skier, these uphill techniques can be practiced first on the flat, then on a gradual incline before attempting a steeper hill.

1. On a moderate incline, practice setting an edge as might be used in side stepping. Emphasis should be on rolling the ankle so weight is on the inside of the downhill ski and on the outside of the uphill ski. Practice climbing 10 to 12 steps.
2. The same exercise may be used for the herringbone as previously described. However, note the weight is set on the inside of each ski as the step is made.

Moving Downhill

Once the skier reaches the top of a hill it is usually necessary to go down. On slight inclines the skier may go straight down, but on steeper hills it becomes necessary to slow down and even to turn in some manner to avoid running into an obstacle. At times the best way to slow down is simply by sitting down. Before you used this method, however, make sure you know how to assume a standing position once again.

In moving downhill, it is important to remember a few key points. First, the weight must be centered or slightly forward over the skis; if not, loss of balance and a fall might result. Secondly, the hands must be held in front of the body so that the weight is placed properly over the skis. If the hands are allowed to fall behind and to the back of the body, they cause the weight to shift backward, thus resulting in a loss of balance and control. Finally, the skier should prevent the poles from dragging behind or becoming snagged in the snow, on a bush, or on any obstacle, because this would also result in a loss of balance and possible fall.

Straight Running.   As the name implies, in straight running the skier goes straight down a hill. For the beginning skier, this technique is used on hills with a gradual incline. Remembering the points previously discussed, the following cues are important.

▶ **Learning Cues**

1. Body weight is over the center of the skis; the skis are shoulder width apart.
2. The knees must be flexed, the upper body is bent at the waist, hands held in front, head up and

FIGURE 17-14   The step turn. Note the head and shoulder drop in the direction of the turn.

looking ahead, poles tucked under the arms, parallel to the skis.

Snow Plow—Snow Plow Turn.   An easy method to learn for slowing down is the snow plow. To slow down, the skis are pushed apart at the tails and weight is transferred to the inside edges; the tips remain 6 to 8 inches apart forming a V. To turn in this position, the weight is merely transferred to the inside of one ski.

▶ **Learning Cues**

1. The knees are flexed more than normal as the body is lowered slightly. By exerting pressure through the inside of the heels, the ski tails are pushed outward, while the ski tips remain close together.
2. Body weight is slightly forward; pressure is placed on the inside edges of the ski by moving knees inward and slightly rolling the ankles.

3. To turn in this position merely transfer more weight to the inside of one ski, and you will turn in the opposite direction. Pressure to the inside of the left ski will result in a right turn, and vice versa.

Step Turn.   A step turn is frequently used to change direction, to go around a corner, or to avoid an object on the ground (Figure 17-14). The turn is executed from a glide, while running straight downhill or while on the flat. The skis should be flat preparatory to initiating the turn. The steps themselves are a series of short steps, tips leading to the side, rather than wide steps. If going downhill, the stepping action is quicker than on a slight incline.

▶ **Learning Cues**

1. Turn the head and drop the shoulder slightly in the direction of the turn.
2. While lifting the tip of the inside ski, shift the weight from the outside ski stepping on to the inside ski in the direction of the turn.
3. For tighter turns, quicken the steps.
4. Keep the hands in front of the body throughout the movement.

▶ **Practice Suggestions:** Downhill Techniques

Begin developing the downhill techniques on a gradual slope before moving on to a steeper slope.

1. On a long gradual hill begin by first straight running. Execute a snow plow with tails apart, then allow skis to return to a straight run position, then repeat snow plow. Practice using this combination several times.
2. For snow plow turns, place stakes on a long gradual hill several feet apart and practice turning around one to one side and then another to

the other side. Practice until you feel comfortable turning in both directions.

3. For the step turn, use stakes to design a course that forces you to step in different directions while moving on the flat and downhill.
4. Practice getting up from a fall while on the flat and while on a hillside. Emphasis should be on assuming a good base of support (crouch position) and use of poles.

WAXING

The art of waxing becomes more important as the skier's approach becomes more serious. Waxing is optional on the waxless ski but it is essential on the waxable ski. For the waxless ski (fishscale pattern or step pattern—see Figure 17-2), you may apply a base wax to the whole surface and a glide wax on the tips and tails of the skis. The base wax is applied with a hot iron and then ironed on evenly onto the surface. Care must be taken to move the iron quickly over the surface so as not to burn the base. The glide wax may be rubbed on by hand then smoothed down with a cork. Most recreational skiers will never need to wax their waxless bottomed skis.

For waxable skis a two-wax system is recommended: one for snow conditions below freezing and the other wax for above freezing temperatures. The wax is applied to the kicker zone of the ski so that the ski will grip when pressure is applied to that area but will release and glide smoothly when the pressure (kick) is completed. Manufacturers have color-coded the waxes to give the best results at varying snow temperatures. Usually the green to blue colored waxes, which are harder waxes, are used for lower temperatures while the red and violet colored waxes, which are softer, are used for higher temperatures.

For the beginning skier using waxable skis, it is recommended that the base wax be applied at the ski shop at the time of purchase. For subsequent care, a ski wax kit can be purchased containing all the equipment needed. Such a kit should contain two to three kicker waxes and two to three glide waxes, a scraper to remove old wax, and a cork to smooth the surface.

MODIFICATIONS FOR SPECIAL POPULATIONS

Orthopedically Impaired

1. Use additional supports (similar to outriggers for downhill skiing) when traversing across the countryside.
2. Ski on level surfaces as much as possible.

Mentally Impaired

Few modifications are needed. Use of peer teachers is advised. Make sure students have developed good cardiovascular fitness prior to cross-country ski units.

Sensory Impaired

1. For blind skiers use tracked snow trails whenever possible (approximately 3 to 4 inches deep tracking).
2. Use peer system, possibly tethering the blind skier to the sighted partner.

SAFETY AND COURTESY

1. Check equipment before you begin to ski, make sure it is in proper working condition.
2. Use good judgement when skiing with people of lesser ability. Make sure all people are familiar with the trail and ski within their physical limits and on terrain appropriate to their level of skill.
3. Get yourself in good physical condition several weeks before engaging in a vigorous touring or racing program.
4. If skiing on a course that has pre-made tracks, let faster skiers have the right of way.
5. Be aware that the wind chill factor can make the air feel much colder then the actual temperature, therefore causing the danger of frostbite. Cover and protect extremities—ears, nose, fingers, and toes are especially vulnerable.
6. Dress appropriately for the prevailing conditions. Remember that as the temperature falls, wet clothes are very uncomfortable. Wear a hat. One third of the body's heat loss is lost through the head.
7. Wear a good pair of sunglasses on bright, sunny days to cut the glare and prevent possible snow blindness.
8. If touring all day long, carry an emergency kit that contains ski wax, extra clothing, a wax candle, matches or lighter to start a fire, high energy food bars, and duct tape for temporary repair or broken ski tips.
9. If skiing alone, let someone know where you are going and the route you'll be skiing on.
10. When skiing in rural areas, request permission of the property owner before crossing someone's land.
11. Ski under control at all times; if you find yourself going too fast, sit down.
12. Ski in areas free of traffic, including automobiles and snowmobiles.
13. When in a crowd, be careful with your ski poles; the pointed tips can cause injury.

TERMINOLOGY

Alpine skiing Downhill and slalom skiing as opposed to cross-country or Nordic skiing.

Bale A metal device that presses the sole of the boot over three pins, thus securing the boot to the ski.

Basket Circular portion, usually made of plastic, near the bottom end of the ski pole that prevents the pole from sinking too deeply into the snow.

Binding Metal or plastic device for fastening the boot to the ski.

Camber The curved portion built into all skis that touches the snow when force is applied and lifts off when weight is lifted. The ski appears bowed as it lies flat on the ground.

Diagonal stride A skier's gliding action that resembles walking as it is executed.

Fishscale A type of surface resembling fishscales found on the bottom of waxless skis.

Gaiter A water repellent covering that fits over the boot, ankle, and lower leg. It is designed to keep snow out of the boot.

Groove Indentation that runs the length of the bottom of the ski allowing the ski to run straight.

Herringbone A technique used to climb uphill that leaves a V pattern on the snow.

Kick The force (push) that is applied during the stride, allowing the skier to glide on the snow.

Kick turn A technique used to change direction 180° while standing still on the flat or hillside.

Klister A type of sticky wax used on the bottom surface of a ski. Klister is the Norwegian name for paste.

Layering Wearing loose layers of clothes over undergarments so that the skier may easily add on for extra warmth or remove excess if too warm.

Nordic skiing Cross-country skiing and ski jumping.

Pin binding A type of toe binding that has three pins that are projected into the sole of the boot, securing the boot to the ski.

Pole plant Action in which the poles are put into the snow at a particular place and during a particular time.

Setting an edge A technique used to prevent a skier from slipping by angling the edge of the ski into the hillside.

Side step A technique used to climb a hill on skis. The skis are parallel to each other as the skier steps up along the length of the ski.

Snow plow A technique used to slow the skier down while going downhill by spreading the tails and keeping the ski tips close together.

Step A type of ski bottom design found on waxless skis resembling a series of steps.

Tail The back or end portion of a ski.

Tip The front end or leading point of a ski.

Track The trail that is left by skis as the skier moves through the snow. These may be machine made.

Traverse Movement back and forth across the face of a hill; the technique may be done uphill or downhill.

Wax A petroleum-based product applied to the bottom of a cross-country ski that enable the ski to grip and also to slide.

SELECTED REFERENCES

Baldwin, N. *Skiing Cross Country.* Toronto: McGraw-Hill Ryerson Limited, 1977.

Brady, M. *Cross-Country Ski Gear.* Seattle: The Mountaineers, 1987.

Caldwell, J. *The New Cross-Country Ski Book.* 8th ed. Lexington, MA: The Stephen Greene Press, 1987.

Endestad, A. and Traford, J. *Skating for Cross-Country Skiing.* Champaign, IL: Leisure Press, 1987.

Foss, M. and Garrick, J.G. *Ski Conditioning.* New York: John Wiley & Sons, 1978.

Gillette, N. and Dustal, J. *Cross-Country Skiing.* 3d ed. Seattle: The Mountaineers, 1987.

Hall, W. *Cross-Country Skiing Right.* San Francisco: Harper and Row, Publishers, 1985.

Heller, M., ed. *The Skier's Encyclopedia.* New York: Paddington Press Ltd., 1979.

Jensen, C.R. *Winter Touring: Cross-Country Skiing and Snow-Shoeing.* Minneapolis, MN: Burgess Publishing Company, 1977.

Lederec, W.J. and Wilson, J.P. *Complete Cross-Country Skiing and Ski Touring.* 2d ed. New York: W.W. Norton and Company, Inc., 1975.

Masia, S. *Cross-Country Ski Maintenance and Repair.* Chicago: Contemporary Books, Inc., 1987.

Sheahan, C. *Cross-Country Skiing.* Chicago: Contemporary Books, Inc., 1978.

Thornton, P. *Contemporary Cross-Country Skiing.* Chicago: Contemporary Books, Inc., 1978.

Audio-Visual Materials

Available from The Travelers Film Library, One Tower Square, Hartford, CT 06115. *I Hope I Get a Purple Ribbon* (1977). Featuring Bill Koch—silver medalists, 1976 Olympic Games. (16 mm sound film. 15 min.)

Available from The Travelers Film Library, One Tower Square, Hartford, CT 06115. *It's as Easy as Walking* (1975). (16 mm sound film. 10 min.)

Available from Modern Talking Picture Services, 5000 Park St., North, St. Petersburg, FL 33709. *Skiing Is Believing.* (16 mm sound film. 24 min.)

Pyramid Films, P.O. Box 1048, Santa Monica, CA 90406. *If You Can Walk.* (16 mm, 3/4 or 1/2 video, 14 minutes). Techniques of natural stride.

PBS Video, 475 L'Enfant Plaza, SW, Washington, D.C., 20024. *Introduction and Diagonal Skiing* (3/4 or 1/2 inch video, 29 minutes). An overview of cross-country skiing and diagonal stride. *Turning and Review* (3/4 or 1/2 inch video, 29 minutes). Three most successful turns and review of other techniques.

RMI Media Productions, 2807 W. 47th St., Shawnee Mission, KS 66205 (1/2 inch VHS or Beta video, 45 mintues). Overview of cross-country skiing including equipment selection and other skills.

18 SOCCER

OBJECTIVES

▶ Identify and put into practice the rules governing the game.
▶ Practice and then execute the basic skills including kicking, passing, trapping, heading, tackling, the throw-in, and goalkeeping.
▶ Discuss and employ basic offensive and defensive strategy and tactics.
▶ Identify and discuss the nature of the game including player responsibilities, field markings, and player positioning.
▶ Identify and use basic terminology associated with the game.

NATURE AND PURPOSE

Soccer is played by eleven players from each team. The game starts at midfield with a free kick called the kick-off as each team is in its own half of the field. The offensive objectives are to maintain possession of the ball, keep the ball wide until near the goal, and then get the ball in front of the opponent's goal where a player can propel it between the uprights, beneath the crossbar and completely across the goal line for a score. The ball may be propelled with any part of the body except the hands and arms; however, the foot, body, and head are the main parts of the body used.

The defense's main objectives are to contain the opponents and the ball, forcing excessive passes, mark (guard) opponents in scoring position, tackle the opponent, taking the ball away whenever possible, funnel the ball to the middle of the field toward their own goal, and concentrate in front of their goal when the ball is in scoring position. The goalkeeper provides great assistance to the defense by being allowed to use the hands to contact the ball; and he also attempts to clear the ball away from the scoring area by throwing, punting, or drop-kicking it.

Systems of play are comprised of attackers (strikers/wings/forwards) midfielders (linkmen/halfbacks) and defenders (stopper/sweeper/fullbacks). The attacker's primary contribution to the system is scoring. The midfielders support the offense and are the first line of defense. The defenders support the midfielders and are the last line of defense. The defender's primary objective is defending against the opponent's attack. Systems are numbered from the defenders forward (example 4-2-4) depending upon the number of players comprising each of the three lines excluding the goalkeeper.

The game is continuous with no timeouts allowed, and time is stopped only for an injury, a temporary suspension of play by the official, the end of a period, or a score.

The players use basic skills of kicking, trapping, dribbling, heading, tackling, and throwing (where allowable) to propel or control the ball. The game is low scoring due to the difficulty of executing the skills, plus the nature of some rules.

The game requires constant adjustments by all the players and calls for short sprinting plus slower jogging. Good physical conditioning is necessary. The constant activity, use of the big muscle groups, large numbers competing, and low equipment expense make the game highly suitable for competitors of all ages and sexes.

FIELD OF PLAY

A regulation field measures 100 to 120 yards in length and 65 to 75 yards in width (Figure 18-1). The dimensions and areas can easily be modified to suit the number, age, and sex of the participants. The field can be made longer or shorter and various grids can be applied (as discussed later on) to provide practice areas for modified games.

In the list below, the numbers correspond to the numbers in the diagram of Figure 18-1.

1. *End Line.* When the ball goes out of play over this line it is put in play with either (a) goal kick (offense last touched the ball) or (b) corner kick (defense last touched the ball).
2. *Goal Area*—the area where the ball is placed for the defending team to take a goal kick. It is placed on the front line of the area in that half field in which the ball went out of play.
3. *Penalty Area.* Restriction area where (a) the goalie is allowed to play the ball with the hands; (b) the offensive team has to stay out of when the

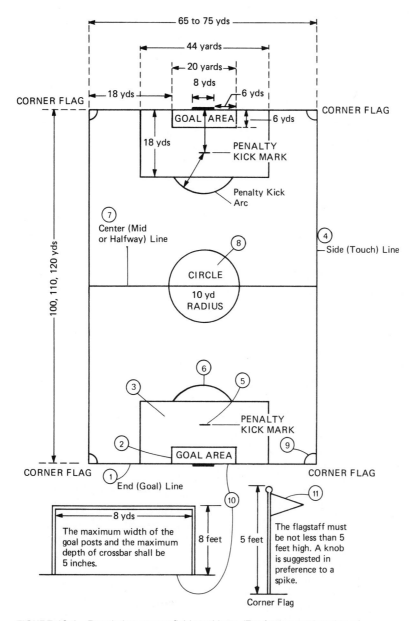

FIGURE 18-1 Regulation soccer field markings. (For further explanation of numbers, see text.)

defending team is taking a goal kick; (c) on the goal kick the ball must be kicked out of this area for the ball to be legally in play; (d) if a foul committed in this area by the defending team results in a *direct free kick*, then a *penalty kick* is awarded to the team fouled; (e) players from both teams must stay outside this area on a penalty kick with the exception of the goalie and the person taking the penalty kick.

4. *Side or Touch Line.* A ball going out of bounds over this line is put in play with a throw-in by the opposite team which last touched the ball.

5. *Penalty Kick Mark*—the spot where the ball is placed when a penalty kick results.

6. *Penalty Kick Arc.* This arc is a ten-yard radius from the ball, and players from both teams must stay behind it. On a penalty kick both teams (except one offensive player and the goalie) must be out of the penalty area and at least ten yards from the ball.

7. *Center, Mid, or Halfway Line.* This line (a) insures that both teams are in their own half of the field on the kickoff, and (b) is used to help regulate the offside rule.

8. *Center Circle*—a ten-yard radius circle to restrict players of the defending team on the kickoff. They must stay out of the circle until the ball is contacted.

9. *Corner Arc.* One yard from each corner there is a corner arc. The ball is placed on this arc when the offensive team is taking a corner kick.
10. *Goal Line*—the line between the uprights of the goal. When the whole ball crosses it below the crossbar, either on the ground or in the air, a goal results.
11. *Corner Flag.* The flag is at least five feet high and located in each of the four corners to assist in locating the boundary lines.

EQUIPMENT

The only equipment absolutely necessary for playing soccer are a ball and two goals. There are many makes and price ranges of soccer balls manufactured today. The molded ball with a rubber bladder, nylon wound carcass, and compressed weatherproof leather or synthetic panels is recommended. Goals can be purchased or may be constructed of 2 × 4s or pipe. Soccer shoes, shin guards and nets for the goals may be added when progressing from physical education class to intramural to inter-scholastic competition levels. Gym shoes may be substituted for soccer shoes, thick magazines for shin guards, and chain link fencing for nets. The fact that the game can be played by a large number of players at very little expense makes it particularly appealing. Competition apparel is not a major factor. Colored jersey vests and game jerseys are inexpensive. For pants, gym shorts, sweatsuits, or game trunks may be worn.

BASIC RULES

Kickoff.   At the beginning of the game, choice of ends and the kickoff are decided by the toss of a coin. The ball is placed in the center of the field on the half-way line, and the team kicking off plays the ball forward from the line. The player usually kicks the stationary ball legally (one circumference of the ball) forward to his teammate, attempting to maintain control of the ball. All players from both teams are in their own half of the field with the defending team at least ten yards from the ball. A goal cannot be scored from the kickoff.

Fouls.   Fouls and misconduct committed during the course of play result in a free kick to the offended team. The severe infractions, which are most often injurious, result in a direct free kick, meaning a goal can be scored directly from that kick. A direct free kick foul occurring in the penalty area and against the defending team results in a penalty kick, the most severe infraction. Less severe infractions result in an indirect free kick, meaning someone else must contact the ball following the kick before a goal can be scored. When making a free kick, the opponents must be ten yards from the ball, unless standing on their own goal line between the uprights, until the ball is kicked. The ball must be stationary on the free kick, must travel the circumference of the ball to be in play, and may not be re-contacted by the kicker until someone else touches it.

Direct Free Kick Offenses

Offenses for which a direct free kick is awarded are:

1. Handling the ball; intentionally contact the ball with the hands or arms. This includes the goalies when outside the penalty area.
2. Holding an opponent with the hands or arms.
3. Pushing an opponent; includes the hands or arms.
4. Striking or attempting to strike an opponent; the goalie is also not allowed to use the ball to strike a player.
5. Jumping at an opponent.
6. Kicking or attempting to kick an opponent.
7. Tripping or attempting to trip an opponent.
8. Using the knee on an opponent.
9. Charging an opponent violently or dangerously; includes the goalie in the penalty area or from the rear unless being obstructed.

All direct kicks awarded to the attacking team in the penalty area are penalty kicks.

Indirect Free Kick Offenses

Offenses for which an indirect free kick is awarded are:

1. A player playing the ball a second time before it is played by another player at the kickoff, on a throw-in, on a free kick, on a corner kick, or on a goal kick (if the ball has passed outside the penalty area).
2. A goalkeeper carrying the ball more than four steps or the goalie delays getting rid of the ball.
3. A substitution or re-substitution being made without reporting to the referee, or a substitute replacing the goalie not informing the referee and then handling the ball in the penalty area.
4. Persons other than the players entering the field of play without the referee's permission.
5. Dissenting by word or action with a referee's decision.
6. Ungentlemanly behavior. For persistent infringement of the rules, a warning, or expulsion may follow.
7. Dangerous play by raising the foot too high or head too low while attempting to play the ball, thus endangering a player.
8. Resuming play after a player has been ordered off the field.
9. Offside.

10. Charging illegally (not violent or dangerous).
11. Interfering with the goalkeeper or impeding him in any manner until he releases the ball, or kicking or attempting to kick the ball when it is in his possession.
12. Obstruction other than holding.
13. Player leaving the field of play during the progress of the game without the consent of the referee.

Physical Contact. Body contact is allowed provided it is legal. A legal charge consists of a gentle nudge (not violent or dangerous), shoulder to shoulder, in an upright position, at least one foot contacting the ground, the arms close to the sides of

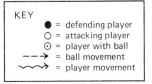

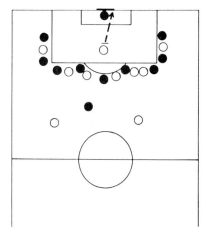

FIGURE 18-4 Penalty kick.

the body, and playing the ball at the exact moment (Figure 18-2). The body may not be used as an obstacle to shield an opponent from getting to the ball unless actually playing the ball at that moment. This is obstruction (Figure 18-3), and allows for an opponent legally to charge the person obstructing, provided the contact is not violent or dangerous.

Penalty Kick. The penalty kick (Figure 18-4) is taken from any spot on the penalty mark, and all players except the kicker and the goalkeeper must be outside the penalty area. The goalkeeper must stand, without moving the feet, on the goal line between the goal posts until the ball is kicked. For any infringement by the defending team the kick is retaken, if a goal does not result. On an infringement by the attacking team, other than the player making the kick, the kick shall be retaken if a goal results. An infringement by the player making the kick results in an indirect free kick by the opposing team at the spot where the violation occurred.

Goal Kick. The ball is in play as long as it is not totally across the boundary lines (goal line or side line), either on the ground or in the air. When it goes out of bounds over the goal line, the ball is put in play either with a goal kick (last touched by the attacking team) or a corner kick (last touched by the defending team). A ball put out of bounds over the side line by a player is put in play with a throw-in by the opponents.

On the goal kick, the ball is placed on the front line of the goal area in that half of the field nearest to where it crossed the goal line (Figure 18-5). Any player on the team may take the kick. It is kicked from the ground. The opposing players remain out-

FIGURE 18-2 Legal charge.

FIGURE 18-3 Legal obstruction. Note use of body to protect the ball while playing it.

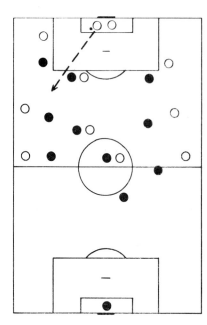

FIGURE 18-5   Goal kick.

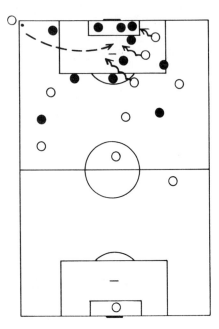

FIGURE 18-6   Corner kick.

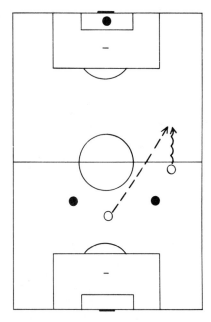

FIGURE 18-7   Player is in own half of field—*not offside.*

side the penalty area until the ball is kicked, and the ball must travel beyond the penalty area for it to be in play. The kick is retaken for any infringement.

Corner Kick.   The corner kick is taken by the offense from the arc in that half of the field nearest to where the ball crossed the goal line. A goal may be scored directly from the corner kick (Figure 18-6).

Throw-in.   The throw-in is taken from where it went out of play. It is thrown equally with both hands on the side of the ball from a point behind the head and delivered directly over the head. Both feet must remain on the ground during the throw and be either in contact with the side line or outside the field of play.

Offside.   The players must be concerned with their position in reference to the ball as play progresses. An offside infraction is called if a player is nearer the opponent's goal line than the ball at the moment the ball is played, with limited exceptions. The offside rule is for assisting the defending team so that the offense will not be able to have players continually lurking in front of the goal. This would lead to an unskilled game with team strategy consisting of no more than long, uncontrolled kicks from one end of the field to the other, and back again.

A player nearer the opponent's goal line than the ball at the moment the ball is played is considered *offside* (Figure 18-8B) unless: (1) he is in his own half of the field of play (Figure 18-7); or (2) there are two opponents nearer their own goal line than he (Figure 18-8A); or (3) the ball last touched an opponent; or (4) he received the ball directly from a dropped ball by the referee, a goal kick, a corner kick, or a throw-in. A player in an offside position does not have to be penalized except if he is gaining an advantage by his

position, seeking to gain an advantage, or interfering with an opponent. Once offside, the only way for a player to put himself onside again is if: (1) an opponent next contacts the ball; or (2) he is behind the ball when it is next contacted by his teammates; or (3) there are two opponents near their goal when he is in an advanced position of the ball, and the ball is played to him by his teammates. The key factor for offside is always the position of the player in relation to the ball at the moment the ball is contacted.

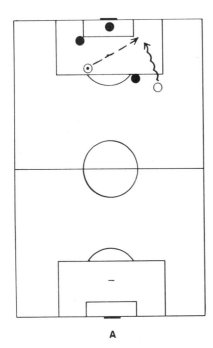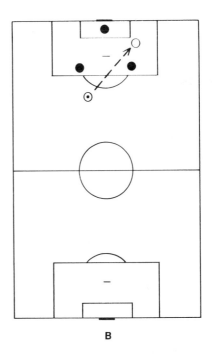

A   **B**

FIGURE 18-8 (A) Two opponents are nearer their own goal line at the moment the ball is played, *plus* the receiver is behind the ball at that moment—*not offside.* (B) Two opponents are *not* nearer their goal line—*offside.*

Dropped Ball. Temporary stopping of play while the ball is still playable results in the game restarting with a dropped ball. Two opponents face each other and the referee standing between them drops the ball to the ground for either to contact. It is dropped where the ball was when play stopped unless in the penalty area. Then it is brought to the nearest point outside the penalty area and dropped. Common reasons for a dropped ball occurring are: (1) simultaneous contact by opponents causing the ball to go out of bounds, (2) temporary stopping for injury, (3) the ball becoming deflated, or (4) simultaneous fouls by both teams.

Goalkeeper. When the ball nears the scoring area, the goalkeeper enjoys certain privileges not granted to other players while in the penalty area. He may: use his hand and arms to stop a ball from scoring; take four steps with the ball in his possession; punt, throw, or drop-kick the ball; and he is free from interference by opponents while in possession of the ball. He loses these privileges when outside the penalty area.

Scoring. A goal is scored when the whole of the ball passes over the goal line, between the goalposts, and under the crossbar, provided it has not been thrown, propelled by hand or arm, or carried by a player of the attacking side (Figure 18-9). If a member of the defending team, other than the goalie, deliberately deflects the ball with his hand or arm attempting to stop a goal, it should be scored a goal if it crosses the goal line between the uprights.

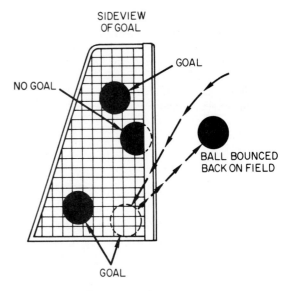

FIGURE 18-9 Scoring a goal.

Goals may also be scored on "direct free kicks," penalty kicks, and corner kicks. A goal counts one point for the team scoring the goal. After a goal is scored, a kickoff is made at the center of the field by the team scored against. Teams change ends after each regular and extra period.

Time and Players. The length of the game, number of substitutes, and when substitutes are allowed to enter the game are rules that vary depending upon the age and ability levels of the players. The organizations governing competition provide rule guides; however, there are only minor differences in them. Men and women are playing by basically the same rules regardless of the organization, and quite often at an early age (6 to 11), the game is played co-ed.

SUGGESTIONS FOR MODIFIED PRACTICE GAMES AND AREAS

Figure 18-10 is a grid model showing various ways of modifying a regulation field to provide areas of different sizes. The larger the area the more competitors possible. Examples are 2 on 1, 3 on 1, 2 on 2, 3 on 2, 3 on 3, 4 on 2, 4 on 3, 4 on 4, 5 on 3, 5 on 4, 5 on 5, etc. A modified goal, objective, or soccer strategy and tactic are used in the games. Cones, flags, or other players are used as two-sided goals. These may be placed opposite each other on the end line of the area, slightly on the field with space behind them or in the middle of the area. One, two, or more goals may be used.

Combining grids allows for actual games with modified field sizes. An example is using grid D, E, and F together, placing a goal on the side line of the field and centered in the middle of the area. The size of the field is now 96 feet by 225 feet, where an actual game might consist of 6 on 6, 7 on 7, or 8 or 8. Two games may be played at once if grids G, H, and I are used similarly.

Combining areas A through F provides an even wider field, whereby more players can compete in an across field game, as in the foregoing example. The same area (A through F) is used to practice offense (attackers and midfielders) versus defense (goalie, defenders, and midfielders) playing half field as on the regulation field. Scoring objectives are: the offense gets one point for scoring a goal, hitting the goal posts, or causing the goalkeeper to field the ball. Defense scores one point if they get the ball past the halfway line under their control.

Here are some other suggestions for playing games within a restricted area: a given number of consecutive passes without losing the ball receives a point; allow only one contact per player; allow no more than two contacts per player; after receiving the ball the player must out-dribble an opponent; the receiver of a pass must take the ball (pass or dribble away from) his own goal before it next goes forward; every other pass must be in the air; no pass above knee height. The possible modifications are endless and dependent upon what skill or strategy one wants to stress.

SUGGESTED LEARNING SEQUENCE

Beginning Level

A. Stretching and running
B. Basic rules
C. Fundamental skills
    1. Kicking
        a. Inside of foot push pass
        b. Instep
    2. Trapping (Receiving)
        a. Sole of the foot
        b. Inside of the foot
        c. Chest
    3. Dribbling
        a. Inside of the foot
        b. Outside of the foot
    4. Heading; Power standing
    5. Tackling: Front
    6. Throw-in: Standing
    7. Goalkeeping
        a. Catch—roll or bounce
        b. Catch—waist or chest
        c. Catch—head or above
        d. Punt
D. Strategies
    1. Tactics
        a. Possession
        b. Space—receiving ball
    2. Group
        a. Superiority around ball
    3. Team
        a. Communication
        b. Functional training combining two or more positional lines

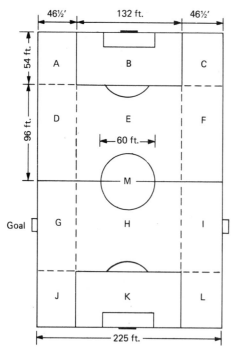

FIGURE 18-10 Grid for setting up practice areas.

E. Principles
  1. Attacking
    a. Depth/Support
    b. Width
    c. Penetration
  2. Defending
    a. Delay
    b. Depth/Support
    c. Width
    d. Balance
F. Systems
  1. W formation
  2. M-W formation
  3. Defensive style—zone
  4. Offensive style—static positioning, long pass and short pass
G. Restarts
  1. Corner kick
  2. Goal kick
  3. Throw-in
  4. Kickoff

Intermediate Level

A. Partner stretching and interval training
B. Review beginning unit
C. Fundamental skills
  1. Kicking
    a. Outside of foot
    b. Lofting the ball
  2. Trapping (Receiving)
    a. Outside of foot
  3. Dribbling
    a. Screening
    b. Sole of the foot
  4. Heading: Power jumping
  5. Tackling: Side
  6. Throw-In: Running
  7. Goalkeeping
    a. Catch—fall to side
    b. Tip
    c. Throw—overhand
D. Strategies
  1. Review beginning unit
  2. Tactics
    a. Space-creating
  3. Group
    a. Space-restricting
    b. Tempo
  4. Team
    a. Rhythm
    b. Functional training involving tactical passing restrictions
E. Principles
  1. Attacking
    a. Mobility
    b. Improvisation
  2. Defending
    a. Concentration
    b. Control

F. Systems
  1. 4-2-4
  2. 3-3-4
  3. Defensive style—diagonal and man to man
  4. Offensive style—dribbling and fast/slow
G. Restarts
  1. Indirect free kicks
  2. Direct free kicks
  3. Defensive wall

SKILLS AND TECHNIQUES

The fundamentals of soccer are dribbling, heading, trapping, kicking (shoot or pass), tackling, throwing, and goalkeeping. Because the game of soccer is primarily a kicking and trapping game, it is essential that players master the technique of controlling the ball without use of the hands or arms. In observing good soccer players, one sees that they control the ball and keep it reasonably close to their bodies when passing or advancing it down the field. The ball is kept close to the ground and not kicked into the air where it is difficult for the player to keep possession and control.

When learning or teaching each of the skills, the following factors are important for understanding problems—their causes and corrections:

  1. Alignment to Ball
    a. Position the body early in preparation to contact the ball.
    b. Position at the best spot in the line of flight for making initial contact.
    c. Prepare the contact surface at the proper angle required for optimum execution.
    d. Be as stable as possible.
  2. Base
    a. Position the foot/feet for optimum stability.
    b. Position the foot/feet so that the contact surface can be at the proper angle for execution.
    c. Position the grounded foot/feet in the direction the ball is to be propelled or received.
  3. Whole Body Position
    a. Position of specifically the feet, knees, hips, shoulders, arms, and head before, during, and after ball contact.
  4. Power/Absorption

  Power
    a. Ball contact surface—speed of ball.
    b. Joints providing force—range of motion and speed of motion.
    c. Proper line of force (see #5).
    d. Total body parts alignment as they relate to the desired trajectory.
    e. Follow-through (see #7).

  Absorption
    a. Ball contact surface—speed of ball.
    b. Joints involved in receiving force.

c. Proper line of receiving force (see #5).

d. Total body parts alignment as they relate to receiving the trajectory and force of the ball.

e. Direction (away from ball) of body parts used for absorbing the ball.

5. Line of Giving/Receiving Force

a. Correct direction of all body parts related to the desired trajectory, rotation (spin), and final destination of the ball.

6. Ball Contact

a. Surface and angle of body part used to make contact.

b. Exact spot on the ball to contact for accomplishing the desired end result.

c. Alignment to ball (see #1).

d. Base (see #2).

e. Whole body (see #3).

f. Power/absorption (see #4).

g. Line of giving/receiving force (see #5).

7. Follow-through

a. The full range of motion (arc) of the primary power joints used and the exact point at which to stop in order to provide the desired power plus trajectory to the ball.

b. When receiving the impetus (trapping) of the ball, the primary joints used in recoiling, giving, or absorbing which lead to cushioning the impact—follow-through away from the line of flight of the ball.

Each of these factors will be considered as we discuss the learning cues for performing each specific skill or technique. Either a *B* (Beginning) or *I* (Intermediate) is indicated with each skill or technique to designate the appropriate ability level for presenting that skill. Where suitable, verbal learning cues are given in capital letters.

Kicking (Pass or Shot)

Kicking is primarily used for passing, shooting, and clearing. The rotation (spin) on the ball denotes proper or improper contact. Different parts of the foot can be used to contact the ball.

▶ **Learning Cues:** Inside of Foot Push Pass (B)

1. *Alignment to Ball.* Quickly position as near the direct flight (180°) of the ball as possible—ALIGNMENT.

2. *Base.* Place grounded foot toward target, position it to the side of the ball approximately 6 to 12 inches and either even with or slightly behind the ball (Figure 18-11A), depending upon desired flight (on the ground or in the air)—GROUNDED FOOT. Knee slightly flexed.

3. *Whole Body Position.* Contact foot raised with toe pointed out—TOE OUT, knee pointed out—KNEE OUT, and ankle joint locked at 90-degree angle—ANKLE LOCKED. Draw leg backward from the hip

FIGURE 18-11   Inside of foot push pass.

in a straight line. Raise the contact leg to the rear bending the knee until the lower leg is close to parallel with the ground with the inside of the foot facing the ground—COCKED POSITION. Position head directly above ball (to keep ball on ground) or slightly behind the ball (to loft off ground)—HEAD. Hips and shoulders near 90° to approaching ball with slight pivot out as contact leg is drawn back. Arms comfortable, away from body for balance (Figure 18-11).

4. *Power.* Power results from the height that the contact foot is raised off the ground (Figure18-12B), speed that the contact leg is snapped forward to meet the ball, speed of the approaching ball, correct ball/foot contact (hard surface), and the amount of follow-through.

5. *Line of Giving Force.* The foregoing power items applied in the correct line depend upon the approaching flight of the ball and the desired final destination. The correct line involves the body alignment to the ball (as near 180° as possible), direction the grounded foot is pointed (Figure 18-12A), straight linear (180°) cocking of contact leg, and straight linear snap down plus follow-through of that leg—LINE OF FORCE.

6. *Ball Contact.* The correct contact surface is the hard area near the heel of the foot and ankle area (Figure 18-12B) with the inside of the foot facing the approaching ball. The ball is contacted near its midline and either high, middle, or low depending upon the desired speed and trajectory.

7. *Follow-Through.* The height the contact foot and

FIGURE 18-12   Inside of foot push pass. Note leg, ankle, and knee of contact foot.

FIGURE 18-13   Instep kick. Note toe, ankle, and knee of contact foot.

leg are allowed to lift after contact depends upon the desired trajectory and/or force.

▶ **Learning Cues:** Instep Kick (B)

1. *Alignment to Ball.* Approach the path of the ball from a 45° angle.—ALIGNMENT.
2. *Base.* Same as Inside of Foot Push Pass except the grounded foot is approximately 10 to 18 inches to the side of the ball—GROUNDED FOOT. Knee flexed.
3. *Whole Body Position.* Contact foot lifted with toe pointed down—TOE DOWN, knee rotated in—KNEE IN, and ankle joint locked as near 180° with the lower leg as possible—ANKLE LOCKED (Figure 18-13). Lift heel upward toward the buttocks—COCKED POSITION. Hip extends and rotates slightly. Position head directly above ball (to keep ball on ground) or slightly behind ball (to loft off ground)—HEAD. Hips and shoulders near 90° to approaching ball with slight pivot out as contact leg is drawn back. Arms comfortably away from body for balance.
4. *Power.* Power results from the height that the contact foot is raised—HEEL RAISED, speed that the contact leg is snapped forward to meet the ball—SPEED, speed of the approaching ball, correct ball/foot contact, and the amount of follow-through.
5. *Line of Giving Force.* The foregoing power items applied in the correct line depend upon the approaching flight of the ball and the desired final destination. The approach angle of the body to the flight of the ball approximates 45°. The grounded foot is pointed toward the intended destination (Figure 18-13A) as the remainder of the power joints naturally correct to a direct alignment with the desired line of flight.
6. *Ball Contact.* The correct contact surface is the

hard area on the top of the arch (Figure 18-13B). The ball is contacted near the midline and either high, middle, or low depending on the desired speed and trajectory.

7. *Follow-Through.* The height the foot and leg are allowed to lift is dependent upon desired trajectory and/or force.

▶ **Learning Cues:** Lofting the Ball (I)

1. *Alignment to Ball.* Same as Instep Kick.
2. *Base.* The grounded foot is approximately 10 to 18 inches to the side of the ball and slightly behind it. Knee flexed.
3. *Whole Body Position.* Same as Instep Kick, except that the head is positioned slightly behind the vertical plane of the ball—HEAD BACK (Figure 18-14).

FIGURE 18-14   Lofting the ball with an instep kick. Note body angle, low contact with ball, and head behind ball.

4–7. Power, Line of Giving Force, Ball Contact, Follow-Through: all same as Instep Kick.

▶ **Learning Cues:** Outside of Foot Kick (I)

1. *Alignment to Ball.* Same as Inside of Foot Push Pass.
2. *Base.* Same as Inside of Foot Push Pass.
3. *Whole Body Position.* Contact foot lifted with the toe extended down and rotated inward—TOE DOWN AND IN, knee rotated in—KNEE IN, and ankle joint locked—LOCKED ANKLE. Lift heel backward and upward toward the buttocks—COCKED POSITION (Figure 18-15).

FIGURE 18-15   Outside of the foot kick. Note toe, ankle, and knee of contact foot.

FIGURE 18-16   Outside of the foot kick and dribble. Note toe, knee of contact leg, and contact surface.

4–5. Power and *Line of Giving Force*: Same as Inside of Foot Push Pass.
6. *Ball Contact.* The correct contact area is the hard area on the top outside surface of the foot (Figure 18-16). The ball is contacted near the midline and either high, middle, or low depending upon the desired trajectory and speed.
7. *Follow-Through.* Same as Instep Kick.

Trapping

Many surfaces of the body can be used to trap (catch) the ball. Trapping means controlling a ball that is received by a player. There is "immediate" or "deflect" trapping. The first denotes control of the ball right where the player receives it, while the second means redirecting the ball close to the receiver (3 to 4 feet) to avoid an on-rushing opponent. When a body trap is used, a foot trap usually follows in order to "settle" the ball to the ground.

▶ **Learning Cues:** Sole of Foot Trap (B)

1. *Alignment to Ball.* Quickly position as near to a direct line (180°) with the path of the ball as possible—ALIGNMENT.
2. *Base.* Body weight is totally supported by the grounded foot as the contact leg is raised with the sole facing the approaching ball.
3. *Whole Body Position.* Ankle of contact foot flexed (90°) with toe higher than heel, toe up, providing a wedge-like surface for ball contact. The contact leg and foot are extended in front of the body, reach out, as the grounded leg provides support with a slight flexion of the knee. Hips and shoulders near 90° to approaching ball. Arms slightly away from body to provide balance and stability.
4. *Absorption.* The ball at contact is cushioned by slightly flexing the knee of the contact leg, slightly flexing the knee of the support leg with a slight pike at the waist which moves the head forward toward the ball—GIVE.
5. *Line of Receiving Force.* The foregoing absorption factors are applied as near a direct line with the path of the ball as possible.
6. *Ball Contact.* The ball is contacted on the top and slightly to the rear by the sole of the foot. The contact foot approximates a 45° angle with the ground providing a wedge between the sole of the foot and the ground (Figure 18-17).
7. *Follow-Through.* There is negative follow-through as the contact leg and foot at impact give in the same direction that the ball is traveling in order to stop the ball.

▶ **Learning Cues:** Inside of Foot Trap (B)

1–3. Alignment to Ball, Base, and *Whole Body Position*: same as Inside of Foot Push Pass (Figure 18-18).

FIGURE 18-17 Sole of the foot trap.

FIGURE 18-19 Inside of the foot trap. Note grounded foot, position of ball, ball/foot contact, and toe and knee position of contact leg.

FIGURE 18-18 Inside of the foot trap. Note alignment to ball, base, whole body position.

4. *Absorption.* The force of the ball is cushioned by the soft relaxed contact surface, the wedging of the ball against the ground by the contact foot—WEDGE, and the movement of the contact leg away from the path of ball at about the same speed of the approaching ball—GIVE.

5. *Line of Receiving Force.* The foregoing absorption factors applied in the correct line depend upon the path of the ball and the desired final destination for the ball. The correct line involves the body alignment to the ball (as near 180° as possible), direction the grounded foot is pointed, angle of the contact foot, and direction the contact leg is moved upon impact.

6. *Ball Contact.* The correct contact surface is the soft area on the inside of the foot near the arch. The ball is contacted on the top and back wedging it to the ground to the rear of the grounded foot for "immediate" control (Figure 18-19). It is contacted nearer the bottom and back (imparting back spin) in advance of the grounded foot for "deflecting" the ball away from but close to the body.

7. *Follow-Through.* The contact leg lowers the foot on the ball wedging it (immediate control) or the leg and foot made a relaxed, sweeping action "deflecting" the ball away from but close to the body.

▶ **Learning Cues:** Chest Trap (B)

1. *Alignment to Ball.* Quickly position as near to a direct line (180°) with the path of the ball as possible.

2. *Base.* The feet are in a staggered stance with the body weight evenly distributed—STANCE.

3. *Whole Body Position.* The knees are flexed, hips thrust forward bending backwards, shoulders back further than the hips, placing the upper chest near parallel with the ground, the head away from the body for balance—BACKBEND (Figure 18-20).

4. *Absorption.* Upon ball contact, the knees flex deeper allowing the chest to "give" quickly, absorbing the impact.

5. *Line of Receiving Force.* Same as #4 above. The ball rebounds off the chest in a low upward trajectory, falling to the ground near the feet. Turning the shoulders at impact causes the ball to rebound to the side of the body if desired.

FIGURE 18-20   Chest trap.

FIGURE 18-21   Outside of the foot trap.

6. *Ball Contact.* The contact surface is the high flat part of the chest just below the throat.
7. *Follow-Through.* Following contact and rebound, quickly stand straight and prepare to "settle" the ball to the ground by using one of the foot traps—SETTLE.

▶ **Learning Cues:** Outside of Foot Trap (I)

1. *Alignment to Ball.* Same as Sole of the Foot Trap. The path of the ball is to the outside of the grounded foot—approximately 6 to 12 inches.
2. *Base.* Body weight is totally supported by the grounded leg while the contact leg is off the ground.
3. *Whole Body Position.* The contact leg reaches across and in front of the grounded leg—REACH ACROSS, with the ankle rotated inward and down preparing the outside of the foot for contact. The upper body leans—LEAN, at an angle in the direction the ball is to be deflected. The arms are away from the body for balance.
4–5. *Absorption* and Line *of Receiving Force.* The sweeping action of the contact leg from one side of the body to the other—SWEEP, absorbs force and controllably deflects the ball in the desired direction (approximately 90°) away from the approaching flight of the ball. The ankle rotates out with a flicking action—ANKLE FLICK.
6. *Ball Contact.* The contact surface is the outside of the foot and the contact is high on the ball. The ankle which is rotated inward and downward before contact makes a forceful outward rotation at impact—ANKLE FLICK, flicking the

ball to the side of the body as the whole contact leg sweeps across the body (Figure 18-21).
7. *Follow-Through.* The contact leg sweeps across and in front of the body in the direction that the body is leaning providing controlled re-direction to the ball.

DRIBBLING

The skill of dribbling involves very controllably propelling the ball with the feet in an effort to move the ball to another area without relinquishing possession to another player. Different surfaces of the foot can be used to dribble.

▶ **Learning Cues:** Inside of Foot Dribble (B)

1. *Alignment to Ball.* The body is directly behind the ball prior to contact.
2. *Base.* The grounded foot is behind and to the inside of the ball while the other foot is slightly off the ground for contact.
3. *Whole Body Position.* The body is in a continuous running action making repetitive contacts with either foot (Figure 18-22).
4. *Power/Absorption.* The contact surface (inside of the foot) can provide either force or absorption depending upon how close to the body one wants to keep the ball.
5. *Line of Giving/Receiving Force.* The speed of the running action provides force at contact. Contacting high on the ball takes away force and keeps the ball close, contacting near the middle applies, and contacting low on the ball lifts the ball which is *not* desired.
6. *Ball Contact.* The toe of the contact foot is pointed out; knee out, foot slightly off the ground, and sole parallel to ground. The angle of the contact surface depends upon the path desired for the ball after impact.

FIGURE 18-22   Inside of the foot dribble.

7. *Follow-Through.* There is a continuous running action with repetitive contacts by either foot, TAP-TAP, propelling the ball along the ground in a controlled action.

▶ **Learning Cues:** Outside of Foot Dribble (B)

1–3. *Alignment to Ball, Base,* and *Whole Body Position.* All same as Inside of the Foot Dribble.
4. *Power/Absorption.* The contact surface (outside of the foot) can provide either force or absorption depending upon how close to the body one wants to keep the ball.
5. *Line of Giving/Receiving Force.* Same as Inside of the Foot Dribble.
6. *Ball Contact.* The toe of the contact foot is pointed in and extended down with the knee inwardly turned. The contact surface is high on the outside of the foot near the ankle joint. The angle of the contact surface depends upon the path desired for the ball after contact (Figure 18-23).
7. *Follow-Through.* Same as Inside of the Foot Dribble.

▶ **Learning Cues:** Screening (I)

1–2. *Alignment to Ball* and *Base.* Same as Inside of the Foot Dribble.
3. *Whole Body Position.* The body and ball are under definite control as the body is used to screen the opponent from the ball. Slight leaning contact against the opponent aids in protecting the ball plus determining the path the opponent desires to take to reach ball (Figure 18-24).
4. *Power/Absorption.* None.
5. *Line of Giving/Receiving Force.* Light leaning force against the opponent.
6–7. *Ball Contact* and *Follow-Through*—depends upon which dribbling technique (inside, outside,

FIGURE 18-23   Outside of the foot dribble.

or sole of the foot) the player decides to use to keep away from the opponent. These techniques are often used in combination to feint the opponent prior to breaking away.

Heading

The head is used to play the ball when shooting, passing or clearing the ball. Beginners use the *standing* approach; intermediates use the *jumping* play.

FIGURE 18-24   Screening. Note leaning body contact.

FIGURE 18-25   Power heading—standing position.

▶ **Learning Cues:** Power Heading, Standing (B)

1. *Alignment to Ball.* Quickly position as near as possible to a direct line (180°) with the path of the ball.
2–3. *Base* and *Whole Body Position.* Same as Chest Trap (see Figure 18-20).
4–5. *Power and Line of Force.* From the foregoing position the whole body snaps forward—SNAP (Figure 18-25). The upper body starts forward as the arms are vigorously thrust backward—ARMS, the weight transfers more to the front foot and the neck snaps—NECK SNAP, thrusting the head toward the ball. All are directed in a straight line toward the approaching ball.
6. *Ball Contact.* The contact surface is near the hair line on the forehead. The contact on the ball is dependent upon the desired trajectory and target. Low ball contact propels the ball upward, middle contact propels the ball straight forward parallel with the ground, while high ball contact propels the ball downward to the ground.
7. *Follow-Through.* All power components continue forward following contact providing continued force and direction.

▶ **Learning Cues:** Power Heading, Jumping (I)

1. *Alignment to Ball.* Same as Power Heading, Standing. Position in the arc of the trajectory where the ball can be contacted with a maximum height jump (Figure 18-26).
2. *Base.* A two-foot takeoff provides stability while suspended in air. A running one-foot takeoff

FIGURE 18-26   Power heading—jumping.

provides height in jumping. Use both where desirable.
3. *Whole Body Position.* The arms are close to the side, the back arches, and the neck cocks in preparation for contact.
4. *Power.* The proper contact surface, back, neck, and proper jump timing assist with power as the upper body snaps forward to meet the ball while suspended in mid-air.
5–6. *Line of Giving Force* and *Ball Contact.* Same as Power Heading, Standing.

7. *Follow-Through.* Same as Power Heading, Standing. A two-foot landing after execution of the skill is necessary for stability.

Tackling

The tackle is a skill used for taking the ball away from an opponent and maintaining control of the ball following that confrontation. Beginners use the frontal approach; for intermediates tackling may be from the side.

▶ **Learning Cues:** Front Tackle (B)

1. *Alignment of Ball.* Quickly position as near as possible to a direct line (180°) with the path of the approaching player and ball (Figure 18-27).
2. *Base.* From a running approach the grounded foot is positioned near and to the side of the ball as the full body weight is supported by that foot.
3. *Whole Body Position.* The head is above or slightly in front of the ball, grounded foot and flexed knee. The arms are down and close to the body, and the hips are behind the ball. All are in a forward learning position. The contact foot is slightly raised backward with the toe and knee out.
4. *Power.* The knee of the contact leg snaps forward as the contact foot blocks the ball—BLOCK, at the exact same instant that the opponent makes contact. Do not kick ball but block it attempting to both simultaneously tie-up the ball.
5. *Line of Giving Force.* At that instant of contact the near shoulder contacts the opponent with a gentle nudge. The straight contact leg is pushed/pulled forward from the groin—DRAG, as the whole body leans into the opponent attempting to knock him off balance.
6. *Ball Contact.* The ball is contacted exactly in the middle with the inside of the foot (see Figure 18-12) at the exact time the opponent makes contact, blocking the ball.
7. *Follow-Through.* The whole body leans into the opponent as the contact foot lightly rolls over the top of the ball causing it to roll over the opponent's foot and propelling it behind the opponent.

▶ **Learning Cues:** Side Tackle (I)

1. *Alignment to Ball.* The approach angle is from the side at approximately 90° with the path of the player (Figure 18-28).
2. *Base.* Same as Front Tackle. The grounded foot is firmly planted in a direct line (180°) with the path of the player and ball.
3. *Whole Body Position.* The firm plant of the grounded foot and transfer of total body weight to that foot allows the body to correct itself, facing the oncoming player as in the front tackle. (Refer to Front Tackle.)

FIGURE 18-27   Front tackling.

FIGURE 18-28   Side tackling. Note 90-degree approach angle prior to pivot and contact.

4–7. *Power, Line of Giving Force, Ball Contact, Follow-Through.* Same as Front Tackle.

Throw-In

The throw-in is the only time that players, other than the goalkeeper, can use their hands to propel the ball. This is allowable only when the ball goes out of bounds over the touch line.

▶ **Learning Cues:** Standing Throw-in (B)

1. *Alignment to Field.* Face in the direction that you intend to deliver the ball.

FIGURE 18-29   Throw-in—standing or running.

FIGURE 18-30   Kneeling catch—roll or bounce ball.

2. *Base.* Either a parallel or staggered stance can be used. The staggered stance (Figure 18-29) provides best stability for a forceful throw.
3. *Whole Body Position.* From the stance the back arches and arms raise the ball directly over and to a position behind the head.
4. *Power.* The snap forward of the arms, wrists, and upper body provides power.
5. *Line of Giving Force.* All power factors are delivered in a straight line as the body weight transfers to the front foot. The back foot must stay in contact with the ground throughout the throw.
6. *Ball Contact.* The hands must be on the side of the ball and the ball delivered equally with both hands.
7. *Follow-Through.* See #5.

▶ **Learning Cues:** Running Throw-in (I)

1. *Alignment to Field.* Same as Standing Throw-in.
2. *Base.* A run prior to delivery with a skip step followed by a stride (staggered) stance is used.
3–7. Same as Standing Throw-in.

Goalkeeping

The goalkeeper uses skills for fielding and for clearing the ball. The hands may be used while in the penalty area. Catches are made in different positions, depending on how the ball arrives. Clearing involves either throwing or kicking skills.

▶ **Learning Cues:** Kneeling Catch—Roll or Bounce (B)

1. *Alignment to Ball.* Quickly position in a direct line (180°) with the path of the ball.

2. *Base.* Kneeling (Figure 18-30), the knee of one leg and foot of the other are placed on the ground on opposite sides of the path of the ball for stability and blocking purposes. Standing (Figure 18-31), the feet are placed together in a direct path with the flight of the ball.
3. *Whole Body Position.* Kneeling, the hands and arms are extended downward in front of the body to receive the ball. The lower leg of the kneeling limb is placed at an angle (45° or greater) directly behind path of ball to block it if it gets past the hands. The head is directly above the ball and the shoulders are 90 degrees to the path of the ball. Standing, the upper body bends over at the waist with both legs straight. The hands and arms are extended downward in front of the legs to receive the ball. The head is directly over the ball and the shoulders are 90 degrees to the path of the ball.
4. *Absorption.* The soft contact surface (hands) makes initial contact as the ball is curled to the forearms, biceps, and chest.
5. *Line of Receiving Force.* The movement of the contact surface and absorption factors away from the line of flight at about the same speed as the ball assists in receiving the force.
6. *Ball Contact.* The little fingers of both hands are close together, all fingers are spread and palms are facing the approaching ball. This surface contacts the ball below its center bringing it to the forearms, biceps, and chest in one smooth curling action.
7. *Follow-Through.* Immediately stand up for balance and stability.

FIGURE 18-32 Catch—waist or chest high ball.

the impact immediately on the body while simultaneously curling the hands and arms around the ball as in catching a rolling ball. A slight jump in the air at contact also aids in absorption.

5–6. *Receiving Force* and *Ball Contact.* Same as catching a rolling or bouncing ball.

7. *Follow-Through.* Bring the knee forward for protection against approaching players, if necessary (Figure 18-32).

▶ **Learning Cues:** Catch—Ball Head High or Above (B)

1. *Alignment to Ball.* Same as catching a rolling or bouncing ball (Figure 18-33).

FIGURE 18-33 Catch—ball head high or above.

FIGURE 18-31 Standing catch—roll or bounce ball (front and side views).

▶ **Learning Cues:** Catch—Waist or Chest High Ball (B)

1. *Alignment to Ball.* Same as catching a rolling or bouncing ball.
2. *Base.* The feet are even in a parallel stance.
3. *Whole Body Position.* The hips and shoulders are parallel with the goal line. The hands and arms are extended together in front of the body reaching forward for the ball.
4. *Absorption.* A ball traveling at a slower seed is cushioned the same way as when catching a rolling or bouncing ball by first contacting the hands, forearms, biceps, and finally chest. A fast approaching ball is cushioned by taking some of

2. *Base.* From a parallel stance raise the knee of one leg forward while the weight is supported on the other (exactly the same if a jump is required).

3. *Whole Body Position.* The hips and shoulders are parallel with the goal line, while the arms extend upward and forward to the desired height for fielding the ball.

4. *Absorption.* The soft contact surface (hands) makes initial contact as the ball is quickly brought to the chest area for protection.

5. *Line of Receiving Force.* Movement by the contact surface and arms is away from the line of flight at the same speed as the approaching ball.

6. *Ball Contact.* The thumbs of both hands are close together, all fingers are spread apart and the palms are facing the approaching ball. This surface contacts the ball near its center and brings the ball to the chest area in one smooth action.

7. *Follow-Through.* Land with two feet in a wide stride stance and lower the hips to a medium standing position for balance and stability.

▶ **Learning Cues:** Catch—Fall to Side (I)

1. *Alignment to Ball.* With the ball rapidly approaching to the side, drop to the ground on the side of the body, attempting to place either the hands or body in alignment with the ball blocking it (Figure 18-34).

2. *Base.* From a parallel stance the ball-side leg is folded and extended behind the other foot dropping the whole body to the ground on its side.

3. *Whole Body Position.* The body weight is supported on its side and the arms are extended as far as necessary for intercepting the ball.

4–6. Same as catching the ball above the head.

FIGURE 18-34 Catch—fall to side. Note hands behind ball.

FIGURE 18-35 Tip—one or two hands.

7. *Follow-Through.* As the ball is brought to the chest area, both knees are brought forward curling around the ball for protection.

▶ **Learning Cues:** Tip (I)

1. *Alignment to Ball.* Same as catching a rolling or bouncing ball.

2–3. *Base and Whole Body Position.* Same as catching a ball above the head.

4–5. *Power* and *Line of Giving Force.* The contact surface (one or two hands) thrusts upward and backward deflecting the ball over the crossbar.

6. *Ball Contact.* The ball is contacted on its bottom area with the heel of the palm(s) as the wrist(s) is flexed for deflecting the ball upward and backward (Figure 18-35).

7. *Follow-Through.* The knee is brought forward for protection, and the landing is on two feet for stability.

▶ **Learning Cues:** Punt (B) (Figure 18-36)

1. *Alignment to Ball.* The ball is held with both hands in front of the body.

2. *Base.* From a walking or running motion the body weight is transferred to one foot while the other prepares to kick the ball.

3. *Whole Body Position.* The kicking leg is brought behind the body with a high heel raise as the arms are extended in front with the ball in the hands preparing to drop it.

4. *Power.* The proper contact surface, height that the contact foot is raised behind the body, speed

FIGURE 18-36 Punt.

FIGURE 18-37 Overhand throw.

that the contact leg is snapped forward to meet the ball as it is dropped, and amount of follow-through all provide power.

5. *Line of Giving Force.* The foregoing power factors applied as near as possible to a 180° angle with the intended flight provide the line and amount of force.

6. *Ball Contact.* The ball is contacted in the back/bottom area. The closer to the ground that the ball falls prior to contact the lower its trajectory. The contact surface is the top hard area of the foot (instep).

7. *Follow-Through.* The contact leg continuing to lift following contact provides both height and force as the body weight is supported by the grounded foot.

▶ **Learning Cues:** Overhand Throw (I)

1. *Alignment to Ball.* The ball is held near the shoulder at the side of the thrower.

2. *Base.* A medium stride stance is used.

3. *Whole Body Position.* The ball is held in one hand and brought behind the body about head high with the arm flexed (Figure 18-37). The non-throwing arm is extended in front of the body for balance. The knees are slightly flexed. The hips and shoulders are slightly rotated toward the throwing arm.

4. *Power.* The distance that the ball is brought behind the body, speed that the throwing arm is brought forward and the non-throwing arm is brought back, and follow-through of the throwing arm plus upper body all provide power.

5. *Line of Giving Force.* The foregoing power factors applied in a straight line provide maximum force and the desired direction.

6. *Ball Contact.* The ball is held in the palm of the throwing hand and at the back/bottom of the ball.

7. *Follow-Through.* As the ball is released overhand, the throwing arm continues forward and the body bends forward providing force and direction.

PLAYING STRATEGY

Skilled execution of the techniques blended with knowledge of principles, tactics, and systems lead to a winning combination in soccer. *Principles* are factors which lead to skillful organized controlled play. *Tactics* denotes the execution of techniques and application of principles in a competitive situation. These fall into categories of individual, group, and team. *Systems* refer to the formational placement of players on the field where they apply techniques, principles, and tactics.

Principles

The basic principles are possession and space. Possession can be by one's own team (attack) or by the opponents (defend). The knowledgeable use of space when attacking or defending is the basis for successful play. The field size (space), understanding of the importance of each third of the field, attack principles and defense principles provide the initial foundation for team play.

Space.   The position of players on the large (75 yd. × 120 yd.) field area presents a variety of available spaces. When in possession of the ball, the objectives are to attack the space behind, between, or in front of the opponents or to create new spaces by forcing them to move. The defensive objective is to deny the use of these spaces. The larger the space the more time a player has to maintain possession leading to more controlled play.

Strategic Field Areas.   The field is divided into thirds (Figure 18-38). The following factors, when applied in each area, lead to systematic team coordination.

Defend

1. Ball is distributed wide immediately upon possession.
2. Always provide support behind teammate with ball.
3. Do not pass ball across goal mouth.
4. Do not give the ball away.
5. Control pass to midfield area as quickly as possible.
6. When in trouble clear ball: (a) to midfield, (b) out of bounds over sideline, (c) to goalie, (d) over end line (as a last resort).

Midfield

1. Slow down tempo of ball and players.
2. Maintain control.
3. Diagonal cross field flow of ball.
4. Back pass to supporting players—reverse field to opposite side.
5. Penetrate to attack zone.
6. Keep ball wide.
7. Overlap extra players for numerical superiority.

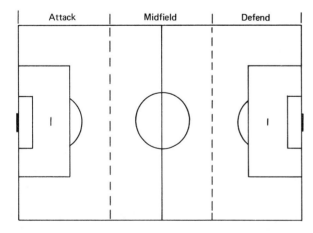

FIGURE 18-38 Strategic field areas.

Attack

1. Wide passes for control plus spread defense.
2. Penetrate with ball when possible.
3. Center or cross ball in front of goal mouth, preferably in the air.
4. Short passes, one/two touch contact.
5. Back pass to maintain possession.
6. Shoot whenever possible.
7. Pressure the ball when it is lost.

Offensive Principles.   As illustrated in the diagrams (Figure 18-39), the following principles aid the attacking team:

1. *Width*—distributing the ball wide spreads out the defense, opening larger areas for penetrating by either the ball or another player.
2. *Depth/Support*—10- to 15-yard positioning ahead or behind the ball provides additional possible passing angles and enhances possession.
3. *Penetration*—the ball that penetrates past an opponent toward the end line is the most threatening pass to him. The deeper the controlled penetration the better.
4. *Mobility*—the movement by players without the ball to different positions can provide superiority around the ball, create surprise, and create new situations to which the opponents must adjust.
5. *Improvisation*—the ability to adjust to ever-changing situations during the course of the play.

Defensive Principles.   As illustrated in the diagrams (Figure 18-40), the following principles aid the defending team:

1. *Delay*—positioning in front of the player with the ball so that the ball cannot make immediate penetration, thus gaining the important defensive ingredient: time.
2. *Depth/Support*—positioning beside and behind teammates restricting the space that the ball/opponent might move.
3. *Balance*—the spread of players across the field protecting all areas.
4. *Concentration*—retreating by all defensive players funneling to the goal scoring area causing congestion.
5. *Pressure*—forcing mistakes through aggressive play.
6. *Control/Restraint*—applying all other principles of defense, awaiting the best opportunity for winning the ball; also not committing and being beaten by either the ball or the player.

Tactics and Practice Suggestions

The execution of techniques and application of principles in a competitive situation is called tactics. These may be either individual, group, or team.

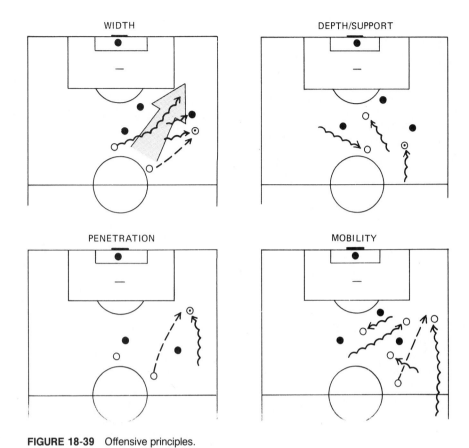

FIGURE 18-39 Offensive principles.

FIGURE 18-40 Defensive principles.

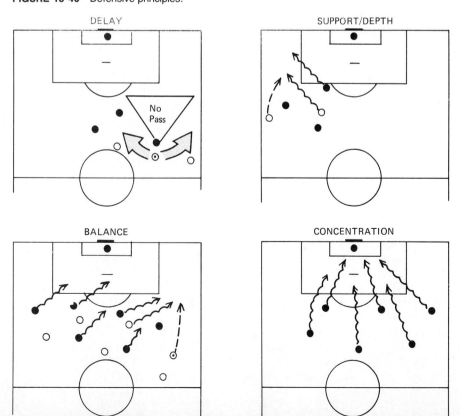

Individual.   A player with the ball has the opportunity to dribble, pass, or shoot, and only has possession of the ball approximately two minutes of a 90-minute game. Developing technique and proficiency in the foregoing skills is important; however, it is more important to learn what to do for the other 88 minutes when one does not have the ball. One must learn how to use the available space for receiving the ball, how to create new space for either the ball or a teammate, and how to apply the principles of attacking or defending.

Group.   The basic soccer objective of superiority around the ball initiates group tactics. When superiority is gained, the factors of using space, creating space, restricting space, and controlling tempo (time) are applied in small side games. Small side games (2 on 1, 2 on 2, 3 on 1, 3 on 2, 3 on 3, etc.) in restricted areas provide excellent opportunities for learning individual and group tactics.

Team.   The grouping of a larger number of players leads to team tactics. Organizing restrictive games often with two lines of players (for example, 4 attackers and 3 midfielders versus 2 midfielders, 4 defenders, and the goalkeeper) requires additional continuity.

Playing within the boundaries of the suggested one-third field areas (see Figure 18-38), the players can concentrate upon the factors governing systematic team coordination. Communication becomes critical since more players are involved. Short one-word cues aid in communication. Using cue words such as *square, back, through, lead, leave, touch, carry, turn, settle*, etc., lets teammates know what to do with the ball.

Special rules in such competitions help reinforce specific tactics. Examples of special rules are: allow only one or two touches per player; a back pass must be used before a penetrating pass; no passes over 15 yards; after receiving a pass the player must dribble past an opponent; all passes must be longer than 15 yards; no passes above knee high; all passes above the head; etc.

The next step in developing playing strategy is the application of principles and tactics within a specific system.

Systems

The formational placement of players on the field is called a system (Figure 18-41). The players are numbered starting with the defenders (fullbacks), midfielders (halfbacks) and then attackers (forwards). The goalkeeper is not included in the numbering. The first attempt to develop new systems occurred when the five forwards of the 2-3-5 system changed their relative positions thus forming either a W or M due to their alignment with each other on the field. Since that first change many new systems have evolved, and all systems have

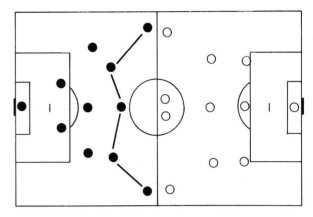

FIGURE 18-41   A systems alignment at kickoff. Number 2-3-5 (W) versus 3-3-4.

strengths and weaknesses. Each evolved due to the specific abilities and knowledge of the players involved. The choice of which system to use should always depend upon those two factors—abilities and knowledge.

Style.   Within a system there are varying styles of play. Offensive styles are long pass, short pass, fast, slow, static positioning, improvisational movement, and dribbling. Defensive styles are zone, man to man, switching man to man, rotational, and diagonal.

Many current coaching books discuss principles, tactics, and systems in more detail. The Selected References section lists several books for those requiring additional information.

Dead Ball Situations

When the ball goes out of play or there is an infraction of the rules the game restarts from a dead ball situation. This allows a team the opportunity to initiate set plays. Goal kick, corner kick, kickoff, throw-in, indirect and direct free kicks provide such an opportunity. The defending team also has time to prepare. There are many such plays and plans.

References in coaching books can provide a variety of set plays for dead ball restart situations.

Player Positional Responsibilities

Traditionally the player positions were called forwards, halfbacks, fullbacks, and goalkeeper. In recent years the three basic lines are referred to more commonly as attackers, midfielders and defenders. Each line has specific responsibilities related to that particular position. Listed below are the basic responsibilities for each line. It is pointed out that differing systems of play demand varying responsibilities, and Selected References can provide further information.

Attackers

(The forward line players who include wings, insides (strikers), center forward, or other teammates who overlap into the attacking area.)

1. Scoring by shooting (head-foot).
2. Setting up scoring opportunities by dribbling to commit an opponent; center or crossing the ball in the air into the penalty area; running to create a new space for the ball or a teammate and to receive the ball; distributing the ball strategically and quickly wide, backward, or forward.
3. Performing offensive restarts such as direct, indirect, and corner kicks in scoring area.
4. Pressuring the opponents immediately upon their gaining control.
5. Positioning for counterattacks upon regaining possession of the ball.

Midfielders

1. Supporting the attackers on offense.
2. Redistributing the ball wide, forward, or backward upon gaining possession for sustaining offense.
3. Shooting outside the penalty area.
4. Overlapping into attack area for additional strength or surprise.
5. Retreating, delaying the opponents upon their gaining definite control of the ball.
6. Challenging for a loose ball when there is a 50/50 chance of gaining possession.
7. Receiving goal kicks, both offensive and defensive.
8. Taking a majority of the throw-ins.
9. Defending against opponent's corner kicks.
10. Positioning for counter attacks upon regaining control of the ball by one's own defenders or goalkeeper.

Defenders

1. Supporting midfielders when attacking.
2. Challenging for ball at midfield when there is a 60/40 chance of gaining possession.
3. Retreating, delaying the opponents upon their gaining definite control of the ball in midfield area.
4. Funneling toward the goal and concentrating in the scoring area.
5. Supporting each other when challenging for the ball.
6. Clearing (kick or head) the ball out of the scoring area and when possible out of the defensive one-third.
7. Keeping balance across the field; not allowing weakened areas.
8. Positioning wide for counterattacking.
9. Protecting the goal when the goalkeeper leaves the goal mouth.
10. Forming walls for protecting against free kicks.
11. Assisting or taking goal kicks.
12. Overlapping occasionally for added superiority or surprise.
13. Defending against corner kicks.
14. Taking free kicks in defensive one-third.
15. Sprinting to goal when beaten by both the ball and man.

MODIFICATIONS FOR SPECIAL POPULATIONS

Orthopedically Impaired

1. Contact the United States Cerebral Palsy Athletic Association (USCPAA) in Westland, Michigan for the rules of Wheelchair Team Handball. This game originated as Wheelchair Soccer.
2. Allow students using crutches, canes, and/or walkers for ambulation to move the ball up and down the field or court with their assistive devices.
3. Modify the soccer game using a large cageball instead of the regular soccer ball. The large cageball can be moved up and down the court by students in wheelchairs.

Mentally Impaired

1. Contact local Special Olympics for their soccer manuals.
2. Move from simple to complex instructions and rules of the game as the unit develops. Follow similar guidelines for skill development.
3. Keep playing sessions short allowing for frequent rest periods. Fitness levels are generally low for the student with mental retardation.

Sensory Impaired

1. See modification for Orthopedically Impaired, #3 above.
2. Use sighted peer teachers and play as tethered partners. Tether the students at the wrist.
3. Minimal modifications are needed for the deaf and/or hearing impaired.

TERMINOLOGY

Center A pass from the outside of the field near the side line into the center.

Charge The body contact between opponents which may be either illegal or legal.

Chip The lofting of the ball into the air using the instep kick technique: contacting the ball very low causing it to loft quickly with back spin.

Clear Playing (kick or head) the ball a great distance attempting to move it out of a danger area.

Corner kick A direct free kick awarded to the attacking player on the corner arc when the defending team last played the ball over their own end line.

Cross   A pass from the outside of the field near the end line to a position in front of the goal.

Dead ball situation   The organized restarting of the game following the stopping of play.

Direct free kick   A free kick from which the kicker may immediately score from that initial contact.

Dribble   The technique of the player self-propelling the ball with the foot so that he maintains control while moving from one spot to another.

Drop ball   The method used for restarting the game after temporary suspension of play when the ball is still playable.

Goal area   The rectangular area in front of the goal where the ball is placed for a goal kick.

Half-volley   Contacting the ball just as it hits the ground after being airborne.

Head   The technique of playing the ball with the head.

Indirect free kick   A free kick from which player other than the kicker must contact the ball before a score can result.

Kickoff   The free kick that starts play at the beginning of the game, after each period, or after a score.

Obstruction   The illegal use of the body to shield an opponent from reaching the ball.

One-touch   Immediately passing a ball being received without stopping it.

Penalty area   The large rectangular area in front of the goal where the goalkeeper is allowed to use the hands to play the ball.

Penalty kick   A free kick awarded for a Direct Free Kick foul in the penalty area against the defending team.

Settle   The act of taking a ball that is off the ground and getting it settled on the ground so that it is rolling and no longer bouncing.

Square pass   A pass that is directed toward the side of a player.

Tackle   A technique for taking the ball away from the opponents.

Through pass   A pass that penetrates between and past the defenders.

Throw-in   The technique used for restarting the game when the ball goes out of play over the side line.

Touchline   The side line of the field.

Trap   The technique used for receiving the ball, bringing it under control.

Two-touch-receiving   (Trap) a ball and immediately re-passing it.

SELECTED REFERENCES

Coerver, W. *Soccer Fundamentals for Players and Coaches.* 2nd ed. Englewood Cliffs, NJ: Prentice Hall, 1986.

Hargroves, A. *Skills and Strategies for Coaching Soccer.* Champaign, IL: Leisure Press, 1990.

Lurbacher, J.A. *Fun and Games for Soccer Training.* Champaign, IL: Leisure Press, 1987.

Nelson, R. *Soccer.* Dubuque, IA: Wm. C. Brown, 1986.

Robson, B. *Soccer Skills.* New York: Sterling Publishing Co., Inc., 1989.

Schellecheidt, M. *Youth League Soccer Skills.* North Palm Beach, FL: The Athletic Institute, 1989.

Thomson, W. *Teaching Soccer.* Minneapolis, MN: Burgess Publishing Co., 1980.

19 SOFTBALL

THIS CHAPTER WILL ENABLE YOU TO:

▶ *Identify the basic equipment needed in softball and understand the rules pertaining to it.*
▶ *Understand the rules of slow-pitch and fast-pitch games.*
▶ *Demonstrate the skills of batting, baserunning, sliding, fielding, throwing, pitching, and catching; and of playing the infield and outfield positions.*
▶ *Identify drills and lead-up games for the teaching of skills.*
▶ *Identify the terminology necessary to understand the game.*
▶ *Observe the procedures to make the game safe for participants.*

NATURE AND PURPOSE

In 1887 an indoor version of the game of baseball was developed by George Hancock of Chicago, Illinois. He used smaller playing dimensions and a larger and softer ball. The game became extremely popular and was moved outdoors. This game, softball, is now played by over 30 million adults and youths in the United States as well as in many nations throughout the world. Almost 5 million youths are estimated to participate in youth softball programs, making softball the most popular youth sport.[1] Participation in softball games ranges from informal games at picnics, in parks, in backyards, and on the streets to formal leagues sponsored by schools, playgrounds, recreation departments, churches, and industrial organizations. The traditional forms of softball games included in league play are fast pitch, 12-inch slow pitch, and 16-inch slow-pitch games. With the variety of types and modifications of the basic game of softball, the game can be enjoyed by men and women of all ages. Softball is considered to be one of the safest sports for all ages.[2]

EQUIPMENT AND CLOTHING

Bats. The official softball bat is round and made of one piece of hardwood or bonded wood. Plastic, bamboo, or metal are also acceptable. The bat's maximum measurements are 34 inches in length, 2¼ inches in diameter at its barrel end, and 38 ounces in weight. Bats must be free of rivets, pins, rough or sharp edges, or any form of exterior fastener; metal bats must be free of burrs. The handle requires a safety grip of cork, tape (not smooth plastic tape), or composition material, and the bat must be marked "Official Softball" by the manufacturer.

Balls. A 12-inch ball is used for fast-pitch and men's and co-ed slow-pitch softball. An 11-inch ball is used for women's slow pitch games. A larger 16-inch ball is also used for some slow-pitch games. The official 12-inch ball must be a smooth-seam concealed-stitch or flat-surfaced ball from 11⅞ to 12⅛ inches in circumference, and weigh from 6¼ to 7 ounces. [The official 11-inch and 16-inch balls have relative size and weight specifications.]

Gloves. Gloves (which have fingers) may be worn by any player, but mitts (which have no fingers) may be used only by the first baseman and catcher. The pitcher's glove must be a solid color other than white or gray. Multicolor gloves are acceptable for all other players, but gloves with white or gray circles on the outside resembling a ball are illegal.

Shoes. Shoes may have canvas or leather uppers or similar materials. The soles may be either smooth or have soft or hard rubber cleats. Ordinary metal sole and heel cleats may be used if the spikes on the plates do not extend more than ¾ inch from the sole or heel of the shoe. Shoes with rounded metal spikes are illegal. No metal spikes are allowed in any division of youth or co-ed play.

Protectors. Masks, throat protectors, and helmets must be worn by all catchers during a game and by anyone who is warming up a pitcher. Masks should be checked to be sure the wire eye opening is smaller than the bat barrel. Youth fast-pitch softball catchers must also wear shin guards and body protectors. Body protectors are recommended for slow-

---

[1] S.D. Houseworth and F.V. Rivkin. *Coaching Softball Effectively* (Champaign, IL: Human Kinetics Publishers, Inc., 1985), p. 3.

[2] M.E. Kneer and C.L. McCord. *Softball: Slow and Fast Pitch*, 4th ed. (Dubuque, IA: Wm. C. Brown Publishers, 1987), pp. 1–2.

pitch games as well. Helmets are required to be worn by all adult fast-pitch players and youth fast- and slow-pitch offensive players. The helmets must be of similar color with double ear flaps. Helmets are not allowed for defensive players except the pitcher and the catcher and for medical purposes.

Uniforms.   All players on a team must wear uniforms identical in color, trim, and style. Ball caps are considered part of the uniform and are required for all players under U.S. Slow-Pitch Softball Association (USSSA) rules and in Amateur Softball Association (ASA) rules for male players including the catcher. Caps, visors, and headbands are optional for female players but may not be mixed on a team. All female players are not required to wear headwear, but for those players who do so, the headwear must be alike. Plastic visors are not allowed as headwear.

PLAYING FIELD

The regulation playing field is 60 × 60 feet square (Figure 19-1). The accompanying indications of the required distances for fast pitch and slow pitch are used in the majority of age groups. For official distances for specific age groups, consult a current ASA softball rule book. Ground or special rules establishing the limits of the playing field may be agreed upon by leagues or opposing teams whenever backstops, fences, stands, vehicles, or other obstructions are within the prescribed area.

The home plate is made of rubber or other suitable material and is a five-sided figure, 17 inches wide across the side facing the pitcher, 8½ inches long on the sides parallel to the inside lines of the batter's box, and 12 inches long on the sides of the point facing the catcher.

The pitcher's plate is made of wood or rubber and measures 24 inches long and 6 inches wide. The top of the plate must be level with the ground; the front line of the plate measures the following distances from the outside corner of home plate: male fast-pitch and slow-pitch and female slow-pitch—46 feet; female fast-pitch—40 feet.

The bases other than home plate must be 15 inches square and made of canvas or other suitable material and not be more than 5 inches thick. The bases should be securely fastened in position. A dou-

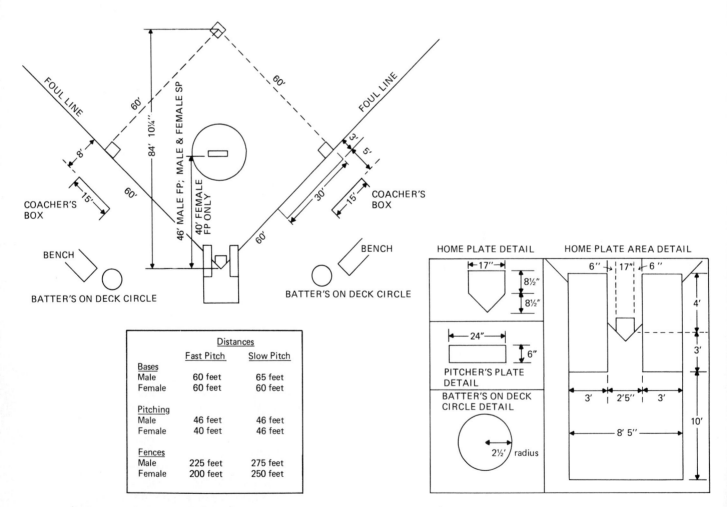

Distances		
	Fast Pitch	Slow Pitch
Bases		
Male	60 feet	65 feet
Female	60 feet	60 feet
Pitching		
Male	46 feet	46 feet
Female	40 feet	46 feet
Fences		
Male	225 feet	275 feet
Female	200 feet	250 feet

FIGURE 19-1 Softball field, official dimensions.

ble base may be used at first base. This base is 15 by 30 inches. The half of the base in fair territory is white and the half of the base in foul territory is orange.

Laying Out a Diamond

The following directions are for laying out a diamond with 60-foot bases and a 40-foot pitching distance. Determine home plate position by running a line in the direction desired for the diamond. Place a stake at the corner of home plate nearest the catcher. Tie a cord to the stake with knots or other markings at the following distances: 40 feet, 60 feet, 84 feet 10¼ inches, and at 120 feet.

Place the cord along the direction line without stretching it. Place a stake at the 40-foot mark. This is the front edge of the pitching rubber. Also drive a stake at the 84 feet-10¼ inches mark. This is the center of second base.

Now place the 120-foot mark on the center of second base. Hold the cord at the 60-foot mark and walk to the right of the direction line. When the cord is taut, drive a stake at the 60-foot mark. This is the outside corner of first base. Walk across the field and do the same thing to mark the corner of third base.

SUGGESTED LEARNING SEQUENCE

A. Nature and purpose of softball
B. Conditioning—exercises and drills for developing muscular strength, speed, agility, coordination, and balance.
C. Safety suggestions. Moving people and moving objects can create hazards; therefore, from the first day, safety precautions must be adhered to without fail.
D. Basic game concepts
   1. Field of play and player positions
   2. Equipment
   3. Safety
E. Skills and techniques
   1. Catching
   2. Throwing
      a. Grip on ball
      b. Arm motion
      c. Body movement
   3. Fielding the ball
      a. Ground balls
      b. Fly balls
   4. Batting
      a. Grip on bat
      b. Stance
      c. Stride
      d. Rotation of body and arms
      e. Follow-through
   5. Bunting
      a. Grip on bat
      b. Stance
      c. Direction of bunt

   6. Baserunning
   7. Sliding
   8. Pitching and catching
F. Rules—start with those essential to play the game and expand in depth and comprehensiveness as playing ability increases.
   1. Terminology
   2. Playing field
   3. Equipment
   4. Players and substitutes
   5. The game
   6. Pitching regulations—fast- or slow-pitch, for whichever game is being taught
   7. Batting
   8. Baserunning
   9. Dead ball—ball in play
G. Playing strategy. The fast-pitch game utilizes many strategies of baseball, whereas the slow-pitch game is the adaptation of field positions to batting strengths and/or weaknesses.

SKILLS AND TECHNIQUES

While adaptable for general recreational use, softball is a game that demands a good performance of certain fundamental skills and techniques. Enjoyment from participation in the game intensifies as skills improve. Skill techniques are described followed by short cues to use in teaching each of the skills. Practice suggestions include drills and lead-up games to enhance skill development.

Catching

Catching the ball is a fundamental skill that must be mastered before other skills are attempted.

▶ **Learning Cues**

1. *Watch the ball* into the hands or glove.
2. Fingers up and thumbs together for balls chest high or higher. Fingers down and little fingers together for balls waist high and lower.
3. Relax the fingers and arms.
4. On contact with the ball absorb the force by bringing the ball close to the body: "give with the ball."

▶ **Practice Suggestions**

1. Provide each student with a ball. The students toss the ball up in the air and catch it, trying to toss the ball higher and higher and still be able to catch it.
2. A student tosses the ball up in the air and everyone claps and counts until the ball comes down and is caught. Take turns to see who can get the most claps.
3. Catch balls thrown by a partner from short range. Initially use foam balls or whiffle balls to

eliminate fear of being hurt. Gradually increase the distance.

4. Catch balls a partner throws high, low, and to each side.

Throwing

Throws should be made quickly, accurately, and to the correct base or fielder. Players should be able to throw using an overhand, sidearm, or underhand motion. But spend more time on the overhand throw because with it one can attain the greatest accuracy. The sidearm throw imparts a side spin on the ball that causes it to curve.

▶ **Learning Cues**

1. Grip ball across a seam with index and second fingers (all four fingers if hand is small), thumb underneath, and third and fourth fingers to the side (see Figures 19-2 and 19-3).
2. Point elbow away from body as arm moves backward (Figure 19-4).
3. Move body weight to foot on same side (rear foot) and rotate trunk in that direction.
4. Keep wrist extended until just before release.
5. Push off with the rear foot and step with the other foot in the direction of the intended throw.
6. Rotate hips, trunk, and shoulders as arm comes forward.
7. Lead with the elbow and snap the wrist as the ball is released opposite the peak of the cap.
8. Throwing arm continues across the body for the *follow-through*.
9. Use a natural rhythmical movement.

FIGURE 19-4   Overhand throw—as arm moves backward, point elbow away from the body.

▶ **Practice Suggestions**

1. Throw to a partner. Start with a short distance and then increase that distance. Throw to a specified target on the partner such as the chest. Vary the target and the speed of the throw. Stay at a distance until accurate for four out of five throws (preferably all five).
2. Throw at a target from various distances.
3. Throw to different bases from different field positions.
4. Play "Beatball." A runner stands at home plate and a catcher has a ball, preferably a soft ball. On a signal the runner begins running the bases. The catcher throws the ball to third base. The ball is relayed from third to second base and then to first base and home plate. The runner scores one point for each base touched before the ball returns to home plate. *Variation:* Allow the runner to continue around the bases until the ball reaches home plate prior to the runner on the same trip around the bases. Place a maximum of three trips around the bases.

Fielding Ground Balls

The ability to field ground balls is crucial to the success of any defense. With proper guidance most players can learn to field routine ground balls successfully and improve their ability to field cleanly hard hit balls and bad bounces.

▶ **Learning Cues**

1. Prior to the pitch assume ready position with the feet parallel and wider than shoulder width

FIGURE 19-2   Two-finger grip for adults.

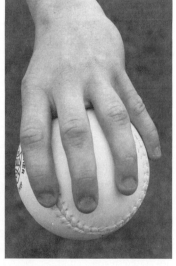

FIGURE 19-3   Four-finger grip for children.

FIGURE 19-5 Fielding ground ball position.

apart. Flex the knees and hips and place the hands close to the ground.
2. When possible, move forward ("charge") the ball when it is hit.
3. Stay in front or get in front of ground balls. This enables you to handle them if they take bad bounces to the left or right.
4. Field ground balls with the feet in a stride position, knees slightly bent, and the body crouched (Figure 19-5): *wide stance.* On hard-hit balls it may be advisable to close the feet or drop to one knee to block the ball.
5. Catch a ground ball just as it leaves the ground on a bounce or after it has reached the peak of its bounce.
6. Keep the body and glove low on ground balls and move upward to make the catch. One can move more quickly upward and since the body is already low, more bad bounces may be blocked by the body or glove.
7. Keep the glove open and *watch the ball into the glove.*

▶ **Practice Suggestions**

1. Slowly roll ground balls between partners.
2. Increase the speed of the rolls and then increase the distance between partners.
3. Toss ground balls to the right and to the left of the partner.
4. Field ground balls with a partner tossing balls at varying speeds and in different directions.
5. Field ground balls hit by a partner at varying speeds and directions. Throws can be made to a catcher next to the hitter or to a base.
6. Play "Pegging First." One team is at bat and the other is in the field. Using a fungo bat, each bat-

ter hits the ball on the ground and runs to first base. If the batter reaches first before the ball, one point is scored. All members of the batting team bat before teams change positions.

Fielding Fly Balls

Catching fly balls can be a difficult skill for beginners to learn. Once the basic catching skill is mastered, judging the ball's speed and distance must be learned in order to field fly balls.

▶ **Learning Cues**

1. Get *under the ball* as quickly as possible. *Use two hands.*
2. To catch a ball hit over the head and to the right or left, pivot on the foot on the ball side, turn and run diagonally backward, and watch the ball over the shoulder opposite the ball side.
3. Relax the fingers slightly and have the hands and arms *give with the ball* as it is caught to reduce the force of impact.
4. Catch the ball, when possible, close to the throwing side so that the throwing arm can move into position for the throw as soon as possible.
5. Watch the ball into the glove.
6. Know where to throw the ball before you catch it, and then move quickly to accomplish the throw *after the catch.*

▶ **Practice Suggestions**

1. Catch fly balls thrown by a partner. Gradually increase the distance.
2. Catch fly balls hit by a partner. Throw to a relay person, or directly to a catcher next to the hitter, or to a player at a base.
3. Play "Five Hundred." Using a fungo bat, one player hits to a group of fielders. Fielders score successful catches. A fly ball is worth 100 points; a ground ball, 50 points; and a catch on a first bounce, 50 points. If a catch is tried and missed, the respective number of points is deducted. A player scoring 500 points exchanges with the batter.

Batting

The key to offensive softball lies in effective batting—a complex motor task—coupled with base running.

▶ **Learning Cues**

1. The basic position has the batter standing in the batter's box with feet slightly more than hip width apart, knees relaxed and flexed slightly, and with the body bent slightly forward at the hips.

2. The bat is gripped by the handle in such a manner that the second joints of each finger on each hand are in alignment (Figure 19-6).

3. Before hitting, the bat is held in a position over the rear shoulder with the forearm (closer to pitcher) fairly straight and raised so that the elbow is chest high. The back arm is bent slightly with the elbow away from the body (Figure 19-7).

4. The forward leg should *step forward toward the pitcher,* and during the swing the weight should shift over to the front leg which should be straight.

5. In executing the swing, the body, arms and bat first rotate slightly away from the pitcher. This gives the bat more distance over which to gain momentum and enables the body to exert more torque in hitting.

6. Rotate the hips as the bat comes forward, the arms should straighten, the wrists should straighten forcefully just before the ball is hit, and should continue to straighten very forcefully as the ball is hit.

7. The trunk and hips rotate until the batter almost faces the pitcher, and the ball is struck about half an arm's length in front of the shoulder that is closer to the plate (Figure 19-8).

8. The rear foot initiates a push forward but should maintain contact with the ground as the ball is hit.

9. *Watch the ball* from the time the pitcher has it until just before hitting the ball.

10. Swing only at pitches in the strike zone.

▶ **Practice Suggestions**

1. Strike the ball from a stationary tee or from a rope suspended overhead.

2. Using a fungo bat, hit fly balls, line drives, and ground balls.

3. Have partner toss ball from a distance of two to three yards to the side (about a 45-degree angle). Can hit the balls into the playing field or into a fence.

4. Get in groups of four or five with batter, pitcher, and two or three fielders. Hit ten or fifteen pitches and rotate. Position groups for safety.

Bunting

This is an effective offensive weapon in the fast-pitch game but is illegal in slow-pitch softball. Although the fielders are closer to the batter in softball than in baseball, it takes just as much time to field and throw a softball as a baseball. Therefore, the batter in softball should have a slight advantage over the baseball player in using the bunt as a means to reach first base safely.

FIGURE 19-6 Batting grip.

FIGURE 19-7 Batting stance.

FIGURE 19-8 Batting position at contact with ball.

FIGURE 19-9 Bunting position.

▶ **Learning Cues**

1. The initial stance is the same as for hitting because it is most effective as a surprise maneuver, and its declaration must be withheld as long as possible.
2. Just before the pitcher releases the ball, the batter should pivot on the front foot and bring the back foot forward parallel with the front foot so that the batter is facing the pitcher and is near the front of the batter's box.
3. The knees should be bent and the body should crouch low, especially on low balls. Move the body up and down and maintain bunting stance rather than moving the arms for high and low pitches.
4. The arms bring the bat downward to a position parallel with the ground in front of home plate and perpendicular to the ball's line of flight. As the bat comes down, slide the top hand up the bat to a position beyond the center of the bat where the thumb and index finger grasp the bat on the rear side to avoid having the fingers hit. Arms should be half flexed (Figure 19-9).
5. By flexing one arm a little more while extending the other arm, the ball may be guided down either the first or third base lines.
6. The ball should contact the bat slightly above the top hand.
7. The arms should give slightly as the ball hits the

bat to keep the ball from rebounding too far into the playing field.
8. Keep the bat higher than the ball and hit the top half of the ball so that the ball is more likely to be hit downward.

▶ **Practice Suggestions**

1. In front of a mirror, practice turning from batting stance to bunting stance.
2. Bunt balls that a partner tosses slowly.
3. Bunt to a glove placed on the ground at various positions.

Baserunning

In running the bases, follow the base lines and avoid making wide turns when rounding a base. The proper method is to pull out about three feet from the base line a couple of strides before reaching the base, and then by timing your steps, hit the inside corner of the base with the left foot. As the left foot hits the base, the body twists slightly to the left so that the right foot will land just beyond the next base line. The runner comes back to the base line and continues (see diagram, Figure 19-10).

When advancing from first to second, watch the third base coach for directions. The coach is usually in a better position to see the entire field of play and tell the runner whether to stop at second or continue on to third base. Since the runner must remain on his or her base until the ball leaves the pitcher's hand (fast pitch) or reaches home plate (slow pitch), a sprinter's stance (Figure 19-11) should be taken

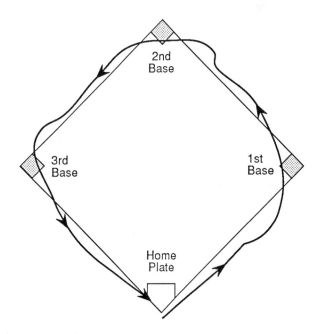

FIGURE 19-10 Path for running bases.

FIGURE 19-11   Sprinter's stance.

FIGURE 19-12   Hook slide.

with one foot on the base in readiness for a quick departure (whether on a steal or a batted ball).

▶ **Practice Suggestions**

1. Run the bases after hitting in batting practice.
2. Practice hitting the ball and starting for first base.
3. Practice starting from a base with the sprinter's stance.

Sliding

To avoid injury, no one should attempt sliding without prior instruction and practice in the technique. Knowing how to slide correctly will also prevent overrunning a base.

The *hook slide,* which is the most popular, is performed by sliding on a thigh and hip with the body leaning away from the base. When sliding on the right hip and thigh, the base is hooked with the left toe, and the right leg is either bent under the left leg with the right toe pointing backward (to keep from getting caught in the ground) or is extended forward in the air (to prevent the spikes from catching in the ground and injuring ankles and knees). The left leg is raised slightly off the ground and as the body, which is slightly to the right of the base line, approaches the base the toe hooks onto the base (see Figure 19-12). It is important to start the slide soon enough so that by the time the toe hooks the base,

FIGURE 19-13   Bent-leg slide.

the body's momentum is slow enough to avoid pulling the toe off the base.

The *bent-leg slide* is used by players who wish to get to their feet quickly in order to advance to another base on an overthrow or misplay. In this slide the player slides on the bent underneath leg with the upper leg making contact with the base (Figure 19-13). The forward momentum of the slide is utilized to raise the body to an upright position after making contact with the base.

The *head-first slide* is often used when it becomes necessary to return to a base. The use of a head-first slide in any other situation should be strongly discouraged.

▶ **Practice Suggestions**

1. Practice in a gym, on wet grass, or in a sliding pit. Wear long pants and socks, no shoes.
2. Judge one another on technique.
3. Slide for a square marked on the grass.
4. Slide into a base opposite catch made by a partner who receives toss from another player. Rotate.

Pitching

The success of a winning team depends largely on the consistency of its pitching. A good pitcher must have control and command a variety of pitches that can be used whether playing slow-pitch or fast-pitch softball. Special movement requirements are outlined under "Pitching Regulations" in the Basic Rules given below.

Slow Pitching.   Place the foot on the throwing arm side on the front of the pitching rubber. The opposite foot is behind the throwing arm-side foot. The throwing arm is brought behind the body in an underhand, pendulum motion. The opposite foot steps toward home plate. The arm is swung forward with the fingers under the ball. The ball should be released about shoulder high, which helps to attain the 12-foot arc and to drop the ball over the plate (see Figure 19-14). Lower releases tend to flatten the pitch and give it more velocity. Varied spins as well as different speeds on the ball should be developed to keep the batter mixed up in the timing of the swing.

Fast Pitching.   Several different types of deliveries are possible including a sling shot or half windmill and a windmill. The beginning stance for each delivery is the same as for slow pitching except that the back foot must be in contact with the pitching rubber. The half windmill is the same motion as slow pitching but faster and the release is by the hip with a snap of the wrist. A windmill involves moving the pitching arm through a full circle. The body is twisted away from the batter at the top of the swing. As the arm begins the downward swing, the hips are

FIGURE 19-14   Pitching delivery, slow pitch.

rotated to a position facing the batter. The leg on the throwing side pushes forcefully against the pitching rubber as the ball is released at the hip with a strong wrist snap (see Figure 19-15).

▶ **Practice Suggestions.**

1. Throw to a partner who moves the target around the strike zone.
2. Throw to a target—such as an old mat tacked on a wall, fence, or backstop. In slow-pitch place an empty bucket, milk crate, or circle on the ground as a target.
3. Play "Pitcher vs. Pitcher." Two players work together. One pitches and the other catches. The pitcher pitches to an imaginary batter. The catcher calls balls and strikes. The "batter" is either struck out or walks. "Runners" advance as additional "batters" become "runners." One player continues to pitch until three "batters" are out then the players exchange positions. The winner is the pitcher with the fewest "runners" scoring.

Playing Catcher

The catcher is frequently called the "defensive center of the infield" because the catcher handles all the pitched balls and is in a position to see all the infield proceedings. The catcher should call the player's name on infield flies, tell the fielder of a

FIGURE 19-15 Windmill pitching sequence.

bunt where to throw, and keep all players informed of the number of outs. He or she gives the pitcher the signal for the type of pitch to be thrown, gives a target to throw to, makes every effort to block wild pitches with runners on base, and makes plays at home plate. The catcher assumes a squat position as close to the batter as possible without interfering with the swing and with the weight forward on the balls of the feet so that quick movements in any direction can be made. In making a throw, bring the ball up to a position behind the ear, step forward with the left foot, and throw by bringing the arm for-

ward quickly and with a strong wrist snap just prior to release.

Playing First Base

The first-base player in fast-pitch softball must always be alert for fielding a bunt as it is used frequently. The field position for this is in toward home plate 10 to 20 feet; a greater distance is used with no one on base and a shorter distance with a runner on first and a double-play possibility. In slow-pitch the playing position is approximately 10 feet behind the base but varies in depth and distance from the foul line according to the strength or weakness of the batter. To be in a position to receive a throw from another fielder, run quickly to the base when the ball is hit and assume a position facing the fielder with the heels touching the inside edge of the bag. The first-base player should shift the body according to the direction of the throw. When the throw is to the left (toward home plate), bring the toe of the right foot to the edge of the bag by the left heel and then step toward the ball with the left foot. Reverse the procedure for a throw on the right (toward the outfield).

▶ **Practice Suggestions**

1. Do the footwork without catching until it is an automatic response.
2. Have partner toss balls to both sides of the base.
3. Have fielders throw balls to base.
4. Have coach hit ground balls to fielders and let them throw to first base.
5. Field bunts and ground balls hit to various spots in the first base area.
6. Practice catching fly balls in the vicinity of first base.

Playing Second Base and Shortstop

The fielding position for the second-base player is approximately 15 feet from second base toward first base and about 12 feet behind the baseline. The position varies with the strength and weakness of the batter. One should attempt to field all batted balls to the first-base side of second base. On a double-play situation from the third-base side, one should move quickly toward the base in a path that puts second base between the person fielding the ball, and the second-base player. Time the move so that the ball is caught as the right foot hits the bag; step forward with the left foot toward the infield and first base to avoid the baserunner; and with a pivot, throw to first base.

The shortstop takes a field position similar to the second-base player's position but closer to third base; the position varies with the strength and weakness of the batter. One should attempt to field all batted balls to the third base side of second base. On a double-play situation, move quickly to the base in a direct line with second base and the player fielding the ball. Time the move to catch the ball just before reaching the bag; step to the outfield side with the left foot; drag the right foot across the bag; and pivot and throw to first base. Both the shortstop and second-base player can stop just before they reach second base, catch the ball and touch second base with the left foot, push back with that foot, landing on the right foot, and then pivot and throw to first base.

▶ **Practice Suggestions**

1. Field ground balls hit to various positions and with varying speeds.
2. Move across the bag and throw to first base.
3. Make the step-back-and-throw maneuver.
4. Complete the double-play situation after fielding ground balls.
5. Make the double-play with a runner moving with the hit ball.
6. Tag runners stealing second base.
7. Catch infield fly balls.

Playing Third Base

The position of the third-base player in fast-pitch is similar to that of the first-base player—be in a position to field bunted balls by playing in toward home plate 10 to 20 feet, depending on the game situation. Attempt to field all batted balls hit down the third-base line and as many as can be reached hit to the second-base side, as the momentum developed by moving in that direction should aid the throw to first base.

▶ **Practice Suggestions**

1. Field bunted balls and throw to first base and second base.
2. Field batted balls hit to various positions and with varying speeds. Throw to first base and to second base.
3. Field batted balls and practice the double-play situation.
4. Catch pop-ups in the vicinity of third base.
5. Tag runners stealing third base.

Playing the Outfield

The position of the outfielders should enable them to cover their area from the infield to the fence, and it should vary according to the strength and weakness of the batter. The overhand throw is used when throwing to the infield because it is usually more accurate due to the fact that side spin is not put on the ball, which causes it to curve. Use the techniques for fielding ground balls and fly balls.

▶ **Practice Suggestions**

1. Catch fly balls hit to various positions, including over one's head.
2. Field ground balls hit to various positions.
3. Make throws to second base, third base, home plate, and to a relay player. Do the same with players running the bases.
4. Throw to targets at the various bases.

PLAYING STRATEGY

Fast-pitch softball permits most of the team strategies used in baseball. It is varied according to any given game situation and the philosophical beliefs of the coach. One difference is that the second-base player covers first base on bunts rather than the pitcher. The winning team will be the one that not only masters individual fundamentals but functions as a unit in the execution of team plays. In slow-pitch softball there are no offensive plays, since a baserunner cannot leave the base until the pitched ball reaches home plate and cannot advance until the ball is hit or the batter is walked.

BASIC RULES

The rules of softball are patterned after those of baseball, making it very similar to the parent game. Pitching and several rules concerning field dimensions and equipment are different. A brief summary of the rules is given below, but players should study a copy of the Official Rules in order to become familiar with all regulations governing the game.

The games of slow-pitch softball and fast-pitch softball have many similarities: the ball must be pitched underhand, the game is 7 innings long, the purpose is to get on base and score runs. The major difference, as the names imply, is in the speed of the pitched ball. In slow-pitch softball, the ball must be thrown underhand with a specific arc (6 to 12 feet), whereas in fast-pitch softball the ball is thrown underhand in a straight line with great velocity—much like a baseball. Other differences are noted below.

Slow-Pitch	*Fast-Pitch*
No bunting	Bunting
No stealing bases	Stealing bases
Runners may leave the base after the ball crosses home plate	Runners leave base after the pitcher releases the ball
10 players per team	9 players per team
65-foot base paths (Males)	60-foot base paths
60-foot base paths (Females)	
Recommend a mask and chest protector for the catcher	Require a mask and chest protector for the catcher

Game Regulations

The purpose of the game is to score more runs than the opponent. A regulation game consists of 7 innings or 6½ innings if the team second at bat has scored more runs than its opponent. The umpire may call (terminate) a game if five or more complete innings have been played or the team second at bat has scored more runs than the other team has scored in five or more innings. The score of a forfeited game shall be 7–0 in favor of the team not at fault.

Players and Substitutes

A team consists of 9 players in fast-pitch, 10 players in fast-pitch with a Designated Player (DP), and 10 players in slow-pitch. A team must have the required number of players to start or continue a game. A substitute may take the place of a player whose name is on the team's batting order. Any of the starting players, including a DP, may be withdrawn and re-enter once, provided such a player occupies the same batting position whenever he or she is in the line-up. A player, other than the starting line-up, removed from the game may not participate in the game again except as a coach. The DP may be used for any player provided it is made known prior to the start of the game and his or her name is indicated on the line-up sheet. The DP must remain in the same position in the batting order, may enter the game on defense, and may be substituted for at any time by a player who has not yet been in the game.

Pitching Regulations

Fast-Pitch. In fast-pitch, the pitcher must take a position with both feet firmly on the ground and in contact with, but not off the side of, the pitcher's plate. Before pitching, the pitcher must come to a full and complete stop for a least one second and not more than ten seconds, facing the batter with both shoulders in line with first and third base and with the ball held in both hands in front of the body. The pitcher may not take the pitching position without the ball. The pitcher may use may wind-up in the delivery provided there is no stop in the forward motion or reverse in the direction of the arm swing. The release of the ball and the follow-through of the hand and wrist must be forward past the straight line of the body, and, when the arm passes the body in the forward swing, the hand shall be below the hip and the wrist not farther from the body than the elbow. The pitcher shall not take more than one step which must be forward toward the batter (within the length of the pitcher's plate), simultaneous with the delivery of the ball, and the pivot foot must remain in contact with the pitcher's plate until the stepping foot has touched the ground.

Slow-Pitch. In slow-pitch, the pitcher can take the pitching position with one or both feet touching the pitcher's plate, but both the pivot and non-pivot foot must be within the length of the pitcher's plate. A full stop must be made for 1 second and not more than 10 seconds with one or both hands holding the ball in front of the body and the shoulders in line with first and third base preliminary to pitching. The pivot foot must remain in contact with the pitcher's plate until the pitched ball leaves the hands. It is not necessary to step, but if a step is taken, it must be forward toward the batter within the length of the pitcher's plate. The pitch shall be released at a moderate speed (umpire's decision—if warned about excessive speed and the act is repeated, the pitcher shall be removed from the pitcher's position for the remainder of the game), and at a perceptible arc of at least 6 feet and no higher than 12 feet from the ground.

Batting Regulations

The batter shall take a position within the lines of the batter's box and may be called out for stepping on home plate or having the entire foot touching the ground completely outside the lines of the batter's box when the ball is hit. A batter is removed from further participation in the game if an illegal bat is used. Players must bat in regular order as indicated in the starting line-up. Batting out of order is an appeal play, and if the error is discovered while the incorrect batter is at the plate, the correct batter must replace the incorrect batter and assume the ball and strike count. If the error is discovered after the incorrect batter has completed the turn at bat and before there has been a pitch to another batter, the player who should have batted is out, and the next batter is the player whose name follows that of the player declared out. Any runs scored are cancelled, and base runners must return to bases held when the incorrect batter came to plate. If the error is not discovered until after a pitch is made to the next batter, no one is declared out and all play is legal.

A strike (fast-pitch) occurs when the ball passes over any part of home plate and is between the batter's armpits and the top of the knees when in a natural batting stance. In slow-pitch the strike zone is over any part of home plate between the batter's higher shoulder and the knees when in a natural batting stance.

A foul tip is a foul ball which goes directly from the bat, not higher than the batter's head, to the catcher's hands and is legally caught. In fast-pitch the ball is in play and baserunners may advance at their own risk. In slow-pitch the ball is dead.

The batter is declared out when an infield fly is hit with baserunners on first and second or on first, second, and third with less than two out (infield fly rule). The batter is also called out in slow-pitch when the ball is bunted, is hit with a downward chopping motion, or is hit foul after the second strike.

Baserunning Rules

Baserunners must touch the bases in regular order and if forced to return while the ball is in play, the bases must be touched in reverse order. Two baserunners may not occupy the same base simultaneously. The runner who first legally occupied the base shall be entitled to it and the other baserunner must return or be put out. A baserunner is out when he or she: (a) runs more than three feet from a direct line between bases in regular or reverse order to avoid being touched by the ball in the hand of a fielder; (b) passes a preceding baserunner before that runner has been put out; (c) leaves a base to advance before a caught fly ball has been touched provided the ball is returned to a fielder who touches that base while holding the ball, or a fielder with the ball touches the baserunner before returning to the base; (d) fails to keep contact with the base until a legally pitched ball has been released by the pitcher in fast-pitch (whether on a steal or batted ball); (e) fails to keep contact with the base until a legally pitched ball has reached home plate in slow-pitch (batted ball only). A pitcher in slow-pitch who desires to walk a batter intentionally may do so by notifying the Plate Umpire who shall then award the batter first base.

Dead Ball Rules

The ball is dead and not in play under the following circumstances: (a) on an illegally batted ball; (b) when the batter steps from one box to another as the pitcher is ready to pitch; (c) on an illegal pitch; (d) when a pitched ball touches any part of the batter's person or clothing; (e) when a foul ball is not caught; (f) when a baserunner is called out for leaving a base too soon; (g) when any part of the batter's person is hit with a batted ball while in the batter's box; (h) when a blocked ball is declared; (i) when a wild pitch or passed ball in fast-pitch goes under, over, or through the backstop; and (j) in slow-pitch after each strike or ball.

Scoring Regulations

A base hit results when a batted ball permits the hitter to reach first base safely when no fielding error is involved. A base hit shall not be recorded when a baserunner is forced out by a batted ball, or would have been forced outside, except for a fielding error.

Sacrifices are scored when with less than two out the batter advances one or more baserunners with a bunt and is retired at first base, or when a run is scored by advancing runners after a fly ball is caught.

Assists are scored to each player who handles the ball in any play or series of plays which results in a put-out, but only one assist is credited to a player in any one put-out.

Put-outs are credited to players who catch a batted fly ball, catch a thrown ball that retires a baserunner, or touch a baserunner with the ball while the runner is off the base.

Errors are recorded for the player who commits a

misplay that prolongs the turn at bat of the batter or the life of the baserunner.

A run batted in (RBI) is a run scored because of: (a) a safe hit; (b) a sacrifice bunt or fly; (c) an infield put-out or fielder's choice; (d) a baserunner forced home because of interference, or in fast pitch the batter being hit with a pitched ball, or the batter being given a base on balls; and (e) a home run and all runs scored as a result.

Winning and Losing Pitcher

A pitcher is credited with a win if he or she starts and pitches at least 4 innings and the team is not only in the lead when the replacement occurs but remains in the lead the remainder of the game. When a game is ended after 5 innings of play and the starting pitcher has pitched at least 3 innings and the team scores more runs than the other team when the game is terminated, he or she shall be declared the winner. A pitcher shall be charged with a loss regardless of the number of innings pitched if replaced when the team is behind the score and the team thereafter fails to tie the score or gain the lead.

MODIFICATIONS FOR SPECIAL POPULATIONS

Orthopedically Impaired

1. Contact the National Wheelchair Softball Association (see Paciorek and Jones, 1989).
2. Allow students using crutches, canes, and/or walkers to strike the ball from a stationary position, e.g., batting tee balanced on a traffic cone.
3. Use plastic bats and balls, e.g., whiffle ball.

Mentally Impaired

1. Contact local Special Olympics for their softball manuals.
2. Play "one-base" softball, where batter runs to only first base and not first, second, third, and home. Add additional bases as skills and concepts of the game improve.
3. Do not play "three out"; allow all players from one team to hit before exchanging offensive and defensive positions.

Sensory Impaired

1. Contact the United States Association for Blind Athletes for the rules of "Beep Baseball."
2. Construct modified guidelines with jump ropes from home plate to first base for blind and/or visually impaired.
3. Strike the ball from a stationary position, e.g., batting tee, and instruct the runners to move to an auditory cue, e.g., bell or buzzer at first base.
4. Minimal modifications are needed for the deaf and/or hearing impaired.

SAFETY PROCEDURES

The following procedures should be observed to minimize the possibility of accidents and injuries.

1. Organize throwing and catching warm-up drills in parallel lines. Adjacent players should be a safe distance apart. When a ball is missed, it should be retrieved and the student should return to the line before making a throw to the partner.
2. The receiver should indicate the target before any ball is thrown.
3. Players should wear proper protection (helmets, masks, gloves, etc.) at all times.
4. Perfect sliding techniques before using them. Always avoid unnecessary slides.
5. Anchor bases firmly to the ground.
6. Students should swing bats only in designated areas, and no one should be allowed to enter batting areas.
7. Have batting practice organized so that one group does not hit toward another group.
8. Grip the bat tightly so it will not slip from the hands. Keep the hands dry and only use bats with the proper safety grip. After batting, *drop* the bat, do not throw it.
9. Players of teams waiting to bat should be in a specific safe area.
10. Keep equipment organized and in the dugout. Do not leave it scattered around or in the playing area.
11. Keep the playing area clear of rocks, depressions, obstructions, or any foreign objects.
12. To avoid collisions, learn the correct procedure for calling for fly balls and for covering bases.
13. Organize drills so that students are facing away from the sun.

TERMINOLOGY

Appeal play   A play upon which an umpire cannot make a decision until requested by a player or a coach.

Assist   Fielding credit for a player who throws or deflects a batted or thrown ball in which a put-out results, or would have resulted except for a subsequent error.

Battery   The pitcher and the catcher.

Batting average   The number of hits divided by the times at bat.

Blocked ball   A batted or thrown ball that is touched or stopped by a person not engaged in the game, or which touches any object that is not part of the official equipment or official playing area.

Blooper   A batted fly ball that goes just over the head of the infielders and just in front of the outfielders.

Cleanup hitter   The number four batter in the batting order, a position usually occupied by the team's heaviest hitter.

Control   The ability of a pitcher to throw the ball to a desired area when pitching.

Count The number of balls and strikes on the batter.

Cut-off A throw from the outfield that is intercepted by an infielder for the purpose of throwing out a runner other than the intended runner.

Double play Two consecutive put-outs occurring between the time the ball leaves the pitcher's hand and its return to the pitcher.

Error A misplay or mistake by the defensive team that results in prolonging the turn at bat of the batter or the time on base of the baserunner.

Fielder's choice The batter is safe because the defensive player elected to retire a preceding baserunner.

Force out An out as a result of a defensive player with the ball tagging a runner or the base to which the baserunner must go because the batter became a baserunner.

Fungo bat A lightweight bat used in hitting balls to fielders during practice.

Grand slam The batter hits a home run with the bases loaded.

Hit A ball hit in such a way that the batter or preceding baserunners are not retired by good defensive play.

Hot corner The third base area.

Infield fly A fair fly ball that can be caught by an infielder with runners on first and second, or first, second, and third, before two are out. The batter is declared out by the umpire.

Keystone sack The second base area.

On deck The player in line to follow the batter at the plate. The place for waiting is the "On-deck circle."

Overthrow A thrown ball that goes into foul territory beyond the boundary lines of the playing field on an attempt to retire a runner who has not reached or is off a base.

Passed ball A legally delivered pitch that should have been held or controlled by the catcher, which allows a baserunner to advance. A dropped third strike that permits the batter to reach first base in fast pitch is an error, not a passed ball.

Put-out An out credited to the fielder who last handles the ball on a play that retires the batter or a baserunner.

Running squeeze A play where the runner on third base starts for home with the pitch because he knows the batter is going to bunt the ball.

Sacrifice bunt A play where the batter bunts for the ball to advance a baserunner and is thrown out at first base, or would have been if the ball was played properly.

Sacrifice fly A fly ball that is caught and after which a baserunner crosses home plate to score a run.

Safety squeeze A play where the baserunner on third base starts for home after the batter bunts the ball.

Switch hitter A batter who bats both right- and left-handed.

Texas leaguer Same as a *Blooper.*

Wild pitch A legally delivered pitch so wide or low or high that the catcher cannot stop or control the ball, which allows a baserunner to advance.

SELECTED REFERENCES

Blakemore, C., Hawkes, N., and Burton, E. *Drill to Skill: Teacher Tactics in Physical Education.* Dubuque, IA: Wm. C. Brown Publishers, 1991.

Craig, S. and Johnson, K. *The Softball Handbook.* Champaign, IL: Leisure Press, 1985.

Houseworth, S.D. and Rivkin, F.V. *Coaching Softball Effectively.* Champaign, IL: Human Kinetics Publisher, Inc., 1985.

Ivankovich, M. *The Strategy of Pitching Slow Pitch Softball.* Maple Glen, PA: Author, 1985.

Johnson, C.P. and Wright, M. *The Woman's Softball Book.* New York: Leisure Press, 1984.

Kneer, M.E. and McCord, C.L. *Softball: Slow and Fast Pitch.* 4th ed. Dubuque, IA: Wm. C. Brown Publisher, 1987.

Linde, K. and Hoehn, R.G. *Girl's Softball: Complete Guide for Players and Coaches.* West Nyack, NY: Parker Publishing Company, Inc., 1985.

NAGWS Softball Guide. Current ed. The American Alliance for Health, Physical Education, Recreation, and Dance. 1900 Association Dr., Reston, VA 22091.

Official Softball Rules. (current ed.). The International Joint Rules Committee on Softball. P.O. Box 11437, Oklahoma City, OK.

Paciorek, M.J. and Jones, J.A. *Sports and Recreation for the Disabled.* Indianapolis, IN: Benchmark, Inc., 1989.

Potter, D.L. and Brockmeyer, G.A. *Softball: Steps to Success.* Champaign, IL: Leisure Press, 1989.

Reach, J. and Schwartz, B. *Softball Everyone!* Winston-Salem, NC: Hunter Textbooks, Inc., 1989.

Whiddon, N.S. and Hall, L.T. *Teaching Softball.* New York: Macmillan Publishing Company, 1980.

Audio-Visual Aids

Athletic Institute, 200 Castlewood Dr., N. Palm Beach, FL 33408 (16mm films, 3/4" and 1/2" videotapes, and filmstrips.)

Aims Media, Inc., 6901 Woodley Ave., Van Nuys, CA 91406 (16mm films, 3/4" and 1/2" videotapes, 8mm silent cartridges)

Champions on Film, 745 State Circle, Ann Arbor, MI 48104 (S8mm silent cartridges)

Clearvue, Inc., 5711 N. Milwaukee Ave., Chicago, IL 60646

Eye Gate Media, 3333 Elston Ave., Chicago, IL 60616

Phoenix/BFA Films and Video, Inc., 470 Park Ave. South, New York, NY 10016 (16mm films, 3/4" and 1/2" videotapes, S8mm silent cartridges, S8mm cartridge with optical sound)

Universal Education and Visual Arts, 100 Universal City Plaza, Universal City, CA 91608 (S8mm silent cartridges)

University of Nebraska, Instructional Media Center, University of Nebraska Extension Division, Lincoln, NE 68508 (16mm films)

20 SPEEDBALL

THIS CHAPTER WILL ENABLE YOU TO:

▶ Identify and put into practice the rules governing the game.
▶ Practice and then execute the basic skills including kicking, passing, catching, trapping, dribbling, and aerial ball conversions.
▶ Identify differences and similarities of skills, rules, and strategies found in other sports.
▶ Discuss and employ basic offensive and defensive strategies and tactics.
▶ Identify and use basic terminology associated with the game.

NATURE AND PURPOSE

The game of speedball is a combination of the skills, rules, and strategies of soccer, basketball, and football. It is a vigorous, continuous-motion activity involving running (sprinting and jogging) and changes of direction (dodging, cutting, stopping, restarting). It is played outdoors on a football or soccer size field by teams of 11 players, yet with limited modifications it can be played indoors in smaller areas and with fewer players.

Originally a men's activity, the game was modified for women's participation and has evolved into a sport that men and/or women can play by the same set of rules. Speedball is an adaptable game and the leader can alter the rules to meet individual preferences.

The object of the game is to propel a ball to the opponent's end of the field and score points. The ball is propelled either as a ground ball (soccer skills) or an aerial ball (basketball and football). The skills involved are kicking, passing (hands or feet), catching, trapping, and dribbling.

In advancing the ball the offense attempts to score either by a field goal, touchdown, drop kick, penalty kick or end goal. The defenders attempt to impede the attack by guarding. Players on both teams are organized into forwards, halfbacks, fullbacks, and a goalkeeper as in soccer.

EQUIPMENT

The only necessary equipment is a ball and two goals. The regulation speedball is slightly larger than a soccer ball, but a soccer ball, which is more readily available, is most often used. Any type of goal (soccer, football, field hockey, team handball, etc.) can be used, but the soccer and football goals

(uprights extending from the ground up) are most often available. The regulation goal is 18 feet wide for women and 18 feet 6 inches for men.

FIELD OF PLAY

A football, soccer, or field hockey field can be used. The regulation fields for men and for women are shown in Figure 20-1. The field consists of a middle/halfway line, restraining lines, end zone/penalty area, penalty kick mark, end lines, goal lines, and sidelines.

Middle/Halfway Line. This line is used on the kickoffs to insure that the team taking the kick is in its own half of the field.

Restraining Line. The opponents of the team taking the kickoff must stay behind this line until the ball is contacted. In men's rules the ball must travel beyond (10 yards) the restraining line on kickoff, or be touched by an opponent before those taking the kickoff can replay the ball.

End Zone/Penalty Area. The size of this area varies in men's and women's play. The area has four purposes: (1) A ball thrown from the field of play, across the goal line, and caught in the end zone by the team attacking that end results in a score (touchdown as in football). (2) Any "contact foul" (women) or "personal foul" (men) committed in this area and against the team defending that end results in a penalty kick. (3) On a penalty kick no player from the defending team except the goalie can be in this zone. (4) A legal attempt to score on a ground ball within this area by the offense results in an end goal if it crosses the end line but not in the goal (men's rules only).

Penalty Kick Mark. This is the spot to place the ball for taking a penalty kick.

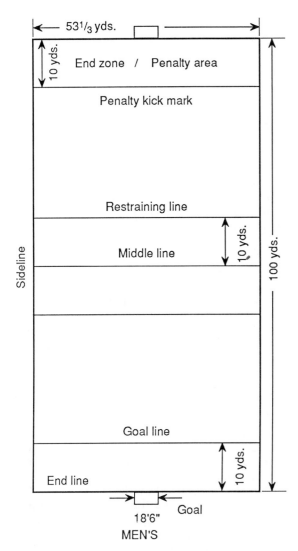

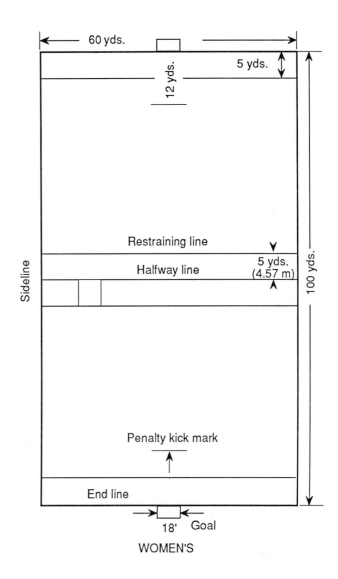

FIGURE 20-1 Men's and women's speedball fields.

End Line. This line serves as a boundary, and when the ball goes out of bounds without scoring, it is put back in play by the opposing team from that spot. The end line can also determine an end goal in men's rules (see End Zone/Penalty Area, purpose #4). On a penalty kick the defensive players stand behind this line.

Goal Line. This line separates the field of play from the end zone/penalty area. On a penalty kick players stand behind the goal line so that they are not in the penalty area.

Sideline. This is a boundary line, and when the ball goes out of bounds it is put back in play with a throw by the opposing team from that spot.

BASIC RULES

Although there are two sets of official rules for men's and women's competition (for sources, see Appendix A), separate rules are no longer necessary. The following is a combined and simplified set of rules.

Scoring

The regulation methods for scoring are listed in Figure 20-2 and described below. The points can be adjusted to meet the needs of varying age groups or for emphasizing specific skill usage. From experience most individuals elect to overuse the "touchdown" method of scoring. Adding a higher point value than the one listed for a "field goal" leads to players using their kicking skills more often, thus de-emphasizing throwing and catching. Another suggestion is that the "end goal" method of scoring be eliminated.

Field Goal: propelling the ball with the feet or body (no hands or arms) into the goal—identical to a legal soccer score.

FIGURE 20-2. Speedball scoring—official and recommended

	Men's	Women's	Recommended
Field goal	3	2	3
Drop kick	2	3	2
Touchdown	1	2	1
Penalty kick	1	1	1
End goal	1	X	X

Touchdown: throwing the ball across the goal line to a teammate who catches it in the end zone/penalty area—similar to a football touchdown.

Drop Kick: drop kicking the ball over the goal crossbar from outside the end zone/penalty area.

Penalty Kick: free kicking the ball as a result of a personal contact foul against the defending team when in their own penalty area. The ball is kicked from the penalty kick mark into the goal. It is suggested that the ball be placed on the ground (men's rules) similar to a soccer penalty kick rather than drop kicked (women's rules).

End Goal: the offense kicking the ball over the end line from within the end zone/penalty area without the ball going into the goal (men's rules). It is suggested that this method of scoring *not* be used, but instead the opponents receive a pass/kick-in from the spot where the ball went over the end line.

Violations, Fouls, and Penalties

There are some variations and some similarities in the official rules for men and women pertaining to violations, fouls, and penalties. Men's rules classify infractions as violations, technical fouls, and personal fouls, while women's rules identify individual fouls and team fouls. Many of the infractions are identical but are listed according to their own specific classification. The penalties for infractions vary according to the severity of the infraction. The following list combines the infractions and classifies them as either fouls (severe) or violations (less severe).

Violations

(M = Men's; W = Women's rules prior to combining.)

1. A ground ball touched with the hands or arms (M&W).
2. Taking too many steps with ball—two steps if received while running and one step while standing (M&W).
3. More than one aerial dribble per possession (M&W).
4. Holding the ball more than three seconds (W).
5. Kicking or kneeing a fly ball before catching it (M).
6. The offense drop-kicking the ball in the defense's penalty area (W).

7. The offense throwing the ball to a teammate when both are in the defense's penalty area (W).

Violation Penalties

1. A violation outside the penalty area results in an indirect free kick at the spot of the infraction (W). See Soccer, "Fouls—Indirect Free Kick."
2. A violation inside the opponents' end zone/penalty area gives the opponents a free kick or throw from the end line nearest the infraction (W).
3. A violation inside one's own end zone/penalty area results in an indirect free kick by the opponents at the spot of the infraction (W).

Fouls

(M = Men's; W = Women's rules prior to combining.)

1. Illegal contact with opponents
   a. Kicking (M&W)
   b. Pushing (M&W)
   c. Tripping (M&W)
   d. Holding (M&W)
   e. Blocking (M&W)
   f. Charging (M&W)—see Soccer, Charge for legality
   g. Hacking (W)
   h. Obstruction (W)—See Soccer, "Obstruction" for legality
   i. Unnecessary roughness (M)
2. Illegal substitution (M&W)
3. Unnecessary delay of game (M&W)
4. Taking more than three time-outs (M&W)
5. Having more than 11 players on the field (M&W)
6. Unsportsmanlike conduct (M&W)

Foul Penalties

1. A body contact foul (#1a–1i) by the defending team in their own penalty area/end zone results in a penalty kick by the opponents (M & W).
2. A body contact foul (#1a–1i) occurring other than in one's own penalty area/end zone results in an indirect free kick by the opponents (W).
3. A non-contact foul (#2–#6) results in a penalty kick to the offended team (M&W).
4. A double foul results in a jump ball at that spot unless the fouls were behind the goal line. When behind the goal line, the jump ball takes place on the goal line nearest where the fouls occurred (W).

Length of Game

Speedball is played in quarters with intervals between each quarter and at the half. The time for each play period and for intervals can be modified to suit the physical abilities of the participants.

Kickoff

The ball is kicked from the ground forward from the middle line. All members of the kicking team remain behind the middle line until the ball is contacted. The receiving team remains behind the restraining line until contact.

Men's and women's rules differ on the kickoff and either choice is acceptable. Men's rules dictate that the ball must be kicked forward beyond the restraining line or touched by an opponent before the kicking team can play it. Women's rules are identical to a soccer kickoff (see soccer, "Kickoff"), but also allow the play to be turned into an aerial ball by lifting it with the feet to the hands of a teammate (not to self).

Playing the Ball

Ground Ball. The ball, when on the ground (rolling, bouncing, or stationary), is played as in soccer with skills of dribbling, kicking, heading, or trapping. In order for the ball to be thrown it must first be brought from the feet immediately into the hands.

Aerial Ball. The legal conversion of a ground ball using the feet to lift or kick it into the hands is called an aerial ball. When in the hands it can be thrown, passed, and caught as in football and basketball. The ball can be air dribbled to oneself only one time each new possession. The air dribble consists of throwing the ball in the air and relocating to regain possession by catching it. On the air dribble, steps do not count while the ball is in the air. A player is legally allowed one step with the ball when holding it if obtained while standing, or two steps if running prior to receiving it. Additional steps are illegal and are called traveling. Holding the ball with the hands for more than three seconds without giving up possession is illegal. This speeds up the game and is a rule which can be modified.

Physical Contact. Rules allow for the same body contact as in soccer (see Soccer, "Physical Contact") when the ball is on the ground. With the ball in the hands, guarding as in basketball (see Basketball, "Fouls") is appropriate. Other personal contact fouls were identified in the foregoing listing of speedball fouls.

Jump Ball (toss-up, tie-ball). Two opponents simultaneously holding the ball results in a jump ball. Likewise, if it is not possible to decide which team put the ball out-of-bounds, a jump ball is held. The format is the same as in basketball with two opponents facing each other and jumping to tip the ball which is tossed between them. All other opponents must be at least 5 yards away on the toss-up. The ball remains as an aerial ball off the tip provided it does not contact the ground in which case it is considered a ground ball.

Out-of-Bounds. A ball going off the field of play over the sideline is put back in play with a throw (overhand, underhand, two hands, one hand, etc.). A ball over the end line is either thrown or kicked into play.

Free Kick. Certain identified infractions result in a free kick which is identical to soccer (See Soccer, "Fouls") except that the opponents only need to be 5 yards from the ball. The kick is taken at the spot of infraction. It can be turned into an aerial ball. Indirect free kick means that someone must touch the ball prior to a score.

Penalty Kick. Certain foul situations previously identified result in a penalty kick which is a free kick. The ball is placed on the penalty kick mark (line), and one of the offended team members is allowed a free kick to score a field goal against the opposing team goalie. The offensive team members position outside the defenders' penalty area. The defensive players, aside from the goalie, position either behind the end line or outside the penalty area.

Goalkeeper. The goalie primarily defends the goal against the field goal attempts. The goalkeeper is bound by the same rules as all other players with no special privileges or rules.

SUGGESTED LEARNING SEQUENCE

A. Stretching and running
B. Basic rules
C. Fundamental skills
  1. Passing
    a. Soccer—inside of foot, instep kick, lofting the ball and punt
    b. Basketball—chest, overhead and baseball
    c. Football—forward
    d. Speedball—drop kick
  2. Catching/Trapping
    a. Soccer—sole of foot, inside of foot, outside of foot and chest
    b. Basketball—two hands above and below the waist, pivoting
    c. Football—over the shoulder
  3. Heading
    a. Soccer—standing and jumping
  4. Dribbling
    a. Soccer—inside and outside of foot
    b. Speedball—aerial
  5. Individual defense
    a. Soccer—tackling from the front and side
    b. Basketball—guarding and denial of ball
    c. Football—pass defense
  6. Personal conversion to aerial
    a. Speedball—roll up, two foot lift and one foot lift
  7. Goalie
    a. Soccer—catch waist, chest and above head; falling catch; tip; throw and punt.

D. Strategies
   1. Offense
      a. Soccer—possession, superiority around the ball, creating space, tempo, communication, depth/support, width, penetration, mobility and improvisation.
      b. Basketball—cutting, fakes/feints, attacking a man to man and zone defense, fast break.
      c. Football—dodging, faking and change of pace.
   2. a. Soccer—pressure, depth/support, width, balance, delay, concentration and control.
      b. Basketball—player to player, fast break and zone.
      c. Football—pass defense.
E. Systems
   1. Style—long or short pass, static positioning, aerial or ground ball, man to man or zone.
   2. Formations—(M or W as in soccer), V or inverted V.
F. Restarts
   1. Kick off
   2. Throw-in
   3. Free kick
   4. Penalty kick

SKILLS AND TECHNIQUES

Only a few skills are specific to speedball. The majority of the skills needed are described in the basketball, soccer, and football chapters. The skills from these sports are identified below, and a review of these sections will prepare the speedball player for skilled participation.

Basketball Skills: pivoting; chest pass; overhead pass—one-hand overhead pass (baseball); two-hand catch and holding the ball; cutting; individual defense against a player with the ball, player without the ball and denial defense.

Soccer Skills: inside of foot pass; instep kick; lofting the ball; sole of foot trap, inside and outside of foot trap; chest trap; inside and outside of foot dribble, heading, standing, and jumping; tackling from front and side; goalkeeping—catching ball waist, chest and above head plus falling to side, tip, punt and overhand throw.

Football Skills: forward pass and over-the-shoulder catch.

Aerial Conversions

Ball control and scoring opportunities are enhanced by having the ball in the hands. The ball must go from the feet directly into the hands for it to be a legal aerial ball. This may happen as a result of punts, soccer style kicks, and drop kicks. An individual can convert a ground ball to an aerial ball by using either a roll-up, two-foot lift, or one-foot lift.

▶ **Learning Cues—Roll-Up**

1. Stand erect with the ball wedged evenly between the feet (Figure 20-3A).
2. Bend at the waist so the back is parallel with the ground.

| A | B | C |

FIGURE 20-3 Roll-up: (A) wedged ball, (B) rolling ball up leg, (C) converting to an aerial ball by grabbing it with hands.

3. Extend the arms downward and perpendicular to the ground.
4. Place pressure on the bottom half of the ball with the inside of one foot, rotate the knee outward and roll the ball up the inside ankle and calf of the opposite leg (Figure 20-3B).
5. Grab the ball off the foot and leg with the hand converting it to an aerial ball (Figure 20-3C).

▶ **Practice Suggestions**

Wedge the ball with the inside of both feet and roll the ball up and down one lower leg by applying more pressure with the foot opposite that leg. Do not attempt to pick up the ball at this point, but repeatedly roll it up and down the leg to get the feeling so that control is not lost. Progress next to bending over to grab the ball off the foot and leg with the hands. Gradually attempt to speed up the whole process.

▶ **Learning Cues—Two-Foot Lift**

1. Stand erect with the ball wedged evenly between the feet as in Figure 20-3A.
2. Hop up, keeping the ball wedged evenly between the feet and lifting it higher toward the hands.
3. In the air, lean forward extending the arms and hands downward to grab the ball from the feet (Figure 20-4A).
4. Catch the ball and land on two feet with the converted aerial ball ready to pass it (Figure 20-4B).

▶ **Practice Suggestions**

Wedge the ball with the inside of both feet and hop in the air attempting to lift the ball as high as possible. Keep the body erect and do not yet attempt to lean over to grab the ball. Continue this exercise, attempting to bring the ball higher each time. Progress next to leaning over to grab the ball with the hands before it drops to the ground.

▶ **Learning Cues—One-Foot Lift**

1. Stand erect with one foot extended in front of the body and the sole of that foot applying light pressure on the top of the ball (Figure 20-5A).
2. Apply more pressure on the top of the ball with the sole of the foot, and roll the ball quickly toward the body.
3. Place the toe of the foot rolling the ball under the rotating ball to lift it upward.
4. Bend forward at the waist, extend the arms and hands downward and lift the ball with the toe toward the hand (Figure 20-5B).
5. Catch the ball with two hands as it is lifted waist high into the air (Figure 20-5C) converting it to an aerial ball.

A

B

FIGURE 20-4 Two-foot lift: (A) lifting the ball to convert to an aerial, (B) catching the ball from lift.

A   B   C

FIGURE 20-5   One-foot lift: (A) rolling ball backward, (B) lifting backward rolling ball with toe, (C) catching the ball from the toe lift.

▶ **Practice Suggestions**

In an erect position, reach forward with an extended leg and apply pressure with the sole of the foot on the ball. Roll the ball backward and forward keeping foot pressure on it to get the feeling of rolling. Gradually, on the backward roll, apply more pressure causing rapid rotation on the ball as that foot releases from the ball. Next, attempt to place the toe of that foot quickly under the ball and lift the ball as high as possible into the air without catching it. Try to lift it at least waist high. Finally, repeat all of foregoing and lean forward to catch the ball. Once consistency is obtained, attempt to use the one-foot lift on an approaching ball that is already rolling toward the participant.

Drop Kick

The drop kick is used as one method for scoring. It can also be used to kick the ball a great distance similar to punting, except that a drop kick tends to have a lower trajectory, which adds distance to the kick.

▶ **Learning Cues**

Refer to the Soccer chapter learning cues on punting (see Figure 18-36). Cues 1–5 apply to speedball. The following techniques differ for drop kicking.

6. *Ball Contact.* The ball is contacted with the instep (hard top surface) of the foot immediately

upon the ball touching the ground (bounce). The contact is in the back/bottom surface of the ball. The higher the contact surface on the ball, the lower the trajectory of the ball, and vice-versa.

7. *Follow-Through.* A short follow-through by the contact leg results in a low trajectory, and a long one results in a higher trajectory.

▶ **Practice Suggestions**

Face a wall 10 yards away and drop the ball, attempting to drop kick it with a low trajectory (no higher than the head). Allowing the ball to bounce too high from the ground results in a high trajectory, so attempt to contact the ball the instant it contacts the ground. Gradually attempt to kick the ball higher without sacrificing accuracy. Alternate between high and low trajectories to reinforce the timing of ball/ground/foot contact.

PLAYING STRATEGIES

The placement of players on the field assists continuity in offense and defense. Speedball players consist of forwards, halfbacks, fullbacks, and a goalkeeper, and their responsibilities are the same as in soccer. The basic strategies are for the players to position systematically on the field, maintain possession of the ball, propel the ball toward the opponent's goal line, and score points.

Offense

A quick reference to the Soccer chapter will prepare participants for offensive play. Note especially the information on space; strategic field areas; offensive principles; individual, group, and team tactics; and styles of play.

One difference in speedball offense is that there are several methods for scoring. One method (touchdown) can be accomplished any place along the entire width of the field while others (field goal and drop kick) can only be accomplished at the goal in the middle of the field. Converting an aerial ball to a ground ball for a field goal attempt provides an opportunity to score more points. Due to this, the ball in the middle of the field near the goal is a good offensive strategy specific to speedball.

Since ball control and possession are easier in speedball than soccer, and there is no offside rule, it is an advantage to have many players in front of the ball to increase penetration and scoring opportunities. Passers should immediately attempt to locate in advance of the ball upon relinquishing possession.

Varying the ways the team attempts to score makes it more difficult for the opponents to defend against the offense.

Defense

The Soccer chapter identifies defensive principles that apply to speedball. The player-to-player defense is imperative in speedball since the offense can use the aerial ball, which leads to ball control. Defenders must be close to their assigned individual to disrupt the offensive advantage. Quick transition from offense to locating the assigned individual one is to guard is extremely important. The defenders need to know where their opponents are at all times and be close enough to protect against a pass.

The aerial ball rules in speedball make it important that the defender positions far enough away from the player with the ball so that the player cannot air dribble quickly getting behind the defender. The offensive player cannot move very far on one air dribble and has only three seconds to get rid of the ball. If the aerial ball is converted to a ground ball by the offense, the defender should immediately pressure the opponent and get closer so as to destroy control and reduce the chances of making a long kick or shot on goal.

Systems

The placement of players on the field and their responsibilities reflect systematic cohesion among teammates. The team systems indicated in the Soccer chapter are appropriate for speedball. Field balance is important for either offensive or defensive success and a system provides this. The system utilized is dependent upon what the opponents use and/or the strengths and weaknesses of one's own team.

MODIFICATIONS FOR SPECIAL POPULATIONS

See modifications listed in Soccer and Team Handball.

TERMINOLOGY

Aerial ball   A ball that has been thrown or propelled into the air by the feet and that can legally be played with the hands.

Air dribble   A ball tossed to oneself in an attempt to relocate.

Double foul   Two opponents simultaneously committing a foul which results in a jump ball (toss-up).

Dribble   Propelling the ball with the feet (soccer) so that the individual maintains control while moving.

Drop kick   The skill of dropping the ball from the hands to the ground and kicking it upon ground contact; also a method of scoring.

End goal   A score resulting from the offense kicking the ball across the opponent's end line while in the penalty area (men's rules).

Field goal   A score resulting from the offense propelling the ball, as in soccer (no hands or arms), into the opponent's goal.

Foul   An infraction of the rules that is penalized severely.

Free kick   An unguarded kick from the ground such as penalty kick, kickoff, or indirect free kick.

Goalkeeper   The player responsible for protecting the goal against the field goal.

Ground ball   A ball that cannot be touched by the hands but must be propelled as in soccer by dribble, kicking, heading, etc.

Guard   The act of defending against an opponent.

Indirect free kick   A free kick in which someone other than the individual making that kick must touch the ball before it can go into the goal.

Infraction   A breach of the rules.

Jump ball (Toss-up)   Tossing the ball between two players who jump to tip the ball restarting play.

Kickoff   A free kick at the middle line at the start of the game, following a score, following suspension of play each period.

Kick-up   The conversion of a ground ball to an aerial ball.

One-foot lift   The skill of converting a ground ball to an aerial ball by rolling and lifting it with the foot.

Pass   Propelling the ball, with either the hands or feet, to another player.

Penalty kick   A free kick to attempt a field goal as a result of a foul.

Punt   The skill of immediately kicking the ball after dropping it from the hands.

Roll-up   The skill of converting a ground ball into an aerial ball by rolling it up the leg with the foot and grabbing it with the hands.

Throw-in   Putting the ball back in play after it has gone out of bounds over the sideline.

Touchdown   A score made when a teammate throws the ball to a partner who catches it in the opponent's end zone/penalty area.

Trapping   The skill of receiving (catching) the ball with the foot or body to bring it under control.

Traveling   Taking too many steps with the ball in the hands: one step if received while standing and two if while running.

Two-foot lift   The skill of converting a ground ball to an aerial ball by hopping to lift the ball to oneself.

Violation   An infraction of the rules that is not severely penalized.

SELECTED REFERENCES

Meyer, M. and Schwarz, M. *Team Sports for Girls and Women*. Philadelphia, PA: W.B. Saunders Co., 1980.

Musher, C. *Team Sports for Girls and Women*. Princeton, NJ: Princeton Books. 1983.

Phillip, J. and Wilkerson, J. *Teaching Team Sports*. Champaign, IL: Human Kinetics. 1990.

21 SWIMMING, DIVING, AND WATER EXERCISE

THIS CHAPTER WILL ENABLE YOU TO:

▶ *Understand and apply the principles of safety involved in aquatic-related activities.*
▶ *Understand the fundamental skills, biomechanics of swimming and progressions utilized in the beginning through intermediate levels of swimming and diving.*
▶ *Identify and correct common errors of learning swimmers and divers.*
▶ *Understand and participate in the benefits of water exercise.*
▶ *Participate in and contribute to aquatic games and contests.*

NATURE AND PURPOSE

Aquatic activities are among the leading forms of recreation in the United States. Over 75 million Americans enter the water in some form of recreational aquatic activity each year. An estimated 7,000 drownings occur annually in the United States. Many of these result from the inability to swim or from preventable accidents. These statistics indicate the importance of knowing how to swim; in fact, a knowledge of basic swimming skills may be life saving. The goal of physical educators who teach swimming and diving in our schools is to provide sound information to students who wish to utilize our nation's recreational aquatic facilities.

There are other advantages to be derived from swimming in addition to increased safety in the water. Participants may improve their cardiorespiratory fitness levels. Many aquatic activities may benefit those unable to jog or otherwise restricted from land activities due to physical handicaps, because the body's natural buoyancy in water reduces strain in the knee and hip region. Flexibility, agility, balance, and strength can be improved with regular participation in water activities.

EQUIPMENT

Most of the equipment needed for instruction, activities, and aquatic games is generally found in and around aquatic facilities. A well-equipped aquatic program would include but is not limited to the following: kickboards, pull buoys, float belts, Personal Flotation Devices (PFD's), masks, fins, snorkels, water volleyballs (rubber) and net, water polo equipment (balls, hats, flag, goals), inner tubes, rescue equipment (reaching pole, ring buoys throw bag, backboard, head immobilizing device, cervical col-

lars, pocket masks, first aid kit, rescue tubes, rescue board, shepherd's crook, whistles), water basketball and goals, various types of floatable toys, hula hoops, rubber diving bricks and rings, resolite mats, and net bags for equipment storage.

A hose or water source other than the pool's should be available to rinse all equipment at the end of each session, and a preventive maintenance program should be developed to help keep all equipment in good working order. A planned equipment replacement and expansion budget should be instituted.

AQUATIC SAFETY STANDARDS AND ACCIDENT PREVENTION

1. *Instructor Certification.* In most states the Board of Education requires that the public school teacher teaching in the pool be currently certified as an American Red Cross Water Safety Instructor or equivalent. An acceptable equivalent is the YMCA's progressive swimming instructor certification.
2. *Lifeguards.* A trained lifeguard certified through the American Red Cross or YMCA lifeguarding program must be on duty at water side for the duration of the activity, and may not be assigned any other duties than guarding the participants during the time they are in the water. If the school budget does not provide for a lifeguard, the teacher or coach may not also act as a lifeguard, which requires a specific certification.
3. *Risk Assessment.* The Aquatic Council to the National American Association of Health, Physical Education, Recreation and Dance established risk assessment procedures for aquatics in the AAHPERD publication, Principles of Safety in Physical Education and Sport. Some of the

topics to be considered in a risk assessment include: design safety, hazard identification, maintenance, state regulations, pool checklists, remedial maintenance protocols, supervision/instruction, record keeping, insurance, and emergency accident management procedures.

4. *Pool Safety Checklist.* Pool safety is achieved only through a continuous program of quality supervision, maintenance, and inspection by trained and knowledgeable aquatic professionals. A pool safety checklist should be developed for the facility and should be used on a regular basis. The different areas of responsibilities may be assigned to different individuals according to their daily duties.

5. *Emergency Accident Plan and Equipment.* (a) The pool must have: a telephone accessible to the lifeguard and instructor with emergency numbers posted, a first aid kit, towels, blankets, and an easily accessible emergency entrance/exit able to accommodate ambulance personnel and equipment. (b) A written emergency plan should be posted, and records of staff rehearsals kept on file. The local Emergency Medical Services System should be consulted and utilized in the development of the emergency plan and subsequent rehearsals.

6. *Attention.* The instructor should have all equipment for the lesson moved to the pool edge prior to the participants' entry into the water. The lifeguard or instructor should not handle phone calls or other interruptions until the exit of all students from the water. It only takes 20 to 60 seconds for a swimmer to drown.

7. *Divide and Conquer.* In classes with swimming students of many different skill levels, the instructor should test students along the shallow end of the pool and divide them into groups according to their skill level; beginner, intermediate, or advanced. The advanced students can then assist the instructor. The advanced students will gain valuable insight to their own swimming by assisting in the instructional process. This may also entice these students into moving toward obtaining their water safety instructor certification in the future. The instructor should set aside time at the end of the class period to work with the advanced students on advanced skills, while beginners and intermediates practice basic skills unassisted, yet supervised. This strategy works well with the middle school ages and up. However, for the elementary students, the divide and conquer strategy will differ.

First of all, the swimming instructors should request for prior grouping of students so that they teach beginners in one class period, intermediates in another class period and so forth. Also, the instructor(s) should indicate what the appropriate student/instructor ratios are for the different skill levels. Recommendation:

> Beginners 10/1 Maximum
> Advanced Beginners 15/1 Maximum
> Intermediate 20/1 Maximum

If classes cannot be set up this way, the instructors must go to the divide and conquer method within the class period. Since many students of elementary age may not be able to stand even in the shallow end, it once again becomes imperative to have assistance in the pool classroom. A rule to which there can be no exception is to work with the student one on one. Stress that the students may not leave the wall and maintain constant vigilance with the students on the wall. If the school is combined with older grade levels, utilize older volunteer students from study hall or activity periods to assist the teacher.

FUNDAMENTAL SKILLS, KNOWLEDGE, AND TECHNIQUE PROGRESSIONS

The teaching of aquatic-related skills in our schools since the advent of the YMCA and American Red Cross programs traditionally has been one of "assembly line" like instruction. A recent contrast to this approach comes in the contemporary prescriptive aquatic instruction or a developmental approach. This approach is based on the principles common to movement education. Both of these approaches should be given consideration and aligned with the goals of the particular instruction program offered at the institution.

This section outlines basic knowledge which many of the swimming/aquatic skills utilize. This section will include: methods of instruction, biomechanical/hydrodynamic principles related to swimming, effective pool use, water entry and exit, water orientation, bobbing and safety bobbing, buoyancy and floating, gliding, kicking, strokes, basic diving mechanics, and basic dives.

Teaching Methodology

Teaching of swimming skills successfully is dependent upon the instructor's knowledge of mechanics, student readiness, the student's desire to practice, and the instructor's ability to communicate constructive observations. The method used to teach swimming is dependent on two factors: (1) the complexity of the skill to be learned and (2) the motor ability of the learner. For simple skills with average to above average ability, the whole method of teaching is used (verbal description, demonstration, and swimming of the whole stroke). For complex skills the part method (breakdown of skill into body position, kick, armstroke, breathing, coordination) should be used. For assessment of swimmer's ability, a whole method is recommended as it allows the instructor to establish the overall ability of the class and ascertain levels of student fear. Where fear is not evident and swimmers are of average ability, swimming skills would be classified as simple and the whole method of instruction should be used.

Biomechanical Principles of Swimming

It is essential that the instructor understand how the biomechanics of the stroke affect swimming efficiency. A swimmer's forward progress through the water is affected by many factors—in particular, propulsion, resistance, and buoyancy.

Propulsion. The propulsive force is created by the different hand positions, pulls, and kicks utilized by the swimmer. Regardless of the stroke used, the hand should be held firm, slightly cupped and the fingers relaxed but close together. The hands follow an elliptical pattern as opposed to a straight line. In the underwater phase of all strokes, the pull arm(s) come to a bent arm position, minimizing up and down movements in the water. Propulsion in all strokes must be optimized to overcome the laws of inertia. Other important laws of movement include the law of acceleration whereby the swimmer must apply an equal force (even stroke) in the direction in which the force acts. A variation in application of force will be required in strokes other than the front and back crawl strokes. The law of action/reaction which states that every action has an equal and opposite reaction, is also critical to the swimmer. For example, if a swimmer's armstroke in the front or back crawl is wide and sweeping, then the swimmer's legs and trunk will move in the opposite direction thereby creating more resistance.

Resistance. Often referred to as drag resistance is the combination of forces which slows a swimmer's forward progress. Frontal resistance is created by the water directly in front of the body: The more vertical the body is in the water, the greater the frontal resistance. Skin function resistance is created by the water that is flowing immediately next to the body. Tail suction, or "eddy" resistance is caused by poorly streamlined body parts creating a momentary void in the water, making the body pull or suck water with it. All three of these resistance factors can be reduced by streamlining the body during all phases of strokes and turns.

Buoyancy. Various physical factors affect an individual's ability to float, among them bone size, fat tissue, muscular development, weight distribution, and lung capacity. A swimmer with dense bone structure and heavy muscle tissue will tend to sink lower in the water than a person with a higher body fat percentage. This explains why some swimmers will float better than others.

The center of buoyancy is that point of the body around which it rotates in the water. The center of buoyancy is located higher in the body than the center of gravity. In general, on land a female's center of gravity is in the hip region and a male's is in the lower rib area. In the water, however, the center of buoyancy is generally located much higher in males than in females, likely due to the more dense leg structure of the male. This information is important when teaching floating and gliding skills, and explains why men find it more difficult to float and glide horizontally than do women. Another reason is that men float lower in the water, which requires them to overcome greater frontal resistance and skin friction due to the greater submerged body surface.

Getting Started—Effective Pool Use

Efficiency of pool use is necessary when classes are large. Beginner classes offer more restraints than advanced classes due to the use of only shallow water. The instructor will need to be in the water with the beginning level swimming, while in teaching more advanced swimmers, he or she may wish to be on the deck. In both situations, it is recommended that instructors utilize the width of the pool for teaching and making corrections. Demonstrations should be done while swimmers are standing on the deck with the demonstrator in the water. If the pool has windows, the students watching the demonstration should have their backs to the windows. These two recommendations allow students to get a better view of the demonstration by reducing glare.

Students need to be reminded that most accidents in the pool area occur on the pool deck and during water entry and exit. Reminders should be given at the beginning and throughout each pool session that students should enter by sitting on the pool side and slipping into the water or jumping in feet first facing outward. Students should exit the pool by using the ladders.

SUGGESTED LEARNING SEQUENCE

Beginning Swimming

A. Water orientation
B. Holding positions
   1. Entry
   2. Front
   3. Back
   4. Drafting
   5. Streamlining on front
   6. Streamlining on back
C. Skills
   1. Bubble bobs
   2. Safety bobbing
   3. Front float

4. Back float
5. Front glide
6. Back glide
7. Front glide with kick
8. Back glide with kick
9. Front beginner stroke
10. Back beginner stroke
11. Jump from wall (shallow water)

Intermediate Swimming

A. Strokes
    1. Front crawl
    2. Elementary backstroke
    3. Back crawl
    4. Breaststroke
    5. Sidestroke

Diving

A. Types of dives (in order of difficulty)
    1. Slide-in dive
    2. Sitting dive
    3. Kneeling dive
    4. Scale or tip-in dive
    5. Shallow push dive
    6. Deep push dive
    7. Forward standing dive (1 meter)
    8. Standing back dive (1 meter)

BEGINNING SWIMMING

Water Orientation

Beginning students may approach their first swimming session with great anxiety. It is important that the instructor create an atmosphere conducive to learning under these circumstances. The following gradual steps should be taken with the beginner swimmers. Instructors should demonstrate all skills immediately prior to students' attempt.

1. Sit on pool side with feet and lower legs in the water.
2. Use hands to splash water on themselves.
3. Slide into shallow water and remain holding the wall. Instructor may need to assist students into the pool.
4. Sink into water and pull the warm blanket of water over the shoulders.
5. Instructor—demonstrate bubble blowing with chin and lips in the water. Student's turn!
6. Bubble blowing from mouth and nose.
7. Face completely immersed—with bubbles.
8. Head under.

NOTE: The student should be asked to do these skills, never forced. Remember fear levels may be high, the peer pressure of classmates doing the skill should be ample external motivation. Student readiness will determine the level of accomplishment.

Holding Positions

1. Entry. The beginning swimmer may need assistance entering the water. This is particularly true if they cannot touch the bottom. The instructor reaches under the armpits of the student and lowers him or her from a sitting position on the deck into the water. Students should be reminded to hold onto the wall.

2. Front. The front holding position, to be used when instructing the front float, front glide, etc., is best accomplished by having the student cross one hand over the other and place both hands in one of the instructor's hands. The student's arms are then extended at the elbow and as the student stretches to the glide position, the instructor places his or her opposite hand on the student's hip (Figure 21-1).

FIGURE 21-1 Holding position for front/prone glide.

FIGURE 21-2   Holding position for back/supine glide.

3. Back.   The back holding position provides the student with security when learning the back float, back glide, etc. The student places both hands on the wall, pushes the abdomen toward the wall, and places the head back toward the instructor. The instructor cradles the head in one hand while reaching to the small of the back with the other. The student is instructed to straighten the elbows and to keep an arch in the back (Figure 21-2).

4. Drafting.   This skill helps students gain confidence in their ability to float. The student is held in either the front or back holding position directly perpendicular to the instructor. The instructor begins to move backward while pulling the student along. Once the student is moving, the instructor in-

termittently reduces support or, depending on the student's confidence level, lets go. The student's body will be pulled by inertia toward the instructor and follow in his or her wake (Figure 21-3).

5. Streamlining on the Front.   Streamlining helps reduce water resistance. The most important part of this skill is the grab of the hands. While standing, students place both hands over their heads. Without grabbing their hands, they should try to squeeze their ears with their arms. Then, contrast this by having students place one hand over the other and lock the thumb of the top hand over the bottom hand. Now, squeeze the ears again. Students should note that they are much stronger with hands locked into position. Once accomplished, have stu-

FIGURE 21-3   The transition from backglide holding position to drafting.

dents sink into the water, push off into a front or prone glide keeping arms straight, hands locked, finger tips pointed, and body in line.

6. Streamlining on the Back. This can be accomplished in the same manner as the frontal streamlining, just turned over. However, when floating on the back, most beginning students find it easier to leave hands and arms straight down at the sides. This is acceptable at the beginning level.

Beginner Skills

1. Bubble Bobs. The student holds the wall with both hands approximately shoulder width apart. Submerge and blow bubbles toward the wall. This should be done systematically at the beginning of each class, and students should build to about two sets of ten rhythmic bubble bobs. Emphasis is placed on blowing out under water, taking a breath above water, keeping eyes open during both phases, and not wiping face with hands.

2. Safety Bobbing. Once the student is comfortable with bobbing, safety bobbing can be taught. The instructor takes students one at a time into water slightly over their head. Practice at 5 feet from the wall and have student bob to wall systematically and rhythmically, bouncing from the bottom and pushing toward the wall. The instructor should assist as much as needed.

3. Front Float. Students can achieve a front float once they are comfortable putting their face in the water. With minimal support from the instructor, student allows legs and arms to dangle in the water with the face in. Breath should be exhaled slowly from mouth and nose.

4. Back Float. With minimal support from the instructor, the student lays head back in the water while pushing hips and abdomen toward surface gently; arms are extended laterally and knees are bent.

5. Front Glide. From the front holding position have student push gently away from the wall. Once moving, remove support hand from hip and then from hands. If student is comfortable in attempting, and can push from the wall in the streamline position and can maintain glide for 5 to 10 seconds, move on to the front glide with kick.

6. Back Glide. Generally, students are less comfortable in the supine position. The instructor needs to assess student readiness before attempting any removal of support from the back holding position. To start, have student ease off the wall in the back holding position; request that the student make eye contact with the instructor and keep the belly up. Drafting can be used to increase student's confidence.

7. Front Glide with Kick. The flutter kick (freestyle) should be first practiced on the wall using the wall holding technique shown in Figure 21-4. Simultaneous practice of the kick and head position for breathing can be done as shown. Once a satisfactory kick is established, the student may push off the wall in the streamline position, glide (5 feet) and begin kicking. The kick should generate from the hip area with knees flexing slightly and toes pointed on the downbeat; kick is finished with a straight leg. The foot then moves upward until the heel breaks the water surface. Legs are alternated. The kick should not splash water. Proper head position is

FIGURE 21-4 Flutter kicking with head in breathing position.

accomplished with the water line at the middle of the forehead.

8. Back Glide with Kick. The backstroke kick (flutter) is accomplished by allowing the foot to first sink in the water about 12 inches by bending the knees. The upbeat, which is the propulsive phase, is done by straightening the leg. The foot should not come out of the water but the leg and toes do come near the surface. This maintains proper body position. The student eases off the wall on the back, glides (5 feet) and begins a gentle backstroke kick. Arms should remain at side. Proper head alignment is indicated by the chin being slightly up and the water line just over the ears.

9. Front Beginner Stroke. This stroke is taught when the front glide with kick can be done for 10 seconds. The stroke consists of the front glide with kick and an armstroke. The armstroke is accomplished by alternating arms from the streamlined position to the thigh. The arms are moved in perfect alternation with an underwater recovery and pull, push, slice, reach action. The pull phase is initiated by pulling down and back on the water with the hand from the overhead position. Then, keep the elbow high and begin a bend at the elbow. The hand then passes down the centerline of the body. Once the hand passes mid-chest a pushing action is made toward the feet. The hand should be angled so that the palm is facing and pushing toward the feet. Breathing can be accomplished by turning the chin to either shoulder. The breathing is timed so that when the hand of the desired breathing side is in the push phase, the chin should be turned to the shoulder of the breathing side. The breath pattern should be such that the student blows bubbles into the water with the face in, completes the exhaling phase when the mouth exits the water, and inhales with the mouth out of the water. Immediately after taking the breath the student turns the head so that the face is in the water and begins to exhale. The breath is not held.

10. Back Beginner Stroke. The student streamlines from the wall in the back streamline position (arms down), glides (5 feet) and begins the backstroke kick. Simultaneous arm movement is started by running the thumbs up the sides of the body to the shoulders and then extending laterally. Palms should face the wall the body came from and using straight arms, push the water toward the feet and hands to the hips, the start position. Arm cycle is repeated after a short glide. ARM CUE: Up, Out, Together, Glide.

11. Jump from the Wall (Shallow Water). This activity can be very exciting for the beginner. Although the skill is relatively easy, safety precautions must be given. Advise students not to turn around toward the wall when jumping into the pool. It's a good idea to assist the swimmer for the first

FIGURE 21-5 Instructor assisted jump from wall.

few jumps. The instructor stands facing the student, holds hands with the student, either right to left or left to right, then turns so that the student does not jump on top of the instructor (Figure 21-5). Students should look at the area where they are going to enter the water. The instructor can enhance this by placing the free hand in this area so that the student may spot it.

INTERMEDIATE SWIMMING

Before moving on to the intermediate level, students must thoroughly understand and be able to demonstrate the beginner skills in the previous section, and be able to swim approximately 2 widths of the pool. The intermediate skills described in this section will enable students to be more proficient in the water.

Stroke Skills

It would be helpful to review the section on the biomechanics of swimming and apply the principles to the teaching of the strokes. Similarities will be found among the strokes in propulsive force, pull patterns, rhythmic breathing patterns, and high elbow positions.

Front Crawl. The fastest of the strokes and also the one preferred for fitness swimming activities is the front crawl (freestyle). This stroke is characterized by the crawling motion of the arms.

1. The *arm cycle* is similar to that described in the beginner stroke, except that the arm recovery is above the water. The hand enters the water in front of the head, extending straight up from the shoulder and entering with the thumb and forefinger side first (30-40 degrees pitch). Upon entry the arm should be extended fully forward and slightly downward. The catch of the stroke begins with the fingers pointing downward toward the bottom as the wrist and elbow begin to flex. Keeping the elbow above the hand the swimmer begins to pull the body forward across the hand. The palm of the hand should face the wall the swimmer came from, the hand should move down the centerline of the body, and the elbow should bend to approximately 90 degrees to provide maximum leverage. The push phase is the final underwater stage and is accomplished by extending the elbow and pressing the hand to the thigh.
2. The *recovery* begins with the hand turning to the little finger side, by the thigh, and slipping out of the water. The elbow is lifted to a 90-degree angle at the elbow joint above the water, and the finger tips are carried close to the water surface to the entry point. ARMSTROKE CUES: Slice, Down the Hill, Up the Hill, Push to Thigh, High Elbow, Slice.
3. The *freestyle kick* is identical to the front kick in the beginner section with a six-beat rhythmical pattern to stroke cycle.
4. Breathing is accomplished to either side with the head beginning the turn during the push phase of the armstroke to that side. The breath should not be held during any part of the stroke cycle.

Elementary Backstroke. The elementary backstroke is a resting stroke that provides the swimmer with an opportunity to relax and breathe continuously.

1. The *arm cycle* is identical to that described in the beginner backstroke. The kick now becomes an inverted breaststroke kick instead of a flutter kick.
2. The inverted *breaststroke kick* is learned by sitting on the edge of the pool with legs together and extended over the water. Drop the heels to the pool wall by bending the knees. Keeping the knees close together (less than 6 inches) curl ankles away from each other and toes toward surface of the water. The propulsive phase is accomplished by straightening the legs and pushing water with the insoles of the feet. KICK CUES: Drop, Curl, Together.
3. Overall coordination begins with the thumbs up the side of the body to shoulder level while the heels drop at the knee (Up); the arms reach lateral while the ankles and toes curl up and out

(Out); the pull begins slightly ahead of the extension of the legs; and hands touch thighs as toes come together (Together). CUE: Up, Out, Together, Glide.
Note: Hips, knees, and chest should remain in alignment throughout the entire stroke.

Back Crawl. The back crawl is the second fastest competitive stroke and is characterized by the crawling motion in the supine position.

1. The *armstroke* of the back crawl begins with a straight arm entry of the little finger side of the hand, arms length, above the head (Karate Chop). The fingertips turn toward the bottom and sweep downward. The catch of the water takes place by an upward rotation of the hand and a bend of the elbow. The pull is an elliptical pattern and can be described as arm wrestling the water. The final underwater phase is a push downward and toward the feet. Arms alternate simultaneously.
2. The recovery begins by letting go of the water and bringing the hand out of the water with thumbs up. The arms remains straight during the above water phase, and the shoulder shrugs past the cheek. CUE: Karate Chop, Fingertips Down, Catch, Arm Wrestle, Push, Let Go, Thumb Up, Straight Arm, Shrug, Little Finger.
3. The kick is a six-beat flutter on the back similar to the beginner backstroke.

Breaststroke. The breaststroke can be used as a resting stroke although it is one of the four competitive swimming strokes.

1. The armstroke of the breaststroke differs from the front and back crawl in that the arms do not alternate, and the recovery is underwater. The armstroke begins with the body in the streamlined position. The hands separate and press outward in a sculling motion. The hands rotate as the elbows bend slightly and move to an inward sweep. This phase ends as the hands come together beneath the chin. The hands then move upward and forward to the streamlined position with forearms close together. This movement can be described as drawing a heart on the pool bottom with the finger tips and then cutting the heart in half as the arms recover and extend forward.
2. Breathing takes place during the pull phase of the armstroke and is done simply by lifting the chin to water level. The breath should not be held during any phase of the stroke.
3. The kick is accomplished by taking the inverted breaststroke kick that was learned for the elementary backstroke and turning it over. A slight difference to be noted is the heels should be pulled to the buttocks and the knees should not be pulled toward the abdomen.

4. The coordination of the stroke starts with the streamline, arm pull, breathe, extend arms and recover heels to buttocks simultaneously, kick and glide into the streamlined position. *Hint:* Students may have trouble getting back to the streamlined position and holding it for the glide. Have students grab the thumb on the extension phase of the arms and hold the thumb until their toes touch from the kick, then glide, then separate and angle hands for pull. CUE: Hold Thumb, Pull, Breathe, Grab Thumb, Extend Arms, Kick, Toes Touch, Glide, Pull.

Sidestroke.   The side stroke is the stroke of choice used in lifeguard rescues. The side stroke uniquely allows a rescuer to carry a victim comfortably and efficiently.

1. The arm cycle begins with the body on either side with the top arm (trailing arm) extended over the hip and the bottom arm (leading arm) extended forward. The ear in water (bottom ear) lies on the shoulder of the leading arm, and the water line runs down the cheek with the mouth out of the water. Arms move simultaneously with leading arm sweeping downward and inward (Pull) in line with the body while the trailing arm slices to position under the chin. The hands near each other, and the leading arm begins to slice forward as the trailing hand sweeps downward, backward, and upward (Push) in close proximity to the abdomen and finishing at the thigh.
2. The kick used in the sidestroke is the scissors kick, characterized by the scissor motion. The standard scissors kick begins with top leg resting on the lower with knees straight and toes together and pointed. This is the start and end position. Legs are bent at the knees and drawn in line to the hips with heels toward buttocks.

The top leg and bottom leg separate simultaneously, with top leg forward, bottom leg backward, knees slightly flexed, and toes pointed, to the stride position. Legs can then be straightened to the glide position, producing propulsion with the back of the top leg and the front of the bottom leg.

3. The overall timing begins in the glide position on the side; as the pull takes place the heels are drawn up, as the hands meet the legs separate to stride, then the push and kick occur together, and the stroke finishes with a glide. CUE: Pull and Draw, Push and Kick, Glide.

Diving

Diving from the pool deck, dock, springboard, or platform can be exciting and exhilarating. Unfortunately, diving can also be dangerous if not taught and executed properly. It is estimated that 95 percent of all the diving injuries each year occur to the untrained diver and in less than 5 feet of water. This fact should make students and instructors follow proper progressions and make sure of the proper water depth in diving. The recommended depth for teaching diving from deck level is 9 feet or greater. The recommended depth for teaching from a 1 meter springboard is 12 feet or greater with the board extending 6 feet over the water and a landing area of the 12-foot depth extending forward 20 feet from the end of the board.

The following dives should be taught in sequence to ensure diving safety among participants. Dives must be taught in appropriate depth water.

1. Slide-in Dive (9 feet deep).   This is the most basic of all dives. The instructor has the student lie face down on a smooth resolite mat (preferred) or on the side of the deck with arms extended overhead and body slightly arched (Figure 21-6). The instruc-

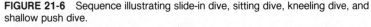

FIGURE 21-6 Sequence illustrating slide-in dive, sitting dive, kneeling dive, and shallow push dive.

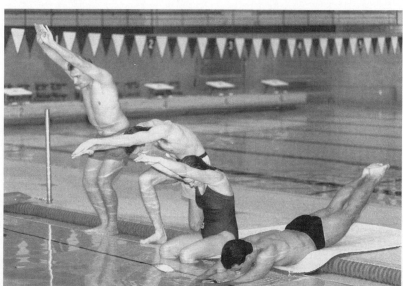

tor then holds the student's ankles, lifts the legs and slides the student into the water. The student holds the body rigid and adjusts angle of entry by raising or lowering the arms and hands. If the student points the fingertips to the bottom, a deep dive will result; if the student raises fingertips and points to the other side of the pool, a shallow/distance dive will result.

2. Sitting Dive (9 feet deep). The sitting dive is the next in the sequence shown in Figure 21-6. Head position and arm position are essential. The early learning phase should consist of the chin being on the chest, arms over ears and should remain in this position throughout the dive. This position will minimize the probability of smacking the chest and abdominal area. As the student becomes more accomplished, he or she will be able to adjust head and arm position to achieve desired depth or distance of dive. The instructor may assist from in water by holding the student's fingertips and leading them down into the water.

3. Kneeling Dive (9 feet deep). The student positions on one knee with toes of opposite foot over the pool edge (Figure 21-6). Arms are extended overhead in the streamlined position, and the chin is placed on the chest. Initially the student simply pivots over the knee and enters the water. As skill and readiness increase, the student can push with the foot of the non-kneeling leg. Instructor can assist in the same manner as the sitting dive.

4. Scale Dive or Tip in (9 feet deep). The scale dive begins from the standing position with arms placed overhead and in the streamline position. The diver then performs a gymnastic type scale and balances with one leg vertical and one leg horizontal. The instructor may assist the student by lifting the horizontal leg. The student pivots around the foot of the vertical leg and while keeping knees straight, brings legs together with toes pointed as he or she enters the water fingertips first. Emphasis should be placed on keeping the chin on chest and keeping the vertical pivot leg straight.

5. Shallow Push Dive (9 feet deep). The shallow push dive starts with hands together in front of the body at waist level. The toes of both feet are over pool edge and knees are bent (Figure 21-6). The student begins the dive motion by extending the arms over the water surface, extending legs straight and pushing with the ankles. Emphasis should be placed on getting heels higher than the head to achieve a fingertip head first entry.

6. Deep Push Dive (9 feet deep). The deep push dive is used for reaching the bottom of the pool rapidly. As in all dives emphasis should be placed on keeping the arms overhead entering the water to prevent the head from striking the bottom or another object in the water. Additionally, the diver

should always check the areas for swimmers or other obstacles before diving.

The diver begins in a more vertical position than in the previous dive. Arms are overhead in the streamline position, knees and hips are flexed, and toes are over the edge of the pool. The emphasis is on springing or jumping the hips up as the head and arms move downward toward the water. Once the diver is in the air, he or she must extend the body into a straight position to enter the water vertically and be projected to the pool bottom. It is helpful if the diver maintains a very slight pike at the hips upon entry so that the legs are not flopped over and the back arched.

7. Forward Standing Dive from the One-Meter Spring Board (12 feet deep). This dive is performed in a similar manner as the deep push dive from the deck. The only notable difference is instead of jumping forcefully, the diver should utilize the spring of the board by extending the legs and riding the board to achieve maximum height. Body position upon entry should be stretched and rigid as shown in (Figure 21-7).

8. Standing Back Dive from the One-Meter Spring Board (12 feet deep). The back dive may cause some anxiety among students and instructors. But if proper safety precautions and instructional techniques are followed carefully, attempts will be more successful and less subject to trial and error or injury. The diving board must extend 6 feet over the water, and the depth from the end of the board back to the wall must be at least 12 feet, the distance of the diver's underwater path. Backward and inward dives should not be attempted from the pool side or from backyard pool diving boards because the diver may hit the pool wall.

The diver needs to understand that he will pivot around the tip of the board at his heels and that it is essential to keep straight legs. Also, the diver must realize that the body will follow the head and that the head must stay back with eyes looking for the water. The diver then places the arms above the head, arches the lower back slightly, looks up at the hands, and falls head and shoulders first while keeping legs straight.

The instructor assists the diver by placing student in proper body alignment. The instructor then places one knee against one of the student's knees to keep him from bending the leg, and assists him in clearing the board. To maintain balance the instructor must stand in the stride position. The instructor's hands are placed on the student's sides level with the small of the back. The student is cued with Fall, and the instructor manages rate of fall by extending the arms. The instructor then moves hand positions to spot the diver by going to the back of the calf and adjusting the diver for a vertical entry (Figure 21-8).

FIGURE 21-7   Standing dive from 1-meter board; water depth, 12 feet.

FIGURE 21-8 Standing back dive with instructor spotting from 1-meter board; water depth, 12 feet.

WATER EXERCISE

Water exercise is one of the nation's fastest growing fitness activities. There are many advantages to this exercise venue. It is only in water that three-dimensional resistance to movement is possible. This provides improved muscle tone and joint stability. Water also provides smooth resistance that is accommodating over the full range of motion. The participant in water exercise is buoyed up by the water which provides protection from injuries often associated with land exercise. This factor allows almost complete elimination of injurious ballistic stress on joints, connective tissues, and muscles. Water training allows the participant to simulate almost any sport movement, and if proper program is adhered to for 20 to 30 minutes, three times a week, there can be an aerobic training effect for the heart and circulatory system. Clearly, therefore, water activity holds great value for rehabilitation, and in fact many individuals who cannot walk, run, or make ballistic movements on land can do so in the water.

Although it is recommended that participants know how to swim, it is not necessary that they have deep water swimming ability, since water exercise can be taught completely in the shallow water. However, if water exercise classes wish to utilize deep water for conditioning, it is recommended that the instructor screen participants for deep water swimming ability.

Equipment

Cassette player, audio cassette, battery microphone, and amplification equipment.

SUGGESTED LEARNING SEQUENCE FOR WATER EXERCISE

A. The Instructor
   1. The instructor should teach from the pool deck. This allows students to see the techniques and allows the instructor to see students' performance. Additionally, this enables the instructor to access any audio-visual equipment which may be in use.
   2. The instructor's demonstration on deck must be slowed to allow the students who are in the water to keep pace with the instructor.
   3. Select music with lyrics appropriate for the students' age group.
   4. Music tempo should correspond to the students' ability to keep pace and to the desired physiological response, i.e., warm-up, aerobic, etc.
B. The Participant
   1. Appropriate swimwear should be worn (bathing suits). Cut-offs, gym shorts, and T-shirts should not be allowed.
   2. Participants may wish to wear aqua sock type footwear to support the arches and protect the balls of the feet.
   3. Participants should take a soap shower and discard any chewing gum, candy, etc., before entering pool.
C. Teaching Techniques
   1. Water should be approximately chest level for most exercises (3½ to 5 feet deep).
   2. Some participants may prefer to remain in the shallower water and squat down to chest level, this will increase their stability. Others may wish to reduce stability by standing in deeper water. Each participant should find a comfortable depth in which to achieve maximum desired results.
   3. When exercising, the body weight should move in the same direction as the motion of desired area being exercised; i.e., if arms are moving forward, body weight should be moving forward.
   4. Leg position is the key to stability. Depending on the exercise goal, the feet should position either shoulder width apart (straddle) or one foot in front, one foot in back (stride).
D. Exercises

Table 21-1 lists a number of common exercises that can be done in the water to work out muscle groups affected by each. Many other variations are of course possible. Water exercises are limited only by one's imagination and creativity. Instructors can readily select or design exercises to meet specific needs.

SAFETY CONSIDERATIONS

All swimming activities require a lifeguard on duty.

A. For Progressive Swimming Levels
   1. Encouraged behavior:
      Soap shower
      Proper swimwear
      Care for others' safety
      Cooperation with lifeguards
   2. Discouraged behavior:
      Diving from starting blocks
      Diving from poolside into less than 9 feet of water
      Running, pushing, or other unsafe acts
      Swimming in spring board diving area
      Food, gum, or drinks in pool area
B. For Spring Board Diving
   1. Divers must pass deep-water swim test.
   2. Check area in front of diving board.
   3. One person on diving board at a time.
   4. No excessive bouncing.
   5. Exit diving area promptly to nearest ladder.
   6. Difficult dives must be supervised.

TABLE 21-1 Water Exercises for Various Muscles

Name	Muscle Group	Body Position	Foot Position
UPPER BODY			
Push / pull	Chest / back / arms	Standing / wall	Straddle
Push-down / pull-ups	Shoulders / upper arm	Squat	Straddle
Lateral pull / press	Shoulders / upper chest & back	Squat	Straddle
Horizontal flys	Shoulders / upper chest & back	Standing	Stride
Front raise / press back	Shoulders / upper chest & back	Standing	Stride
Water punches	Upper arms	Squat	Stride
Arm circles	Shoulders / trunk	Squat	Straddle
Arm rowing	Upper back / trunk	Squat	Stride
Single arm circle	Shoulders	Standing / wall	Straddle
TRUNK			
Trunk rock	Abdomen / lower back	Standing	Straddle
Waist circles	Abdomen / lower back	Standing	Stride
Grapevine / cross kick	Abdomen / lower back	Standing / wall	Straddle
LEGS			
Walking / running	Buttocks	Standing / wall	Stride
Alt. leg kick-straight	Buttocks / thigh	Standing / wall	Stride
Alt. leg kick-bent	Buttocks / thigh	Standing / wall	Stride
Lat. leg kick-straight	Inner / outer thigh	Standing / wall	Straddle
Lat. leg kick-bent	Inner /outer thigh	Standing / wall	Straddle
Squat-tuck jumps	Abdomen / thigh	Squat	Straddle
Knee lifts	Abdomen / thigh	Squat / wall	Straddle
Roundhouse hor. kicks	Buttocks / abdomen / lower back	Standing / wall	Straddle
Leg circles front / back	Buttocks / thigh	Standing / wall	Straddle
Hamstring / quad. curls	Thigh	Standing / wall	Straddle
Shuffle / run	Abdomen / thigh	Standing	Stride

7. Reserve 3-meter diving boards for competitive use only.

C. For Water Exercise
   1. Permanently attach the pool safety life line which separates the shallow and deep water sections.
   2. Before embarking on any physical fitness program, participants should consult a physician.
   3. Minimal instructor certification includes: WSI, First Aid, and Cardiopulmonary Resuscitation Certification.
   4. Instructor must understand physiological concepts of conditioning as they pertain to the aquatic environment which differs considerably from land aerobic activity.

Failure to comply with the above stated safety considerations may result in serious or fatal injury!

MODIFICATIONS FOR SPECIAL POPULATIONS

Orthopedically Impaired

1. Use flotation devices, e.g., inner tubes, to play water games in shallow depths.
2. Use kickboards for stability in vertical positions.

3. Provide assistive stability with peer teachers positioned behind student stabilizing the trunk at the waist.
4. Use hand paddles attached with elastic for striking games.

Mentally Impaired

1. Keep all activities in the shallow end until student has complete understanding of the rules of the game or task.
2. Keep your instructions very short and to the point, avoiding excessive directions.
3. Use peer teachers providing manual assistance until student has complete understanding of the rules of the game or task.

Sensory Impaired

1. Use peer teachers (see #3 in Mentally Impaired).
2. Visually impaired should be allowed additional practice prior to initiating game or task.
3. Use cue cards (symbols) to change directions for the deaf and/or hard of hearing.
4. Use color codes (cue cards) to represent change in sequence and/or directions for the game or task.

SELECTED REFERENCES

American Alliance for Health, Physical Education, Recreation and Dance (1987). *Principles of Safety in Physical Education and Sport.* Reston, VA, 1987.

American Red Cross. *Swimming and Aquatics Safety.* Washington, D.C.: Author, 1981.

American Red Cross. *Lifeguard Training.* Washington, D.C.: Author, 1983.

Gabrielsen, M.A. *Swimming Pools, A Guide to Their Planning, Design, and Operation.* Human Kinetics, Champaign, IL, 1987.

Johnson, R.L. *YMCA Pool Operation on Location, YMCA of the USA.* Chicago, IL, 1990.

Maglischo, E.W. *Swimming Faster: A Comprehensive Guide to the Science of Swimming.* Chico, CA: Mayfield Publishing, 1982.

Torney, J. and Clayton, R. *Aquatic Organization and Management.* Minneapolis, MN: Burgess, 1982.

United States Diving. *U.S. Diving Safety Manual.* Indianapolis, IN, 1990.

22 TEAM HANDBALL

THIS CHAPTER WILL ENABLE YOU TO:

▶ *Identify and demonstrate the basic skills associated with team handball.*
▶ *Develop at least one practice formation for each of the basic skills: pass, catch, throw, and dribble.*
▶ *Understand and demonstrate simple rules and regulations.*
▶ *Understand and demonstrate free throw, penalty throw, corner throw, throw-in, and throw-off.*
▶ *Identify and name the positions of players.*

NATURE AND PURPOSE

Team handball may be played indoors or outdoors by children or adults of both sexes. Team handball employs fundamental motor skills such as running, throwing, catching, jumping, and defensive and offensive strategies similar to the motor skills used in basketball, soccer, and hockey.

The object of the game is to pass and/or dribble the ball toward the opponent's goal and then shoot the ball into the goal. The ball is played primarily with the hands; however, any portion of the body above the knee can be used to play the ball.

COURT, EQUIPMENT, PLAYERS

The Playing Area

1. The playing area (indoors or outdoors) should be a rectangular surface with dimensions of 126 to 147 feet in length, and 60 to 73 feet in width (Figure 22-1). For a physical education class, a basketball court can easily be adapted to an indoor playing court by taping the goal-area line and the free-throw line.
2. The goal area is a semicircular space marked off by the goal-area line which is drawn in front of the goal at a distance of 20 feet, with a radius of 20 feet from the back inside edges of the goal posts.
3. The free-throw line is drawn as a broken line parallel to and 10 feet beyond the goal-area line.
4. The penalty-throw line is 3 feet 3 inches long and is drawn at a distance of 23 feet from the goal.
5. The goal is in the middle of each goal line and measures 6 feet 7 inches in height and 10 feet in width. If possible, a loose net, measuring 2 feet 8

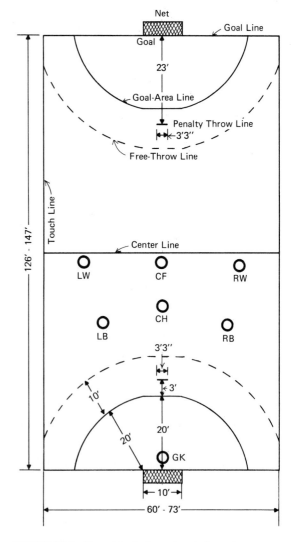

FIGURE 22-1 Team handball court and players' positions.

inches at the top and 3 feet 3 inches at the bottom, should be attached behind the goal post. For a physical education class, two poles, such as volleyball or badminton poles, with a rope tied across them will serve as a goal.

The Ball

A round ball is used that will vary in weight and circumference according to the age and sex of the players. For males over age 15, the ball should weigh from 15 to 19 ounces and be 23 to 24 inches in circumference; for females and boys under age 15, the ball should weigh 11½ to 14 ounces and measure 21 to 22 inches around. For physical education classes, a playground ball or volleyball will serve the purpose of the game. However, basketballs and soccer balls should not be used.

Players

Each team consists of 7 players (6 court players and 1 goalkeeper) with 5 additional players for substitution. The positions of players are designated as goalkeeper, center half, right and left backs, center forward, and right and left wingers (see Figure 22-1).

BASIC RULES

Duration of the Game

1. Playing times for a regulation game will vary depending upon the age and sex of the players: for men—two periods of 30 minutes with an interval of 10 minutes; for women and junior males—two periods of 25 minutes with an interval of 10 minutes; and for all other players—two periods of 20 minutes with a 10-minute interval.
2. The winning team from referee's coin toss has the choice of either the end, defense, or offense.
3. By referee's whistle, the game must start at the center of the court only by passing the ball to another teammate. All players must be within their own half of the court at the beginning.
4. After each goal is scored, the other team will always start the game at the center of the court.
5. A goal cannot be scored directly from the throw-on.

Playing the Ball

1. The ball can be played in any manner with any part of the body except below the knee. (For violation of this rule a free throw is awarded to the opposition.)
2. The ball cannot be held for more than three seconds if the player is not moving. (Otherwise, a free throw is awarded to the opposition.)
3. The ball can be bounced once or repeatedly with either hand while moving or standing—like a dribble in basketball.
4. Once the ball has been seized with one or both hands, it must be played off within three seconds or after three steps have been taken. (Otherwise, free throw is awarded to the opposition.)
5. Any ball that touches a referee and/or goal post is still playable.
6. Players cannot dive for rolling balls that are on the ground.
7. The ball may be continuously rolled on the ground with one hand.
8. When the ball has passed the touch line, the ball can be put into play by the other team as in basketball, and the throw-in should take place from the point where the ball crossed the touch line.
9. If the ball is touched by a defensive player except the goalkeeper, and travels across the goal line outside the goal, a corner throw is awarded to the attacking team.

Approach to Opponent

Players are not permitted to:

1. Block an opponent with arms, hands, or legs. (Free throw is awarded to opposition.)
2. Hold, hit, push, run into, or jump at the opponent, throw oneself down in front of or endanger an opponent in any other way. (Free throw is awarded to opposition.)
3. Throw the ball intentionally at an opponent or execute a dangerous feint by moving the ball toward the opponent. (Free throw is awarded to opposition.)

The Goal Area

1. No player except the goalkeeper may enter the goal area.
2. A player of the defending team, providing the entry is intentional and for the clear purpose of defense, shall have a penalty throw (23 feet) awarded to the attacking team.
3. There shall be no penalty if a player enters the goal area after playing the ball.
4. Inside the goal-area line the ball belongs to the goalkeeper. No other player shall touch a ball that is lying, rolling, or being held by the goalkeeper inside this area.
5. The ball shall neither be thrown into one's own goal area nor to the goalkeeper. (Penalty throw is awarded to the opposition team.)
6. A ball in the air is not considered to be in the goal area.

The Goalkeeper

1. So long as the goalkeeper remains inside the goal area, the goalkeeper is allowed to defend

the goal in every possible way, including kicking the ball with the feet while the ball is moving toward the goal or is inside the goal area.

2. The goalkeeper is allowed to leave the goal area without the ball. When he or she does, the same rules apply to the goalie as to the rest of the team.

3. The goalie may not touch a ball that is lying or rolling outside the goal area.

Scoring

1. A goal is made when the ball has passed the goal line inside the goal with its *entire* circumference.
2. A goal made by the defending team is also scored as a goal.
3. After every goal is made, the other team should start the game from the center of the court.

Penalty Throw

1. When the offensive player has lost a clear chance of scoring by the defensive player's foul, the offensive player shall be awarded a penalty throw from the 23-foot line.
2. During a penalty throw no other player except the goalkeeper shall be allowed between the goal area line and the free-throw line.
3. The penalty throw shall be aimed directly at the goal.

Free Throw

1. All violations of the rules, except the penalty throw, shall have a free throw awarded to the opposing team.
2. All free throws are taken from the point where the violation occurred except a violation between the free-throw line and the goal-area line, in which case the free throw shall be taken at the free-throw line.
3. During a free throw, players of the defending team shall stand 10 feet away from the player having the free throw.
4. A goal may be scored directly from a free throw.

SUGGESTED LEARNING SEQUENCE

Team handball is an activity that can be learned very quickly. It may be played at all levels by both sexes and on a coeducational basis. A basic game can be played at an early stage of the physical education class; offensive and defensive formations and styles of play may be added as the level of skill increases. It is important to discuss terminology, rules, skills, and strategies at a time when most appropriate and meaningful to the discussion of a particular concept.

A. Purpose of the Game
B. Skills and Techniques. The skills of passing, shooting, and dribbling are best taught in combination with each other.
   1. Passes for short distances
      a. Bounce
      b. Close Hand-Off
      c. Hook
      d. Chest
      e. Shovel
      f. Overhead
   2. Passes for medium distances
      a. Ground
      b. Jump
      c. Shoulder (baseball)
      d. Side Arm
   3. Catching
   4. Dribble
   5. Shooting
      a. Jump Shot
      b. Dive Shot
      c. Underhand Shot
      d. Reverse Shot
      e. Side Throw
      f. Lob Shot
      g. Penalty Throw
   6. Goalkeeping. Goalkeeping should be started early in the sequence. A few minutes practice each day will add to the quality of the game.
C. Playing Strategies
   1. Offensive
   2. Defensive
D. Rules. Discuss the rule when most applicable to a given situation or skill.
E. Terminology. Terms should be discussed as they arise in the normal progression.

It is recommended that scrimmage time be included in early lessons. The length of scrimmage time will increase as the unit progresses.

SKILLS AND TECHNIQUES

The basic skills to be discussed in this section are passing, catching, dribbling, and shooting.

Passing

Passing is the most important element of team handball. It allows a player to move the ball quickly and accurately so as to advance the ball and set up scoring opportunities. Team handball passing fundamentals are quite similar to those utilized in basketball.

▶ **Learning Cues**

1. The speed of the receiver as well as the distance between the receiver and the passer will deter-

mine how hard the ball should be thrown and the type of pass to be used.

2. For practice purposes the non-throwing arm should be pointed in the direction of the throw. (In actual game situations, more deception must be used so that the individual does not "telegraph" his pass.)
3. Use finger-tip control to ensure a more consistently accurate pass.
4. Maintain proper balance and distribution of body weight to ensure a more accurate pass. Shift your weight from the back to front foot, maintaining momentum behind the ball for a crisp pass. (Don't throw a pass when you are off balance except in improvised or emergency situations.)
5. Step forward with the leg opposite to throwing arm.
6. Snap your wrist upon release.
7. Select a pass which is appropriate for a specific situation.
8. After you pass always be ready to penetrate the defense and await a return pass.
9. A properly thrown pass will usually enable your teammates to catch the ball more easily.
10. A generalized rule to keep in mind when passing the ball is always to make a threatening motion (feint) to score before passing to a teammate.

Passes can be divided into three categories characterizing the distance, trajectory, and type (arm form) of the throw.

Short Distance Passes. Passes which are normally used in short distances include:

1. *Bounce*—The ball should be thrown so that it bounces approximately three feet in front of the receiver. The receiver should move toward the ball and try to catch it on the short hop (as in baseball) in such a manner that he is immediately prepared to throw the ball.
2. *Close Hand-Off (front and back)*—In this pass (which usually occurs in close quarters around the goal area) the player merely hands the ball to a teammate in a manner similar to an "end-around" (reverse) play in football. Deception is of utmost importance in this pass. It should be used only after considerable practice and by players who are very familiar with each other since the chance for error is much greater than most other passes.
3. *Hook*—This pass is very useful when a player is closely guarded by two or more players. It can also be used when a player is in the air for a jump shot. The player simply releases the ball at the top of his or her jump to a teammate who might be penetrating toward the goal. This pass is the same as the "hook shot" in basketball.
4. *Chest (push)*—This pass should be one of the most frequently used in short distances. It is one

of the most accurate passes and relatively simple to learn. The same fundamentals can be applied as the two-hand chest pass.

5. *Shovel (scoop)*—This pass is less frequently used than those passes described thus far. The player picks a low ball upon the short hop and remains in a crouched position while quickly tossing the ball (underhand) to a teammate.
6. *Overhead (two hands)*—One of the methods of putting the ball back into play after it has crossed one of the side lines. The throw is taken by a player of the team which did not cause the ball to go out. The player making the throw must have both feet touching the surface outside the sideline and throw in to the playing area with one or two hands in any manner.

Medium Distance Passes. Passes which are normally used in medium distances include:

1. *Ground ("roller")*—When all other passing lanes are blocked it may, on occasion, be appropriate to roll the ball between a defender's legs. Also, when there is a "scramble" for a loose ball on the court and a player can't control the ball completely, he or she can roll it to a nearby teammate.
2. *Jump*—When normal passing lanes are impeded, a player can use this pass by jumping into the air and releasing the ball in a manner similar to the shoulder throw.
3. *Shoulder (baseball)*—When throwing, the player should not attempt to grip the ball as if it were a baseball. Rather, allow the ball to rest in the hand with a flexed wrist and fingers spread wide enough to cover as much of the ball surface as is comfortably possible.
4. *Side Arm*—This pass is the same as the shoulder pass except the positioning and action of the throwing arm may be likened to a three-quarters and/or "submarine" pitching motion as in baseball. The length of stride for the lead leg should correspond (approximately) to the length of the pass. For a right-handed throw the right foot can remain in place (with weight back), and the left foot can stride forward simultaneously with the arm-throwing motion.

Catching

An accurate throw will result in an accurate catch.

▶ **Learning Cues**

1. Whenever possible, players are to catch the ball with two hands to ensure best control.
2. The player should always attempt to catch the ball with his finger tips spread. Whenever possi-

ble the ball should not be allowed to make contact with the palms.

3. The elbows should be flexed and the body relaxed to absorb the impact of a hand-thrown ball.

4. Whenever possible the player should move forward to meet the ball, maintaining eye contact with the ball as it comes into the hands.

5. Upon receiving a pass, a player should be immediately prepared to shoot, dribble, or pass the ball again.

Dribble

In team handball the dribble is used to advance the ball up the court when a player is not closely guarded and to gain "rhythm" when attempting to move the ball for purposes of attacking the goal or setting up a possible scoring play. Because of their strong basketball orientation, most Americans have a tendency to dribble too much in team handball.

The dribble is similar to that used in basketball except that the player may take three steps when the ball is seized by either one or both hands. When the ball is seized, it must be played off within three steps or three seconds.

Shooting

The primary objective of attacking the goal in team handball is to score. Shooting will not occur in team handball as frequently as in basketball. Players must learn to be patient and work for a good opportunity to score a goal. This does not mean that players should be overcautious, as team handball is an aggressive game in which the offense must continuously attack the goal and generate its own scoring opportunities.

▶ **Learning Cues:** Basic Shooting Principles

1. The shooter must have a definite throwing direction in mind prior to releasing the ball. Shots blocked and easily caught by the goalie often result in fast-break 2-on-1 situations for the opposing team. The most vulnerable shooting lanes are the high and low corners of the goal mouth. It is generally agreed that shots directed to the lower corners of the goal have greater scoring percentages.

2. The momentum of the shooter should always be toward or perpendicular to the goal.

3. The use of deception is of utmost importance. The shooter should attempt to draw the goalkeeper toward one corner of the goal and depending upon the commitment of the goalkeeper, the player should aim his shot for the opposite corner.

4. The shoulder pass is the most frequently used in team handball shooting.

a. The ball is held behind the head with the arm cocked to hide the ball from the goalie and make it more difficult for defensive players to take the ball away.

b. The non-shooting arm remains forward to ward off defenders and assist in maintaining balance.

c. The shot should be released with a snap of the wrist and follow-through (as in throwing a football or baseball).

5. Many foot movement patterns can be utilized in team handball shots, including hop steps, crossover steps, and running steps. New players are encouraged to experiment with different step and dribble combinations which fit their individual abilities.

Specific Shots and Their Uses

Jump Shot. This shot simply involves the use of the shoulder throw (pass) in which the ball is released at the height of the jump, with the momentum of the body directed toward the goal rather than falling away. By jumping high in the air the player is able to see the goal more clearly and determine the direction of his shots (Figure 22-2).

Dive Shot. This shot also utilizes the shoulder throw. The shooter stretches his body out and directs his momentum toward the goal. The ball is released

FIGURE 22-2 The jump shot.

at the last possible moment and as close to the goal mouth as possible.

▶ **Learning Cues**

1. The weight is evenly distributed on both feet as the shot is initiated.
2. The body is leaning, moving in a position parallel with the floor.
3. The upper body is thrust upward in a diving action toward the goal.
4. Snap the wrist and release the ball quickly.
5. Break the fall with your chest and both hands positioned at your side about chest level.

Underhand Shot. The side arm or three-quarter pitching motion is used in this shot. The right-handed thrower turns (twists) the left side toward the goal. To generate increased power, a crossover step is used with the push-off coming from the rear foot. This shot is used when upper scoring lanes are cut off by the defense. The shot is on a low trajectory with a continuous follow-through.

Reverse Shot (circle). This shot is used around the goal area when the defender is playing behind and/or overplaying to the shooting side (Figure 22-3). When you are unable to execute a normal shoot, lower your center of gravity (bend knees), fake to the strong (normal shooting) side, turn and quickly pivot away from the strong side on your right foot (if you are right-handed), releasing the ball in a side-arm motion (Figure 22-4). (This is similar to the initial backward motion in the discus throw.) As the ball is released, body momentum should be directed toward the goal.

Side Throw (twister). This is a relatively weak shot, but with the proper element of surprise it can be successful. Most frequently it is used in close to the goal area when an attempted shot with a regular shoulder throw is stopped by a defender. If you are right-handed, drop your left shoulder, step across your body with your right foot, then execute the same arm motion described for the reverse shot with body momentum directed toward the goal.

Lob Shot. This shot is often used in a 1-on-1 fast break situation and also in certain 2-on-1 situations. When the goalie comes out to challenge, the offensive player lobs the ball over his head into the goal, or to his teammate if this is a 2-on-1 situation. Timing is of utmost importance in the execution of this shot.

Penalty Throw. This throw is taken at the 23-foot penalty-throw line. It is a 1-on-1 situation with the goalie as the only defender. The goalie may move about and come within 10 feet of the penalty line. The player who is awarded the penalty throw cannot move his foot or touch the penalty line until the ball is released. The offensive player has three seconds in which to shoot from the time the referee blows the whistle to begin the throw. The type of

FIGURE 22-3   Setting up for the reverse shot: fake to one side.

FIGURE 22-4   Reverse shot, release with side-arm motion.

shot normally utilized in this situation is the shoulder or side throw. The other players must remain outside the free throw line area until the shot is taken. They should strategically position themselves around the goal to be ready for a blocked shot which might possibly rebound out into the area of play.

▶ **Practice Suggestions—Basic Skills**

Drills for team handball basic skills—passing, catching, and dribbling the ball—are similar to those in basketball. Therefore, basketball drills should be utilized to practice the basic skills, particularly passing, catching, and dribbling the ball with the following points in mind:

1. The ball is much smaller than the ball used in basketball. Therefore, the ball can be easily handled by either one or both hands.
2. It is permissible to take a maximum of three steps or three seconds with the ball in either one or both hands. For example, after catching the ball from another player, you may take three steps and start dribbling. When you stop dribbling, you must either pass or shoot after taking no more than three steps or three seconds.

Goalkeeping

The goalkeeper is the most important defensive player in team handball. The goalie should have quick hands and feet, be fearless of the ball, and be able to throw the ball well in initiating fast break plays. The main task of goalkeeping is to stop the ball by any manner possible. The goalie can use any part of the body to deflect shots. Within the goal area there is no restriction on how many steps the goalie may take or the time the ball may be held. Without the ball, the goalie may become a court player at any time; in that case all rules applying to court players apply to the goalie.

▶ **Learning Cues:** Goalkeeping Fundamentals

1. The goalie should know the position of the ball on the court at all times.
2. The goalie should maintain a low center of gravity with weight evenly distributed on the balls of the feet.
3. In blocking shots, the goalkeeper's palms should always face out toward the field of play. The hands should be relaxed enough to "give" with a shot to keep it under control in the area and not allow the ball to rebound back out onto the field of play.
4. Low shots in close to the goalie's legs should be fielded (blocked) in a manner similar to an infielder fielding a ground ball.
5. On shots that are low and to the side, the goalie should stride to the side with hands and outside foot stretching simultaneously to block the ball.
6. Similar to the goalkeeping used in hockey or soccer, the goalie should move out away from the goal mouth in an attempt to cut down the best shooting angles.
7. On high hard shots the goalie should not try to catch the ball, rather he should deflect the ball over the top of the goal.
8. In defending against the penalty shot, the goalie should move out toward the 23-foot penalty line to cut down the shooter's angle.
9. The goalie should always play one foot out from the goal line to avoid a self-scored goal.
10. When the goalie recovers a blocked or missed shot, he returns the ball to play by means of a "throw-out." In this instance, the ball is free and

the defense can try and intercept the pass out and score directly.
11. It is recommended that the goalie wear a protective supporter, long pants, and a long-sleeved shirt to cut down on the "sting" of blocked shots.

PLAYING STRATEGIES

Various defensive and offensive strategies are described below. These can be understood better and developed further with reference to similar team sports such as soccer, basketball, field hockey, and football.

Defensive Formations

When the ball is lost, all players of the team become defensive players with certain defensive responsibilities according to the defensive strategies employed. Generally, defensive strategies are divided into (1) man-to-man defense; (2) zone defense, and (3) a combination of the two. In defensive play, a player should always attempt to keep the opponent in front of him or else the opponent should be slightly overplayed to the shooting arm side. ("Stay between your man and the goal" is a general rule to follow.)

Man-to-Man Defense. Each defensive player must cover one designated player of the attacking team regardless of whether he has the ball or not. The offensive player is continually blocked off and hindered in attacking actions.

Zone Defense. Each defensive player is responsible for protecting a particular area against the attacker. Zone defense may require less running, but it requires more teamwork to be effective.

Combinations

6-0 Defense (Figure 22-5). Six court players stand alongside and in front of the goal-area line, each having the specific responsibility to protect a certain area. The players must coordinate with each other to cover any space that may be left uncovered when a defensive player attempts to attack an opponent with the ball. Taller players should be placed in the center of the defensive zone and shorter players on the outside.

5-1 Defense (Figure 22-6). The 5-1 concept is similar to that of a box and 1 defense used in basketball. Five players stand in front of the goal-area line. One player, pulled out to the free-throw line, has the two assignments of covering the man with the ball and/or covering a good shooter. This player, who frequently originates the fast break, must be an all-round athlete.

4-2 Defense (Figure 22-7). Four defensive players are positioned on the goal-area line and shift

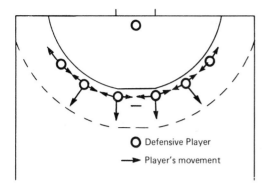

FIGURE 22-5 The 6-0 defensive formation.

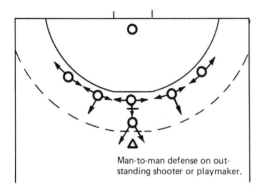

Man-to-man defense on out-standing shooter or playmaker.

FIGURE 22-6 The 5-1 defensive formation.

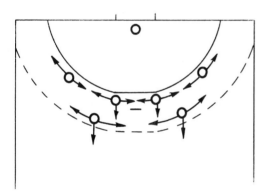

FIGURE 22-7 The 4-2 defensive formation.

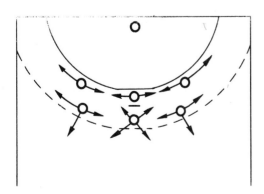

FIGURE 22-8 The 3-3 defensive formation.

as a unit. Two defensive players move out to the free-throw line in order to concentrate on intercepting passes and harassing the ball handlers to prevent their taking the most advantageous routes toward the goal area. These two players not only have to protect the central axis, but also are responsible for filling in gaps between defensive players behind them.

3-3 Defense (Figure 22-8). Three defensive players stand on the middle of the goal-area line, and the other three players stand in front of the free-throw line. These three players as a unit have to shift toward the attacking point of the offensive team to protect against long-distance shootings. This formation is vulnerable against the team having shots from angles, and requires a capable goal-keeper.

Offensive Formations

In the deployment of any offensive alignment, every effort should be made to utilize the entire of-fensive floor area. Fast continuous movement must be maintained at all times. Upon receiving a pass, every player should make a motion of threatening to score whenever in scoring range. In order to spread out the defense as much as possible, it is important that players maintain good spacing and that most plays be initiated from approximately 40 feet. Drib-bling should be avoided if possible and the ball should be passed quickly between players. Effective screening (similar to that used in basketball) is a key to the success of most offensive patterns. Screens and double screens can be improvised from any of the offensive formations presented. The following represent some common offensive formations.

2-4 Offense. This is the most frequently uti-lized offensive formation in team handball. In this formation, the two backcourt players are situated at around 40 feet. The wing players are spread out wide for the best possible shooting angles. The circle run-ners are strategically positioned between the two wing players at 20 feet. A variety of offensive maneu-vers can be initiated from this basic offensive pat-tern. This offense will spread out most zone defenses and allow opportunities for scoring between the de-fensive players.

3-3 Offense. This offense is also effective in spreading out the coverage of a zone defense. If a team possesses three strong shooters, this is an ex-cellent offensive formation to employ. Constant movement of the ball is essential, and each player must threaten to score each time he receives a pass.

1-5 Offense. This offensive formation can best be employed by a team which has some strong inside players who are very physical. Effective inside screening is the key to a successful 1-5 offense. It is of utmost importance that one player always stays back to guard against a possible fast break.

1-3-2 Offense. One back court player is situated around 40 feet as a playmaker; three players are placed around the middle of the free-throw line; and two players become outside and circle runners between the free-throw line and the goal-area line.

The back court player passes the ball to make a play. The three middle players attempt to block defensive players by whatever means to create an opportunity for the two circle runners to make effective shooting chances. The two circle runners must constantly move and feint to confuse defensive players and at the same time make a good shot into the goal.

MODIFICATIONS FOR SPECIAL POPULATIONS

Orthopedically Impaired

1. Contact the United States Cerebral Palsy Athletic Association in Westland, Michigan for the rule book on Wheelchair Team Handball.
2. Set up a stationary game for those students with severe mobility problems.
3. Use a balloon or beachball instead of a handball for those students unable to catch and throw.
4. Place able-bodied students on scooters.

Mentally Impaired

1. Create smaller groups to avoid confusion.
2. Allow students to move the ball up the field in any possible manner; e.g., with one or two bounces.
3. In early sessions, emphasize offensive and defensive transitions rather than playing skills.

Sensory Impaired

1. Blind players may be tethered with sighted partners.
2. Do not allow defensive players within 10 feet of offensive partners; this will help promote more movement.
3. Designate blind or visually impaired students as attackers in stationary positions. They must attempt a shot on goal once every two trips down the field by their team.
4. Minimal modifications are needed for the deaf or hearing impaired.

TERMINOLOGY

Corner throw   When the ball is played over his own goal line by a defending player (except the goalkeeper) on either side of the goal, the game is restarted by means of a throw from the corner of the court by one of the attacking players. The player must place one foot on the corner and throw the ball in, using either hand.

Court player   Member of the handball team actually playing on the court, except the goalie.

Dive shot   A means of trying to score a goal by launching the entire body into the air toward the goal in an attempt to gain more distance.

Free throw   A throw awarded to the opposing team when the other team is in violation of certain rules of the game.

Free-throw line   The broken line parallel to the goal-area line at an extra distance of 10 feet; from this line, free throws awarded near the goal area are taken.

Goal   A goal is considered scored when the ball has passed wholly over the goal line between the uprights and underneath the crossbar of the goal.

Goal area   The area of the playing court inside and including the goal-area line.

Goal-area line   The semicircular line drawn in front of and on either side of the goal.

Goalkeeper (goalie)   The player who is allowed to play freely inside the goal area to defend the goal.

Goal line   The line forming the end of the court which runs between the uprights of the goal and meets the sidelines at the corners of the court.

Penalty throw   A shot attempted by any offensive player when an offensive player is prevented from making a clear goal-scoring chance by foul means. The player attempting the penalty throw is required to make a direct attempt to score a goal from the penalty-throw line.

Referee's throw   A ball bounced by the referee to restart the game after an interruption of play caused by players of both teams committing simultaneous infractions of the rules or if the game has been interrupted for some other reason.

Throw-in   The method of putting the ball back into play after it has crossed one of the sidelines. The throw is taken by a player of the team which did not cause the ball to go out. The player making the throw must have both feet touching the surface outside the sideline and throw the ball into the playing area with one or two hands in any manner.

Throw-off   The means the goalkeeper takes of throwing the ball onto the court after obtaining possession of the ball in his goal area.

Throw-on   The method of putting the ball in play at the start of the game and after a goal is scored. The throw is made from the center of the court.

Throw-out   Same as a throw-off except that defensive players may place themselves at the goal-area line.

SELECTED REFERENCES

Handbook of the International Handball Federation. Basle, Switzerland, I.H.F., 1960, p. 88.

International Handball Federation. *Information Bulletin.* Basle, Switzerland: International Handball Federation, Nos. 16 and 95, 1972.

Korsgaard, R., and Park, S.J. "Codified Rules of Team Handball." Ball State University, Muncie, IN, 1970.

Neil, G.I. *Modern Team Handball: Beginner to Expert.* Montreal, Canada: McGill University, 1976.

Official U.S. Team Handball Rules. Jayfro Corp., P.O. Box 400, Waterford, CT 06385.

United States Team Handball Federation (USTHF), 10 Nottingham Road, Short Hills, NJ 07078.

United States Team Handball Federation Business Office, 1750 E. Boulder, Colorado Springs, CO 80909.

23 TENNIS

THIS CHAPTER WILL ENABLE YOU TO:

▶ *Select tennis equipment that will be appropriate for you.*
▶ *Demonstrate the proper grips and techniques for the following strokes: serve, return of serve, approach shot, forehand, backhand, volley, lob, overhead.*
▶ *Understand the scoring procedures and the basic rules of play.*
▶ *Identify the playing courtesies, safety considerations, and basic terminology associated with tennis.*

NATURE AND PURPOSE

Tennis has always appealed to both sexes, young and old. Many consider it to be one of the best forms of corecreational sports. The pace can be adjusted to the players' abilities ranging from a mild form of exercise, to a strenuous test of strength and endurance. Speed, agility, coordination, and endurance can be developed, and indeed are needed, to play even a recreational game of tennis.

The game of tennis can be played either as singles or doubles. The singles game has two participants, one individual opposing the other. The doubles game has four participants, two individuals teaming up to compete against another team of two. The doubles court is 9 feet wider than the singles court, having a 4½ foot alley on each side of the singles court (Figure 23-1).

The basic rules are the same for men's and women's tennis. To start the game, the server stands just behind the baseline to the *right* of his or her center service line, and puts the ball into play by striking it in the air in such a manner that it lands in opponent's right service court. The server has two chances to put the ball into play. The ball that does not land in the proper service court is called a "fault" and is not played. A served ball that touches the net during flight and lands in the proper service court is called a "let"; a let is not counted as a fault nor is it played, but is served again.

The receiver must return the serve to the server's court on its first bounce. The rally continues until one of the players fails to return the ball, either on the fly or after the first bounce within the boundaries of his court.

When the point has been completed, the server stands just behind his baseline and to the *left* of the center service line and serves to his opponent's left service court, continuing to alternate left and right after each point until the game is completed. Upon completion of the game, the server becomes the receiver. Players change sides at the completion of each odd-numbered game.

In doubles, each player serves a game in turn—first a member of one team, then a member of the other team, and so on. The same order of serving is kept throughout the set.

Scoring

Points in tennis are called Love, 15, 30, 40, Deuce, Advantage, and Game.

0, or nothing, is called Love.

First point won by a player is called 15.

Second point won by a player is called 30.

Third point won by a player is called 40.

Fourth point won by a player gives him Game, provided his opponent does not have more than 30 (2 points).

If each player has won three points (40-all), the score is Deuce. The next point won by a player gives him Advantage. However, if he loses the next point, the score is again deuce. When either player wins two *consecutive* points following the score of deuce, the game is won by that player. The server's score is always given first. The score should be called loudly and clearly after every point.

In scoring, the player who first wins six games wins a *set*, unless both players have won five games; then it takes an advantage of two games to win, so the score could be 7–5, or 8–6, or 9–7, and so on.

In scoring the *match*, the player first winning two sets is generally declared the winner. In professional tennis matches, the winner of three sets is declared the winner of the men's match, while in the women's game the winner of two sets is declared the winner of the match. For example, match scores could be 6–0, 6–3, 6–2; 9–7, 4–6, 10–8; 2–6, 6–4, 6–4;

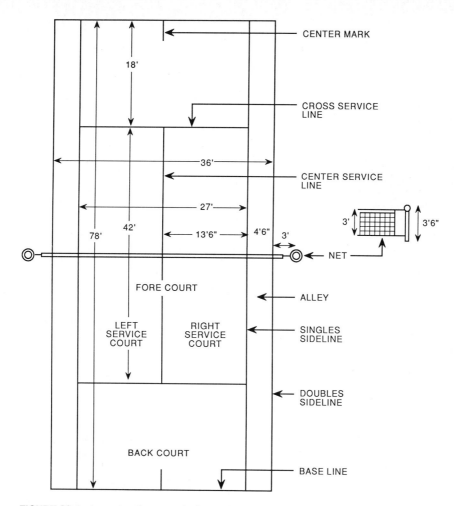

FIGURE 23-1 Lawn tennis court, singles and doubles.

6–1, 6–1, 6–3; 4–6, 6–4, 6–4, 6–4; 6–0, 5–7, 7–5, 2–6, 8–6.

The VASSS scoring system (Van Alen Simplified Scoring System) is used today in most tournaments. There are two major aspects to this system. The first, and most popular, is the "nine-point sudden death tie-breaker," which takes effect when the game score is tied at 6 games all. At such times, the best 5 of 9 points are played to determine the winner of the set. The serving order continues, but now each player serves two points at a time until one player wins five points. Players change sides of the court after the fourth point. If the score becomes tied at four points all, the receiver dictates into which service court the ninth point is served. The second aspect of VASSS is termed the "no-add" rule: when the game score is tied at deuce (3–3) the next point wins the game. Again, the receiver dictates into which service court the no-add point should be played.

SELECTION OF EQUIPMENT

The selection of proper equipment is of utmost importance to the beginning tennis player as well as to the professional player. With good equipment the beginning player can eliminate many handicaps, and thereby get more enjoyment from mastering the fundamental skills.

Tennis Rackets

In selecting the racket, give consideration to the weight, balance, grip size, stringing, and quality of the frame (Figure 23-2). Rackets are manufactured in three different weights: light, medium, and heavy; they range from about 11 to 15 ounces. Women tend to prefer light rackets while men usually select medium or heavy racket frames. The "feel" of the racket as you swing it should be the most important consideration in choosing a new racket. When shopping you should make this comparison test and also take into account differences in materials and manufacture.

Most rackets are 27 inches long and measure 9 inches across the racket face. Currently, tennis rackets are being manufactured in different lengths, with oversized racket heads, and using various combinations of wood, aluminum alloy, steel, magnesium, fiberglass, and graphite. Choose a racket of good quality, with a frame sturdy enough to withstand at least four or five restringings. Cheap

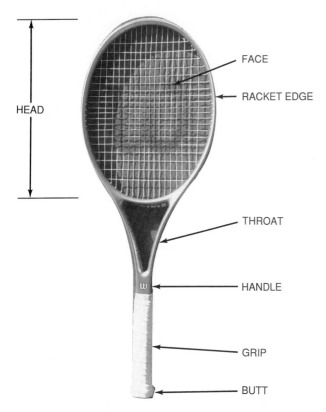

HEAD

FACE

RACKET EDGE

THROAT

HANDLE

GRIP

BUTT

FIGURE 23-2   Parts of a tennis racket.

rackets soon lose their shape and are usually not a good long-term investment.

Basically, there are two types of strings: gut and nylon. Gut strings are more expensive but also more resilient and pliable. This type is preferred by most tournament players. Gut requires more care than nylon and is vulnerable to humidity and wetness. Nylon strings do not have the elasticity of gut, but still are very comparable in play. Also nylon strings are more durable, impervious to dampness, and less expensive. Nylon is very adequate for the beginning player.

When you are purchasing a racket, the retailer will usually want to know your preference for string tension. The greater the tension (or tightness), the less control the player tends to have. Also, the racket frame cannot withstand as many restringings when it is strung tightly. The recommended string tension for beginning and intermediate players is between 55 and 57 pounds.

Rackets are manufactured to be evenly balanced, head-heavy, or handle-heavy. Head-heavy rackets are preferred by players inclined to be ground strokers or base line players. Handle-heavy rackets are used by individuals who are predominantly net players. It is suggested that beginners select an evenly-balanced racket to start with.

Another important factor in choosing an appropriate racket is the size of the grip. Grips usually

range in circumference from 4 to 5 inches. The proper grip size depends upon the user's hand size, and selection may require professional assistance. If the individual grips the racket in an Eastern forehand grip (described below), the thumb should come just past the first knuckle of the middle finger. Correctly fitting a grip is of the utmost importance.

Tennis Balls

Most tennis balls are pressure-packed with compressed air and marked with numbers for identification. Manufactured according to United States Tennis Association (USTA) specifications, a ball must weigh two ounces, measure 2½ inches in diameter, and have a wool-felt covering.

Tennis balls are also produced to be court specific. Some are made especially for hard courts (asphalt or cement) by having more felt on the ball's cover. Others are made for soft court play on such surfaces as clay or grass.

OFFICIAL RULES

1. Server and Receiver.   The players shall stand on opposite sides of the net; the player who first delivers the ball shall be called the server, and the other the receiver.

2. Delivery of Service.   The service shall be delivered in the following manner. Immediately before commencing to serve, the server shall stand with both feet at rest behind the baseline, and within the imaginary continuations of the center-mark and sideline. The server shall then toss the ball by hand into the air and before it hits the ground strike it with his racket. The server is not permitted to touch the court inside the baseline until after the racket has made contact with the ball.

3. From Alternate Courts.   In delivering the service, the server shall stand alternately behind the right and left courts, beginning from the right in every game. The ball served shall pass over the net and hit the ground within the service court, which is diagonally opposite.

4. Faults.   The service is a fault if the server commits any breach of rules 2 or 3; if he misses the ball in attempting to strike it; or if the ball served touches a permanent fixture (other than the net) before it hits the ground. However, if he tosses the ball without making an effort to hit it, there is no fault.

5. Ball in Play Until Point Decided.   A ball is in play from the moment at which it is delivered in service. Unless a fault or a let is called, it remains in play until the point is decided.

6. Player Hinders Opponent.   If a player commits any act, either deliberately or involuntarily, which, in the opinion of the umpire, hinders his opponent in making a stroke, the umpire shall in the first case award the point to the opponent, and in the second case order the point to be replayed.

7. Ball Falling on Line. A ball falling on a line is regarded as falling in the court bounded by that line. Good ball.

8. Good Return. It is a good return:
  a. If the ball touches the net, posts, cord or metal cable, strap, or band, provided that it passes over any of them and hits the ground within the court;
  b. If a player's racket passes over the net after he has returned the ball, provided the ball passes the net before being played and is properly returned;
  c. If a player succeeds in returning the ball, served or in play, which strikes a ball lying in the court.

9. When Players Change Sides. The players shall change sides at the end of the first, third, and every subsequent alternate game of each set, and at the end of each set unless the total number of games in such set be even, in which case the change is not made until the end of the first game of the next set.

10. Doubles, Order of Service. Decided at the beginning of each set. The pair who have to serve in the first game of each set shall decide which partner shall do so and the opposing pair shall decide similar for the second game. The partner of the player who served in the first game shall serve in the third; the partner of the player who served in the second game shall serve in the fourth. The order of serving may be changed following the completion of any set.

11. Doubles, Order of Receiving. Decided at the beginning of each set. The pair who have to receive the first game shall decide which partner shall continue to receive the first service in every odd game throughout that set. The opposing pair shall likewise decide which partner shall receive the first service in the second game and that partner shall continue to receive the first service in every even game throughout that set. The order of receiving may be changed following the completion of any set.

A complete staff of officials for a tennis match includes a referee, an umpire, a net-court judge, and at least seven linesmen. However, most dual matches are played with only a referee or, at most, a referee and an umpire.

SUGGESTED LEARNING SEQUENCE

In the beginning stages it is important to stress that the learner acquire the ability to hit the ball consistently across the net. Early drills and skill development should focus on gaining familiarity with the basic stroke mechanics and racquet skills. Students should be introduced to all strokes as quickly as possible; much time will be spent developing consistency in both the stroke and return of the tennis ball.

The following outline includes everything one would need to cover; the sequence might vary from teacher to teacher.

A. Basic Racket Skills
  1. Stance and basic foot movement—side-to-side, forward and backward
  2. Grips—Eastern and Continental
B. Strokes
  1. Forehand and Grip
  2. Backhand and Grip
  3. Service
  4. Return of Service
C. Rules and Etiquette (best to introduce when directly related to skill or strategy being taught)
D. Volley
E. Lob
F. Singles Game—focus on consistently returning the ball into the court
G. Doubles Game—regular and mixed

SKILLS AND TECHNIQUES

The Grip

The importance of a proper grip cannot be stressed enough. There may be adjustments made in a player's swing, but a proper grip will last a player for a lifetime.

Special names have been given to the forehand grips, based upon the position of the palm against the racket handle:

When the palm sits upon the top right side, the grip is called the *Continental* (Figure 23-3). This grip requires a strong wrist and is used by some professionals for both forehand and backhand strokes.

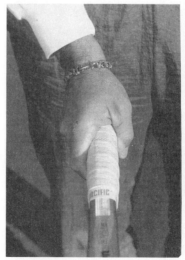

FIGURE 23-3 Continental grip (front and back views).

When the palm sits on the back side of the handle, it is called an *Eastern* grip (Figure 23-4). The palm and the racket face are on the same plane, which gives the sensation of hitting the ball with the palm of your hand. This is the most common grip and the one strongly recommended in this chapter.

When the palm rests on the bottom of the handle, so that the palm points at the sky, it is called a *Western* grip (Figure 23-5). This is the least common grip, although some players use it to great advantage.

Eastern Grip. This being recommended for the forehand, it will be the only grip described in detail. A teacher without an extensive tennis background can't go wrong by suggesting this grip.

If you are right-handed, start by holding the

FIGURE 23-4 Eastern grip (front and back views).

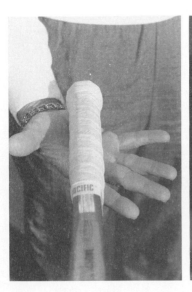

FIGURE 23-5 Western grip (front and back views).

throat of your racket with your left hand so that the racket face is vertical to the ground. Then hold the racket at waist level with the right palm vertical and your fingers pointing slightly downward at approximately a 45-degree angle. The thumb should overlap and lie next to the middle finger, with the index finger spread. Now hold the racket out away from you and look at the top edge of your racket and the top edge of your right palm to see if they are both absolutely vertical. If you play this game correctly you'll rarely hit a shot that requires the racket to vary more than 10 degrees from the vertical position.

Eastern Backhand Grip. The backhand grip advocated in this chapter is the Eastern backhand grip. This is attained by putting the palm on the top of the racket; the knuckle of the index finger rides the top right ridge, and the thumb can be placed either behind the racket or underneath. This grip position provides the most stability and requires the least amount of wrist adjustment in order to provide a vertical racket head at impact.

Strokes

All the strokes are described in terms of a right-handed player's actions. There are some general principles that the player must be aware of:

1. Spin of the Ball. The direction in which the ball spins is determined by the trajectory taken by the racket before and after contact with the ball. If the racket comes from below the ball, is vertical at impact, and finishes above the ball, topspin (low to high) will be attained. If the racket starts above the ball and sweeps down to the ball, underspin (high to low) will be attained.
2. Nearly every successful hit is accomplished with a vertical racket head. A player *does not* come over the ball for topspin or under the ball for underspin!
3. With the exception of the serve and overhead, all strokes in this chapter will be hit with a locked wrist. The swing will come from the shoulder and not the wrist.

The Serve

The serve is the first ball hit in every point. The motion is very similar to that of a baseball pitcher's throwing motion. A good way to start teaching the serve is just to watch the student throw the ball over the net. Have the student pretend the ball is the racket and don't be satisfied until the perfect motion is attained.

Many beginners prefer to use the regular forehand grip to hit a basic "flat" serve, but intermediate and advanced players should use the Continental grip, halfway between the Eastern forehand and Eastern backhand, in order to facilitate greater ball rotation with less stress on the wrist.

FIGURE 23-6   The service sequence.

To attain a good service motion it is necessary to coordinate two movements simultaneously—the ball toss and the action of the racket. The toss is made by holding the ball near the finger tips, with the palm up, and then releasing the ball upwards with all fingers letting go at the same time.

Achieving spin on the ball is an important aspect of serving. There are three kinds of serves recommended:

1. *Flat.* A totally flat serve is a myth because every ball has some amount of spin. This serve has the least amount of spin and is attained by snapping the wrist up and forward through the middle of the ball.
2. *Slice.* Very much like a curveball in baseball. The racket face must move across the backside

of the ball on an almost horizontal plane thus producing sidespin. Using the face of a clock as a reference, the righthander would hit from 9 o'clock to 3 o'clock.
3. *Topspin.* The principle of applying topspin on a serve is basically the same as on a forehand or backhand. Swing from low to high and brush the back side of the ball at about a 45-degree angle. On the imaginary clock hit from 8 o'clock to 2 o'clock.

The Serve Motion.   Figure 23-6 shows the sequence of motions involved in the service (refer to views A–E):

A. Ready Position. It is important to be totally relaxed before attempting to serve. The feet are shoulder width apart, and the front shoulder is pointing in the direction the ball will be served.

B. To start the motion, the player's arms go down together and then start up together. Also begin to lean forward slightly.

C. Position C is crucial. At this point the ball is released and shoulder rotation must begin. The racket is slightly above the shoulder, and the tossing arm is pointing toward the right net post so the toss will be 10 to 12 inches to the player's right. Height of the toss is 18 inches out of outstretched tossing arm. The object of the shoulder rotation is to let the right shoulder replace the position of the left shoulder. Weight at this point is mainly over the front foot with both feet still in contact with the ground.

The racket is forming a loop behind the player's back. The racket *does not* scratch the back but forms a loop. This loop is accomplished by maintaining a loose arm and rotating the shoulders at the proper time. If the racket is hitting or touching the student's back at any time, the motion is out of sync.

D. Point of Contact. At impact the arm should be extended but not necessarily at the peak of one's reach (depending on spin desired). The chin is held upward, and for optimal power both feet should be in contact with the ground though weight should have transferred forward. Notice that contact is made to the right of the player's head and in line with the hitting shoulder.

E. Follow-through. The right shoulder has replaced the position of the left shoulder, and the player's momentum following impact has brought the back foot a step into the court. If the player wishes to serve and volley, this will naturally become the first step toward the net. If not, the participant may step back and rally off of the baseline.

Serve and Volley. The footwork recommended for serve and volley are to step with the right foot, left foot, right foot, and then bring both feet into alignment (Figure 23-7). The closer you can get to the service line the better.

▶ **Learning Cues**

1. No fancy movements. Just relax and take your time.
2. To toss the ball, hold the ball with the finger tips and not the palm.
3. The toss must fit into the motion.
4. Chin up and hit up and out. This is true for all serves.
5. Think positive. Picture in your mind a successful serve before starting the motion.
6. Shoulder rotation and *not* the strength of the arm is the main source of power.
7. Hit the second serve with the same motion as the first—just with more topspin.

▶ **Practice Suggestions**

1. Hit buckets of balls at specific targets to each service court.
2. Before serving, determine the spin to be desired (flat, slice, topspin), and then evaluate your success accordingly.

FIGURE 23-7 Footwork for serve and volley.

FIGURE 23-8 Loop backhand sequence.

Loop Backhand

Figure 23-8 illustrates the sequence of motions involved in executing the loop backhand (refer to views A–F).

A. Ready Position. In a good ready position the player's feet are shoulder length apart and knees slightly bent. Elbows are winged out, and the racket position is at a 45-degree angle to the ground. Note that the player is now holding the racket with an Eastern forehand grip.

B. Backswing. The first move, once determining the ball is coming to the backhand side, is to turn the shoulder and change the grip simultaneously. The grip recommended is the Eastern backhand. The body should be turned enough so that the back of the shoulder is pointing at the oncoming ball.

C. Position viewed from behind. Notice how low the racket is and also that the racket face is slightly tilted downward. The arm is a radius and if the racket is to be vertical at impact and the wrist remain locked throughout the swing, the racket face must be tilted downward at this point. The left hand may be used to help push the racket downward, but this is optional.

D. Three movements happen simultaneously in this photo. The right foot steps into the ball, the racket drops to the bottom of the loop, and the knees bend to a crouch position. The racket must be below the level of the oncoming ball if topspin is to be achieved.

E. Impact with the Ball. The racket face is vertical and the arm is extended well in front of the body (8 to 10 inches in front of the right foot). Eyes are focused right on the point of contact. Knees have lifted upward so as to help lift the ball up (topspin), and the hips have rotated toward the net. Body weight has transferred forward slightly before impact.

F. Follow-through. Following impact let the racket face and knuckles follow the flight of the ball until the arm is fully extended. Freeze at this point and check to make sure that your weight is forward and over your front foot, and also the racket should form an archway. If one were to drop the shoulder straight down, the racket should still form a perfect hitting position.

▶ **Learning Cues**

1. Change grip and pivot body as early as possible.
2. Cradle the throat of the racket with the left hand—don't let the hitting arm take a solo.
3. Concentrate on bending the knees and getting low. The legs are a tremendous source of power.
4. Work hard to swing easy.
5. Reach forward and out away from the body for contact.
6. Keep the wrist locked.
7. Let the knuckles of the hitting hand be the guide for direction. As the knuckles go, so goes the racket head.
8. Reach out and upwards for the follow-through.
9. Always check the follow-through at the completion of a swing.
10. While the body is lifting, the head must remain stationary. Leave head and eyes glued on point of impact.

▶ **Practice Suggestions**

1. Hit backhands toward a specific target area either from a ball machine or from someone feeding from across the net.
2. Hit off of a backboard.

Loop Forehand

Figure 23-9 shows the loop forehand sequence (A–F):

A. Ready Position. The feet are shoulder length apart and knees slightly bent. Elbows are winged

out, and the racket is at a 45-degree angle to the ground. The player is holding the racket with an Eastern forehand grip.

B. Backswing. Turn the shoulders so that the back of the left shoulder is pointing toward the oncoming ball. It is important that this movement happens well before the ball crosses the net. Note that racket head is at eye level. The left hand is held in front of the body for balance and may also be an aid on the follow-through.

C. The backswing as seen from behind. The racket should never go back any farther than as shown.

D. Bottom of the Loop. Three movements happen simultaneously in this photo. The left foot steps forward, the racket and knees drop down together. Notice that the racket face is turned slightly downward. The arm is a radius, and if the wrist is to remain locked and the racket be vertical at impact, then the racket face must be tilted slightly downward at this point.

E. Impact with the Ball. The racket face is vertical, and the player's eyes are focused on the point of contact. Legs are lifting upward and hips are turning forward. Body weight has been transferred forward to the left foot.

F. Follow-through. There are two important points on the follow-through. One, the palm of the hitting hand should be pointing toward the intended target. Two, the hitting arm should be extended until the shoulder and chin touch, as shown in the photo. Also, the legs are totally extended, and all weight is on the left foot.

▶ **Learning Cues**

1. Rotate both shoulders together when turning the body.
2. Keep the wrist firm and let the palm be the guide for direction.
3. Synchronize the movement of the racket and body.
4. Keep the swing short. Don't let the racket get lost behind the body.
5. Power is generated from the leg lift and hip rotation—not just the arm.
6. On completion of the follow-through, the palm should face the intended target and the player's chin and hitting shoulder should touch.
7. Always check the follow-through at the completion of the swing.
8. While the body is lifting, the head must remain stationary. Leave head and eyes glued on point of impact.

▶ **Practice Suggestions**

1. Hit forehands toward a specific target area either from a ball machine or from someone feeding from across the net.
2. Hit off of a backboard.

A   B   C

D   E   F

FIGURE 23-9 Loop forehand sequence.

Lobs

With some practice the lob stroke should resemble the forehand and backhand ground strokes as much as possible. To conceal the lob, remember to turn the front shoulder and have a loop swing identical with the forehand and backhand ground strokes. This also means running to the ball with the racket head up and already back. But instead of turning the racket face down as the racket drops, work on a bevel (slight backward tilt) and lifting the ball high into the air using the opponent's baseline as a target.

Figure 23-10 shows the ready position for the overhead smash. The motion from this point is exactly like that of a flat serve. When teaching, stress keeping the chin up through contact and also reaching up for the ball.

FIGURE 23-10 Ready position for overhand smash.

Backhand Volley

The sequence of motions recommended for backhand volley are illustrated in Figure 23-11.

A. Ready Position. The player is waiting to determine the direction of the ball; he is holding the racket with an Eastern forehand grip.
B. Backswing. The player pivots the body and changes his grip. Actually, there is little or no backswing. The racket should always remain out in front of the body. Notice how the left elbow is held high to keep the racket face on line with the ball.
C. Contact and Follow-through. The key points here are:
   1. The racket head must remain above the wrist.
   2. The ball is contacted well in front of the body —8 to 10 inches.
   3. The arm and racket form a V.
   4. The player's head, racket head, and ball should all be on the same plane. During the follow-through, the racket head should remain above the wrist and ideally the racket face should follow the flight of the ball to gain depth on the volley. The follow-through is very short. From an instructional standpoint, it is good technique to try to have the student freeze the racket right at the point of impact to assure that the wrist isn't breaking.

A   B   C

FIGURE 23-11 Motion recommended for backhand volley.

A	B	C

FIGURE 23-12 Motion recommended for forehand volley.

Forehand Volley

The sequence of motions recommended for forehand volley are shown in Figure 23-12 (A–C).

A. Ready Position. The player assumes a ready position; he is holding the racket with an Eastern forehand grip.
B. Backswing. The player pivots the body striving to get the shoulders sideways to the net. The racket should go back as far as the body turn takes it, yet never be out of the player's peripheral vision. The less backswing the better.
C. Contact and Follow-through. Reaching forward to the ball, impact should take place slightly in front of the left shoulder. The nature of the swing will give the ball natural underspin. Do not break the wrist or chop at the ball. The arm and the racket form a V and the player's head, racket head, and the tennis ball should be at the same height at contact. During the follow-through keep the wrist firm, try to keep the racket face in line with the ball. Do not let the racket head drop if at all possible.

▶ **Learning Cues for Volleys**

1. Always step forward and attack the volley. Also, change the grip when necessary.
2. Use little or no backswing.
3. Contact well out in front of the body especially on backhands.

4. Keep the wrist locked.
5. Finish with racket head above the wrist.
6. Use the knuckles for direction guidance on the backhand and the palm on the forehand.

▶ **Practice Suggestions**

1. Hit off a ball machine or a feeder with a specific target in mind.
2. Alternate hitting a forehand and then a backhand to get used to changing the grip.
3. Hit off of a backboard.

Backhand Return of Serve

The suggested technique for backhand return of serve is analyzed in Figure 23-13.

A. Ready Position. Player should be up on his toes, slightly leaning forward, and holding an Eastern forehand grip.
B. Player pivots the body sideways while changing the grip to an Eastern backhand. The backswing is very short, the emphasis being on a blocking motion similar to the volley.
C. Contact and Follow-through. At this point it is crucial that the returner has stepped forward and is reaching out to contact the ball 8 to 10 inches in front of the body. This shot is hit with underspin. Concentration should be on putting the ball back in play rather than on hitting a winner. The follow-through is the same archway as described in the backhand ground stroke.

A   B   C

FIGURE 23-13 Suggested technique for backhand return of serve.

Forehand Return of Serve

The suggested technique for forehand return of serve is illustrated in Figure 23-14.

A. Ready Position. Remember to keep the elbows raised and be ready to move forward.
B. Rotate both shoulders sideways while limiting the length of the backswing. Hold the racket face on the level of the ball and remember that a blocking motion similar to a volley is desired.
C. Contact. The ball is met just in front of the player's left shoulder. A step forward as well as body weight transfer is important. The shot is hit with slight underspin with emphasis on putting the ball back in play.
D. Follow-through. This position is the same as described on the forehand ground stroke.

▶ **Learning Cues**

1. Start with a forehand grip rather than in between the two grips.
2. Short backswing, long follow-through.
3. Wrist locked.
4. Always try to have feet forward, never backward.
5. Contact ball in front of body, especially on the backhand.
6. Follow-throughs are the same as ground strokes.

▶ **Practice Suggestions**

Have a fellow participant practice serves while you hit returns to a specific target area. Alternate between both service courts.

PLAYING STRATEGY

To be effective, strategy must be an automatic response to a given set of conditions. The problem with beginners is that there are no "givens." Therefore, it is suggested that beginners not worry about strategy and concentrate on getting the ball back over the net one more time than their opponent. This sounds terribly feeble but that's how Bjorn Borg's and Chris Evert's coaches explained it to them at an early age. A player needs to "own" or "control" certain shots before he or she can become worried about strategy. Of course, if at all possible you should hit to your opponent's weakness whenever the chance arises. The best advice for beginning players is to be able to laugh at the mistakes they make and have fun learning. Things we learn with pleasure we don't forget!

MODIFICATIONS FOR SPECIAL POPULATIONS

Orthopedically Impaired

1. Follow rules from National Wheelchair Tennis Association and allow wheelchair users two bounces before a return shot is required.
2. Tether a ball to an assistive device, e.g., walker, crutch, for mobility impaired students.
3. Use a larger size ball or one made of different material, e.g., nerf ball.
4. Use velcro strapping to secure racquets to hand during play.
5. Use flat paddle-type boards secured to hand with a velcro strap during play.

A

B

C

D

FIGURE 23-14 Suggested technique for forehand return of serve.

6. Commercial extension devices are available for amputees and others with grip limitations.
7. See modifications mentioned for Handball/ Racquetball, Chapter 14.

Mentally Impaired

1. Have students throw the ball back and forth across the net to develop the concept of the game.
2. Reduce the court size, net height, and court coverage responsibility.

3. Use one-walled courts or stations in the gymnasium.

Sensory Impaired

1. Individual considerations need to be made on the appropriateness of tennis for the blind. Lead-up games such as Goalball help the students develop the concept of defending their side of the court. Similar to modifications for racquetball, the instructor might allow the student to roll or throw an audio ball against a wall to

practice movement and appropriate positioning. Place small bells inside whiffleballs and use as audio ball.

2. Minimal modifications would be needed for the deaf or hard of hearing. Instructional considerations include use of sign language, videos, pictures.

ETIQUETTE

To make the game more enjoyable for yourself and for others, you should follow certain court courtesies or rules of etiquette. If one of your tennis balls rolls into another court, wait until the players on the court have finished their rally before asking for your ball. When you return someone's ball that has rolled into your court, roll the ball back to the player asking for it instead of trying to gain some stroking practice. If they are engaged in playing a point, roll the ball back against the screen out of their field of play. If your opponent is interfered with in any way during the play for a point, stop the play, call a "let," and then play the point over. You call lines on your side of the net and let your opponent call lines on his side. When leaving or entering the courts, do not walk behind a player playing a point. Wait until the rally is over, then quickly cross the rear of the court close to the back screen.

HELPFUL HINTS

1. Keep your eye on the ball at all times.
2. Strive for accurate placement rather than speed.
3. Always play the game to win, but if you go down in defeat, give your opponent due credit.
4. Play to your opponent's weaknesses.
5. When calling the score, always call the server's score first.
6. Keep your weight on the balls of both feet so you can move in any direction with ease and speed.
7. Acquire an understanding of the fundamentals of stroking, and practice faithfully to master them.
8. Notice how your opponent strokes the ball so when he or she uses the chop or slice stroke you can play the bounce accordingly.
9. Turn your body sideways to the net on all ground strokes.
10. When stroking the ball, avoid stiff leg action by keeping the knees loose and relaxed.
11. On ground strokes, return the ball deep into the opponent's back court near the baseline.
12. On ground strokes, attempt to hit the ball at waist level and on the rise.
13. Hit the ball squarely on the strings of the racket face by hitting "through" the ball instead of chopping under it.

14. The follow-through of the racket is in the direction of the intended flight of the ball.
15. After completing each stroke, return to a ready position, facing the net and loosely grasping the throat of the racket with the left hand to facilitate change of grip if necessary.
16. Well-placed lobs out of reach of the net rusher will help keep him or her away from the net.
17. When serving, attempt to get the first serve in the proper court as often as possible. Stress control and accuracy if a second serve is necessary and concentrate on getting the ball into the proper service area.
18. The server should always have two balls in his or her possession before starting the service.
19. The receiver should not retrieve or return the ball if the opponent's first serve is a fault, but should remain in receiving position so the server can immediately follow with a second attempt.
20. Devote periodic practice sessions to correcting specific weaknesses.

SAFETY CONSIDERATIONS

1. Warm up sufficiently before starting strenuous play.
2. If injured, stop and report injury to the instructor.
3. Remove rings, bracelets, watches, and other objects which may cause bruises and cuts.
4. Check the playing surface for glass, nails, stones, slippery spots, etc.
5. Stay in line, on mark, or in your own area when swinging or hitting.
6. Control your emotions; do not throw the racket or hit a ball in anger.
7. Shout a warning when there is danger of a ball hitting someone.
8. Avoid showing off and "horseplay."
9. Be aware of the distances between the baselines and walls, fences, screens, etc.
10. When playing in excessive heat, make sure to drink plenty of fluids.

TERMINOLOGY

Ace A ball served and untouched by the opponent's racket.

Advantage (Ad) Scoring term: the next point won after the score is "deuce."

Alley The 4½ foot strip on either side of the singles court, used to enlarge the court for doubles.

Approach shot A shot hit inside the baseline while approaching the net.

Backcourt The area between the service line and the baseline.

Backhand Strokes hit on the left side of a right-handed player.

Backspin Spin acquired on a ball dropping from a vertical position, which forces the ball to bounce back toward the hitter.

Backswing The beginning of all ground strokes and service motion requiring a backswing to gather energy for the forward swing.

Baseline The end line of a tennis court, located 39 feet from the net.

Break Relates to the act of winning a game in which the opponent serves.

Center mark Short mark that bisects the baseline.

Center service line The line perpendicular to the net which divides the two service courts.

Center strap A strap placed at the center of the net and anchored to the court to facilitate a constant 3-foot height for the net at the center.

Center stripe Same as the center service line which divides the two service courts into halves.

Chip Refers to the short chopping motion of the racket against the back and bottom side of the ball.

Chop Used in the same manner as "chip" by many. Refers to the placement of backspin on the ball with a short high to low forward swing.

Cross-court A shot hit diagonally from one corner of the court over the net into the opposite corner of the court.

Cut off the angle To move forward quickly against an opponent's cross-court shot, allowing the player to hit the ball near the center of the court rather than near the sidelines.

Deep (depth) A shot that bounces near the baseline on ground strokes and near the service line on serves.

Default A player who forfeits his or her position in a tournament through failure to play a scheduled match.

Deuce Scoring term used when the game score is 40-40.

Dink A ball normally hit very softly and relatively high to ensure its safe landing.

Double fault When the server has served two serves out of bounds on the same point.

Doubles line The outside sideline on a court—used in doubles only.

Down-the-line A shot hit near a sideline which travels close to, and parallel to, the same line from which the shot was initially hit.

Drive An offensive shot hit with extra force.

Drop shot A ground stroke hit in such a manner as to drop just over the net with little or no forward bounce.

Drop volley A volley hit in such a manner as to drop just over the net with little or no forward bounce.

Error A mistake made by a player during competition.

Face The hitting surface of the racket.

Fault A serve that lands out of bounds or is not hit properly.

Flat shot A ball hit in such a manner as not to rotate when traveling through the air.

Foot fault Illegal foot movement before service, penalized by the loss of that particular serve. Common foot faults are: stepping on or ahead of the baseline before the ball has been contacted, and running along the baseline before serving.

Forecourt The area between the net and the service line.

Forehand The stroke hit on the right side of a right-handed player.

Frame The rim of the racket head plus the handle of the racket.

Game Scoring term when a player wins 4 points before his opponent and holds a minimum 2-point lead.

Grip That portion of the racket which is grasped in the player's hand.

Ground stroke Any ball hit after it has bounced.

Half-volley A ball hit only inches away from the court's surface after the ball has bounced.

Hold serve To win your own serve. If you lose your own serve, your serve has been "broken."

Let (ball) A point that is played over because of some kind of interference.

Let serve A serve that touches the net tape and falls into the proper square and is played over.

Linesman A match official who calls balls "in" or "out."

Lob A ball hit sufficiently high to pass over the outstretched arm position of the net player.

Lob volley A shot hit high into the air from a volleying position.

Love Scoring term: zero points or games.

Match A contest between two or four opponents.

Match point The point immediately preceding the final point of a match. The player who holds this point is said to be serving for match point.

Midcourt The area in front or in back of the service line of the playing court.

Net ball A ball that hits the net and falls back on the same side as the hitter.

Net man The player who has gained position at the net and is prepared to volley.

No man's land A general area within the baseline and proper net position area; when caught in that area, the player must volley or hit ground strokes near his feet.

Offensive lob A ball hit just above the racket reach of an opposing net player.

Open face racket A racket whose face is moving under the ball. A wide open racket face is parallel to the court surface.

Overhead A shot hit from a position higher than the player's head.

Overhead smash A shot hit extremely hard from a position higher than the player's head.

Overhitting Putting too much force into each shot.

Pace The speed of the ball.

Passing shot A shot that passes beyond the reach of the net player and lands inbounds.

Placement A shot hit inbounds and untouched by the opponent.

Poach To cross over into your partner's territory.

Racket face The hitting surface of the racket.

Racket head Top portion of the racket frame which houses the strings.

Rally   The act of hitting balls back and forth across the net. A rally includes all shots other than the serve.

Receiver   The player about to return the opponent's serve.

Retrieve   Normally refers to a fine defensive shot in response to an opponent's well-placed offensive shot.

Server   The player initiating play.

Service line   The end line of the service courts running parallel to the net.

Set   Scoring term: The first player to win six games with a minimum two-game lead has won a set.

Set point   The point which, if won, will give the player the set.

Sidespin   A ball hit and rotating on a horizontal plane.

Signals in doubles   Signaling your partner that you are going to poach at the net.

Singles line   The first sideline closer to the center mark and running the entire length of the court.

Slice   Motion of the racket head going around the side of the ball and producing a horizontal spin on the ball.

Tape   The band of cloth or plastic running across the top of the net.

Telegraphing the play   To indicate the direction of one's intended target before actually hitting the ball.

Topspin   The clockwise rotation of the ball at a 90° angle.

Touch   The ability to make delicate soft shots from several positions on the court.

Twist   A special rotation imparted to the ball during the serve, causing the ball to jump to the left (of right-handed server).

Umpire   The official used in tournament play to call lines.

Underspin   A counterclockwise spin placed on the ball by catching the backside and bottomside of the ball with the racket head.

Volley   To hit the ball in the air before it has bounced on the court.

SELECTED REFERENCES

Braden, V. and Bruns, B. *Tennis for the Future.* Boston: Little, Brown and Company, 1977.

————————————. *Teaching Children Tennis the Vic Braden Way.* Boston: Little, Brown and Company, 1980.

Brown, J. *Tennis: Steps to Success.* Champaign, IL: Leisure Press, 1989.

Gould, D. *Tennis Anyone?* 4th ed. Palo Alto, CA: Mayfield Publishing Company, 1986.

Kraft, E. *The Tennis Teacher's Guide to Group Instruction.* Princeton, NJ: United States Tennis Association, 1989.

Kriese, C. *Total Tennis Training.* Grand Rapids, MI: Masters Press, 1988.

Parks, B.A. *Tennis in a Wheelchair.* National Foundation of Wheelchair Tennis, 1988.

USTA Schools Program. Princeton, NJ: United States Tennis Association. Latest ed.

USTA Recreational Tennis Curriculum. Princeton, NJ: United States Tennis Association, 1989.

Audio-Visual Materials

Brentwood Productions, P.O. Box 49956, Los Angeles, CA 90049. (203) 472–0868. *Strokes* (Tennis fundamentals). 12.5 minutes, 16mm film.

Oklahoma State University, Audio Visual Center, Stillwater, Oklahoma 74078, (405) 624–7216, or Pennsylvania State University, Audio Visual Services, Special Services Building, University Park, Pennsylvania 16802, (814) 865–6314. *Tennis: Basic Tactics for Doubles* and *Tennis: Basic Tactics for Singles.* (Basic strategy for both singles and doubles.) 13 minutes each, 16mm film.

United States Tennis Association National Film Library, 707 Alexander Road, Princeton, NJ, provides many rentals: *The Winner's Edge—Tennis* (45 minutes, VHS); *Fair Game: Tennis Played by the Rules* (basic rules, scoring, customs and traditions covered—18 minutes, VHS or 16mm film); *Practice for Tennis* (drills and methods for improving stroke production—20 minutes, 16mm film); *Tennis in a Wheelchair* (18 minutes, VHS); *Tennis Our Way* (with Vic Braden, Stan Smith and Arthur Ashe —2½ hours, VHS); and many others. Write to the USTA for complete listing of rental tapes and films.

Vic Braden Tennis College, 22000 Plano Rd., Trabuco Canyon, CA 92670. *Vic Braden Tennis Training Films*: Forehand Drive (5¼ min.); Backhand Drive (4¼ min.); Half Volley (4¼ min.); Approach (4¼ min.); Forehand Volley (5 min.); Backhand Volley (4¾ min.); Basic Serve (5¼ min.); Overhead (4 min.); Advanced Serve (5¼ min.); The Lob (4 min.); Ball Rotation (4¾ min.); Footwork (4 min.); Singles Strategy (3¼ min.); Doubles Strategy (3¼ min.).

24 TRACK AND FIELD

THIS CHAPTER WILL ENABLE YOU TO:

▶ Understand the learning sequence for the hurdling, jumping, and throwing events.
▶ Demonstrate and perform basic skills and techniques of various running, hurdling, jumping, and throwing events.
▶ Set up a training program for a participant in various running and hurdling events.
▶ Identify the basic terminology used in the sport of track and field.
▶ Identify the basic rules of the sport.

NATURE AND PURPOSE

The more than thirty different track and field events in the Olympic Games involve walking, running, jumping, and throwing. Each requires different combinations of sports fitness (endurance, strength, speed, flexibility) and motor skills to be successful. Yet this great variety of events requiring these different combinations of natural and acquired abilities gives practically every individual, no matter what body size, shape, or form, the opportunity to participate successfully. Often young boys and girls do not realize they have the natural ability to become successful in track and field until they give it a try. Many track and field stars "discovered themselves" in a physical education class or intramural sport. In fact, participants can easily assess their natural abilities of strength, speed, endurance, and power by performing specific tests. These talent tests could include a 30-meter timed sprint, standing long jump for distance, vertical jump for height, five alternate leg bounds for distance, 5-kg shot tossed backward overhead for distance, or an 800-meter timed run.

EQUIPMENT

The equipment required in track and field varies with the events. Proper equipment is important and can affect the learning of skills and technique as well as help to reduce injuries. Lighter-weight throwing implements for shot or discus should be used for smaller and younger athletes. For the beginning hurdler, modified hurdles using light-weight wooden rods placed upon small cones or bricks and easily displaced should be used instead of heavy solid hurdles. In the high jump, a soft foam pit made from gymnastic mats or high jump mats is essential. The cross bar should be of soft plastic rather than solid metal.

Spiked shoes must be worn not only for safety but for optimal performance, particularly in the jumping events. For the elite performer, shoes designed specifically for the various events may be purchased.

Track and field shorts, shirts, and warm-up suits vary in price depending upon the quality of the material. These can be purchased from catalogue suppliers, sporting goods or department stores.

BASIC RULES

Sprinting

1. One false start disqualifies a runner.
2. A starter may not touch on or over the line before the firing of the gun.
3. Some part of each foot must be in contact with the track in the blocks.

Relay Races

1. The baton must be passed inside the 20-meter passing zone.
2. The baton must be carried in the hand throughout the race.
3. After passing the baton, the runner may not interfere with an opponent.

Hurdling

1. Entire body must pass over the hurdle.
2. A hurdler may not interfere with a hurdler in another lane.

High Jump

1. The jumper must make a jump from one foot.
2. Three trials are allowed at each height.
3. Displacing a bar, passing under it, crossing the line of the bar extended, or leaving the ground shall count as a foul and trial.

Long Jump

1. Touching in front of scratch line or passing the line extended shall count as a foul and trial.
2. The jump shall be measured at right angles to the board and at the point of landing closest to the take-off.

Triple Jump

1. During the hop and step phase the free leg must not touch the ground.
2. The legal measurement of a jump is the same as described in the long jump.
3. A scratch jump is the same as described in the long jump.

Shot Put

1. Touching on top or outside of circle or toe-board with any part of the body constitutes a foul.
2. The thrower must enter and leave by the back of the circle.

Discus Throw

1. The discus must be thrown within a 60-degree sector (45-degree in college). As in shot put, after entering the ring, the thrower must pause before starting.
2. The thrower may not touch any part of a painted line, or the top of a band used to outline part of the ground outside the circle.

SUGGESTED LEARNING SEQUENCE

The running and field events described in this chapter may be taught in any order, taking into account the particular student needs, the time available, and the type of facilities available. It is, however, important to follow a simple-to-complex progression leading up to the completion of a skill. Other important keys to successful learning include positive reinforcement through feedback and using good learning cues.

In all instances, rules, hints, cues, and terminology should be introduced only when significant to the learning progression and when dealing with the particular event. Safety considerations are of prime importance during the initial stages of learning.

A. Orientation
  1. Safety considerations
  2. Discussion of equipment
  3. Importance of warm-up and cool-down
B. Rules, Skill Development, Terminology, Specific Safety Instructions are given in connection with the particular event.
C. Running Events
  1. Sprinting
  2. Middle/Long Distance Running
  3. Relays
  4. Hurdling

D. Field Events
  1. High Jump (Flop Style)
  2. Long Jump
  3. Triple Jump
  4. Shot Put
  5. Discus Throw

SPECIFIC SAFETY INSTRUCTIONS

Sprinting

1. Warm up thoroughly before starting.
2. Don't jump or lunge at the finish tape.
3. Don't take starts after a hard training session.

Relay Races

1. After passing the baton, remain in your lane until all others have passed.
2. Pass the baton to opposite hands, right to left or left to right, to avoid a collision.

Hurdling

1. Warm up and stretch well before hurdling.
2. Never attempt to go over a hurdle from the wrong direction.

High Jump

1. Make certain the pit is positioned correctly.
2. Don't jump without spiked shoes, to prevent slipping.
3. Use a heel cup or heel pad to prevent bruises.

Long Jump

1. Keep the landing pit area soft and smooth.
2. Wear jumping shoes with heel cups or rubber pads in take-off heel.

Triple Jump

1. Wear heel cups or rubber pads in both jumping shoes.
2. Keep the landing pit area soft and smooth.

Shot Put

1. Roll the shot back to the circle—don't throw it back.
2. Practice in a protected area.

Discus Throw

1. Make sure the implement and the throwing surface are dry.
2. Never throw the discus in any other than the specified direction.

SKILLS AND TECHNIQUES

Sprinting

While speed or sprinting ability is largely determined by inherited traits—the white muscle fiber composition of the body—a sprinter's innate speed can be greatly improved through technique work and training. Technique work involves improving a sprinter's start, ability to lift ("change gears"), and ability to relax, thereby sustaining speed.

The Start. The placement of the starting blocks is essential to a good start. Most sprinters favor the medium start. In this start, the front block is set in approximately 2-foot lengths from the starting line, and the back block 3- to 4-foot lengths. These distances may vary according to the sprinter's body structure, height, and length of limbs.

The starting commands are "on your marks" and "set" and the firing of the gun.

In the on-the-mark position, the hands are parallel to the starting line, the arms are shoulder width apart, the dominant leg is forward in the blocks with the opposite knee resting on the track, and the head is relaxed. After assuming this position, the sprinter will then slide or roll forward until the shoulders are over or in front of the starting line with the pressure being on the knee and finger tips.

On "set" the sprinter raises the hips until slightly higher than the shoulders. In this position the knees are parallel or at a slight angle to the track. The sprinter feels good power in both legs in this position if the blocks are spaced properly. The head is relaxed with no tension on the neck (Figure 24-1).

At the gun the sprinter concentrates on good sprint form: opposite arm/opposite leg action while keeping the driving angle low and forward (Figure 24-2). It is important that the sprinter's movement be forward, not upward, which is the result of the proper "set" position.

Lifting. After coming out of the blocks, the sprinter concentrates on lifting, or "shifting gears," by driving the knees high, which will continue acceleration. This action continues until the sprinter has reached maximum speed, somewhere between 30 to 40 meters, at which time an upright running position and full running stride length will have been achieved.

Free-Wheeling. In this phase, which is also referred to as floating, the sprinter works to sustain speed through total body relaxation. Total relaxation is achieved by running tall while keeping the hands, arms, and jaws loose, and the shoulders down to reduce tension in the antagonistic muscle groups of the neck (Figure 24-3).

The Finish. The sprinter drives or runs through the tape at the finish in regular sprint form and does not attempt to jump or lunge.

▶ **Practice Suggestions—Training Workout**

In training for the sprinting events, quality work is important over quantity work. Basic sprint training should include: *long sprints* consisting of 200 to 250 meters for the 100 meters, 250 to 300 meters for the 200 meters, and 500 to 600 meters for the 400

FIGURE 24-1 An excellent "set" position is demonstrated by the two sprinters.

FIGURE 24-2 At the gun, these two sprinters demonstrate good sprint form and drive forward out of the blocks.

FIGURE 24-3 Free-wheeling. A 400-meter sprinter displays total relaxation, which is important in sustaining speed.

TABLE 24-1 A Weekly Training Program for Sprinting Events

	100 Meters	200 Meters	400 Meters
Monday	4 × 250m at 95% effort/ walk 8 min.	3 × 300m at 95% effort/ walk 10 min.	2 × 600m at 90% effort/ walk 15 min.
Tuesday	baton work; 8–10 × 30–40m gun starts	baton work; 8–10 × 75m gun starts (around turn)	8–10 × 150m gun starts (around turn)
Wednesday	5–6 × 75m at allout/ walk back for recovery	6 × 150m at allout/ walk back for recovery	2–3 × 300m at race pace
Thursday	baton work; 5–6 × 20–30m gun starts	baton work; 6–8 × 50m gun starts	5–6 × 100m at 95% effort
Friday	Meet	Meet	Meet
Saturday	1–2 miles easy distance golf course	1–2 miles easy distance golf course	2–4 miles easy distance golf course
Sunday	Rest	Rest	Rest

meters; *medium sprints* consisting of 50 to 75 meters for the 100 meters, 100 to 150 meters (around turn) for the 200 meters, and 300 to 350 meters for the 400 meters; and *short sprints* with the gun consisting of 20 to 30 meters for the 100 meters, 50 to 75 meters for the 200 meters, and 100 to 150 meters for the 400 meters. A weekly competitive season training program is given in Table 24-1. Each of the workouts should be preceded by a good warm-up which includes stretching and flexibility exercises, easy running, and sprint drills, and should be followed by a good cool-down of easy running and stretching.

▶ **Practice Suggestions—Sprinting Skills**

1. *High Knee Drill.* Running 20 to 30 meters with knees lifted so that thighs are at least parallel to the ground. Emphasize quality lifting; the drill should not be hurried. The vertical action is fast, but the horizontal movement forward is slow.
2. *Block Drill.* Sprinter A gets into the blocks in the "on the mark" position. Sprinter B stands facing him with hands on shoulders of sprinter A. Upon continued hand pressure, sprinter A comes to "set" position. On the command "go" from sprinter B, sprinter A drives out of the blocks, concentrating on driving the arms and lifting the knees while sprinter B continues to offer resistance.
3. *Figure Four Drill.* Running 20 to 30 meters, the sprinter concentrates on the heel coming up under the buttocks as the foot comes off the track, this will elevate the knee parallel with the track.
4. *Sprint-Float-Sprint Drill.* The sprinter runs 150 meters, running the first 50 working hard, the next 50 meters floated (relaxed running), and the last 50 meters working hard. The sprinter runs the floated 50 meters within one second of

the hard 50 meters by concentrating on good sprint form and relaxation, so as not to decelerate.

Middle and Long Distance Running

Middle distance races include the 800-meter, 1500-meter, and mile races. Long distance races include the 3000-meter steeplechase, 5000-meter, 10,000-meter, and marathon races. Running form in these events is not significantly different from the sprinting events except that as the speed of a runner is reduced, the stride length becomes shorter, the body is more erect, and the foot strikes more on the heel in landing.

In training for these events it is important to train both energy systems of the body—the aerobic and anaerobic.

Aerobic Training. This type of training, which improves a runner's endurance or stamina by increasing the ability to take in and utilize oxygen, is accomplished through runs of 3 to 10 miles or longer at different tempos (speeds). An easy tempo involves relaxed recovery running; a brisk tempo involves running at steady state or oxygen balance; and hard tempo involves running beyond steady state but not allout. Using all three tempos in a run produces a type of training called *Fartlek* (Swedish for "speed play") or playing with speed. Early training should include only easy and brisk tempo runs for several weeks; later, hard tempo and hard Fartlek runs with hills may be alternated with easier runs. An example of this pattern of training is given in Table 24-2.

Anaerobic Training. This type of training, which improves the body's ability to run while under oxygen debt, is best developed through intermittent or interval type training. Interval training consists of running a number of short distances at a given

TABLE 24-2   An Aerobic Training Program

Sunday	Long and easy (10 miles, easy tempo)
Monday	Intense (6 miles, hard tempo)
Tuesday	Active rest (5 miles, brisk tempo)
Wednesday	Intense (7 miles, hard Fartlek)
Thursday	Active rest (4 miles, brisk tempo)
Friday	Intense (5 miles, hard tempo)
Saturday	Active rest (8 miles, brisk tempo)

pace, interspersed by 1 to 5 minutes of rest or jogging fixed distances. For example: 8×200 meters at 30 sec/jog 200 meters. Interval training is used basically to develop race rhythm and for sharpening speed.

▶ **Training Workout Suggestions**

A weekly competitive season aerobic/anaerobic training program is outlined in Table 24-3.

Relays

There are two types of relays: *sprint relays* (400, 800, 1600 meters) and sprint medley (200, 400, 800 meters) and *distance relays* (3200, 6000) and distance medley (400, 800, 1200, 1600 meters). Four runners compete for a team, each running an equal distance (except in medley relays), and pass a baton to the next runner. The baton must be exchanged within a 20-meter exchange zone. There are two general methods of exchanging the baton, the *blind pass* and the *visual pass*.

Blind Pass.   The blind pass is used in sprint relays. In this exchange the outgoing runner stands in a good sprint position at the back of the 10-meter

fly zone located beyond the 20-meter zone (see Figure 24-4). The runner stands on the low side of the lane if the baton is to be received in the right hand, and the high side of the lane when the baton is to be received in the left hand. When the incoming runner hits a predetermined mark on the track, called the "go mark," the outgoing runner leaves, concentrating on good sprinting action. This "go mark" may vary by 5 to 8 meters and is established by a trial and error method. The baton is exchanged at a given point in the zone, preferably in the last 10 meters of the 20-meter passing zone, without the receiver looking back. The exchange is made by the incoming runner extending the baton forward as far as possi-

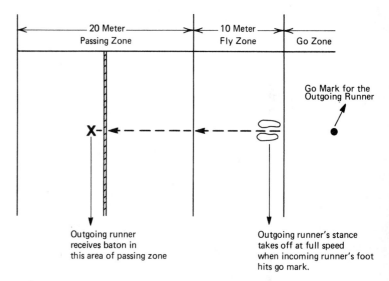

FIGURE 24-4   The blind pass, used for all sprint relays.

TABLE 24-3   A Weekly Competitive Season Aerobic/Anaerobic Training Program

	800 Meters	1500 Meters	5000 Meters
Sunday	6 miles (easy tempo)	8 miles (easy tempo)	10 miles (easy tempo)
Monday	1 mile (easy tempo) 2×600m at race pace/ walk 5 min.; 15 min. (easy tempo)	2 miles (easy tempo) 5×800m at slower than race pace/jog 400 m; 20 min. (easy tempo)	3 miles (easy tempo) 4×1200m at race pace/ jog 600m; 25 min. (easy tempo)
Tuesday	40 min. (brisk tempo)	50 min. (brisk tempo)	60 min. (brisk tempo)
Wednesday	2 miles (brisk tempo) 4×400m at faster than race pace/walk 4 min.; 15 min. (easy tempo)	3 miles (brisk tempo) 8×400m at race pace/ jog 200m; 25 min. (easy tempo)	4 miles (brisk tempo) 12×400m at faster than race pace/jog 200m; 35 min. (easy tempo)
Thursday	20 min. (brisk tempo) 4×200m at 90% effort/ jog 200m	30 min. (brisk tempo) 6×200m at 90% effort/ jog 200m	50 min. (brisk tempo) 8×200m at 90% effort
Friday	20 min. (easy tempo)	30 min. (easy tempo)	40 min. (easy tempo)
Saturday	Meet	Meet	Meet

FIGURE 24-5 These two relay runners demonstrate excellent hand-off technique in the 400-meter sprint relay.

ble and placing the baton downward into the receiver's opposite hand, which has been extended backward, palm up (Figure 24-5).

Visual Pass. The visual pass is used in all distance relays. It enables the outgoing runner to judge the speed and fatigue of the incoming runner. In this exchange, the outgoing runner, who is turned toward the inside of the track facing the pole lane, stands on the high side of the lane and receives the baton in the left hand, palm up. Upon receiving the baton the runner immediately transfers it to the right hand.

▶ Practice Suggestions—Sprint Relay Drills

1. *Standing Hand-Slap.* Two relay runners standing in their hand-off positions and moving their arms in a running motion slap or touch hands on command "reach" or "hand."
2. *Running Hand-Slap.* This drill is the same as the standing hand-slap, but with the two relay runners now running at a slow pace. With extended practice the runners gradually progress to running at a faster pace through the exchange zone practicing this technique.
3. *Four Runner Baton Drills.* After mastering the first two drills, progress to using all four relay runners and a baton. First standing still and then running, the runners gradually increase the pace. The relay runners should be staggered to the right or left, according to the receiving hand. Care must be taken to keep the proper spacing between runners to allow good extension of the passing and receiving arms.
4. *One-on-One Drill.* Two relay runners, first starting at 10 meters apart and running at 75 percent speed, move through the passing zone using a hand-slap. The outgoing runner takes off when the incoming runner hits a "go mark." This drill progresses by gradually increasing the speed of the two relay runners and their distance apart

from each other. This drill teaches the runners to "attack" the passing zone and helps to establish a correct "go mark."

Hurdling

Hurdling is rhythmical sprinting and should be done with as little deviation from sprinting as possible. Clearing a hurdle is a *run over* action, not a jumping movement, and all hurdling is taught with this concept in mind. (Figure 24-6).

The physical attributes of height or good leg split, speed, flexibility, and coordination along with the mental qualities of courage, patience, and concentration are important for success in hurdling.

▶ Learning Sequence

One of the best ways to teach hurdling is the "sticks and bricks" method developed by Geoff Dyson of Great Britain. Different size cones using dowel rods could also be used. In this method the hurdler progresses through the following steps:

1. Each individual sprints as fast as possible for 20 to 25 meters maintaining a consistent rhythm and stride pattern.
2. Teach each person the proper foot positioning at the starting line: left foot back and right leg forward, which results in a left lead leg over the hurdle. Using this position the hurdler sprints the entire distance once again.
3. Teach the beginners to run 8 steps to the first hurdle. Have every person sprint allout, counting aloud through 13 steps. The 8th step will be on the right foot. This is done three times to develop a constant stride pattern.
4. After the third sprint, place a stick midway between the 8th and 9th strides. Have everyone run through again; place a stick on the ground between the 12th and 13th strides. Emphasize a smoother, unbroken rhythm. Have them run through once again; place a stick between the 16th and 17th strides.
5. Place two bricks flat on the ground for each stick, putting the ends of the sticks on the bricks. Have each person sprint over these twice, gradually increasing the height by turning the bricks and adding a second brick.
6. When the stick reaches 24 inches above the ground, introduce specific hurdling techniques: proper lead leg, trail leg, and arm action, by means of a wall drill.
7. Wall Drill—first part: work on the proper lead leg and arm action. The hurdler, standing a few feet from a wall, starts by lifting the lead knee and leg toward the wall, letting the weight fall forward. The leg is planted on the wall at hurdle height, the chest drops down toward the knee, and the opposite arm is driven toward the opposite leg.

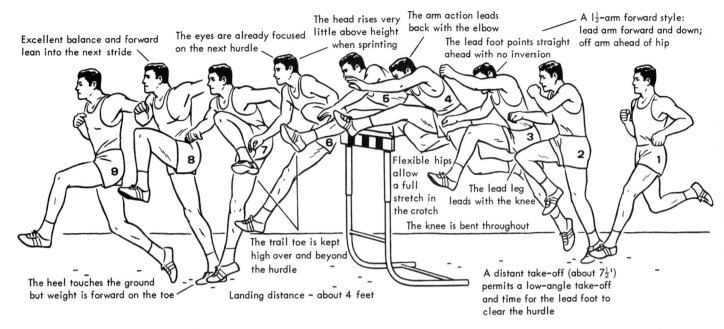

Excellent balance and forward lean into the next stride

The eyes are already focused on the next hurdle

The head rises very little above height when sprinting

The arm action leads back with the elbow

The lead foot points straight ahead with no inversion

A 1½-arm forward style: lead arm forward and down; off arm ahead of hip

Flexible hips allow a full stretch in the crotch

The lead leg leads with the knee

The knee is bent throughout

The heel touches the ground but weight is forward on the toe

The trail toe is kept high over and beyond the hurdle

Landing distance – about 4 feet

A distant take-off (about 7½') permits a low-angle take-off and time for the lead foot to clear the hurdle

FIGURE 24-6 Recommended form in the high hurdles. (From J. Kenneth Doherty, *Modern Track and Field.* Englewood Cliffs, NJ: Prentice-Hall, Inc., 1953.)

8. Wall Drill—second part: work on the trail leg. Standing facing the wall, the hurdler leans forward with both hands against the wall, the trail leg is brought up under the armpit and reaches out for a long step forward.

9. The next step is to walk over a 24-inch hurdle using these proper lead leg, trail leg, and arm actions.

10. The last step is to run over a 30-inch hurdle gradually increasing the speed of running into full effort as correct hurdling form is executed.

Hurdle Start. The hurdle start differs from the regular sprint start in that the hurdler must come up to the running position sooner. A high hurdler will take 7 or 8 steps to the first hurdle; an intermediate hurdler 21, 22, 23, or 24 steps. The hurdler who takes an odd number of steps to the first hurdle will have the same leg forward in the blocks as leads over the hurdle. With an even number of steps, the lead leg over the hurdle is the back leg in the blocks. The hurdler determines the lead leg by attempting to hurdle with each leg. The one most comfortable should be the lead leg.

Running Between the Hurdles. In the highs a hurdler must take 3 steps and in the intermediates 13, 15, or 17 steps. The intermediate hurdler can use a 14- stride pattern if the lead leg is alternated. The hurdler must concentrate on good sprint action between the hurdles, running up on the balls of the feet, knees high, and arms driving hard with relaxation. Good sprint rhythm between the hurdles is important. The hurdler should never gallop or overstride, which often is caused by not getting a good step off the hurdle with the trail leg.

Learning Cues

1. In the lead leg action, lead with the knee, not the foot.
2. Keep the trail leg flat, toe out, and bring it up high under the armpit and out.
3. The opposite arm/opposite leg action is used over the hurdle.
4. Sprint through the hurdle, rather than jumping over the hurdle.

▶ **Practice Suggestions—Hurdling Drills**

1. *Wall Drill.* (See Learning Sequence: 7 and 8, above.)
2. *Lead Leg Over Hurdles.* Performed with the lead leg over the side of four to six hurdles spaced 7 to 9 meters apart for the three-stride rhythm or 9 to 13 meters apart for a five-stride rhythm. The hurdle height varies from 12 to 36 inches.
3. *Trail Leg Over Hurdles.* Same as the preceding lead leg drill, except only the trail leg passes over the hurdle.

Table 24-4 presents a weekly competitive season training program for hurdling. Each of these workouts is preceded by a good warm-up consisting of specific hurdling flexibility and stretching exercises, easy running, and sprint work, and is followed by a good cool-down of easy running and stretching.

High Jump (Flop Style)

The flop or back layout style of jumping, originated by the 1968 Olympic champion Dick Fosbury, is currently used by the majority of high jumpers. The

TABLE 24-4 Hurdling—A Weekly Competitive Season Training Program

	110m Hurdles	400m Hurdles
Sunday	2 miles (easy tempo)	3–4 miles (easy tempo)
Monday	Go over flights of 7, 6, 5, 4, and 3 hurdles 3 times each 1 × 400m at full effort	Go over flights of 8, 6, 4, and 2 hurdles, from blocks, working on stride pattern at race pace
Tuesday	"Five-step" 5 hurdles, 2–3 times 3–4 × 150m at 90% effort/walk back for recovery	2 × 300m at full effort
Wednesday	Go over 5 flights of hurdles (70 meters) 5 times at full effort 1 × 300m at full effort	Go over flights of 5, 4, 3, 2, and 1 hurdles at race pace
Thursday	5–6 gun starts over 2 hurdles 3–4 × 100m at 90% effort/walk back for recovery	4 × 200m at 90% effort
Friday	Easy stretching and jogging "Five-step" 3 hurdles, 2–3 times	3–4 gun starts over 1st hurdle working on stride pattern
Saturday	Meet	Meet

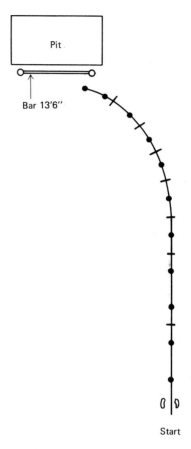

FIGURE 24-7 The "J" approach used in the back layout (flop style) high jump.

technique can be broken down into three phases: approach, plant/take-off, and bar clearance.

1. *Approach.* The "J" approach is used by most jumpers. This is a run of 3, 4, or 5 strides straight ahead, then 3, 4, or 5 strides on a curve (see Figure 24-7). Speed is important in the approach, so the jumper must lean to the inside of the arc in order to maintain velocity into the bar.
2. *Plant/Take-Off.* The next-to-last stride is longer to enable the jumper to lower the center of gravity for the jump. The last stride (take-off) is from the outside foot farthest from the bar and is shorter so that the body is in a lean back position. The free knee leg is kicked upward and coordinated with an upward swing of the arms. The kick combined with the curved approach and the take-off foot planted toward the left standard causes the jumper's back to rotate toward the bar at take-off. As the take-off is being executed, the jumper should look over the inside shoulder.
3. *Bar Clearance* (layout position). During bar clearance, the lead knee remains up with the plant by catching up to it. The legs are spread with the knees out in a "frog" position and the feet together. The hands are placed alongside the body. There is a laying back of the head and

an arching of the back until the bar passes along the back and hips. At this point the chin is tucked down to the chest so that the body folds up in an L-position.

▶ **Learning Sequence**

1. The important plant/take-off techniques are learned first with the jumper performing a series of 3- and 5-stride approach jumps away from the pit on a curve. The center circle on a basketball court or the arced lines on the turns of the running track can be used.
2. The jumper then transfers the same 3- and 5-foot approach to the pit with the bar set at a lower height. The take-off is approximately one arm's length from the bar.
3. The approach is developed next with the jumper running the "J" approach gradually building from 7 to 9 strides. After take-off from this approach, the jumper can execute a scissors jump to a sitting position, followed by a back landing position and an upper back landing position.

▶ **Learning Cues**

1. Approach the bar fast but relaxed with good sprint technique.

2. Use the same speed for all heights.
3. Quicken the last two strides and lower the hips.
4. Plant the foot farthest from the cross bar, heel first, and at an approximate 15-degree angle to the bar.
5. Drive the lead knee upward at take-off.
6. At clearance keep the legs apart, "frog" position, and squeeze the buttocks muscles together.
7. Drop the chin to the chest after the hips pass over the bar.

▶ **Practice Suggestions—Drills**

1. Plant/Take-off Drill (described in Learning Sequence)
2. Approach Drill (described in Learning Sequence)
3. Clearance Drill. Stand on a small box at the edge of the pit with your back to the pit. Jump up and backwards, working on the clearance technique.

Long Jump

The long jumper must possess good sprinting speed, a rhythmic, consistent stride pattern, and powerful jumping ability. The basic technique of the long jump can be broken down into four phases: the run-up, plant/take-off, flight, and landing.

1. *The Run-up or Approach.* During the approach the jumper must get to the take-off board with maximum controlled speed and be in a position to lift. Therefore, relaxation and consistency of stride length are important during the approach. To ensure that the jumper hits the take-off board with consistency, checkmarks are established in the following manner:
   a. The jumper, one stride from the take-off board, runs 12 to 16 strides in the opposite direction of the jumping pit until the same foot that is to hit the take-off board lands on the track.
   b. The jumper continues with 4 to 5 run throughs in this direction until the take-off foot hits consistently at the same point.
   c. The jumper then places a checkmark at that point and standing one stride away hits the mark with the take-off foot.
   d. Now running toward the jumping pit the jumper makes 4 to 5 run throughs until hitting the board consistently.
   e. The checkmark may be moved forward or backward depending on whether the jumper is over or under the take-off board.
2. *Plant/Take-off.* Like in the high jump, the next-to-last stride is a longer, settling stride preparing for the lift. The last stride is shorter, and the take-off hits in a heel-toe action. The free leg comes through as in a normal running stride.
3. *The Flight.* After leaving the board the jumper can use one of three types of techniques in the air: the hitch kick, hang, or sail. The *hitch kick* is done with a run-in-the-air action (see Figure 24-8). The *hang* is performed by letting the legs hang down, the hips are forward, and the upper body back. In the *sail* the legs are tucked up under the body. The purpose of these flight positions is to prevent forward rotation and to get good leg extension in landing.
4. *The Landing.* Important in landing is getting good leg extension. This can only be achieved when the flight positions are done correctly. Upon landing impact the jumper must work through the jump in order not to sit back. This is accomplished by dropping the chin to the chest and driving the arms back forcefully behind the body.

▶ **Learning Sequence**

1. Begin by teaching the plant/take-off rhythm. To practice this rhythm the jumpers work on 3-step approach jumps, counting out loud as they step

FIGURE 24-8   Recommended form in long jump, using a modified hitch kick.

1—2–3 (long, short, short), which gives them the proper rhythm.
2. Next, a split leg jump into the pit is added to the 3-step approach jumps.
3. Progress to a 5-step approach with the split landing.
4. The last step is jumping off an 8- to 10-inch box on the plant/take-off, followed by flight and landing.

▶ **Learning Cues**

1. Work for a consistent stride pattern in the approach using a gradual, uniform acceleration.
2. Run-up off the take-off foot with 1—2–3 rhythmical last 3 strides.
3. At take-off, drive the free leg knee up and push the hips forward.
4. After take-off the hips remain forward, and the arms are used for good balance (Figure 24-9).
5. Work through the jump and land with good leg extensions, sweeping the arms backward to prevent falling back.

▶ **Practice Suggestions**

1. *Pop-ups*. Repeat 3- to 5-stride jumps working on the 1—2–3 rhythm.
2. *Flight Pop-ups*. Repeat 3- to 5-stride jumps from a box, working on the flight in the air technique, the sail, hang, and hitchkick.

FIGURE 24-9 This NCAA All-American long jumper uses excellent in-flight technique after leaving the take-off board.

3. *Landing and Extension Pop-ups*. Repeat 3- to 5-stride jumps from a box, concentrating on correct landing procedures as to leg extension, collapsing of the knees, and driving the arms back forcefully.

Triple Jump

Formerly called the "hop, step, and jump," the triple jump is an event requiring good speed, great leg strength, and excellent coordination. Proper knee action, with thighs parallel to the ground, and equal rhythm, are the keys to good performance.

The technique in the triple jump can be broken down into the approach, plant/take-off, flight, and landing.

1. *Approach*. To ensure hitting the take-off board with consistency, check marks are established using the same method as in the long jump. However, the approach is slower and more controlled than in the long jump.
2. *Plant/Take-off*. Since the movement at take-off is more forward than upward as compared to the long jump, the jumper does not need to settle or gather at take-off. The take-off foot is planted flat with the center of gravity directly over the foot.
3. *Flight*. The first phase of the flight is the hop. The *hop,* or first jump, is performed by bringing the take-off leg forward after it has fully extended from the take-off board. The thigh of the hopping leg is held parallel to the ground; the hopping foot lands flat in preparation of the next phase. The *step,* or second jump, is performed by bringing the free leg forward and parallel to the ground, riding it forward until there is a good thigh split (Figure 24-10). The third phase, or *jump,* utilizes the same technique as described in the long jump. However, the hang or sail should be used rather than the hitch kick as there is less time to perform the action.
4. *Landing*. The landing techniques are the same as those used in the long jump, except that some jumpers sit out in landing rather than falling forward as in the long jump.

▶ **Learning Sequence**

1. Standing on one foot, the jumper performs a standing triple jump saying out loud "same, other, both," which refers to the landing leg or legs.
2. The jumper progresses to 3-stride and then 5-stride short approach run jumps. Cones are placed at equal distances for each phase of the jumps so that the jumper keeps a rhythmical pattern and equal distances.
3. Once proper technique is mastered, these short run jumps are transferred to the runway and jumping pit.

FIGURE 24-10 Excellent technique in the second phase of the triple jump ("the step") is demonstrated by this triple jumper.

▶ **Learning Cues**

1. Run-off the board emphasizing jumping out, not up, and keeping the legs low.
2. The body remains upright throughout the jump.
3. Work through each phase of the jumps with active heel first or mid-foot landings.
4. Coordinate the arms with the leg action to maintain speed throughout the jumps.
5. Keep the rhythm even during all three phases of the jump.

▶ **Practice Suggestions**

1. *Rhythm Drills.* Use short 5- to 7-stride approach runs working on the equal length of each phase and overall rhythm.
2. *Power-Bounding Drills.* Short 25- to 50-run intervals, on soft surfaces, hopping on either one leg or the other.
3. *Box Drills.* Box drills are done jumping on or over various size boxes. As technique improves the boxes can be moved farther apart.

Shot Put

The world record for shot put distance has been increased through improved techniques and greater emphasis on speed, strength, and explosive power training. Today, putters use one of two styles of throwing: the glide (O'Brien) and the spin (discus-turn).

Glide Style. With the putter facing opposite the direction of the throw, the thrower glides (shifts) across the circle, lifts the shot with the back, hips, and legs, and then explodes with the arm. In learning this technique, it is important to keep the legs and hips ahead of the upper body and throwing arm, thus utilizing the stronger, larger muscle groups of the lower body.

In learning this shot technique, it is helpful to think of the circle as the face of a clock with the twelve o'clock position at the back, and two lines dividing the circle in four equal parts: one a line of direction, the other, a cross line.

1. *Grip.* The weight of the shot is placed where the fingers meet the palm of the hand. The thumb and little finger support and guide the shot. The three middle fingers are used for power.
2. *Shot Placement.* The shot is held against the neck under the jaw bone underneath the ear.
3. *Starting Position.* The putter stands at the back of the circle with the right foot in the eleven o'clock position on the line of direction. The putter keeps the eyes focused on a focal point in the back of the circle, with the non-throwing arm and shoulder kept square and held back.
4. *Glide.* From the starting position, the body weight drops down over the right leg, raising the left leg. The left leg makes an easy swinging motion toward the throwing direction. At the same time the right leg begins its pushing action across the circle. This is a ball-to-heel motion that causes a stretching action, not a hopping or jumping movement. As the body weight moves toward the front of the circle, the right leg snaps underneath the thrower to the middle of the circle in the nine o'clock position. The left leg lands at the same instant in the five o'clock position just to the left of the line of direction.
5. *Throwing (Power) Position.* This position at the front of the circle is called the power position; it is the key to a successful throw. Hitting this position correctly for a right-handed thrower means the feet and hips are turned to the left side of the circle, the head faces the back of the circle, body weight is over the right leg, and the right and left legs are bent.

▶ **Learning Sequence**

1. Since 80% of the distance in the throw comes from the leg and the trunk, begin with standing power position throws emphasizing the rotation of the right foot-knee-hip.
2. Next, the glide across the ring is developed with concentration on getting the bent right leg up under the body, and keeping the shoulders square to the back of the circle, which insures a leg/trunk throw.
3. The finish of the throw emphasizes an explosive right leg drive over a braced left leg.

▶ **Learning Cues**

1. Keep the shot against the neck in the movement across the circle.
2. Leg and hips lead and shoulders remain square to the back of the circle in the glide across the circle.
3. Right leg is snatched up under the body quickly in the glide across the circle and must remain bent.
4. Use concentration and explosive action from the power position—with the force coming from the ground up, legs, hips to shoulders, and then the arm.

▶ **Practice Suggestions**

1. *Standing Throw Drill.* Execute standing throws from the power position concentrating on perfect technique and leg/trunk force.
2. *T-Drill.* From a standing position, the thrower drops down in a T-position as if starting the throw.
3. *A-Drill.* From the standing T-position, the thrower drops down and kicks the left leg until the thrower's body is in the A-position.
4. *Cross Bar Drill (right leg).* With arms draped over a cross bar, the putter snaps the right leg under; the cross bar prevents the shoulders from turning.
5. *Cross Bar Drill (left leg).* With arms draped over a cross bar, the putter concentrates on driving the left leg low and to the toe-board without turning the upper body.

   Spin Style. In the spin (discus-turn) style, the thrower makes a 1¾ spin as in the discus throw. The thrower must accelerate across the circle gradually in order to hit the power position. As in the glide style, the legs and hips lead the throw, and the shot is held against the neck at the jaw.

Discus Throw

As in the shot put, world distance records for the discus have increased with improvement in techniques and greater emphasis on speed, strength, and explosive power training.

1. *Grip.* The thrower holds the discus on the last crease of the fingers with the fingers spread or the first two fingers placed together.
2. *Preliminary Swings.* The thrower begins by standing at the back of the circle with the back opposite to the direction of the throw. With the legs bent slightly and the weight on the balls of the feet, the thrower initiates several preliminary swings shifting the weight from the right foot to the left as the discus is swung back and forth in a horizontal plane.
3. *Turn.* At the end of the final swing to the right, with the discus as far back as the thrower can

reach, the thrower prepares to enter the turn, pivoting over the left leg. The right leg is picked up and moves in an arc toward the front of the circle as the left leg drives forward. The legs and hips are kept ahead of the shoulders as the turn is performed.

4. *Power Position.* After the right foot lands in the middle of the circle, the thrower keeps pivoting until the left leg lands slightly bent. The thrower is now in a power position with the legs bent and the shoulders and the throwing arm back in a torqued position.
5. *Follow-Through.* The right hip drives through as the bent legs drive upward and the weight shifts to the left leg. The throwing arm is whipped through by this powerful leg/trunk action.

▶ **Learning Sequence**

1. The grip and release are taught first. The thrower, legs bent, flips the discus in the air or bowls it on the ground, making sure the discus comes off the index finger in a clockwise rotation (for a right-handed thrower).
2. The standing throw is taught next. In the power position, with the bent right leg at the nine o'clock position and the left leg at the six o'clock position, the thrower, shoulders torqued and throwing arm back, performs a series of standing throws. Concentration is on a right foot/right hip action beginning the initial movement of the throws.
3. The step back throw is now introduced. The thrower, standing in the center of the circle with the feet together, steps back with the left leg while sinking on the right, which achieves a power position. From this power position the thrower performs a series of throws.
4. The thrower is now ready for the 1¼ turn throw. Standing at the rear of the circle sideways to the direction of the throw, the thrower transfers weight to the left foot, pivots, and using a running sprint across the circle, lands in a good power position. From this position the thrower performs the throw.
5. After mastering this progression, the thrower can learn the 1¾ turn discus throw.

▶ **Learning Cues**

1. Keep the throwing arm up at shoulder level throughout the turns.
2. Before starting the turns, the shoulders and throwing arm are torqued back as far as possible.
3. The shoulders remain level during the turns and the legs bent.
4. Legs and hips always lead, which creates a "leg throw."

▶ **Practice Suggestions**

1. *Flip and Bowling Drills.* Used to teach the release, these drills are best learned with partners.
2. *Swing Drill.* With discus taped to the hand, practice the weight shift for the preliminary swings and getting the discus all the way back.
3. *Line-Turn Drill.* Facing the direction of the throw, the thrower pivots or turns on the right foot ending up for a power position throw. To simulate the discus throw, cones may be used in this drill.
4. *Standing Throw Drills.* With a traffic cone or any other soft, weighted object, the thrower, with feet together and back facing opposite to the throw, steps with the right foot into the power position, practicing leg/hip pop throws.

MODIFICATIONS FOR SPECIAL POPULATIONS

Orthopedically Impaired

1. Contact the National Wheelchair Athletic Association (NWAA), United States Cerebral Palsy Athletic Association (USCPAA), United States Les Autres Sports Association (USLASA) for their information on track and field.
2. Hold mock track and field meets in the gymnasium using modified equipment, e.g., toss bean bags instead of shot puts; suspend a rope between two standards and throw nerf balls over rope to simulate the high jump; vary the height of the rope.

Mentally Impaired

Contact local Special Olympics for their track and field manuals.

Sensory Impaired

Contact the American Athletic Association of the Deaf (AAAD) and/or United States Association of Blind Athletes (USABA) for their track and field manuals.

TERMINOLOGY

Aerobic running   Running done at low intensity speeds so that oxygen intake and oxygen output are the same; therefore, this type of running can be sustained for a long period.

Anaerobic running   Running done at great intensity speeds so that oxygen intake is less than oxygen output; therefore, this type of running can only be sustained for a short period.

Anchor leg   The last leg for a runner on a relay team.

Baton   The stick that is passed from one relay runner to another.

Blind pass   A nonvisual baton exchange used in sprint relays.

Crossbar   The bar which a high jumper or pole vaulter must clear.

Discus   One of the field events in track and field in which a cylinder-like object is thrown. The weight and size of the discus may vary according to the age of the participants.

False start   Moving or jumping before the gun is fired.

Fartlek   Swedish term for "speed play," a type of training in which a runner varies running speeds over a long distance, usually in a forest, golf course, or other non-track area.

Flight   The in-the-air techniques for the long jump and triple jump.

Flop style   The style of high jumping in which the jumper's back passes over the bar.

Fly zone   The 10-meter zone outside the passing zone used by the outgoing runner to get a flying start.

Gather   In jumping events, the settling or lowering of the hips during the last few strides prior to take-off.

Heat   Preliminary race whose winners qualify for the semi-finals or finals.

Hitch kick   A running-in-the-air action during flight in the long jump, used to prevent forward rotation.

Interval training   A type of running training containing four variables: the number of repetitions, distance, tempo of run, and rest interval.

Passing zone   The 20-meter zone in which the baton in a relay must be exchanged (passed).

Relay leg   The distance each runner travels in a relay.

TAC   The Athletics Congress, the governing body of track and field in the United States.

Take-off board   The board from which the long jumper takes off.

Throwing sector   The specified arc in which a thrown implement must land.

Toe-board   A board, in the form of an arc, on which or over which the shot-putter must not step.

Trial   An attempt in a field event.

Visual pass   The pass used in the distance relays in which the outgoing runner visually watches the incoming runner during baton exchange.

SELECTED REFERENCES

Gambetta, V. *Track and Field Coaching Manual.* 2nd ed. Champaign, IL: Leisure Press, 1989.

Bowerman, W.J. and Freeman, W. H. *High Performance Training for Track and Field,* 2nd ed. Leisure Press, 1991.

Doherty, J.K. *Track and Field Omnibook,* 4th ed. Los Altos, CA: Track and Field News Press, 1985.

National Collegiate Athletic Association. *Official Track and Field Guide,* current ed. New York: National Collegiate Athletic Bureau.

National Federation of State High School Athletic Associations. *Track and Field Rules,* current ed. Washington, D.C.

Powell, J.T. *Track and Field Fundamentals for Teacher and Coach,* 3rd ed. Champaign, IL: Stripes Publishing Company, 1971.

Periodicals

Track and Field News. 2570 E. Camino Real, Suite 606, Mountain View, CA 94040.

Track and Field Quarterly Review. 1705 Evanson St., Kalamazoo, MI 49008.

Track Technique. (Available through *Track and Field News*)

Audio-Visual Materials

The following videos and cassettes can be ordered through *Track and Field News:*

1988 Olympic Track and Field (Men)

1988 Olympic Track and Field (Women)

Bill Dellinger's Championship Track and Field (17 cassettes)

Women's Track and Field Video Series (9 videos)

Rick Sloan's Men's Track and Field guides

25 VOLLEYBALL

THIS CHAPTER WILL ENABLE YOU TO:

▶ Describe the nature and adaptability of volleyball.
▶ Apply basic skills in modified practice games.
▶ Describe and execute in game play the skills of overhand pass, forearm pass, serve, spike, and blocking.
▶ Describe, discuss, and put into practice the rules of power volleyball during a game or match.
▶ Describe play in power volleyball using the correct terminology associated with the sport.

NATURE AND ADAPTABILITY

Volleyball is an adaptable team sport which may be played by various numbers of players (from 2-on-2 to 6-on-6); by all-male, all-female, or mixed teams; with net height adjustments for men, women, co-ed, or age group differences; and using a variety of playing surfaces (wood, rubberized material, sand, or grass).

Volleyball is a net game and a rebound sport in which, following the initiation of play (serve), the ball may not visibly come to rest. Each team is allowed a maximum of three contacts before the ball is returned across the net. A player may not play the ball twice in succession.

The basic objective of the game is to keep the ball, which is served over the net, from contacting the floor on your side and to return it so that it contacts the floor on the opponents' side before they can return it. Skillful, organized play involves using the three allowable contacts to pass, set, and attack the ball (offense). The opponents attempt to block the ball at the net before it crosses, dig it if the ball evades the block, or pass a nonforcefully returned ball skillfully making the transition back onto offense. The continuous cycle repeats until the rally is terminated; hence, either a point is scored (serving team only) or a side-out is awarded with the opponents earning the right then to serve. The sequence is repeated until one team reaches 15 points with at least a 2-point advantage.

Since all players on the team must rotate one position clockwise each time they earn a side-out assures that one-half of the time individual players have restrictions concerning net play. This controls domination of the net by taller players and requires that each individual become a more complete player possessing a variety of skills and techniques.

There are five basic skills, each having a variety of techniques. The air skills of attack and block are normally performed in the attack area near the net while the ground skills of forearm pass, overhand pass, and serve are utilized while in contact with the playing surface.

Teams involving six players use organized systems for serve reception, attack coverage, defense, and offense. The organized game involves specialization using the individual talents and skills of the players such as setters, attackers, passers, etc.

The flexibility in number of players, sexes, equipment adjustments, and playing surfaces allows for individual preference and for selecting a variety of competition levels. Due to its adaptability volleyball may be played on any level—from recreational to national, international, and professional.

EQUIPMENT

Volleyball is an inexpensive activity. The player's equipment is minimal requiring only rubber-soled shoes and possibly knee pads (individual preference) for hard playing surfaces or for safety. A ball, net, and net supports are the only other equipment necessary. Volleyballs are available in different sizes, weights, and coverings. The recommended covering is either synthetic leather or leather with a molded carcass. Care should be taken in selecting a ball that is not too hard and that meets the abilities of the players.

THE COURT

The court (Figure 25-1) is divided into equal halves separated by a center line and net. Each half has a front court attack area which restricts back row players from attacking or blocking in that area.

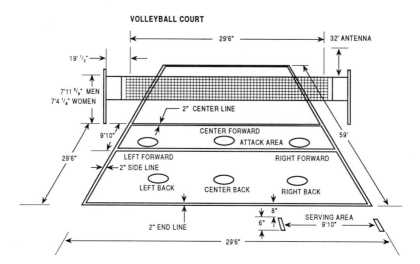

FIGURE 25-1 The official volleyball court markings and dimensions.

There is a serving area in the right back of each half court for determining where the serve is legally initiated. The boundary lines are considered a part of the court; thus, a ball landing on these lines is considered inbounds.

Nets should extend at least one foot on each side of the court (32 feet), have 4 inch square mesh openings, and a flexible cord or cable running through a 2 inch wide white band at the top. The net supports should be located at least 19½ inches outside the sideline, and be anchored securely enough to allow the net to be safely stretched tight without any sag below the required height. Supports with easily adjustable settings assist in quickly varying net height.

The net height is adaptable for differences in player size, sex, and team composition. Men's regulation height is 7 feet 11⅝ inches and women's is 7 feet 4⅛ inches. A ball contacting the net within the boundaries of the court is considered playable except if it is on the serve. In regulation play, antennas extend upward from the net directly above the sideline to assist in determining whether the ball crossed the net within the court. A ball contacting the antenna is out of play.

BASIC RULES

Players and Rotation. When the ball is not in play, the players must remain in the proper rotation order which establishes the sequential service order. Proper rotation order (6 on 6) establishes three front row and three back row players (Figure 25-2). The back row players may not legally enter the front court attack area to block or attack the ball over the net. When the ball is dead, players may not overlap with a player who is in an adjacent position. "Adjacent" refers to the player in the corresponding

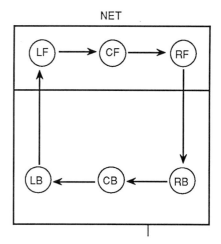

FIGURE 25-2 Team position and rotation.

position on the opposite row (example: center back with center front), plus the teammate(s) next to that player on the same row (example: center back with *both* left back and right back). The players all rotate one position clockwise following a rally in which they win the right to serve (side out).

Serve. The player who rotates to the right back position serves or if at the start of the game is the first server. The serve is initiated from within the serving area (see Figure 25-1) and behind the boundary line. The objective is to serve the ball across the net into the opponent's court. It is a fault (illegal) if the ball contacts the net, or the antenna, or does not land in the court.

Playing the Ball. Each team has a maximum of three contacts each time the ball crosses into their court. A ball contacting the block does not count as one of the three allowable contacts. No player may play the ball twice in succession, except if they contacted the ball as a blocker.

The ball may not visibly come to rest; if it does it is considered a held ball (fault). A held ball frequently results when a player uses the hands in executing an overhand pass. The ball may not be guided, lifted, or pushed in an effort to redirect it, nor may the ball contact any part of the body below the waist.

Net Play. A player may not contact any part of the net or it is a fault. A ball contacting the net is considered playable other than on the serve. A player may reach across the net to contact the ball on the opponent's side provided it was attacked by the opponent. Likewise, a player may cross the net when attacking the ball provided part of it was on the attacker's side when it was contacted. Opponents simultaneously blocking the ball may result in a held ball, which is then replayed with no point scored (play over).

A player may contact the ball on the opponent's side *underneath* the net while attempting to save the ball. The boundary line below the net separating the court restricts players from stepping into the opponent's area. Standing on the line is legal as long as part of the foot is in contact with the line. Any other part of the body on the floor and across the line is illegal.

Scoring. The serve starts play, and the objective is to keep the ball from contacting one's own floor and without violating the rules, rally until the opponents fail. When the team serving wins the rally a point is scored. If not serving and the rally is won by the nonserving team, they earn a side out, rotate, and serve next. The first team to score 15 points and ahead by at least 2 points, wins the game. A match consists of either winning 2 out of 3 or 3 out of 5 games.

SUGGESTED LEARNING SEQUENCE

Beginning Level

A. Running, stretching and explosive sprinting/jumping.
B. Introduction—Nature and Purpose
C. Basic Rules
D. Fundamental Skills
  1. Movement skills
    a. Low Position
      1. Shuffle step
      2. Forward/backward
    b. Medium Position
      1. Shuffle step
      2. Run lateral/forward
      3. Backpedal
  2. Serve
    a. Underhand
    b. Overhand floater
  3. Forearm Pass
    a. Serve reception
    b. Free-ball pass
    c. Side to target
    d. Back to target
  4. Overhand Pass
    a. Set forward
    b. Free-ball pass
  5. Attack
    a. Spike roll
    b. Spike
E. Strategies
  1. Use 3 contacts
    a. Pass to center front—8′ × 8′
    b. Set to left front
    c. Spike roll/spike
  2. Make opponents play the ball
  3. Serve in court 80%–90%
F. Systems
  1. Five-person, "W" serve reception pattern
  2. Free-ball defense
  3. 6–6 or 4–2 offense
G. Play Modified Games (instant winner)
  1. 1 on 1, 2 on 2, 3 on 3
  2. Small court—½ wide front court
  3. Toss on serve
  4. Vary type of contact required

Intermediate Level

A. Running, partner stretching, and explosive sprinting/jumping
B. Review Beginning Unit
C. Fundamental Skills
  1. Serve
    a. Overhead floater
      1. Deep
      2. Short
  2. Forearm
    a. Dig
      1. Stride and slide
  3. Overhand Pass
    a. Set backward
  4. Attack
    a. Spike
      1. Power angle
    b. Lob
      1. Dink
      2. Roll
  5. Block
    a. One blocker
    b. Two blockers
D. Strategies
  1. Serve–weak opponent/deep corners
  2. Dig to middle of court 15 × 15 ft.
  3. Set forward and backward—12 to 15 ft. high to 3 × 3 ft. target
  4. Spike cross court and lob over block-short.
  5. Block
    a. Take away cross court
    b. No hole between blockers

E. Systems
    1. Repeat beginning unit
    2. Spiker coverage
    3. 2–1–3 defense
    4. 4–2 or 5–1 offense
F. Play modified games and 6 on 6
    1. Modifications (point on each serve—5 points winner stays.
        a. Court ½ wide, full length 3 on 3—must use 3 contacts.
        b. Full court 4 on 4 (3 back, 1 at net)—no block.
    2. Full game—6 on 6 with no modifications.

SKILLS AND TECHNIQUES

Volleyball comprises five basic skills: forearm pass, overhand pass, serve, attack, and block. Each skill uses a variety of techniques which players need as they progress from beginning to advanced levels of competition.

The ball handling skills—*forearm pass* and *overhand pass*—and their associated techniques constitute at least two-thirds of the ball contacts during play. The *serve* often dominates play both positively and negatively at the beginning to intermediate levels and is a crucial skill because the rules allows a team to score only while serving. The *attack* adds offense and power to the game but can only be utilized when the ball handling skills become accurate and consistent. The *block* is used only when the opposing team consistently attacks the ball from a point near or above the net, forcefully driving it downward into one's court.

Forearm Pass

The forearm pass (also called "pass," "bump," or "dig") with its associated techniques is the most frequently used ball handling skill. It is utilized to pass the serve, play balls below the waist, play hard driven balls, and contact balls located far from the player. Employing this skill avoids official ball handling violations.

▶ **Learning Cues**

1. Feet are shoulder width apart, in a stagger stance (heel-toe relationship), and the body weight is forward on the inside front half of each foot with the heels slightly off the ground (Figure 25-3).
2. Knees are flexed approximately 90 degrees, inside the feet and in front of the toes.
3. Upper body is in a front leaning position with waist flexed approximately 90 degrees and the shoulders in front of the knees.
4. Hands are connected by pressing the pads of both thumbs together with the base of the

FIGURE 25-3 Body position for the forearm pass.

thumbs even and level. The grip is relaxed with the hands extended downward. Several methods for clasping the hands together (back of one hand across palm of other, interlock fingers, fist of one hand cupped by fingers of other) are acceptable as long as they follow the foregoing (Figure 25-4).
5. Arms reach out in front of the body, elbows rotate inward together and are locked exposing the fleshy part of the forearm. The arms are parallel with the thigh of the leading leg. Attempt to align with the approaching ball as near as possible to the midline of the body.
6. Ball contact is on the fleshy part of the forearm approximately 2 to 6 inches above the wrist. The trajectory angle of the rebound is dependent upon the angle of the forearms. The eyes focus on the ball until contact and following rebound.
7. Force is provided to the ball when needed by a slight bunting action of the arms, extension of the legs, and body lean toward the intended target. A hard driven ball from the opponents might require absorption of the force at contact by dropping of the forearms upon contact as a cushioning effect.

▶ **Practice Suggestions**

Use the part method for learning to isolate and reinforce correct contact. Start on one knee, leaning forward and bunt a controlled tossed ball back to a partner standing 10 feet away. Establish accuracy standards to check progress and to motivate. Repeat, except from the correct whole body position. Next, add lateral shuffle steps prior to toss. Finally, attempt to pass the ball repeatedly back and forth between partners who are 15 feet apart. When control is achieved, move to small court to play modified small side competitive games (see Modified Games).

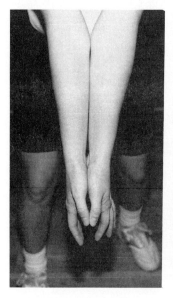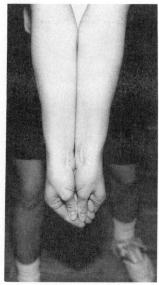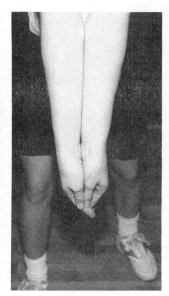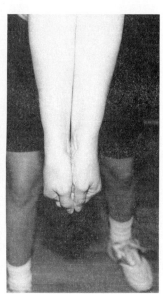

FIGURE 25-4 Hand position and forearm surface.

Overhand Pass

The overhand pass is the most controllable of the ball handling skills. It is used for accurately passing any ball above the head to a teammate and for the setting technique of passing the ball to an attacker with specific height, trajectory, and placement. Ball/hand contact and precise alignment with the ball make the skill more susceptible to official ball handling violations.

▶ **Learning Cues**

1. Feet, knees, and upper body (same as Forearm Pass, # 1, 2, and 3).
2. Align ball with the forehead hairline (Figure 25-5).
3. Arms are raised, elbows flexed (90 degrees) at approximately chin height, and the hands are equally positioned six inches above the forehead with the wrist flexed back (Figure 25-6).
4. Fingers and hands are spread into the shape of the approaching ball, thumbs pointing toward the nose and wrist flexed back. The thumbs are approximately three inches apart and the index fingers about twice as far apart.
5. Ball contact is on the inside edge of the first digital areas of the thumbs, index, middle, and ring fingers, and the ball is allowed to almost slide through with the hands on the side.
6. Force is initiated by the thighs, ball/hand contact is made and finally the arms are extended fully. The synchronized action is THRUST (thighs)—CONTACT (hands)—EXTEND (arms) for the correct, smooth, and sequential action. Weight finishes forward on the front (right) foot with all body action directed toward target.

FIGURE 25-5 Body position and alignment to ball on overhand pass.

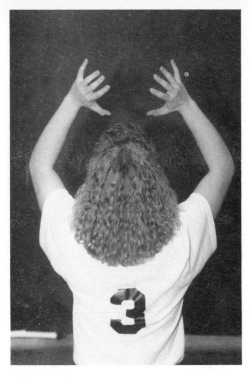

FIGURE 25-6 Arms, hand shaping, wrist flex, and finger/thumb position prior to overhand contact.

FIGURE 25-7 Whole body ready position prior to overhand contact.

▶ Practice Suggestions

The part method aids in the development of the many aspects for skillful execution of the overhand pass. Start on the left knee with the right foot forward in a kneeling position. Place the arms and hands in the correct position for receiving the ball (see Learning Cues #3 and #4). The ball is tossed accurately and gently into the hands by a partner who is just three feet away. Play the ball six feet straight up so it drops on the tosser's head. Use the "force" sequence of CONTACT-EXTEND to play the ball (see Learning Cues #5 and #6). Next, assume a full squat position and duplicate the foregoing playing it 10 feet high. The "force" sequence now entails THRUST-CONTACT-EXTEND to play the ball.

When accuracy and synchronization are established, stand in a medium ready position (Figure 25-7) to receive a ball tossed from a partner 10 feet away. Adjust to the tossed ball and play it 10 feet high, returning it to the tosser. Finally, attempt to volley the ball repeatedly with a partner and move to modified small side competitive games (see Modified Games) when control and accuracy is achieved.

Serve

A consistent serve is important because only the serving team can score. The serve has an expected success rate that is 80 to 90 percent higher than the other skills because the server tosses the ball to himself rather than receiving the ball from another player. Equally important is the fact that the serve is the first opportunity a team has to put the opponent at a disadvantage. The overhand floater serve provides both power and consistency (Figure 25-8).

FIGURE 25-8 The overhand floater serve.

▶ **Learning Cues**

1. Stand or step and stride with the opposite foot from the striking arm (left foot for right-handed person). That lead foot is positioned 2 feet in front of the back foot and is pointed directly toward the intended target. The stride starts as the ball is tossed into the air.

2. The toss is made in front of the striking shoulder and at contact is in front of the striding body parallel to the front foot. The ball is tossed low (1 to 2 feet above head height) for controlled accuracy. A two-handed spin free toss aids accuracy.

3. The striking arm action on the toss resembles an overhand throwing motion (Figure 25-9). As the ball is released (approximately shoulder level) on the toss, the arm flexes, elbow draws back at shoulder height, the upper body rotates so that the non-striking shoulder is in a leading position and the alignment of both shoulders is approximately 45 degrees with the back line of the court. The elbow snaps forward ahead of the wrist, and the forearm accelerates in preparation for ball/hand contact.

4. The wrist of the striking arm is tense and locked, the hand open wide presenting a flat contact surface, and the ball is aggressively contacted with the bottom half (heel) of the hand at a point slightly higher than head level.

5. Velocity is generated by the elbow snap throwing the forearm forward, and the ball accelerates rapidly as it is contacted with the hard surface (heel) of the hand.

6. Body weight transfers to the front foot, and the forearm of the striking arm is immediately stopped at contact producing a recoil action.

7. Body balance is maintained as both feet remain in contact with the floor and all movement is directly at the target on the follow-through.

▶ **Practice Suggestions**

Practice the toss and stride (Cues #1 and #2), letting the ball drop to the floor. The ball should land to the side of the body, in front of the striking shoulder, and parallel with the front foot.

Progress to the whole skill with a partner. Students stand 10 feet from the net on opposite sides. The ball is tossed and served at the net (1 to 3 feet above) on a straight line using the up-stretched arms and hands of the partner to check accuracy. Observe the served ball to make sure it is not rotating in flight but floating spin-free.

Gradually move back from the net maintaining (a) a straight line trajectory, (b) spin-free (floater) flight, and (c) accuracy. The greater the distance the more emphasis on providing force to ball contact

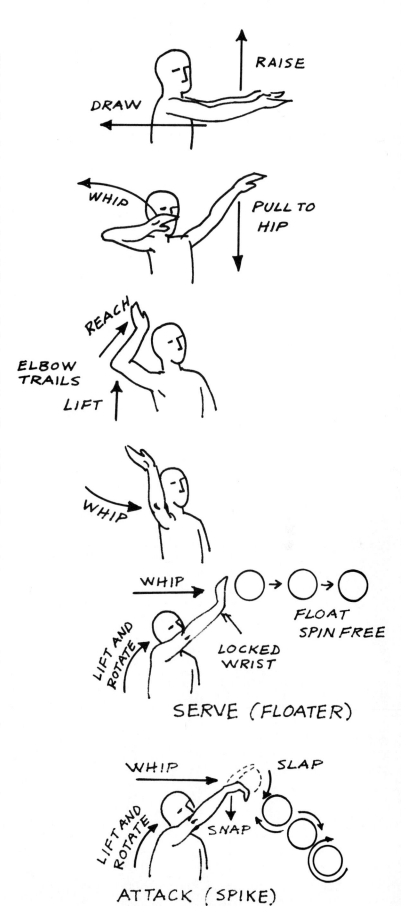

FIGURE 25-9 The striking arm action for the overhand serve and the attack (ball/hand contact and wrist action are different).

(Cues 3–6). Continue moving back until the serve can be initiated legally from behind the back line.

Attack

The attack is used in aggressive play against the opponents to keep them from returning the ball or making a transition to return it aggressively. The types of attack are the spike, lob, and drive, with the emphasis on performing these techniques from as high a position off the floor as possible.

The *spike* is contacted above the midline and at the back of the ball, attempting to impart top spin and drive the ball downward into the opponent's court. The *lob* is contacted below the midline and at the back of the ball, attempting to play it up over the block. The *drive* is contacted in the middle back of the ball, attempting to propel it off the blocker's hands.

In beginning to intermediate levels of play one does not consistently receive a ball from teammates in a manner which allows time to jump and attack the ball. The technique of the *spike roll* provides an intermediate step between returning the ball easily (free ball) to the opponents and jumping to spike the ball downward into the opponent's court. It also gives a short player an opportunity to attack the opponents even though that player may be unable to contact the ball above the net.

▶ **Learning Cues**

Spike Roll

1. Align with the ball so that it is dropping directly above the striking arm's shoulder.
2. The feet are in a stagger stance (see the first sentence in Serve Learning Cues #1).
3. Both arms lift above the head. The shoulders rotate approximately 45 degrees with the non-striking arm in a leading position (Figure 25-10A). The nonstriking arm fully extends and points at the descending ball. The striking arm, in a motion resembling an overhand throw, flexes at the elbow as it draws back at shoulder height.
4. The nonstriking arm starts the hitting action by pulling toward the hip on that side as the striking arm's elbow snaps forward simultaneously lifting higher. The hand and forearm of the striking arm move from a lead position of the elbow to a position trailing it. The hand is open, fingers spread, and wrist flexed back fully (Figure 25-10B).
5. The firm, open hand is thrown at the ball with initial contact made on the bottom back quarter of the ball with the palm simultaneously snapping the wrist forward (SLAP and SNAP). The hand goes from a below ball initial contact to one at follow-through, which is over the top. This imparts the essential top spin on the ball (Figure 25-10C).

| A | B | C | D |

FIGURE 25-10   Spike roll: (A) both arms positioned to strike, (B) non-striking arm pulls down and striking arm elbow snaps forward, (C) open hand contacts the bottom back quarter of the ball, (D) SLAP ball, SNAP wrist and finish in high position.

6. Body weight transfers to the front foot, and the striking arm finishes in an extended high position with the wrist fully snapped forward, fingers pointing toward the ground upon completion (Figure 25-10D).

7. Body balance (see Serve, Learning Cue #7).

Spike

1. The approach to jump is started from a point approximately 12 feet from the net, depending on the length of the attacker's stride. It is an angular approach directly to where the ball is descending, the angle dependent upon the approach position (left, center or right front) and the handedness of the attacker. A right-handed person's approach is 45 degrees toward the net from the left front (LF) position and increases moving to the remaining positions (CF & RF). A left-handed player also makes a 45-degree angle in approaching from the opposite side (RF), the angle increasing when in CF and LF positions. Figure 25-11 shows the approach to jump sequence.

2. The footwork consists of four final steps: a short step with the same side foot as the striking arm (Figure 25-11A), followed by an elongated running stride with the opposite foot (Figure 25-11B), followed by an almost simultaneous step, step/close gathering for a maximum vertical jump (Figure 25-11C & D). The length of the second step depends on the desired distance and speed. The next step, step/close is a breaking heel plant rocking to the balls of the feet for a two-footed take-off in the jump. The feet are 8 to 10 inches apart on the step/close with the foot opposite the striking hand ahead of the other foot (Figure 25-11D). The legs flex approximately 90 degrees for maximum jumping thrust.

3. The arms assist in providing force for jumping. They function identically during the approach and are extended straight, behind and nearly parallel to the floor at the two-footed take-off (Figure 25-11D). The arms thrust vigorously forward and upward for lifting force as the legs thrust for the vertical jump (Figure 25-12A).

4. The take-off point aligns the body with the ball so that it can be contacted 6 to 18 inches in front of the body and in front of the striking shoulder.

5. The arm action for striking starts as the body leaves the floor (see Spike Roll, Cues #3 and #4 and Figure 25-12B).

6. The firm open hand is thrown at the ball with initial contact made on the top back quarter of the ball (Figure 25-12D) with the palm simultaneously snapping the wrist forward (SLAP and SNAP) (see Figure 25-9). This imparts top spin on the ball and drives it downward toward the opponent's court.

7. The simultaneous coordination of the arm and leg action while suspended in air provide force and body control. The arm action is performed as the legs are flexed and then vigorously snapped down providing a piking action by the upper and lower body (Figure 25-12C).

8. The legs are flexed upon contacting the floor to prevent injury and to regain stability.

Lob

1. The approach, footwork, arm action, alignment to ball, upper and lower body coordination, and landing are identical to the spike (see Spike, Cues 1–5 and 7). The only difference is the ball/hand contact.

2. Ball/hand contact is made in the lower back quarter of the ball causing it to take an upward trajectory over the block. As the hand comes forward on the striking action, the fingers and thumb are formed to make contact with the surface of the ball with the first digital area of each. The contact is referred to as a "dink," which is the most common type of lob used at the beginning to intermediate level of play.

A   B   C   D

FIGURE 25-11 Spike. Approach footwork and arm positions prior to jump in attack (right-handed).

FIGURE 25-12   Attack: (A and B) actions of whole body in take-off, (C) striking motion, (D) ball/hand contact.

Drive

1. As with the lob, the only difference between the drive and the spike is the ball/hand contact.
2. The ball is contacted in the middle back causing it to take a trajectory parallel with the floor and deflecting off the blocker's fingers. The hand contact as in the spike is with the firm open surface of the palm but driving the ball straight ahead instead of downward.

▶ **Practice Suggestions**

The ball/hand contact (SLAP) is developed by holding the bottom of the ball firmly with the nonstriking hand. Position the ball at arms length

in front of the striking shoulder and at head height. With the striking arm hanging straight down at the side, initiate the correct arm action by lifting it straight forward and upward until it is beside the ball. Use the throwing action (see Spike Roll, Cues #3 and #4) and ball/hand contact (see Spike Cue #6) to aggressively "slap" the back/top quarter area of the ball developing the feeling of the palm contact.

Repeat the foregoing but hit the ball downward out of the holding hand to the floor. Stand 6 feet from a wall so that the ball hits the floor and then rebounds off the wall. Emphasize the ball/hand contact and power component (wrist snap) for force-SLAP and SNAP. Finish with the striking arm high and fully extended with the palm facing the floor and fingers pointing down.

Next, toss the ball in front of the striking shoulder using both hands to toss it precisely 4 feet high. Both arms extend up as if jumping (see Spike Roll, Cue #3) and duplicate the complete arm action (Cues #3 and #4) contacting the ball (see Spike Cue #6) driving it to the floor as in the foregoing.

Next toss and jump off 2 feet, repeating the foregoing arm lift, striking action (both arms), and ball/hand contact.

Practice the approach footwork (see Spike Cues # 1, 2, and 3) toward the net and mimic the correct striking arm actions previously described without using a ball. Next, place a tennis ball in the striking hand and repeat the approach, footwork, jump, and arm action throwing the tennis ball over the net with an aggressive wrist snap. Emphasize the SNAP and a high straight arm finish of the throwing arm.

Proceed to hitting a volleyball over the net. A partner, with side to net and three feet from net, tosses the ball 12 feet straight up so the attacker can approach, jump, and attack the ball. The tosser stands on the attacker's hitting arm side careful to use a two-hand underhand toss such that the ball goes straight up and down directly in alignment with the attacker's striking arm. The tosser gradually moves laterally away from the attacker, tossing higher (15 to 18 feet) with a trajectory that drops in alignment with the approach path of the attacker.

Block

The block is used to counter a forceful attack defensively. This is accomplished by jumping and positioning the hands above and over the net, decreasing the area available for the attacker to drive the ball downward forcefully into the blocker's court. The use of two blockers on one attacker increases the area of the block, conversely decreasing the court area available for a downward attack. Defensive systems are developed around the block.

Not every attack calls for blocking since the attacker controls the path of the attack. The objective of the block, aside from reducing the area an opponent can attack, is to render the ball unreturnable while it is in the opponents' court. The success rate for effective blocking is low and negative outcomes are possible. Therefore the decision on whether or not to block is governed by the attacker's ability to drive the ball downward into the court from a position near or above the net.

▶ Learning Cues

Ready Position (Figure 25-13A)

1. The feet are in a parallel stance, shoulders parallel to the net. Stand 6 to 12 inches from the net with knees slightly flexed for quick movement.
2. The hands are positioned between the net and the body at shoulder height with fingers spread and palms facing the net.
3. The elbows are flexed and touching the rib cage with the forearms perpendicular to the floor.
4. The back is straight.

Jump

1. The knees flex to near 100-degree angle for a quick and maximum jump (Figure 25-13B).

FIGURE 25-13 Block: (A) ready position, (B) knee flex, (C) net penetration and piking action.

A

B

C

2. Thrust off from the floor equally with both legs and thrust the arms straight upward parallel with the net.
3. As the hands clear net height, gently push them across as far as possible, careful not to touch the net (Figure 25-13C). Position the outside hand slightly toward the court to deflect the ball inward.
4. Pike slightly at the waist for balance and power (Figure 25-13C).
5. Upon descending, gently withdraw hands, returning them in front of the shoulders.
6. Upon floor contact, bend the knees to absorb shock and for balance. Pivot away from the net following the direction of the ball.

Movement Footwork

1. To adjust 3 to 6 feet laterally use one to two shuffles steps keeping hands up, feet parallel, and shoulders parallel to net prior to jumping.
2. A longer adjustment requires a step, run, and plant footwork:
   a. *Step.* Take a step with the foot nearest the ball, pointing the foot toward the sideline.
   b. *Run.* The shoulders rotate from a parallel position to perpendicular as the trail leg takes a running stride for distance and speed toward the sideline.
   c. *Plant.* Both feet hop into a plant with both returning to a parallel position of toes toward the net. The hop is a breaking of momentum as knees flex for a vertical jump.
3. The hands remain in the "ready" position throughout all footwork prior to jumping.

▶ Practice Suggestions

Blocker stands facing a partner three feet away who is holding a volleyball firmly with arms fully extended upward. In a standing "ready" position the blocker thrusts the arms upward surrounding the held ball to assume ball/hand contact. Next, duplicate the foregoing with both players squatting to jump prior to arm action and ball/hand contact. Movement footwork can be added plus a net between partners.

Using a net between partners, the blocker assumes the "ready" position directly in alignment with the partner who is standing three feet away from net. The partner self tosses the ball and jumps to spike (see Spike Practice Suggestions) the ball into the hands of the blocker, who has jumped to intercept it on the spiker's side of the net. Add two blockers to the foregoing drill.

MODIFIED GAMES

It is not necessary that a skill be mastered nor that all skills be taught before playing on the court. When players can adjust to a moving ball and perform the whole skill, it is time to play modified games on the court.

Modifications can be made in a variety of criteria: court size, height of net, number and alignment of players, number of contacts allowed, type and combinations of skills, special rules for desired outcomes, etc. The games should have an immediate winner/loser so that everyone is participating quickly without waiting.

Games provide motivation, enjoyment, teamwork, communication skills, strategy, and most of all, immediate feedback on performance. Following is an example:

Court: ½ court wide and 10 ft front (10 × 15).
Players: 2 on 2
Rules:

1. Immediate winner of the rally; winner moves to winner's side of the net; losers move to end of waiting line; two new players challenge winners.
2. Play starts with an easy toss (serve) from the challengers to the winners.
3. Must make *two* contacts only.
4. First contact *must* be forearm and second contact *must* be overhand.
5. On each contact that player *must* call "mine" (communication) prior to contact.
6. Rally continues until play terminates—rules broken or ball not returned.
7. A point is scored if the players on the "winner's side of net" win. If challengers win rally, they change to "winner's side of net" to have an opportunity to score a point, and their opponents rotate out to the end of the waiting line (NOTE: Have no more than 8 persons per ½ court—two volleyball courts equal 32 players).
8. Losers chase the ball. Each waiting couple has a ball.
9. First to accumulate 5 points wins game.
10. Option: Change partners each time the losers go to end of line. Each player would then carry individual score forward instead of a team score.

PLAYING STRATEGIES

Offensive Play

Offenses in power volleyball have developed widely in the last several years. While the techniques of passing and spiking have changed relatively little, the methods by which the spike is obtained vary greatly.

In most beginning programs or physical education classes, the 6–6 offense would be the simplest to administer. In this offense all six players spike when rotating to the spiking positions and any of them will also be setters when rotating into a setting position. The 4–2 offense is very similar, except that four members of the team are basically spikers and two

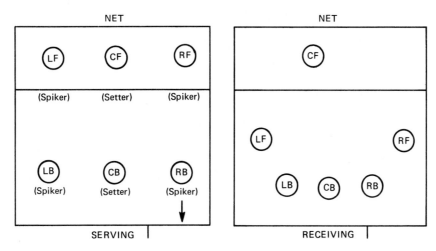

FIGURE 25-14 The 4-2 offense: (A) serving, (B) receiving.

members are used essentially as setters. For the alignment of the 4–2 offense, see Figure 25-14A.

The 4–2 offense can certainly be used in physical eduation classes. It allows smaller players to develop skills as setters and become an integral part of the volleyball team. Although relatively simple, the 4–2 offense includes some of the concepts used in the more complex 5–1 and 6–0 offenses.

In preparing to receive a serve (Figure 25-14B), players face the server in a semi-crouched position, prepared to return the ball with a forearm pass. Every attempt is made to direct the first pass to the center front position (setter, either with or without switching) with an arc of 12 to 16 feet. This high pass gives the setter ample time to get to the ball. The setter positions under the ball and faces the direction he or she plans to set the ball for the spiker.

The setter attempts to pass or "set" the ball 6 to 10 feet above the net, 2 to 3 feet from the net, and near the sideline. This sideline set gives the spiker three advantages: (1) the center blocker has a greater distance to travel; (2) the spiked ball may rebound back out of bounds; and (3) a ball spiked diag-

onally across court has a greater area in which to land for a point.

Team coverages on the spike for the 4–2 offense are shown in Figure 25-15.

It is necessary for the spiking team to form a "cup" around the spiker to protect against a blocked spike that returns immediately back into their court. The players not in the cup follow the ball, looking for a ball that is blocked high and deep.

When the offensive team is serving, the front line players are close to the net in preparation for the blocking of a spike (Figure 25-16).

Defensive Play

Defenses in power volleyball may vary as widely as the offenses, but the primary job of the defense is to offset the spiking action of the opponents. This can be done by blocking and rejecting the ball or controlling it on your own side of the court, which results in a passing-setting-spiking combination.

Players move to base defensive positions when the ball goes into the opponent's court (Figure 25-

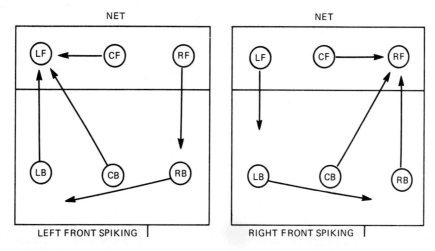

FIGURE 25-15 Coverage for the spiker in the 4-2 offense when serving.

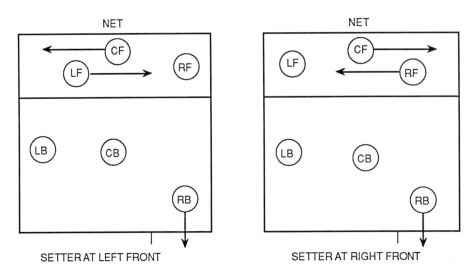

FIGURE 25-16 Switiching the setter in the 4-2 offense when serving.

17A). Switching positions between players is usually done to capitalize upon any specialization skills. For example, at the beginning level the setter might switch to the center front position to set.

Player-Back Defense

The player-back or 2-4 defense provides good deep coverage with four players stationed near the court's perimeter and two men blocking. The starting positions and areas covered by each player are shown in Figure 25-17B. The blockers attempt to

protect more against the sideline spike by the positioning of the block. This defense is used by a team whose players are not particularly tall but very quick and agile.

Player-Up Defense

The player-up or 2-1-3 defense is shown in Figure 25-18. The player that is "up" is the center back who moves to a position behind the block and covers all dinks, or deflections that fall short. The blockers attempt to protect against a crosscourt spike by es-

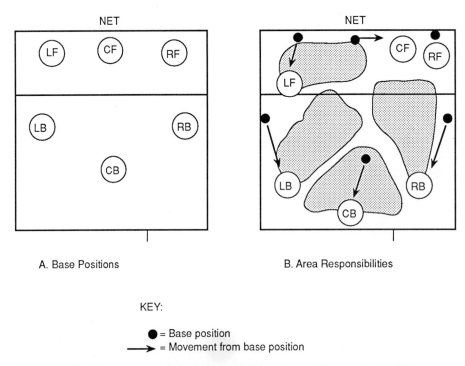

A. Base Positions   B. Area Responsibilities

KEY:

● = Base position
⟶ = Movement from base position

FIGURE 25-17 The player back/2-4 defense: (A) base positions, (B) area responsibilities.

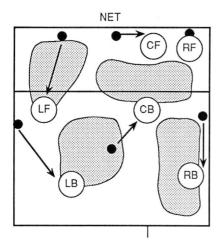

FIGURE 25-18 The player up/2-1-3 defense and area responsibilities.

tablishing their block to the inside of the spiker. It is hoped that the spiker will attempt to hit down the line where the right back defensive player is waiting. This defense would be used by a team that is tall and blocks well.

Serve Reception

The five-person "W" formation is used at the beginning level. It provides complete coverage of the court (Figure 25-19). The front row setter positions near the net in each of the three rotation positions in order to set the second contact. The setter is careful not to be out of position by overlapping with a teammate who is in an adjacent position until contact is made on the serve. Upon contact the setter quickly positions with the right side to the net approximately 12 feet from the right sideline, keeping the middle of the court in front where the passed ball descends.

MODIFICATIONS FOR SPECIAL POPULATIONS

Orthopedically Impaired

1. Contact the United States Amputee Athletic Association (USAAA) for information on sitting volleyball for individuals with a spinal cord injury.
2. Instead of volleyball use a beachball or balloons.
3. Use a rope for the net, and lower the height.
4. For students with severe mobility problems, play a modified game of tetherball.

Mentally Impaired

1. Contact local Special Olympics for their volleyball manuals.
2. Play lead-up game of Newcomb to develop concept of the game. Newcomb is played like volleyball except the players are allowed to throw and catch the ball.
3. See suggested modifications for Tennis.

Sensory Impaired

1. Individual considerations must be taken into account as to the appropriateness of volleyball for the blind and visually impaired.
2. Minimal modifications are needed for the deaf and/or hearing impaired.

TERMINOLOGY

Attack Any method used to return the ball across the net in an attempt to put the opponents at a disadvantage.

Ball handling Execution of any passing fundamental.

Block The process of intercepting the ball, just before or as it crosses the net. A block may be executed by any front row player.

Bump (See Forearm pass)

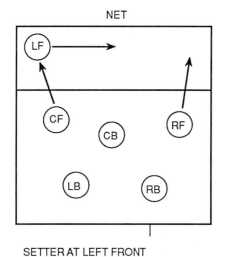

SETTER AT LEFT FRONT

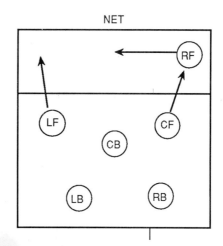

SETTER AT RIGHT FRONT

FIGURE 25-19 Five-person "W" formation serve reception.

Court coverage The court assignment of each player on defense.

Dig An emergency pass, usually used to defend a hard-driven attack.

Dink A soft shot off the fingertips used to lob the ball over the block.

Double foul Infraction of rules by both teams during the same play.

Drive An attack contacted in the center that attempts to hit the ball off the blocker's hands.

Fault An infraction of the rules.

Forearm pass A pass made off the forearms. Used to play served balls, hard-driven spikes, or any low ball.

Free ball A return of a ball by the opponent that may easily be handled.

Front court The playing area in which it is legal to block or attack.

Held ball A ball that is simultaneously contacted above the net by opponents and momentarily held upon contact.

Kill An attack that cannot be returned directly as a result of that attack.

Lob A soft attack that is contacted in the back bottom quarter of the ball causing it to take an upward trajectory.

Overhand pass A pass made by contacting the ball above the head with the finger pads.

Overlap An illegal foot position, when the ball is dead, with an adjacent player putting one out of position.

Play over The replay of a rally due to a held ball or the official prematurely suspending play. The server reserves with no point awarded.

Point A point is scored when the receiving team fails to return the ball legally to the opponents' court.

Rotation Shifting of the players clockwise upon gaining the ball from the opponents.

Serve The method of putting the ball in play over the net by striking it with the hand.

Set The placement of the ball near the net to facilitate attacking.

Setter Player assigned to set the ball.

Side out Side is out when the serving team fails to win a point or plays the ball illegally.

Spike A ball hit with top spin and a strong downward force into the opponents' court.

Spiker Player assigned to attack the ball.

Spike-roll An attack that first takes an upward trajectory using the spiking actions (with or without jumping).

Topspin (Overspin) Imparting of a forward spin to the ball during the serve, spike, or spike roll.

SELECTED REFERENCES

Bertucci, B. *The AVCA Handbook*. Grand Rapids, MI: Masters Press, 1987.

Bertucci, B. and Hippolyte, R. *Championship Volleyball Drills Volume 1*. Champaign, IL: Human Kinetics Publishers, Inc., 1984.

Frazer, S.D. *Strategies for Competitive Volleyball*. Champaign, IL: Leisure Press, 1988.

Goebel, K. and Kluka, L. and D. *Competitive Volleyball Drills*. Logan, UT: Kelcon, Inc., 1989.

Gozansky, S. *Championship Volleyball Techniques and Drills*. Englewood Cliffs, NJ: Prentice Hall, 1983.

Iams, J. *New, Competitive Volleyball Games*. Evanston, IL: Sports Support Syndicate, 1990.

Kiraly, K. *Championship Volleyball*. New York: Simon & Schuster Inc., 1990.

Pederson, J. and Loggins, V. *Bump, Set Spike*. Chicago, IL: Contemporary Books, Inc., 1986.

Scates, A. *Winning Volleyball*. Boston: Allyn and Bacon, Inc., 1990.

Scates, A. *Winning Volleyball Drills*. Dubuque, IA: W.C. Brown Publishers, 1984.

Schaafsma, F. and Heck, A. *Volleyball for Coaches and Teachers*. Dubuque, IA: W.C. Brown Publishers, 1985.

Selinger, A. and Ackerman-Blount, J. *Arie Selinger's Power Volleyball*. New York: St. Martin's Press, 1986.

Viera, B. and Ferguson, B.J. *Volleyball Steps to Success*. Champaign, IL: Human Kinetics Publishers, Inc., 1989.

Periodicals

American Volleyball. American Volleyball Coaches Association, 122 Second Ave., Suite 201, San Mateo, CA 94401.

Coaching Volleyball. Human Kinetics Publishers Inc., 1607 N. Market, Champaign, IL 61820–2200.

Volleyball. Western Empire Publications, Inc., 950 Calle Amanecer, Suite C, Box 3010, San Clemente, CA 92672.

Audio-Visual Materials

Beginning Girls' Volleyball—Individuals' Skills. Truckee River Studios, P.O. Box 1040, Alamo, CA 94507. VHS or BETA.

Beginning Girls' Volleyball—Team Tactics. Truckee River Studios, P.O. Box 1040, Alamo, CA 94507. VHS or BETA.

Men's Volleyball. Truckee River Studios, P.O. Box 1040, Alamo, CA 94507. VHS or BETA.

USA Volleyball. Athletic Institute, 200 Castlewood Dr., N. Palm Beach, FL 33408. ½" VHS.

Women's Volleyball - Series I. Truckee River Studios, P.O. Box 1040, Alamo, CA 94507. VHS or BETA.

26 WEIGHT TRAINING

THIS CHAPTER WILL ENABLE YOU TO:

▶ Identify and compare the key points associated with Olympic lifting, powerlifting, athletic weight training, and bodybuilding.
▶ Identify the differences and similarities among weight lifting equipment.
▶ After practice, demonstrate the various skills and techniques necessary to execute the various weight training lifts.
▶ Identify and discuss facts and myths related to female weight lifting.
▶ Identify the necessary safety concerns of weight training.
▶ Become familiar with basic terminology required to carry out a successful weight training program.

NATURE AND PURPOSE

During the past two decades, the effectiveness of carefully planned weight training as a method of improving body development and sports performance has been accepted on the basis of well-controlled studies. Although being musclebound, having reduced localized muscle endurance, and loss of speed and agility were once thought to result from weight training, such claims have no physiological basis.

Much may be gained from the systematic and intelligent application of modern weight training principles. Using the principle of overload (taxing the muscles beyond their normal daily activities), coupled with progressive resistance through a full range of motion appears to be the most effective means of acquiring dynamic strength. The closer the weight lifting movement simulates the actions in sports, the greater the transfer of strength to motor performance. Weight lifting is also an excellent way to develop flexibility, provided the exercise is executed through the entire range of motion. Muscle enlargement does not reduce muscle endurance, because an increase in capillarization usually accompanies the cross-sectional increase of muscle fibers, which helps to delay the onset of fatigue. Weight training does not necessarily affect cardiorespiratory endurance unless movements are executed for this specific purpose. Increasing the cardiorespiratory endurance requires specific training. To achieve this, heart and respiratory rates must be intensely increased and maintained at higher than normal resting values for a duration of time. Systematic weight training that applies the principles of resistance, overload, and specificity will have positive effects on motor performance parameters and contribute to successful participation in sports.

Many individuals become involved in weight training as a means of gaining or losing weight. The use of weight training is of greater benefit to gaining body weight than to losing it. This is due to the activities' physiological effect upon the body. The overload principle causes proteins to be readily incorporated into the muscle thus increasing muscular mass (hypertrophy), while on the other hand the energy expenditure of weight lifting is too low to be of much benefit in body weight reduction. However, the overweight person may want to include weight training as part of a reduction program to increase body tone while reducing with diet and an aerobic program.

Many centers of rehabilitation find the use of weights valuable in developing weak or injured muscles, strengthening underdeveloped muscles, or rebuilding muscles affected by atrophy following casting or hospitalization.

EQUIPMENT

Variable Resistance Machines

This type of weight training machine is manufactured by many companies under a variety of trade names. The most widely used are the Universal Gym (Figure 26-1), Nautilus (Figure 26-2), Cybex (Eagle), and Paramount. These units consist of weight stacks connected by pulleys or cams to levers of lifting bars. The levers and pulleys allow a variable resistance through a fixed and oftentimes limited range of motion. While this type of equipment is available in separate units, it may also be found in a jungle gym arrangement on which several athletes can work out at one time. Weight training machines offer a number of conveniences and time saving features which appeal to the coach as well as the lifter. These machines may be placed within restricted space and offer the safety of confined weight stacks which are

FIGURE 26-1   The Universal Gym, a widely used variable resistance machine.

FIGURE 26-2   The Nautilus pullover torso machine.

not features of traditional "free weights." Since the amount of resistance can be changed rapidly by a pull of a pin in the stack, the amount of time required to complete a training session is also greatly reduced over free weights. One great disadvantage to all machines is in the transfer of strength gains to performance. While the machines can offer great safety, they also remove the interaction between the weights and the lifters needed to balance or coordinate movements while lifting. This interaction is of greatest importance for maximum benefit to performance. However, when time is a restricting factor, training on machines has been found by many coaches to be an excellent way to maintain strength in-season.

Isokinetic Equipment

Probably the most talked about and misunderstood equipment available today are isokinetic devices. The term "isokinetic" means "moving at a constant speed." These machines require no weights as the resistance felt from this equipment is self-generated. The machines are capable of being set at a variety of training velocities. If the athlete is capable of moving through a range of motion which approaches this velocity, then resistance is felt through that range. If the velocity is not reached, resistance is not felt. For this reason to train on these devices requires a highly motivated athlete with constant supervision. The significance of training at a variety of velocities is found in the physiology of the muscle fibers. Since muscle fibers are of a fast and slow nature, it is felt that training at fast and slow speeds will increase recruitment of these fibers.

The value of isokinetic devices in rehabilitation is well founded. The Orthotron (Figure 26-3) and Cybex 340 (Lumex Inc.) are most commonly used for rehabilitation while the Mini Gym is used for sports training. One problem with isokinetic devices is that

FIGURE 26-3 The Orthotron isokinetic machine.

they do not relate well with other forms of strength training. There is also doubt as to their effectiveness in building muscular bulk.

Free Weights

The oldest forms of weight training have been done with free weights. There are two types: the Olympic form and the standard one-inch barbell. A well-equipped training room will have both types of bars. The Olympic bar offers more balance, is more durable, and is a must for power and Olympic lifts. If properly used with supervision from an experienced lifter, free weights offer the most substantial strength program available. The cost of equipment is low, but the risk may be high with improper accessory equipment or lack of supervision.

Other Equipment

The following items may become necessary to the lifter of free weights as the training becomes more intense.

Lifting Belt. The lifting belt is made of thick leather and is used to give physical support to the lower back and moral support to the mind. There are two types of belts: training and competition. The training belt is five inches wide and gives a wide support to the lower back. The competition belt is four inches wide and may not exceed this in Olympic and power lifting. The belt is generally worn with free weight squats and cleans.

Lifting Straps. Lifting straps are loops of leather or canvas belting about one inch wide. The straps are placed around the hands and then under and around the bar. With an overhand grip the lifter

secures the strap, and the bar is held tightly to the hand. Straps are used with dead lifts and cleans for training only. Lifting straps may not be used in competition.

Knee Wraps (Super Wraps). Wraps are long, three-inch wide strips of tough elastic material. They are worn extremely tight around the knee to add spring to the rebound phase of the squat and clean. They are needed only with heavy weights and may be worn in competition.

Super Suits. Super suits are made of tough elastic material and look like wrestling gear. The suit gives support and spring to the body during heavy squats and cleans. They are generally not worn in training but are normally always worn in competition.

THE FEMALE WEIGHTLIFTER

The fundamentals, techniques, and training programs described in this chapter are directed at both sexes. The female athletes need strength training every bit as much as their male counterparts, if not more. Competitive power lifting and bodybuilding are also becoming very popular among women across the country. Coeducational weight training classes offer no problems in terms of training programs; in fact, they are very effective ways of destroying weight lifting myths concerning females.

Myth: Women are not as strong as men.
Fact: Through elementary school, middle school, and well into high school, females are as strong if not stronger than their male counterparts, although with age and training men will surpass women pound for pound.

Myth: Women should execute lifts differently because they are built differently.
Fact: Anatomical differences in bone and muscle are so slight that they have no bearing on lifting technique.

Myth: Women will become extremely muscular if they lift heavy weights.
Fact: Women can increase strength up to 70 percent with little change in physical appearance. It is the male hormone (testosterone) which causes the noticeable hypertrophy in men. Most women have such small amounts of this hormone that bulk muscularity is next to impossible. Women bodybuilders who do show extreme hypertrophy have (1) very low body fat, (2) unusually high levels of testosterone, or (3) may take anabolic steroids (a testosterone-like drug).

Myth: Women (as well as men) are concerned that their muscles will turn into fat if they stop working out.
Fact: Just as lead cannot turn into gold, muscle cannot turn into fat. Muscle generally atrophies (be-

comes smaller) when training ceases. People who appear to have become fat after they stopped training may not have changed their eating habits and consequently may be gaining weight.

Myth: Women should not train during various stages of the menstrual cycle.

Fact: The overwhelming majority of female athletes report no adverse effects on performance due to this physiological process.

Most women who have begun training with weights find they have gained the following benefits:

1. Increased physical strength improves their performance in sporting events.
2. There is a decrease in overall body fat while developing muscular tone.
3. There is an improvement in self-image and a feeling of well-being.

SUGGESTED LEARNING SEQUENCE

Weight training as part of a physical education program should be approached as a skill-oriented class and not merely as an activity. Weight training requires an overall philosophy, the development of techniques, and the ability to execute the skills of each lift.

A four-day-a-week lifting program is recommended which splits the various lifts into two groups. Monday and Thursday lifts emphasize legs and back while Tuesday and Friday lifts emphasize upper body. If time restricts the number of lifts that can be accomplished, then some leg and back lifts may be done on Monday and some may be done on Thursday. The same arrangement can be used with the upper body lifts. A practical approach for utilization of equipment would be to split the class into two groups containing subgroups of three students (matched for strength, if possible). By doing this, one group can do Monday/Thursday lifts on Tuesday and Friday, thus allowing the proper amount of time needed to execute a proper program. The subgroups of three students lift as a team and are responsible for spotting each other when this is required. Each member of the subgroup should complete a set before any member repeats a set.

The following instructional approach is recommended:

1. Students should be informed of the various forms of strength training and how they differ.
2. Each lift should be demonstrated to the student with emphasis placed on key points as well as safety factors. Students should also understand the purpose of each lift. (Olympic lifts may be omitted from the demonstration as they are not part of the training program.)

3. If the course meets five times a week, the non-lifting day should be devoted to instruction about related areas (stretching techniques, aerobic exercises, guest speakers or lifters).
4. Begin the lifting schedule as soon as techniques have been demonstrated and safety tips have been emphasized.

Outlined below is a basic plan which may be adopted as is or with modifications. If this plan does not meet the needs of your program, many different lifting schedules may be found in the books listed in the reference section. This program may be done almost entirely on variable resistance machines (Universal Gym), totally with free weights, or in combination. Students should begin with an amount of weight which can be handled through the recommended number of repetitions. The first set should be lighter than the second or third set. The student may increase the weight in a set when there is no longer difficulty in completing the last few reps of the second or third set.

FW = Free Weights; VRM = Variable Resistance Machines

Monday and Thursday Lifts:

EXERCISE	SETS	REPS
Back		
Dead lifts (FW)	2	5
Bent over rows (FW)	2	10
Lat pull overs (FW)	2	10
Lat pull downs (VRM)	2	10
Biceps and Forearms		
Barbell curl (FW or VRM)	2	8
Reverse curl (FW or VRM)	2	8
Legs		
Squats (FW)	1	10
	1	5
Leg lunge (FW)	2	10
Leg press (VRM)	2	10
Leg extensions (VRM)	2	10
Leg curls (VRM)	2	10
Calf		
Donkey calf raise	2	15
Dorsal flexion	2	15
Abdominals		
Sit-ups	2	15 (may vary)

Tuesday and Friday Lifts:

EXERCISE	SETS	REPS
Power cleans (FW)	3	5
Shoulders		
Military press front (FW or VRM)	2	10
Military press back (FW or VRM)	2	10
Dumbbell shrugs (FW)	2	10

Chest

Bench Press (FW or VRM)	3	5
Incline Bench Press (FW)	3	5

Triceps

Lying triceps extensions (FW)	2	10

Calf
Same as Mon/Thur

Abdominals
Same as Mon/Thur

SKILLS AND TECHNIQUES

The correct lifting form is essential not only for obtaining quick results but also for safety.

The Grip

The overhand, palms down, grip is used in practically all exercises. The thumbs may be hooked underneath the bar or in some instances, as in the bench press, may remain on the same side of the bar as the other fingers. This requires more balance and is not recommended to the novice lifter.

The underhand grip is the exact opposite of the overhand grip, with palms placed upward under the bar. This grip is used in executing the curl maneuver.

The alternating grip, with one hand palm down and the other hand palm up, is favored for dead lifts. Regardless of style, the hands must be spaced evenly on the bar in order to execute the lift properly as well as provide safety.

When involved in Olympic or power lifting, the use of chalk on the hands is recommended. The chalk will increase the bar/hand friction, thus facilitating a better grip.

The Feet

When the bar is being lifted from the floor, as in cleans or dead lifts, place the toes approximately under the bar with the feet spread about one foot apart. The feet should always be in the same line although the distance between them may vary. Many beginners have the fault of not starting close enough to the bar; consequently, when they start the lift the bar swings toward the feet instead of going straight up. Many experienced lifters find that a slight angling outward, not more than 15 degrees, of the feet is a more comfortable and efficient lifting style. This is a technique which should be developed as the lifter improves.

Breathing

Breathing should come naturally during the course of the exercise, letting the body regulate the

FIGURE 26-4 The overhand grip.

FIGURE 26-5 The underhand grip.

FIGURE 26-6 The alternating grip.

demand. Forced gasping and hyperventilating (rapid puffs of breath) only interfere with proper breathing and may even lead to lightheadedness. The best pattern of breathing is to inhale during the lifting phase and to exhale with the return movement. As the weight increases, many lifters find it more effective to take one deep breath and hold it through the repetition of the lift. The lifter should never hold a breath for more than one repetition. This puts undue pressure on the body cavities as well as the blood vessels of the head. Getting a purple face in the weight room will not improve your lifting ability.

The Bar and Body Placement

A technique which is of utmost importance in a weight room is lifting a bar from a power rack or squat stands. Injuries which occur during this phase of lifting with free weights can most always be traced back to carelessness on the part of the lifter. To properly place your body under the bar to execute a lift, check the following items:

1. The bar should be no higher than the shoulder nor more than three to four inches below the shoulder.
2. Grip the bar evenly and space your hands wider than your shoulders.
3. Move under the bar in such a way that the midpoint of the bar is on line with your backbone.
4. The bar should rest on the base of the neck and the shoulders.
5. If the muscles of the neck and shoulders lack mass to cushion the bar, foam pads or towels should be wrapped around the bar so as to protect the bony parts of the back. This is extremely important for young lifters and as a rule is a good policy for women to follow.
6. By bending at the knees, align your body as vertically as possible under the bar.
7. With the head up, lift straight up with hip and leg power to a vertical position.
8. Step backwards out of the rack no more than 2½ feet.
9. With spotters on both ends of the bar, execute the lift.
10. Rerack the weights by stepping back into the rack, with alignment by spotters, and set the weight down.

TRAINING PROGRAMS

As weight training has come of age and specificity has become a recognized factor in a successful program, it has become difficult to recommend training programs without knowing what equipment is available and what purpose the program will serve. There are recent publications which speak to many specific programs in weight training. For this reason specific programs will not be proposed but rather comments concerning programs will be presented. For training manuals, refer to the references at the end of the chapter.

Light Conditioning Programs

These types of programs cover the broadest range of weight trainers from in-season athletic pro-

grams to the programs typically offered to the general public at health clubs. The programs generally consist of a three-day-a-week lifting routine. All of the basic lifts would be done at this time with a brief stretching and warm-up followed by one set of 10 to 15 reps of the various lifts. This is the "circuit or circus" training approach, also known as the "get them in—get them out" routine. This approach is a lifelong battle which gives non-dramatic results.

Heavy Conditioning Programs

Programs in this area are practiced by a smaller group of lifters containing pre-season athletes, power lifters, Olympic lifters, and bodybuilders. The programs run from a four- to seven-day week with muscle groups worked rather than the entire body. The average workout would be around two hours; however bodybuilders, prior to a contest, may actually train on a split-day routine, thus doubling the workout time. This is a very effective program if you can afford the time. The general rule followed in heavy training is to thoroughly overload and exhaust the muscle each time it is trained with at least one day between training of that muscle group again. Overtraining in heavy programs is a real problem, and it affects different people at different times. Constant muscular pain with a loss in strength are the warning signs. The large muscle groups are the first to be affected, especially the lower back.

A heavy training program, although there is much variation, may consist of a 5×5 approach of 5 sets with 5 reps, not including a warm-up or stretch. A current variation of the 5×5 approach is to include one day of extremely high rep work at around 50 to 60 percent of maximum.

An important point concerning heavy training for sport specificity is that the movements of the sport should also be done before or after the lifting. This will allow new motor skills to develop with the new strength gains.

DESCRIPTION OF TRAINING GROUPS

Olympic Lifting

Olympic lifting requires strength, power, and quickness. In competition there are two lifts: the two-hand snatch and the two-hand clean and jerk. Training for competition requires explosive lifts such as power cleans as well as bench press, military press, and parallel squats for strength development. Olympic lifters are also concerned with muscular endurance and often include running in a training regime. Although Olympic lifting is an Olympic sport, its popularity in this country has dropped off dramatically in past years. This drop-off is due to several reasons:

1. The reluctancy of lifters to adopt modern training techniques.
2. The lack of experienced strength coaches.
3. A new emphasis on power lifting.
4. The acceptance of bodybuilders in society.

In competition the competitor attempts to lift the heaviest weight he can in each lift, and the individual with the highest total is declared the winner in his body weight class as established by the Amateur Athletic Union.

Two-Hand Snatch

1. Place the bar on the floor horizontally in front of the lifter.
2. Grip the bar with both hands, palms down, at least shoulder width apart.
3. With the legs bent, drive with the legs and pull with the arms until the bar is supported vertically above the head with straight arms.
4. The lifter may split the legs or squat with the weight in order to achieve the vertical arm position. The lifter must stand erect upon completion of the lift.
5. The lifter must stand motionless with feet in the same line to be judged a good lift.

Two-Hand Clean and Jerk

1. Place the bar horizontally on the floor in front of the lifter.
2. Grip the bar with both hands, palms down, at least shoulder width apart.
3. The bar is brought to the shoulder from the floor in one continuous motion with bent or split legs.
4. The bar may rest on the chest while the feet must return to the same line with straight legs before continuing with the jerk.
5. By bending the legs and then extending them and the arms vertically, bring the bar to a vertical extension above the head.
6. The lift is complete when the lifter is motionless with the weight vertical above the head and feet on the same line.

Power Lifting

While flexibility and explosive power are of utmost importance in Olympic lifting, power lifting relies mainly on sheer strength. Although technique is important, the power lifts are easier to master than the Olympic lift. The power lifts are the bench press, the parallel squat, and the dead lift. As in Olympic lifting, the competitor attempts to lift the greatest amount of weight in each lift. The largest total lifted wins the individual weight class. The competition begins with the parallel squat, and the lifter must have one of three attempts judged good to continue into the other lifts. While power lifting is not an Olympic sport, it is very popular in the United States with women as well as men.

Bench Press *(see Figures 26–7 and 26–8)*

1. The lifter lies horizontally with head, trunk, and buttocks on the bench.
2. The palms are placed up against the bar with the thumb placed on the same side as the other fingers or hooked on the opposite side. Placement of the hands may not exceed 32 inches between forefingers.
3. The bar is pressed vertically to straight arm length and held for two seconds.
4. The bar is lowered to the region of the chest but may not sink into the chest.
5. The bar is then raised evenly to a vertical position without moving the trunk, buttocks, or feet. Movement is grounds for disqualification.

FIGURE 26-7 Starting position for proper execution of the bench press.

FIGURE 26-8 The bar is lowered to the chest region with the back flat on the bench.

FIGURE 26-9 Starting position for the parallel squat.

FIGURE 26-10 With the back flat, the weight is lowered to a position where the thighs are parallel to the floor.

FIGURE 26-11 Begin the dead lift close to the bar, back flat and head up.

Parallel Squat (see Figures 26–9 and 26–10)

1. Begin in an upright position with the bar resting across the shoulders.
2. The head should be held up.
3. The back should be flat with the small of the back kept arched.
4. The feet are 12 to 16 inches apart and in the same line.
5. Keeping the back straight, squat slowly with the weight until the tops of the thighs are parallel with the floor.
6. From the squat position, drive with the legs and hips to an upright position. The small of the back should remain arched slightly so as to prevent leaning, which may lead to injury.

Dead Lift (see Figures 26–11 and 26–12)

1. Place the bar on the floor horizontally in front of the lifter.
2. Begin in the squat position, thighs parallel to the floor, head up, feet 12 to 14 inches apart and back flat.
3. The palms are placed on the bar approximately shoulder width apart, using a palms down grip or an alternating palms up, palms down grip.
4. The lift may also be done with the increasingly popular "sumo" style. The only difference is that the feet are spread widely apart, 36 to 40 inches, with the hands placed about 14 inches apart.
5. With the arms straight and the back flat, drive upward with leg and hip strength.
6. Pull with the back once the bar is past the knees.
7. The lift is complete when an upright body position is attained.

FIGURE 26-12 End the dead lift standing erect.

Training includes a few other lifts besides those which would strengthen secondary muscle groups involved in the power lifts. These lifts will be discussed in the next section. For information concerning training schedules for Olympic and power lifting, consult the references listed at the end of the chapter.

Bodybuilding

Bodybuilding for men and women is an activity which is growing rapidly in this country. Reasons for this are many, although media coverage and the popularity of self-improvement are the main contributors. Bodybuilding is as much an art form as it is a sport and may well be called a form of kinetic sculpture. Bodybuilders are not concerned with muscular strength, although all maintain a strength which matches their muscular size. They do not train with the specificity needed for a particular sport activity, yet all are athletic. Bodybuilders train with weights to achieve muscularity with symmetry. This requires a multitude of lifts which are variations of the lifts described in the weight conditioning section. Rather than attempt to describe each of these lifts in detail, the reader is referred to the literature suggested at the end of the chapter.

Weight Training Conditioning

Weight training in the pre-season and during the season is important for every athletic team or conditioning class. The key to a successful weight training program is specificity and supervision. Specificity means that the program should be designed to fit the needs and movements of the athlete. Supervision by a strength coach or a member of the teaching/coaching staff is important from a safety standpoint as well as a means of building morale. This section will describe a number of the lifts commonly used in building a strength program. It will not, however, attempt to put together any programs for different sports. For this type of information, the Selected References will be helpful.

Behind the Neck Press. This is an excellent exercise for the development of the shoulders, especially the deltoid group. The exercise may be done with a barbell or with a machine (Figure 26-13).

1. With the barbell resting behind the head on the shoulders, inhale and press the weight to a vertical position above the head (Figure 26-14).
2. Lower the weight until it nearly touches the shoulders behind the head and exhale.
3. The exercise may be done standing or seated.

The Military Press. Again this is an excellent lift for shoulder development and may be done with free weights or on a machine (Figure 26-15).

FIGURE 26-14 Raise the bar to a vertical position above the head.

FIGURE 26-15 Starting position for the military press.

FIGURE 26-13 Begin the behind the neck press with the barbell resting in this position.

1. With the barbell resting on the chest, inhale and press the bar to a vertical position above the head (Figure 26-16).
2. Lower the weight until it nearly touches the chest and exhale.
3. The exercise may be done standing or seated.

Bent Over Rowing. Rowing has long been used as an overall back developer. It will add thickness and width to the "lats" while developing strength very quickly. This exercise must be done with a barbell.

1. Place the barbell horizontally on the floor in front of the lifter (Figure 26-17).

FIGURE 26-16 Raise the bar to a vertical position above the head.

FIGURE 26-17 Starting position for bent over rowing.

FIGURE 26-18 Raise the bar to this height to complete the lift.

2. Bend at the hips and grip the bar palms down, shoulder width apart. Bend the knees slightly to remove hamstring tension.
3. With the back stationary and flat, pull the bar to the chest (Figure 26-18).
4. Slowly lower the bar to near the starting position (bar need not touch the floor).

The Bench Press. Much controversy continues as to which muscle gains the principal benefit from this exercise. Most biomechanic experts would agree it primarily exercises the anterior deltoid and triceps with the pectoralis major a secondary mover. To put more emphasis on the "pecs," the incline bench press may be incorporated in advanced training programs.

The correct procedure for the bench press has been outlined earlier under power lifting. It should be emphasized at this point that athletes, trainers, and coaches who recommend benching by bouncing the weight off of the chest or arching the back and pushing with the legs to achieve the lift are toying with injury. Many coaches boost their athletes' bench press achievements by actually teaching the bounce and arch as part of the lift. The athlete will gain more physiologically and mentally if taught the proper technique in this exercise. The lift should be done with free weights and spotters, but may also be done on a machine.

Upright Rowing. This lift is often done to supplement training for Olympic lifting. The front deltoids and the trapezius musculature are thoroughly exercised. The lift must be executed with a barbell and may be done explosively or at a slower speed.

1. Grip the bar palms down, about shoulder width apart.

2. Begin by standing with the bar held at the level of the thighs.
3. Pull the bar straight up the front of the body to the area of the chin (speed may vary).
4. Slowly return the bar to the front of the thighs.

Dumbbell Lat Pullover. This is a lift for all sports from tennis to the shotput. The exercise is designed to work the musculature of the back and rib cage. For this reason it should be included in all training regimes for track events. The pullover should be done with a dumbbell but may be done with a light barbell. Traditional lat work is done on some form of lat pull down machine and will not be described in this text.

1. Lie crossways on a flat bench with only the upper shoulder region supported by the bench (Figure 26-19).
2. The knees should be bent with the feet flat on the floor.
3. The buttocks should dip slightly to keep an arch in the small of the back.
4. Grip the weight by cupping the hands in such manner that the palms are against the weight plates. This will cause the weighted ends to be in an up-and-down position.
5. Extend the arms vertically so that the weight is over the face (Figure 26-20).
6. Lower the weight slowly in an arch so as to miss the head until the weight is nearly touching the floor behind the bench.
7. Return the weight to the vertical position slowly by contraction of the lats, keeping the arms nearly locked out.

The Barbell Curl. The curl is well known to anyone who has ever touched a weight. The exercise

FIGURE 26-19   Start the dumbbell lat pullover with hips low and shoulders flat on bench.

FIGURE 26-20   Keeping the hips low, raise the arms to a vertical position above the head.

FIGURE 26-21   Begin the barbell curl with the bar in front of the thighs and the elbows at the sides.

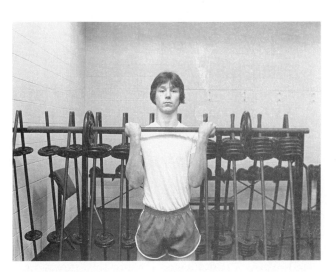

FIGURE 26-22   Contract the biceps and raise the bar in an arch toward the shoulders.

builds the biceps, and is tremendously overused, especially by teenage boys. It is most often used to increase the size of the arms for visual rather than functional reasons, and therefore should be considered a bodybuilding exercise. Coaches will generally have little trouble getting males to do an arm workout. The lift may be done with a straight barbell, a bent (E-Z curl) barbell, dumbbells, or machines. All provide slightly different results in terms of appearance.

1. Grip the bar palms up, about shoulder width apart (Figure 26-21).

2. Begin with the bar in front of the thighs and the elbows kept at the sides.
3. Contract the biceps so that the bar moves in an arch toward the shoulders (Figure 26-22).
4. Slowly lower the bar against gravity to ensure a good stretch to the starting position and repeat.

The Reverse Curl.   The reverse curl is done to strengthen the forearm and biceps. The lift is most effective when done with a barbell.

1. Grip the bar with palms down, about shoulder width apart (Figure 26-23).
2. Start with the elbows at the sides and the bar in front of the thighs.
3. Move the bar in an arch toward the shoulders (Figure 26-24).
4. Lower the bar to starting position and repeat.

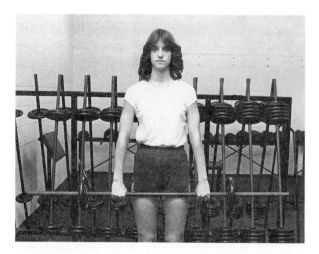

FIGURE 26-23   Begin the reverse curl with palms down.

FIGURE 26-24   Contract the biceps and raise the bar in an arch toward the shoulders.

FIGURE 26-25   Begin the donkey calf raise with heels lower than toes.

FIGURE 26-26   Complete the lift by raising up on toes.

Donkey Calf Raise. When traditional calf machines are not available, the donkey calf raise will give the best all round calf development. This exercise is done with a partner and does not involve weights. The partners should be approximately the same weight.

1. Place the feet on a calf board (2 × 4 on 2 × 4 blocks) with the balls of the feet on the board and the heels off the board (Figure 26-25).
2. Bend at the waist until the back is flat while supporting the body weight on a chair or bench.
3. The partner should sit on the exerciser's back, on the hips if possible.
4. The lifter should then lift up as far as possible onto the toes (Figure 26-26).
5. Once the toes are locked out, lower the heels until they pass beyond the calf board, and then repeat.

The Parallel Squat. The parallel squat, described in the power lifting section, is the ultimate exercise for leg development. It has long been used to develop strength and size in the leg. Done properly the parallel squat will give very quick results. The current belief held by many coaches that the parallel squat will damage the knees is both biomechanically and medically unfounded. The use of a bench for the athletes to squat on is very popular but not necessary. In fact, bouncing up and down on the bench may lead to more serious injuries due to aggravation of the spine. If safety is the reason for bench use, the problem can be eliminated by using spotters at both ends of the bar or by the use of safety squat racks.

Leg Lunge. The lunge is done to strengthen the thigh and is an exercise that might be used as a means of stretching prior to doing squats. The motion of the lunge should be mastered without weights before actual weighted lifts.

1. Begin the lift with the bar resting across the back (Figure 26-27).
2. Take a lunging step forward, about three to four feet, so that the rear knee dips and touches the floor (Figure 26-28).
3. Return then to an upright, starting position.
4. Balance is of utmost importance with this lift, and any amount of weight should be worked up to gradually.

Dumbbell Shrugs. The shrug is probably the best exercise for development of the trapezius and neck muscles. It is a must for additional training in the power lifts. The lift may also be done with a straight bar; however, the best results are obtained with the dumbbell.

1. Begin the exercise with dumbbells in both hands and arms at the sides (Figure 26-29).
2. Raise the shoulders as far as they will go towards the ears (Figure 26-30).
3. Hold that position for a three count and relax.
4. The lifter may also roll the shoulders while executing the lift.

Lying Triceps Extensions. The triceps extensions work to strengthen the posterior portion of the arm. This exercise should be done as a secondary lift with the bench press. The exercise may be done with a bar or a machine.

1. Lie on your back on a flat bench.
2. Grip the bar, which should be behind your head on the floor, with a palms up position about 12 inches apart.
3. Raise the bar such that it is positioned vertically over the face with the arms locked out (Figure 26-31).
4. Lower the bar from the elbows while keeping the upper arm in a near vertical position. The bar

FIGURE 26-27 Begin the leg lunge in this position.

FIGURE 26-28 Lunge forward with a straight back until opposite knee touches the floor.

FIGURE 26-29 Begin the shrugs with dumbbells at the sides.

FIGURE 26-30 Keeping the arms straight, shrug the shoulders upward.

FIGURE 26-31 Triceps extensions begin with bar held vertically over the face, arms locked out.

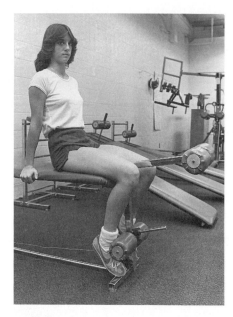

FIGURE 26-33 Begin the leg extension in this position.

FIGURE 26-32 Bar is lowered to position behind the head and then raised to vertical position.

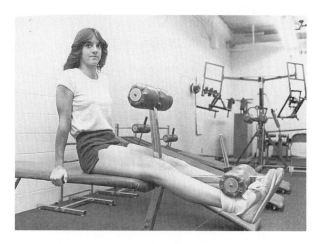

FIGURE 26-34 Extend legs so they are parallel with the floor.

should be lowered to the forehead or just beyond the head (Figure 26-32).

5. Extend the forearm back to the vertical position.

Leg Extensions. The leg extension works directly on the quadriceps muscle group. The exercise can be done with a weight boot but most workout areas are now equipped with extension machines. The leg extension is generally part of a rehabilitation program for people who have weak knees or who have recently undergone surgery.

1. Sit on the bench of the extension machine and put your feet behind the lower pad so that your toes point out. You should sit so that you are leaning slightly back (Figure 26-33). This will put the quadriceps at the optimal angle for maximum extension.

2. Hold on to the sides of the bench and raise the lower weighted bar so that your legs are parallel to the floor (Figure 26-34).

3. If the lifter cannot achieve full extension, there is too much weight on the machine.

4. Slowly lower the weight to the starting position.

The Leg Curl. The leg curl is a most effective way of strengthening the hamstring muscles of the upper leg. Unless the athlete is on a good parallel squat program, there is a tendency for the "quads" to become too strong in relationship to total quad/hamstring strength. While the exercise may be done with weighted boots, most workout areas are equipped with leg curl machines.

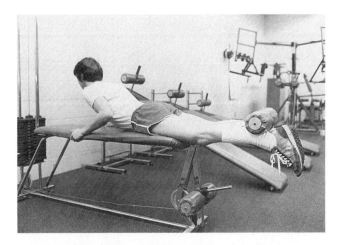

FIGURE 26-35 Begin the leg curl in this position.

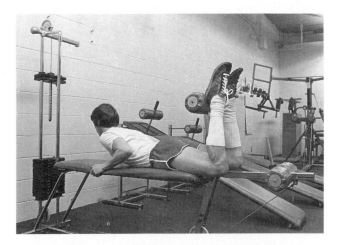

FIGURE 26-36 Flex the legs so they are vertical to the floor.

1. Begin by lying stomach down on the machine and position the heels behind the heel pad (Figure 26-35).
2. Prop yourself up slightly with your elbow so as to keep the hamstrings as prime movers of the lift.
3. Contract the hamstrings and attempt to touch the heels on the buttocks (Figure 26-36).
4. Slowly return to the starting position and repeat.

Dorsal Flexion of the Foot. A group of muscles on the front of the lower leg are generally forgotten about in training except by bodybuilders. Yet it is this musculature that causes many athletes a great deal of trouble in the form of shin splints. While the exact cause of all shin splints is not known, it generally results from an overdeveloped calf muscle and an underdeveloped anterior tibial muscle (front of the lower leg). This condition is found in many runners and may also result from prolonged wearing of high heels. The exercise is simple and really requires no equipment other than what may already be found around the home.

1. Begin in a seated position with the feet hanging freely above the floor.
2. A weighted device is hung from the toes so that resistance is felt. The weight may be as simple as a bucket filled with water or sand, which allows the amount of resistance to be altered easily.
3. Contract the foot so as to bring the toes up (Figure 26-37) and point to the knee (active dorsal flexion).
4. Relax the foot and repeat (Figure 26-38). Repetition is the key to this exercise.

The Power Clean. The power clean is probably the most total body lift that can be successfully executed short of the clean and jerk. More than any other single lift, the power clean will significantly improve the vertical jump with greater total body strength. All training programs should include the clean to some intensity. The lift must be done with free weights, preferably Olympic weights. The sequence is shown in Figure 26-39, A–E.

1. Begin with the bar horizontally at the feet of the lifter.
2. Grip the bar, palms down, about shoulder width apart.
3. The feet should be placed inside the hands so as to provide a firm base of support.
4. Squat low as in the beginning dead lift position.
5. The head should be up with gaze fixed toward the ceiling.
6. Drive with the hips and legs to lift the bar from the floor.

FIGURE 26-37 Contract the foot and point the toes upward.

FIGURE 26-38 Relax the foot and let the toes point downward.

(A) The power clean starting position.

(B) Initial pull phase should not be rapid.

(C) Rapid acceleration phase—note extension onto the toes.

(D) The bar has lost momentum—time to move under it.

(E) The catch phase—knees are bent.

FIGURE 26-39
The power clean.

7. Continue to drive with the legs as the bar gains acceleration and as the bar passes the knees, pull with the back and shoulders.
8. As the bar reaches the chest region it will begin to lose momentum.
9. At this point the body needs to move slightly under the bar as the elbows drive forward under the bar to catch the weights on the chest. This arm movement should be somewhat passive as this is not a reverse curl. If the lifter must reverse curl the weight, the weight is too heavy or there was insufficient momentum in the drive phase.
10. The lifter will find it necessary to bend at the knees in order to achieve the correct catch position. When bending occurs, stand erect with the weights before lowering them to repeat.

▶ Learning Cues

To ensure a successful training lift in the clean, be sure to follow these instructions:

1. The bar should move almost vertically up the front of the body.
2. This is an explosive lift; therefore, rapid acceleration of the bar is important.
3. Do not jerk the weight from the floor with the arms, rather drive it up with the legs.
4. Extend up on the toes when possible to increase leg drive force.
5. Do not actively reverse curl the bar back to the chest.

DRUG EDUCATION

Anabolic Steroids and Weight Training

Anabolic steroids are protein-building drugs that are used by some weight training individuals for effects that are believed to enhance performance. These drugs may be legally prescribed only by physicians and veterinarians. Anabolic steroids are used in conjunction with weight training because they increase weight and because there is evidence that they help induce muscle hypertrophy (enlargement of individual muscle fibers which results in increased muscle mass). They are also credited with enhancing endurance, improving recovery time, and increasing aggressiveness, but none of these claims has been objectively proven. Many of the drugs used come from black market sources. Since there is no regulation of these sources, counterfeit and deliberately misidentified anabolic steroids have become a widespread problem. The health risks of anabolic steroid use are not well known. There is little medical information on the effects of anabolic steroids at the doses used by weight training individuals. However, their link with the development of liver tumors and a consistent decrease in HDL-cholesterol with increased LDL-cholesterol is well documented. The change in cholesterol fractions has been identified as a significant risk factor for heart disease. The health risks associated with anabolic steroid use are likely to increase the larger the dose and the longer the use.

MODIFICATIONS FOR SPECIAL POPULATIONS

Orthopedically Impaired

1. Follow the same guidelines used for able-bodied students with the following adaptations:
   a. Do not allow students with cerebral palsy to move the resistance too ballistically. Ballistic type movements will increase flexor tone for students dominated by spasticity, therefore concentrate on less resistance and more range of motion.
   b. Make sure the brakes on all wheelchairs are locked prior to lifting.

   c. For spinal cord injured students be sure to identify the level of injury and consult with an adapted physical educator and/or physical therapist prior to initiating a program.
2. Consult your local fitness clubs for commercial equipment modified for the physically impaired.
3. Wrist weights, weighted sand bags, and other homemade equipment make great modified equipment for fitness training.

Mentally Impaired

1. Fitness levels for the mentally impaired are generally very low; it is important to start a weight training program very slowly. Take time to build a solid base, and increase resistance very slowly in the early stages of the program.
2. Minimal modifications are needed; however, use of peer teachers, improvement charts, T-shirt clubs, etc., are excellent incentives for the student.

Sensory Impaired

1. Maintain close supervision of blind or visually impaired students during a lifting program.
2. Use weight machines for increased safety precautions with the blind or visually impaired.
3. Deaf or hard of hearing students require minimal adaptations. Visual cues need to be established for starting and stopping a lifting session while working out with a large number of students in a small area.

SAFETY IN THE WEIGHT ROOM

1. Stretching exercises and a warm-up should precede the training program.
2. Until you are familiar with the movements involved with the lift, do not attempt a great amount of weight on the bar.
3. Collars should always be used on the bars, and they should be secure.
4. Keep adequate distance between the lifters and the equipment in the training room.
5. Always use spotters on the squats and the bench press.
6. Avoid dropping weights any place other than on a lifting platform. Also avoid banging the weight stacks on machines up and down.
7. It is always best to unload both sides of a weight bar partially before removing the final batch of weights.
8. When weight plate racks are available, replace all weights after use.

TERMINOLOGY

Barbell A steel bar 5 to 7 feet long on which circular iron plates of known weight may be placed.

Cheating A lift that is executed with the addition of muscle groups other than the prime movers involved in the lift.

Clean The power clean or beginning phase of the clean and jerk.

Dumbbell A short barbell, 12 to 16 inches, with fixed or removable weight plates.

"Lats" The latissimus dorsi muscles of the back.

Overload principle Progressively increasing the intensity of the workouts over the course of the training program.

"Quads" The four quadriceps muscles of the thigh front.

"Pecs" The pectoralis major muscles of the chest.

Rep Repetition or the continuation of identical motions.

Set The completion of a predetermined number of repetitions.

Specificity The development of a training program aimed at increasing one's ability to succeed in a particular skill.

Spotter An individual responsible for the safety of the lifter. Generally two spotters are used, one at each end of the bar, in lifts such as the squat and the bench press. They are not used in Olympic lifts.

SELECTED REFERENCES

Fleck, S.J., and Kraemer, W.J. *Designing Resistance Training Programs*. Champaign, IL: Human Kinetics Books, 1987.

Lombardi, V.P. *Beginning Weight Training*. Dubuque, IA: Wm. C. Brown Publishers, 1989.

Martens, R.; Christina, R.W.; Harvey, J.S.; and Sharkey, B.J. *Coaching Young Athletes*. Champaign, IL: Human Kinetics Books, 1981.

Riley, D.P. *Strength Training by the Experts*. Champaign, IL: Leisure Press, 1982.

Stone, W.J. and Kroll, W.A. *Sports Conditioning and Weight Training*. Boston, MA: Allyn and Bacon, Inc., 1980.

Williams, M.H. *Beyond Training: How Athletes Enhance Performance Legally and Illegally*. Champaign, IL: Leisure Press, 1989.

Organizations

The National Strength and Conditioning Association, 300 Old City Hall Landmark, 920 O Street, Lincoln, NB 68508.

27 WRESTLING

THIS CHAPTER WILL ENABLE YOU TO:

▶ Identify and discuss the key features of a wrestling match.
▶ Identify the differences in equipment, weight classes, and strategy between high school and collegiate wrestling.
▶ Identify rule differences between high school and collegiate wrestling.
▶ Describe the offensive and defensive strategies utilized in wrestling.
▶ Identify the basic terminology associated with the sport of wrestling.

NATURE AND PURPOSE

There are two worldwide styles of wrestling—the "Greco-Roman" and the "free- style"—both of which are represented in the Olympic games. In America we use a variation of the free-style, in which the wrestlers start in an upright position and one attempts to pin the shoulders of the other to the mat for one second (two seconds in high school). This style of wrestling, as practiced in the schools and colleges of this country, is commonly called "catch-as-catch-can."

All matches occur on a protective mat 32 ft. square or 32 feet in diameter (Figure 27-1). A smaller circle 10 feet in diameter is located at the center of the mat, and this is where the opposing wrestlers begin to wrestle.

Matches last for 6 minutes in high school and 7 minutes in college. High school matches are divided into three 2-minute periods; college matches are divided into a 3-2-2-minute system. There are no rest periods between periods.

The first period always begins with both opponents in a standing position and facing each other with their lead foot in contact with the starting line located within the small circle at the center of the mat. This is the "neutral position."

The second and third periods can begin in one of three positions: (1) neutral, with both wrestlers standing and neither in control of the other; (2) a "referee's position," in which one wrestler is in a down-man position and the other in a top-man position; or (3) an "optional offensive starting position," whereby the top man positions himself on either side or to the rear of his opponent (supporting all his weight on both feet, one knee or both knees) and places his hands on his opponent's back with thumbs touching.

If during the course of the match neither wrestler is able to successfully pin his opponent's shoulders to the mat for the required one second (two seconds in high school), the winner may be determined by a point system.

There are five ways to score points against an opponent:

1. *Takedown*	2 points
2. *Escape*	1 point

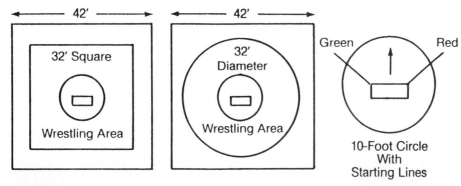

FIGURE 27-1 Wrestling mat.

3. *Reversal*   2 points
4. *Near fall*   2 or 3 points
5. *Time advantage (college)*   1 point

Weight Classification. In order for two wrestling opponents to be evenly matched in size, weight classifications have been developed to allow opponents to wrestle at the same approximate weight.

HIGH SCHOOL	COLLEGE
103 lb.	118 lb.
112	126
119	134
125	142
130	150
135	158
140	167
145	177
152	190
160	Heavyweight (177–275)
171	
189	
275	

Wrestling uses various types of holds involving throws, lifts, and twists. Strength is an important asset but not a prerequisite. A wrestler must also have quickness, physical conditioning, and a knowledge of leverage points.

BASIC RULES

Certain rules differ between high school and collegiate wrestling. To win a fall, the shoulder blades of one's opponent must be held in contact with the mat continuously for one full second in college wrestling and for two seconds in high school.

Any hold may be used except the following, which are considered dangerous to the safety of one's opponent:

ILLEGAL HOLDS

Hammerlock above a 90° angle
Twisting hammerlock
Full nelson
Front headlock without the arm
Headlock without the arm
Straight head scissors
Overhead double arm bar
Over-scissors
Strangle holds
Body slams
Twisting knee lock
Key lock
Bending, twisting, or forcing the head or any limb
    beyond its normal limits of movement
Locking the hands behind the back in a double arm bar
    from the neutral position
Full back suplay from a rear standing position
Arm holds used for punishment alone

If no fall (pin) is secured, the decision goes to the contestant who has scored the most points during a match.

THE MATCH: TIMING AND SCORING

Contestants begin the match from a standing position, facing one another. When a contestant takes his opponent to the mat within the first period limit (3 minutes college, 2 minutes high school), they continue to wrestle until a fall is declared or until the time limit is reached.

If neither contestant secures an advantage position (a wrestler who is in legal control of his opponent) before the time limit has elapsed, the remaining time is divided into two periods of mat wrestling. The referee flips a coin, and the winner of the "call" chooses one of the three re-starting positions described above, or he can "defer" this choice to his opponent. If he defers the choice to his opponent at the start of the second period, he becomes the wrestler with the "choice" at the start of the third period. If a fall takes place during the second period, the match is ended and there is no third period.

Team Point System for Dual Competition (High School and College)

1. *Fall (pin)*	6 points
2. *Forfeit*	6 points
3. *Default*	6 points
4. *Disqualification*	6 points
5. *Technical Fall* (by 15 points or more)	5 points
6. *Decision*	
(by 8–14 points)	4 points
(by less than 8 points)	3 points
7. *Draw*	2 points

Individual Scoring System

1. *Takedown* (2 points)—For each takedown of opponent to mat and securing an advantage position.
2. *Escape* (1 point)—Escape from a disadvantage position (a wrestler being legally controlled by his opponent) to a neutral position.
3. *Reversal* (2 points)—Reversal from a disadvantage position to an advantage position.
4. *Near Fall* (2 points)—The defensive wrestler is held in a high bridge or on both elbows for two seconds; both shoulders of the defensive wrestler are held within 4 inches of the mat or less; or, when one shoulder of the defensive wrestler is touching the mat and the other shoulder is held at an angle of 45 degrees or less, for less than 5 seconds.
5. *Near Fall* (3 points)—Same situation as #4, but wrestler is held in this position for 5 seconds or more.

6. *Time Advantage* (College: 1 point)—One minute or more of net accumulated time in the advantage position.
7. Points may also be scored if an opponent is stalling, commits certain technical violations, or applies an illegal hold.
8. A fall terminates the match, and all points scored up to that point are disregarded.

SUGGESTED LEARNING SEQUENCE

A. Nature and purpose of wrestling
B. Conditioning aspects. Plan drills and exercises relating to wrestling movements.
C. Basic wrestling aspects
   1. Wrestling area
   2. Equipment
   3. Safety
   4. Sportsmanship and courtesy
D. Rules
E. Skills and techniques. Any teaching sequence may be followed, but skills should be taught in combination whenever possible.
   1. Escapes and reversals
      a. Referee's position
      b. Sit out and turn in
      c. Outside switch
      d. Sit out and turn out
      e. Stand-up with inside leg
   2. Breakdowns and rides
      a. Near arm, tight waist, into double wrist ride
      b. Head lever and tight waist
      c. Near ankle and cross face
      d. Far ankle and near waist
   3. Pinning combinations
      a. Half nelson
      b. Arm bar and half nelson
      c. Cross face cradle
      d. Near side cradle
   4. Stance and Drop-step
      a. Square stance
      b. Lead foot
   5. Takedowns
      a. Double-leg
      b. Single-leg
      c. Fireman's roll
F. Strategies. Offensive as well as defensive wrestling concepts should be introduced as early as possible so that skills can be practiced during the wrestling match.
G. Wrestling matches

SKILLS AND TECHNIQUES

Starting/Restarting Positions

At some time during a match the contestants may go off the mat with one contestant in a position of advantage over his opponent. When this occurs, the wrestlers will be restarted from either the "referee's position" or the "optional starting position." These positions may also be used to start the second or third periods.

Referee's Position. The "bottom" man (defensive wrestler) assumes a stationary position on his hands and knees facing the referee and keeping both knees on the mat at the rear starting line. The heels of both hands must be on the mat in front of the forward starting line (Figure 27-2). The wrestler on top being in legal control of his opponent is said to have "a position of advantage" while the wrestler on the bottom being legally controlled by his opponent is said to be in "a position of disadvantage."

FIGURE 27-2 The referee's position, right and left views.

FIGURE 27-3 Optional starting position, front and side views.

The "top" man (offensive wrestler) assumes a position on one or both knees to the side of his opponent. The near arm is placed loosely around the defensive wrestler's waist, and the palm of the other hand is placed on the back of the near elbow. The chin and neck are placed on the midline of the opponent's back.

Optional Starting Position. The top man positions himself on either side or to the rear of his opponent (supporting all his weight on both feet, one knee, or both knees) and places his hands on his opponent's back with thumbs touching (Figure 27-3).

On signal from the referee, both wrestlers begin. The bottom man's objective is to execute a reversal and gain a position of advantage. The top man's objective is to turn the opponent over and hold his shoulders to the mat for the time required to secure a fall. The systematic procedure for attaining this objective is to break his opponent down and then work for a fall.

ESCAPES AND REVERSALS

There are numerous moves available to the wrestler in the bottom position enabling him to escape from or reverse an opponent. To facilitate these movements the wrestler must possess an astute sense of balance, timing, explosiveness, and deception. It is particularly important to maintain a good base of support, and to prevent getting one's arms or legs "tied up." The wrestler who masters these skills will have a distinct advantage over his opponents.

Sit Out and Turn In (Figure 27-4)

▶ **Learning Cues**

1. Bottom man assumes referee's position.
2. Wrestler steps up with outside leg and grasps wrist of opponent's far arm.
3. Sit through with inside leg and maintain grasp of arm.
4. Pivot on inside shoulder and hip to face opponent.
5. Bring free arm upwards to prevent opponent from following.
6. Grasp opponent around waist with free arm and go behind.

Outside Switch (Figure 27-5)

1. Assume bottom man referee's position.
2. Bring inside arm across body to release grip of opponent.
3. Shift weight to inside hand and outside foot while lifting knee of outside foot off mat.
4. Pivot on outside foot and sit through bringing inside leg towards side of outside foot.
5. Throw outside arm over outside arm of opponent and place into crotch of opponent, swinging wide to apply pressure against opponent's shoulder.
6. Pull opponent forward while pivoting on hip that is closer to opponent, thereby coming to a top man position.

FIGURE 27-4   Sit out and turn in.

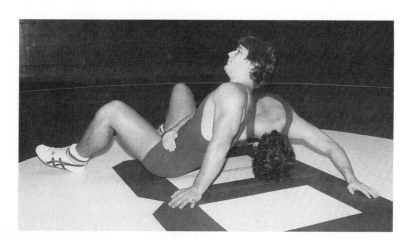

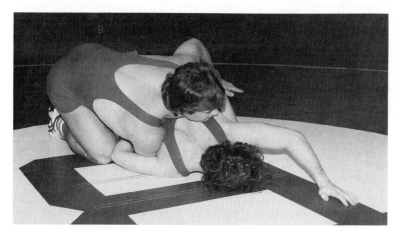

FIGURE 27-5   Outside switch.

Sit Out and Turn Out (Figure 27-6)

1. Bottom man assumes referee's position.
2. Wrestler steps up with outside leg.
3. Sit through with inside leg.

4. Arch your back while pivoting on outside shoulder and hip.
5. Face opponent.

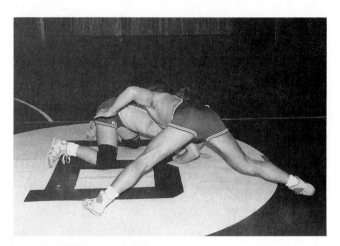

FIGURE 27-6 Sit out and turn out.

FIGURE 27-7 Stand-up with inside leg.

Stand-up with Inside Leg (Figure 27-7)

1. Assume bottom man referee's position with partner on top.
2. On signal, thrust weight upward and backward into opponent while stepping up with inside leg.
3. Grasp opponent's outside arm at wrist with your outside hand, and come to a standing position and push opponent's hand to side.
4. Pivot away until facing opponent.

▶ **Practice Suggestions**

1. Without partner, assume bottom man referee's position. At reduced speed execute step-by-step progression of the sit out and turn in, outside switch, side roll reversal, and stand-up.
2. Same as #1; on signal execute the escape, a reversal, or stand-up at normal speed.
3. Assume referee's position, with partner assuming passive role. Execute the escape, a reversal, or stand-up at reduced speed.
4. Same as #3, except partner offers resistance. Execute on signal the escape, a reversal, or stand-up at normal speed.

BREAKDOWNS AND RIDES

Breakdowns are maneuvers for pinning an opponent. To secure a fall, the wrestler must be able to break down his opponent and maintain control to prevent a reversal. Realizing that the opponent has four bases of support, the wrestler must take away one of these bases in order to initiate a breakdown. By breaking the opponent down to a prone position, the wrestler destroys his opponent's base of support and eliminates his likelihood of escape, thereby making a fall possible.

A ride is a method for maintaining the opponent in a prone position by utilizing various holds and leverage points.

Near Arm, Tight Waist Breakdown and Double Wrist Ride (Figure 27-8)

1. Assume a top man referee's position.
2. At the whistle, tighten waist control and break down opponent's near arm at elbow, pulling in towards waist.
3. Shift weight forward and against opponent's hips to facilitate breakdown to prone position.
4. Maintain weight on top of opponent and grasp wrist of opponent's near arm with both hands (double wrist ride) to maintain control.

Head Lever and Tight Waist Breakdown (Figure 27-9)

1. Assume referee's position with partner.
2. On signal, slide hand on elbow to wrist, and tighten waist control.
3. Place head in opponent's near armpit and drive forward, pulling arm backward and to side.
4. Shift weight forward and drive opponent towards removed base of support to prone position.

Near Ankle and Cross Face Breakdown (Figure 27-10)

1. Assume referee's position.
2. On signal, remove hand from waist and grasp opponent's near ankle. With near arm execute cross face by reaching across opponent's face and grasping far arm above the elbow.
3. Lift ankle and break down far arm, driving weight forward and towards removed base of support, to prone position.

FIGURE 27-8   Near arm, tight waist breakdown into double wrist ride.

FIGURE 27-9   Head lever and tight waist breakdown.

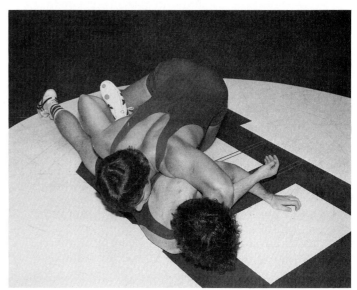

FIGURE 27-10   Near ankle and cross face breakdown.

Far Ankle and Near Waist Breakdown (Figure 27-11)

1. Assume referee's position.
2. On signal, reach with far arm to opponent's far ankle and grasp.
3. Place near arm around waist of opponent, lift far ankle.
4. Drive weight perpendicular to opponent towards removed base of support to prone position.

▶ **Practice Suggestions**

1. With partner, assume referee's position, partner in passive role. Execute breakdown in step-by-step progression at reduced speed.

2. Same as #1, but execute breakdown at normal speed.
3. Same as #1, except partner offers resistance; execute breakdown at normal speed.

Counters to Breakdowns

Near Arm, Tight Waist.   On whistle, defensive wrestler moves near arm towards far arm and "posts." Far hand grasps opponent's hand around waist and wrestler sits out.

Head Lever, Tight Waist.   Defensive wrestler turns near arm inward with palm up. Drop elbow to mat while pivoting inward to free arm.

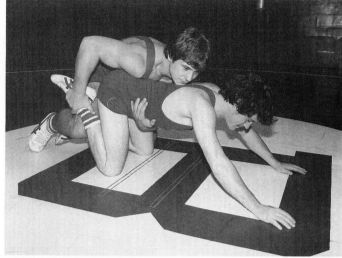

FIGURE 27-11 Far ankle and near waist breakdown.

Near Ankle, Cross Face. Defensive wrestler straightens leg to free from grasp. With free hand reach up and grasp arm of opponent at waist and pull arm off, releasing grip.

Far Ankle, Near Waist. Defensive wrestler straightens leg or reaches back with far hand to grasp opponent's hand. Then post the foot he controls and push hips into him until grasp is released.

PINNING COMBINATIONS

Once the opponent has been broken down to a prone position the wrestler's objective is to secure a fall in order to win the match outright. Various pinning combinations are utilized to position the opponent on his back to facilitate the fall.

Half Nelson (Figure 27-12)

1. Assume a prone position with double wrist ride.
2. Wrestler crosses over to other side of opponent, but maintaining double wrist ride.
3. Slide near hand under opponent's near arm, place wrist on opponent's head, and move to position perpendicular to opponent.
4. Pry opponent's arm upward sliding arm around head and turning under.
5. Drive forward, turning opponent to his back and lifting his head. Maintain wrist lock and prone position.

▶ **Practice Suggestions**

1. Assume prone position with partner in double wrist lock. Execute step-by-step progression of

FIGURE 27-12   Half nelson.

pinning combination at reduced speed with partner maintaining passive role.
2. Same as #1, but execute pinning combination at normal speed.
3. Same as #1, except partner offers resistance; execute pinning combination at normal speed.

Arm Bar and Half Nelson (Figure 27-13)

1. Assume prone position in head lever ride or double wrist ride.
2. With near arm, slide under opponent's near arm until hand is on shoulder in perpendicular position.
3. Cross over to other side of opponent, while maintaining arm bar, to perpendicular position from opponent.
4. Slide free hand under opponent's near arm to a half nelson.
5. Drive weight forward, prying arm upwards and turning opponent onto his back.

Cross Face Cradle (Figure 27-14)

1. Assume prone position with a cross face on opponent.

2. Grasp opponent's far leg behind knee.
3. Drive head of opponent towards his knee by walking around the head towards far knee and lock hands.
4. Wrestler turns opponent towards him onto opponent's back.
5. With far leg, lock opponent's free leg. Slide near leg under opponent's hips.

Near Side Cradle (Figure 27-15)

1. Assume referee position.
2. Wrestler moves near arm on elbow to a position over the opponent's head, with the elbow joint resting on the back of the neck.
3. Other hand moves from waist to around opponent's near leg at knee joint.
4. Lock the hands in front of the opponent's chest, and force him downwards and leg upwards.
5. Wrestler brings right leg up and sits through onto hip, thereby turning opponent onto his back.
6. Once opponent is on back, wrestler continues pivoting until on top of opponent, and then returns to a prone position perpendicular to opponent.

FIGURE 27-13   Arm bar and half nelson.

FIGURE 27-14 Cross face cradle.

▶ **Practice Suggestions**

1. With partner maintaining a passive role, assume a referee's position. Execute the pinning combinations in step-by-step progression at reduced speed.
2. Same as #1, but execute pinning combination at normal speed.
3. Same as #1, except partner offers resistance: execute pinning combination at normal speed.

Counters to Pinning Combinations

Half Nelson.   Defensive wrestler locks arm of offensive wrestler above elbow. Drive elbow to the mat and throw near leg high and across top wrestler's body into a pinning situation.

Half Nelson and Arm Bar.   Defensive wrestler turns body away from opponent and keeps head high. Straighten far arm to counter arm bar. Pull hand off neck to counter half nelson.

Cross Face Cradle.   Defensive wrestler locks his legs and then straightens legs while turning to a prone position to break grip of opponent.

Near Cradle.   Defensive wrestler brings free leg forward and plants near arm firmly on mat. Sit through hand while throwing head back into opponent's armpit to break grip.

THE STANCE AND THE DROP-STEP

The stance may vary according to the individual preference of the wrestler. Two basic stances are utilized: the square stance and the lead-foot (stagger) stance. It is important in the stance to use a sliding step rather than a crossover step in execution of movement from side to side.

Square Stance (Figure 27-16A)

1. Feet are shoulder width apart and parallel.
2. Knees and hips are flexed.
3. Head held in an upright position, the back straight at a slight angle from the waist.
4. Elbows close to the sides, hands in front, with palms facing the mat.
5. Weight on the balls of the feet, and equally distributed.

Lead-foot (Stagger) Stance (Figure 27-16B)

1. One foot slightly forward of the other foot, shoulder width apart.
2. Knees and hips flexed.
3. Head and back in same position as in square stance.

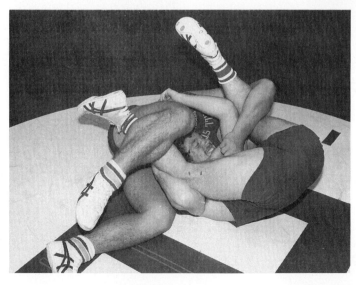

FIGURE 27-15   Near side cradle.

A

B

FIGURE 27-16 (A) Square stance, (B) lead-foot stance.

4. Hands in front with elbows close to body, palms facing downward.
5. Weight on the balls of the feet, and equally distributed.

▶ **Practice Suggestions—Stances**

1. Place class in evenly spaced lines. Assume a square or lead-foot stance. On the signal, move them to the right, left, forward, or backward.

Drop-step (Figure 27-17)

In order for a wrestler to be effective on his feet and to gain control over an opponent he must be able to penetrate the defense of the opposing wrestler. Penetration allows the wrestler to lift an opponent off his base of support, thereby neutralizing his balance and power. The drop-step is an effective maneuver used to penetrate the opponent's defense.

1. Using a lead foot, step and stretch as deep and as far as possible.
2. Lower chest down near knee of front leg.
3. Move back foot up behind front foot.
4. Head in upright position, back straight over front knee.
5. Weight over front foot.

FIGURE 27-17 Drop-step.

6. Elbows next to body, hands in front, palms pointing downward.

▶ **Practice Suggestions**

1. Align wrestlers in line, shoulder to shoulder, all facing the opposite side of the mat. On signal, wrestlers lead with one foot and steps into drop-step pattern. Trail leg follows and stomps mat, then proceeds to step through with that leg. Continue drill across entire length of the mat. Do 8 to 10 repetitions.
2. Facing a partner standing 6 feet away, begin drop-step pattern and penetrate into partner, chest against partner's thighs. Straighten back and lift partner off mat; still on your knees, carry him four or five steps.

TAKEDOWNS

The takedown is a maneuver used by a wrestler in a neutral position to take his opponent to the mat and gain control. Takedowns are frequently used in wrestling offense, and good wrestlers are very proficient at this skill. The takedown consists of three components: the set-up, penetration, and the follow-through.

Double-Leg Takedown (Figure 27-18)

1. Drop-step towards opponent, penetrating as deep as possible.

FIGURE 27-18 Double-leg takedown.

FIGURE 27-19 Single-leg takedown.

Single-Leg Takedown (Figure 27-19)

1. From wrestling stance, perform drop-step, stepping to side of opponent.
2. Place head to inside of hip, shoulder against leg, arms locked around leg.
3. Lift leg of opponent and come to a standing position, head against inside of opponent's thigh.
4. Exert force downward and away from opponent's one base of support, causing opponent to fall to mat.
5. Move to a position of control.

▶ **Practice Suggestions**

1. With partner in passive wrestler role, execute double-leg and single-leg takedown maneuvers in step-by-step progression at reduced speed.
2. Same set-up, execute double-leg or single-leg takedown at normal speed.
3. Same set up, execute series of feints prior to performing the double-leg or single-leg takedown. Partner offers resistance.

Fireman's Roll Takedown (Figure 27-20)

1. Assume collar-bicep tie-up position with partner.
2. Execute drop-step into partner, lead leg between partner's legs, knee of trail leg on mat.

2. Place chest against opponent's thighs, head to outside of legs against the hip.
3. Wrap arms around thighs and lock hands.
4. Lift opponent and turn towards side opposite of head; return opponent to mat on his side.
5. Move to a position of control.

FIGURE 27-20   Fireman's roll takedown.

3. Duck head under arm of partner, cradling neck into armpit.
4. Maintain grasp of bicep, place other hand around near leg, and lift off mat.
5. Pivot onto outside hip and side, carrying partner over your shoulders.
6. Turn partner to his back and maintain a chest-to-chest, perpendicular position.

▶ **Practice Suggestions**

1. With partner, place hand on collar of partner, with other hand grasping bicep on opposite side. Maintain a side stance and move about using hands to maneuver partner from side to side and forward and backward as set-up prior to take-down.

2. From bicep-collar tie-up, execute fireman's roll to point of lift, at reduced speed, then at normal speed.
3. Same set-up, execute entire fireman's roll at reduced speed, then at normal speed. Partner offers resistance.

Counters to Takedowns

One effective defense against another wrestler is by utilization of the hands to ward off attempts at control. As another maneuver, once the opponent penetrates the hands the wrestler must sprawl on top of the opponent whereby the hips are dropped and the legs are thrown back. This reduces the effectiveness of the opponent's penetration. A third line of defense calls for the wrestler to maintain a square position to the opponent, and execution of a cross face or quarter nelson will enhance this maneuver.

STRATEGIES

1. Warm up thoroughly prior to the beginning of your match.
2. Sound knowledge of fundamentals, top physical condition, and a strong desire to win are the ingredients necessary for success in wrestling.
3. Learn to wrestle in series; that is, if one move does not work, try another immediately, or if it does work, follow-through to the pin.
4. Be aggressive.
5. Make the opponent wrestle your style of wrestling.
6. Explosive moves are more effective than slower ones. Learn not to rely on strength when it can be avoided, or else you will tire yourself unnecessarily.
7. Learn to set up your maneuvers. Your chances of making them work are many times better when you surprise your opponent.
8. Move in the direction in which your opponent has the least support.
9. The best time to gain an advantage is just as your opponent relaxes or is slightly off-balance from countering another move.
10. Stay off your back.

SAFETY

1. A physical examination prior to the wrestling season is imperative.
2. Do not participate when you have infections or injuries. Wait until they are cleared by a competent physician.
3. Use protective equipment as needed, such as headgear and kneepads.

4. Keep the nails short and the hair clean and at appropriate length. Do not wear jewelry of any kind or other objects that might injure you or your opponent.
5. Be sure there is adequate room for the workout; more injuries occur as a result of rolling onto or falling over other pairs than from wrestling with an opponent.
6. Be sure the surrounding areas are properly padded and that no physical hazards exist in the facilities or equipment.
7. Be sure you are properly conditioned before beginning to compete.
8. Warm up properly. The neck muscles especially, should be exercised prior to wrestling, as they are ordinarily little used.
9. Do not compete in an obvious mismatch. This applies both to size and ability.
10. Remember the basic rule: Anything that endangers life or limb is illegal in amateur wrestling.
11. Roll when you fall, learn which maneuvers are likely to be most hazardous, and, insofar as possible know when to resist the opponent's pressure and when not to.
12. Be sure all injuries are promptly and properly treated.
13. Keep mat and clothing as clean as possible.

PLAYING COURTESIES

1. Refrain from engaging in excessively rough play as it may cause injuries and ill feelings.
2. Refrain from questioning the referee's decisions.
3. Don't swear or throw equipment.
4. Always shake the opponent's hand at the conclusion of the match regardless of the outcome.
5. Encourage other team members to do as well as they can during their matches.

MODIFICATIONS FOR SPECIAL POPULATIONS

Orthopedically Impaired

1. Students using wheelchairs might arm wrestle.
2. Mobility limited students might engage in some form of Tug-of-War.

Mentally Impaired

Minimal modifications would be needed.

Sensory Impaired

1. Try blindfolding the sighted students in class and start in the referee's position.
2. Minimal modifications would be needed for the blind, visually impaired, and/or deaf and hard of hearing.

TERMINOLOGY

Advantage position A wrestler being in legal control of his opponent is said to have "a position of advantage."

Bottom position A four-point stance assumed at the start of a period or when the referee signals a restart. A position of disadvantage.

Breakdown A maneuver in which the wrestler in the position of advantage forces the opponent flat to the mat.

Bridge Supporting one's weight on the feet and head, with the back arched, thus keeping the shoulders away from the mat.

Control One wrestler is positioned in such a way that his opponent is immobilized or restrained.

Counter A block or a movement that prevents the execution of a maneuver by the opponent.

Cradle A pin hold executed by pulling the opponent's head and leg together and holding his shoulders to the mat.

Cross face A maneuver used either as a counter or as an offensive breakdown by reaching across the side of the opponent's face and grasping his opposite arm just above the elbow.

Disadvantage position A wrestler being legally controlled by his opponent is said to be in "a position of disadvantage."

Double-leg takedown A takedown performed by gaining control of both of the opponent's legs.

Escape Coming from a position of disadvantage to a neutral position.

Fall Holding both of the opponent's shoulders to the mat simultaneously for one or two seconds. Same as a pin. This terminates a match.

Half nelson A means of turning the opponent to his back by prying an arm upward, using his head as a fulcrum.

Head lever A means of breaking the opponent to the mat by exerting pressure with the head on his arm at the armpit, at the same time pulling backward on the corresponding wrist.

Near fall A position in which the offensive wrestler maintains his opponent in a controlled pinning situation.

Neutral position Both wrestlers face each other on their feet or knees with neither maintaining control.

Posting The act of placing a hand firmly on the mat and using it as a base of support for the body.

Potentially dangerous holds Holds that may cause injury when used legally.

Optional starting position A starting position that may be used for the opening of the second or third periods and for all restarts not from a neutral position.

Referee's position A starting position whereby the wrestlers assume a top man and bottom man position as directed by the referee.

Reversal A means of scoring by moving from a position of disadvantage to a position of advantage.

Ride A method used to maintain "a position of advantage" by utilizing various holds and leverage points.

Set-up A maneuver whereby a wrestler tries to gain an advantage by feinting, pushing, pulling, or making noises to distract an opponent.

Single-leg takedown A maneuver used by an attacking wrestler to gain control of one of opponent's legs.

Sit-out A maneuver from a position of disadvantage (bottom man) for the purpose of either escaping or reversing. The wrestler sits, throwing his legs in front of him, and turns quickly.

Stalemate An interlocking position in which neither wrestler can improve his situation.

Stalling An action or inaction whereby a wrestler does not make an honest attempt to wrestle aggressively or stay in the circle.

Stance Positioning the legs and feet in various positions while standing to enhance mobility or stability.

Stand-up An escape executed by standing up from a bottom man position.

Suplay Illegal takedown whereby the wrestler picks up his opponent around the waist and falls backward in an attempt to put the opponent's shoulders to the mat.

Switch A reversal executed by bottom man by applying leverage near the opponent's shoulder and sitting out to side.

Takedown A maneuver for taking the opponent down to the mat and attaining control over him.

Top position Wrestler is above and behind the bottom wrestler, with one arm encircling the waist and another placed on the elbow of the near arm. A position of advantage.

Unnecessary roughness A technical violation during a match. Opponent is awarded 1 point.

SELECTED REFERENCES

Dotson, B.; Evans, S.; and Freeman, F. *Concepts in Wrestling: The Idea Book.* Champaign, IL: Leisure Press, 1984.

Dziedzic, S. *The United States Wrestling Syllabus.* Champaign, IL: Leisure Press, 1983.

Hellickson, Russ and Baggot, Andrew. *An Instructional Guide to Amateur Wrestling.* New York: The Putman Publishing Company, 1987.

Hopke, S.L. and Kidder, W. *Elementary and Junior High School Wrestling.* Cranbury, NJ: A.S. Barnes and Co., Inc., 1977.

Jarman, Tom and Hanley, Reid. *Wrestling for Beginners.* Chicago: Contemporary Books, Inc., 1983.

Johnston, J.K.: Dalgewicz, C.; and White, D. *Wrestling: Skills and Strategies for the Athlete and Coach.* New York: Hawthorn Books, Inc., 1979.

Keith, Art. *Successful Wrestling.* Champaign, IL: Leisure Press, 1990.

Martell, W. *Teaching Kids to Wrestle.* Champaign, IL: Leisure Press, 1984.

APPENDIX A

▶ *Sources of Rules*

The following national organizations, athletic associations, and companies publish rules and guides on various sport activities. Some of the national organizations have regional and state affiliates where rules can be obtained. For further information, check the telephone directory for the nearest office in your area.

NATIONAL ORGANIZATIONS

Amateur Athletic Union of the United States (AAU)
3400 West 86th St.
P.O. Box 68207
Indianapolis, IN 46268

National Association for Girls and Women in Sport (NAGWS)

American Alliance for Health, Physical Education, Recreation and Dance (AAHPERD)
1900 Association Drive
Reston, VA 22091

National Collegiate Athletic Association (NCAA)
U.S. Hwy 50 and Nall Ave.
Box 1906
Shawnee Mission, KS 66222

National Federation of State and High School Athletic Associations (NFS)
7 South Dearborn St.
Chicago, IL 60603

OTHER ORGANIZATIONS, ASSOCIATIONS, AND COMPANIES

Angling
American Casting Education Foundation
P.O. Box 51, Nashville, TN 37202

Federation of Fly Fishers
P.O. Box 1088, West Yellowstone, MT 59758

National Association of Handicapped Outdoor Sportsmen, Inc.
R.R. 6, Box 25, Centralia, IL 62801

Archery
National Archery Association of the United States
1750 East Boulder St., Colorado Springs, CO 80909–5778

National Field Archery Association
R.R. Box 514, Redlands, CA 92373

American Archery Council
23 E. Jackson Blvd., Chicago, IL 60604
(Indoor Target)

Special Olympics International
1350 New York Ave. NW, Suite 500, Washington, DC 20005

Badminton
(*See* National Organizations—NAGWS of AAHPERD)

United States Badminton Association
501 W. Sixth St., Papillion, NE 68046
(USBA has modification of rules for special populations)

Basketball
See National Organizations—AAU, NCAA, NAGWS, NFS

Amateur Basketball Association of the United States of America
1750 East Boulder St., Colorado Springs, CO 80909

Federation Internationale de Basketball Amateur
19 Rugendasstrasse, 800 Munich 71, West Germany

National Wheelchair Basketball Association
C/O Dr. Stan Labanowich
110 Seaton Building, University of Kentucky
Lexington, KY 40506

Bicycling
Federation International Amateur de Cyclisme
Via Dei Campi Sportivi 48 00197
Rome, Italy

Special Olympics International Sports Director
Dan McCarthy, Director of Cycling
237 Alpine Ave., Boulder, CO 80302

United States Cycling Federation
1750 Boulder St., Colorado Springs, CO 80909

Bowling
See National Organizations—NAGWS of AAHPERD

American Bowling Congress and Women's International Bowling Congress
5301 South 76th St., Greendale, WI 53129

American Wheelchair Bowling Association, Inc.
Daryl L. Pfsiter, Executive Secretary
N54 W15858 Larkspur Ln., Menomonee Falls, WI 53051

American Blind Bowling Association
C/O Ron Beverly (National Secretary/Treasurer)
77 Bame Avenue, Buffalo, NY 14215

Cross-Country Skiing

Federation Internationale de Ski
Worbstrasse 210, 3073 Gumligen, Berne, Switzerland

National Handicapped Sports & Recreation Association
(Executive Headquarters)
4405 East-West Highway, Bethesda, MD 20814

United States Ski Association
1750 East Boulder St., Colorado Springs, CO 80909

Fencing

See National Organizations—NAGWS of AAHPERD

Amateur Fencer's League of America
601 Curtis St., Albany, CA 94706

Federation Internationale d'Escrime
32 Rue de la Boetie, 75008 Paris, France

International Stoke Mandeville Games Federation
Mr. Theo van Leeuwen, Chairman, Wheelchair Fencing
Draadzegge 14, 2318 zm Leiden, Netherlands

Ludwig Guttman Sports Centre for the Disabled-Stoke
Mandeville
Harvey Rd., Aylesbury
Bucks, HP21 8PP, United Kingdom

United States Fencing Association
1750 East Boulder St., Colorado Springs, CO 80909

Field Hockey

See National Organizations—NAGWS of AAHPERD, NFS,
NCAA

United States Field Hockey Association
1750 East Boulder St., Colorado Springs, CO 80909–5773

Football—Touch and Flag

See National Organizations—NAGWS of AAHPERD

Athletic Institute
200 Castlewood Dr., North Palm Beach, FL 33408–5697

Rules for the Blister Bowl Wheelchair Football Tournament are
available by writing to:
Santa Barbara Recreation Department
P.O. Box Drawer P-P, Santa Barbara, CA 93102

Golf

National Amputee Golf Association
Bob Wilson, Executive Director
P.O. Box 1228, Amherst, NH 03031

U.S. Golf Association
Liberty Congress Road, Far Hills, NJ 07931

Gymnastics

See National Organizations—AAU, NCAA and NAGWS of
AAHPERD

Federation International de Gymnastique
Juraweg 12, 3250 Lyss, Switzerland

Special Olympics International Sports Director
Ms. Kate Faber-Staff Liaison (Gymnastics)
Director of Gymnastics
69 Bretan Rd., Brick Township, NJ 08723

United States Gymnastics Federation
201 S. Capitol Ave., Suite 300, Indianapolis, IN 46225

Handball and Racquetball

See National Organizations—AAU

American Amateur Racquetball Association & National
Wheelchair Racquetball Association
815 North Weber, Suite 203, Colorado Springs, CO 80903

Canadian Racquetball Association
#13–1381 Pleasant Lane, Victoria, British Columbia
Canada, V9B 5J7

U.S. Handball Association
4101 Dempster St., Skokie, IL 60076

United States Wheelchair Racquet Sports Association
Chip Parmelly
1941 Viento Verano Dr., Diamond Bar, CA 91765

Horseshoes

National Horseshoe Pitchers Association of America
9725 Palm St., Bellflower, CA 90706

Orienteering

Orienteering Services
Box 1604, Binghamton, NY 13901

United States Orienteering Federation
P.O. Box 1444, Forest Park, GA 30051

Pickle-Ball

Pickle-Ball, Inc.
801 N.W. 48th St., Seattle, WA 98107

Racquetball

See Handball

Soccer

See National Organizations—NCAA, NAGWS of AAHPERD,
NFS

Amputee Soccer International
P.O. Box 7161, Seattle, WA 98177

Federation Internationale de Football Association
Case Postale 85, 8030 Zurich, Switzerland

Soccer Association for Youth
P.O. Box 921, Cincinnati, OH 45201

Special Olympics International Sports Director
Mr. Dwain Hartzler, Director of Soccer, Goshen College,
Goshen, IN 46526

United States Soccer Federation
1750 East Boulder St., Colorado, CO 80909

Softball

See National Organizations—NAGWS of AAHPERD

Amateur Softball Association
2801 N.E. 50th St., Oklahoma City, OK 73111

Federation Internationale de Softball
2801 N.E. 50th St., Oklahoma City, OK 73111

National Beep Baseball Association
Dr. Ed Bradley, President
9623 Spencer Highway, LaPorte, TX 77571

National Wheelchair Softball Association
Jon Speake, Commissioner
P.O. Box 22478, Minneapolis, MN 55422

Speedball

See National Organizations—NAGWS of AAHPERD

Swimming

See National Organizations—AAU, NCAA, NAGWS of
AAHPERD

United Stated Diving, Inc.
Pan American Plaza, 201 South Capital Ave.
Indianapolis, IN 46225

Federation Internationale de Natation Amateur
208–3540 West 41st Ave, Vancouver, British Columbia
Canada V6N 3E6

United States Swimming, Inc.
1750 East Boulder St., Colorado Springs, CO 80909

United States Swimming, Adapted Swimming Committee
Libby Anderson, Chairperson
4660 Natalie Dr., San Diego, CA 92115

Table Tennis

American Wheelchair Table Tennis Association
Ed Morrison, President
166 Haase Ave., Paramus, NJ 07652

International Table Tennis Federation
53 London Road, St. Leonards-on-the-sea
Sussex Tn37 6AY, Great Britain

United States Table Tennis Association
1750 East Boulder St., Colorado Springs, CO 80909

Team Handball

See National Organizations—NAGWS of AAHPERD

Federation Internationale de Handball
Lange Gasse 10, 4052 Bale, Switzerland

Special Olympics International Sports Director
Mary Phil Dwight, Team Handball Development Coordinator
Northern Michigan University, Meyland Hall
Marquette, MI 49855

United States Team Handball Federation
1750 East Boulder St., Colorado Springs, CO 80909

Tennis

See National Organizations—NAGWS of AAHPERD

Federation Internationale de Tennis
Church Road, Wimbledon, London SW19 5TF Great Britain

National Foundation of Wheelchair Tennis
Brad Parks, Executive Director
940 Calle Amancer, Suite B, San Clemente, CA 92672

Special Olympics International Sports Director
Randall S. Hester, Director of Tennis
United States Tennis Association
707 Alexander Rd., Princeton, NJ 08512

United States Tennis Association
1212 Avenue of the Americas, New York, NY 10036

USTA Center for Educational & Recreational Tennis
729 Alexander Rd., Princeton, NJ 08540

Track and Field

See National Organizations—AAU, NCAA, NFS, NAGWS of
AAHPERD

The Athletic Congress of the USA
P.O. Box 120, Indianapolis, IN 46202

International Amateur Athletic Federation
3 Hans Crescent, Knightsbridge
London, SW1 0LW, Great Britain

Special Olympics Sports Director for Athletics
Special Olympics International
1350 New York Ave., NW Suite 500, Washington, D.C. 20005

Volleyball

See National Organizations—NFS, NAGWS of AAHPERD

Federation Internationale de Volleyball
7 Place Chauderon, 1003 Lausanne, Switzerland

Ontario Wheelchair Sports Association
333 River Road, Otawa, Ontario
Canada K1L 8H9

Special Olympics International Sports Director
Ms. Ruth Nelson, Director of Volleyball
7743 Bles Ave. ''B'', Baton Rouge, LA 70810

United States Volleyball Association
1750 East Boulder St., Colorado Springs, CO 80909

Weight Lifting and Training

See National Organizations—AAU

National Strength and Conditioning Association
P.O. Box 81410, Lincoln, NE 68501

United States Weightlifting Federation
Colorado Springs, CO 80910

Wrestling

See National Organizations—NFS, NCAA

Federation Internationale de Lutte Amateur
AV. Ruchonnet 3, CH-1003
Lausanne, Switzerland

United States Association for Blind Athletes
Dr. James Mastro, Director for Blind Wrestling
Braille Sports Foundation
7525 North St., St. Louis Park, MN 55426

U.S.A. Wrestling
225 S. Academy, Colorado Springs, CO 80910

APPENDIX B

▶ How to Conduct Tournaments

TYPES OF TOURNAMENT DRAWINGS

Various kinds of bracket arrangements may be used in conducting tournament competition. The type of elimination is usually determined by several factors: (1) type of activity, (2) number of entries, (3) amount of playing time, (4) playing space and equipment, (5) age of participants, (6) officials available.

With a large number of entries it is sometimes desirable to run a combination tournament, for example, a double elimination—single elimination tournament. The winners of the double elimination brackets compete in a single elimination tournament to determine the ultimate champion.

Number of Byes. The first step before making a drawing for the bracket arrangement is to determine the number of entries.

When the number of competitors is 4, 8, 16, 32, 64,128, or any higher power of 2, they shall meet in pairs. When the number of competitors is not a power of 2, there shall be byes in the first round. For example: if there are 13 entries, a bracket of 16 with three byes is required. The purpose of having byes is to bring into the second round a number of competitors that is a power of 2. To determine the number of byes, subtract the number of competitors from the next higher power of 2; to determine the number of competitors in the first round, subtract the number of byes from the total number of competitors. If the byes are an even number, half of them shall be placed at the top of the draw and half at the bottom of the draw; if they are an uneven number, there should be one more bye at the bottom than the top. The byes at the top half shall be the names drawn first. The next names drawn shall be placed in the first round. The byes in the bottom half are drawn last.

Seeding the Draw. It is a common practice to select the best teams or individuals and place them in the bracket so that they will not meet in the early rounds of the play. Two or more entries may be seeded—usually the four best are selected in a sixteen name bracket and eight in a thirty-two name bracket. The seeded entrants are usually placed in the 1st, 5th, 9th, 13th, etc., bracket positions. The No. 1 and 4 seeded teams are generally placed in the first and fifth positions of the top bracket and the No. 2 and 3 seeded teams in the ninth and thirteenth positions of the lower bracket, or No. 1 and 3 in the upper with No. 2 and 4 seeded teams in the lower half.

Single Elimination Tournament

If the contestants are of equal strength or their strength is not known, have a drawing for positions in the bracket. If the strength is known, seed the best teams so they will not meet in the early rounds. Place the seeded entries in the 1st, 5th, 9th, 13th, etc., positions.

All byes must occur in the first round of play. The total number of games played is always one less than the number of entries. To determine the number of games that the winner would have to play, count the powers of two in the number of entries; e.g., with 32 entries the winner plays 5 games.

Double Elimination Tournament

Two defeats eliminate an entry in this tournament. The losers in the first rounds move into the losers' bracket. The teams which advance farthest in either bracket meet each other in the final game. Should the winner of the losers' bracket defeat the winner of the first-round bracket, the teams are rematched for the championship when one team will have lost two games.

Byes are distributed in the first round of the

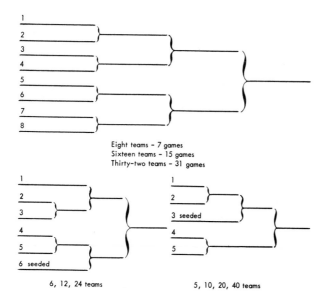

Eight teams – 7 games
Sixteen teams – 15 games
Thirty-two teams – 31 games

6, 12, 24 teams   5, 10, 20, 40 teams

original elimination brackets as in a single elimination tournament, but in the first round of the losers' brackets byes must be arranged to avoid giving a second bye to an entry that has already had a bye. Also, at all stages of the losers' bracket, avoid pairing entries that have met in earlier rounds, if possible.

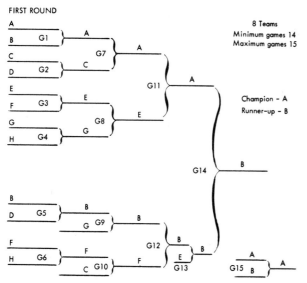

FIRST ROUND

8 Teams
Minimum games 14
Maximum games 15

Champion – A
Runner-up – B

Formula for total number of games, with N representing Number of entries $2(N-1)$ = Minimum Games to Play; $2(N-1) + 1$ = Maximum Games to Play.

This type tournament is seldom used unless the entries are eight or less in number. If more than eight entries, double the process and the two winners meet for the title.

Consolation Tournament

There are two types of general use: the consolation type tournament is generally used only when the number of entries is 8 or 16. In No. I bracket arrangement, only the losers in the first round of play compete for consolation title. In No. II, the losers in all the rounds except the final of the upper bracket compete for 3rd and 4th place.

In both tournaments every team plays at least two games before being eliminated.

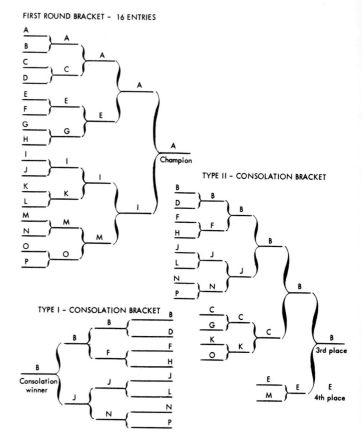

FIRST ROUND BRACKET - 16 ENTRIES

TYPE II - CONSOLATION BRACKET

TYPE I - CONSOLATION BRACKET

Round Robin Tournament

In this simple but efficient method, each team plays every other team once with the final standing determined on a percentage basis.

The following formula will apply to any number of teams, whether the total is odd or even. With an odd number of teams there is the same number of rounds; with an even number of teams there is one less number of games than teams.

For Odd Number of Teams. Assign a number to each team and then use only the figures in drawing the schedule. For example, in a league with 7 teams start with 1, putting down figures in the following order:

7	6	5	4	3	2	1
6–1	5–7	4–6	3–5	2–4	1–3	7–2
5–2	4–1	3–7	2–6	1–5	7–4	6–3
4–3	3–2	2–1	1–7	7–6	6–5	5–4

Note that the figures go down on the right side and up on the left. No. 7 draws a bye in the first round and the others play as indicated. With an odd number of teams, all numbers revolve and the last number each time draws a bye.

For Even Number of Teams. With an even number of teams the plan is the same except the position of No. 1 remains stationary, and the other numbers revolve about it until the original combination is reached. For example, with 8 teams:

1–2	1–8	1–7	1–6	1–5	1–4	1–3
8–3	7–2	6–8	5–7	4–6	3–5	2–4
7–4	6–3	5–2	4–8	3–7	2–6	8–5
6–5	5–4	4–3	3–2	2–8	8–7	7–6

In essence there are two things to remember: (1) with an even number of teams, No. 1 remains stationary and the other numbers revolve; (2) with an odd number of teams, all numbers revolve and the last number each time draws a bye.

Ladder Tournament

In a ladder tournament the competition is arranged by challenge, and the tournament requires a minimum of supervision. A player may challenge either of the two players above him in the ladder. If the challenger wins, he exchanges places with the loser in the ladder. All challenges must be accepted and played at an agreed time. Players draw for positions in the ladder; a starting and closing date for the tournament must be announced. Each player carries his handicap against all players, in case handicaps are used.

```
┌──────────────────────┐
│    TABLE TENNIS       │
│  1 _____   │
│  2 _____   │
│  3 _____   │
│  4 _____   │
│  5 _____   │
│  6 _____   │
│  7 _____   │
│  8 _____   │
│  9 _____   │
│ 10 _____   │
└──────────────────────┘
```

Pyramid Tournament

The pyramid tournament is similar to the ladder tournament except the design allows for more participating and challenging. After the original drawings are made, any player may challenge any other player in the same horizontal row. If he wins he may then challenge anyone in the row above—the two change places in the pyramid.

TABLE A-1. Tournament Schedule Calculator

Teams Entered	Byes Top	Byes Bottom	SINGLE ELIM. No. Games	DOUBLE ELIM. No. Games	ROUND ROBIN No. Games
4	0	0	3	6 or 7	6
5	1	2	4	8 or 9	10
6	1	1	5	10 or 11	15
7	0	1	6	12 or 13	21
8	0	0	7	14 or 15	28
9	3	4	8	16 or 17	36
10	3	3	9	18 or 19	45
11	2	3	10	20 or 21	55
12	2	2	11	22 or 23	66
13	1	2	12	24 or 25	73
14	1	1	13	26 or 27	91
15	0	1	14	28 or 29	105
16	0	0	15	30 or 31	
17	7	8	16	32 or 33	
18	7	7	17	34 or 35	
19	6	7	18	36 or 37	
20	6	6	19	38 or 39	
21	5	6	20	40 or 41	
22	5	5	21	42 or 43	
23	4	5	22	44 or 45	
24	4	4	23	46 or 47	
25	3	4	24	48 or 49	
26	3	3	25	50 or 51	
27	2	3	26	52 or 53	
28	2	2	27	54 or 55	
29	1	2	28	56 or 57	
30	1	1	29	58 or 59	
31	0	1	30	60 or 61	
32	0	0	31	62 or 63	

Diagrams reproduced courtesy of Wilson Sporting Goods Co.

APPENDIX C

▶ *Athletic Field and Court Diagrams*

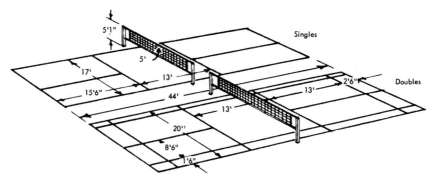

BADMINTON COURT

Measure to outside edge of boundary lines

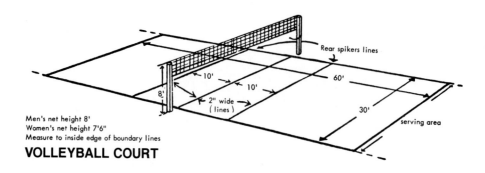

Men's net height 8'
Women's net height 7'6"
Measure to inside edge of boundary lines

VOLLEYBALL COURT

BASEBALL DIAMOND

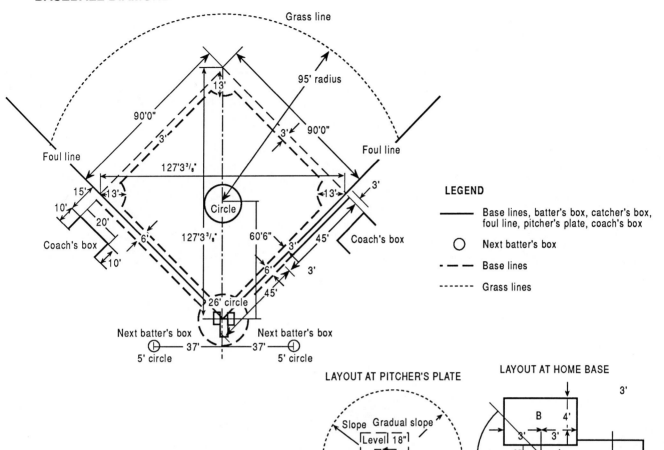

LEGEND

——— Base lines, batter's box, catcher's box, foul line, pitcher's plate, coach's box

◯ Next batter's box

– – – Base lines

········· Grass lines

LAYOUT AT PITCHER'S PLATE

LAYOUT AT HOME BASE

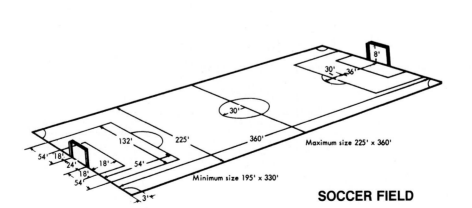

SOCCER FIELD

BASKETBALL COURT

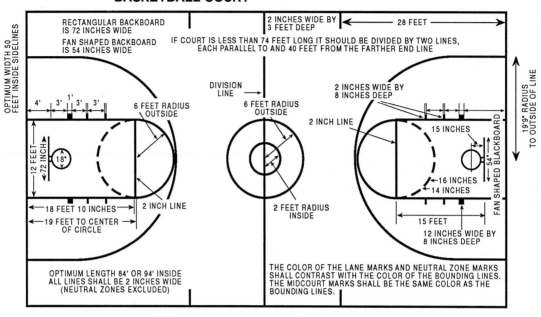

RECTANGULAR BACKBOARD IS 72 INCHES WIDE

FAN SHAPED BACKBOARD IS 54 INCHES WIDE

OPTIMUM WIDTH 50 FEET INSIDE SIDELINES

2 INCHES WIDE BY 3 FEET DEEP

28 FEET

IF COURT IS LESS THAN 74 FEET LONG IT SHOULD BE DIVIDED BY TWO LINES, EACH PARALLEL TO AND 40 FEET FROM THE FARTHER END LINE

DIVISION LINE

6 FEET RADIUS OUTSIDE

6 FEET RADIUS OUTSIDE

2 INCHES WIDE BY 8 INCHES DEEP

19'9" RADIUS TO OUTSIDE OF LINE

2 INCH LINE

15 INCHES

12 FEET

72 INCH

18"

54"

FAN SHAPED BLACKBOARD

2 FEET RADIUS INSIDE

16 INCHES
14 INCHES

18 FEET 10 INCHES

2 INCH LINE

15 FEET

19 FEET TO CENTER OF CIRCLE

12 INCHES WIDE BY 8 INCHES DEEP

OPTIMUM LENGTH 84' OR 94' INSIDE ALL LINES SHALL BE 2 INCHES WIDE (NEUTRAL ZONES EXCLUDED)

THE COLOR OF THE LANE MARKS AND NEUTRAL ZONE MARKS SHALL CONTRAST WITH THE COLOR OF THE BOUNDING LINES. THE MIDCOURT MARKS SHALL BE THE SAME COLOR AS THE BOUNDING LINES.

Left end shows large backboard for college games.

MINIMUM of 3 FEET
Preferably 10 feet of unobstructed space outside. If impossible to provide 3 feet, a narrow broken 1" line should be marked inside the court parallel with and 3 feet inside the boundary.

SEMICIRCLE BROKEN LINES
For the broken line semicircle in the free throw lane, it is recommended there be 8 marks 16 inches long and 7 spaces 14 inches long.

Right end shows small backboard for high school and Y.M.C.A. games.

BASKETBALL BACKBOARDS

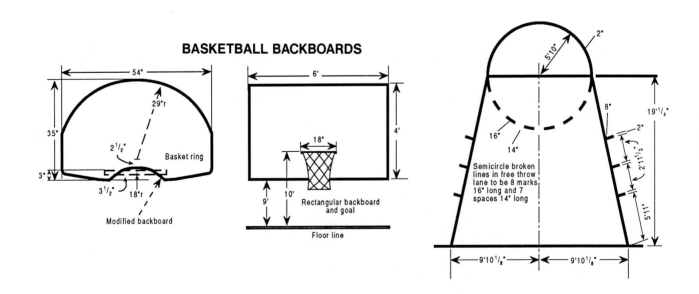

54"

29"r

35"

2 1/2"

Basket ring

3"

3 1/2"   18"r

Modified backboard

6'

18"

4'

9'   10'

Rectangular backboard and goal

Floor line

5'10"

2"

8"

16"

14"

2"

2'11 1/2"

5'11"

19'1 1/4"

Semicircle broken lines in free throw lane to be 8 marks 16" long and 7 spaces 14" long

9'10 1/8"   9'10 1/8"

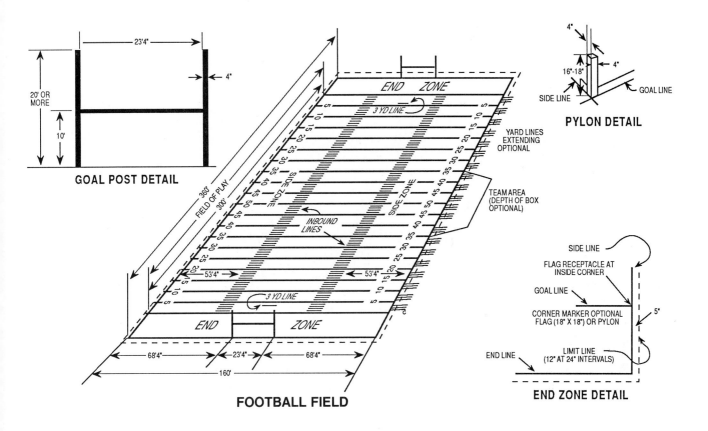

GOAL POST DETAIL

FOOTBALL FIELD

PYLON DETAIL

END ZONE DETAIL

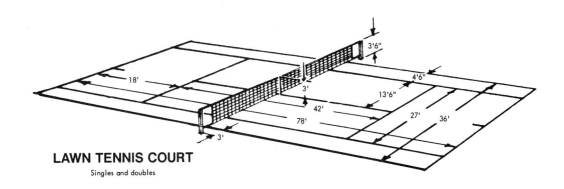

LAWN TENNIS COURT

Singles and doubles

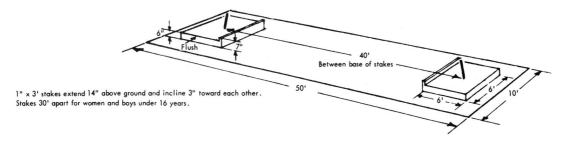

1" x 3' stakes extend 14" above ground and incline 3" toward each other.
Stakes 30' apart for women and boys under 16 years.

HORSESHOES

FIELD HOCKEY

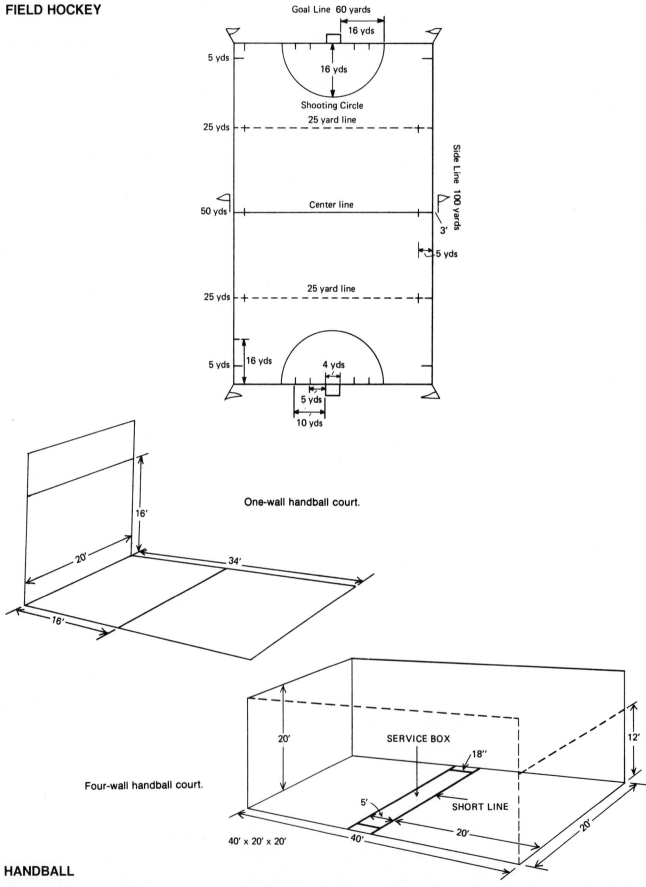

Goal Line 60 yards

16 yds

5 yds

16 yds

Shooting Circle

25 yard line

25 yds

Side Line 100 yards

50 yds

Center line

3'

5 yds

25 yard line

25 yds

16 yds

4 yds

5 yds

5 yds

10 yds

One-wall handball court.

16'

20'

34'

16'

Four-wall handball court.

20'

SERVICE BOX

18''

12'

5'

SHORT LINE

40' x 20' x 20'

40'

20'

20'

HANDBALL

SOFTBALL FIELD

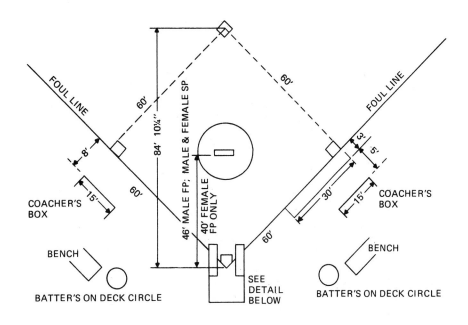

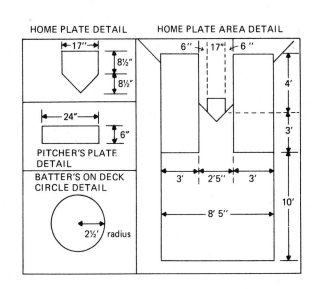

HOME PLATE DETAIL

17″

8½″

8½″

PITCHER'S PLATE DETAIL

24″

6″

BATTER'S ON DECK CIRCLE DETAIL

2½′ radius

HOME PLATE AREA DETAIL

6″ 17″ 6″

4′

3′

3′ 2′5″ 3′

8′ 5″

10′

	Distances	
	Fast Pitch	Slow Pitch
Bases		
Male	60 feet	65 feet
Female	60 feet	60 feet
Pitching		
Male	46 feet	46 feet
Female	40 feet	46 feet
Fences		
Male	225 feet	275 feet
Female	200 feet	250 feet

APPENDIX D

▶ *Sources of Audio-Visual Materials*

Audio-visual materials should be considered as an integral part of the instructional program, and not as entertainment or something to be used on rainy days. Audio-visual materials are supplementary aids to enhance the teaching process. The following sources have physical activity films, video tapes, and other materials.

AAHPERD
1900 Association Dr.
Reston, VA 22091

Academy Entertainment
1 Pine Haven Shore Road
Shelburne, VT 05482

Advantage Video
1246 NW 122
Portland, OR 97229

Aetna Life & Casualty
Public Relations Resources, DA23—D. Harper
Hartford, CT 06156

AIMS Media (Attn: W. Sherman)
6901 Woodley Ave.
Van Nuys, CA 91406

Ambrose Video Publishing Company
381 Park Avenue S. Suite 1601
New York, NY 10016

American Film Registry
831 South Wabash Avenue
Chicago, IL 60605

Anargyros Film Library
1813 Fairborn Avenue
Los Angeles, CA 90025

Association Films
561 Hill Grove Ave.,
La Grange, IL 60525

Athletic Institute
200 Castlewood Dr.
North Palm Beach, FL 33408

Audio Film Center
2138 E. 7th St.
Mt. Vernon, NY 10550

Avis Films
2408 WS. Olive Avenue
Burbank, CA 91506

BFA Educational Media/Phoenix Films
468 Park Avenue South
New York, NY 10016

Boston University Film Library
765 Commonwealth Ave.
Boston, MA 02215

Brandon Films, Inc.
200 West 57th St.
New York, NY 10019

Bureau of Audio-Visual Instruction
University of Wisconsin
P.O. Box 2093
Madison, WI 53701

Carousel Films, Inc.
1501 Broadway
New York, NY 10036

Castle Films Division
1145 Park Avenue
New York, NY 10036

Champions on Film and Video
P.O. Box 1941
Ann Arbor, MI 48106

Chicago Tribune Motion Picture Bureau
435 N. Michigan Ave.
Chicago, IL 60611

Chronicle Video
2855 Mitchell Drive
Suite 225
Walnut Creek, CA 94598

Churchill Films
662 North Robertson Boulevard
Los Angeles, CA 90069

Coronet/MTI Films/Video, Inc.
108 Wilmot Road
Deerfield, IL 60015

Educational Activities, Inc.
P.O. Box 392
Freeport, NY 11520

Educational Screen and A-V Guide
434 S. Wabash Ave.
Chicago, IL 60605

Educators Guide to Free HPER Materials
Educators Progress Service
Randolph, WI 53956

Encyclopedia Britannica Educational Corporation
425 North Michigan Avenue
Chicago, IL 60611

Film Associates
11559 Santa Monica Blvd.
Los Angeles, CA 90025

Films, Inc.
5547 N. Ravenswood Avenue
Chicago, IL 60640–1199

Film Trends
8060 Melrose Avenue
Los Angeles, CA 90046

Golden Door Productions
Tenth & Parker
Berkeley, CA 94710

Health Alert
123 4th St. NW
Charlottesville, VA 22901

Indiana University
Audio Visual Center
Bloomington, IN 47405

International Film Bureau, Inc.
332 S. Michigan Ave.
Chicago, IL 60604

Johnson-Nyquist Productions, Inc.
23854 Via Fabricante, D-1
Mission Viejo, CA 92691

Journal Films
909 W. Diversey Parkway
Chicago, IL 60614

Karol Media
22 Riverview Drive
Wayne, NJ 07470–3191

Kent State University
Audio Visual Center
Kent, OH 44244

Lee Tennis Products
999 Grove St.
P.O. Box 1909
Charlottesville, VA 22903

Library of Congress Catalog
Motion Pictures and Filmstrips
Building 159 Navy Yard Annex
Washington, D.C. 20541

Maryland Public Television
Program Circulation Manager
Owlings Mill, MD 21117

McGraw-Hill Film
1221 Avenue of Americas
New York, NY 10036

Modern Talking Picture Service
5000 Park Street, North
St. Petersburg, FL 33709

National Foundation of Wheelchair Tennis
1541 Red Hill Road, Suite A
Tustin, CA 92680

Official Sports Films, Inc.
400 Leslie St.,
Elgin, IL 60120

Oklahoma State University
Audio Visual Center
Stillwater, OK 74078

Peak Performance, Inc.
P.O. Box 2829
Duxbury, MA 02332

Penifield Productions, Ltd.
35 Springfield St.
Agawam, MA 01001

Pennsyvlania State University
Audio Visual Services
Special Services Building
University Park, PA 16802

Rarig Film Service, Inc.
834 Industry Drive
Seattle, WA 98188

Rolex Watch U.S.A., Inc.
665 5th Avenue
New York, NY 10022

School Film Service
549 West 123rd St.
New York, NY 10027

Scope Productions
P.O. Box 206
Ahwahnee, CA 93601

Society for Visual Education, Inc.
1345 Diversey Parkway
Chicago, IL 60614

Sportlite Films
230 North Michigan Avenue
Chicago, IL 60601

Sports Films and Talents
12755 State Hwy. 55
Minneapolis, MN 55441

Sports Investors, Inc.
6 East 39th St.
New York, NY 10016

Sports World Cinema
P.O. Box 17022
Salt Lake City, UT 84117

SyberVision Systems, Inc.
6066 Civic Terrace Avenue
Newark, CA 94560

Teaching Film Custodians, Inc.
25 West 43rd Street
New York, NY 10036

Trans World International
The Pier House
Strand on the Green
London W4 3NN
England

University of Colorado
Academic Media Services
Box 379
Boulder, CO 80309

University of Kansas
Media Services
Lawrence, KS 66045

US Olympic Committee
Department of Education Services
1750 East Boulder Street
Colorado Springs, CO 80909–5760

APPENDIX E

▶ Selected National Health Objectives for the Year 2000

Healthy People 2000: National Health Promotion and Disease Prevention Objectives, a report released in 1991 by the U.S. Department of Health and Human Services, outlines national strategies for improving the health and well-being of the nation over the next decade.[1] Many of the objectives presented in this report can be accomplished or reinforced through sound programs in health and physical education. Outlined below are specific objectives in a selected number of categories. For each topic we have grouped the objectives pertaining to (1) health status, (2) risk reduction, and (3) services and protection.

A. PHYSICAL ACTIVITY AND FITNESS

Health Status Objectives

1. Reduce coronary heart disease deaths to no more than 100 per 100,000 people.
2. Reduce overweight to a prevalence of no more than 20 percent among people aged 20 and older and no more than 15 percent among adolescents aged 12 through 19.

Risk Reduction Objectives

1. Increase to at least 30 percent the proportion of people aged 6 and older who engage regularly, preferably daily, in light to moderate physical activity for at least 30 minutes per day.
2. Increase to at least 20 percent the proportion of people aged 18 and older and to at least 75 percent the proportion of children and adolescents

aged 6 through 17 who engage in vigorous physical activity that promotes the development and maintenance of cardiorespiratory fitness 3 or more days per week for 20 or more minutes per occasion.
3. Reduce to no more that 15 percent the proportion of people aged 6 and older who engage in no leisure-time physical activity.
4. Increase to at least 40 percent the proportion of people aged 6 and older who regularly perform physical activities that enhance and maintain muscular strength, muscular endurance, and flexibility.
5. Increase to at least 50 percent the proportion of overweight people aged 12 and older who have adopted sound dietary practices combined with regular physical activity to attain an appropriate body weight.

Services and Protection Objectives

1. Increase to at least 50 percent the proportion of children and adolescents in 1st through 12th grade who participate in daily school physical education.
2. Increase to at least 50 percent the proportion of school physical education class time that students spend being physically active, preferably engaged in lifetime physical activities.

Note: Lifetime activities are defined as those that may be readily carried into adulthood because they generally require only one or two performers. Examples include swimming, bicycling, jogging, and racquet sports. Also counted as lifetime activities are vigorous social activities such as dancing. Competitive group sports and activities typically played only by young children, such as group games, are excluded.

---

[1] *Healthy People 2000,* U.S. Department of Health and Human Services (Pub. No. (PHS) 91–50213), 1991.

3. Increase community availability and accessibility of physical activity and fitness facilities as follows:

Facility	2000 Target
Hiking, biking, and fitness trail miles	1 per 10,000 people
Public swimming pools	1 per 25,000 people
Acres of parks and recreation open space	4 per 1,000 people (250 people per managed acre

4. Increase to at least 50 percent the proportion of primary care providers who routinely assess and council their patients regarding the frequency, duration, type, and intensity of each patient's physical activity practices.

B. NUTRITION

Health Status Objectives

1. Reduce coronary heart disease deaths to no more than 100 per 100,000 people.
2. Reduce overweight to a prevalence of no more than 20 percent among people aged 20 and older and no more than 15 percent among adolescents aged 12 through 19.

Risk Reduction Objectives

1. Reduce dietary fat intake to an average of 30 percent of calories or less and average saturated fat intake to less than 10 percent of calories among people aged 2 and older.
2. Increase complex carbohydrate and fiber-containing foods in the diets of adults to 5 or more daily servings for vegetables (including legumes) and fruits, and to 6 or more daily servings for grain products.
3. Increase to at least 50 percent the proportion of overweight people aged 12 and older who have adopted sound dietary practices combined with regular physical activity to attain proper body weight.

Services and Protection Objectives

1. Achieve useful and informative nutrition labeling for virtually all processed foods and at least 40 percent of fresh meats, poultry, fish, fruits, vegetables, baked goods, and ready-to-carry-away foods.
2. Increase to at least 5,000 brand items the availability of processed food products that are reduced in fat and saturated fat.
3. Increase to at least 90 percent the proportion of restaurants and institutional food service operations that offer identifiable, low-fat, low-calorie food choices, consistent with the *Dietary Guidelines for Americans*.
4. Increase to at least 90 percent the proportion of school lunch and breakfast services and child care food services with menus that are consistent with the nutrition principles in the *Dietary Guidelines for Americans*.
5. Increase to at least 75 percent the proportion of the nation's schools that provide nutrition education from preschool through 12th grade, preferably as part of quality school health education.

C. TOBACCO

Health Status Objectives

1. Reduce coronary heart disease deaths to no more than 100 per 100,000 people.
2. Slow the rise in lung cancer deaths to achieve a rate of no more than 42 per 100,000 people.
3. Reduce cigarette smoking to a prevalence of no more than 15 percent among people aged 20 and older.
4. Reduce the initiation of cigarette smoking by children and youth so that no more than 15 percent have become regular cigarette smokers by age 20.
5. Increase to at least 50 percent the proportion of cigarette smokers aged 18 and older who stopped smoking cigarettes for at least one day during the preceding year.
6. Reduce to no more than 20 percent the proportion of children aged 6 and younger who are regularly exposed to tobacco smoke at home.
7. Reduce smokeless tobacco use by males aged 12 through 24 to a prevalence of no more than 4 percent.

Services and Protection Objectives

1. Establish tobacco-free environments and include tobacco use prevention in the curricula of all elementary, middle, and secondary schools, preferably as part of quality school health education.
2. Increase to at least 75 percent the proportion of worksites with a formal smoking policy that prohibits or severely restricts smoking at the workplace.
3. Enact and enforce in all 50 States laws prohibiting the sale and distribution of tobacco products to youth younger than age 19.
4. Increase to 50 the number of States with plans to reduce tobacco use, especially among youth.
5. Eliminate or severely restrict all forms of tobacco product advertising and promotion to which youth younger than age 18 are likely to be exposed.

D. ALCOHOL AND OTHER DRUGS

Health Status Objectives

1. Reduce death caused by alcohol-related motor vehicle crashes to no more than 8.5 per 100,000 people.
2. Reduce drug-related deaths to no more than 3 per 100,000 people.

Risk Reduction Objectives

1. Increase by at least 1 year the average age of first use of cigarettes, alcohol, and marijuana by adolescents aged 12 through 17. (Baseline: age 11.6 for cigarettes, age 13.1 for alcohol, and age 13.4 for marijuana in 1988)
2. Reduce the proportion of young people who have used alcohol, marijuana, and cocaine in the past month, as follows:

Substance/Age	2000 Target
Alcohol/aged 12–17	12.6%
Alcohol/aged 18–20	29.0%
Marijuana/aged 12–17	3.2%
Marijuana/aged 18–25	7.8%
Cocaine/aged 12–17	0.6%
Cocaine/aged 18–25	2.3%

Note: The targets of this objective are consistent with the goals established by the Office of National Drug Control Policy, Executive Office of the President.

3. Reduce the proportion of high school seniors and college students engaging in recent occasions of heavy drinking of alcoholic beverages to no more than 28 percent of high school seniors and 32 percent of college students.
4. Reduce alcohol consumption by people aged 14 and older to an annual average of no more than 2 gallons of ethanol per person.
5. Increase the proportion of high school seniors who perceive social disapproval associated with the heavy use of alcohol, occasional use of marijuana, and experimentation with cocaine, as follows:

Behavior	2000 Target
Heavy use of alcohol	70%
Occasional use of marijuana	85%
Trying cocaine once or twice	95%

Note: Heavy drinking is defined as having 5 or more drinks once or twice each weekend.

6. Increase the proportion of high school seniors who associate risk or physical or psychological harm with the heavy use of alcohol, regular use of marijuana, and experimentation with cocaine, as follows:

Behavior	2000 Target
Heavy use of alcohol	70%
Regular use of marijuana	90%
Trying cocaine once or twice	80%

Note: Heavy drinking is defined as having 5 or more drinks once or twice each weekend.

7. Reduce to no more than 3 percent the proportion of male high school seniors who use anabolic steroids.

Services and Protection Objectives

1. Provide to children in all school districts and private schools primary and secondary school education programs on alcohol and other drugs, preferably as part of quality school health education.
2. Extend to 50 States legal blood alcohol concentration tolerance levels of .04 percent for motor vehicle drivers aged 21 and older and .00 percent for those younger than age 21.

E. MENTAL HEALTH AND MENTAL DISORDERS

Health Status Objectives

1. Reduce suicides to no more than 10.5 per 100,000 people.
2. Reduce by 15 percent the incidence of injurious suicide attempts among adolescents aged 14 through 17.
3. Reduce to less than 10 percent the prevalence of mental disorders among children and adolescents.
4. Reduce to less than 35 percent the proportion of people aged 18 and older who experienced adverse health effects from stress within the past year.

Risk Reduction Objectives

1. Increase to at least 30 percent the proportion of people aged 18 and older with severe, persistent mental disorders who use community support programs.
2. Increase to at least 20 percent the proportion of people aged 18 and older who seek help in coping with personal and emotional problems.
3. Decrease to no more than 5 percent the proportion of people aged 18 and older who report experiencing significant levels of stress who do not take steps to reduce or control their stress.

F. EDUCATIONAL AND COMMUNITY-BASED PROGRAMS

Health Status Objective

1. Increase years of healthy life to at least 65 years.

Risk Reduction Objective

1. Increase the high school graduation rate to at least 90 percent, thereby reducing risks for multiple problem behaviors and poor mental and physical health.

Services and Protection Objectives

1. Increase to at least 75 percent the proportion of the Nation's elementary and secondary schools provide planned and sequential kindergarten through 12th grade quality school health education.
2. Increase to at least 50 percent the proportion of postsecondary institutions with institutionwide health promotion programs for students, faculty, and staff.
3. Increase to at least 75 percent the proportion of people aged 10 and older who have discussed issues related to nutrition, physical activity, sexual behavior, tobacco, alcohol, other drugs, or safety with family members on at least one occasion during the preceeding month.
4. Establish community health promotion programs that separately or together address at least three of the Health People 2000 priorities and reach at least 40 percent of each State's population.

G. HEART DISEASE AND STROKE

Health Status Objectives

1. Reduce coronary heart disease deaths to no more than 100 per 100,000 people.

Risk Reduction Objectives

1. Increase to at least 50 percent the proportion of people with high blood pressure whose blood pressure is under control.

    Note: People with high blood pressure have blood pressure equal to or greater than 140 mm Hg systolic and/or 90 mm Hg diastolic and/or take antihypertensive medication. Blood pressure control is defined as maintaining a blood pressure less than 140 mm Hg systolic and 90 mm Hg diastolic. In NHANES II and the Seven States Study, control of hypertension did not include nonpharmacologic treatment. In NHANES III, those controlling their high blood pressure without medication (e.g. through weight loss, low sodium diets, or restriction of alcohol) will be included.

2. Increase to at least 90 percent the proportion of people with high blood pressure who are taking action to help control their high blood pressure.
3. Reduce the mean serum cholesterol level among adults to no more than 200 mg/dL.
4. Reduce dietary fat intake to an average of 30 percent of calories or less and average saturated fat intake to less than 10 percent of calories among people aged 2 and older.
5. Reduce overweight to a prevalence of no more than 20 percent among people aged 20 and older and no more than 15 percent among adolescents aged 12 through 19.
6. Increase to at least 30 percent the proportion of people aged 6 and older who engage regularly, preferably daily, in light to moderate physical activity for at least 30 minutes per day.
7. Reduce cigarette smoking to a prevalence of no more than 15 percent among people aged 20 and older.